Sport
and
Society

SERIES EDITORS

Benjamin G. Rader

Randy Roberts

A list of books in the series appears at the end of this book.

The New
American
Sport History

The New American Sport History

Recent Approaches and Perspectives

Edited by S. W. Pope

UNIVERSITY OF ILLINOIS PRESS
Urbana and Chicago

©1997 by the Board of Trustees of the University of Illinois
Manufactured in the United States of America
1   2   3   4   5   C   P   5   4   3   2   1

This book is printed on acid-free paper.

Library of Congress Cataloging-in-Publication Data
The new American sport history : recent approaches and perspectives /
   edited by S. W. Pope.
         p.   cm.—(Sport and society)
      Includes bibliographical references and index.
      ISBN 0-252-02264-5 (cloth : alk. paper).—ISBN 0-252-06567-0
   (paper : alk. paper)
      1. Sports—United States—History.   2. Sports—United States—
   Historiography.   3. Sports—Social aspects—United States—History.
   I. Pope, S. W. (Steven Wayne), 1962–.   II. Series
   GV581.N48   1997
   796´.0973—dc20   96-6137
                                                             CIP

For my grandparents:
James, Georgia, Walter, and Ella

Contents

═══

Acknowledgments

I wish to thank several people who helped bring this book to fruition. William Baker introduced me to the field of sport history, supervised my doctoral dissertation, and critiqued early versions of the introductory essay. This book would not have been conceived without his unfailing inspiration. I've also benefited immeasurably from Stephen Hardy's knowledge of sport history and cultural theory—this book is much sounder as a result. Allen Guttmann and Elliott Gorn read and commented on an early draft and have been generous sources of support and encouragement the past two years. I appreciate Richard Wentworth, director and editor in chief of the University of Illinois Press, for his unwavering dedication to this work since its inception three years ago. I'm grateful to the Sport and Society series editors—Benjamin Rader, for his enthusiasm and astute suggestions during the early stages of the project; and Randy Roberts, for his advocacy and sage advice in the latter phase. Theresa L. Sears, Veronica Scrol, and Robert Schneider of the University of Illinois Press conscientiously attended to the logistical and copyediting details. My friend Mark Dyreson graciously secured the assistance of Elizabeth Taylor and Wendy Weese of Weber State University for the preparation of the final manuscript. And finally, I thank my wife, Cathy, who not only typed lengthy endnotes but, more substantively, comforted my psyche throughout the process.

Grateful acknowledgment is made to the various editors and publishers for permission to reprint, sometimes in slightly altered form, the following essays in this collection:

Chapter 1, "Sports through the Nineteenth Century," reprinted from *The Encyclopedia of American Social History*, ed. Mary Kupiec Cayton, Elliott J.

Gorn, and Peter W. Williams, vol. 3, pp. 1627–42. Copyright © 1993 by Charles Scribner's Sons. Used by permission of Charles Scribner's Sons, an imprint of Simon and Schuster Macmillan.

Chapter 2, "The Early Years of Baseball, 1845–60," reprinted from *A Sporting Time: New York City and the Rise of Modern Athletics, 1820–70,* by Melvin L. Adelman, pp. 121–42. Copyright © 1986 by the Board of Trustees of the University of Illinois. Used by permission of the University of Illinois Press.

Chapter 3, "In the Beginning Was the Rule," reprinted from *Reading Football: How the Popular Press Created an American Spectacle,* by Michael Oriard, pp. 25–56. Copyright © 1993 by the University of North Carolina Press. Used by permission of the publisher.

Chapter 5, "Gender and Sporting Practice in Early America, 1750–1810," reprinted from *Journal of Sport History* 18 (1911): 10–30. Used by permission of the North American Society for Sport History.

Chapter 6, "Sport and the Redefinition of Middle-Class Masculinity in Victorian America," reprinted with a new title from *International Journal of the History of Sport* 8 (1991): 5–27. Used by permission of the publisher, Frank Cass and Co.

Chapter 7, "The 'Amazon' and the American 'Lady': Sexual Fears of Women as Athletes," reprinted from *From "Fair Sex" to Feminism: Sport and the Socialization of Women in the Industrial and Post-Industrial Era* (1986), ed. J. A. Mangan and Roberta J. Park, pp. 282–98. Used by permission of the publisher, Frank Cass and Co.

Chapter 8, "Sports and Eros," reprinted from *Women's Sports: A History,* by Allen Guttmann, pp. 258–65, 313–15. Copyright © 1991 by Columbia University Press. Used by permission of the publisher.

Chapter 9, "The Meanings of Prizefighting," reprinted from *The Manly Art: Bare-Knuckle Prize Fighting in America,* by Elliott J. Gorn, pp. 129–47, 277–84. Copyright © 1986 by Cornell University. Used by permission of Cornell University Press.

Chapter 10, " 'Oy Such a Fighter!': Boxing and the American Jewish Experience," reprinted from *Ellis Island to Ebbets Field: Sport and the American-Jewish Experience,* by Peter Levine, pp. 144–69, 306–8. Copyright © 1992 by Peter Levine. Used by permission of Oxford University Press.

Chapter 11, "Muscular Marxism and the Chicago Counter-Olympics of 1932," reprinted from *International Journal of the History of Sport* 9 (1992): 397–410. Used by permission of the publisher, Frank Cass and Co.

Chapter 12, "Selling Sport and Religion in American Society: Bishop Sheil and the Catholic Youth Organization," reprinted with a new title from *Inter-*

national Journal of the History of Sport 10 (1993): 233–41. Used by permission of the publisher, Frank Cass and Co.

Chapter 13, " 'Great Speed but Little Stamina': The Historical Debate over Black Athletic Superiority," reprinted from *Journal of Sport History* 16 (1989): 158–85. Used by permission of the North American Society for Sport History.

Chapter 14, "Entrepreneurs, Organizations, and the Sports Marketplace," reprinted from *Journal of Sport History* 13 (1986): 14–33. Used by permission of the North American Society for Sport History.

Chapter 15, "Mediated Spectatorship," reprinted from *Sports Spectators*, by Allen Guttmann, pp. 127–46, 207–10. Copyright © 1986 by Columbia University Press. Used by permission of the publisher.

Chapter 16, "The 'Visible Hand' on the Footrace: Fred Lebow and the Marketing of the Marathon," reprinted from *Journal of Sport History* 19 (1992): 244–56. Used by permission of the North American Society for Sport History.

Chapter 17, "The Quest for Self-Sufficiency and the New Strenuosity," reprinted from *Journal of Sport History* 18 (1991): 255–66. Used by permission of the North American Society for Sport History.

The New
American
Sport History

Introduction
American Sport History—Toward a New Paradigm

S. W. POPE

Sport has been described in literature and recorded in engravings, sculpture, and paintings for thousands of years by some of the world's greatest artists and writers. During the past century the task of interpreting the significance of sport has been the domain of journalists, cartoon artists, cultural critics, and filmmakers. The best popular works have been informative, entertaining, and occasionally sophisticated investigations of sport's connection to broader historical, cultural, and intellectual trends—like H. G. Bissinger's excellently done *Friday Night Lights* and Steve James's recent documentary *Hoop Dreams*.[1] This should be no surprise since, as the sport-studies scholar Stephen Hardy writes in a review of Stephen Fox's exemplary popular history of American sport, "Not only do sports rehearse fundamental human movements, passions and characters in recurring, unpredictable scripts," they also provide a dynamic, accessible window into politics, economics, gender, race, class formation, ideology, religion, and virtually any other topic.[2]

Curiously, scholars have only recently grasped this. Prior to the 1940s, most scholars ignored the history of sport because most of them considered it a frivolous, ancedotal research interest that added little to the coherent national (political) narratives. Sport history only became a bona fide field of intellectual inquiry during the past three decades. Ironically, sport languished as a physical, rather than a mental, activity—outside the traditions of classroom and intellectual discourse—in American academe for nearly a century, despite its prominence at the nation's leading universities. There were, however, several noteworthy attempts by early sport historians to situate their work within larger societal dialogues and paradigms.[3]

The first sixty years of American sport historiography generally followed the influential "frontier" paradigm. Frederick Paxson initiated this trend in a 1917 article for the *Mississippi Valley Historical Review*. Paxson argued that as the frontier receded and new pressures arose from rapid industrialization, sport as a new "safety valve" provided a needed release for a new generation of urban Americans. The new American urbanites created leisure activities to compensate for their lost traditional, rural recreations. The fact that "American society learned to give instead of crack" throughout a half-century of severe economic dislocations and class warfare, Paxson wrote, proved the success of safety valves like sport in mediating the tensions of a transforming society.[4]

In 1931 Jennie Holliman incorporated Paxson's thesis but recast the history of American sport to demonstrate its earlier, intimate developments along English and Native American lines. Americans' obsession with sports and games, in other words, *preceded* industrialization and the closing of the frontier by two centuries. Holliman's contemporary Lewis Mumford, however, suggested something quite different. Although sport was a tangential concern for his pioneering work on urban and technological history, Mumford argued that the rise of American sport was a direct reaction against the mechanization, division of labor, and standardization of life in a "machine civilization."[5]

During the politically charged World War II years, historians gave the sport-frontier paradigm a new ideological twist: the frontier experience was unique in the annals of human history, and thus Americans were an "exceptional" people. Historians emphasized how sport reflected America's superior institutions and preserved the nation's open, democratic character. During the pivotal transition from an agrarian to an urban-industrial society, "no other country and no other age," wrote Foster Rhea Dulles, "had ever had a wider choice of amusements open to the masses." Diligent in his use of primary sources, Dulles sketched a cogent chronicle of collegiate and professional sport, as well as the less formally organized games and pastimes of the first two-and-a-half centuries of America. The accessibility of sport and leisure signaled to Dulles that "[American] democracy had come into its heritage."[6]

The most distinguished sport historian of the 1950s and early 1960s, John Rickard Betts, fused the ideological assumptions of consensus historians with a savvy grasp of business and technological history. Betts argued that resourceful industrial capitalists expanded opportunities for mass sporting participation by building the necessary facilities, manufacturing standardized sporting goods, and providing cheaper, more efficient modes of transportation. Moreover, Betts established new standards for the study of nineteenth-century sport journalism, changing ideas about health and exercise and the impact of technology. To be fair, there were professionally trained historians who published books and articles on sport history prior to the mid-1960s—most notably Harold Seymour and David Voigt's histories of baseball—but most of the academic interest in the subject inhered in physical-education departments, whose practitioners' lackluster efforts failed to attract the attention of historians, American studies scholars, or social scientists.[7]

American sport history emerged as a recognized subdiscipline in the early 1970s, a time when historical scholarship itself changed dramatically. The Vietnam War, the civil rights movement, and the women's movement undermined the prevailing atmosphere of consensus, belief in progress and prosperity, and self-righteousness in both academe and larger American society. A new generation of historians raised on a steady diet of commercialized mass culture, challenged many of the prevailing social and cultural assumptions in the craft. In particular, those who came of age in a society rife with social and political conflict rejected the notion that a history rooted in the ideas and actions of an elite group of politicians, lawyers, and intellectuals could speak for the rest of American society. Armed with new assumptions, questions, and topics, the "new" historians shifted their attention from political events and ideas to collective processes and the experiences of everyday life.[8]

The new American social history derived from two basic European intellectual trends. The first grew out of the influential French journal *Annales*, whose editors and contributors believed that historians should incorporate all of the human and social sciences in their studies so as to recreate the totality of the past. The other principal influence behind American social history came from the British Marxists, who also turned away from traditional political history to analyze the relationships between intellectual, economic, social, and cultural developments. They focused on social groups rather than individuals, and, most significantly, emphasized "human agency"—the ways in which ordinary people made their own history. Above all, they were concerned with the rise of global capitalism and the resulting class struggle as the primary engine of historical change. Complementing these two schools of thought was the important influence of anthropologists and sociologists, particularly Max Weber, Clifford Geertz, Norbert Elias, and Michel Foucault, who expanded historians' understanding of such concepts as society, community, modernization, culture, and power. Sport historians borrowed liberally from anthropology and sociology and examined the relationships between sport and social structures.

Between the mid-1970s and the mid-1980s, sport historians transformed their infant field beyond recognition. Investigations into the socially constructed ideas of racial, religious, regional, ethnic, class, and gender subcultures generated new areas of specialization within both social history and the sport history subfield. Following historian Robert Wiebe's lead, sport scholars probed the importance of urban sport in Americans' search for "order" and "community." The most important work of the new American sport history was Allen Guttmann's *From Ritual to Record,* which linked the older concerns about the consequences of sport in the transition from a rural, agrarian to an urban, industrial society with the newer emphasis on sport in Americans' search for community.[9]

Most sport historians worked within one of the dominant scholarly paradigms—modernization theory—to investigate the meanings of the transition from a rural and agrarian society to an urban and industrial one in different times and locales. Modernists elevated Weberian "traditional" and "modern" ideal social types. Traditional society was characterized by stability, localism, unspecialized social roles, and paternalistic social hierarchies—all of which demonstrated little variation over time. Modern society, theorists posited, is dynamic, cosmopolitan, technological, mobile, industrial, and constantly modified by rational thought. Societies "modernize" as they shed the former qualities and adopt the latter ones. Guttmann synthesized the basic elements of this pivotal decade's literature into a modernist paradigm that brought global dimensions to the emerging field of sport history. Published two years after Richard D. Brown's influential work on pre–Civil War American history, Guttmann's imaginative *From Ritual to Record* not only paralleled contemporary historiographical tendencies critical of class-conflict explanations but also contributed to the broader modernist literature by setting the "modern" mania for records within a historical context dating back to ancient ritual. Whereas "traditional" sport was unorganized, tied to local religious customs, and interwoven with agrarian rhythms, "modern" sport, according to Guttmann, is marked by its secularity, bureaucratization, specialization, and quantification—all of which make it historically unique.[10]

Although ancient, medieval, and Renaissance societies had rich (and sometimes sophisticated) sporting cultures, the last three centuries contain the most important historical development—namely, the transformation of traditional agrarian pastimes into the commercial spectacles of urban-industrial societies. Rules, records, roles, facilities, and equipment have become much more formal, precise, and rational. For instance, the annual Shrovetide football matches in fifteenth- and sixteenth-century England had no real boundaries, formal rules, or limits on team size. By contrast, today's brand of football has established rules, standardized equipment and facilities, carefully plotted tactics, well-defined positions and roles, and myriad statistics and records to quantify and compare performance across time and space. These developments illustrate Guttmann's modernization-of-sport thesis, which continues to provide a framework for understanding the cultural, historical, and geographical development of sport.[11]

Modernist syntheses, however, quickly drew trenchant criticism.[12] Although many critics failed to demonstrate the paradigm's systemic limitations, most convincingly exposed modernization as an ahistorical construct that distorted the past by emphasizing structure at the expense of human agency. By the 1980s, such arguments had become standard fare within the historical profession. Scholars were particularly critical of the modernist paradigm's failure to address why things did not change, how specific ideas and lifestyles became dominant while others were relegated to the dustbin of history as a result of social-class interaction—issues well-established in the field of social and cultural history by the early 1980s.[13]

Several sport historians broached the issue of class and power as it applied to the struggle for "social control" in early twentieth-century America. The key works analyzed interactions between middle-class social reformers and urban working-class groups and debated whether reformers' efforts to use sport actually represented altruism or an insidious desire for social control to divert class-conscious impulses.[14] Sociologist Richard Gruneau brought a more rigorous theoretical approach to this critique. Working within the British Marxist cultural-studies tradition, he analyzed sport within the objective historical conditions of capitalism, and granted sport a degree of autonomy for its ability to express and dramatize a wide variety of social-class aspirations. Gruneau's work suggested that sports are social practices based on the forces and relations of production, and are therefore susceptible to challenge and redefinition by workers, women, and ethnic and racial groups.[15] Simultaneously, a new generation of social historians analyzed leisure as a medium of class domination and resistance.[16] Despite such efforts, however, most American sport historians remained loyal to the legacy of modernization and conventional, functionalist historical approaches until the mid-1980s.[17]

Since then sport historians have been less concerned with conventional periodizations, institutional developments, and the effects of urbanization, technology, and modernization and have focused instead on the more inclusive themes of class, gender, race, and ethnicity that currently define the parameters of social and cultural history. Moreover, recent works in sport sociology challenge historians to synthesize theoretical issues of the new social and cultural history into a new framework that reconciles modernization with the Marxist and *Annales* traditions. In short, the field of American sport history needs a new paradigm that does justice to the past decade's conceptual innovations. Many practitioners recognize this larger challenge, but only Stephen Hardy has attempted to articulate a comprehensive one.

Hardy suggests that although historians have primarily focused on sport *transformations,* one can discern "long residuals" from the past—continuities in forms and meanings that have crossed time and context.[18] In an earlier work he discussed something called the "Sportgeist"—representing a kind of *longue durée* (i.e., slow-moving, persistent wave of historical time) in the *Annales* (particularly Fernand Braudel) tradition—which embodied a set of potential tensions: competition (victory vs. "fair play"), creativity (freedom vs. regimen), physicality (moderation vs. aggression), and achievement (community vs. individual). In brief, the Sportgeist represents the internal, transhistorical properties of sport. In Hardy's model the Sportgeist is surrounded by other structures: social-class relations, gender and race relations, economic systems, and geography. As individuals or cultures practice sport, according to his paradigm, they make choices and thereby animate a particular version of the Sportgeist.[19]

Most American sport historians find Hardy's theoretically rigorous Hegelian-Braudelian paradigm confusing and esoteric. Its innovative approach, however, in the words of Melvin Adelman, "mandates an escape from the vision of sport history as another variation of social history"—an important contribution, to be sure. Still, apparently unhappy with the Sportgeist, Hardy has recently refined his approach by emphasizing "long residuals"— practices that tie the present to the past—in modern sport history: craft and community; the persistence of gambling; the framing of games within festival, carnival, and spectacle; and the erotic appeals in athletic performance. As he explains, "Periodicity in historical analysis is terribly important in the analysis of sport's contents, forms and relations, for in any given period there will always be a dialectic of incorporation and resistance. Social transformation is not an unfolding, evolutionary process [e.g., "modernization"], but a process that takes place over contested terrain."[20] These basic theses need to be taken more seriously by sport historians in order to move the field toward a new, more dynamic paradigm. The following overview will address some of these concerns.

National Culture

The rise of an American sporting culture took shape in the booming eighteenth-century coastal cities of the middle colonies, which became early centers of urban, commercialized spectacles. Horse racing, cockfighting, and rough-and-tumble brawling united men in a shared patriarchal culture and evoked particular visions of masculinity. Only in the mid-nineteenth century, however, did a coherent sporting ideology evolve, as a Victorian Protestant avant-garde reconciled a deeply rooted ambivalence toward traditional recreations with the prospects of using sport as a moral force. Linking athletic activity to the middle-class values of discipline, order, self-reliance, human perfectibility, and productivity, the emergent Muscular Christian defense of sport not only justified the explosion of sport around mid-century, it also popularized a new bourgeois, industrial morality and redefined "appropriate" male public behavior.[21]

As industrial capitalism increasingly segregated work from play, strenuous sport, according to Elliott Gorn, "helped men slough off defeatist attitudes, replicate the heroism of their fathers, and gear up for battle in new arenas" [e.g., the Spanish-American War]—reaffirming that "strength, aggressiveness, and the will to win were the fundamentals of life." It was within this context that Theodore Roosevelt articulated a distinctly Anglo-Saxon sporting ideology for a maturing industrial nation that elevated "the purposeful athleticism of modern sports," whereby "spectator sports became largely a private male space, filled with heroic competition and virile deeds." By the late 1890s, the structural and ideological framework for the national sporting culture was firmly ensconced in American society.[22]

The invention of a sporting ideology, however important, was only part of the story. The pivotal nineteenth-century episodes were the development of specifically "American" sports. Baseball's rapid growth during the early 1860s enabled it to surpass cricket as the nation's leading ball game, and prompted journalists to insist that it was the national game, reflecting the American character and temperament. Initially played by middle-class gentlemen, baseball was quickly dominated by skilled urban workers, and by the Civil War had spread to a range of social groups. Challenging the orthodox view that early baseball was a "middle class" sport by persuasively documenting that the game was dominated by skilled urban craftsmen and small shopkeepers who had significant control over their own work processes, Melvin Adelman (as well as Steven Gelber and Warren Goldstein) has shown how the game flourished in a fraternal, artisanal culture in which players placed great importance on occupational, political, and ethnic associations. Adelman also attends to the importance of an emergent generation of sports journalists (most notably Henry Chadwick) who assured their countrymen that baseball was not only a manly pastime, but a bona fide American sport.[23]

Between the 1870s and the 1920s, sport evolved from primarily localized activities to nationally organized, commercialized spectacles. Rooted in the material, social, and political realities of the age, sport dramatized fundamental ideas in American society. During a period of rapid social and political change, sport became a powerful medium for national self-identification as well as a metaphor for bourgeois values. Institutionalized sports and the discourses accompanying them were promoted by emergent social groups to rally social cohesiveness, sustain power structures, and legitimize nationalist sentiments.[24]

The key forum for solidifying the national sporting culture around the turn of the century was collegiate football. Michael Oriard documents the critical series of rule changes that transformed English rugby into American football during the 1880s to illustrate how a handful of representatives from elite universities controlled and shaped the new sport at its moment of development. The early years of football, in Oriard's words, exposed "the messy relations and complicated distribution of power among 'producers' and 'consumers' of culture." Unlike the advocates of baseball, who propagated the Doubleday creation myth, the founding fathers of football apparently felt no need for mythic narratives of national identity, much less any hope that the game would provide them. Nevertheless, as Oriard demonstrates, after football's haphazard beginnings such narrative possibilities quickly emerged and effectively transformed a game to be played into a spectacle to be watched and read about. Focusing on the writings of the "father of American Football," Walter Camp, Oriard illustrates how football promoters exploited the narrative possibilities of the game to create a national audience. Reflecting the growing importance of the daily sports page, most Americans, he claims, learned this new game through newspaper narratives and not at the ballfield before the turn of the century.

Mark Dyreson analyzes the role played by Progressive Era middle-class spokesmen in articulating a new sports ideology that reconciled their class interests with the new imperatives of corporate capitalism and revitalized their ability to influence the larger body politic. Transmuting their particular class values into universal ones, bourgeois sport advocates posited the idea of "life as a game" as an organizing principle that suggested the connections between the well-ordered body and the well-ordered political culture.[25] The history of American sport consciousness cannot simply be a history of players and spectators. It must also scrutinize the role of what Italian theorist Antonio Gramsci termed "organic intellectuals"—those cultural experts whose duty it is to define what is "legitimate." Dyreson's sport protagonists are those intellectuals who, in the words of cultural historian Andrew Ross, "patrol[ed] the ever-shifting border of popular and legitimate taste, supervise[d] the passports, the temporary visas, . . . and the deportation orders, and who occasionally made their own adventurous forays across the border." In other words, as Dyreson's essay suggests, at the heart of the story about intellectuals' relationship to sport is a structural connection between knowledge and power.[26]

Gender and the Body

The historical study of gender is one of the most thriving research fields today.[27] The pioneering work of feminist historians Gerder Lerner, Natalie Zemon Davis, Joan Kelly, and others shifted attention away from the Great Women approach to a broader orientation that highlights the diversity of women's historical experience. While many feminists cling to essentialist notions, the field of gender studies has diversified to demonstrate how ideas about sexual difference are socially constructed and vary according to historical context.

The field of sport history has paralleled this larger field of women's studies. Sport historians initially characterized the development of women's sporting practices as a simple reflection of timeless patriarchal dominance, with only marginal consideration of class, racial, and ethnic differences. During the past decade, however, the once-dominant "separate spheres" paradigm has shifted to an interactive view of social processes and gender relations that illuminates class, ethnicity, and race along with gender and sexual orientation. No longer is the focus predominantly on exceptional women who participated in the male-dominated public arena or on the ways in which women uniformly conformed to the ideological dictates of public and private spheres; rather, as Patricia Vertinsky has written, the new emphasis is on the extent to which women's lives actually corresponded to idealized versions of womanhood prescribed for them, and on women's culture rather than women's "place."[28]

The most important early theoretical contribution to this debate came from Jennifer Hargreaves, whose neo-Marxist, Gramscian orientation led her to conclude that although sport has historically been a male preserve, male domination has never been static or complete. Rather, "Some men and women support, accommodate to, or collude in existing patterns of discrimination in sport that are specific to capitalism and to male domination, while other men and women oppose them and struggle for change." This focus on the importance of hegemony directs attention to social class as a primary determinant of women's involvement in sport—and away from "women" as a unified, unproblematical category.[29]

Nancy Struna pioneered the study of women's involvement in colonial sport and leisure. The broader literature of the eighteenth century suggests that sport was connected to an early consumer revolution as Americans began to produce and consume far more leisure practices than their predecessors. Although sporting practice was largely a privileged-white-male phenomenon, Struna's research in estate inventories and probate records demonstrates that colonial women participated in a variety of recreations that extended beyond the confines of home and domestic production. Men owned most sporting goods and dominated sporting activities, but middle- and upper-class women were clearly essential to the use of those goods and the construction of male sporting culture—though they continued to be relegated to subordinate positions in nineteenth-century upper-class sports culture.[30]

Women became more active in sport by the end of the nineteenth century. While sport served as an arena in which the social place of women could be delineated, it was also partly formed by those women who spurned the stereotype of the "swooning damsel," donned the habit of the sportswoman, and, gifted with a distinct consciousness, had an impact as a separate constituency of sport. Nevertheless, sportswomen were only a minority among American women, since some shied away from sport by preference and others were effectively banned from it for lack of money and time. The fragmentation among women generally carried over into their sport, and diversity reigned. The growing interest in sport among many women did not produce a unified and simple modification of their identity in American culture, except in the general shift toward a comparatively broader scope of activities and toward the embrace of action itself that was part of the emancipation of women. Women's pleasure in action formed the common ground for the diverse expressions of women's sport, as well as the shared base from which women of sometimes-opposing views lent their endorsement to sport.[31]

Women's unequal sports participation throughout the nineteenth century derived from male fears that they might be challenged in governance of the social order. Steven Riess argues that as concerns about the effeminacy of American culture surfaced and urban reform movements grappled with perplexing social problems, many middle-class men came to embrace sport as a moral character builder and a mechanism to redefine and achieve a transformed masculinity during the late nineteenth century. Beginning in the 1890s women bicycled and played croquet, tennis, golf, and basketball, and shortly thereafter readied themselves for "socially acceptable" regional, national, and international competition.[32] Yet, as some women challenged the "separate spheres" ideology through sport, they encountered the long residual of institutionalized male cultural hegemony. As Donald Mrozek demonstrates, male physicians continued to see themselves as guardians of the moral and physical well-being of women, and used their privileged status to perpetuate traditional assumptions about female physical "propriety." Middle-class men insisted that women's entry into the public sphere to be therapeutic rather than self-expressive. Women who challenged this boundary risked being considered freakish Amazons. As Mrozek argues, public excellence in women's sport lay uncomfortably on the edge of middle-class respectability—women could be more energetic, but the actual opportunities for sportswomen depended on the battles outside the sport arena and inside the minds of men and women where sport was justified.[33]

Allen Guttmann's essay broaches the currently popular subject of body culture—how human beings conceive of themselves physically. Sport sociologists have led the way in showing how physical skill, body images, and body culture are special forms of "capital" and power. As Guttmann notes, scholars have only recently begun to uncover the taboo associations between sport and the erotic. Guttmann suggests that scholars should pay more attention to the ways in which participants and spectators enjoy the eroticism of athletic activity. Contemporary consumer capitalism has profitably exploited the eroticism of modern sport and, as a result, has brought many of these taboos out of the closet. In so doing, the marketeers of contemporary sport have effectively changed traditional notions of the ideal male and female bodies. Feminists often condemn such practices as men using female athletes for their own voyeuristic fantasies, and maintain that female athletes merely collaborate with patriarchal capitalism. Such criticisms fail, however, to deal with the fact that erotic sporting images proliferate in women's magazines, that women are attracted to male sport stars, or that everything is "objectified" in capitalist society.[34]

Class, Race, and Ethnicity

Since the early 1980s, sport historians have debated the relationship of social class to industrialization, urbanization, and modernization. Unlike their British peers, American sport historians' use of class has had a distinctly functionalist hue. The ghost of the Weberian modernizationist approach has precluded serious consideration of class as a social relationship rather than another "category." Sport historian Steven Riess reinforces this tendency in his recent survey of class in sport history. Pronouncing the "death" and marginality of Marxian class analysis to the field, Riess in a functionalist manner dismisses the important theoretical work of Richard Gruneau and John Hargreaves for its "lack" of empirical data and overreliance on "secondary" sources. Although focused on developments outside the United States, Gruneau and Hargreaves incorporated the theoretical insights of Marxists Raymond Williams and Antonio Gramsci to suggest how sport reflected the power relations of capitalism. Both argued that institutionalized sport tended to unify dominant groups and their supporters while disorganizing and fragmenting subordinate ones, whose sporting activities were ultimately subsumed under bourgeois auspices. Despite Riess's denial, these assumptions have become mainstream in the new approaches to the field. Moreover, without refuting this basic thesis, Riess reviews the literature on class and selectively offers praise for Alan Metcalfe, Richard Holt, Hardy, Elliott Gorn, and Roy Rosenzweig—all of whom openly acknowledged their debt to Marxian and neo-Marxian versions of class analysis.[35]

Despite current announcements of the death of "grand theories" like Marxism and postmodernism, most scholars continue to work within such larger paradigms. The relative paucity of theoretically informed work in American sport history speaks more to its practitioners' neglect of scholarly debates than to the inadequacy of such theoretical frameworks. Gorn and Oriard have recently encouraged sport historians to integrate concepts and approaches from the booming field of cultural studies. The fact that most have not is ironic, since cultural studies—the interdisciplinary analysis of history, cultural expression, and power—is exactly where the study of sport is most needed.[36]

Riess gives credit to the influential work of E. P. Thompson, Eric Hobsbawm, Herbert Gutman, and David Montgomery—all Marxist historians—for recognizing the importance of working-class involvement in American sports culture. He also acknowledges that "scholars have gone a long way in the past decade to recover the history, resiliency, and continuity of traditional sport, a sphere over which workers exercised nearly total agency."[37] In fact, Riess's statement—with references to resistance and human agency—could not have been conceptualized without the lingering influence of the "dead" Marxian grand theorists, nor could his admonition that scholars engage Hobsbawm's notion of "invented tradition" and the yet-to-be-explored issues of power and hegemony. Again, Riess simultaneously discounts the utility of Marxian theories of class analysis and elevates the concepts and issues derived from that approach as fruitful areas for future research.[38] This collection embraces his call for more explicit consideration of such topics.

The essays by Gorn, William Baker, and Gerald Gems have a decidedly working-class orientation. The history of middle- and upper-class sport has been ably documented, as Riess's article attests, yet the history of sport and the American working class remains a sideline venture.[39] Future accounts of workers and sport must address not only "bottom-up" perspectives but also workers' interactions with political structures and civil society.[40] For instance, to what extent did dominant political and cultural institutions promote anti-working-class sporting traditions? Did workers' acceptance of sport traditions, imbued with state or bourgeois ideologies, imply working-class acceptance and assimilation? Under what conditions did workers reject the preferred sport forms and ideas? When, if ever, did new sport forms emerge from the negotiation or struggle between working-class factions, or between workers and middle-class socialists?

Gorn explains how prizefighting began as a working-class ritual that dramatized toughness, prowess, and honor—principal features of an underclass masculine identity. Yet, as corporations and bureaucracies engulfed American social life, and immigration, the women's movement, and routinized, alienated labor eroded American male identities during the late nineteenth century, boxing was no longer a distinctly working-class sport; it was absorbed into the hegemonic culture and dramatized the dominant ideas of meritocracy, social mobility, and capitalist rationality. The transformation of boxing depended on the emerging widespread acceptance of "manly" sport by middle-class men. Gorn's essay comes closest to integrating the entire anthology's fundamental concepts. Drawing on folklore, anthropology, sociology, American studies, labor and social history, and gender studies, Gorn seeks to capture the layered and changing meanings that prizefighting had for its practitioners, fans, and opponents.

William Baker demonstrates how the 1932 American Communist Party's "Counter-Olympics" promoted a unique, alternative vision of sport within the larger scheme of conflicting economic and political loyalties that many workers confronted during the Depression. Baker presents clues from rare Communist sources to illuminate how the Labor Sports Union of America's Popular Front drew on a rich tradition of European working-class sport activism to protest bourgeois sport's exploitative, imperialist nature; racial segregation in sport; and the Western sport blockade against the Soviet Union. Ultimately, Communist sport activism netted only marginal results, not only because of the immigrant, "European" sport venue—track and field, gymnastics, and soccer—but also because of the hegemonic mainstream American sport culture.[41]

Immigrants' sporting experience differed from WASP Americans' due to their particular nationalities, social class, degree of acculturation, and concentration in large, crowded cities, where working-class people established ethnic subcommunities to sustain their cultural heritage amidst an alien environment. Despite the prominence of sport in nineteenth-century America, Gorn reminds us in the following chapter, most first-generation male immigrants were not terribly interested as spectators, and if they played a sport at all, it was more likely to be a game from their homeland. Second-generation young people, however, saw athletics as in his words a "powerful sense of belonging to the only culture they knew firsthand." Symbolically, sport provided a dual identity for millions of ethnic Americans. However, embracing the strenuous life was not without conflict; athletics pitted immigrants and their children against middle-class Americans who enlisted sport for urban social reform. Ethnic groups responded to capitalists' and social reformers' use of sport for assimilation by maintaining European sporting traditions that often challenged WASP conventions, such as Sunday sport and alcohol-accompanied athletic contests. Non-"American" sports like soccer, cricket, hurling, Gaelic football, and gymnastics preserved and reinforced ethnic cultural solidarity. German Turners, Czech Sokols, Polish Falcons, and other immigrant sport clubs maintained close ties to the nationalistic objectives of their parent countries, which often obstructed easy assimilation and sometimes clashed with the dominant social order.[42]

Peter Levine astutely situates the Jewish sporting experience in a nuanced understanding of twentieth-century American culture. Sport emerged as a "middle ground"—a complex cultural activity shaped by "interactions between generations of Jews as well as between ethnic and majority cultures that involved both the adaptation of traditional practices to new American settings and the transformation of American experiences into ethnic ways." This is precisely what Hardy means by long residuals. And, although Levine does not explicitly identify this process in terms of the struggle for cultural hegemony, the essential dynamics are clearly identified. In an unmistakable revisionist tone, he writes that "sport [as] both actual experience and as symbol, encouraged the active participation of immigrants and their children in shaping their own identities as Americans and as Jews." Clearly, then, sport was neither a tool for manipulating immigrants into American conformity nor a vehicle for social harmony and self-expression. It intersected with both ten-

sions and resolved them in often-contradictory ways. Levine develops this thesis by documenting how boxing uniquely countered the dominant anti-
Semitic stereotypes, defused ethnic tensions, and thereby validated Jewish athletes' American identity.[43]

The relationship between organized religion and working-class sport has
been asserted by historians but not subjected to careful scrutiny.[44] Gerald
Gems analyzes the conservative role of religion in working-class sport
through the career of Bishop Bernard J. Sheil and the Catholic Youth Organization. The CYO provided college scholarships, material goods, medical care,
and travel adventures to promote social mobility, and yet its sport programs
enabled workers to maintain a sense of class without provoking truculent
class consciousness during a volatile period in American history. Sheil deftly
brought working-class Catholic athletes closer to the mainstream by arguing
that religious sport programs had greater influence than class, race, or ethnic
alternatives.

With several noteworthy exceptions, the literature on African-Americans
and sport is dominated by biographies (and collective biographies) of prominent black athletes. Despite the works' generally high quality, the biographical tone has overshadowed needed social and cultural analysis, as well as a
more rigorous conceptualization of race and sport. In this sense, students of
black sport history have been reticent in relating their work to the larger field
of African-American studies. The general literature ably documents black exclusion from white sport but as yet fails to sufficiently analyze the negotiated
struggles between blacks and whites, or the ways in which black athletes were
differentiated from each other by color, class, religion, and political orientation. In other words, future explorations of the African-American sporting experience should transcend reliance on both race as an analytically sufficient
concept and the contributions of extraordinary black athletes, and begin to
think about how various other socially constructed categories have affected
this important dimension of American sport history. Although he disputes my
contention that biography has dominated the study of African-American athletes, the historian Jeffrey Sammons, whose partisan survey of the literature
reviews the field in its entirety, admits that "books on blacks and sport have
been overwhelmingly narrative, largely devoid of theory, rarely pathbreaking,
and often behind the curve." Earlier in his essay, Sammons further confirms
this basic point when he declares that "race is one of the most hotly debated
topics among scholars and one which should be addressed openly, directly, and
cautiously," and that any investigation of " 'race and sport' " that does not question the assumptions inherent in the term "race" "undermine[s] any attempt

to expand understanding of sport history and attract others to the field."[45] Such future research might usefully integrate the work of Lawrence Levine, Eugene Genovese, Leon Litwack, Herbert Gutman, Robin Kelley, and Roger Abrahams, among others.[46]

The journalist Nelson George's study of "black" basketball style suggests some fruitful new directions along such lines. George examines the development of the game from its white, Muscular Christian origins to the racial integration of the National Basketball Association, the contributions of both star and unsung players, and basketball's place in their history of race relations. George argues that innovative passing and dribbling, one-on-one challenges, and slam dunks represent the same "black aesthetic" as jazz and blues music—"individual virtuosity in an ensemble." Unlike its regimented, methodical white counterpart, black basketball, he writes, resonated with a "fluid, no-sweat attitude everybody called 'cool.' "[47]

Riess documents how, in the context of urbanization, blacks used sport along with the church, press, and politics to develop a sense of community in their neighborhoods and provide hopes for social mobility—however illusory—since most were unable to escape urban poverty and the ghetto.[48] Sport played a central role in this newfound black consciousness, but only at a time when political and social groups external to the community organized black sporting life with their own agendas in mind. Capitalists and social-settlement workers infused black-community sport with bourgeois notions of efficiency, worker loyalty, moral uplift, and civic responsibility, in direct opposition to indigent black street culture. This white-created sporting establishment for blacks was curtailed during the Depression due to financial exigencies, leaving a significant cadre of black sports activists with a structure within which they could create a legitimate black sporting establishment. Successful in such efforts, black Pittsburgh, for instance, was to sport what Harlem was to the black cultural renaissance.

Black athletes were forced to cautiously negotiate their inclusion into the white sports establishment. Prior to formal integration of professional and national amateur sport, blacks solidified cultural bonds between their communities and the American mainstream through athletic heroes. During the 1930s and 1940s, for instance, German fascism forced American whites to question their own moral integrity, leading them to elevate the accomplishments of Jesse Owens and Joe Louis as representatives of a tolerant society. Louis's appeal as a bona fide American sport hero ultimately reflected his ability to threaten neither race—thus, according to historians Dominic Capeci and Martha Wilkerson, pleasing various segments in American society who played on his prestige as a means to manipulate public behavior. Like Jackie Robinson, whose negotiation with lily-white major leagues precluded vocal opposition to the status quo, Louis, in the words of Capeci and Wilkerson, "emerged more hero than leader." His historical significance "lay in the symbolism he represented for black and white societies, their ideologies, their struggles, and their assurances of success." In other words, although Louis achieved unprecedented progress for black athletes, his "multifarious hero" status rested on a tacit acceptance of the dominant society.[49]

In addition to their capricious acceptance within white society, black athletes have always been subjected to racial theories of athletic superiority. Recognition of black foot speed runs throughout American sport history, as do questions about and explanations for why they are quicker than white athletes. As historian Stephen Fox has observed, given the power of black stereotypes to mold the thinking of both races, "the idea of black athletic superiority could offhandedly encourage the oldest, most harmful racial myths: the notions that black people were inherently stupid or lazy . . . [since] if blacks had inborn athletic advantages, then perhaps they won without training hard or thinking much, without truly earning their victories." Contemporary explanations provoke controversy, since the issue is framed simplistically: either blacks are inherently faster and springier, or they are spurred to athletic excellence by societal unfairness and the lack of options, or they work and think harder than lesser athletes. Surely all three are true to some degree, Fox concludes, "with the relative proportions varying so much as to render large generalizations impossible."[50]

David Wiggins reviews the political, scientific, and ideological bases that have informed various theories of an alleged relationship between race and athletic ability. Debates about black athletic prowess date back to the early sports world of the nineteenth century. Although omnipresent throughout the first half of the twentieth century, such debates have surged to the forefront of public awareness since the 1960s in the context of outstanding black Olympic performances and African-Americans' increased prominence in professional sport.

Wiggins's essay dramatizes the dangers of essentialist notions of race. "One of the most glaring aspects of the debate down through the years," he writes, has been "the divergent opinions and theories expressed not only between the black and white communities, but among the two groups themselves." The debate crescendoed during the 1980s when two well-known sport "authorities" dispensed orthodox (white) views on national television. In 1982 CBS sports commentator Jimmy "The Greek" Snyder sparked heated controversy when he suggested that physical differences account for athletic performance and related such racial differences to the breeding practices of slave owners. Five years later on ABC's "Nightline" news program, Los Angeles Dodgers vice president Al Campanis acknowledged that blacks were "outstanding athletes," "very God-gifted, and they're wonderful people. . . . They are gifted with great musculature and various other things. They're fleet of foot . . ." but "may not have some of the necessities to be, let's say, a field manager or perhaps a general manager" of a professional sports team.[51] Future studies, however, require scholars to reconcile such comments, however inflammatory, with similar statements made by African-American athletes and intellectuals. Not only did the distinguished Harvard psychiatrist Alvin F. Poussaint argue in 1972 that black men, stripped of their social power, focused their energies on other symbols of masculinity, particularly physical power, but also *Time* magazine discovered a near-consensus among black athletes (most notably O. J. Simpson, Arthur Ashe, and Joe Morgan) in its 1977 survey that physiological differences account for superior black athletic performance.

Markets and Audiences

Contemporary Americans are inundated with visions of the strenuous life. Specialized footwear, chic athletic wear, sport personalities, chiseled male and female "hard bodies," and pulsating sound tracks have become all-consuming images in the nation's cultural landscape. Basketball superstar Michael Jordan has perhaps the most recognized face in the world, just as Muhammad Ali's was twenty years ago. Nike's advertising campaigns capitalized on Jordan's disarming smile and good-guy image to quadruple the company's annual sales of footwear and increase its profits by 900 percent in eight years. Such popular ad campaigns peddle not only sporting goods but also lifestyles and social ideals. Nike's call for America (and the world) to "Just Do It" and tennis player Andre Agassi's declaration for Canon that "Image Is Everything" are cultural statements that reverberate not only in the locker room but throughout society.

Benjamin Rader situates these developments within a historically prescribed context—post–World War II consumerism, alienated labor, rationalized society, corporate sponsorship of fitness and wellness programs, and changing notions of the ideal male and female. Whereas the traditional strenuous life had focused on community imperatives, the new physical orientation of the "me decade" privileged the individual self. As people sought greater control over their lives and personal satisfaction, many turned to strict diets and vigorous exercise to project new socially approved visions of fitness—

tanned, sleek, lean, and muscular bodies, exuding energy, and assertiveness. Bolstered by advertising, rock videos, and film, the new strenuous image has become associated with upward mobility and erotic, physical attraction.[52]

Today most sports depend on purchased commodities. This is essentially a twentieth-century phenomenon. Commercial leisure firms created a mass national market by developing products and images that appealed to many classes and social groups. From the 1890s on, American corporate leaders, cooperating with other elites tied to the growth of national markets, transformed American culture from a republican, Protestant, production-oriented society of thrift and self-denial to a culture preoccupied with consumption, comfort, luxury, and acquisition. This fundamental shift in values and habits derived partially from the "therapeutic ethos," whereby sport entrepreneurs created and legitimized meanings and value for products—what several scholars have termed "cultural and symbolic capital." Moreover, mass production, mass distribution, and an integrated national market—essential for this type of culture—were products of advanced capitalist development.

Beginning in the late 1870s, an American sporting-goods industry emerged and promoted new types of equipment, brand recognition, and a new cultural aesthetic—the consumption of leisure. Although Americans continued to create their own sport, the rising consumer culture idealized the purchase of mass-produced commodities as a great human privilege and goal. Sporting-goods entrepreneurs not only marketed their wares, they also shaped the demand for special game forms through their involvement with nascent sport-governing organizations.[53]

Although the work was pioneered by John Rickard Betts, Stephen Hardy has undertaken more rigorous analysis of entrepreneurs and the sport marketplace. Hardy suggests that sport embodies game forms, services, and goods—and that these distinct components render simple definitions of "sport" hazardous. A handful of rules committees have historically controlled the game forms played by most people; a few manufacturers have supplied the goods at all levels of play; and a limited number of professional groups have established the guidelines for coaching, training, playing, and management techniques. Only by scrutinizing these basic production structures, Hardy argues, can we hope to understand how various sports developed along historically and culturally specific lines.

Allen Guttmann explores the complex subject of sport spectatorship—an important, neglected dimension riddled with contradictory trends, tendencies, and patterns. The section included in this volume is part of a larger, transhistorical study that examines sport spectators' class and gender identities, the actual and ideal motivations of spectatorship, and the types of behavior that have characterized spectators' role. Although we know a fair amount about the ways in which journalists created and reinforced spectatorship patterns, there is surprisingly little literature on the ways in which film and radio stirred visceral passions and extended audiences, and, by so doing, challenged the dominance of the print media during the 1920s and 1930s.[54] Television surpassed radio in the 1950s as the ultimate stage of mediated spectatorship. Televised sport not only elevated a new set of celebrities, it also supplied the action, suspense, and drama to market products, images, and lifestyles. The world's television networks recently paid a total of $633 million to broadcast the 1992 Olympic Games at Barcelona; and thanks to an audience of 3.5 billion consumers, a dozen multinational corporations paid $30 million each to secure worldwide rights for their products linked to the Olympics. International broadcasts via satellite, cable superstations, and pay-per-view television all thrive on sporting events. Yet, as Guttmann maintains, at the dawn of television, owners of sports franchises, international sports officials, and television networks failed to realize what the new medium could do for sport as a worldwide cultural institution.[55]

Pamela Cooper's case study of the New York City Marathon engages some of these crucial issues. She investigates how sport entrepreneur Fred Lebow single-handedly seized control of the emergent marathon event in the mid-1970s and transformed the race, while simultaneously securing widespread corporate sponsorship. Led by the New York Road Runners Club, the 1970s marathon movement incorporated all three of the components that Hardy identifies as constituting the "sport product"—reflecting the new managerial imperatives of advanced capitalism that united sport and economic production.[56] The marathon was marketed as a medically approved, clean-lifestyle activity to educated, upwardly mobile audiences, thus transforming the traditionally working-class sport. Cooper not only unearths a new topic in American sport history, she connects its growth to the exigencies of self-presentation in contemporary culture, and, by so doing, documents how one particular type of marathoning became the dominant style.

———

Now in its late adolescence, American sport history has abundant reasons to take pride in its accomplishments. The following essays are representative of the recent scholarship on sport and American society. Not all topics, sports, and viewpoints are included in this collection. Although the contributors do not collectively agree on theoretical and conceptual issues, their work suggests some common directions. Together they show the usefulness of casting the valuable and growing body of research into a new paradigm that emphasizes the relations and structures among class, culture, gender, race, ethnicity, and national identity in a more nuanced, dynamic fashion.

Notes

1. H. G. Bissinger, *Friday Night Lights: A Town, a Team, and a Dream* (New York, 1990). Both *Friday Night Lights* and *Hoop Dreams* are exceptions to the rule for most nostalgia-driven popular work—consequently, there continues to be a vast gap between what sport scholars do and what the larger public consumes and conceives of as "sport history."

2. Stephen Hardy, "Why We Can't Stop Watching the Boys Play Ball" (review of S. Fox, *Big Leagues: Professional Baseball, Football, and Basketball in National Memory*, 1994), *Boston Globe*, Oct. 30, 1994, B16.

3. See Thomas S. Kuhn, *The Structure of Scientific Revolutions* (Chicago, 1962); David Hollinger's review "T. S. Kuhn's Theory of Science and Its Implications for History," *American Historical Review* 78 (1973), 370–93; Gene Wise, *American Historical Explanations: A Strategy for Grounded Inquiry* (Minneapolis, 1980); Ian Tyrrell, *The Absent Marx: Class Analysis and Liberal History in Twentieth-Century America* (Westport, Conn., 1986); Peter Novick, *That Noble Dream: The "Objectivity Question" and the American Historical Profession* (New York, 1988); and Thomas Bender, *Intellect and Public Life: Essays on the Social History of Academic Intellectuals in the United States* (Baltimore, 1993).

Useful reviews of the "new" social and cultural history include Michael Kammen, ed., *The Past before Us: Contemporary Historical Writing in the United States* (Ithaca, N.Y., 1980); Oliver Zunz, ed., *Reliving the Past: The Worlds of Social History* (Chapel Hill, N.C., 1985); Lynn Hunt, ed., *The New Cultural History* (Berkeley, 1989); and Eric Foner, ed., *The New American History* (Philadelphia, 1990). The most recent synthesis of American sport history is Elliott J. Gorn and Warren Goldstein, *A Brief History of American Sports* (New York, 1993).

4. Frederick L. Paxson, "The Rise of Sport," *Mississippi Valley Historical Review* 4 (1917), 143–68. The other early major works are John A. Krout, *Annals of American Sport* (New Haven, Conn., 1929); and Jennie Holliman, *American Sports, 1785–1835* (1931; Philadelphia, 1975).

5. Lewis Mumford, *The Culture of Cities* (New York, 1938), 428–30. This interpretation was later refined by the influential avant-garde Frankfurt School and adopted by liberal commentators and scholars in the 1960s and 1970s—that sports and mass leisure were deceptive anodynes to counteract the boredom, oppressiveness, and meaninglessness of modern society. For the classic reviews of the Frankfurt School critique of mass culture, see Edward Shils, "Daydreams and

Nightmares: Reflections on the Criticism of Mass Culture," *Sewanee Review* 65 (1957), 587–608; Martin Jay, *The Dialectical Imagination* (New York, 1973); Christopher Lasch, *The Culture of Narcissism: American Life in an Age of Diminishing Expectations* (New York, 1979); and Frederic Jameson, "Reification and Utopia in Mass Culture," *Social Text* 1 (1979), 130–48.

6. Foster Rhea Dulles, *America Learns to Play: A History of Popular Recreation, 1607–1940* (New York, 1940); also see Frederick W. Cozens and Florence Scovil Strumpf, *Sports in American Life* (Chicago, 1953).

7. John Rickard Betts, "The Technological Revolution and the Rise of Sport, 1850–1900," *Mississippi Valley Historical Review* 40 (1953), 231–56. Betts's monograph, written during the 1950s–60s, was published posthumously as *America's Sporting Heritage, 1850–1950* (Reading, Mass., 1974). The state-of-the-art in business and technological history during the period was presented by Thomas C. Cochran and William Miller in *The Age of Enterprise: A Social History of Industrial America* (New York, 1942) and Samuel P. Hays in *The Response to Industrialism, 1885–1914* (Chicago, 1957). See John Higham's critique of consensus historiography in "The Cult of the 'American Consensus,' " *Commentary* 27 (1959), 93–100. For a succinct review of the early American Studies movement, see Gene Wise, " 'Paradigm Dramas' in American Studies," *American Quarterly* 31 (1979), 293–307.

8. For a review of early American social history, see Oliver Zunz, "The Synthesis of Social Change: Reflections on American Social History," in Zunz, ed., *Reliving the Past: The Worlds of Social History* (Chapel Hill, N.C., 1985), 53–114.

9. Two other noteworthy contributions to American sport history during the 1960s were Harold Seymour, *Baseball: The Early Years* (New York, 1960); and David Q. Voigt, *Baseball: From Gentlemen's Sport to the Commissioner System* (Norman, Okla., 1966).

10. Allen Guttmann, *From Ritual to Record: The Nature of Modern Sports* (New York, 1978); Richard D. Brown, *Modernization: The Transformation of American Life, 1600–1865* (New York, 1976). Thomas Bender explores the changing structure and meaning of community (in terms of the tensions between Gemeinschaft and Gesellschaft) in his elegant, concise *Community and Social Change in America* (Baltimore, 1978). For a valuable overview of Guttmann's work, see William J. Baker, "Touching All the Bases: The Record and Ritual of Allen Guttmann," *International Journal of the History of Sport* 8 (1991), 408–16. Melvin Adelman uses modernization theory to explain the structures of nineteenth-century sport in New York in his fine monograph *A Sporting Time: New York City and the Rise of Modern Athletics, 1820–1870* (Urbana, Ill., 1986). Moreover, the leading survey texts by Baker, Richard Mandell, and Benjamin Rader are written in this modernist vein.

11. See hardy's entry on sport in Peter Stearns, ed., *Encyclopedia of Social History* (New York, 1994), 714.

12. Even during its early days of popularity, modernization theory was rejected by many critics for its inherent Western ethnocentric vision of rationality

and progress, and for the ways in which social scientists used it to legitimize cold-war ideology and imperialism. Valuable critiques of modernization in historical scholarship can be found in Tony Judt, "A Clown in Regal Purple," *History Workshop* 7 (1979), 66–94; James A. Henretta, "Modernization: Toward a False Synthesis," *Reviews in American History* 5 (1977), 1293–1322; Christopher Lasch, "Just What the Doctor Ordered," *New York Review of Books,* December 1975; and Daniel Rodgers, "Tradition, Modernity, and the American Industrial Worker: Reflections and Critique," *Journal of Interdisciplinary History* 7 (1977), 655–81. For more sympathetic treatment of modernization's critics, see Peter N. Stearns, "Modernization and Social History: Some Suggestions and a Muted Cheer," *Journal of Social History* 14 (1980), 189–209, and Adelman, "Modernization and Its Critics," in Mary Kupiec Cayton et al., *The Encyclopedia of American Social History* (New York, 1993), vol. 1, 347–58.

13. Although Adelman recognized some of these deficiencies in his "Academicians and American Athletics" article, sociologist Richard Gruneau initiated the critique of modernization from a neo-Marxist perspective in "Freedom and Constraint: The Paradoxes of Play, Game and Sports," *Journal of Sport History* 7 (1980), 68–86, and later, in more developed form, in his "Modernization or Hegemony: Two Views of Sport and Social Development," in Jean Harvey and Hart Cantelon, eds., *Not Just a Game: Essays in Canadian Sport Sociology* (Ottawa, 1988), 9–32. See also Richard Holt, *Sport and the British: A Modern History* (Oxford, 1989), 357–67.

14. The most influential and synthetic work in U.S. history is Paul Boyer, *Urban Masses and Moral Order in America, 1820–1920* (Cambridge, Mass., 1978). For a perceptive, trenchant critique of the "social control" thesis, see Gareth Stedman Jones, "Class Expression Versus Social Control: A Critique of Recent Trends in the Social History of Leisure," *History Workshop* 4 (1977), 162–70.

Key works in American sport history within this approach include Benjamin G. Rader, "The Quest for Subcommunities and the Rise of American Sport," *American Quarterly* 29 (1977), 355–69; Cary Goodman, *Choosing Sides: Playgrounds and Street Life on the Lower East Side* (New York, 1979); Steven A. Riess, *Touching Base: Professional Baseball and American Culture in the Progressive Period* (Westport, Conn., 1980); Dominick Cavallo, *Muscles and Morals: Organized Playgrounds and Urban Reform, 1880–1920* (Philadelphia, 1981); Rader, *American Sports: From the Age of Folk Games to the Age of Spectators* (Englewood Cliffs, N.J., 1983); and Riess, *City Games: The Evolution of American Urban Society and the Rise of Sports* (Urbana, Ill., 1989). For critical reviews of this literature, see Stephen Hardy and Alan Ingham, "Games, Structures and Agency: Historians on the American Play Movement," *Journal of Social History* 17 (1983), 285–302, and Hardy, "Sport in Urbanizing America: An Historical Review," *Journal of Urban History* (1996), forthcoming.

15. The preliminary contours of this interpretation are sketched by Gruneau in "Power and Play in Canadian Social Development," *Working Papers in the Sociological Study of Sports and Leisure* (Kingston, Ont., 1979); Rob Beamish, "Sport and

movements existed throughout Europe during the 1920s and 1930s. See Robert
F. Wheeler, "Organized Sport and Organized Labour," *Journal of Contemporary
History* 13 (1978), 191–210; David A. Steinberg, "The Workers' Sport Internation-
als, 1920–28," *Journal of Contemporary History* 13 (1978), 233–51; John Hoberman,
Sport and Political Ideology (Austin, Tex., 1984), 177–89; and Jones, *Sport, Politics
and the Working Class.*

42. Works on immigrants and sport include Gerald Gems, "Sport and Cultural
Formation in Chicago, 1890–1940," (unpublished Ph.D. dissertation, University of
Maryland, 1989); Gems, "Not Just a Game," *Chicago History* 17 (1989), 4–21; Roy
Rosenzweig, *Eight Hours for What We Will* (New York, 1983); Rader, "The Quest for
Subcommunities"; Gerald Redmond, *The Caledonian Games in 19th-Century Amer-
ica* (Rutherford, N.J., 1971); Hardy, *How Boston Played;* Vincent, *Mudville's Revenge*;
Michael T. Isenberg, *John L. Sullivan and His America* (Urbana, Ill., 1988); Roberta
Park, "German Associational and Sporting Life in the Greater San Francisco Bay
Area, 1850–1900," *Journal of the West* 26 (1987), 47–64; Ralf Wagner, "Turner Soci-
eties and the Socialist Tradition," in Harmut Keil, ed., *German Workers' Culture in
the United States, 1850–1920* (Washington, D.C., 1988); Gary Ross Mormino, "The
Playing Fields of St. Louis: Italian Immigrants and Sport, 1925–1941," *Journal of
Sport History* 9 (1982), 5–16; and Richard Sorrell, "Sports and Franco-Americans in
Woonsocket, 1870–1930," *Rhode Island History* 31 (1972), 117–26.

43. Levine's quote comes from the introduction to his *Ellis Island to Ebbets Field:
Sport and the American Jewish Experience* (New York, 1992), 7, from which his contribution to this volume is excerpted. See also Riess, "The Jewish-American Boxing Experience, 1890–1940," *American Jewish History* 74 (1985), 223–54.

44. Nobody has yet given historical shape to the uneven pattern of conflict
and accommodation that produced the marriage of religion and sport. See
Michael Novak, *The Joy of Sports: End Zones, Bases, Baskets, Balls, and the Consecra-
tion of the American Spirit* (New York, 1976); Shirl Hoffman, ed., *Sport and Religion*
(Champaign, Ill., 1992); and William J. Baker, *Washed in the Blood: Religion and the
Rise of Sport* (New York, forthcoming).

45. Sammons, " 'Race' and Sport: A Critical, Historical Examination," *Journal
of Sport History* 21 (1994), 203–78; his critique of my review of John M. Carroll's
Fritz Pollard: Pioneer in Racial Advancement (*Journal of Sport History* 19, 1992,
266–68) appears on pp. 253–54; his quotes included above are on pp. 254, 255 of
that essay.

46. Lawrence Levine, *Black Culture and Black Consciousness: Afro-American Folk
Thought from Slavery to Freedom* (New York, 1977); Eugene Genovese, *Roll, Jordan,
Roll: The World the Slaves Made* (New York, 1974); Leon Litwack, *Been in the Storm
So Long: The Aftermath of Slavery* (New York, 1979); Herbert Gutman, *The Black
Family in Slavery and Freedom* (New York, 1976); Roger Abrahams, *Singing the Mas-
ter: The Emergence of African-American Culture in the Plantation South* (New York,
1992); Robin Kelley, " 'We Are Not What We Seem': Rethinking Black Working-

Class Opposition in the Jim Crow South," *Journal of American History* 80 (1993), 75–112; and Kelley, *Race Rebels: Culture, Politics, and the Black Working Class* (New York, 1994).

For recent surveys of the social history of African-Americans, see the Daniel C. Littlefield and Quintard Taylor contributions in Cayton et al., *Encyclopedia of American Social History*, 811–54; and Darlene Clark Hine, ed., *The State of Afro-American History: Past, Present, and Future* (Baton Rouge, 1986).

47. George, *Elevating the Game: Black Men and Basketball* (New York, 1992). Also see Jeff Grenfield, "The Black and White Truth About Basketball," *Esquire*, October, 1975, 170–71, 248; David Leviathan, "The Evolution and Commodification of Black Basketball Style," *Radical History Review* 55 (1993), 154–64; Ronald Rodano, "Jazz, Modernism, and the Black Creative Tradition," *Reviews in American History* 21 (1993), 671–78; and compare with Burton Perreti's *The Creation of Jazz: Music, Race, and Culture in Urban America* (Urbana, Ill., 1992).

48. Riess, *City Games*, 93–123.

49. Dominic Capeci and Martha Wilkerson, "Multifarious Hero: Joe Louis, American Society and Race Relations During World Crisis, 1935–1945," *Journal of Sport History* 10 (Winter 1983), 5–25.

50. Fox, *Big Leagues*, 316, 347.

51. See Phillip M. Hoose, *Necessities: Racial Barriers in American Sports* (New York, 1989).

52. Harvey Green, *Fit for America: Health, Fitness, Sport and American Culture* (Baltimore, 1986); Dyreson, "The Emergence of Consumer Culture and the Transformation of Physical Culture: American Sport in the 1920s," *Journal of Sport History* 16 (1989); and Hardy, " 'Adopted by All the Leading Clubs': Sporting Goods and the Shaping of Leisure, 1800–1900," in Butsch, ed., *For Fun and Profit*, 71–101.

53. On sports journalism, see Betts, *The American Sporting Heritage;* Oriard, *Reading Football;* and Baker, "Press Games: Sportswriters and the Making of American Football," *Reviews in American History* 22 (1994), 530–37. Patrick Trimble analyzes early sports films in "Babe Ruth: The Media Construction of a 1920s Personality," in Pope and R. Moss, eds., "Sport and Leisure in North America," *Colby Quarterly* (special issue), spring 1996, forthcoming.

54. On television and sport, see Benjamin Rader, *In Its Own Image: How Television Has Transformed Sports* (New York, 1984); Joan Chandler, *Television and National Sport: The United States and Britain* (Urbana, Ill., 1988); Ron Powers, *Supertube: The Rise of Television Sports* (New York, 1984); Jim Spence and Dave Diles, *Up Close and Personal: The Inside Story of Network Television Sports* (New York, 1988); and Randy Roberts and James Olson, *Winning Is the Only Thing: Sports in America Since 1945* (Baltimore, 1989), 95–131.

55. See Alfred Chandler, *The Visible Hand: The Managerial Revolution in American Business* (Cambridge, Mass., 1977).

56. The classic text of this development is Christopher Lasch, *The Culture of Narcissism: American Life in an Age of Diminishing Expectations* (New York, 1979); see also Jeremy Howell, "Meanings Go Mobile: Fitness, Health and the Quality of Life Debate in Contemporary America" (Ph.D. dissertation, University of Illinois, 1990), and Howell, " 'A Revolution in Motion': Advertising and the Politics of Nostalgia," *Sociology of Sport Journal* 8 (1991), 258–71.

PART 1
NATIONAL
CULTURE

1

Sports through the Nineteenth Century

ELLIOTT J. GORN

Sports as we know them are a very recent phenomenon. Not until the end of the nineteenth century did many of the features we take for granted become part of sports. Indeed, our usage of the word is rather new. In the eighteenth century, "sport" would more likely have been used in a phrase like "sporting man," or an individual might have been called a "sport." Both terms were less than flattering, for an individual so designated was likely a rake, a gambler, a man who lived by his wits. By 1900, however, "sports" connoted athletic games played by professionals or highly trained amateurs under clearly spelled-out rules with masses of paying spectators cheering their favorites in specially built stadia. Events themselves were now supported by businesses or institutions (the National League, the sporting-goods firm of A. G. Spalding and Brothers, Yale University, the National Collegiate Athletic Association, for example), reported in mass-circulation newspapers, and evaluated with statistics. So severed from their folk origins had sports become that one game—basketball—had no past at all; it was simply made up in 1891 by one James Naismith, who worked at the Young Men's Christian Association Training School in Springfield, Massachusetts, as a way to keep athletes in shape between the baseball and football seasons. This essay will trace the transformation of sports from folk games to modern spectacles.

The British Heritage

British colonists seem to have played mainly the games they remembered from their ancestral homeland. Of course North America was not "virgin land"; hundreds of thousands of Indians inhabited the continent. Eastern woodland tribes, for example, played a game colonists called stickball ("lacrosse" for the French), yet the British seem not to have adopted this or other Indian games. Perhaps they felt a need to keep intact all of their folkways in this strange land; and perhaps the Indian game was too alien to them, surrounded as it was by the various tribes' customs and observances. After all, Indians often played stickball and other games within a context of sacred dancing, chanting and drumming, shamanism, dietary restrictions, body painting, pipe smoking, and other ritual practices, all part of a distinct religious worldview.

The English played various games on the eve of colonization, and they held a range of opinions as to the proper place of recreation. No single game was typical, but Richard Carew's description of "hurling" in Cornwall at the beginning of the seventeenth century gives us a sense of what was possible. The countryside for miles around could be the playing field, and the teams consisted of entire parishes:

> Some two or more Gentlemen do commonly make this match, appointing that on such a holyday, they will bring to such an indifferent place, two, three, or more parishes of the East or South quarter, to hurle against so many other, of the West or North. Their goales are either those Gentlemens houses, or some towns or villags, three or four miles asunder, of which either side maketh choice after the neernesse to their dwellings. When they meet, there is neyther comparing of numbers, nor matching of men: but a silver ball is cast up, and that company, which can catch, and cary it by force, or sleight, to their place assigned, gaineth the ball and victory.

To gain the victory, however, men subjected themselves to brutal competition:

> Whosoever getteth seizure of this ball, findeth himself generally pursued by the adverse party; neither will they leave, till . . . he be laid flat on Gods deare earth. . . . The Hurlers take their next way over hilles, dales, hedges, ditches; yea, and thorow bushes, briers, mires, plashes and rivers whatsoever; so as you shall sometimes see 20 or 30 lie tugging together in the water, scrambling and scratching for the ball. . . . (*The Quest for Excitement: Sport and Leisure in the Civilizing Process*. Edited by Norbert Elias and Eric Dunning [1986])

Whichever team carried the ball to its goal—a church, a manor, a parish seat—won the game.

Note that no restrictions on team size existed, that the playing field was the entire countryside for miles around, and that parish membership determined who played on each team. As Carew described it, the game was singularly violent, and such contests no doubt became ready opportunities to settle old personal grudges or larger community rivalries. Gentlemen arranged the matches, and they undoubtedly offered prizes for the winners, along with a feast for all after the game. These were great men, local nobility or gentry, patrons in the community, whose largesse helped secure the loyalty of their baseborn neighbors. Such games were a social glue, binding men together despite an intensely hierarchical social system. Carew added that hurling helped prepare men for war, for the game required that players know the terrain and anticipate their opponents' movements in order to ambush them. He concluded that hurling "put courage into their hearts, to meet an enemie in the face"; but while the game gave men fortitude, it also left them with bloody heads, broken bones, and injuries that might shorten their days. Though Carew did not mention it, hurling left them with something else—a sense of manhood. Sports like this one seem to have been primarily part of male culture. Implicitly, they defined masculinity—aggressiveness, courage, competitiveness—against femininity. This elemental conception of maleness characterized most sports through the nineteenth century.

Carew wrote his description just as popular recreations were becoming a controversial topic. On the one hand, there was the Renaissance tradition, which celebrated England's national love of play. But on the other , there was the rising tide of Puritanism, a theology suspicious of all worldly pleasures that threatened to divert people from their personal confrontation with God. Just when Jamestown, Plymouth, and Boston were settled the controversy boiled over. King James I issued his "Book of Sports" (1618) to reassure his subjects that the crown still approved of their old entertainments:

> Our pleasure likewise is, Our good people be not disturbed, letted, or discouraged from any lawful recreation, Such as dancing, either of men or women, Archery for men, leaping, vaulting, or any other such harmlesse, Recreation, nor from having of May Games, Whitson Ales, and Morrisdances, and the setting up of Maypoles, and other sports. . . . (quoted in Robert W. Malcolmson, *Popular Recreations in English Society, 1700–1850* [New York, 1973], 7)

The "Book of Sports" was a rebuke to the Puritans who insisted that the Sabbath must be spent solely in prayer and quiet introspection. Puritans responded that the very recreations the king praised led away from God to superstition and idolatry, to sin and wickedness. So powerful were the Puritans in many parishes that they refused to promulgate the king's decree. They enforced their pious Sabbath, and also banned as "corrupt" and "pagan" the festivals and saints' days of the Catholic and Anglican calendars.

The middle decades of the seventeenth century saw the triumph of Puritanism under Oliver Cromwell, then its demise during the Restoration of the monarchy. The ideological battles fought in England were part of the heritage of those who initially settled the British colonies. Some who migrated were champions of Puritan piety, but others bore the tradition of country recreations, of feast days, cockfights, and ball games.

Early American Sports

In the Old World and the New, Puritans (or Calvinists) were suspicious of excessive worldly joys. Those who envisioned godly communities in the wilderness found human nature inherently untrustworthy, too much leisure dangerous, and work a holy endeavor. Sober religious folk were determined to keep amusements hedged within useful and moderate bounds, which threatened to constrict until they contained nothing at all. Yet others shaped their visions of the New World by the age-old ideal of a leisured paradise. These individuals dreamed of a toilless and bountiful life, and the English heritage of fairs, feast days, and sports became the palpable expression of the leisure ethic. The seeming boundlessness of the New World stirred their imaginations.

All of England's North American colonies inherited the dual-leisure tradition. Many colonial Virginians held Calvinist beliefs in original sin, predestination, and election; many came from pious middle-class stock. On the other hand, the Massachusetts Bay Colony was plagued by people who rejected Puritan hegemony, and by individuals who would rather play than work. But as a general rule, austerity was stronger in the North, while leisure found fuller expression in the South.

Early Virginia was disproportionately settled by men, and a boom in tobacco growing in the 1620s gave the colony the raucous tone of a mining camp. Drinking, gambling, and many of the pastimes of Old England flourished; with social status unclear and land abundant and unfenced, hunting, fishing, and fowling, sports of the privileged back home, could be enjoyed by all. Within a generation, however, a gentry elite had established itself. Often from well-off families, these men controlled the labor of others through a system of indentured servitude, followed by black chattel slavery. By 1700, the southern colonies constituted a highly stratified society, with a planter elite that styled itself after the English country gentry, a middling group of white farmers, and a large body of black slaves.

The early boom economy, with its lack of settled domestic life, encourage men's willingness to follow bouts of hard moneymaking with interludes of abandon. Later, the rhythms of the plantation, of sowing, tending, and harvesting, encouraged alternating periods of work and idleness rather than regular sustained labor. As the colony settled into a stable, highly stratified pattern late in the seventeenth century, the old English leisure ideal well served Virginia's social alignments. Men in this environment worked hard, but not with the Puritans' regularity, diligence, or sense of the transcendent godliness of labor. For the gentry on both sides of the Atlantic, to celebrate leisure, especially to do so with enormous wagers, was a way to identify themselves as members of a distinct ruling class, regardless of the poverty or ruthless competitiveness of their ancestors.

So several factors came together by the beginning of the eighteenth century to help make play a dominant southern value: the English leisure heritage, the erosion of the Calvinist notion of calling among the most influential men in the South, and the rise of the rural gentry to ruling-class status. But one more element was crucial. Black chattel slavery drove the final wedge between labor and leisure. How could men value hard work unequivocally once labor was inextricably associated with degraded, servile blacks? How pretend that work was ennobling, character-forming, even sanctified in a society whose hardest workers were seen as dangerous, half-civilized heathens, capable of nothing but brutish tasks?

For all of these reasons, sports and games became a major preoccupation in Virginia and the other southern colonies. Games and amusements were important to all classes, but by the end of the seventeenth century, the gentry had the time, motivation, and means for great displays of consumption and conviviality. As class lines became distinct during the new century, roughly two or three hundred tidewater families constituted Virginia's aristocracy. Knit together by kinship ties, they shared a gracious life in which leisure lay at the heart of their class style and identity. Horse racing, cockfighting, and hunting were the great gentry passions. Men also eagerly participated in boating, wrestling, fencing, quoits (something like horseshoes), bowling, and cudgeling (fighting with long sticks).

Educated in England like so many young colonial men, the rich and accomplished William Byrd II (1674–1744), for example, participated in the whole panoply of English sporting customs on his enormous family estate at Westover early in the eighteenth century. He played billiards, laid out a bowling green, competed in cricket, ninepins, and skittles. Wealthy Virginians like Byrd seized every opportunity for merrymaking, including dancing, partying, or gambling over a sociable bottle. Religion and law now buttressed rather than assailed these practices. Ministers of the Anglican church, whose congregations often depended on the patronage of local gentry, offered little resistance to the ethic of leisure, while county courts recognized gambling debts as legally enforceable.

Timothy H. Breen has demonstrated how a horse race among the Virginia gentry facilitated great displays of wealth, personal honor, and patriarchal prestige. The "merry-dispos'd gentlemen" of Hanover County who celebrated Saint Andrews Day in the 1730s with quarter-horse races did so to cultivate social solidarity, vent their competitiveness, and enjoy each other's company. Spectators could observe their betters, provided they "behave themselves with Decency and Sobriety, the Subscribers being resolved to discountenance all Immorality with the utmost Rigour." As Breen points out, however, what made horse races so central to southern culture was the dramatic tension between control and abandon. On the one hand, events should be orderly, reflecting the good harmony of the new society; they should be moderate, not leading men to licentiousness or excess; and they should not become too distracting from productive endeavors. But on the other hand, sport as a vehicle for displays of prowess, wealth, and status encouraged men to compete recklessly, to drink, gamble, and assert themselves as if their very social position, even their masculinity, were in question. Time and again, governors and legislators inveighed against the disorderliness that accompanied horse races, but this failed to stop men from impulsively betting entire fortunes on a single race.

Before long, the southern gentry was building English-style circular tracks; importing thoroughbred horses; retaining breeders, trainers, jockeys, and stablemen (often blacks); and generally making racing a central symbol of upper-class life. The gentry, however, did not monopolize popular recreations. Various groups might mingle at a single event. Just as in the example of hurling by Richard Carew, great men would initiate contests and lesser ones would receive their largesse. Thus Elkanah Watson described a raucous cockfight in Southampton County, Virginia, at which there were "many genteel people, promiscuously mingled with the vulgar and debased" (*Men and Times of the Revolution; or, Memoirs of Elkanah Watson*, edited by Winslow C. Watson, 2d ed. [1856], pp. 300–301).

Yet on other occasions, events were more segregated. Observed Philip Vickers Fithian one Easter, "Negroes now are all disbanded till Wednesday morning and are at Cock Fights through the County"; a week later he noticed "a ring of Negroes at the Stable, fighting cocks" (*Journal and Letters of Philip*

Vickers Fithian, 1773–1774, edited by Hunter Dickinson Farish, new ed. [1957], pp. 91, 96). Blacks even continued some of the games of Africa in the slave quarters. Moreover, poor and middling whites claimed leisure space for themselves. They held their own races, cockfights, and bear baits; they hunted and fished for pleasure as well as game; they even staged their own ferocious, eye-gouging battles. Nonregular working rhythms of plantations, farms, and market towns enabled individuals to find time for such activities. The hours taken in the middle of work could expand to days for annual events such as the "Public Times," held every spring and fall for court and assembly sessions at the county seats. Mid-eighteenth-century Williamsburg, for example, grew to three times its normal population during these events, as individuals watched or participated in horse races, plays, dancing, fiddling, acrobatics, wrestling, and other pleasures.

Whether describing them as leisure-loving or lazy, many commentators have declared that southerners developed a distinct regional ethic, one that rejected labor as the all-consuming goal of life. When they esteemed commerce and enterprise at all, it was less because piling up wealth contained religious or moral value than because productivity facilitated the good life. While gentlemen-planters were not a hereditary aristocracy, they took their cue from great landed Englishmen, embracing sociability, gracious living, and personal polish as core values. Conspicuous consumption rather than rational savings was the hallmark of the region, because displays of luxury and fine living were markers of a man's status in society. Above all, we must not view the southern ethic as aberrant or unique. Irregular working rhythms, conspicuous display, love of finery, and games and sports all had deep roots in Western cultures. The compulsion to work steadily and regularly, to make leisure a subordinate value accepted only for its ability to increase one's capacity for labor, and to divide work and play into separate, compartmentalized realms were the novel ideas.

The settlers of New England and the middle colonies were also heirs to the dual-leisure tradition. Yet the North proved a more austere climate for traditional recreations. About 1627, Thomas Morton, a renegade from Puritan society, led a band of like-minded settlers to the edge of Plymouth Colony, and there defied his pious neighbors. William Bradford (1590–1657), governor of Plymouth, accused Morton of atheism and paganism—categories that Puritans tended to conflate. Bradford described the renegades' revels: "They also set up a maypole, drinking and dancing about it many days together, inviting the Indian women for their consorts, dancing and frisking together like so many fairies, or furies, rather . . . as if they had anew revived and celebrated the feasts of the Roman goddess Flora, or the beastly practices of the mad

Baccanalians" (*Of Plymouth Plantation: 1620–1647,* edited by Samuel Eliot Morison [1952], pp. 205–6). Morton taunted his Pilgrim neighbors, and they finally responded; in 1628 they cut down the maypole, arrested Morton for selling arms to the Indians, and shipped him back to England in irons.

Generally, however, conflicts over popular recreations took less dramatic forms. In 1621, Bradford had to deal with some new settlers who objected to working on Christmas Day (the Pilgrims of Plymouth, indeed, the Puritans in general, considered Christmas celebrations part of the pagan hangover of the Catholic church). The governor decided not to force these people to work against their consciences, but when he and the others returned from their labors that day; they found the newcomers "in the street at play, openly; some pitching the bar, and some at stool-ball, and such like sports." Bradford took away their sporting toys, not because they played, but because they did so openly: "If they made the keeping of it (Christmas) a matter of devotion, let them keep their houses; but there should be no gaming or revelling in the streets" (p. 97). At least the appearance of a godly community would remain, and the diligent not be tempted from their labor.

Dissenting Protestants, Puritans among them, did not object to all recreations. They allowed innocent amusements like simple ball games, played in moderation; hunting and fishing provided food; martial sports like cudgeling or swordplay taught skills useful to the defense of the settlements; sociable activities like cornhuskings, or spinning or quilting bees, were encouraged. But they drew the line at recreations that violated the Sabbath, encouraged passion, or smacked of the old pagan excesses. The true test of recreations was their usefulness; proper leisure helped people live righteously by serving useful ends, ends that included refreshing them for work. Thus, even as he condemned profane or promiscuous dancing, Increase Mather stated, "The Prince of Philosophers has observed truly, that Dancing and Leaping, is a natural expression of joy; So that there is no more Sin in it, than in laughter, or any outward expression of inward Rejoycing" ("An Arrow Against Profane and Promiscuous Dancing," [1684] excerpted in Perry Miller and Thomas Johnson, *The Puritans: A Sourcebook of Their Writings,* vol. 2 [1938], p. 411).

This spirit of moderation grew out of the Puritans' dominant theology, Calvinism. After the fall from Eden, they believed, all humankind was tainted with sin. In his mercy, God, through Christ, saved a small number from eternal damnation. In other words, the Lord had predetermined the fate of all people, saving a few for reasons only He understood, damning the rest. Since their fates were predestined, it followed that earthly efforts had no impact on people's futures. Nor could one know for sure whether one was among the elect. Still, through constant self-scrutiny, an individual might discover evidence of Christ's grace. Leading an upright life according to God's laws was a sign—albeit a tenuous one—of salvation.

For the Puritans, an upright life meant far more than merely observing ritual forms. Their idea of "calling"—that laboring diligently in one's worldly occupation was a religious observation—infused daily business life with religious significance. The hardworking farmer or tradesman did the Lord's bidding as surely as the writer of sermons. Work was pleasing to God and it followed that success in one's earthly endeavors might just be a sign of inner grace. But even while individuals strove to succeed in the world, they must never overvalue the material fruits of success. Signs of salvation, not the good life, were what one sought in pursuing one's calling. Even as men's labor bore fruit, they must never cherish the comforts of life; their eyes must always be on the Lord. Above all, the bond between piety and labor meant that play could never be unequivocally valued in its own right. Whereas southern life turned men away from seeing work as a transcendent value, northerners eyed leisure with suspicion.

It would be a mistake, however, to interpret northern ideas about sports, play, and leisure purely from the Puritan viewpoint. A more accurate depiction would see this cluster of Protestant ideas as a presence that sometimes dominated the northern colonies, sometimes was challenged by less-than-pious groups, but always made itself felt. In Massachusetts and New England, but also among the Dutch Calvinists of New York and the Quakers of Pennsylvania, ideas like calling and worldly asceticism tempered people's commitment to play. Moreover, the Protestant ethic did not simply fade with the seventeenth century, but rather washed over communities in successive waves. The various religious awakenings that swept through people's lives from the mid-eighteenth through the early nineteenth centuries always contained a powerful element of Protestant self-control, an austerity that cast suspicious glances at those too immersed in the passions of the world. Indeed, even a deist and man of the world like Benjamin Franklin could not escape the earnest spirit of improvement, the suspicion of frivolity, that was his Protestant heritage.

Nonetheless, the English leisure tradition survived in the North: neither harsh frontier conditions nor Puritan hegemony obviated pleasures of the flesh. Crossroads taverns, community gatherings like elections or muster days, and marketing times tied to rural life were all loci of traditional games. What failed to emerge out of the old folkways was an ethos of leisure conferring social rewards, a cultural challenge to the Puritan work ethic, a way of life like that of the southern gentry which assumed that humans worked to play rather than played so they might work.

One exception to this rule emerged in the eighteenth century in cities like Boston, New York, and Philadelphia. Here an urban gentry began to form, consisting partly of British colonial officials and military officers, partly of newly prosperous merchants, and partly of men of landed wealth who lived and governed from the city. In Philadelphia, for example, such a group rivaled the pious Quakers in political clout. The Philadelphia gentry forged group identity through common membership in such organizations as the Mount Regal Fishing Club, the Dancing Assembly, the Gloucester Hunting Club, and the Jockey Club. In New York, too, balls, plays, dances, horse races, and cockfights were important venues where the new urban elite came to identify with each other. But not only the elites of growing cities were active in leisure pursuits. Tavern keepers, to attract customers, tradesmen and laborers among them, became pioneer promoters of recreations. They provided dart boards and bowling greens; they brought bulls and bears to confront pit bulls; they built rings for cockfights; and they held the stakes for various forms of gambling. By the mid-eighteenth century, then, cities were becoming the focus of a whole new realm of leisure. Here, where individuals were most oriented to the marketplace, recreations took their first steps toward commercialization.

Perhaps it is best to speak of various sporting heritages during the colonial era. By the last quarter of the eighteenth century, sporting events at their most organized might attract a few thousand spectators, rich and poor, mostly white, mostly male, watching thoroughbreds, for example, race for high stakes. Such an event would likely pit two local elites against each other, would be held on a track with grandstands built by a rich jockey club, would even be an annual occasion. But at the other extreme, and certainly more common, would be events centered in the countryside and small towns, where the vast bulk of the population lived. Most common were activities like hunting and fishing, where leisure and labor cannot even be distinguished from each other. The most likely form of "sport" might be simple ball games, played according to uncodified rules with available equipment in pastures or clearings. Folk games and recreations were part of communal preindustrial life; they grew out of face-to-face relationships, and expressed the tensions and cohesiveness of particular localities.

The Antebellum Era

In June 1802, the grand jury sitting in Philadelphia received a petition against Hart's racecourse, a local institution: "This English dissipation of horseracing may be agreeable to a few idle landed gentlemen, who bestow more care in training their horses than educating their children, and it may be amusing to British mercantile agents, and a few landed characters in Philadelphia; but it is in the greatest degree injurious to the mechanical and manufacturing interest, and will tend to our ruin if the nuisance is not removed by your patriotic exertions" (quoted in John Thomas Scharf and Thompson Westcott, *History of Philadelphia 1609–1884* [1884], p. 940). The petition was signed by 1,500 mechanics and 1,200 manufacturers, which in that era generally meant craftsmen who worked in their homes or shops with the aid of families and perhaps an apprentice or journeyman.

The petition was filled with code words: Dissipated idle gentlemen who train horses rather than educate their children will ruin manufacturers without the jury's patriotic exertions. Here is a classic example of republican ideology, that set of ideas that helped drive the colonies to rebel against England, and to form a virtuous commonwealth. On one side, the idleness and dissipation of merchants and landed characters; on the other side, producers motivated by the spirit of hard work. Selfishness, luxury, corruption, in the republican lexicon, versus self-restraint, virtue, communal improvement. The racetrack became a symbol of a serious social and ideological schism.

Sports and leisure, as we have seen, had always had a conflicted history. During the revolutionary era, the Continental Congress outlawed games, sports, the theater, all of the usual amusements, as unfit for a virtuous people embarking on independence. Horse racing returned after the war, but the problem of proper versus improper amusement sharpened during the nineteenth century. The old republican tradition that had emphasized individual self-restraint in the name of communal welfare lived on long after the revolution. But as American society increasingly came under the sway of capitalism and the liberal ideology that accompanied it, sports and leisure were not immediately liberated from old prejudices. On the contrary, the newfound freedom of Americans to transact business during the antebellum era was accompanied by singularly stern cultural strictures that demanded rigid adherence to tough rules of personal conduct.

Historians have documented a transformation in the American economy that occurred largely during the first half of the nineteenth century. Agricultural production shifted from an orientation toward semi-subsistence and local consumption to market production. Especially with the opening of new lands, the development of inland waterways, and the building of new transportation systems, increasing numbers of farmers produced staples that they sold in national and international markets. Even more important for our purposes, cities burgeoned as centers of trade and manufacturing, while the methods of making goods were transformed. Machine production was part of this process, as was the increasing concentration of productive property in fewer hands, and the growing pull of the marketplace.

The Philadelphia petitioners against Hart's racecourse represented the old, preindustrial economy, in which apprentices learned a trade, and, with luck, finally became skilled master craftsmen and proprietors of their own shops. This system was part of a household economy that produced goods for local markets. Work and family were often contiguous: apprentices lived in the master's houses, family members labored alongside the head of the household, and this patriarchal extended family was seen as the font of public order.

The new system was much more recognizably part of the modern capitalist order. Old words like apprentice and journeyman hung on, but working relationships were transformed: employers paid wages or piece rates (as low as they could get away with) to individuals who sold their labor for as much as they could command. Trades were rationalized, the size of firms expanded, and the possibilities of workers ever becoming independent property owners diminished. One tendency that accompanied these changes was the destruction of old craft skills; it was to owners' advantage to break down the production process into simple tasks that required cheap, easily replaceable workers. Moreover, entrepreneurs now found themselves much less burdened with fellow feeling for their employees; young workers lived in boardinghouses until they married and started their own families. The new order was based far less on customary or paternalistic relationships, much more on contractual ones.

This new organization of society—of productive relationships—had ideological implications. The old Protestant ethic was very serviceable in the new order. Protestantism's emphasis on stable, sober, dependable behavior was useful to a society whose organization of work increasingly demanded time, thrift, and intense specialization of tasks. Sheer productivity for its own sake had religious sanction, while landlords, speculators, and merchants were sometimes seen as manipulators of markets, accumulators who produced nothing while living extravagantly. For the new middle class, delayed gratification and moral certitude were the cornerstones of society. The economies and social relationships in different parts of the country were not all transformed at once; but the total result, certainly by the middle of the nineteenth century, was a thoroughly changed society. By then, national markets, mass print media, telegraphy, steamships, railroads, voluntary associations, and, above all, a powerful consensus of values bound most white, northern, Protestant middle-class Americans together. For want of a better term, we can label the ascendant national culture that accompanied social and economic change Victorian.

Like the Puritans, Victorians would never argue that wealth was a sure sign of moral worth, but they did believe in a connection, or in the sociologist Max Weber's term, an "elective affinity" between prosperity and good morals. Capitalists and Evangelicals—often the same people—feared idleness, craved regularity, practiced self-control, and idealized usefulness. The millennial hopes of preachers, the belief in eternal life, in spiritual perfectibility, were as real to the saints as the profits that accrued from temperance, thrift, and hard work. Choosing Christ and controlling social stress were part of a single process; converting employees saved souls and secured a reliable labor force; establishing urban missions helped prepare for the millennium and assured a stable business climate. Business and religion were bound together with an earnest tone of moral certitude.

Victorianism, again like Puritanism, contained seeds of repression for popular recreations. Whereas for the Puritans a sociable dram or a local lottery for a good cause were acceptable, the new Evangelicals often condemned such practices as sinful, insisting on an unprecedented level of asceticism. Virtually every recreational outlet was condemned at one time or another, from cockfighting to checkers, from horse racing to croquet. All leisure activities potentially fostered the evils of drinking, gambling, swearing, idleness, and Sabbath breaking. Declared a Congregational magazine, the *New Englander,* in 1851, "Let our readers, one and all, remember that we were sent into the world, not for sport and amusement, but for labor; not to enjoy and pleasure ourselves, but to serve and glorify God, and be useful to our fellow men." In a similar vein, William A. Alcott warned youthful readers in his *Young Man's Guide* (1833), "Everyman who enjoys the privilege of civilized society, owes it to that society to earn as much as he can, or in other words, to improve every minute of his time. He who loses an hour or a minute, is the price of that hour debtor to the community. Moreover, it is a debt which he can never repay." Even in the West, where the constraints of civilization supposedly were left behind, and the South, where the slave system encouraged an ethic of leisure, Victorianism found staunch adherents, and the wilder the sports, the more strenuous reformers were in suppressing all that stood in the way of the City of God and the progress of man.

Yet there were powerful countertrends. The same transformations that gave rise to the Victorian ethic of hard work and sober self-control also created an environment potentially conducive to popular recreations. By divorcing work from the extended family of shop and farm, the new capitalist order freed men and women not only to labor as best they could, but also to spend their leisure time according to their own lights. One of the constant refrains heard from antebellum reformers regarded the dangers of young people roaming the streets, free to go to theaters, gambling houses, dance halls, bars, and other places of recreation.

By midcentury a distinct working-class subculture had emerged in American cities, especially New York, and for young unmarried men, sports were an important part of that subculture. A cluster of images captures the scene: the volunteer fire companies where men gathered to drink, play cards, and occasionally display their heroics as firefighters; ward-bosses in city politics who knew how to distribute largesse and secure elections with the aid of ballot-box stuffers and strong-arm enforcers; the Bowery in New York (and little Bowerys in other cities) where theaters packed in the crowds for melodramas, and working-class men donned the distinctive dress of the "Bowery B'hoy"; taverns where men treated each other to round after round of drinks, and where sporting events like cockfights, bare-knuckle boxing matches, or bull baits were arranged or staged.

Beyond the working-class and immigrant sporting underground, there were other factors contributing to the rise of sports. Steam-power printing, telegraphy, and the penny press all could be used to disseminate sporting news. America's first sporting magazine appeared in the second decade of the nineteenth century, and there were three new magazines in each of the next three decades, four in the 1850s, and nine in the 1860s. The *Spirit of the Times* became a main source of sporting news beginning in the 1830s, but before long, cheap working-class daily newspapers like the *New York Herald* covered sports with depth and regularity. Steamboats and railroads carried runners, or boxers, or thoroughbreds to matches; manufacturers marketed cricket bats, billiard tables, and archery equipment; telegraph lines flashed news of important contests. Perhaps most important, cities grew at an unprecedented pace during the antebellum era—nine had populations over 100,000 by 1860—creating a new potential market for popular entertainment like sports. Although America remained predominantly rural, cities, as nodes of production and distribution, had growing cultural influence.

Increasingly, recreation was transformed into entertainment, a sort of cultural goods to be purchased with earnings. Minstrel shows, melodramas, popular museums like P. T. Barnum's in New York (1842), circuses, pleasure gardens, and sporting events all became cultural commodities. Control of thoroughbred racing in this era passed from the hands of landed gentlemen to promoters who organized yearly meetings and standardized rules; boxing came into its own, as fight organizers coined money chartering trains and boats to transport fans to the scenes of battle; and by the 1850s the old folk game of baseball developed clubs and leagues that began charging admission to games and paying players. Pedestrianism, as foot racing was called, came as close as any sport to the modern athletic events of today. Wealthy socialite John Cox Stevens initiated the commercialization with a challenge in 1835 to pay $1,000 to the first man to run ten miles in under an hour. Roughly 30,000 spectators showed up at the Union Race Course on Long Island to watch a field of runners take up the challenge. Over the next twenty-five years, crowds up to 50,000 would cheer as runners competed for purses as large as $4,000. In an era when the average laborer earned something around $200 a year, the contests were irresistible to young athletic men, some of whom made a living traveling from race to race.

But athletics on this scale remained rare. Some sports, harness racing prime among them, displayed important "modern" characteristics—standardized rules, the keeping of statistics, regular schedules, and so forth—and some events attracted massive coverage and paid athletes handsomely. The $10,000 championship prizefight between Yankee Sullivan and Tom Hyer in 1849 is a good example. But mass spectator events remained rare. Professionalism was still unusual, profits secondary, organizations informal, and scheduling irregular. Sports as a commodity were in their infancy, far from the regular, profitable, well-managed, repeatable spectacles of the twentieth century.

Voluntary association more than money motivated this early stage of sports development. This was certainly true of most events in which working-class men watched or participated. Often their contests played out ethnic rivalries, especially Irish versus native-born. Similarly, young Germans who migrated to America after the abortive revolution of 1848 brought their Turner societies over from the old country. These organizations (the name comes from Turnerbund, literally "gymnastic society") blended nationalism, anticlericalism, and utopian socialism. As part of their program of universal education to prepare men for political and social democracy, the Turner groups placed great emphasis on gymnastic training and sponsored competitions of athletic skill. Similarly, Scottish immigrants in the 1850s replicated their track-and-field events in the Caledonian games. In these and other cases, ethnic groups helped perpetuate their identity through sports, even as outsiders sometimes attended competitions as spectators. Sports, then, could become a point of solidarity for foreign groups in an alien environment.

Men of the upper class, too, organized new sporting institutions. Metropolitan, university, and union clubs both symbolized and buttressed class prerogatives, reinforcing elite styles of dress, speech, and values, while creating new social and business networks. In the two decades before the Civil War, cricket, racquet, yacht, and rowing clubs began to spring up as exclusive men's organizations. The ubiquitous John Cox Stevens, for example, founded the New York Yacht Club in 1844, which attracted some of the city's leading men. When Stevens's yacht, *America,* defeated eighteen British rivals in the first America's Cup Race (1851), other cities quickly organized their own yacht clubs, and these spun out webs of social activities, including balls and cruises. Boat clubs, crew teams, and regattas arose at prestigious Ivy League colleges, and in 1852, Harvard and Yale oarsmen competed in the nation's first—albeit informal—intercollegiate athletic contest. The embryonic alliance between sport and capitalism is especially clear in this example, because the Boston, Concord, and Montreal Railroad sponsored the regatta and paid all of the expenses as a business promotion.

Baseball also first became organized around the club ideal, and we still refer to multimillion-dollar businesses as "ball clubs." Folk versions of baseball had been around for centuries, but in 1845, the New York Knickerbocker Baseball Club became America's first organized team. Merchants, professionals, clerks, and a handful of tradesmen were members of the club during its first fifteen years. By 1858, sixty teams affiliated together as the National Association of Base Ball Players. In part their goal was to prevent the sport from becoming a vulgar commercial spectacle. Early on, clubs tried to assure the social status of the game by excluding men lower down on the pecking order, by keeping the game open mainly to society's upper half. Certainly every mechanic and laborer could not take off whole afternoons for practice as the National Association clubs did, nor could they afford the elaborate banquets that followed games. But a ball, a bat, and an empty lot were easily procured, and before long, firefighters, policemen, teachers, bartenders, and others organized their own clubs all over America. Some of the working-class teams were so good they began charging admission to their games and paying players. Betting, drinking, and boisterous cheering often accompanied these games. Distasteful as the low-caste game was, amateur clubs quietly conceded to professionalization when they purchased the services of "ringers."

By the Civil War sports had grown more prominent than ever in American life. Some of the games we recognize in the twentieth century—baseball, boxing, track and field prime among them—were no longer purely folk events. An occasional horse race, especially one pitting a thoroughbred from the North against one from the South, might even attract as many as 50,000 people and dominate the news for a few days. But if sports proliferated in this era, they were neither highly organized nor well integrated into the larger society. The permanent arenas, regular schedules, massive coverage, compulsive record keeping, and high salaries we associate with modern sports were largely missing. Above all, still absent was an ideology of sports appropriate for a modern, capitalist, bourgeois society.

As the antebellum era came to a close, however, the outline of such an ideology was beginning to appear. The same nationalism that encouraged some to define Americans' mission as virtuous hard work caused others to wish for a nation of vigorous, physically fit men. Oliver Wendell Holmes, Sr., was one who sounded the alarm: "I am satisfied that such a set of black-coated, stiff-jointed, soft-muscled, paste-complexioned youth as we can boast in our Atlantic cities never before sprang from loins of Anglo-Saxon lineage ... " ("The Autocrat of the Breakfast-Table," *Atlantic Monthly* 1, no. 6 [1858], 881). Like many others of the northern intellectual and social elite—Thomas Wentworth Higginson, Catherine Beecher, Horace Mann, Ralph Waldo Emerson, Walt Whitman among them—Holmes began calling for vigorous exercise for American youth. But these early sports advocates were careful to denounce raucous dissipations. The spirit of improvement, the progress of the race, the innocence of play were their ideals.

An avant-garde of clergymen, journalists, and reformers began the chant. Henry David Thoreau believed that "the body existed for the highest development of the soul" (Bradford Torrey and Francis H. Allen, eds., *The Journal of Henry David Thoreau*, vol. 1 [1962], p. 176), so he advocated not stuffy exercises like calisthenics, nor artificial games like baseball, but activities that immersed one in nature, such as walking, swimming, and rowing. Drawing on romantic faith in human perfectibility, men like Walt Whitman began to view the body as divine, and reformers like the Unitarian minister William Ellery Channing advocated wholesome recreations as part of the larger reform agenda. These early "muscular Christians," as they were sometimes called on both sides of the Atlantic, could advocate recreations with missionary zeal. Declared Frederic W. Sawyer in his influential *Plea for Amusements* (1847): "The moral, social, and religious advancement of the people of this country, for the next half century, depends more upon the principles that are adopted with regard to amusements generally, and how those principles are carried out, than to a great many other things of apparently greater moment" (p. 291). Sawyer argued that moral amusements could displace immoral ones—gymnasiums, for example, supplanting smoke-filled billiard halls. While more orthodox individuals scoffed at such suggestions, the tide seemed to be running in favor of liberal reformers and religionists. In colleges, the sons of America's elites began to participate in the earliest intercollegiate athletic competitions. Amherst, Brown, Yale, and Williams led the way. But in the popular imagination, too, bodily health took on new importance. The Cincinnati *Star in the West*, 6 December 1856, for example, declared it as sinful to neglect the body as the spirit or intellect: "God made man to develop all his faculties to the highest possible degree—to stand erect with broad shoulders and expanding lungs, a picture of physical and moral perfection."

These first glimmerings of modern sports were highly gendered—broad shoulders and expanding lungs were "manly" ideals—and while some reformers like Catherine Beecher recommended athletics for young women, the overwhelming emphasis of these early years was on sports for men. In important ways, the language of the new athletic advocates was infused with the rigid gender definitions of bourgeois culture. Sports, it was said, taught independence, self reliance, courage, discipline—qualities valued in the rough-and-tumble world of business. In domestic ideology, so prominent in the popular culture of this era, women were to domesticate men, but this civilizing process, some feared, threatened to blunt masculine assertiveness in the social, political, and economic spheres. The same society that produced unprecedented quantities of consumer goods associated consumption with femininity and self-denial with manliness. Commercial success, love of luxury, soft living threatened to overwhelm masculine virtues in a sea of goods; spartan and manly sports, a few advanced thinkers seemed to be suggesting, might offer a way out of this trap. Advocating sports in the schools, the New York *Spirit of the Times* declared on 20 June 1857: "The object of education is to make men out of boys. Real live men, not bookworms, not smart fellows, but manly fellows."

So the antebellum era wove several strands of sporting life. In rural areas, gentry sports and country amusements continued. The growing cities witnessed the flowering of a working-class culture that highly valued athletic prowess, especially when expressed in the form of ethnic rivalry. While the dominant chord of middle-class Victorianism, especially among Evangelicals, was in opposition to leisure and play, new voices were just beginning to be heard that advocated sports in the name of bourgeois ideals, and as a way to reform the unwashed masses. In the middle decades of the nineteenth century, then, the very structure of society, with its emerging classes, strict division of labor, glimmerings of a consumption ethic, and sharp separation of work time from nonwork time, opened up new opportunities for sports. And a justification for sports began to emerge, clustered around virtuous, bourgeois manliness: gymnastics gave men endurance, baseball promoted discipline, cricket taught self-control. In coming decades, such ideas would flood the nation.

Sports in the Gilded Age

In 1810, a free black American, Tom Molineaux, fought for the boxing championship of all England. Britons feared the prowess of this foreigner, yet were reassured by the skill of their champion, Thomas Cribb. The fight proved a great one, and the English press covered the event in minute detail. In America, on the other hand, the bout was scarcely noted. While boxing was the "national sport of England," few people on these shores had ever even heard of prizefighting; there simply was no interest in such an event here. Yet half a century later, when an American of Irish extraction, John C. Heenan, ventured to England to fight for the title against Tom Sayers, the American press exploded with coverage. Newspapers might condemn the illegal match (all prizefighting was illegal in this era), but they covered it round by round.

The interest in sports that characterized the antebellum era—an efflorescence of working-class events like boxing matches that at once expressed a class sensibility and ethnic divisions; the rise of baseball initially as a genteel middle- and upper-middle-class game; the very first intercollegiate athletic competitions between boys from elite schools; and harness races, which Oliver Wendell Holmes, Sr., praised for their democratic virtues, and which were distinctly modern in their emphasis on fixed rules, record keeping, and equality of entry—grew at an unprecedented pace during the Gilded Age. By the last decade of the nineteenth century, sports as we know them today had been born. And that birth was attended by the whole range of modern institutions we associate with urban-industrial America, bureaucratic structures, corporate organizations, capitalist ideologies, urban development.

By bringing men together in enormous numbers, the Civil War afforded unprecedented opportunities for sports. Between battles, men boxed, played baseball, and raced horses, often for the first time in their lives. More important, the war speeded the transformation of American society. The nation's capacity for manufacturing and distributing goods expanded, communication and transportation networks thickened, the organizational structure of society grew more sophisticated. As American capitalism matured with the century—as the division between those who owned the means of production and those who labored for wages grew deeper—images of stern competition, of winning the race of life, of survival of the fittest, took on en-hanced ideological meaning. Athletics were readily enlisted in the cause of new social alignments.

The problem of moral sports in a Christian land did not go away. Some commentators maintained a hard line against all forms of frivolous amuse-ments. More commonly, ministers and urban reformers gave renewed sup-port to wholesome recreations. Thus, Henry Bergh (1811–1888) called for healthful and invigorating sports to replace cock mains, dogfights, bear baits, and boxing matches. Bergh substituted for the singular "sport"—a rowdy, one who defied social custom—the plural "sports," meaning rational and useful athletic activities. Dogfights and cock mains still found large and enthusiastic audiences, especially in the tradition-bound South and in polyglot cities like New York and New Orleans. The reformers never fully had their way with rural or working-class people. Nonetheless, new sports like baseball—not ex-actly a deacon's first choice, but better than prizefighting—grew extremely popular in working-class communities, as men organized countless teams and leagues.

The most important institutional form of the new physicality was the Young Men's Christian Association (YMCA). Originally founded in England, the "Y" gave youths a refuge against the temptations of the metropolis. Here Christian fellowship, intellectual stimulation, and wholesome physical exer-cise supplanted the loneliness of boardinghouses and the evils of commercial amusements. Where urban life threatened good morals and communal order, YMCAs and similar organizations upheld these old ideals. The "Y" repre-sented a rejuvenated, muscular, middle-class ethos. By 1869, San Francisco, Washington, and New York City all had "Y" gymnasia; within twenty-five years, there were 261 YMCA gyms scattered across America. Religious lead-ers like Washington Gladden and Henry Ward Beecher praised the "Y" for of-fering sports like baseball, football, swimming, calisthenics, bowling, and weight lifting in a wholesome and clean atmosphere. The underlying as-sumption of "Y" programs was that supervised athletics promoted religious and moral goals. Simply put, it made more sense to teach physical training un-der Christian auspices, imparting the values of fair play, cooperation, and good sportsmanship, than to have young men roam the streets. Gymnasia countered the licentiousness of pool halls; men who did calisthenics did not bet on horse races; clean sports engendered leadership, discipline, and tough-mindedness for capitalist society.

The "Y" movement was an early and prominent example of a widespread rehabilitation of sports that took place after the Civil War. Yet the proliferation of such urban institutions was testimony to the resiliency of the working-class ways that the reformers wished to change. No doubt, some laboring men were persuaded that the Christian athlete was on the road to bourgeois respectability and social mobility. Others probably participated in "wholesome" athletics some of the time, but also patronized beer gardens, dance halls, gambling parlors, saloons, burlesque houses, and the disreputable sports that were part of that culture. The public-parks movement that swept the cities late in the nineteenth century provides a fine example of how men found their own paths. As antidotes to moral anarchy, vice, and corruption, city planners developed landscaped parks for public leisure. Clear brooks, lush trees, and blue skies were moral agents, they believed, which would improve the temperament of workers and elevate their thoughts. Parks could mollify class antagonism, planners argued, for here rich and poor came together in harmonious communion with nature. Unfortunately, rather than passively soaking up virtue, the urban multitudes came with beer, bats, and balls, ignored the "keep off the grass" signs, and had a rollicking good time.

But the efforts of neither the moral reformers nor their opponents ultimately were decisive in the rise of sports. More important was the commercialization of culture. Between the Civil War and the turn of the century, baseball became the acknowledged "national pastime," boxing under new rules exploded in popularity, football grew into a college mania, and basketball took firm root in urban athletic clubs. In addition, tennis, golf, and bicycling swept over the upper middle class in waves of popularity, while laborers started their own semiprofessional and amateur leagues in various team sports. Organizational and business structures arose to regulate and rationalize new activities. If sports in that era were rudimentary compared to today, the games themselves and the structures that supported them were in place by the end of the nineteenth century.

Despite a vertiginous boom-and-bust cycle, this era left many workers with a little more disposable time and money than previously, especially those in the burgeoning white-collar sector. The old work ethic was in part a victim of its own success. As the economy slowly solved the age-old problem of insufficient productive capacity, and as work increasingly came to be thought of as a distinct realm of life, Americans were left with gaps of time to fill. Put another way, America's exploding productive capacity was changing people's perceptions of time. The dawning economy of potential abundance—where supply of aggregate goods and services might exceed demand—necessitated the stimulation of new wants and desires. The emergent ethos of play, of having fun, of "letting go" made a virtue of necessity.

New social conditions, then, transformed consciousness as well as material life. Production had shifted away from individuals' making objects for themselves and their communities, toward nameless workers' making goods for unseen others in return for cash. Now leisure more than ever revolved around the abstract concept of monetary exchange. Although Americans continued to create their own entertainment, the emergent national culture idealized the purchase of mass-produced commodities as a great human privilege and goal. Homegrown recreations competed for attention with mass entertainment, and the latter increasingly dominated and structured the former. To purchase leisure—to be a spectator at a ball game, or buy a bicycle or a baseball mitt—was to partake of a new cultural hallmark, the consumption of leisure. Entrepreneurs were quick to come in: A. J. Spalding began mass-producing sporting goods; newspaper tycoons like William Randolph Hearst for the first time printed entire sports sections; and authors like Gilbert Patten (creator of Frank Merriwell) coined money for themselves and their publishers by churning out formula fiction.

Sports were integrally tied to the transformation of life in a mature capitalist economy. Cities became the foci of new activities not just because overcrowding militated against old traditional amusements, but because the city was where the comodification of life was most pervasive; in cities, people were already learning the cycle of desire, pleasure, and more desire that came with the ethic of consumption. Moreover, new technologies opened up recreational possibilities: pneumatic tires facilitated the bicycle craze of the 1880s and 1890s, motion pictures allowed countless fans to see prizefights, electric lightbulbs illuminated grand new downtown arenas. And sports were becoming firmly entrenched in American business culture. By the 1870s, for example, baseball had already been hit with strikes, blacklistings, and combinations to restrain trade. The team owners who founded the National League in 1876 soon wrested control of the game from the players, destroyed rival clubs, took over the apprenticeship system (the minor leagues), and instituted the reserve clause, which denied players the right to sell their labor to other franchises. Owners had, in short, attained what businessmen elsewhere strove for with varying degrees of success—controlled markets that minimized risk.

Both professional and amateur sports were part of the larger organizational revolution. League schedules were established, national rules promulgated, and regulatory bodies like the National Collegiate Athletic Association and Amateur Athletic Union formed. By the 1880s, professional baseball generated millions of dollars each year in revenue, and a prosperous franchise could draw 5,000 spectators per game. Moreover, sports became interlocked

with the larger world of business. A successful local team brought trade to hotels, restaurants, and bars; a new stadium meant jobs in construction, maintenance, and concessions. And sports replicated the structures of modernity.
The keeping of statistics, the rational measurement of means and ends, bureaucratic organizations—all permeated American life, including sports.
Sports also articulated the dominant ideologies of an advanced democratic
capitalist society—meritocracy, scientific worldview, equal competition, victory through brains, pluck, and hard work. Sports were a metaphor for life:
that is, for the life of males in a modern capitalist country.

Still, it would be a mistake to view sports as simply one more manifesta-
tion of a modernizing juggernaut. Older, more traditional sports such as boxing and cockfighting thrived in the late nineteenth century and appealed to
ancient ideals of honor. Despite the structure of new professional and amateur sports, a subculture of raucous old pastimes continued to thrive.
Modernization theory does capture the most striking trend in sports
development—toward bureaucratic structures, rationalized play, quantifiable
results. The problem is that these trends were often so mixed with seemingly
antimodern ones. Richard Kyle Fox, for example, owner of the *National Police
Gazette* during its heyday in the 1880s and 1890s, used the most modern business techniques to promote traditional sport; his publication, brilliantly rationalized in production and distribution, was filled with misogyny and racism,
hardly the stuff of an egalitarian society.

Indeed, while reformers argued that sports taught the ideal of equal opportunity, the fact is that the playing fields of athletics, like those of life, were
never level. Exclusive organizations like the New York Athletic Club—and
every major city had exclusive athletic clubs by the end of the century—allowed only the most wealthy and powerful men to join. While workers might
become interested in the outcome of a Harvard-Yale football game—indeed
while those schools might even employ a "ringer" or two to assure victory—
colleges remained elite institutions, effectively closed to the majority of Americans. To the extent that prestigious colleges did open up in this era, sports
were part of the process by which the children of an industrial elite that was
pushing its way into the most powerful positions in American life dispelled the
boredom of the rigid old classical curriculum. Finally, the late nineteenth century saw the proliferation of exclusive country clubs and elite watering places
like Newport, Rhode Island, and Saratoga, New York, that brought wealthy
people together in play while excluding all lesser folk.

At high-amateur and professional levels, sports did admit whole new
groups of people as spectators and participants. Yet a majority of Americans
were largely left out. First, while there were some important gestures toward

women's sports during this era, domestic ideology, notions of female delicacy, and lingering Victorian prudishness kept most women from active interest in things athletic. Gender roles still defined men as active, women as passive, and the operative metaphors of sports all tended toward patriarchy. Tough competition, physical violence, the importance of winning, teamwork—sports as metaphor did not just reflect masculine ideals, they helped constitute and define those ideals. Competing, achieving, and winning were at the very core of late Victorian notions of manhood, so sports not only excluded women, they helped define and give shape to a masculine world that feared or devalued or mystified all that it regarded as feminine.

Ethnically, too, athletes in this era contained a strong streak of exclusivity. While sports had become an important symbol of American culture, most men of the immigrant generation probably were not terribly interested as spectators, and if they played sports at all, it was more likely to be games from their homelands. The children of immigrants, however, found in athletics a powerful sense of belonging to the only culture they knew firsthand. Symbolically, sports provided a sense of dual identity. Thus heavyweight boxing champion John L. Sullivan espoused both Irish nationalism and American patriotism, and he literally cloaked himself in both the Stars and Stripes and the emerald green when he entered the ring. For Irish-Americans who had long suffered severe discrimination, Sullivan represented not only glittering success, but also the possibility of identifying with both America and Ireland. In the twentieth century, baseball players like Joe DiMaggio and Hank Greenberg repeated this pattern for new immigrant groups.

The situation for blacks, however, was different. Despite the rhetoric of "may the best man win," by late in the nineteenth century, the openings that had existed in early professional sports closed down almost entirely. During the 1890s, African-Americans were systematically barred from major-league baseball, resulting in the formation of the all-black Negro leagues until Jackie Robinson reintegrated baseball after World War II. Moreover, boxing champion John L. Sullivan simply refused to fight black opponents, though the strongest contender during the late 1880s was an Australian black named Peter Jackson. Even in the now obscure but then quite popular sport of bicycle racing, African-American Marshall W. "Major" Taylor was the best cyclist in the world during the 1890s, yet he was excluded from major races. So in the late nineteenth century—an era of lynching and Jim Crow legislation, of the most virulent racism since Reconstruction—the sporting meritocracy proved meretricious at best. Access to organized sports was generally restricted by race and gender, and often by class.

Nevertheless, the sporting ideology that had become a commonplace of the late Victorian era was a powerful cement in American culture. Those excluded from the mainstream still created a sporting space with games and leagues of their own. Equally important, the ideas associated with sports—universal rules, fair play, utter seriousness in a frivolous cause, measurable performance, the joy of physical excellence, the tension of keen competition, the expertise of spectators—were constantly spreading into the larger national culture. Not for all Americans, but for increasing numbers of them, sometimes even crossing deep social chasms, sports were becoming a kind of national language or currency, a set of shared practices, values, and experiences so common as to become invisible as air.

In 1892, roughly a century after the illegal sport of boxing first appeared in America, William Lyon Phelps, professor of English at Yale, was reading the daily newspaper to his blind father, a Baptist minister. The old outlaw prizefighting was in the news, and Phelps read the headline "Corbett Defeats Sullivan," then turned the page, assuming the elderly Victorian gentleman would not be interested. Phelps Senior leaned forward and said to his son, "Read it by rounds."

2

The Early Years of Baseball, 1845–60

MELVIN L. ADELMAN

Between 1845 and the outbreak of the Civil War, baseball evolved from a simple, informal child's game into an organized sport with standardized rules. The formation of the National Association of Base Ball Players in 1857, the increasing press coverage of baseball, the rising spectator interest, the emergence of statistics, and the appearance of baseball's first guidebook in 1860 further exemplified the modernization and growing popularity of the sport during these years.

Baseball propagandists have long sought to give the sport a pastoral image, but from the outset organized baseball was an urban product.[1] In the pre–Civil War years New York City and Brooklyn virtually dominated the development of baseball, even though numerous northeastern cities boasted their own teams, as did a handful of midwestern and southern cities. In fact, by 1860 a baseball club had been established as far west as San Francisco, although the "New York game" triumphed over all other styles of play.

The emergence of baseball as an organized sport can be traced to a dozen clubs that sprang up in Manhattan and Brooklyn between 1845 and 1855, beginning with the Knickerbocker Base Ball Club. In 1842 several gentlemen in search of outdoor exercise and social enjoyment had gathered at a vacant lot at the corner of Twenty-seventh Street and Madison Avenue in Manhattan to play a child's ball game. The growth of the city's residential and commercial community eventually forced them to seek another playing field further north, and after three years of unorganized play Alexander J. Cartwright, Jr., recommended the establishment of a permanent club and promised to recruit more members. The team accepted Cartwright's proposal, drew up a constitution, devised rules for the game, and secured a permanent site at Elysian

Fields in Hoboken, New Jersey, for a fee of seventy-five dollars per year for both the field and the dressing room.[2]

Historians universally accept the Knickerbockers as baseball's pioneer club, even as many of them recognize the existence of earlier teams. Those teams, they are quick to note, were either unorganized, in existence for only a few years, or played some other variation of baseball, such as town ball. One of the pre-Knickerbocker teams, known as the New York Club, did attract more interest than the others, but as Henry Chadwick wrote in 1861 the Knickerbockers deserved "the honor of being the pioneer of the present game of Base Ball." Interest in the New York Club derived mainly from its one-sided, 23-1 victory in 1846 over the Knickerbockers, in what was once believed to be baseball's first match. The New York Club's crushing victory indicates that their players were not novices; in fact, Duncan F. Curry, the first president of the Knickerbockers, later claimed that several of the opposing players were experienced cricketers.[3]

Several references in the *New York Herald* late in 1845, unnoticed by other historians, provide further insights into the New York Club and the early history of organized baseball. On October 21 the *Herald* noted an upcoming match between the New York Club and a team known as the Brooklyn Club. The newspaper did not report the outcome of what must now be considered the first interclub contest, but four days later it indicated that in a rematch the New Yorkers had defeated the Brooklyn squad, 37-19.[4] In a more revealing statement the *Herald* reported on November 11 that members of the New York Club were gathered on its diamond at Elysian Fields to mark the team's second anniversary, making it clear that they had been meeting regularly since 1843. The fact that they played at Elysian Fields and probably paid a rental fee suggests that they were organized, although not, in all likelihood, to the same degree as the Knickerbockers with their formal constitution.[5]

As the sport's first important and long-term club, existing until 1882, the Knickerbockers served as the organizational model for the multitude of baseball teams that emerged in the 1850s. Its major contribution was the establishment of the basic patterns and rules of baseball. A far cry from the rules that now govern the sport, these early rules were certainly more sophisticated than the ones used in the child's game of baseball. Today's fans would find the Knickerbocker game both crude and amusing, yet they would recognize it as baseball.[6]

The Knickerbocker Base Ball Club generally has been portrayed in the literature as a group of urban gentlemen with a certain standing in the community who sought to restrict the game of baseball to their own kind. More

a social club than a sports team, the Knickerbockers supposedly felt that con-
geniality on the field and postgame dinners were as important as winning. In
spirit and tone they were more akin to upper-class sportsmen, such as cricketers and tennis players, than later ball players with their win-at-all-cost philosophy. Many writers also believed that the Knickerbockers sought to
establish themselves as the social arbiters of baseball, following the example
set by the Marylebone Cricket Club.[7]

This popular portrayal contains some grain of truth, but it is marked by inconsistencies and is based on limited evidence that suffers from serious gaps in
the literature. Available biographical information and economic data on New
York ball players, while scarce, do permit a profile of the social class of the
Knickerbockers if we examine their known occupations and extrapolate from
what they were not. The majority between 1845 and 1850 had white-
collar jobs, yet only slightly more than one-third of the forty-four ball players
whose occupations could be identified were involved in commerce and finance,
a far lower percentage than among members of the St. George Cricket Club,
for example. Doctors and lawyers constituted one-fourth of the club members,
and the remaining two-fifths engaged in nonmanual, but less financially re-
warding, occupations, with clerks and similar lower-level white-collar workers
making up slightly less than one-sixth of baseball's first organized team.

The occupational structure of the Knickerbockers indicates that the members were drawn at least from the middle class, but there is no evidence to support the contention that on the whole they were from the city's upper class or
were wealthy urban gentlemen. Certainly, some men in the club were financially well-to-do, such as Benjamin C. Lee, whose father, James, was an honorary member and worth an estimated $20,000 in 1845. Another member, J.
Paige Mumford, was the son of a well-known merchant; however, his father was
worth only $3,000 in 1845, enough for a comfortable, but hardly an opulent,
lifestyle.[8] Thus, while some of the Knickerbockers may have come from the
upper-middle class, the majority appear to have been prosperous middle-class
New Yorkers, much like Alexander Cartwright, at whose suggestion the club
was formed. A few years prior to leaving the city in 1849, Cartwright, who had
been a clerk, and his elder brother had opened a bookstore.[9]

In terms of social class, then, the Knickerbockers hardly conformed to the
typical image of status-seekers. Nor did the intent of the club or its initial action reveal a desire to limit baseball to the upper-middle class. Rather, the sole
purpose seems to have been engaging in an activity that promoted health,
recreation, and social enjoyment among the members. The most striking fea-

ture of the Knickerbocker Club during its early years is the almost total absence of outside competition, suggesting that these men attached limited importance to baseball per se. After the game against the New York Club in 1846, the Knickerbockers did not engage in contests with any other clubs until 1851. They neither emulated the semiorganized New York Club, which played several games against a group of Brooklyn cricketers, nor followed the lead of New York's first cricket club in challenging teams outside the city. While the Knickerbockers adopted their own rules, they must have been aware that numerous variations of baseball had long been played in the Northeast. Yet club records reveal no effort to find out if gentlemen elsewhere had organized baseball clubs. In an important but unpublished piece of research, Robert Henderson helps us understand why the Knickerbocker Club made no apparent effort to engage in friendly contests with other teams: the club was itself on the verge of collapse during the early years because many of its members often failed to show up for schedule practices.[10] The club's condition and the casual attitude of its members contrast sharply with the popular contention that the Knickerbockers sought to become the social arbiters of the sport.

Another problem with the prevalent view is that it does not explain why there was no mention of baseball in the press until 1853, with the exception of a few references to the New York Club in 1845. The absence of information cannot, however, be interpreted as any one group's desire for exclusivity, since status confirmation involves not the absence of publicity but quite the opposite, its demonstration. This was clearly the pattern in all upper-class sports.[11] The failure of the Knickerbockers to ensure public recognition of their organization probably indicated a defensive posture toward involvement in baseball. Given their social status and the prevailing attitude toward ball playing, their reaction is not surprising; after all, they were grown men of some stature playing a child's game. They could rationalize their participation by pointing to the health and recreational benefits of baseball, but their social insecurities and their personal doubts concerning the manliness of the game inhibited them from openly announcing the organization.

A rash of baseball clubs came into existence in the New York City area between 1850 and 1855, probably in response to the increasing encouragement of many forms of outdoor recreation and with the example of organized cricket already a decade old. The Washington Club, later renamed the Gotham Club, began playing around 1850 on the field of the St. George Cricket Club in Harlem. Several members had played on the New York Club in 1846, indicating that they were not novices and strongly suggesting that prior to 1850 other adult men besides the Knickerbockers played baseball, if only informally and on an irregular basis.[12] In 1851 the Washington squad challenged the Knickerbockers to a home-and-home series. The annual contests between the two clubs attracted some public interest, and in 1853 both the *Spirit* and the *New York Mercury* reported briefly on one of the games.[13] Three more clubs—the Eagle, the Empire, and the Baltic—were organized in Manhattan during 1854 and 1855, while seven teams were formed in Brooklyn. The Excelsiors, Brooklyn's first baseball club, were organized in December 1854 by John H. Suydam and several of his friends, who had witnessed a contest between the Knickerbockers and Eagles that fall.

The Eckford Club was the second organized squad in Brooklyn. Historians maintain that the club, composed of shipwrights and mechanics who could keep practice only once a week (in contrast to other teams that met twice weekly), marked the first break with the Knickerbockers' notion of baseball as a gentlemen's game.[14] While formation of this club undeniably symbolized a change in the economic and social composition of baseball players in the early years, the extent of that change has been grossly exaggerated. For example, individuals who worked in New York's shipyards, the center for such construction in the United States and, at times, the world, were the best-paid craftsmen in the city. These shipwrights had been able to insulate themselves from the kinds of social and economic changes that undermined the pay and prestige of artisans in other crafts, in general earning a sufficient annual income to allow them to live within reach of the middle class. It is also significant that between 20 and 25 percent of the Eckford members were employed in nonmanual occupations.[15] Thus, there do not appear to have been radical economic differences between members of the Eckford and Knickerbocker clubs, although clearly there were social differences. But did these translate into varying behavioral patterns?

While we can never be sure, several interrelated factors suggest that members of the Eckford Club belonged to the segment of the working class that held many middle-class values. The presence of white-collar workers on this largely manual-skilled team was in part an extension of the paternalistic relationship between master shipbuilders and their workers, but it was also an indicator of shared beliefs, as was the selection of the club's name. Henry Eckford, a Scotch-Irish immigrant, was New York's richest and most successful shipbuilder in the antebellum period. By identifying with him, these craftsmen gave testimony to their faith in middle-class values, especially upward mobility. One final point: when the issue of professional baseball first emerged in the late 1850s, Francis Pidgeon, president of the Eckford Club, opposed compensation for players, maintaining that the game was for pleasure, not profit.[16]

To ascertain more precisely the social class of Brooklyn and New York ball players we must examine in some detail their types of occupations during different time periods.[17] Between 1850 and 1855 most ball players engaged mainly in nonmanual forms of employment (see table 2-1). No unskilled workers were on baseball teams in either city; but skilled craftsmen made up about one-fourth of the players, a fact that indicates widespread knowledge of the game at this early stage and further confirms the absence of an effort to restrict baseball to the "better class." However, there were striking occupational differences between ball players of the two cities. There is no clear-cut reason for this, since both groups had access to the same kinds of jobs.[18] Indeed, it may have been only a temporary development, because the differences were less evident during the next fifteen years. Brooklyn players still came from more plebeian backgrounds, a trend that no doubt persisted as a result of the greater availability of open space on which to play. Even more critical, perhaps, was the fact that Brooklyn's economic growth did not keep pace with its population, which increased from about 7,000 in 1820 to slightly less than 100,000 three decades later. Moreover, in contrast to the cosmopolitan nature of New York City, Brooklyn retained much of its small-city atmosphere; hence, its ball players were more likely to be drawn from middle-level occupations.[19]

Baseball's growth in the mid-1850s corresponded with, and was stimulated by, the coverage it was receiving in the *Spirit* and some daily newspapers. Beginning in 1853 the press provided brief reports of contests, usually no more than three or four lines, often accompanied by a crude box score; they also noted the formation of new clubs. In response to the increasing number

Table 2-1. Occupational Structure of Area Baseball Players, 1850–55

	New York City		Brooklyn		Combined	
	N	%	N	%	N	%
Professional–High White-Collar	26	41.9	9	28.1	35	37.2
Low White-Collar–Proprietor	28	45.2	9	28.1	37	39.4
Skilled Craftsman	8	12.9	14	43.8	22	23.4
Total	62		32		94	

of baseball clubs in the metropolitan area, the *Spirit* published the Knicker-bockers' rules in 1855, along with a diagram of the playing field.[20] The *Herald*, impressed with the rising number of clubs, maintained that baseball "bids fair to soon be as popular as the favorite game of cricket," an opinion that was shared by the *Spirit* despite its close ties with cricket: "The interest in the game of Base Ball appears to be on the rise, and its bids fair to become our most popular game." That prediction proved absolutely correct.[21]

Baseball grew tremendously in the five years prior to the Civil War, replacing cricket as the nation's leading ball game. From only a dozen clubs in Brooklyn and New York in 1855, the number of organized teams increased eightfold in just three years, to seventy-one in Brooklyn and twenty-five in Manhattan. Counting ball clubs already formed in nearby New Jersey, Westchester County, and on Long Island, there were over 125 teams in the metropolitan area. It is impossible to say exactly how many people played baseball in the neighboring cities. The *Herald* claimed in 1859 that there were more members in Brooklyn and New York City baseball clubs than in all the other clubs combined. The statement is no doubt inaccurate, but it reflects the extent to which the press was awed by the surging popularity of baseball.[22]

The rapid increase in the number of clubs and contests created the need to clarify and codify the various rules of the game. At the end of the 1855 season the *Herald* reported that a preliminary meeting was held as the first step toward creating a central governing body for baseball, but the absence of a follow-up story indicates that nothing apparently came of it. *Porter's Spirit* noted in October 1856 that a convention of baseball clubs to amend the rules seemed imminent. In December of that year the Knickerbockers, in an effort to "promote additional interest in baseball," and quite possibly because they were prodded by other clubs, called for a convention of teams from New York City and vicinity. Delegates from fourteen clubs, all from Manhattan and Brooklyn, met in 1857 and elected Dr. Daniel D. Adams of the Knickerbockers as president. They reconfirmed the rules of baseball's pioneer club with one major change: adoption of the nine-inning game (instead of ending a contest when a team scored twenty-one runs, or aces). The most significant debate, however, revolved around the Knickerbockers' proposal that to retire the batter the ball be caught on the fly instead of on the first bounce. The delegates rejected such a change and continued to do so every year until 1863, despite wide support in the press.[23]

The presidents of New York's four oldest clubs—Knickerbocker, Gotham, Eagle, and Empire—called another meeting in 1858, and the number of clubs represented increased to twenty-six. The convention adopted the name National Association of Base Ball Players (NABBP), even though all the teams represented came from what is currently New York City, with the exception of one team from New Brunswick, New Jersey.[24] The association basically reconfirmed the rules established the previous year and elected new officers. The Knickerbockers were conspicuous by their absence from the executive council, leading baseball historians to erroneously interpret this as a blunt rejection of the club and its effort to be the social arbiter of the sport.[25]

Again, the events simply do not support the contention that the Knickerbockers were trying to become baseball's equivalent to the Marylebone Cricket Club. In 1857 they decided to restrict their contests to those clubs who practiced on their grounds at Elysian Fields, a policy chastised in a letter to *Porter's Spirit*.[26] I contend that the Knickerbockers' desire for the company of their own kind when playing baseball illustrates that for them the game continued to perform mainly a social rather than a competitive function. In fact, they showed no desire to govern baseball, even though as the oldest club and the sport's earliest rule maker, new teams and the press looked to them for leadership. Instead of consolidating these advantages into a position of power, the Knickerbockers shied away from asserting any leadership role whatsoever.

While some disenchantment existed with the Knickerbockers' lack of leadership, their failure to be elected to any "national" office in 1858 was not the product of a revolt from below by "democratic" delegates disenchanted with their supposed aristocratic policies. The new association officers all came from clubs with occupational structures similar to the Knickerbockers'. Of the NABBP's six executives, there were three lawyers, a doctor, a merchant, and one whose occupation could not be ascertained. William H. Van Cott was a deserving choice as president of the NABBP, having been a member of the Gotham Club since at least 1851 and its president since 1856; he also wrote the first letter to the press about baseball in 1854.[27] Contrary to charges by later scholars, the press did not comment on the absence of the Knickerbockers from the executive council, and baseball's pioneer club articulated no displeasure with the outcome of the election. Moreover, they were not totally eliminated from a position of influence: from 1858 to 1862 Dr. Adams served as the head of the important NABBP rules committee.

Popular opinion aside, the Knickerbockers' attitude toward other clubs was clearly revealed in a debate over the admission of junior clubs.[28] When the convention overwhelmingly rejected the credentials of these young men, by a 34-to-8 vote, the press unanimously disapproved. *Porter's Spirit* blamed the outcome on "a clique of men" who have "plenty of money, and a proportionate lack of strength of body and energy of spirit . . . [and who] wish to make the game a means of showing off their figures in fancy dress, and their wealth in fancy dinners." The paper recommended that the junior clubs call their own convention, and in 1860 thirty squads established the National Association of Junior Baseball Clubs.[29] Not only was Adams among the handful of men who supported junior clubs, but he wrote the minority report favoring admission of all teams. While the Knickerbockers preferred to participate in sports with their own social peers, they clearly did not want to restrict the growth of baseball in any way, nor emerge as the equivalent of the Marylebone Cricket Club.[30]

The formation of the NABBP was pivotal in the history of the sport, "marking the close of one baseball era and the beginning of another, in which the players and their representatives would meet annually in convention to revise the rules, settle disputes and control their own game."[31] Although often weak and ineffective, baseball's first centralized organization governed the sport for the next thirteen years. By the eve of the Civil War, membership in the NABBP had increased to over sixty clubs, the majority still being from New York and vicinity, again illustrating that organized baseball was concentrated in this region. As the sport's popularity spread rapidly in the 1850s, clubs were established in most northeastern cities and in other parts of the country. While the NABBP did not reflect baseball's growing national character until after the Civil War, the 1859 election of Henry Schrivner of Baltimore's Excelsior Club as the association's second vice-president symbolized the growing presence of non–New York teams.[32]

Although one of the functions of the NABBP was to centralize the rules of baseball, the *Spirit* noted in 1859 that differences still existed in how the game was played in the East. Within several years, however, the New York–style game emerged triumphant. The earlier organization of the sport in New York City and the establishment there of the NABBP naturally contributed to this development, but the major reason that this particular style dominated was that it was used in America's sports-communication center, where all the national sports journals were located.[33] This centralization of the rules did little to alter the style of play, however. Prior to the Civil War baseball remained essentially a hitter's game, as demonstrated by the number of runs scored (frequently at least twenty per team).

Despite the primitive play, a fair degree of sophistication began to emerge in terms of the execution of the game. One correspondent to *Porter's Spirit* noted that during a run-down infielders should throw the ball as seldom as possible and the pitcher should occupy the uncovered base; and in case a runner attempted to steal third base, the shortstop should back up the third baseman to safeguard against an errant throw by the catcher. There were no called balls and strikes, but the same writer pointed out that "many think that a ball that will curve as it approaches the striker is much more difficult to bat than one that takes a straight course."[34] There were numerous other suggestions as to how to make baseball a more "scientific" sport, such as a recommendation in the press that ball players specialize at one position.[35] Yet the change most frequently advocated—and the one most hotly contested—was the adoption of the fly rule, universally endorsed by sports journalists. Their rhetoric and sharp denunciation of the NABBP for failing to act suggests that the controversy went beyond merely refining the game. Underlying their advocacy of a more skillful sport were the inevitable comparison with cricket and the question of the manliness of baseball.

The Knickerbocker Club first proposed the fly rule, quite possibly the brainchild of James Whyte Davis, at the 1857 convention.[36] Opponents maintained that catching a fly ball hurt the player's hands and would make baseball too much like cricket. *Porter's Spirit* denied that such catches were injurious and countered that many ball players were former cricketers anyway. It urged that the fly rule not be rejected merely because it was used in cricket and then based its support of the rule on nationalistic considerations: "What an Englishman can do, an American is capable of improving upon."[37] This invocation of patriotism is not surprising since baseball was already being described as the national pastime and its supporters were painfully aware of the fact that it required less skill than the English game of cricket. However, the need to make baseball a more skillful sport went beyond nationalism. A more important motivation for support of the fly rule was to remove from baseball the vestiges of its heritage as an unmanly child's game.[38] One journalist commented that an important improvement in the match he watched was "several fine catches being made on the fly, instead of the child's play, 'from the bound.'" The change proved "not only more manly, but adds very much to the quickness of perception, and nerve and determination, which makes up the necessary qualifications of a complete fieldsman, either at Base Ball or Cricket."[39]

Baseball propagandists pointed to the healthful benefits to be derived from their brand of outdoor recreation, and even more than cricketers they emphasized the moral benefits as well. One sports journal went so far as to suggest that baseball clubs were an "important and valuable adjunct to the church, inasmuch as a healthy bodily condition is undoubtedly essential to the enjoyment of a peaceful and religious state of mind."[40] However, virtually absent from the discussion of baseball's positive social contributions were references to its role in instilling character values, an argument that was used to confirm the manliness of cricket. The fact that the press ignored the same theme indicates that they were unsure of the manliness of baseball despite repeated claims to the contrary.

Rule changes, especially in the early stages of a developing sport, derive from an effort to meet the contingency of new and changing situations. Yet arguments in support of the fly rule ran counter to the basic direction of change in baseball—to create a balance between offense and defense. "What is more annoying to an admirer of good fielding," *Porter's Spirit* wrote in advocating adoption of the fly rule, "than to see a splendid hit to the center field, such as would merit a home run, entirely nullified by the puny effort of waiting until the force of the ball is spent on the ground and then taking it on the bound."[41] The idea of penalizing a good hit by allowing an easier catch was justification enough for changing the rule, but the focus here and elsewhere was always on fielding and the improvement of this phase of the game, not really on the disadvantages to the hitter. This approach is surprising, but since baseball was already overwhelmingly a hitter's game, supporters adopted this argument.

Besides the absence of any structural reason for the fly rule, there is another perplexing problem with the press's support of this innovation. In their analyses of the popularity of baseball and cricket they conceded that cricket was the more complex and scientific sport but that baseball was more popular because it was "more simple in its rules, and a knowledge of it is more easily acquired."[42] Then why tamper with a good thing, especially since the stated objective of ball playing was to beckon the city dweller into the outdoors for healthful exercise? This desire to make the national pastime more difficult further demonstrated the need to make it a more manly sport.

In 1859 the Knickerbocker Club decided to use the fly rule during its contests. The press noted that the experiment clearly proved the superiority of the rule and its positive influence on the sport, and they fully expected it to be passed at the next convention. Although Van Cott, the NABBP president and a longtime opponent of the fly rule, shifted his position "out of courtesy to those gentlemen who seem so earnestly to believe that it would be a desirable improvement," efforts to approve the change failed again and continued to fail for another three years.[43] Henry Chadwick and other sportswriters repeatedly chastised the delegates for failing to adopt the innovative rule, insisting that

THE EARLY YEARS OF BASEBALL, 1845–60   69

the players themselves desired a more skillful game. Whether true or not, the momentum was clearly swinging in favor of change. Other clubs began experimenting with the fly rule as players became more proficient fielders, in part through concurrent participation in cricket. The NABBP finally passed the fly rule prior to the 1864 season, by which time organized baseball had changed dramatically.[44]

————

Symbolic of the growing participant and spectator interest in baseball in the late 1850s was the arrangement of an all-star match in 1858 between players from New York City and Brooklyn clubs. Besides attempting to discover which area had the better players, the series served to show off the sport (as is still the case in the annual confrontation between the National and American leagues). The Fashion Course was rented for the best-two-out-of-three series because it was a neutral site and, more important, because it could accommodate thousands of spectators. To cover expenses an admission fee was charged, making it the first time Americans paid to see a baseball game.[45]

The first game was scheduled for July 13 but was postponed on account of rain, even though nearly 2,000 spectators were on hand. Rescheduled for a week later the initial game in the series drew an "immense concourse" and was a closely contested event, with the play on both sides of the "very highest order." Brooklyn jumped to a 7-1 lead in the third inning, but the New Yorkers rallied to tie the score in the fourth and then outscored their opponents 7-4 in the fifth. Each team scored two runs in the sixth and one in the seventh, then Brooklyn pushed across four runs in the top of the eighth to lead, 18-17. New York countered with five runs, and when they held their opponents scoreless in the ninth they took a one-game lead in the series. The second game, played a month later, attracted a somewhat smaller crowd. Both squads made changes in their lineups. Brooklyn jumped to a 17-3 lead after four innings and coasted home to an easy 29-8 win. The entered the deciding game as a slight favorite, although none of the contests attracted heavy betting. The teams changed lineups once again, with the Brooklyn players coming solely from the Atlantic (six players) and the Eckford (three players) clubs. The Brooklynites scored twice in the top of the first inning, but the New Yorkers countered with seven runs and never relinquished their lead, winning 29-18.[46]

The press agreed that the all-star games had been a huge success and were "extremely favorable to the progress and popularity of the game of Base-Ball."

While the New York City players drew first blood in the battle, Brooklyn teams would dominate the sport in the decade that followed, revenging the 1858 defeat in 1861 and winning baseball's unofficial championship from its inception in 1861 until 1867.[47] In a display of boosterism and civic pride, long an integral part of American sport, the Brooklyn *Eagle* proudly told its readers, "Nowhere has the National game of Baseball taken a firmer hold than in Brooklyn and nowhere are there better ballplayers." Given the area's inferiority complex, overshadowed as it was by the giant across the river, it is not surprising that the newspaper was especially pleased when a team from Brooklyn was victorious over a New York City club. "If we are ahead of the big city in nothing else," the *Eagle* wrote, "we can beat her in baseball."[48]

By the end of the 1850s the national pastime had made significant advances both in the New York metropolitan area and throughout the country, although baseball contests remained purely local affairs. The Excelsior Club of Brooklyn broke with this policy prior to the start of the 1860 season when it announced a two-week tour to play teams in the western part of the state. The *Eagle* responded favorably to the idea, noting that "the excursion would not only be an exceedingly pleasant and enjoyable one but it would add greatly to the advances of the popularity of the game in every locality visited." Baseball's first extended road trip proved to be successful as the visitors easily won all six games against less experienced teams. Returning to Brooklyn the Excelsiors took on the Atlantics in a match described as a battle to decide the best baseball team in America. The expected classic confrontation between two equally matched teams turned into a rout, with the Excelsiors manhandling the Atlantics, 23-4, before a huge crowd estimated at 6,000–8,000. The next day the *Eagle* reported that the Atlantics never looked worse and the Excelsiors never looked better. Fresh from victory the Excelsiors went on another tour, going as far south as Baltimore and continuing to attract considerable interest despite one-sided victories over hometown heroes.[49]

The impact of the Excelsior Club on baseball went beyond the interest its tours generated or its success on the field. The club represented changes that were already underway in baseball as a result of the growth of the sport and the increasing competitiveness of the game. Initially composed of the merchants and clerks who formed the club for the benefits to be derived from healthful exercise, the team was totally revamped between 1857 and 1860 as winning took on greater importance and symbolic meaning. Newer and better players were added in a merger with another Brooklyn club, by the decision of two members of the New York Cricket Club to join the baseball team, and with the recruitment of four players from the Star Club, a leading Brooklyn junior squad.[50] Yet with all these changes the Excelsior Club was still considered a club for gentlemen. Many of the new recruits came from respectable families, although the starting nine included players whose economic and social standings placed them below other members. While talent was by no means the sole criterion for membership, it was clearly a major factor in the recruitment of some players.

Of the new Excelsior players none was more important as both a ball player and a symbol of baseball's future than James Creighton, the sport's first superstar, whose arrival in 1860 turned a good team into a powerful one. A reporter for the *Eagle* heard so much about Creighton's prowess as a pitcher that he felt compelled to go see him perform. He noted that the nineteen-year-old threw a "speed ball," but as speed alone was not difficult to hit, he also curved the ball. The reporter claimed that Creighton delivered his pitches "within a few inches of the ground and they rose up about the batsman's hip, and when thus delivered, the result of hitting at the ball is either to miss it or send it high in the air."[51]

Creighton was not only the sport's first premier player, he was, more significantly, baseball's first professional player. How the Excelsior Club compensated him, whether in money or a job, is unknown, but why they chose to violate the NABBP ban against paid players is easier to comprehend. Apparently the young man was from a respectable middle-class family, and considering that his father was only a clerk at city hall, his social standing was probably higher than his economic one. The Creightons were most likely down on their luck, and the Excelsiors agreed to compensate their star pitcher because he lost time at work when on tour and because they had no fear that he would succumb to the evils often associated with professional athletes. While Creighton is the only known baseball professional in the pre–Civil War years, other players probably received gifts or at least had their dues paid by grateful club patrons.[52]

After returning from their southern trip the Excelsiors played the Atlantics again, this time losing in a close game, 15-14. The third, tie-breaking game drew a record crowd of 14,000–20,000, but the contest never reached a conclusion. With the Excelsiors leading 8-6 in the sixth inning their captain pulled the team off the field to protest the unruly behavior of the Atlantic fans after several close calls.[53] While the press absolved both teams of the incident, the deportment of the crowd was symptomatic of the growing rowdyism, excessive questioning of umpires' decisions, and especially gambling and partisanship.[54] "If admirers of this manly pastime desire its future welfare," the *Eagle* pointed out, "they should at once proceed to adopt stringent rules among the various clubs, *against betting on the results of matches played,* for it is unquestionably a regard for their pockets alone that led the majority of those pecuniary interested in the affair to act in the background manner that they did." The *Clipper* saw the problem of gambling as part of "the *spirit of faction* that characterises a large proportion of the community, and in which the foreign element of our immense metropolitan population, and their native offspring especially, delights to indulge."[55] Such problems would continue to plague not only baseball but all highly competitive (especially team and spectator) sports. These problems derive from the shift in the intent of the activity from play to sport, where the seriousness of the process yields to the seriousness of outcome. This shift becomes especially charged when victory takes on communal significance and importance.

———

Despite these difficulties the press insisted that the 1860 baseball season "may justly rank as the most brilliant one in the brief annals of our national game."[56] The rapid and continuing growth of the sport naturally led observers to seek out its cause, which they attributed to the inexpensiveness and simplicity of the game; the health and moral benefits derived from the activity; and the familiarity of many Americans with the game from their childhood and its association with boyhood frolics. By the outbreak of the Civil War the press had also adopted a fourth, and eventually dominant, explanation for baseball's popularity—namely, that baseball expressed and was suited for the American character and temperament.[57] Ever since then writers have sought to explain baseball's special place in American life. Most have relied on the nebulous idea of baseball's relationship to the national character, although several have focused on other, more interesting interpretations. For example, Allen Guttmann maintains that the major reason for baseball's preeminent position among American sport is its place in the cycle of seasons and its tendency toward extreme quantification.[58] While such explanations contain some validity, they do not provide, even collectively, a satisfying framework for understanding why baseball has long been America's number-one sport.

The most important factor in explaining baseball's leadership role is its emergence as a popular pastime at a critical juncture in the history of American athletics. Baseball was not the first organized sport, the first successful spectator sport, nor the first sport to enjoy widespread popularity. However, it was the first sport to take advantage of the changing attitude toward athletics. More than any other sport of its day baseball fulfilled the requirements of the new sporting universe created by the changing social and urban environment of the antebellum period. The rapid spread of baseball clubs illustrated "a great popular want" for outdoor recreation,[59] and while other sports could have served this need, few had baseball's advantages. Not only was it inexpensive, but it combined individual play within a team setting. It is no coincidence that there was an increasing emphasis on team, at the expense of individual, sports with the shift from premodern to modern sport. While several factors shaped this development, one contributory reason was that team sports more readily served the character-value argument so important to the justification of athletics.[60]

The unquestioned acceptance of baseball as the national pastime contributed greatly to its preeminent position in the sports world. Both the absence of an entrenched competitor and timing played a vital role here. As early as 1857 the *Spirit* claimed that baseball "must be regarded as a national pastime," yet organized baseball at that time was confined to the New York metropolitan area, although various children's forms of the game were well known throughout the country. This premature description might have reflected a certain parochialism on the part of the New York–based sports journal, but the desire to promote an American sport was probably the real reason for this contention. In an article entitled "National Sports and Their Uses" the *Times* argued that strenuous athletic activity was necessary to combat the physical degeneracy of urban residents and that the more extensive participation in sport in England was responsible for Britons' longer lifespan. "To reproduce the tastes and habits of English sporting life in this country is neither possible nor desirable," the newspaper maintained, but "to develop analogous tendencies of an original and specific character appropriate to our national trials and opportunities is both very possible and desirable." A statement in *Porter's Spirit* clearly suggested that baseball "ought to be looked upon in this country with the same national enthusiasm" as cricket in England because "there should be some game peculiar to the citizens of the United States." Its advocacy of baseball was not based on the fact that the sport was manly, healthful, or a pleasure to the young, since that would "say nothing specifically in its praise, because all movements of the body in the open air are so." Instead, *Porter's Spirit* rested its support for baseball on the belief that the time had come "that some attempt was made to set up a game that could be termed a 'Native American Sport.' "[61]

The search for a national pastime grew out of the sporting revolution of the antebellum period. As with other cultural forms, the maturation of sport in this country led to the desire on the part of Americans to emancipate their games from foreign patterns. Such nationalistic overtones were already present in harness racing, but this nonparticipatory sport could not emerge as a symbol of an athletic movement with healthful exercise as its major rationale. Since baseball filled the bill, the press prematurely dubbed the game the national pastime, a symbol of, and spur to, America's athletic changes.

The erroneous popular belief that baseball was indigenous to America facilitated the contention that baseball was indeed the national pastime. Robin Carver had delineated the relationship between baseball and the English game of rounders as early as 1839 in his *Book of Sport*. While the children's book was quite popular, many adults were probably unfamiliar with its content, while others no doubt forgot or ignored the relationship. Many Americans innocently presumed that the game was native to this country since they had been playing it for so long and since rounders attracted no public attention in England.[62] As baseball gained in popularity, however, a letter to the *Herald* in 1859 pointed out that English schoolboys had played baseball under the name of rounders for more than a century, and the following year Henry Chadwick, an English-born sportswriter living in America, also noted baseball's English origins. Given Chadwick's authoritative position and the presence of Englishmen on the baseball diamond, the reassertion that baseball evolved from rounders went virtually unchallenged until years later, when Albert G. Spalding and his self-appointed commission sought to purify the game through the propaganda of the Abner Doubleday Myth.[63]

Having raised doubts as to just how American the national pastime was, Chadwick immediately reassured his adopted countrymen that "this invigorating exercise and manly pastime may be now justly termed the American game of Ball, for though of English origin, it has been so modified and improved of late years in this country, as almost to deprive it of any of its original features beyond the mere groundwork of the game." Significant changes in baseball had already taken place, but that any Englishman could easily recognize the game as a variation of rounders indicates that such a claim was a bit premature. Chadwick clearly felt that Americans needed a sport they could call their own and that baseball was well suited as the national pastime because it was peculiarly adapted to the American character. He never insisted, however, as many writers did, that baseball was an inherently better game than cricket—it was simply an excellent way to popularize physical education and a healthy outdoor sport.[64] His argument, adopted by other writers, contained elements of the truth, for a radical change in the character of the sport had taken place—if not by 1860, then clearly by 1870. As a "game" form baseball was not a native product but had evolved from earlier ball games of which rounders was its most direct ancestor. As a "sport" form baseball was indigenous to America, for it was in this country that baseball was organized and the rules standardized. In essence, while baseball originated as an English game, it became an American sport.

The acceptance of baseball as the national pastime and the perception of it as the embodiment of the American temperament was critical to its long-lasting preeminent position. While criticism of baseball was evident even after 1870, it mostly concerned the professional game. By 1900, when college football first came out from behind ivy-covered walls, criticism of baseball had not only abated but the sport was unquestionably accepted as one of America's finest democratic institutions. In 1919 the eminent philosopher Morris Cohen claimed that baseball was the American religion. Indeed, thanks to a pervasive and popular ideology and mythology, baseball had an incalculable head start over any of its serious sports rivals.[65]

Through all this the press never hesitated to point out its contribution to the growth of baseball as a national sport. Although that view was self-serving and slightly exaggerated it was not entirely without merit. Increasing coverage of the sport in the 1850s corresponded with the growing number of clubs and contests and the public desire for such news. The press, especially sports journals such as Porter's Spirit and the Clipper, disseminated information on how to play the game, how the clubs were organized, what the various teams in New York City and vicinity, and the country as well, were doing—in other words, they publicized the game. Baseball reporting made only minor advances during this period as newspapers continued to provide only brief summaries of contests and crude box scores that merely detailed the runs and outs made by each player. By the end of the 1850s, however, sports journals began to compile annual statistics of players and teams, as they did for cricket, as a means of assessing performances.[66] The pre–Civil War period also saw the rudimentary beginnings of a baseball literature. In 1857 a frequent correspondent to Porter's Spirit noted that many cricket books existed and that one was needed for baseball, too. Beadle's Dime Base-Ball Player, edited by Henry Chadwick and published in 1860, was the first annual guidebook for the sport; approximately 50,000 copies were sold. Essentially a rehash of Chadwick's newspaper articles, the guidebook discussed the origins of baseball, published the NABBP rules, provided statistics from the previous year, and offered a brief statement as to the physical and moral benefits of baseball.[67]

The occupational structure of New York City and Brooklyn ball players changed significantly with the rising popularity of the sport. Baseball shifted from an upper-middle–middle-class game to one dominated by men from the middle–lower-middle classes. While professional–high white-collar and low white-collar–proprietor workers made up slightly more than three-quarters of the ball players of these neighboring cities between 1850 and 1855 (see table 2-1), the latter group, along with skilled craftsmen, composed roughly the same proportion during the next five-year interval (see table 2-2). This change was almost directly related to the increasing percentage of skilled craftsmen and the declining proportion of professional–high white-collar workers. The evidence clearly indicates that baseball in Brooklyn and New York City had become a broadly based sport by the outbreak of the Civil War, although unskilled workers, roughly one-third of the work force of each city, remained virtually absent from the diamond. It should be further noted that roughly half of the skilled craftsmen were connected with crafts that were able to minimize the negative impact "metropolitan industrialization" had on a large section of New York's skilled craftsmen. Besides those in the shipping industry, discussed earlier, ball players in both cities worked in the printing, construction, and especially the food industries (one-sixth of all New York ball players were in the food industry, while one-tenth of all Brooklyn players engaged in food-related occupations, including ten men from the Atlantic Club). While many of the skilled workers came from the more prosperous crafts, the fact that one-sixth of all New York and Brooklyn ball players worked at jobs where they barely earned a living wage testifies to the broad appeal of the national pastime.[68]

The general membership of New York City and Brooklyn baseball clubs was from the middling ranks, but middle- to upper-middle-class men were elected officers of these clubs: over three-quarters of them were from the two higher-status occupational groups (see table 2-3). The 12.9 percent difference between baseball officers and total club membership resulted almost exclusively from the shifting proportion of professionals and skilled craftsmen. This

Table 2-2. Occupational Structure of Area Baseball Players, 1856–60

	New York City		Brooklyn		Combined	
	N	%	N	%	N	%
Professional–High White-Collar	41	21.9	31	18.2	72	20.2
Low White-Collar–Proprietor	83	44.4	73	42.9	156	43.7
Skilled Craftsman	61	32.6	63	37.1	124	34.7
Unskilled Worker	2	1.1	3	1.8	5	1.4
Total	187		170		357	

Table 2-3. Occupational Structure of Area Baseball Club Officers, 1856–60

	New York City		Brooklyn		Combined	
	N	%	N	%	N	%
Professional–High White-Collar	23	33.8	21	30.0	44	31.9
Low White-Collar–Proprietor	34	50.0	28	40.0	62	44.9
Skilled Craftsman	11	16.2	21	30.0	32	23.2
Total	68		70		138	

change was evident in both cities, although Brooklyn officers, like Brooklyn ball players, had more plebeian backgrounds. NABBP delegates between 1857 and 1860 held even more lucrative jobs (see table 2-4). Since officers and delegates were a more visible group, they were more easily identifiable—constituting probably no more than one-fourth of the membership, they accounted for 41.5 percent of the known ball players. When baseball's nonofficer membership is examined, the sport's middle-class character emerges even more clearly (see table 2-5). Between 1856 and 1860 only one-eight of the nonofficers were drawn from the more prestigious and lucrative occupations; the remaining players were divided roughly equally between the next two groups, with only a minute percentage being unskilled workers.

Although variations existed between officers and nonofficers there were no differences between members who participated in ball games and those who did not. The occupational structure of the ball players who engaged in at least one game (on the first team of their respective clubs) during this five-year

Table 2-4. Occupational Structure of Area NABBP Delegates, 1857–60

	New York City		Brooklyn		Combined	
	N	%	N	%	N	%
Professional–High White-Collar	14	43.8	6	35.3	20	40.8
Low White-Collar–Proprietor	12	37.5	7	41.2	19	38.8
Skilled Craftsman	6	18.8	4	23.5	10	20.4
Total	32		17		49	

Table 2-5. Occupational Structure of Nonofficer Members of Area Baseball Clubs, 1856–60

	New York City		Brooklyn		Combined	
	N	%	N	%	N	%
Professional–High White-Collar	16	14.4	10	10.2	26	12.4
Low White-Collar–Proprietor	45	40.5	43	43.9	88	42.1
Skilled Craftsman	48	43.2	42	42.9	90	43.1
Unskilled Worker	2	1.8	3	3.1	5	2.4
Total	111		98		209	

interval was remarkably similar to the total membership (compare tables 2-6 and 2-2). Active participants—those who participated in four first-team games during any one year, or ten games in five years—varied significantly from the general membership (see table 2-7). Skilled craftsmen made up nearly half the ball players of the two cities who engaged frequently in baseball contests, with 40 percent of these men employed in the food industry. The next highest occupational group constituted another 36.1 percent of the active participants, with clerks (and similar workers) accounting for 40 percent of this group. Thus, clerks and food-industry workers together made up one-third of the active participants, while those engaged in the most and least lucrative occupations together made up less than one-sixth of the city's leading ball players.

By the mid-1850s baseball in New York City and Brooklyn began to slip from the polite hands of the urban gentlemen, becoming a sport for all social

Table 2-6. Occupational Structure of Area Baseball Players, 1856–60

	New York City		Brooklyn		Combined	
	N	%	N	%	N	%
Professional–High White-Collar	21	11.9	13	18.1	34	20.2
Low White-Collar–Proprietor	40	41.7	28	38.9	68	40.5
Skilled Craftsman	33	34.3	29	40.3	62	36.9
Unskilled Worker	2	2.1	2	2.8	4	2.4
Total	96		72		168	

Table 2-7. Occupational Structure of Active Area Baseball Players, 1856–60

	New York City		Brooklyn		Combined	
	N	%	N	%	N	%
Professional–High White-Collar	8	17.8	3	7.9	11	13.3
Low White-Collar–Proprietor	18	40.0	12	31.6	30	36.1
Skilled Craftsman	18	40.0	22	57.9	40	48.2
Unskilled Worker	1	2.2	1	2.6	2	2.4
Total	45		38		83	

classes, with the notable exception of unskilled workers. On the playing field, clerks, a select group of proprietors, and skilled craftsmen in particular dominated the sport. The high percentage of craftsmen among baseball's active participants, especially in Brooklyn and even before the commercialization and professionalization of the sport, indicates that they were not lured to baseball by these later developments; instead, their presence in large numbers was vital to the emergence of this later stage.

Several factors contributed to the involvement of skilled craftsmen in baseball. The inexpensiveness of the sport and the fact that they could easily engage in it without disturbing their work schedules (or, in the case of ball players who worked in the food industry, had occupations that were completed by midday) facilitated participation. A high percentage of baseball's craftsmen, most notably those in the shipping and food industries, engaged in occupations where the relationship between master craftsmen and their employees was generally good. In fact, one possible reason for the considerable number of ball-playing members from the butcher community is that master craftsmen in this industry may have promoted and sponsored clubs. Clearly, these men were frequently the officers and NABBP delegates of clubs composed of butchers.[69]

Most important of all, craftsmen had a rich sporting heritage in general, especially among those artisans who belonged to the group Bruce Laurie describes as "traditionalist." New York butchers were typical of this group, known as lusty chaps who glorified in their stamina and physical prowess. While they engaged in a variety of sports, baseball held a special attraction for them and for other artisans. Unlike other sports they participated in, such as boxing and animal sports, which were illegal, publicly castigated, and usually conducted surreptitiously, baseball was socially respectable and favorably reported on in the press. Participation in baseball thereby provided butchers with an arena to demonstrate that they were part of the respectable community at a time when they had an unrivaled reputation for forming gangs and for drunken carousing. One reason master craftsmen in this industry, who were regarded as respectable, sober, and substantial, may have promoted baseball clubs among their employees was to counterbalance this negative image and to provide an alternative recreation to those frequently engaged in.[70] Finally, baseball offered artisans a vehicle for enhancing their prestige and influence within their own communities, which had long appreciated and rewarded physical prowess and sporting success. With the growing popularity of baseball, artisans also could win prestige within the large community of players and fans, thereby further enhancing their standing in their own communities. Thus, it was a search for fame rather than fortune that initially attracted these workers to baseball.

The game of baseball made significant advances in the fifteen years after the Knickerbockers organized the first club. Now a popular participant and spectator sport, baseball was well on its way toward modernization by the outbreak of the Civil War. The growth of the game and the rapid advances it made, especially between 1855 and 1860, set the stage for the tremendous changes that would occur during the next decade.

Notes

1. For a discussion of baseball's pastoral image, see Allen Guttmann, *From Ritual to Record: The Nature of Modern Sports* (New York: Columbia University Press, 1978), 100–106; Bruce Catton, "The Great American Game," *American Heritage* 10 (April 1959): 16–25; Richard C. Crepeau, "Urban and Rural Images in Baseball," *Journal of Popular Culture* 9 (1975): 315, 318–24; Murray Ross, "Football and Baseball in America," in John T. Talamini and Charles H. Page, eds., *Sport and Society: An Anthology* (Boston: Little, Brown, 1973), 103–104; Steven A. Riess, *Touching Base: Professional Baseball and American Culture in the Progressive Era* (Westport, Conn.: Greenwood, 1980), 227–68.

2. For the formation of the Knickerbockers, see Harold Seymour, *Baseball*, 2 vols. (New York: Oxford University Press, 1960–71), 1:15; Robert W. Henderson, *Ball, Bat and Bishop: The Origin of Ball Games* (New York: Rockport, 1947), 161–62; Charles A. Peverelly, *The Book of American Pastimes* (New York, 1866), 339–40; Al-

bert G. Spalding, *America's National Game* (New York: American Sports, 1911), 47–88.

3. Henry Chadwick, ed., *Beadle's Dime Base-Ball Player*, 6 vols. (New York: Beadle, 1860–65), 2:6. Also see Seymour, *Baseball*, 1:6, 18, 33; Henderson, *Ball*, 146–47, 161, 168; Spalding, *America's National Game*, 55; Irving A. Leitner, *Baseball: Diamond in the Rough* (New York: Criterion, 1972), 31–32; Harold Peterson, *The Man Who Invented Baseball* (New York: Scribner, 1969), 76–77. For Curry's view thirty-one years after the contest, see Alfred H. Spink, *The National Game* (St. Louis: National Game, 1910), 56.

4. *New York Herald*, October 21, 25, 1845. For further discussion of this theme and an examination of the composition of the Brooklyn Club, see Melvin L. Adelman, "The First Baseball Game, The First Newspaper References to Baseball and the New York Club: A Note on the Early History of Baseball," *Journal of Sport History* 7 (Winter 1980): 132–35.

5. *Herald*, November 11, 1845. In 1865 Alexander J. Cartwright wrote that the Knickerbockers were baseball's first club, "for the old New York Club never had a regular organization." See his letter to Charles Debost in Peterson, *Man Who Invented Baseball*, 175. The statement suggests that the New Yorkers had some organization even if they lacked the formality of the Knickerbockers.

6. Henderson, *Ball*, 162, 167, 196; Seymour, *Baseball*, 1:17–20, 38.

7. For the conventional wisdom about the Knickerbockers, see Peverelly, *American Pastimes*, 340; Seymour, *Baseball*, 1:15–17; David Q. Voigt, *American Baseball*, 2 vols. (Norman: University of Oklahoma Press, 1966–70), 1:8; Spalding, *America's National Game*, 65–69; John A. Krout, *Annals of American Sport* (New Haven, Conn.: Yale University Press, 1929), 117–18; Foster R. Dulles, *A History of Recreation: America Learns to Play* (New York: Appleton-Century-Crofts, 1965), 187; Leitner, *Baseball*, 33.

8. For the view that the Knickerbockers were from the upper class, see Leitner, *Baseball*, 33; Spalding, *America's National Game*, 51, 66; Robert Smith, *Baseball* (New York: Simon and Schuster, 1947), 37; Robert Boyle, *Sport—Mirror of American Life* (Boston: Little, Brown, 1963), 16. None of the Knickerbockers were among, or descendants of, the wealthiest 1,000 New Yorkers in 1845. See Edward Pessen, "The Wealthiest New Yorkers of the Jacksonian Era: A New List," *New York Historical Society Quarterly* 54 (1970): 161–72. Harold Seymour notes that the Knickerbockers were professional men, merchants, and white-collar workers. While he never suggests that they were from the upper class, he parallels baseball's early years with the effort of the upper class to restrict other sports to its own social class. He further asserts that one fact that contributed to baseball's popularity was that "the upper class had given their imprimatur to the game." See *Baseball*, 1:16, 31. A major drawback of Seymour's discussion of the Knickerbockers is that he considers the club's development between 1845 and 1860 in a singular analysis. Although certain similarities in policies and practices persisted throughout these fifteen years, changes naturally

occurred as a result of shifting membership and the overall growth of the sport. Seymour draws data for his analysis of the club members from the membership rosters for 1859 and 1860, which also give the year each member of those two teams joined the club. Since many of the Knickerbockers between 1845 and 1850 were no longer club members in 1859 and 1860, his analysis can hardly be accurate in terms of the occupational structure of baseball's pioneer team during its early years. Voigt's examination of social class among the Knickerbockers is similar to Seymour's. See *American Baseball*, 1:8.

9. Peterson, *Man Who Invented Baseball*, 53, 90–106, 164–76. When the Knickerbockers were formed in the 1840s they were not men of absolute leisure but rather from the mercantile class. See *Wilkes' Spirit of the Times* 19 (January 23, 1869): 359.

10. Robert W. Henderson, "Adams of the Knickerbockers," unpublished manuscript in the New York Racquet and Tennis Club. The Knickerbocker club book reveals no effort to arrange a baseball game, although they did play intersquad contests during this period. See Knickerbocker Base Ball Club of New York, "Game Book, 1845–1868," 5 vols., Manuscript Room, New York Public Library.

11. Elite social clubs indicate the desire of men of eminence to "proclaim their status, to identify to peers and inferiors as dramatically as possible." See Edward Pessen, *Riches, Class, and Power Before the Civil War* (Lexington, Mass.: Heath, 1973), 229.

12. *Porter's Spirit of the Times* 1 (January 3, 1857): 293, 3 (November 7, 1857): 148; Preston D. Orem, *Baseball, from Newspaper Accounts* (Altadena, Calif., 1961), 10.

13. *Spirit of the Times* 23 (July 9, 1853): 246; Orem, *Baseball*, 10–11; Leitner, *Baseball*, 37.

14. *Porter's Spirit* 1 (January 10, 1857): 309; Spalding, *America's National Game*, 59–61; Leitner, *Baseball*, 38–39; Seymour, *Baseball*, 1:23–24; Dulles, *Recreation*, 187.

15. For a discussion of New York shipwrights, see Sean Wilentz, *Chants Democratic: New York City and the Rise of the American Working Class, 1788–1850* (New York: Oxford University Press, 1984), 134–37, 405–7. For the economic status of shipwrights in Philadelphia, see Stuart Blumin, "Mobility and Change in Ante-Bellum Philadelphia," in Stephan Thernstrom and Richard Sennett, eds., *Nineteenth Century Cities: Essays in the New Urban History* (New Haven, Conn.: Yale University Press, 1969), 168–69. The occupations of only eight of the eighteen Eckford players who appeared in the 1855 box scores could be identified. Of these players, four were nonmanual workers (two clerks, a doctor, and a merchant), so if every other player was a manual worker, then 22.2 percent of the club members would have been nonmanual workers.

16. *Porter's Spirit* 6 (March 26, 1859): 52; Chadwick, "Scrapbook," 26 vols., Spalding Collection, New York Public Library, vol. 3. Henry Eckford was among

the wealthiest 300 New Yorkers in 1845. See Pessen, *Riches,* 323. For a typology of the different working-class groups and attitudes, see Paul Faler, "Cultural Aspects of the Industrial Revolution: Lynn, Massachusetts, Shoemakers and Industrial Morality," *Labor History* 15 (1974): 367–94; Bruce Laurie, *Working People of Philadelphia, 1800–1950* (Philadelphia: Temple University Press, 1980).

17. For the method used to collect and collate the data, and the problems that arose, see the appendix.

18. I compared the Brooklyn work force, compiled from the *Census of the State of New York for 1855* (Albany, 1857), 178–95, with Carol Kaestle's work on New York for the same year. See *The Evolution of an Urban School System: New York City, 1750–1850* (Cambridge, Mass.: Harvard University Press, 1973), 201–202. The largest variation between the economic universes of the two cities was 6.7 percent, for common laborers; no other category had a difference larger than 2 percent.

19. For the development of Brooklyn, see Henry R. Stiles, *A History of the City of Brooklyn,* 3 vols. (Brooklyn: Subscription, 1867–70).

20. *Spirit* 25 (May 12, 1855): 147; Seymour, *Baseball,* 1:33.

21. *Herald,* November 3, 1854; *Spirit* 25 (June 2, 1855): 181.

22. *Herald,* July 20, 1859. For a contemporary view of the growth of baseball, see ibid., December 22, 1856; *Brooklyn Eagle,* August 2, 1858; *Porter's Spirit* 1 (September 6, 1856): 13, 3 (December 5, 1857): 212; *Spirit* 26 (January 3, 1857): 558; *New York Times,* July 14, 1858.

23. *Herald,* December 7, 1855; *Porter's Spirit* 1 (October 11, 1856): 93. Also see ibid., 2 (March 7, 1857): 5; *Herald,* December 22, 1856; *Spirit* 26 (January 3, 1857): 558, (January 31, 1857): 603. For the relationship between the expanded number of teams and games and the formation of a national association, see Chadwick, *Beadle's Dime* (1860): 9.

24. *Herald,* March 14, 1858; *Porter's Spirit* 4 (March 20, 1858): 37; *Spirit* 28 (March 20, 1858): 65; Henry Chadwick, "Scrapbook," vol. 7.

25. Spalding, *America's National Game,* 70; Voigt, *American Baseball,* 1:8–9; Krout, *Annals,* 118; Seymour, *Baseball,* 1:35–36.

26. *Porter's Spirit* 3 (October 31, 1857): 132, (September 5, 1857): 4; (January 16, 1858): 309, 2 (March 7, 1857): 5; *Spirit* 26 (January 31, 1857): 603.

27. For the view that the events at the 1858 convention were a democratic revolt, see Krout, *Annals,* 118; Spalding, *America's National Game,* 67–70. Voigt leaves the impression that the 1858 convention was a palace revolt. See *American Baseball,* 1:8–9. For Van Cott's letter, see *Spirit* 24 (December 23, 1854): 534; *Tribune,* December 19, 1854.

28. The term "junior club" was given to those teams whose delegates were less than twenty-one years old. With the passage of time it came to connote teams that were composed mainly of boys and young men (usually ages fourteen to twenty-

one). The NABBP had no age restrictions for members of senior clubs as long as they were not delegates. Most senior teams had some players who were less than twenty-one years old.

29. *Porter's Spirit* 4 (March 20, 1858): 337. For a similar view, see *New York Clipper* 5 (April 3, 1858): 396. Also see *Herald,* March 14, 1858; *Spirit* (March 20, 1858): 65. For the formation of the National Association of Junior Base Ball Players, see Chadwick, *Beadle's Dime* (1861): 50.

30. *Herald,* March 14, 1858; *Spirit* 28 (March 20, 1858): 56.

31. Seymour, *Baseball,* 1:37.

32. For the growth of baseball outside of the metropolitan area, see ibid., 1:24–29; Voigt, *American Baseball,* 1:9–10; Spalding, *America's National Game,* 62–63.

33. *Spirit* 29 (May 21, 1859): 169. New Englanders had their own version of baseball and in 1858 held their own convention. For a discussion of the New England game, see *Porter's Spirit* 1 (December 27, 1856): 176–77, 4 (May 29, 1858): 196, 3 (October 24, 1857): 117; Leitner, *Baseball,* 21, 46–47; Seymour, *Baseball,* 1:26–28. For the suggestion that the New York game won out because it was a better one than the New England game, see ibid., 1:37–38.

34. *Porter's Spirit* 3 (December 26, 1857): 261, (November 7, 1857): 148, 2 (March 7, 1857): 5.

35. Ibid. 1 (December 6, 1856): 229; *Clipper* 7 (March 31, 1860): 496, 8 (May 26, 1860): 43.

36. Orem, *Baseball,* 16. See *Porter's Spirit* 1 (December 20, 1856): 260 for its recommendation that a game have six outs per inning and that a ball caught on the first bounce would constitute one out but if caught on the fly would count as two outs.

37. *Porter's Spirit* 2 (March 7, 1857): 5.

38. The concept of manliness was critical in overcoming the view that baseball was a game suitable only for children. The press described baseball as manly amusement on numerous occasions but, as was the case with cricket, never precisely defined the term. The strong link to physical prowess and skill found in the cricket argument did not appear in the baseball argument, however, and seriously affected attempts to justify the sport as manly. It also suggests that while the press was certain that cricket was a manly sport, it was not so sure about baseball. For the contention that baseball was a manly sport, see *Porter's Spirit* 1 (January 31, 1857): 357, 4 (April 3, 1858): 68; *Clipper* 7 (February 18, 1860): 349; *Herald,* November 3, 1854, October 16, 1859; *Spirit* 26 (January 31, 1857): 603; *Eagle,* July 28, 1858, August 3, 1859, May 10, 1860.

39. *Porter's Spirit* 1 (November 8, 1856): 165. The Knickerbockers, "with a view of making the game more manly and scientific . . . proposed that no player should be out on a fair struck ball, if it was only taken by the fielder according to the old rule." Ibid. 2 (March 7, 1857): 5.

40. *Porter's Spirit* 2 (June 20, 1857): 245.

41. Ibid. 6 (August 20, 1859): 388; Seymour, *Baseball,* 1:19.

42. *Spirit* 28 (March 27, 1858): 78, 29 (December 3, 1859): 505; *Porter's Spirit* 4 (April 3, 1858): 69, 6 (March 19, 1859): 35.

43. *Clipper* 7 (July 9, 1859): 95; *Porter's Spirit* 6 (July 9, 1859): 292, (August 13, 1859): 372. For Van Cott's statement, see Chadwick, *Beadle's Dime* (1860): 45.

44. Chadwick analyzed the voting at the 1860 convention to illustrate that the players supported the fly rule. He noted that the newly admitted clubs, who voted 26-7 against the proposition, had been responsible for the defeat of the bill by 9 votes. Closer scrutiny demonstrates that among older teams, the fly rule was overwhelmingly desired by only those from Brooklyn. Delegates from clubs in that city voted 18-5 in favor of the bill, but New York City clubs and teams from outside the metropolitan area voted 12-10 and 8-7 against the bill, respectively. See Chadwick, *Beadle's Dime* (1860): 46–47. For the argument that the players favored the fly rule, also see *Porter's Spirit* 3 (January 16, 1858): 308; *Eagle,* August 6, 1860.

45. *Porter's Spirit* 4 (June 12, 1858): 228, (June 26, 1858): 260, (July 17, 1858): 313; *Clipper* 6 (July 24, 1858): 110. Two baseball historians contend that it cost fifty cents to witness the all-star game; the only newspaper reference was to a ten-cent admission fee, with a one-horse vehicle costing an additional twenty cents and a two-horse vehicle costing an additional forty cents. The latter fee structure, rather than a flat rate, was the one commonly used at the New York tracks. See *Herald,* July 11, 1858; Spalding, *America's National Game,* 71; Seymour, *Baseball,* 1:25.

46. *Spirit* 28 (July 17, 1858): 270, (July 24, 1858): 288, (August 21, 1858): 330, (September 18, 1858): 373; *Porter's Spirit* 4 (July 24, 1858): 332; *Times* 14 (July 21, 1858); *Eagle* (July 21, 1858); *Clipper* 6 (July 24, 1858): 110.

47. *Porter's Spirit* 5 (September 18, 1858): 36; *Times* 14 (July 14, 1858); *Clipper* 6 (September 18, 1858): 174. For the supremacy of Brooklyn teams, see *Porter's Spirit* 6 (August 6, 1859): 361; Seymour, *Baseball,* 1:25. For the 1861 all-star game, see *Eagle,* October 3, 22, 1861; Chadwick, *Beadle's Dime* (1862): 40–41; *Clipper* 9 (October 5, 1861): 194, (October 12, 1861): 202.

48. *Eagle,* September 3, March 12, May 10, 1862.

49. Ibid., April 30, July 18, 1860. For the importance of the tour, see ibid., July 9, 13, 1860; Chadwick "Scrapbook," vol. 1; Seymour, *Baseball,* 1:32; Spalding, *America's National Game,* 79–81.

50. For a more detailed discussion of the reconstruction of the Excelsiors, see Melvin L. Adelman, "The Development of Modern Athletics: Sport in New York City, 1820–1870" (Ph.D. dissertation, University of Illinois, 1980), 345–46.

51. *Eagle,* August 6, 1860.

52. For the view of Creighton as the first professional baseball player, see Chadwick, "Scrapbook," vol. 7. Also see Orem, *Baseball,* 26; Seymour, *Baseball,* 1:47–48; Voigt, *American Baseball,* 1:13.

53. *Eagle,* August 10, 24, 1860; *Herald,* August 24, 1860; *Clipper* 8 (August 31, 1860): 154; *Times,* August 14, 1860.

54. *Eagle,* August 27, 1860; *Clipper* 8 (September 8, 1860: 163. For earlier problems, see *Porter's Spirit* 3 (November 28, 1857): 196, (September 5, 1857): 4, 5 (October 30, 1858): 135; *Clipper* 8 (July 21, 1860): 107; Chadwick, *Beadle's Dime* (1861): 53–54.

55. *Eagle,* August 24, 1860; *Clipper* 8 (September 8, 1860): 164. The *Clipper* also noted that the problems of the Atlantic-Excelsior contest were rooted in the different social status of the two teams. The Excelsiors were reportedly American-born merchants and the Atlantics were artisans, many of them Irish-American. Also see *Spirit* 19 (January 23, 1869): 359; Spink, *National Game,* 361.

56. *Eagle,* October 30, 1860; *Clipper* 8 (February 2, 1861): 322.

57. *Herald,* December 22, 1856; *Eagle,* September 18, 1858; *Times,* August 28, 1858; *Clipper* 7 (February 18, 1860): 349; *Spirit* 27 (March 27, 1858): 78.

58. Guttmann, *Ritual,* chap. 4. For problems with Guttmann's view, see Adelman, "Modern Athletics," 376–77, n. 100. For other explanations of baseball's special place in American life, see Catton, "Great American Game," 16–25; Voigt, *American Baseball,* 1:80–96; Riess, *Touching Base,* 221–35; Ralph Andreano, *No Joy in Mudville: The Dilemma of Major League Baseball* (Cambridge, Mass.: Schenkman, 1965), 3–39.

59. *Eagle,* September 1, 1858.

60. Guttmann, *Ritual,* 136–57. For a discussion of the connection between team sports and the character-value argument, see the conclusion.

61. *Spirit* 26 (January 31, 1857): 603; *Times,* June 5, 1857; *Porter's Spirit* 1 (January 31, 1857): 357.

62. Robin Carver, *Book of Sport* (Boston, 1834). For a discussion of Carver's work, see Henderson, *Ball,* 152–60. For the belief in the American origins of baseball, see *Porter's Spirit* 1 (January 31, 1857): 357, 3 (October 24, 1857): 117; *Spirit* 26 (January 31, 1857): 103; *Eagle,* August 3, 1859; *Herald,* December 19, 1854.

63. *Herald,* October 16, 1859; Chadwick, *Beadle's Dime* (1860): 5.

64. Chadwick, *Beadle's Dime* (1860): 5; Chadwick, "Scrapbook," vol. 7.

65. Morris Cohen, "Baseball," *Dial* 19 (July 26, 1919): 57–58; Riess, *Touching Base,* 5–8, 221–33.

66. *Eagle,* May 30, 1864; *Baseball Chronicle* 1 (June 6, 1867); Seymour, *Baseball,* 1:32–34.

67. *Porter's Spirit* 3 (October 24, 1857): 117; Chadwick, *Beadle's Dime* (1860); Seymour, *Baseball,* 1:44.

68. For a discussion of metropolitan industrialization and its impact on New York's various crafts, see Wilentz, *Chants Democratic,* 107–42.

69. Biographical material on New York and Brooklyn baseball players is lacking, but there is some evidence to suggest that wealthier master craftsmen within the food industry were officers of several baseball clubs. For example, Seaman Lichtenstein, the treasurer of the Gotham Club from 1857 to 1859, made his fortune in pickles and went on to become one of the city's most prominent produce

merchants. A lover of fast horses, Lichtenstein was a member of the Elm Park Trotting Association and drove his horses with Cornelius Vanderbilt and other well-to-do gentlemen. See *Times*, December 25, 1902. Robert G. Cornell, an officer of the Baltic Club, was the brother of Charles G. Cornell, a wealthy butcher, carriage maker, and member of the city council. Charles Cornell was also a member of the Elm Park Trotting Association, as well as New York's prestigious American Jockey Club. See S. R. Harlow and H. H. Boone, *Life Sketches of the State Officers, Senators and Members of the Assembly of the State of New York in 1867* (Albany, N.Y.: Weed, Parsons, 1867), 85–86. For the relationship between master craftsmen and workers in the butchery and shipping industries, see Wilentz, *Chants Democratic*, 135–36, 139.

70. Wilentz, *Chants Democratic*, 139; Laurie, *Working People*, 54–60; Alvin F. Harlow, *The Old Bowery Days: The Chronicle of a Famous Street* (New York: Appleton, 1931), 151.

3

In the Beginning Was the Rule

MICHAEL ORIARD

The *how* is easy:

> A scrimmage takes place when the holder of the ball, being in the field of play, puts it down on the ground in front of him and puts it in play with his foot. The man who first receives the ball from the snap-back shall be called the quarter-back, and shall not then rush forward with the ball under penalty of foul.

> If on three consecutive fairs and downs a team shall not have advanced the ball five yards or lost ten, they must give up the ball to the other side at the spot where the fourth down was made. Consecutive means without leaving the hands of the side holding it.

The first statement is Amendment #1, adopted on October 12, 1880, by the Intercollegiate Football Association, agreed to by the representatives from Harvard, Princeton, Yale, and Columbia, convening to refine the four-year-old game. The second statement is Amendment #1 approved by the same body at the convention of October 14, 1882.[1] Together, these two simple rules created American football.

Football had been played informally for decades on American school grounds (chiefly as an aspect of hazing and interclass rivalry) when students from Princeton and Rutgers met in 1869 in the first intercollegiate contest.[2] They more or less followed the rules of the London Football Association—association football, soccer—as it was played in England. This initial contest was followed sporadically over the next five years by others, with all the schools (Columbia, Wesleyan, Yale, Tufts, Trinity, Stevens, and Pennsylvania, as well as the original two, Rutgers and Princeton) playing by soccer rules. With one exception: haughty Harvard stood alone; its "Boston game" allowed running with the ball and tackling, as in the rugby game also played in England. Even among the majority, however, each school devised its own set of rules, to be negotiated when matches were being arranged. The first attempt by American collegians to develop a common code took place in 1873, among Yale, Princeton, Rutgers, and Columbia, but the rules agreed upon served for only that season. In May 1874, McGill University of Montreal visited Cambridge, Massachusetts, for a pair of matches, one by Harvard's rules, the other by the Rugby Union code that the Canadians followed. Afterward, the *Harvard Advocate* declared the rugby game "in much better favor than the somewhat sleepy game now played by our men."[3] The following year, Harvard and Yale met for the first time under a modified rugby code that became known as the "Concessionary Rules," negotiated by representatives of the two schools. In 1876, after Princeton and Pennsylvania had competed under soccer rules, and Harvard and Yale under the concessionary rugby rules, representatives from Harvard, Yale, Princeton, and Columbia met on November 26 to create the Intercollegiate Football Association and finally adopt a common code. Harvard and Yale prevailed in the discussions; having dominated the soccer version of the game since its inception, Princeton agreed to the rugby rules reluctantly. As a sign of the self-interested politicking that has remained a part of intercollegiate football to this day, Yale initially declined membership in the Association but agreed to its rules.

The rules that emerged from this first convention of the Intercollegiate Football Association in 1876 did not vary substantially from the Rugby Union code; the Americans' chief modifications gave greater importance to running and instituted judges and referees.[4] But within just six years, in the two brief declarations quoted above, the architects of intercollegiate football in the United States transformed English rugby into a very different American game. First the creation of the scrimmage, as a substitute for the rugby scrummage (players from both teams massed about the ball, all trying to kick it out to a teammate), gave the ball to one team at a time; then the five-yard rule guaranteed that the team possessing the ball either advanced it or gave it up. Later revisions—rules on scoring, on blocking and tackling, on movement before the ball was snapped, on the number of offensive players allowed behind the line of scrimmage, most crucially on forward passing—were necessary before American football assumed a form in 1912 that we would recognize today as our game. Nonetheless, in the evolution of American football from English rugby, the distance from 1882 to 1993 is less significant than that from 1876 to 1882.

The interesting question is, why these most basic alterations? The evolution of football's rules has left a fascinating record that demands interpretation.

Why Americans' initial preference for the running and tackling rather than the kicking game? Then why our insistence on amending the Rugby Union code once adopted? "American exceptionalism" too often reduces more complex cultural relations, but in this instance a fundamental difference is indisputable. The establishment of officials by the very first rules committee may seem innocuous, but the act has deeply revealing implications. "There shall be two judges," rule #59 stated, "one for each side, and also a referee, to whom disputed points shall be referred, and whose decision shall be final." Parke Davis, an early chronicler of American football, appended an asterisk to this rule, with a note at the bottom of the page: "Entirely new. Under the Rugby Union Code the captains acted as officials."[5] It would be difficult to overstate the significance of this simple rule-plus-footnote. As Davis noted, in the public-school sporting contests of early Victorian England the opposing captains interpreted and enforced the rules. When a single referee was later instituted, his function was to penalize "ungentlemanly conduct"; later, when new rules defined fouls more precisely, at least some traditionalists were outraged. When the penalty kick in soccer was adopted in 1891, one English gentleman sputtered angrily, "It is a standing insult to sportsmen to have to play under a rule which assumes that players intend to trip, hack and push their opponents and to behave like cads of the most unscrupulous kind. I say that the lines marking the penalty area are a disgrace to the playing field of a public school."[6] No American in 1891 could have challenged the need for rules and referees; the only question was, how many of each were needed? The institution of judges as advocates for each team, with a referee as final arbiter, led to incessant wrangling that interrupted games for as much as thirty minutes at a time. The wrangling often began long before the football contest; agreeing on a referee was perhaps the single most important decision to be negotiated when matches were arranged. After several ugly controversies the judges were finally eliminated in 1885, conduct of the game left entirely to the referee. When this arrangement proved unworkable, an umpire was added in 1888, then a linesman in 1894, then a second umpire in 1906 (after an earlier unsatisfactory trial) who became a field judge in 1907. (A back judge and a line judge were added in 1955 and 1972 respectively, to complete our current lineup of officials.)

The rules to be enforced changed and expanded with even more unsettling frequency. One coach complained in 1912 that "the rules of the last year required sixty-five pages and fourteen thousand words to make their meaning clear."[7] To this day, rugby and soccer have relatively few and simple rules and a single referee. American football by now has a small army of officials and rules so detailed as to dazzle a modern Blackstone. (Baseball and cricket similarly differ.) At different times over the past several years, for example, offensive linemen have been forbidden to use their hands or extend their arms in blocking; they have been allowed to use their closed fists or open hands, to extend their arms momentarily or leave them extended, and to deliver blows only to variously specified parts of the defenseman's body. So, too, with other aspects of blocking, tackling, and defending against passes. Efficiency is obviously one goal, to maintain the delicate balance between offense and defense in order to satisfy the fans. But behind the always-present threat to proper balance lies the open assumption that rules in American sport exist to be exploited as much as followed.

What we take for granted today demanded comment, and evoked concern, during the closing decades of the nineteenth century when Americans were learning how to compete on playing fields. The issue was not outright cheating, as in prizefighting and other sports of disreputable "sporting men" that were notorious for their routine crookedness. Taking advantage of the rules was a different matter. Early baseball, which stood higher on the social scale than prizefighting but lacked full respectability until the 1920s, is full of amusing anecdotes of legal assaults on legality: a manager substituting himself as a foul ball sails toward the dugout, just in time to catch it; a catcher throwing his mask a few feet down the first-base line to trip the runner; an outfielder juggling the ball as he trots toward the infield, preventing a runner from advancing on a sacrifice fly. Buck Ewing, a baseball manager early in the twentieth century, summed up this spirit: "Boys," he told his players during a spring-training session on strategy, "you've heard the rules read. Now the question is: What can we do to beat them?"[8]

Many applauded this attitude. Amateur purists decried such practices, but the typical baseball fan admired the "brainy" coach or player who could dream up new tricks for winning. And college boys played the same games. The history of college football in the nineteenth and early twentieth centuries is a chronicle of rules constantly evolving in large part to outlaw tactics the old rules had inadvertently permitted. Having created a scrimmage line in 1880, the early rule makers found themselves continually forced to redefine it. The original intention was to give one team clear possession, but as long as the scrimmage line passed through the center of the ball, each team technically owned half of the football at the beginning of the play. In 1885, a proposal to separate the rush lines by five yards was defeated. In 1886, a new proposal "that the centre rush should be permitted to snap the ball without any interference from opponents" was approved; yet the following year, another rule prohibiting interference with the center snap was necessary, and as late as 1906 still another.[9] Similar tinkering was required for the rules on blocking ("interference"), flying wedges and other "mass" plays, scoring, holding, or giving up the ball, and so on. Until a rule made it impossible, a clever team discovered that it could score repeated touchdowns simply by bunting the after-touchdown goal kick to its own man, who then touched the ball down behind the goal line. The rules themselves, and the contemporary reports on them, were laced with comments of this sort: "the object being to prevent teams from deliberately missing goals in order to make another touchdown, which was possible under prior rules"; and "in order to prevent the prevalent stealing of the ball, the referee shall blow his whistle immediately when the forward progress of the ball has been stopped"; and "Note.—There shall be no shifting of men to evade this rule."[10] The basic problem was summed up by Walter Camp in 1894: "The Rugby code was all right for Englishmen who had been brought up upon traditions as old and as binding as the laws themselves. If a point were in dispute it was at once referred to any veteran and his word stood. No innovation would be tolerated, whether it was barred by the rules or not. And here came the difficulties of American collegians. The rules did not cover half the cases that arose, and the printed rule was the only law, as no traditions existed."[11] Camp sounds defensive here (the pressing issue at the time was the game's brutality); others saw in the constant manipulation of rules a splendid expression of Yankee ingenuity.

Elsewhere I have argued that this attitude toward rules—a recognition of the letter but not the spirit, a dependence on rules in the absence of tradition yet also a celebration of the national genius for circumventing them—expressed an American democratic ethos, a dialectical sense of "fair play" (embracing both "sportsmanship" and "gamesmanship") that was very different from the aristocratic British version.[12] Here, I am more interested in what this rule making and rule breaking tells us about the relations of culture and power. If no single Creator brought American football into being *ex nihilo,* it was a very small group of young men who had complete authority in creating the game *ex rugby.* Two representatives from Columbia joined those from Harvard, Yale, and Princeton for the inaugural rules convention in 1876; until 1894, only Wesleyan and Penn were admitted to this inner circle. Fewer than a dozen young men, all representing elite universities and relatively privileged classes, controlled the game during these crucial early years of its development. At the rules conventions they resisted changes that would in any way restrict their own schools' preferred style of play (this accounts to a considerable degree for the slowness in abolishing the mass-momentum plays that seemed mere brutality to outraged critics). Yet the rules once decreed were repeatedly skirted, even ignored, by the players, forcing further decrees. Later, faculty and college presidents, journalists, legislators, eventually a president of the United States had their say—as did the fans, when the interests of 40,000 spectators at the Thanksgiving Day games began to demand consideration.

In 1893, Walter Camp summed up these conflicting interests within the football community: "The captain usually desires to win that one year, no matter at what expense. The coach sometimes, particularly if he is to continue assisting his college, has the desire to win that year coupled with a hope of developing good material for further victories. The faculty wish the sport to be kept up that it may conduce to the physical and moral well-being of the student. The public, outside of those immediately interested in college affairs, wishes to see an interesting game, and incidentally some of the more public-spirited ones a sport that may make the boys, when they became men of the world, good citizens."[13] And all the while the players were doing whatever they could to win the game of the moment, competing against the rules as well as their opponents. Football games had overlapping yet different "meanings" for each of these groups, who wielded varying degrees of control over the way the games would be played and understood. The early years of football thus illustrate most concretely the messy relations and complicated distribution of power among "producers" and "consumers" of culture.

The creators of American football seem to have had power but little control, as they revised the rules again and again. Consider, in contrast, the astonishing stability of baseball. The distances of 60' 6" from the pitching mound to home plate and 90' between the bases seem almost magical: what worked in the nineteenth century continues to work in the 1990s, despite major changes in equipment, strategy, technique, even the physical abilities of players. Offense and defense remain finely balanced, assisted by only minor tinkering with the strike zone and the height of the pitcher's mound. Most of the time the throw still barely nips the runner at first base after a ground ball to deep shortstop; despite sliders and screwballs and split-fingered fastballs, batters still hit the ball often enough to keep the game interesting. Football even today experiences more dramatic swings from dominating offense to dominating defense, yet the current game seems rock-solid stable compared to its initial half-century. The chronicle of rules made, broken, amended, circumvented, amended again, abused again, in endless cycle, seems to reveal a game that developed without intention, by simple necessity after an initial accident.

Once the scrimmage line and the five-yard rule were instituted (by young men unable to anticipate the consequences), subsequent revisions were required to guarantee them, then to modify them as they became unworkable.

One could argue that only the first decisive break with the Rugby Union—creating the scrimmage and granting possession of the ball to one team—was truly a freely chosen rule. The five-yard rule became necessary when the Princeton teams of 1880 and 1881 played the notorious "block game." The Tiger players realized that they could hold the ball an entire half, as the rules permitted, simply by neither kicking nor fumbling, and so allow the more powerful Yale team no opportunity to score. The graver crisis in the 1890s over football's appalling violence similarly resulted as a matter of course from the addition of legalized "interference" to the possession and five-yard rules, and from a seemingly innocuous rule in 1888 that permitted tackling not just above the waist but also between the waist and the knees. In American football today blockers lead the ball carrier; in rugby, the ball carrier precedes his teammates, tossing the ball back to one of them before he can be downed. Together with forward passing, this legalized blocking most obviously distinguishes the look of American football from rugby. Originally, Americans adopted rugby's "off-side" rule—forbidding any offensive player to run ahead of the man with the ball—but they also routinely violated it. The problem was inescapable: once possession of the ball was given to a single team, every time the ball was snapped to the quarterback, the entire rush line was put offside and legally could do nothing to interfere with the defensive players. From this more or less inadvertent interference, the practice of increasingly intentional and sophisticated kinds of interference quickly developed. The rules conventions of the 1880s returned again and again to this problem: decreeing in 1881, for example, that three warnings for "intentional off-side playing" (that is, interference) meant disqualification, then in 1883 allowing an additional infraction before dismissal, then later in 1883 back to two, in 1884 only one, and so on. Finally, after a recommendation in 1889 that "the side which has the ball can interfere with the body only, the side which has not the ball can use hands and arms as heretofore," interference was at last made legal, and the modern game of blocking emerged. But legalization also meant new possibilities for abuse. For many years blockers were allowed to use their hands against opponents and could push and pull their own ballcarrier. Even more dangerous were flying wedges and other mass-momentum plays (various schemes for attacking a stationary defense with several blockers leading the ballcarrier), which became the dominant offensive strategy in the 1890s, resulting in unprecedented brutality that jeopardized the sport's survival. This course of development seems to have been both accidental and inevitable: possession + five-yards-in-three-plays-for-a-first-down + interference = mayhem. The rules conventions of the 1890s and early 1900s could forget about violations of the offside rule but had to wrestle incessantly to alter this new equation.

In contrast to the murky evolution of interference, the legalization of low tackling in 1888 was a single, clearly defined revision of the rules, but with disastrous unforeseen consequences. Walter Camp proposed the low-tackling rule out of a desire to readjust the balance between offense and defense: fast, shifty runners were difficult to drag down when they could be tackled only above the waist. Instead, low tackling virtually eliminated open-field running, led to increasingly brutal (and boring) mass play, altered the very shape of football players by tilting the advantage overwhelmingly toward sheer bulk, and necessitated the development of padded armor to protect the newly vulnerable players. Even the long hair of football players, a tribal mark that amused observers and provoked countless caricatures in the 1890s, was a consequence of this one rule: long hair became an alternative to the various kinds of headgear that began to appear as protections against head injuries. Memory of a glorious "open game" haunted the debates over football brutality in the 1890s: swift, wiry players spread across the field, passing and kicking the ball to each other, then dashing down the field on heroic jaunts into the end zone. Low tackling seemed to have replaced this style with closely packed behemoths pounding each other for a couple of yards of bloody turf. Such, anyway, was the hyperbolic response of many saddened observers. A single rule transformed the game in unwanted ways.[14]

Football thus developed as much by accident as by design, and the enhanced narrativity that also resulted from the scrimmage and the five-yard rule was equally accidental. Harvard's preference for the running-and-tackling game in the years just preceding the formation of the Intercollegiate Football Association in 1876 seems to have been compounded of equal parts of arrogance and desire for wide-open action. Declining to join Yale and Princeton for a rules convention in 1873, Harvard's captain declared imperiously to the representatives from Yale, "Harvard stands entirely distinctly by herself in the game of football." But he also deigned to explain a bit more fully: "We cannot but recognize in your [soccer-type] game much but brute force, weight, and especially 'shin' element. Our game depends upon running, dodging, and position playing,—i.e., kicking across field into another's hands. We are perfectly aware of our position in regard to other colleges. I assure you we gave the matter a fair discussion last spring. We even went so far as to practice and try the Yale game. We gave it up at once as hopeless."[15] A few weeks later, the contests with McGill confirmed Harvard's preference, only now more in line with English rugby rules.

A simple desire for more open action thus seems to have been the initial impulse; whatever more complex or calculated motives may have contributed are lost to us. And Yale's and Princeton's acquiescing in Harvard's insistence on rugby rules at the formative convention of 1876 seems to have resulted less from preference than from deference to Harvard's preeminence among American colleges, and from a pragmatic view of the possibilities for consensus. Although Yale, not Harvard, became the football powerhouse, Harvard led Yale (and both led Princeton) in the institutional pecking order of the day.[16] All three colleges clung to their athletic independence in various ways throughout this formative period, but Harvard most successfully.

I find no evidence to suggest that the founding fathers of intercollegiate football realized that a nation with little history and less tradition required mythic narratives of national identity, and sensed that football might provide them: the Great American Epic in knickers and canvas jackets. But following the game's nearly haphazard beginnings, these narrative possibilities quickly became evident. It is important to remember that football began as a game to be played, not watched; the initial games drew small crowds from the contending college communities. By the mid-1880s, however, crowds of 10,000 and 15,000 were attending the Thanksgiving Day championship, 30,000 and 40,000 by the early 1890s.[17] This growth, too, occurred more by circumstance than by conscious plan, while the experience of spectatorship itself was more determined by those who managed and publicized the games than by those who played them. Initially, the fans ringed the playing area, restrained at most by ropes or simple fences. When their team scored, they poured onto the field to mob the heroes of the moment, disrupting the contest until they could be herded back to the sidelines. The development of facilities and methods for accommodating 30,000 people at Manhattan Field in New York, or Hampden Park in Springfield, Massachusetts, meant a transition from picturesque semi-chaos to orderly spectatorship. The big game became a social event as well as an athletic contest, as Richard Harding Davis noted in describing the crowd at the Yale-Princeton game in 1895:

> But if Somebody's Sister in one of the grand stands did not get quite as near to the inwardness of what was going forward as did the ex-player and the coaches along the line, she at least witnessed a spectacle that was worth crossing a continent to see. The majority of the spectators yesterday belonged to the class of the unseeing ones. They came because it was the thing to do, just

as they went to the opera to look at the boxes and not to listen to the music, and their interest in Yale and Princeton was perhaps of the slightest, and their knowledge of the game even less. But that did not interfere with their enjoyment of the day or prevent them from rising in their places and shouting as they had never shouted before.[18]

As an activity for a couple dozen young men became a spectacle for thousands, and as the benefits to the universities in both prestige and income became increasingly apparent, those who oversaw the development of the game had to shape it to the desires of viewers as well as participants. Football succeeded as spectacle because the games' own structure made narrative drama possible, but also because these narrative possibilities were exploited by football's promoters.

To trace the emerging consciousness, and exploitation, of football's narrative power I will explore the writings of "the father of American football," Walter Camp, in the remainder of this chapter. Through Camp's writings we have only one man's view of the game during its formative years, but Camp was the man who did most to shape it.

———————

Walter Camp was never an All-American but for thirty-seven years the maker of All-Americans, never a paid coach but the "coach of coaches," never a ruler but the preeminent creator of rules.[19] The son of a middle-class schoolteacher in New Haven, Camp was a star running back at Yale for six years and part of a seventh (1876–82), first as an undergraduate, then as a medical student (the limitation on seasons of eligibility came later, after years of wrangling among the rule makers). More important, after he left medicine and Yale for a career in business, first with the Manhattan Watch Company, then for four decades with the New Haven Clock Company (eventually becoming president and board chairman), Camp continued as graduate adviser to Yale captains for nearly thirty years, serving "as Yale's unofficial, unpaid, unquestioned chief mentor and arbiter."[20] Richard Harding Davis wrote in 1893, "There is only one man in New Haven of more importance than Walter Camp, and I have forgotten his name. I think he is the president of the university."[21] Outside New Haven, among football men he was the game's preeminent spokesman and authority, routinely identified in newspapers and magazines with such epithets as "the leading foot-ball expert in the country" or the "father of football at Yale"; on occasion, with touches of gentle irony, as "the King of American football" or "the great high priest of the grid-iron arena."[22]

Many of the captains and players Camp advised became coaches elsewhere, carrying with them their mentor's methods and ideas. Most important, from 1878 to his death in 1925, Camp served continuously on football's
rules committees, for twenty-eight years as secretary. His views dominated
the early committees in particular. The scrimmage rule of 1880, assigning possession to one team at a time, was his idea, as was the five-yard rule of 1882
(years later, Camp wrote that this rule initially "had no adherents save the man
who proposed it").[23] He proposed eleven players on a side instead of fifteen,
and devised the point-scoring scale, approved in 1883, that with more tinkering became the basis of our modern system. Ironically, though a most gentlemanly sportsman himself, Camp also proposed the legalization of low
tackling in 1888, then through the 1890s fought legislation to eliminate the resulting mass-momentum plays that critics blamed for football's shocking brutality. Losing that battle, Camp then resisted legalizing the forward pass in
1906, the ultimate shift from "mass" to "open" play. But if he yielded reluctantly to the later stages of development (motivated privately by Yale's self-
interest and publicly by a consistent vision that football was preeminently a
team game, not an individual sport), it remains true that American football
was to a considerable degree Walter Camp's creation.

Camp also wrote voluminously: nearly thirty books, over 200 magazine articles, countless newspaper commentaries. Included in these writings are his
reports on the All-American teams he personally selected from 1889 until his
death; beginning in 1898 these were an annual feature in *Collier's Weekly*. Also
included, though less well remembered, are numerous treatises on the emerging game, sometimes directed toward would-be coaches and players, sometimes meant to teach an awakening public what they were witnessing on the
field and, more important, what lay behind the visible action. These writings
provide an invaluable detailed record of Camp's understanding of football's
deeper meanings and significance, his own reading of football's cultural text.
Appearing in major periodicals (*Century, Collier's, Harper's Weekly, Outing, Outlook, Independent*), in the most popular juvenile magazines (*St. Nicholas, Youth's
Companion, Boys' Magazine*), in the major New York daily newspapers, and in
books by major publishers, Camp's ideas, enhanced by his peerless reputation,
had to have a powerful influence on the public's understanding.

Camp's writings reveal no attempt to develop football toward greater narrativity, nor even a conscious understanding that such a quality had uninten-
tionally resulted. Yet his writings also reveal that by the late 1880s Camp
himself recognized that football, both its brief history and the games on the
field, was a cultural text whose meaning he wished to interpret for its grow-

ing audience. Beginning with his earliest essays in *Harper's Weekly* (the era's major middle-class periodical) and *Outing* (its chief monthly devoted to sport and recreation), Camp's own narrative of football's development had a distinct plot: the rationalization and tactical development of the game's action, driven by the object of winning, developed in young men the character and experiences essential for success in America. Camp's master metaphor for football in all his writings was the hierarchically structured, efficiently run industrial corporation, no doubt linked in his own mind with the New Haven Clock Company. That is, in dozens of essays and four major treatises writtin during football's formative years, Camp consistently interpreted the game's meaning and significance from what is essentially a managerial and technocratic perspective.

This perspective might seem merely self-serving: for Walter Camp, a former three-time captain, then Yale's unofficial coach for a quarter-century, football was a game of tactics and leadership rather than physical achievement. Self-serving or not, Camp expressed a view that continues to distinguish American sports—basketball and baseball, as well as football—from the same or similar games elsewhere. In American basketball and baseball, the games are orchestrated from the sidelines, their outcomes frequently attributed to the winning team's superior "bench coach" or "field manager." When Indiana plays North Carolina in college basketball, it's Bobby Knight vs. Dean Smith; in the World Series it's Billy Martin vs. Tommy Lasorda, Tony LaRussa vs. Roger Craig. The tendency is less strong in professional than in college basketball, in baseball than in football; but in relation to European sport the American emphasis on the coaches is striking. And this emphasis is most pronounced in football, where the importance of teamwork is greatest and the players are drilled to execute, with little improvisation, a game plan devised by the coaching staff. Baseball commentators speak of "the book," the unwritten but universally known traditions that dictate most managers' decisions. There is no "book" in football; tactical styles vary from coach to coach, and at least once a decade some coach's innovation has truly expanded the possibilities in the game. From the original "V-trick" and "flying wedge" of the 1890s, to the single wing and double wing and split-T, to the wishbone and shotgun and run-and-shoot, football coaches have repeatedly reconceived the way their game is played.

Initially, coaching during games was forbidden by the rules taken over from the Rugby Union; once the contest began, all decisions were made by the captain on the field. Moreover, the early coaches were unofficial and unpaid, usually graduates returning to the university to advise the captain and help train the new eleven. Through its system of volunteer graduate coaches, Yale had dominated the Harvards and Princetons that continued to depend on student leadership. In addition, as more and more schools and athletic clubs took up the game, they needed coaches from outside because they lacked graduates with football experience (Yale initially provided most of these outside coaches). The professional coach originated at western colleges such as Minnesota and Chicago (where Amos Alonzo Stagg was hired in 1891 with a professor's salary). Not by intention but by necessity, the paid coach emerged as a fixture by the early twentieth century, but only after much agonizing and debate over the intrusion of "professionalism" into amateur sport. The success of the great tacticians of the 1890s and early 1900s, men like Stagg at Chicago, George Woodruff at Pennsylvania, and Henry L. Williams at Minnesota, made the value of professional coaches apparent to everyone. Harvard rarely beat Yale until, against internal resistance at even this late date, it hired its first professional coach in 1905. After several unaccustomed losses to Percy Haughton's teams at Harvard, Yale followed suit a decade later.[24] Having taught the football world the benefits of coaching, Yale accepted the professional coach with great reluctance.

As paid coaches emerged inevitably with the growing importance of winning for the university's prestige, the rule makers did not willingly surrender the game to coaches. Coaches were expected to help the captains organize their teams, train them, and develop strategy; once the games began, the players were to take over, the coaches to become mere interested spectators. A member of Harvard's faculty athletic committee in 1902 spoke for all advocates of amateur purity when he classed "side line coaching" among the "shady practices" that violated true sport. "When eleven young men appear on the football field," he wrote, "it is commonly understood that they are going to win or lose on their own merits, and not with the assistance of some one on the side lines." But he also acknowledge that, unfortunately, sideline coaching was a common practice, difficult for rule makers to prevent.[25]

They tried. American collegians began with a ban on coaching, as was traditional in English sport, but as always they immediately began to circumvent it. A rule in 1892 directed the umpire to prevent coaching from the sideline; another in 1900 forbade coaching during the game by substitutes or anyone else not actually playing; another in 1914 prohibited all persons from walking up and down the sidelines. No doubt the most difficult rule to enforce, instituted in 1917, said that substitutes could not communicate with other members of the team until after the first play (thus preventing them from bringing in instructions from the coach). After the offensive huddle became common, beginning in 1921 when it was introduced by the Illinois team coached by Bob Zuppke, the referee joined the huddle as substitutes entered the game, to assure their silence. Sideline coaching was not officially sanctioned until 1967.[26]

The early restrictions proved to be minor obstacles in the march toward coaching dominance, however. Substitution rules, one of the chief mechanisms by which coaching strategy could be expanded or contracted, changed thirty times in college football's first 100 years. The current intercollegiate rules allowing unlimited substitution (initially permitted in 1941, then restricted in 1953, then restored in two stages, in 1964 and 1973) have brought football coaches' control to new extremes: not just the two-platoon football first made possible in 1941, then again in 1964, but players shuffled in and out of the game to meet increasingly specialized needs determined by huge coaching staffs with their computer-generated strategies. The quarterback who calls his own plays in either college or professional football has become increasingly rare; the computerized efficiency of the Dallas Cowboys under Tom Landry in the 1970s and the "genius" of the San Francisco 49ers' Bill Walsh in the 1980s are recent contrasts in coaching control. How strange it must seem to Americans watching World Cup soccer matches to see that coaching is still not allowed during the contest.[27]

One of the narratives we read in football today, then, concerns a contest between what are seemingly rival corporations, and we can look to Walter Camp for the roots of his narrative—but also for the competing narrative that most directly challenges it. In the 1980s, sportswriters debated whether the Super Bowl victories of the 49ers belonged chiefly to Bill Walsh or to quarterback Joe Montana. When writers argued whether Montana was programmed by Walsh, then plugged into an unbeatable system, or made the system unbeatable himself, they restated competing narratives nearly as old as the game. At the same time that Camp was repeatedly explaining the development of American football in terms of rational efficiency, he was annually celebrating the eleven best football players in the land, not the coaches and captains who devised the tactics but the individual heroes who executed and sometimes transcended them. These dual perspectives and differing purposes point to what Camp explicitly described as distinct audiences and desires: the knowing few intimately involved with the teams, and the rapidly expanding audience of casual fans who came to the games for excitement and spectacle. From its infancy, in short, even in the mind of its principal author, football's cultural text has had competing interpretations.

Throughout his published writings Camp's account of football's development consistently evoked a cluster of ideas: unbound by tradition (alternately a lack or a freedom in Camp's view), and unaided by experienced rugby players who could interpret the rules, the American collegian "took the English rules for a starting-point, and almost immediately proceeded to add and subtract, according to what seemed his pressing needs." The most pressing initial need, according to Camp, was simply for order. The creation of the scrimmage in 1880 meant the elimination of chance (the random exit of the ball from the rugby scrummage) and opened up possibilities for greater "skill in the development of brilliant plays and carefully planned maneuvers." In turn, this initial act led naturally to further rationalizing, the division of labor according to distinct positions. "The same man did not always snap the ball back as he does now," Camp explained in 1891, "but any one of the rushers would do it upon occasion. The men did not preserve their relative positions in the line, and any one of the men behind the line would act as a quarter-back [the man who received the ball from the snap-back]. Such a condition of affairs could not, however, last long where intercollegiate rivalry proved such an incentive to the perfection of play, and the positions of center-rush or snap-back and quarter-back became the most distinctive of any upon the field."[28]

Linking "intercollegiate rivalry" to "the perfection of play" suggests not only that winning mattered more than enjoyment, but also that it contributed to an advance in American achievement. Camp viewed English rugby as chaotic play; he envisioned American football as purposeful work. That is, the model of "perfection" for Camp in late nineteenth-century America was the rationalized, bureaucratic, specialized corporate work force. Rugby distinguished only between rushers and backs. In his writings Camp explained in detail the emergence of end-rushers, tackles, guards, and snap-backs, as well as quarterbacks, halfbacks, and fullbacks, with each position demanding certain skills or qualities: relative degrees of speed, size, strength, agility, and intelligence. And a hierarchy emerged among the positions, a clearly demarcated structure and chain of authority derived from the exigencies of football action, but those exigencies were considerably determined by rules he himself proposed that rewarded organization and tactical skill.

All of the quotations above are from Camp's first book, *American Football* (1891), the first important primer on the new game, but they could as easily have come from his magazine articles earlier and later, or from his other major treatises—*Walter Camp's Book of College Sports* (1893); *Football* (1896), coauthored with Harvard's famous tactician, Lorin F. Deland; and *The Book of Football* (1910)—through which Camp reiterated his fundamental ideas about the development and current qualities of the American game. Camp consistently interpreted football's brief history in terms of an evolution from chaos and primitive physicality (the "nondescript running and kicking" of rugby) toward reason and order (a "scientific contest"),[29] and he cast the current manner of playing the game as the endpoint of that evolution, a reflection of the modern corporate organization. Even in his occasional inconsistency Camp was consistent. Reviewing the season of 1887 for *Outing* magazine, for example, Camp decried the illegal practice of interference (destined "to make great trouble and leave an ugly mark on the American game"), only to embrace it three years later in the same magazine (as "a truly American feature" of the sport) and again the following year (as the essence of team play).[30] Similarly, as interference led to mass-momentum plays, Camp defended them against charges of brutality for some twenty years, then in 1912 casually dismissed mass play as a "serious menace to the sport."[31] Such revisions in detail always served the larger claims of a consistent narrative. Camp belatedly embraced interference because it enhanced team play and increased the coach's tactical options. He defended mass-momentum plays initially because they epitomized highly developed teamwork; as they gave way to "line plunging," the chance of injury was reduced without these options being restricted, so that he could later disdain mass play without sacrificing what he valued most. Football for Camp remained always a game of teamwork and coaching strategy.

On occasion Camp compared football to war, with references to "the football army" and "the kicking or artillery work," and with long discussions of "generalship"—seemingly different qualities from those required for corporate success.[32] *Football* (1896) is particularly laden with such rhetoric, although coauthor Deland is likely its chief source (he developed the king of the mass-momentum plays, the flying wedge, after studying Napoleon's campaigns). In any case, football for Camp was not the *moral* but the *tactical* equivalent of war. Camp's interest in military lay not in the physical and psychological demands on soldiers, but in its lessons for command and strategy; "generalship" (on-the-field leadership, as opposed to pregame strategy) was a different quality altogether from Purple Heart courage. Saluting the first Army-Navy football contest in 1890, Camp made the point that football most closely mimics "the art of war"—*art*, not struggle.[33] Whether writing for himself or with Deland, Camp always placed intellectual above physical requirements. Writing at a time when the brutality resulting from mass-momentum plays was provoking outcries against the game from many directions, Camp's explanation of football tactics—pounding the weak point in the opponent's line, winning by endurance and attrition whenever possible—was peculiarly bloodless. Camp emphasized the tactical advantage of mass play, not what was to his mind the incidental brutality. Football's "great lesson," Camp wrote in the book with Deland, "may be put into a single line: *it teaches that brains will always win over muscle!*"[34]

"Brains" did not have to be evenly distributed throughout the team, of course. Those with brains served the important managerial functions; those without them translated ideas into physical action. As "director of the game" on the field,[35] the quarterback had to have brains, as did the captain, who in the era before paid coaches became common was principally responsible for selecting, training, and directing the team. Camp also reserved a special place for the "graduate adviser," the unpaid coach who met regularly with the captain to develop training methods and game strategy (as Camp himself did with Yale captains from 1882 to roughly 1910). For Camp, football was fundamentally the strategists' and organizers' game, valuable to the players for its lessons in teamwork. In accounts ranging over almost twenty years, Camp repeatedly defined football's past as an era of individualism, its present as the era of team play; the game, that is, always having recently evolved away from a more primitive past into the modern era. In 1891, Camp predicted that the new season would be marked by "the progress of the game through the medium of qualified teachers and coaches." In 1897, he claimed that "team play has more or less replaced individual superiority." In 1909, he contrasted the "probably unequaled style of team play" of Yale's team in 1900 to "the individual brilliancy, and beyond that the individual independence and football initiative" of the team in 1891. In a contest between the two, the 1900 squad would win.[36]

First and last, then, football for Camp was a coach's game, whether the coach was a volunteer alumnus or a hired expert.[37] In *The Book of Football* (1910), Camp's fourth and final major account of the game's history and present state, he summed up the role of the coach most succinctly, as both an inevitable part of football's evolution and an expression of the American spirit:

But where did the coach come from and why did he come? He was developed by the exigencies of the case, and he came because team play began to take the place of ineffective individual effort. The American loves to plan. It is that trait that has been at the base of his talents for organization. As soon as the American took up Rugby foot-ball he was dissatisfied because the ball would pop out of the scrummage at random. It was too much luck and chance as to where or when it came out, and what man favored by Dame Fortune would get it. So he developed a scrimmage of his own, a center-rusher, or snap-back, a quarter-back, and soon a system of signals. One could no more prevent the American college youth from thus advancing than he could stop their elders with their more important and gigantic enterprises. But all these things led to team play, at the sacrifice, perhaps, of individual brilliancy, but with far greater effectiveness of the eleven men in what for them was the principal affair of the moment—the securing of goals and touch-downs.[38]

This passage bristles with loaded phrases: "ineffective individual effort," the American's "talents for organization," the elders' "more important and gigantic enterprises," "the sacrifice . . . of individual brilliancy" for the sake of the team's "greater effectiveness." For Camp, football was a mirror of the corporation, a preparation for corporate success, and itself a corporate activity. Football was work, not play; Camp used such phrases as "the work of the tackle" and "the play of the guard" interchangeably, always to mean the same thing: effort on behalf of a collective purpose, "the principal affair," as he put it, to be "the securing of goals and touch-downs." That goals and touchdowns should be the objective is not self-evident; playing in order to demonstrate one's fitness to assume social and political power granted by birthright is one obvious alternative (this was a primary function of the rugby matches played at British public schools and at Oxford and Cambridge). Or playing for the simple joy of playing, a possibility Camp explicitly rejected in two essays in *Outing* in 1912 and 1913.[39]

These essays were late affirmations of a position Camp had held for more than two decades. He made explicit the relationship between football and modern business civilization as early as 1891, in the opening sentence of an essay in *Harper's Weekly* titled "Team Play in Football": "If ever a sport offered inducements to the man of executive ability, to the man who can plan, foresee, and manage, it is certainly the modern American foot-ball."[40] The closest contemporary analogue to football as Camp understood it was not war but the "scientific management" promoted by Frederick Winslow Taylor, whose time-and-motion studies revolutionized American manufacturing. In fact, the parallels between Camp's advocacy of "team work, strategy, and tactics" and of "scientific planning"[41] and Taylor's "principles of scientific management" are strikingly specific. In a famous paper from this period Taylor identified the four elements of scientific management as Science, Harmony, Cooperation, and Maximum Output. Scientific managers, that is, do four things:

First. They develop a science for each element of a man's work, which replaces the old rule-of-thumb method.

Second. They scientifically select and then train, teach, and develop the workman, whereas in the past he chose his own work and trained himself as best he could.

Third. They heartily cooperate with the men so as to insure all of the work being done in accordance with the principles of the science which has been developed.

Fourth. There is an almost equal division of the work and the responsibility between management and the workmen. The management take over all work for which they are better fitted than the workmen, while in the past almost all of the work and the greater part of the responsibility were thrown upon the men.[42]

Camp's version of scientific management could be summarized in a parallel list: the devising of plays; the training of players for the positions that suit them; the cooperation of coach, captain, and quarterback with the rest of the players so as to assure common purpose; and the distribution of responsibilities according to position and ability. Taylor made a science of organizing physical labor; so did Camp. Taylor distinguished the needs for brain and for brawn, and assigned them accordingly; so did Camp. In one example Taylor explained that stupidity was necessary for the man handling pig iron in a steel plant; in *The Book of Football,* Camp noted that in the positions of guard and center, football provided "an opportunity not afforded in any other sport for the big, overgrown fat boy."[43] Ultimately, Taylor and Camp shared a common vision for the American future.

Camp's condescension toward fat boys was not a careless remark. Later in *The Book of Football,* in the chapter on "General Strategy," he warned captains and coaches that "oftentime it is entirely inadvisable to let the players know what the final outcome of some of the plays is intended to be." As "the material" to be developed by coach and captain, the players as Camp discussed them seem more like equipment than personnel. "The object must be to use each man to the full extent of his capacity without exhausting any. To do this scientifically involves placing the men in such position on the field that each may perform the work for which he is best fitted, and yet not be forced to do any of the work toward which his qualifications and training do not point."[44] Nowhere in the book is there any suggestion that the players might take over the game themselves. Managers assure productivity; coaches and captains win football games.

The Book of Football includes several accounts of victories by Yale due to the graduate adviser's tactical brilliance. Two decades earlier, in the chapter "Foot-ball in America" from *Walter Camp's Book of College Sports* (1893), Camp illustrated the meaning of "pluck" as the key to football success, with the story of "two little chaps" who once played for Yale, at 125 pounds apiece, "together a little over the weight of the varsity snap-back." Realizing that the team that year was overconfident and undertrained, the two players took it upon themselves to mold the scrub team into a force that would challenge the varsity men out of their complacency. Without consulting the captain they began organizing and drilling the scrubs, until they were actually outplaying the "overfed, underworked university players." "These two boys began to show them the way to make use of brains against weight and strength" so successfully that the varsity "speedily developed under this experience into one of Yale's strongest teams." The most telling moment in this anecdote just precedes that triumphant line: "How those two ever got such work out of the rabble they had to handle, no one knows to this day." There were two lessons here: the primary principle that "brains will beat brute strength every time if you give them fair play," but also the secondary one that ingenious management can turn "rabble" into an effective work force.[45]

"Rabble" is a remarkable word. Camp's view of the coach-player relationship was always autocratic, as when, in an 1897 essay, he insisted that "no team will keep always extending itself save under the whip and spur of continual, and many times extremely severe, criticism."[46] The coach, as Camp repeatedly portrayed him, viewed the players from a distance, his outlook shaped by his larger vision and graver responsibilities. As Camp suggested in a 1912 essay, the players in fact constituted the coach's heaviest burden: "I doubt if any really conscientious, capable coach ever reached the end of the second week of fall practice without being pretty well convinced that every big man on his squad was slow and awkward and all the rest were featherweights or too stupid to get a signal even if it were repeated to them twice." As the players develop, credit goes not to them but to the coach: "Meantime the candidates themselves are, if the coaching is good, improving daily in the detail of the work."[47] But "rabble" goes beyond such suggestions of undevelopment. The members of Yale's scrub team undoubtedly had the same sort of Anglo-Saxon and northern European genealogies as the members of the varsity; yet "rabble" during this period usually referred to the growing urban underclass—Irish, Italian, Jewish, black. At its harshest, then, Camp's interpretation of football's cultural text makes the sport seem a model of social control. More typically, Camp seems conscientiously paternalistic: the players are boys, not men, to be molded by their experienced elders. In either case, success in football depends more on coaches than on players.

Yet Camp was also the creator of All-Americans, the man who selected the season's best players for special recognition. Particularly once *Collier's Weekly* showcased the All-American team as an annual feature, selection by Camp was the highest accolade to be won in college football. And as the game acquired its own history, Camp periodically measured present heroes against the "giants" of the past, selecting from the annual lists those names deserving of the highest Olympian honor. In the opening paragraph of "Heroes of the Gridiron," written for *Outing* in 1909, Camp's admiration of the game's great players, both past and present, seems obvious. "Were there really giants in those old football days?" Camp asks rhetorically. "To tell the truth, as one looks back, it certainly seems as if some of those moleskin warriors of other days were indeed veritable Goliaths, not only in prowess but in physique as well. Then as in comparison one comes down the long line of memorable players, the men of the later days loom large and one begins to think that perhaps there are just as many prodigies in the present decade as in those that have preceded it."[48]

The interpreter of football in terms of managers and workers was also the troubadour of individual heroes. But not without some uneasiness. Although his early selections reveal no reservations, over time Camp became strikingly self-conscious, even defensive, about singling out individual players for praise. The explanation may be simple: the greater the distance from his own youth and playing days, and the longer his involvement in various aspects of coaching, the less appropriate may have seemed the conferring of greatness on a handful of twenty-year-olds. But All-Americans also presented a more serious challenge to Camp's advocacy of teamwork and managerial control. Camp's awareness of this challenge is apparent in a variety of ways. In selecting his All-Americans of 1897, for example, he explicitly rewarded those players who illustrated his own values, placing the steady and reliable players on the first team, the more individually brilliant but erratic ones on the second.[49] In this same spirit the essay "Heroes of the Gridiron" concludes by praising "the man who can sacrifice self for the team." Such comments notwithstanding, a contradiction not only emerges from the very notion of All-Americans but also haunts Camp's writings generally. Its source was simply the game itself: for all its tactical possibilities, football also depended then as now on players who executed the game plan and sometimes exceeded its intentions.

This contradiction is played out most fully in Camp's last full-scale account of the sport, *The Book of Football,* in the collisions between its separate chapters (some of which first appeared as essays in *Century* magazine). In "General Strategy," camp reasserted his fundamental values: "But while in American intercollegiate foot-ball, the development of players is of great interest, still more appealing to those who enjoy the sport for its strategical possibilities is the study and development of plays."[50] The chapter opens with a long anecdote of Yale's season in 1900, in which "the graduate" (Camp himself) persuades the captain to adopt a set of plays that he admits will provoke objections among the players and skepticism among observers, but whose success will show by the big games at the end of the season. Indeed, the graduate proves his point: despite a rocky beginning, strategy, together with the players' faith and hard work, ultimately results in lopsided victories over Columbia, Princeton, and Harvard.

The hero of the story, of course, is the brilliant "graduate." But in other chapters Camp concedes more power to the players, singling out numerous star athletes throughout the game's already-rich history. In the chapter "Personality in Football," Camp notes that before 1876 popular interest in the new sport was slight. "Up to that time few besides the players and would-be candidates manifested any desire to witness the games; but in the next decade public interest increased amazingly." Camp's explanation: "The game took on organized methods, individual players became known for their prowess, and the beginnings of marked 'hero-worship' of prominent players could be noted."[51] The simple comma elides the fact that "organized methods" and individual "prowess" refer to radically different accounts of football's meaning. Camp's discussion of star players in this essay is full of defensiveness and reluctant concessions. Athletic heroism is less celebrated than defended, on the grounds that it is not as pernicious as it seems. "So, on the whole, it is not entirely bad that there should be these stars in athletics," Camp wrote, "for most of them acquire their shining qualities through a clean life, practical self-denial, discipline, obedience, unmurmuring pluck, and a good deal of patience."[52] Camp was equally defensive in the book's final chapter, "All-Time, All-America Teams":

> To be chosen a member of the All-American team in foot-ball falls to the lot of few men who have not practised certain virtues, and practised them for several seasons. To their elders it may seem a foolish casting of the limelight upon boys whom, in their maturer view of things, they regard as unable to stand the flattering notice. But if these elders could only know these young men as they are known among their intimates, they would speedily be disabused of the delusion that the boys are in danger of being spoiled in any such fashion. Year after year a boy sees the class ahead of him go out into the world and knuckle bravely down to hard knocks and hard work, sees his own turn coming, and gets a fairer perspective of the relation of things than his timorous elders give him credit for.[53]

Camp's defensiveness is striking. This concluding chapter on All-Americans immediately follows "The Captain and the Coach," where he characteristically approves the sacrifice of "individual brilliancy" for the sake of the "far greater effectiveness of the eleven men" working together as a team. Rationality, efficiency, and the importance of winning: these, according to Walter Camp, made American football a valuable sport. Yet the public cared more about "individual brilliancy." "The Captain and the Coach" is Camp's penultimate chapter; whether by design or not, he gave the final word to the All-Americans.

————

Camp thus seems an author who lost control of his text. Besides being the primary force behind rule making and the organization of intercollegiate football, Camp was the game's most tireless proselytizer and publicity agent. But his success in these roles meant a different kind of failure. "Fifteen years ago," Camp wrote in the *Century* in 1894, "when some of the American colleges were endeavoring against great odds to establish the sport of foot-ball, I undertook the then extremely unpleasant task of begging for space in daily papers, weekly periodicals, and magazines in which to exploit the advantages of the sport. It was hard and thankless work, for the real devotees of the game were few in number, and gibes were many. It took the most zealous efforts of those of us who really cared for the sport to persuade editors occasionally to allow a game to be written up by an actual player." Unfortunately, in Camp's view, the discovery by "parents and the general public . . . that the game was not barbarous, brutal, or demoralizing" had an unintended impact on the game: "During the last two or three years it has become over-popular with the public, and this craze has led it to assume an importance and prominence wholly unsought."[54]

Although the occasion for Camp's essay was the widespread criticism of football's brutality, the larger issue concerned the relationship of the game to its popular audience. Camp envisioned football as the ideal training ground for a managerial elite, and for this he campaigned fervently. He wanted the game to become popular, so that its benefits could be widely shared, but without the inevitable consequences of popularity. The more popular the game became, the more its control by a northeastern elite—the students and graduates of Yale, Harvard, and Princeton—eroded. As football became the object of harsh criticism—for brutality, "professionalism," distorted university priorities, financial excess—Camp repeatedly defended the elite universities that initiated intercollegiate competition, casting blame elsewhere. In this spirit he wrote in 1897, during yet another crisis over brutality on the field, "It is the utter disregard of the interests of the sport itself exhibited by athletic-club teams and some of the more remote college teams [in the Midwest, that is] that keeps up the agitation against football, and furnishes ammunition for those who enjoy a shot at anything prominent in the public eye."[55] The game Camp created, his vision of its place in American life, kept slipping away from him. Having promoted football to an indifferent public, Camp had to come to terms with public desires far from his own. Having once begged for space in the daily papers, Camp came to rue the manner in which the daily papers transformed individual players into celebrities and melodramatized football violence. And having repeatedly insisted that football was a game of team-work, Camp had to confront the fact that the great majority of spectators cared considerably more about feats of individual prowess.

An ambivalent quarrel with his audience runs through Camp's writings. Without spectators, football could not survive; with spectators, football took a different course from the one Camp envisioned. Through hindsight this course seems inevitable. Once American collegians broke with rugby rules over the random way in which the ball was put in play from the scrum, foot-ball developed in the direction of increasing rationalization—toward "scien-tific" football. What this meant by the early 1890s was flying wedges and other forms of mass-momentum play: by intention, the epitome of "scientific" strat-egy (the surest way to gain five yards in three downs with minimal risk of fumbling); by accident, the cause of countless injuries. Moreover, though fascinating to the strategist who devised or at least understood the methods for focusing the greatest offensive force on the weakest part of the defense, mass play was uninteresting to anyone lacking "inside" knowledge of the game. In essays such as "A Plea for the Wedge in Football," Camp continued to champion mass-momentum plays because they rewarded the teams with the most brilliant tacticians and the most disciplined training. At the same time the press, claiming to represent the public, called for their abolition because they were both brutal and boring. Boredom seemed the chief threat in1891, as Camp wrote: "A long run behind a cleverly-moved wedge is by no means unattractive, and it is a play easily understood and appreciated. But close mass work in the centre, crowding down two or three yards at a time, while it may, and sometimes does, entail just as much skill and combined team work, will never appeal in the least to the spectator, and certainly would, if carried to an extreme, disgust him with the game. And the spectator—that is the spectator who has some technical knowledge of the game—is the man whose opinions are likely in the long run to prevail."[56] By 1893 Camp was acknowledging that brutality had become an additional issue: "The public, as represented by the press, agree with the faculties in desiring the elimination of plays wherein the danger is or may become great, and in addition the public desires the open style of play—the more open the better. Spectators wish to see exactly what is being done, and in kicks and individual runs therefore lies their principal interest." Camp grudgingly conceded in this case that momentum plays should be altered, though not banned entirely: "That the spectator wishes them abolished does not of itself prove that such action should be taken, although the college spectator ought to be considered next to the player."[57]

The crux of Camp's quarrel with the public was his desire for control: control of the games' outcomes through a style of offensive play that minimized the risk of losing the ball and maximized intelligence and generalship, control of football's place in the university and in the larger society, control in interpreting the sport's meaning. Football in all these aspects escaped his control—not quite Frankenstein's monster berserk in the countryside, but certainly a creation grown more powerful than its creator. The spectators' desire for open play won out, if only after several years of wrangling. The advantages of sheer weight became increasingly obvious, despite Camp's repeated insistence that brain would win over brawn.[58] Hero-worship prevailed with the greater public, despite Camp's repeated insistence on the value of teamwork. And popularity fed unwelcome "extravagance" and distorted priorities in a variety of other ways. "We want the sport within reasonable bounds," Camp wrote in 1895, "—we want it clean, honest and vigorous, but not spectacular or extravagant."[59] Yet spectacular and extravagant it was. Even the great Thanksgiving Day football games in New York between Yale and Princeton in the 1880s and early 1890s became something very different from what had been intended. Writing in 1894, when these games seemed to have gotten out of hand (enormous crowds, huge gate receipts, the postgame riotous behavior of students in the Bowery theaters), Camp claimed that the colleges had first chosen Thanksgiving simply for the convenience of students on holiday, New York because it was "the place *par excellence* for a neutral ground and a fair field." That the Thanksgiving Day game in the city became considerably more than an extracurricular activity for the players and their classmates was not the fault of the colleges: "The public have come to regard the game as one of the important 'sporting events' of the year, and have attached to it many attributes in themselves undesirable."[60]

Not always, but often enough, "the public" becomes openly the enemy in Camp's writings on football. In early articles, while still needing to play the promoter, Camp more simply and enthusiastically called attention to the game's growing popularity, and he approved all changes that contributed to "the pleasure of the spectators."[61] But as popularity itself began to change the game, Camp developed a more ambivalent attitude. In a 1910 essay he could invoke the spectators as a "moral force" operating for football's good. But in

1913 he bluntly stated: "With the wave of popularity that has seized upon all forms of athletic sport, the spectator has become a great problem."[62]

Camp's loss of control over football's cultural meanings was thus part of a larger loss of control over the game itself. In relation to the questions of power raised by cultural theory, the example of Walter Camp challenges any simple model of manipulation from above. Football experienced no simple populist takeover, of course; in calling the spectator the "great problem" Camp failed to name the entrepreneurs and media that developed and profited from football spectatorship. But once constituted as spectators, ordinary people did in fact exert some control over the sport's development, and even more over its meanings. Spectators became a constituency whose desires had to be accommodated, and an audience that read the game according to its own interests.

Camp's writings also remind us that the power of cultural narratives is not shared, whether equally or unequally, by "authors" and "readers" alone; some of it resides in the text itself. That is, at revealing moments in Camp's writings the game of football itself challenges the meanings that he would impose on it. The best example of this is Camp's account of the 1885 Yale-Princeton game, published initially in the popular children's magazine *St. Nicholas* in 1889, then incorporated into *Walter Camp's Book of College Sports* (1893)—a rare extended anecdote in what is primarily a treatise on football with the usual Campian themes. The story opens in this way: "One of the most magnificent dashes ever made on an American foot-ball field was the run made by Lamar, of Princeton, in the game with Yale which was played upon the Yale field, November 21, 1885." Princeton reputedly had the stronger team that season, but the managerial genius of Peters, the Yale captain who "had done wonders with his recruits," was immediately apparent as the game opened. Stunning Princeton with an early goal, Yale continued to hold its lead well into the second forty-five-minute half and seemed "certain of victory" as the clock wound down, confirming Camp's belief that tactics would defeat mere physical superiority. Camp even uncharacteristically interjected a little novelistic coloring at this point, as he described Princeton's plight: "The sun was low in the horizon, nearly forty minutes of the second half were gone, and no one dared to hope such failing fortunes could be retrieved in the few remaining minutes." But then, with Yale in possession of the ball, Peters faced a crucial decision: he could "continue with the running game and thus make scoring against him impossible and victory certain," or he could "send the ball by a kick down in front of his enemy's goal and trust to a fumble to increase his score." Electing to kick, Peters implicitly defied some sixty previous pages of Camp's advice on proper tactics for achieving victory; but Camp now as storyteller offered no criticism, and he even made what was for him a startling comment: "A kick was surely the more generous play in the eyes of the crowd." Yale's kick was "perfect," but "Lamar, with the true instinct of the born runner," brilliantly eluded two "inexperienced tacklers," broke into the open field, and raced toward the goal line just beyond the grasp of "Peters, a strong, untiring, thoroughly trained runner" and "the captain of a team which but a moment before had been sure of victory." Building dramatic intensity with all of the novelist's devices (rare in his usually flat, prosaic writing), Camp concluded this way:

> How he ran! But Lamar—did he not too know full well what the beat of those footsteps behind him meant? The white five-yard lines fairly flew under his feet; past the broad twenty-five-yard line he goes, still with three or four yards to spare. Now he throws his head back with that familiar motion of the sprinter who is almost to the tape, and who will run his heart out in the last few strides, and, almost before one can breathe, he is over the white goal-line and panting on the ground, with the ball under him, a touchdown made, from which a goal was kicked, and the day saved for Princeton. Poor Lamar! He was drowned a few years after graduation, but no name will be better remembered among the foot-ball players of that day than will his.[63]

There are elements in this remarkable tale that reinforced Camp's managerial master narrative: captain Peters's early success and the vulnerability of inexperienced tacklers most obviously. But what is the reader to make of Lamar's "instinct of the born runner," with its implication of innate physical superiority rather than "pluck" or "brains"? The better team triumphed, not by brains over brawn, but by "instinct," individual brilliance, and the opponent's unwise decision to kick. And what, finally, of Lamar's untimely death, so unexpectedly appended to his moment of heroics? The motif is a familiar one: the fleetingness of fame, the bizarre twists of fate, the athlete dying young. Familiar ideas, but alien to Camp's usually detached, pragmatic analysis of football. Both Lamar's last-second touchdown dash and his shocking death give a romantic conclusion to what began as a lesson in technical efficiency and ingenious leadership.

The contradiction in the essay runs deep. Camp's master narrative of football made a hero of the corporate manager by wedding an older ideal of individual prowess to the requirements of the modern corporation. Camp's exemplary captains and coaches were not bloodless intellectuals but charismatic leaders. In the narrative of the Yale-Princeton game that composite heroic figure is separated into Peters and Lamar—the modern and the antimodern, the corporate manager and the swashbuckling hero—as if the game itself could not sustain the narrative Camp imposed on it by locating all of the necessary virtues in a single figure. Camp complicated matters further when he called Peters's decision to kick a "generous" one. The captain's goal, as reiterated throughout the book's earlier discussion of training and tactics, was to *win*. The wise captain exploited every opportunity, took every advantage— attacking the defense, for example, at its weakest point. Camp's was a democratic sporting ethic that presupposed success would go to those who earned it. For the "generous" captain, on the other hand, winning was less important than the thrill of competition, the satisfaction of playing well, the high principle of sportsmanship. The lineage of the "generous" captain would go back through aristocrats' sons on English public-school playing fields to Renaissance gentlemen for whom style was all-important. Those aristocratic gentlemen did not need to win because they had already "won" at life by virtue of their birth; *how* they played mattered most because the correct manner demonstrated a proper use of their birthright. The "generous" captain in Camp's tale, then, ceases to be the managerial hero, the figure of "pluck," becoming instead a companion to Lamar from a premodern, aristocratic past.

The chief author of American football produced conflicting narratives, apparently without intention. Not just the public audience but the game itself exerted pressure on Camp's narrative of managerial control. Lamar's run became legendary, an event evoked frequently by football reporters in the 1890s and early 1900s as the benchmark against which other great runs were measured. It was remembered not just because of spectators' preference for individual prowess but because of the game's capacity to make the heroic possible. The arrangement of the concluding chapters of *The Book of Football* that I noted earlier—"The Captain and the Coach" followed by "All-Time, All-America Teams"—is ultimately appropriate, then. By juxtaposing the managerial and the heroic aspects of football, Camp touched on a dialectic that informed the game from its beginnings. By assigning the final pages to the exploits of football's greatest heroes, intentionally or not he acknowledged the course football would follow into the future. The culture of celebrity, in sport the singling out of individual heroes from their teammates or mass of competitors, would become conspicuous by the 1920s. The irony of this development, toward which Camp's writings point, should not be lost on us. The hunger for heroes in the modern world is a powerful *antimodern* impulse, but one fed by the most advanced technologies of the mass media and the

techniques of promotion they make possible. Camp's writings also lead to another conclusion: even the most powerful authors of cultural narratives have
limited control over their texts.

Notes

1. Both rules are quoted in the appendix to Parke H. Davis's *Football,* a meet-
ing-by-meeting account of the proceedings of "intercollegiate conventions, conferences, and sessions of rules committees, 1876 to 1911." Davis's book is an
invaluable record of the early evolution of American football and is the major secondary source for my discussion.

2. The best succinct accounts of the rise of intercollegiate football can be
found in Parke H. Davis's book and, among recent histories, in Smith, *Sports and
Freedom,* chaps. 6 and 7. It is a remarkable fact that the only full-scale histories of
intercollegiate football remain the anecdotal one published in 1956 by sportswriter Allison Danzig, *The History of American Football,* and a more recent year-by-
year journal, Tom Perrin's *Football.* Davis in particular is my guide through the
following discussion.

3. *Harvard Advocate,* May 29, 1874, p. 113.

4. Davis, *Football,* p. 467.

5. Ibid.

6. Quoted in McIntosh, *Fair Play,* p. 80.

7. Cochem, "Something New in Football," p. 88.

8. Quoted in Dizikes, *Sportsmen and Gamesman,* p. 311. The baseball anecdotes
are found in Thorn, *A Century of Baseball Lore.*

9. See Davis, *Football,* appendix.

10. Ibid., pp. 470, 494, 497. The first is from an 1883 convention; a nearly identical rule emerged from an 1887 convention as well (p. 475).

11. Camp, "Football of 1893," p. 118.

12. I develop this idea in *Sporting with the Gods,* pp. 10–16.

13. Camp, "Football of 1893," p. 117.

14. On the consequences of low tackling, see Smith, *Sports and Freedom,* p. 90;
and Bergin, *The Game,* pp. 35–36.

15. *Harvard Advocate,* April 3, 1874, p. 58; quoted in Smith, *Sports and Freedom,* p. 74.

16. Smith, *Sports and Freedom,* pp. 76–77.

17. Ibid., pp. 79–80.

18. Davis, "How the Great Football Game Was Played," p. 1.

19. On Camp's importance to football, see Martin, "Walter Camp and His
Gridiron Game"; Smith, "Walter Camp"; and Smith, *Sports and Freedom,* pp. 83–88.

20. Martin, "Walter Camp and His Gridiron game," p. 54.

21. Davis, "A Day with the Yale Team."

IN THE BEGINNING WAS THE RULE 117

22. See *Independent,* March 22, 1900, p. 715; *New York Times,* November 20, 1897, p. 3; and *World,* November 30, 1893, p. 1.

23. Camp, "Methods and Development in Tactics and Play," p. 173.

24. See chap. 11 of Smith, *Sports and Freedom.*

25. Hollis, "Intercollegiate Athletics," pp. 538–39.

26. See Davis, "Evolution of American College Football," in Walsh, *Intercollegiate Football,* pp. 477–79; and Waldorf, *NCAA Football Rules Committee.*

27. As I write, the dominance of coaches may be waning, for basic economic reasons. In professional sport, the rise in players' salaries now means that most coaches and managers earn considerably less than the star players they are supposed to control. Even in professional football, where this increase in players' salaries has been smaller and slower, we now have teams such as the Miami Dolphins paying star quarterback Dan Marino $5 million a year and the coach, Don Shula, $1 million. In college sports, the lure of these huge salaries has increasingly led undergraduates to leave college for the pros before their eligibility expires, with the result that the players' and the coaches' interests at that level are more obviously at odds.

28. Camp, *American Football,* pp. 9–11. Camp had been making the same points since at least 1888 in popular magazines. See, for example, "The American Game of Foot-ball"; and "The Game and Laws of American Football."

29. Camp "The American Game of Foot-ball."

30. Camp, letter to the "Editor's Open Window"; "Football of 1891"; and " 'Interference' in Football."

31. Camp, "The New Football" (*Outlook*), p. 174.

32. Camp, *Walter Camp's Book of College Sports,* pp. 99, 117ff.

33. Camp, "Football of 1891," p. 155. Similarly, Deland was a chess master; for him as well as Camp, war and football were both contests of strategy.

34. Camp and Deland, *Football,* p. iv.

35. Camp, *American Football,* p. 81.

36. Camp, "Football of 1891"; "Football at the Colleges," p. 1161; and "Great Teams of the Past," p. 281.

37. See, for example, Camp, "College Football" (*Outing*); and "The Football Season."

38. Camp, *The Book of Football,* pp. 333–34.

39. See Camp, "Making a Football Team"; and "What Are Athletics Good For?"

40. Camp, "Team Play in Foot-ball."

41. Camp, *Book of Football,* pp. 20, 33.

42. Taylor, *The Principles of Scientific Management,* pp. 36–37.

43. Ibid., p. 60; Camp, *Book of Football,* p. 88.

44. Camp, *Book of Football,* pp. 196, 202, 212–13.

45. Camp, *Walter Camp's Book of College Sports,* pp. 139–41.

46. Camp, "College Football" (*Harper's Weekly*).

47. Camp, "Making a Football Team," p. 141.

48. Camp, "Heroes of the Gridiron," p. 131.

49. Camp, "A Review of College Football."

50. Camp, *Book of Football*, p. 192.

51. Ibid., pp. 137–38.

52. Ibid., p. 140.

53. Ibid., p. 344.

54. Camp, "The Current Criticism of Foot-ball," p. 633.

55. Camp, "Football Notes."

56. Camp, "Football of 1891," p. 154.

57. Camp, "Football of 1893," p. 117.

58. See, for example, Camp, "Football: Review of the Season of 1896," pp. 26–29; and "Football of '97."

59. Camp, "Football of '95," p. 176. See also "Athletic Extravagance"; and "Some Abuses in Athletics."

60. Camp, "The Current Criticism of Foot-ball."

61. Camp, "The American Game of Foot-ball."

62. Camp, "The New Football" (*Outing*), p. 17; and "What Are Athletics Good For?," p. 270.

63. Camp, *Walter Camp's Book of College Sports*, pp. 142–46.

Works Cited

Bergin, Thomas G. *The Game: The Harvard-Yale Football Rivalry.* New Haven, Conn., 1984.

Camp, Walter. *American Football.* New York, 1891.

———. "The American Game of Foot-ball." *Harper's Weekly,* November 10, 1888, p. 858.

———. "Athletic Extravagance: In Training, in Playing, and in Describing." *Outing* 26 (April 1895): 81–84.

———. *The Book of Football.* New York, 1910.

———. "College Football." *Harper's Weekly,* November 27, 1891, pp. 1185–86.

———. "College Football." *Outing* 17 (February 1891): 384–90.

———. "The Current Criticism of Foot-ball." *Century* 47 (February 1894): 633–34.

———. "Football: Review of the Season of 1896." *Outing* 31 (October 1897): 26–33.

———. "Football at the Colleges." *Harper's Weekly,* November 20, 1897, pp. 1161–62.

———. "Football Notes." *Harper's Weekly,* December 4, 1897, p. 1210.

———. "Football of 1891." *Outing* 18 (November 1891): 153–57.

———. "Football of 1893: Its Lessons and Results." *Harper's Weekly,* February 5, 1894, pp. 117–18.

———. "Football of '95: A Forecast of the Season." *Outing* 27 (November 1895): 169–76.

———. "Football of '97: A Forecast of the Season." *Outing* 31 (November 1897): 133–36.

———. "The Football Season." *Harper's Weekly*, October 30, 1897, p. 1090.

———. "The Game and Laws of American Football." *Outing* 11 (October 1888): 68–76.

———. "Great Teams of the Past." *Outing* 55 (December 1909): 281–93.

———. "Heroes of the Gridiron." *Outing* 55 (November 1909): 131–42.

———. " 'Interference' in Football." *Harper's Weekly*, November 19, 1892, p. 1115.

———. Letter to the "Editor's Open Window." *Outing* 9 (January 1888): 379–81.

———. "Making a Football Team." *Outing* 61 (November 1912): 131–43.

———. "Methods and Development in Tactics and Play." *Outing* 37 (November 1900): 171–76.

———. "The New Football." *Outing* 57 (October 1910): 17–25.

———. "The New Football." *Outlook*, September 28, 1912, pp. 171–77.

———. "A Review of College Football." *Harper's Weekly*, December 11, 1897, pp. 1233–34.

———. Some Abuses in Athletics." *Independent*, March 22, 1900, pp. 714–17.

———. "Team Play in Foot-ball." *Harper's Weekly*, October 31, 1891, p. 845.

———. *Walter Camp's Book of College Sports*. New York, 1893.

———. "What Are Athletics Good For?" *Outing* 63 (December 1913): 259–72.

Camp, Walter, and Lorin F. Deland. *Football*. Boston, 1896.

Cochem, E. M. "Something New in Football." *Outing* 61 (October 1912): 88–92.

Danzig, Allison. *The History of American Football: Its Great Teams, Players, and Coaches*. Englewood Cliffs, N.J., 1956.

Davis, Parke H. *Football: The American Intercollegiate Game*. New York, 1911.

Davis, Richard Harding. "A Day with the Yale Team." *Harper's Weekly*, November 18, 1893, p. 1110.

———. "How the Great Football Game Was Played." *Journal*, November 24, 1895, pp. 1–2.

Dizikes, John. *Sportsmen and Gamesmen*. Boston, 1981.

Hollis, Ira. "Intercollegiate Athletics." *Atlantic* 90 (October 1902): 534–44.

Martin, John Stuart. "Walter Camp and His Gridiron Game." *American Heritage*, October 1961, pp. 50–55, 77–81.

McIntosh, Peter. *Fair Play: Ethics in Sport and Education*. London, 1979.

Oriard, Michael. *Sporting with the Gods: The Rhetoric of Play and Game in American Culture*. New York, 1991.

Perrin, Tom. *Football: A College History*. Jefferson, N.C., 1987.

Smith, Ronald A. *Sports and Freedom: The Rise of Big-Time College Athletics*. New York, 1988.

———. "Walter Camp." In *Biographical Dictionary of American Sports: Football*. Ed. David L. Porter. Westport, Conn., 1987, pp. 85–87.

Taylor, Frederick W. *The Principles of Scientific Management*. New York, 1911.

Thorn, John. *A Century of Baseball Lore.* New York, 1980.

Waldorf, John. *NCAA Football Rules Committee Chronology of 100 Years, 1876 to 1976.* Shawnee Mission, Kans., 1975.

Walsh, Christy. *Intercollegiate Football: A Complete Pictorial and Statistical Review from 1869 to 1934.* New York, 1934.

4

Regulating the Body and the Body Politic
American Sport, Bourgeois Culture, and the Language of Progress, 1880–1920

MARK DYRESON

Historians have charted the economic, technological, and social forces that transformed the nineteenth-century United States and challenged the republican tradition and bourgeois notions of order. By the late nineteenth century the old universe of bourgeois history and myth had disappeared. New technologies of social production, new forms of corporate and capitalist organization, new modes of market relations, and new political realities at the local, national, and international levels had destroyed the imagined "self-balancing" world of the old middle classes and brought bourgeois culture to a crisis that threatened its very existence.[1]

Confronted with visions of disorder, American elites and middle classes transformed themselves and expanded their powers. Emerging new middle classes and their elite allies, committed to a historical conception of themselves as the foundation of the American republic, tried to choose a path through formidable obstacles and reconcile the revolutionary implications of technical civilization with the values and cultural logic they had inherited from their social ancestors. They demanded a national culture committed to their visions of progress. They sought to republicanize the processes of industrialization and urbanization, control and mold other social classes, and win the struggle to define modernity. They gave their national culture a dynamic if not always consistent logic, which they championed as universal and progressive.[2]

In an attempt to return to some semblance of balance, late nineteenth- and early twentieth-century American bourgeois culture turned to the regulation of body and mind through organized athletics in an effort to exert control over the processes of history. From the symbol of the well-regulated and disciplined body and mind of the archetypal athlete, bourgeois spokespersons soon spun new explanations and defenses of a well-regulated body politic—a modern civilization that balanced corporate and social needs through the gospel of fair play.

"Few people realize how great is the part played by sport in the life of a nation," surmised Price Collier in an 1898 essay entitled "Sport's Place in the Nation's Well-Being." "Most of us think of the hour or two spent at some form of exercise as a pastime which has little or no bearing upon the political life about us," he asserted. But Collier argued that such a perception was drastically flawed. The sporting life, he insisted, produced precisely the type of citizen needed for national and individual success in the revolutionary conditions that characterized modern life. "It was no mere epigram of the Iron Duke about the playing fields of Eton, and Waterloo," Collier proclaimed. "There was a direct connection, just as there is a direct connection between that hardy, plain-living family of Deweys from Vermont, and Manila," he continued, heralding the hero of the American victory over the Spanish fleet in the 1898 war over Cuba, and implicating athletics as a key factor in the emergence of the United States onto the world stage near the beginning of the twentieth century.[3]

Collier's connection of the "hardy, plain-living" American folk to the practice of the "strenuous life" indicated an important innovation in American political culture. With increasing frequency during the late nineteenth and early twentieth centuries, social commentators identified modern athletic practice with the production and reproduction of a national culture in the United States—a national culture modeled on the bourgeois norms of an emerging and self-conscious new middle class. Sport, in the hands of the architects of the new athletic ideology, was championed as an integral part of any modern and progressive nation's "well-being."

Who were the inventors of the sporting republic? Journalists, politicians, educators, social reformers, and scientists—they fit neatly into the ranks of the self-styled progressive elites who were determined to lead the new middle class in an efficient and, they hoped, painless shift from entrepreneurial to corporate capitalism. Boosters of the sporting republic dotted the progressive spectrum: Theodore Roosevelt and Woodrow Wilson, Jane Addams and Jacob Riis, William James and G. Stanley Hall, Edward Ross and Simon Patten. They made sport a part of their language of progress, constructing a sporting republic around a set of symbols, ideas, and institutions that promoted organized athletics as an essential social force in their struggle to shape modernity. In scientific and technical studies of social problems, in political discourse, in educational theory, and in the daily constructs of the new mass media, the sporting republic represented both a political and a cultural ideal and a definition of the American role in the world. The founding fathers and mothers of the sporting republic insisted that modern nations should employ the regulation and training of body and mind through organized athletics for the production of civic virtue and national vitality.[4]

Organized athletics lent itself to the discourse on the nature of progress since at crucial semiotic junctures political and athletic culture overlapped. Fair play, competition, regulation: as social scientists like Ross used the metaphor of a game to describe the social "rules" of human interaction and politicians like Roosevelt employed the concept of sportsmanship in programs for reshaping the political economy, the symbology of the playing field increasingly shaped American perceptions of the patterns of modernity.[5]

The ideology of physical culture promulgated by Price Collier in articles like "Sport's Place in the Nation's Well-Being" and "The Ethics of Ancient and Modern Athletics" typified the new athleticism that linked the "strenuous life" to the reproduction of middle-class values, the realization of republican political ideals, and the creation of a virtuous citizenry. Indeed, Collier, with an optimism that rivaled the extravagant claims of patent-medicine salesmen, asserted that the creed of the sporting republic would steel its citizens to meet the challenges faced by the United States as it entered the twentieth century: "We have our colonies to govern; we have the poison of the fierce lust of money, for which a wholesome antidote should be provided; we have the rude jostling of the self-advertising social strugglers to beware of; we have in our midst the disease of political corruption, for which a remedy is sorely needed; we have a powerful press to tame; we have the fads in religion and in morals . . . to meet and vanquish; and, though we are taking matters rather gayly in these days of our youth and prosperity, it needs no prophet to foresee that our Hercules will need some hard training to accomplish all his labors successfully."[6]

Of course hard training, one form of the work ethic, was no stranger to the middle-class value system. But corporate capitalism and mass society had altered patterns of work and destroyed the traditional order of economy and society. The relationship of play, games, and sport to civic life attracted a host of commentators and the attention of the American bourgeois in the late nineteenth and early twentieth centuries.[7] Reconciled to the specialization required by industrialism, the new middle classes increasingly located their hopes for an egalitarian realm of social life in leisure, rather than in work. The "amusement problem" soon consumed the attention of social scientists and moral reformers, taking its place next to the "trust problem," the "labor problem," and other maladies of modernism perplexing bourgeois minds.

That perspective made the organization of leisure a central task in the drive to construct a national culture. "The things we do, when we do what we please, are vitally related not only to health, but also to morality, and the whole development of the finer self," proclaimed pioneering play theorist Luther Halsey Gulick to the members of the American Academy of Political and Social Science.[8]

In the formulations of Gulick and like-minded boosters of athleticism, the mere winning of one's daily bread, the drudgery of labor, had been rendered insufficient for making the complete person. Work became a restricted realm, required by modern conditions.[9] "When released from the daily work, the mill we have to tread in order to live, then we strive to become what we would be if we could," surmised Gulick. Play became an arena for pursuing ideals, a fulcrum for building character, an avenue for inculcating ethics. In modern society, claimed Gulick, leisure had become a mass, rather than an aristocratic, reality. That fact, he claimed, was the truly revolutionary consequence of the industrial revolution. "The world has never before seen such equality of opportunity and the possibilities latent in this fact are stupendous," he declared.[10] The ideology of the sporting republic reordered the political understandings of leisure and work in important ways. No longer did the "chosen people" labor in the earth; now they played in green fields.

The Hercules, to use Price Collier's term, which the boosters of the sporting republic promised would be spawned by a national conversion to the gospel of the strenuous life, faced a republic under siege by what appeared from many perspectives to be a host of threats. The new middle class that surged to the forefront of American civilization during the Progressive Era shared a commonality that had as much to do with acceptance of a constellation of ideas and beliefs as with similarities in its relation to the mode of production. As Loren Baritz indicated in a recent study of American bourgeois culture, "Becoming middle class required some accumulation of goods and resources of course. But an altered frame of reference was even more important."[11]

The new middle class included in its frame of reference a historical role as the backbone of the American republic—and, indeed, of all republics and liberal forms of government in the history of Western civilization. *The Independent,* one of the great oracles of middlebrow sentiment in American life, argued that "many of the most important social habits, a great part of the stock which breeds the leaders of intellectual and practical life, and to a great extent that sound habit of mind which leads men to devote themselves to excellent work rather than to sacrifice all other considerations for money rewards, are identified with the middle class."[12] In such a formulation, quite common in progressive commentary, the middle class, unlike the selfish and self-absorbed capitalist and labor interests, became both the "public" that manifested interest in the whole of the commonwealth and the cornerstone of moral civilization. Indeed, an editorial in *The Dial* on "The Middle Class Mind," which on one level condemned bourgeois taste and sentiment, also proclaimed that "the mechanism of society needs a 'governor' to save it from being torn to pieces by its internal energies, and this controlling influence is supplied by the middle class mind."[13]

The public, understood by most progressives in these middle-class terms, served as the congregation to which the "ministers of reform" preached their semi-secularized gospels of progressivism, and the group toward which social technologies that promised, like sport, the creation of a modern republican virtue were aimed. In such a climate social reformers easily transmuted their particular historical values into what they thought were universal values, and prescribed their brand of athleticism as a tonic for producing a classless and harmonious civilization. The vitalistic national culture that the advocates of the new athleticism promised would unite traditional and modern cultural patterns had immense appeal in an era of rapid change, when, as *The Independent* warned, "the middle class of today is by no means the middle class of yesterday," and the middle class of tomorrow faced extinction.[14]

The roots of the sporting republic lay in the same complex of factors that had given rise to the new middle class. The emergence of modern sport coincided with the transformation of American society by successive waves of industrialism. Peter Levine has charted the appearance in antebellum America of the conception of sport as a tool for revitalizing a society that seemed to be fracturing as modernizing forces threatened the foundation of the republican experiment—a seemingly constant, and historically well-founded, lament in republican jeremiads. Child-guidance advisers, health reformers, and Muscular Christians preached—in particular to an urban, middle-class audience—the necessity of athleticism for both individual self-improvement and national survival in an increasingly artificial world. The image of George Washington as an athletic founding father and the popular conception of Andrew Jackson as the personification of activist vigor stood as the symbols of the pre–Civil War connections between strenuosity and political virtue.[15]

From its roots in the antebellum reform movements that addressed the fears and hopes of the new bourgeois elements in American society, the sporting republic emerged forcefully in the late nineteenth century as the national bureaucratic structures that characterized corporate capitalism came increasingly into view and the urbanized, industrialized, professionalized middle class became increasingly self-conscious and powerful. The new economic structures created a curious conflict in bourgeois culture, in particular amongst their progressive political leaders and theorists. They worshiped the material plenitude and comfortable lifestyles that the machine process promised, but they feared the commercial and artificial directions in which their world appeared to be heading. The new middle-class intellectuals, as they transformed the laissez-faire assumptions of classical economic philosophy and decried Adam Smith's invisible hand as a false God, increasingly identified an overly commercial spirit as a fundamental social evil.

Indeed, their fears of a bourgeoisie simplified into base economic creatures and cast adrift in a Hobbesian polity by modern capitalist forces predated the forceful critique of the modern spirit made by Hannah Arendt in *The Origins of Totalitarianism*.[16] Beneath their willing acceptance of progress and the corporate order lurked an uncontrolled fear that blurred for them the lines between social control and social justice.[17] Progressives, middle-class champions of classlessness, argued that the selfish trusts and labor unions that threatened social war suffered from overly acquisitive and hypercompetitive sentiment, and worried about the infection spreading to the middle-class "public." In their search for ways to control the energies of modernization, they invented the sporting republic.[18]

As the progressives redefined the categories of competition, individualism, and regulation and sought to invent a new republicanism for controlling the economic and political conditions of the new order, the new sporting experts redefined athleticism. Modern sport, in progressive theories, offered a way to preserve competition and channel individual talent into socially efficient action. A society organized around industrial and corporate enterprise required the welding of individual striving to group effort. "Unselfishness must be practiced at every turn," preached athletic advocate Francis Tabor in an 1899 sermon on the conduct of true sport. "The strong must help the weak; and the weak must be aroused, that they may not be a drag upon the strong."[19] That same social vision could be found in Lester Ward's sociology or Herbert Croly's political science.[20] The imagery of community employed by the new social scientists to explode the precepts of classical laissez-faire models and their derivatives in the cult of social Darwinism also found frequent display in the literature of the sporting republic. Theodore Roosevelt was unsurpassed in his mastery of the sporting sermonette. He resorted to such imagery frequently in his parables to his political congregation, urging the channeling of individual vitality toward the commonweal.[21]

The boosters of the sporting republic argued that the work ethic, innovation, and perseverance were rewarded on the playing field. But the energy expended in pursuit of excellence required subjugation to the needs of the group in team sports, or to the demands of the event in individual competition. The same dynamic tension between individual energy and group stability forms the basic problem in republican political theory—the need to discover the proper balance between the individual and the community, between liberty and authority. The rigorous competition on the playing field was not, in the progressive conception, the brutal combat of the struggle for survival but the socially accepted striving for common goals. Indeed, John Corbin described sport as an antidote to Darwinian forces. "The bare struggle for existence exacts strength and masterhood," he wrote, "but to live in the fair name of a sportsman it is necessary to rise to spiritual heights."[22]

The transcendental properties of athletics captured the attention of the professional, technical, and managerial leaders of the corporate order as they embraced the machine process and the new business dynamic, but at the same time the potential for an excessively artificial and "inauthentic" commercial civilization repelled them. T. J. Jackson Lears's conception of the antimodern features of the cultural patterns created by the late-nineteenth- and early-twentieth-century American bourgeoisie offers important insights into the nature of modern sport.[23] The modernization paradigm employed to explain the characteristics of modern sport by Allen Guttmann, Melvin Adelman, and others, while useful at some levels, does not come to grips with the hopes and fears that the new middle class brought to the practice of athletics. Guttmann argues forcefully for the secular quality of modern—as opposed to traditional or classical—physical culture, theorizing that more recent versions of athleticism are "not related to some transcendent realm of the sacred."[24] But the ideology of the sporting republic was clearly related to the Christian—and, in particular, the evangelical Protestant—theology that informed the political and social outlook of the new middle class. As denominationalism and sectarianism, scientism and pragmatism increasingly eroded the cultural force of organized religion, the preservation of Protestant ideals and ethics through the process of what Robert Crunden calls "innovative nostalgia" transformed the Puritan ethic into a this-worldly struggle to engineer the Kingdom of Heaven on earth.[25] Morality, long the concern in an older America of local churches and congregations, found a regularized and nationalized conduit for transmitting religiously derived precepts to the middle-class public through the structures of the sporting republic.

Paeans to the moral power of sport, like the Reverend A. E. Colton's "What Football Does," appeared regularly in the Progressive Era popular press. Colton, field agent of the American Bible Society for the New England States, celebrated the education and training that his son received on Boston

High's football team, and stressed the virtues created by a devotion to the strenuous life. Patience, obedience, self-denial, self-control, submergence of self, alertness, the bigness of trifles, endurance, the joys of victory and the sorrows of defeat, courage, cleanliness, scholarship, and, finally, physical perfection—a litany of middle-class values—derived from football, the Reverend thought. "F. B. comes out of the season in prime condition for the hardest kind of tackling and protracted endeavor with languages, physics and mathematics," proclaimed Colton. "Thus we gladly pay our tribute to the great game which is doing so much for developing our young men physically and morally, preparing them for the hard grinding battles of coming days." Colton strikingly avoided direct references to religion, which were rife in the typical expressions of Muscular Christianity, yet his witnessing for the republican virtues produced by football blurred the line between the sacred and the secular. Clearly, he felt that football transcended the realm of the playing field, and taught important lessons for the conduct of life in a competitive world. His essay indicates the increasing appropriation of religious symbolism for secular situations, and the modernist warping of the distinction between the sacred and the profane.[26]

Perhaps the clearest expression of the transcendently modern faith in sport was Princeton professor William Milligan Sloane's history of the ancient and modern Olympics. Indeed, the modern Games are, to use Lears's terminology, perhaps the ultimate example of the misappropriation of symbols for antimodernist purposes in the modern sporting world. Sloane, the original prophet of Olympic idealism in America, a compatriot of Baron Pierre de Coubertin, and the organizer of the first American Olympic expedition to Athens in 1896, contended in his interpretation of classical antiquity that "Greek civilization imposed itself upon the central world by an irresistible moral compulsion." The professor hypothesized that "no single factor so contributed to create this moral force as the Olympic Games."[27] Sloane argued that the modern Olympics had created the same moral force in the twentieth century that he imagined the classical Olympics had created in the ancient world. "The field therefore of the Olympic idea is not merely sportive and social, it is educational and sociological as well," he wrote. "The intercourse of athletes and their friends makes for reciprocal good will and international peace: but in its largest aspect the idea makes for the general uplift and personal purity of untold millions."[28] Sloane's use of language like "sociological" in conjunction with his faith in the transcendental power of Olympism illustrates the innovatively nostalgic thought-forms that underpinned progressivism. Virtue increasingly became the province of sociology rather than theology, and the paradoxes of mixing symbolic forms multiplied.

Of course, virtue and its production, as well as corruption and the battle to prevent it, had long been a stock theme in republican theorizing. The architects of the sporting republic promised that athletics would preserve American civilization from the selfishness of both the plutocrats and the labor radicals, from the increasing artificiality of life and "nervous" exhaustion, from the cities and decadence, and from non-republican ideologies. They also promised that a strenuous life would protect the nation against the usual litany of modern problems: crime and street gangs, illicit sex, alcohol and drug abuse, irresoluteness, and vice of all kinds. Thus the production of a modernized version of civic virtue became one of the key provisions of the sporting republic's constitution.

"A boy who learns to lie and cheat and to deal in subterfuge in football and baseball . . . will follow the same methods in business or professional life when he gets out into the world," admonished Caspar Whitney in an 1897 codification of the athletic ideal. "On the contrary, a boy who learns by his athletic life to do everything he can honorably to win, but to submit cheerfully to defeat rather than indulge in trickery and meanness, will carry the same spirit in all his recreation and work in after life."[29] Whitney recognized what athletic idealists, with the exception of many of the members of the American collegiate athletic establishment, have long admitted: that sport can be misused and perverted.

Still, Whitney and his compatriots had great faith in the power of athletic institutions. Progressive leaders and the middle-class public connected the sporting republic to education and social reform. Francis Tabor argued that athletics was the essential ingredient in a "moral education," and that a teacher could only truly inspire young charges when the lectern was traded for the playing field. There, with the artificial barriers of the classroom removed, teachers could lead by example rather than "precept," and build character through pragmatic lessons. When the playing field became the center of the educational process, "manliness, energy, courage, endurance, all follow,—not because they are *said* to be good, but because they are *seen* to be good, and *felt* to be absolutely essential," insisted Tabor. "The code of honor among true sportsmen is so rigid that truth and fair-dealing become as important as a well-balanced bat or a sound ball."[30] Political and ethical concerns, read the sporting republic's creed, met on the playing field.

Price Collier summed up the virtuous implications of sport for the middle-class public. He claimed that athletics promoted "healthy democracy," and insisted that "every school-boy in these days is taught, not only by his masters, but by the overwhelming influence of schoolfellows, that he may succeed by fair means only." Collier felt that sport promoted healthy democracy by teaching moral principles and a regard for justice "in days of commercial and social scrambling, when the Ten Commandments are mere rungs on the ladder of financial and social success." He considered it "something gained that thousands of our boys are being taught to play with all their might, to play fair, and to win, if they can. A lad who has ten years of such training can scarcely fail to retain something of that same spirit when he comes to take part in the real contests of life." Collier thought that athletic ethics were absolutely essential in the maintenance of American political culture: "Living in the richest and most unkempt country in the world, where standards are mostly tentative, and where the leveling of a democracy offers huge bribes to wealth, to notoriety, and to popularity, the man who holds that it is not everything to succeed, but that whatever happens he must continue his failures in good spirits, is well worth producing, even at the price, in time and money, of teaching him how to play his games."[31]

Such was the paradox of Collier's thought, making an argument against the overcommercialization of the American spirit by directing his logic toward the "cost" of preventive provisions. Cost, production, and efficiency contrasted with ethical considerations and the necessity of republican virtue. Such an ambivalence plagued the new middle classes as they attempted to adapt to, and to shape, the corporate order.[32]

Well, how much does civic virtue cost? The dialectic between economic and moral motives was particularly evident in the public pronouncements and political career of Theodore Roosevelt. Although certainly not from a middle-class background himself, the patrician Roosevelt paradoxically led the new middle classes' seizure of American political culture. He tried, with curious logic, to mix his cost-benefit analysis of the new order—good trusts versus bad ones—with his romantic vision of nationalism and the will to power of the American people.[33]

"Wealthy men who use their wealth aright are a great power for good in the community, and help to upbuild the material national prosperity which must underlie national greatness; but if this were the only kind of success the nation would be indeed poorly off," Roosevelt blustered. He placed the icons of the new middle class, the governors and servicers of the social order—statesmen, soldiers, sailors, explorers, historians, poets, and men of science—in a position much more essential to the "commonweal" than any "mere" businessman. Similar forms of "innovative nostalgia" helped to inform Roosevelt's peculiarly anticommercial corporate philosophy. Roosevelt's historicist sensibilities celebrated the republican tradition in typically middle-class fashion. Rome, in republican times, he much preferred to the Hellenistic

Greeks: the latter were too "mercenary"; the former were far more virtuous. He vigorously celebrated the American republican tradition, and worshiped the progressive demigod Abraham Lincoln. One of the founders of the sporting republic, Roosevelt made bodily vigor and the sporting life essential features of his neorepublican creed.[34]

Roosevelt restated the classical idea of soundness in mind and body as the cornerstone of character building, arguing that republics required citizens of character in order to function and survive. Of course the equation between vigor and virtue was as old as the theory of republicanism in Western civilization. In the preindustrial world republicans had insisted that vigor and independence sprang from agrarian roots. They opposed the symbol of the healthy, moral yeoman farmer to the dissipated, venal city dweller. The republicans sought a middle ground between nature and artifice, a pastoral clime that would nurture physical, political, and moral strength.[35] Roosevelt, despite his nostalgia for the republicanism of tradition, was no mere reactionary. He believed that industrialism and the corporate economy offered an enticing future if the nostalgic features of republicanism could be preserved by progressive innovation. In his statist philosophy he imagined that "alike for the nation and the individual, the one indispensable requisite is character."[36] And, of course, he preached that the strenuous life produced the character required by modern political realities.

In the evolutionary and historical theories of modernity constructed by Roosevelt and contemporary prophets of progress, sport played a crucial role in preserving vitalistic and energetic modes of human action in forms that could be regulated and channeled toward the public good. Roosevelt and his fellow boosters of the sporting republic, like *Outing* editor and popular journalist Caspar Whitney, connected the sporting life to national vigor, and a lack of athletic institutions to national decadence and social malaise. The sporting republic's champions pointed to the nations that *fin de siècle* American perspectives generally regarded as despotic, decadent, and desperate—France, the perennial homeland of overcivilization in Anglo-American tradition; Spain, the country that the yellow press had by 1898 turned into the paradigm of Old World sloth and cruelty; and, of course, the "sick man" of China—as areas where the sporting life was conspicuously absent.[37]

In Japan, Whitney discovered evidence that some Asians were more forward-looking than the dissolute Chinese. "It speaks highly of the sagacity of Japan's nineteenth century latter day sponsors that they should appreciate the peculiar need to Japan of implementing in her boys a taste for healthful and vigorous physical effort, so that when they grow to manhood there

should be a fresher and sturdier mental activity, with its corresponding elevation of ideals," noted Whitney in the course of a globe-trotting voyage of discovery in search of worldwide athletic practices. That Japan had taken what
Whitney called "her progressive strides . . . one of the wisest features of modern civilization—athletics" confirmed for him the common assumption that
the Japanese were on the correct path to modernity. As the United States
moved toward the front rank of world powers, American commentators had
decided that athletic culture was a necessary ingredient in the composition of
modern states and looked to playing fields around the globe for confirmation
of American ideas of power, race, and progress.[38]

The American version of vitalism created by the architects of the sporting
republic was designed to assuage fears that urban, industrial, and commercial
forms of economy could lead, as the republican theorists in premodern conditions had always argued, to corruption, tyranny, and the extinction of rule
by law. Would the new urban America inevitably suffer the same fate? Was the
city still the symbol of evil? The mayor of Chicago, a young city in the early
twentieth century whose mushrooming growth had come to symbolize
agrarian fears of the death of traditional ways of life, told the nation that he
had a method for making cities republican. "If it is desired that the next generation be a namby-pamby one then the boys and girls of to-day should leave
athletics severely alone," warned Mayor Carter Harrison. "To neglect the
body and train merely the mind is, in my judgment, little short of criminal.
The time has come, in my opinion, when cities should officially recognize the
absolute necessity for a broad and systematic plan of physical training for the
children and youth of both sexes," argued Harrison, whose campaign promise
to build more parks in Chicago had helped him gain office. He felt that "the
neglect of this municipal duty in our American cities is really astounding," and
urged, in the typical fashion of urban progressives, the creation of commissions of experts to advise America on how to best provide for the physical culture of its citizens.[39]

Outing's editors portrayed an even more apocalyptic scenario. "Unless we
can make bodily culture keep up with mind culture our civilization cannot
possibly last," they warned. "From this point of view athletics are not the
amusement of an idle hour,—a way of killing a vacation,—they are elemental duties, vital moral laws."[40] The vitalist doctrines of the sporting republic
spoke to those in the new middle class most directly engaged in commerce.
Modern athleticism, claimed William Frederick Dix, "is strengthening physically and broadening mentally these overworked American businessmen. It is

making them saner and better, cultivating their love of fair play and their interests in life." Dix imagined sport as a panacea for modern problems. "As we grow to be better citizens, we learn to ride straight and play fair and hit hard in life. The blood goes coursing through our veins with a new vigor, and the game of life becomes greater and finer and more worth the playing because we are learning the vast benefits of the manly and womanly idea of modern sport."[41] And so the civic ethics of the new citizenship flowed from playing field and gymnasium into company office and corporate boardroom, or so read the manifestos of the sporting republic.

Athleticism, proclaimed the ideology of the sporting republic, produced manliness in men, womanliness in women—although there was much debate about what kinds of gender roles athletics prepared people for. The progressive historian Frederic L. Paxson argued that participation in sport had aided women in their effort to acquire the franchise.[42] Other theorists, from less liberating perspectives, saw sport as an institution to breed healthy race bearers.[43] Price Collier, in rather chauvinistic terms, lumped the political virtues that sport produced under the heading of manliness and then announced: "If our more manly citizens could rule us, then, no doubt, we should be better off."[44] In the political culture of the Progressive Era, vigor and activism attracted votes and won elections. If sport built character in the public, why would the new middle class look to soft leaders? Theodore Roosevelt stood as proof of that political reality. The extremes between the robber barons and the proletariat that consumed so much attention helped camouflage the fact that the first decades of the twentieth century witnessed the triumph of the new middle class in political life. Roosevelt was the quintessential leader, in both the political and cultural realms, of the middle class's rise to power.[45]

Roosevelt became the stock figure of the age of energy, the archetype of "muscular" executive leadership. A *New York Times* reporter once remarked, "ANDREW JACKSON could shoot as well and ride as well as Mr. ROOSEVELT but we doubt if he could have safely faced him with a tennis net between them," thereby elevating Roosevelt to the pinnacle of the list of vigorous presidents in American history.[46] After Roosevelt's election in 1904 to the office he had assumed after William McKinley's assassination, Caspar Whitney blustered from the "Sportsman's View-Point" to *Outing's* readers that Roosevelt had won the presidency not because Republicans elected him, but because "the clean-blooded, wholesome-minded, right-intended people of the country . . . sought the man rather than the elevation of the party." *Outing*, the foremost chronicle of the strenuous life in the turn-of-the-century

United States, commended the nation for choosing a chief executive who was "honest, and courageous, and virile," and committed to the visions of fair play that filled its pages.[47]

But symbols in the political life of energy controlled and channeled toward socially productive ends through athletic endeavor came from both likely and unexpected sources. With the election of 1908 looming, the dynamo Roosevelt foresworn to abdicate his office, middle-class voters found in the unlikely person of 350-pound William Howard Taft a new figurehead for the sporting republic.

Taft, in William Allen White's campaign confessional, appeared as the archetype of the new middle class. Well off but not wealthy, a respected professional in the legal field, he became in White's rendition of his public career the typical American anti-aristocrat. "The independence of America is in that class," surmised White, "for the man who does not need a valet is not much awed by a king." White also believed that Taft was an important transitional figure between the old middle class and the new. "If Taft should be made President of this Republic he would never cease to be in the heart of him a straphanger, a commuter, not of the city, with its crass wealth and biting poverty, nor of the country—but a suburban president, the first of his type." White thought Taft's suburbanism, his neopastoral origins, were a key to his leadership and character. Taft represented the "new type of American from the suburban community, who as a boy knew both swimminghole and pavement, who roamed the woods and fought the north-end gang, who was afraid of neither cows nor cars—that is a new type of man in American politics—a type that must become more and more prevalent as the country grows less and less rural and more and more urban."[48]

Taft became, in White's hands, "a hewer of wood," a sturdy and active replacement for Rooseveltian strenuosity. But not only White, the Grand Old Party's vocal propagandist, thought that Taft would make a good leader for the sporting republic. On the eve of the election, *Outing* published a major essay implicitly endorsing Taft as the candidate to succeed Roosevelt. Entitled "Taft at Yale," Ralph D. Paine's article glorified the presidential candidate's character-building experiences at New Haven. "The Taft who ruled the Philippines, who made Cuba put her house in order, who said the right word at Panama, who was placed at the head of the War Department, who twice refused a seat on the bench of the Supreme Court of the United States, owes somewhat of his genius for doing the day's work with clear-sighted fairness to all men to the old Yale Fence and the democracy it inspired in all who lingered there," believed Paine.

The Yale Fence (the location of campus sporting life before organized athletics at Yale) symbolized the spirit of the playing field, rather than the classroom, at the ancient—by American standards—college. Paine recalled that
the portly candidate had entered Yale as a strapping 225-pound freshman, and
immediately earned the moniker "Solid Bill Taft." His cohorts at Yale included
Walter Camp, future American Olympic Committee treasurer Julian W. Cur-
tiss, and the legendary rower Robert Cook. Although collegiate sport as it was
known in 1908 did not really exist at the Yale of the late 1870s, Taft, in Paine's
account, nevertheless excelled in the vigorous activities that enriched student
life: the freshman "rush" against the sophomore class, the ritualized wrestling
matches, and all the horseplay around the Fence. Paine and *Outing* thought
Solid Bill Taft an adequate athletic replacement for Theodore Roosevelt, and
a political leader who had imbibed deeply of the gospel of fair play.[49]

It was in relation to the concept of fair play that the middle-class ideology
of sport most clearly showed its connection to the political doctrines of progressive republicanism. The progressives hoped, in their naive fashion, that
fair play would be transmitted from American playing fields into society at
large, and they mistook their historical and cultural values for universal ethical principles.[50] They believed that the spirit of playing within the rules would
apply not simply to sporting contests but to corporate endeavors, labor relations, commercial exchange, and the entire range of economic, social, and political processes that composed their historical environment.

"Let me mould the sports of my countrymen, and whomever frame their
laws," quipped John Corbin in a bit of hyperbole typical of athletic boosters
at the turn of the century.[51] His outburst reflected both his faith in the power
of sport to shape culture and the middle-class distrust of the contemporary
legislative process that muckrakers and progressive gadflies had identified as
seriously corrupted.[52] His concern also reflected the analogical reasoning
that related regulation of the body to regulation of the body politic, the rules
and structures of modern athletic contests to the constitutionalism that underlay the American republican tradition.[53] That the Constitution and the en-
shrinement of the principles of rule by law provided equity for all citizens
and factions was a central tenet of early-twentieth-century American political culture—in spite of Charles Beard's broadside into the myths that
shrouded the American democratic faith.[54] As Woodrow Wilson put it during his bid for the presidency in 1912, he could easily solve American problems "if you will give me a fair field and as much credit as I am entitled to,
and let the law do what from time immemorial law has been expected to
do—see fair play."[55]

The idea of life—its economic, political, and social features in particular—
as a game, or games as representations of life, marked one of the central organizing principles of American thought in the late nineteenth and early
twentieth centuries.[56] From the Western novelist Owen Wister's cry "Let the
best man win!" as the heart of the American creed to the sociologist Edward
A. Ross's shorthand for the "scientific" understanding of social practice as "the
rules of the social game," American thinkers used the language and imagery
of the playing field to describe the workings of civil societies.[57] Laws and rules;
legislators and referees; justice and fair play: the analogies indicated the structural levels at which the sporting republic connected the well-ordered body to
the well-ordered body politic.

Woodrow Wilson was an especially deft weaver of athletic and political
semiotics. "America was created to break every kind of monopoly and to set
men free, upon a footing of equality, upon a footing of opportunity, to match
their brains and their energies," he argued while running for president in 1912
in language that reduced the republican experiment to a sporting contest. "I
know, and every man in his heart knows, that the only way to enrich America
is to make it possible for any man who has the brains to get into the game. I
am perfectly willing that they should beat any competitor by fair means; but
I know the foul means they have adopted, and I know that they can be stopped
by law," he asserted, reducing antitrust legislation to athletic jargon. "All the
fair competition you choose, but no unfair competition of any kind," he
promised the American electorate. "America stands for a free field and no favor," he shouted, determined to wed his ideology to the gospel of fair play.[58]
Wilson, who was forced by the new corporate order to abandon the Jeffer-
sonian world of free competition toward which he had led the nation in a
nostalgic lust during the election of 1912 and to come to grips with new
bureaucratic innovations, understood "regulated competition"—the capstone
of the emerging consumer-based corporate economy—as "fair competition."
His ideological confusion ironically helped adjust American attitudes to a new
form of political republicanism that fused the antimodernism of his epoch
into a new and "streamlined" liberal culture.[59]

What was "sport's place in the nation's well-being"? If the question is
viewed from a perspective that, as Clifford Geertz has advocated, conceives of
social life as organized in terms of symbols, then from the vantage point of
the American middle classes—and particularly the progressives who sought to
define and represent their interests—the sporting republic had become a crucial institution in their struggle to regulate American civilization.[60] Once
again, Woodrow Wilson leaves important clues. His 1911 speech to the first

National Conference on Civic and Social Center Development, a group committed to creating sites for athleticism, inculcation of progressive values, adult education, community involvement, and direct democracy, portrayed the progressive state as a team committed to common purpose. Liberty he saw in typically republican fashion: as the coordination of various interests into a communal whole, not by the classical method of an invisible hand or a self-regulating natural principle, but by a modern conception of team spirit. In Wilson's construction, progress flowed from the adjustment of civilization to the new rules of the game.[61]

During the Progressive Era the idea of a sporting republic played an important role in the revitalization of middle-class culture and the adjustment of the bourgeois frame of reference to the realities of corporate capitalism. Athletic analogies helped the concept of government regulation of the economy gain currency by linking political activism to the gospel of fair play and explaining economic theories through playing-field rhetoric. The vitalistic doctrines of the sporting republic combated fears that the urban-industrial environment would doom the nation. A middle-class ideology of strenuosity, designed in part by an elite leadership, shaped political dialogue and expectations, reinvigorated the cult of civic virtue, and placed athletic physical culture in a central position in modern American life. The tropological categories of the new republicanism linked the regulated body with the regulated body politic and defined the idea of economy as a form of game. But the symbolic logic of the new republicanism made one huge assumption: it expected that every social interest would, in the jargon of the strenuous life, play fair. Such a faith would be hard to match with experience. Indeed, such a faith would be hard-pressed to explain the realities of events within the world of modern athletics itself.

Notes

1. There is, of course, a voluminous historiography on the subject, dating from the beginning of the transformation itself as contemporaries sought to make sense out of the process by placing it into a historical context. The question of what it means to become modern has been one of the staples of political philosophy and social criticism in the nineteenth and twentieth centuries. On modernization, industrialization, and the rise of a market economy in the United States, from both specific and broad angles of vision, see Richard Brown, *Modernization: The Transformation of American Life, 1600–1865* (New York: Hill and Wang, 1976); Diane Lindstrom, *Economic Development in the Philadelphia Region, 1810–1850* (New York: Columbia University Press, 1978); Anthony F. C. Wallace,

Rockdale: The Growth of an American Village in the Early Industrial Revolution (New York: Knopf, 1978); Thomas C. Cochran, *Frontiers of Change: Early Industrialism in America* (New York: Oxford University Press, 1981); Thomas Bender, *Toward an Urban Vision: Ideas and Institutions in Nineteenth-Century America* (Lexington: University Press of Kentucky, 1975); Gunther Barth, *City People: The Rise of Modern City Culture in Nineteenth-Century America* (New York: Oxford University Press, 1980); Robert Wiebe, *The Search for Order, 1877–1920* (New York: Hill and Wang, 1967); Kenneth E. Boulding, *The Organizational Revolution: A Study in the Ethics of Economic Organizations* (New York: Harper & Row, 1953); Samuel P. Hays, *The Response to Industrialism, 1865–1914* (Chicago: University of Chicago Press, 1957); James Weinstein, *The Corporate Ideal and the Liberal State, 1900–1918* (Boston: Beacon, 1968); David F. Noble, *America by Design: Science, Technology and the Rise of Corporate Capitalism* (New York: Oxford University Press, 1980).

On republicanism challenged and transformed, see particularly the work on political culture of Paul A. Carter, *Revolt Against Destiny: An Intellectual History of the United States* (New York: Columbia University Press, 1989); Dorothy Ross, "The Liberal Tradition Revisited and the Republican Tradition Addressed," in *New Directions in American Intellectual History*, John Higham and Paul K. Conkin, eds. (Baltimore: Johns Hopkins University Press, 1979); Robert Kelley, "Ideology and Political Culture from Jefferson to Nixon," *American Historical Review* 82 (June 1977), 531–62.

On the changing nature of political culture in the late nineteenth and early twentieth centuries, see Richard L. McCormick, "The Discovery That Business Corrupts Politics: A Reappraisal of the Origins of Progressivism," *American Historical Review* 86 (April 1981), 247–74; David Thelen, *The New Citizenship: Origins of Progressivism in Wisconsin, 1885–1900* (Columbia: University of Missouri Press, 1972); and "Social Tensions and the Origins of Progressivism," *Journal of American History* 56 (September 1969), 323–41; John D. Buenker, John C. Burnham, and Robert M. Crunden, *Progressivism* (Cambridge, Mass.: Schenkman, 1977); Arthur Link and Richard L. McCormick, *Progressivism* (Arlington Heights, Ill.: Harlan Davidson, 1983).

On the crisis of bourgeois culture, see T. J. Jackson Lears, *No Place of Grace: Antimodernism and the Transformation of American Culture, 1880–1920* (New York: Pantheon, 1981); Howard Mumford Jones, *The Age of Energy: Varieties of American Experience, 1865–1915* (New York: Viking, 1970); Robert M. Crunden, *Ministers of Reform: The Progressives' Achievement in American Civilization, 1889–1920* (Urbana: University of Illinois Press, 1984). See also Wiebe, *The Search for Order;* Noble, *The Paradox of Progressive Thought* (Minneapolis: University of Minnesota Press, 1958), and *The Progressive Mind* (Chicago: Rand McNally, 1970); Alan Trachtenberg, *The Incorporation of America: Culture and Society in the Gilded Age* (New York: Hill and Wang, 1982); John F. Kasson, *Amusing the Million: Coney Island at the Turn of the Century* (New York: Hill and Wang, 1978).

2. The distinction between older and newer middle classes has been employed to chart a shift that is as much cultural as it is economic. Descriptions and explanations of the shift appear in most of the fundamental critiques of the modern social order, ranging from the work of Karl Marx and Friedrich Engels to that of Max Weber and Hannah Arendt, and even Alvin Toffler. In American social science, Thorstein Veblen, *The Theory of the Leisure Class* (New York: Macmillan, 1899), and C. Wright Mills, *White Collar; The American Middle Classes* (New York: Oxford University Press, 1953), greatly influenced the basic paradigm. For an interesting survey of the idea of class between the Civil War and the end of the First World War, see Glenn C. Altschuler, *Race, Ethnicity, and Class in American Social Thought, 1865–1919* (Arlington Heights, Ill.: Harlan Davidson, 1982). The drive to construct a nationalized culture is hinted at in many of the works concerned with the American bourgeoisie, particularly Lears's *No Place of Grace* and Trachtenberg's *The Incorporation of America*. H. Wayne Morgan, in *Unity and Culture: The United States, 1877–1900* (Baltimore: Penguin, 1971), offered a provocative essay on the effort to construct a national style in high culture. Less work has been done on the "search for order" in mass culture. One can gain a strong appreciation for the pervasiveness of the bourgeois effort to inculcate its standards from the writings of critics of middle-class efforts at constructing some sort of hegemony. See Randolph Bourne's provocative "The Puritan's Will to Power," *The Seven Arts* I (April 1917), 631–37.

Too often historians overemphasize the deterministic nature of modernization and forget the role that human agency played in the construction of industrial civilization. Too often they stress the economic, technical, and social aspects of modernization as somehow having a reality separate from culture and consciousness. And too often they dismiss ideas as rhetorical camouflage in their anxiousness to get at what people "do" rather than what they "say," forgetting that one of the things that human beings "do" is spend a great deal of their time and energy making systems of explanation in which to ground their behaviors. This study concerns the ideas of republicanism and athleticism and it assumes that ideas matter, that ideology can serve as an honest, if culture-bound, method for turning experience into meaning. The concern with cultural meanings—or, to use an anthropological metaphor, Clifford Geertz's infamous "winks"—debated in national communities of discourse has been nurtured by the reading of, among many others, Carter, *Revolt Against Destiny;* Gene Wise, *American Historical Explanations: A Strategy for Grounded Inquiry,* 2nd ed. (Minneapolis: University of Minnesota Press, 1980); Dominick LaCapra, *History and Criticism* (Ithaca, N.Y.: Cornell University Press, 1985); Edmund S. Morgan, *Inventing the People: The Rise of Popular Sovereignty in England and America* (New York: W. W. Norton, 1988); Clifford Geertz, *The Interpretation of Cultures* (New York: Basic Books, 1973), and *Local Knowledge: Further Essays in Interpretive Anthropology* (New York: Oxford University Press, 1956).

3. Price Collier, "Sport's Place in the Nation's Well-Being," *Outing* 32 (July 1898), 382–88.

4. Roosevelt enunciated his athletic gospel in numerous writings. Perhaps the seminal statement of the code, and its connection with nationalism, can be found in Theodore Roosevelt, "The Strenuous Life," speech before the Hamilton Club, Chicago, April 10, 1899; in Herman Hagerdorn, ed., *The Works of Theodore Roosevelt, Vol. XIII: American Ideals, The Strenuous Life, Realizable Ideals* (New York: Charles Scribner's Sons, 1926), 331. See also Woodrow Wilson, "The Social Center," *Bulletin of the University of Wisconsin Extension Division,* serial no. 470 (Madison, Wis., 1911), 3–15; Jane Addams, *The Spirit of Youth and the City Streets* (New York: Macmillan, 1909); Jacob Riis, "Fighting the Gang with Athletics," *Collier's* 46 (February 11, 1911), 17, and *Battle with the Slum* (New York: Macmillan, 1902). William James sometimes sprinkled sporting metaphors like "second wind" and "warming up" in his essays on mental exertion. See "The Energies of Men," *Essays on Faith and Morals,* Ralph Barton Perry, ed. (New York: Longmans, Green, 1947), 216–37. G. Stanley Hall, who served with varying degrees of success as a teacher to both George Herbert Mead and John Dewey, influenced progressive conceptions of child psychology and its dynamogenic components with his "evolutionary theory" of play. See his *Adolescence: Its Psychology and Its Relations to Physiology, Anthropology, Sociology, Sex, Crime, Religion and Education* (New York: D. Appleton, 1904). See also Simon N. Patten, *Product and Climax* (New York: Huebsch, 1909); Edward A. Ross, *Social Control: A Survey of the Foundations of Order* (New York: Macmillan, 1916).

The literature on late-nineteenth- and early-twentieth-century sport is growing. See in particular Dominick Cavallo, *Muscles and Morals: Organized Playgrounds and Urban Reform, 1880–1920* (Philadelphia: University of Pennsylvania Press, 1981); Allen Guttmann, *A Whole New Ball Game: An Interpretation of American Sports* (Chapel Hill: University of North Carolina Press, 1988), and *From Ritual to Record: The Nature of Modern Sport* (New York: Columbia University Press, 1978); Don S. Kirschner, "The Perils of Pleasure: Commercial Recreation, Social Disorder and Moral Reform in the Progressive Era," *American Studies* 21 (fall 1980), 27–42; J. A. Mangan and James Walvin, eds., *Manliness and Morality: Middle-Class Masculinity in Britain and America, 1800–1940* (New York: St. Martin's, 1987); Donald Mrozek, *Sport and American Mentality, 1880–1910* (Knoxville: University of Tennessee Press, 1983); Steven Riess, *Touching Base: Professional Baseball and American Culture in the Progressive Era* (Westport, Conn.: Greenwood, 1980).

Of course the progressive ideology of sport had many critics and contestants in the struggle to define American physical culture. See in particular Elliott J. Gorn, *The Manly Art: Bare-Knuckle Prize Fighting in America* (Ithaca, N.Y.: Cornell University Press, 1986); Stephen Hardy, *How Boston Played: Sport, Recreation, and Community, 1865–1915* (Boston: Northeastern University Press, 1982); Roy Rosenzweig,

Eight Hours for What We Will: Workers and Leisure in an Industrial City, 1870–1920 (Cambridge: Cambridge University Press, 1983).

5. Symbolic anthropologists have explored the idea that the body and its treatment can give important clues to social relations and cosmology. See Mary T. Douglas, *Natural Symbols: Explorations in Cosmology* (New York: Pantheon, 1970); Victor Turner, *Dramas, Fields, Metaphors: Symbolic Action in Human Society* (Ithaca, N.Y.: Cornell University Press, 1974). Mrozek, in *Sport and American Mentality, 1880–1910*, discusses the connection between the modern desire to regulate energy and modern sporting forms. See also the insightful work of Roberta J. Park, "Biological Thought, Athletics and the Formation of a 'Man of Character': 1830–1900," *Manliness and Morality*, 7–34.

6. Price Collier, "The Ethics of Ancient and Modern Athletics," *Forum* 32 (November 1901), 317–18.

7. See the voluminous count of articles and books on the "amusement problem" offered to the public in Richard Henry Edwards, *Popular Amusements* (1915; rep., New York: Arno Press, 1976).

8. Luther Halsey Gulick, "Popular Recreation and Public Morality," *Annals of the American Academy of Political and Social Science* 34 (July 1909), 33.

9. Thorstein Veblen, *The Vested Interests and the Common Man: The Modern Point of View and the New Order* (New York: Heubsch, 1919).

10. Gulick, "Popular Recreation and Public Morality," 33.

11. Loren Baritz, *The Good Life: The Meaning of Success for the American Middle Class* (New York: Harper & Row, 1989).

12. "The Changing Middle Class," *Independent* 79 (July 27, 1914), 117.

13. "The Middle Class Mind," *The Dial* 55 (August 16, 1913), 99–101.

14. "The Changing Middle Class," 117.

15. Peter Levine, "The Promise of Sport in Antebellum America," *Journal of American Culture* 2 (winter 1980), 623–34; Steven A. Riess, *City Games: The Evolution of American Urban Society and the Rise of Sports* (Urbana: University of Illinois Press, 1989).

16. See Hannah Arendt's chapter entitled "The Political Emancipation of the Bourgeoisie" in *The Origins of Totalitarianism* (New York: Harcourt, Brace & World, 1966), 123–57. On the reconstruction of American social thought in the late nineteenth and early twentieth centuries consult Sidney Fine, *Laissez Faire and the General Welfare State* (Ann Arbor: University of Michigan Press, 1956); David Noble, *The Progressive Mind* (Chicago: Rand McNally, 1970); Daniel Levine, *Varieties of Reform Thought* (Madison: University of Wisconsin Press, 1964); Morton White, *Social Thought in America: The Revolt Against Formalism* (New York: Oxford University Press, 1976); Paul F. Boller, *Freedom and Fate in American Thought: From Edwards to Dewey* (Dallas: Southern Methodist University Press, 1978); Henry Steele Commager, *The American Mind: An Interpretation of American Thought and*

Character Since 1950 (New Haven: Yale, 1950); Henry F. May, *The End of American Innocence* (New York: Alfred A. Knopf, 1959).

17. The concepts of social control and social justice are somewhat problematic since they arise in large part from the ideological arguments of historians who have debated about the nature and existence of progressivism, rather than from the historical context itself. Social control and social justice were intertwined categories in the discourse of the era, and progressives seemed untroubled by control in the name of what they considered justice. For discussions of the problem see Daniel T. Rodgers, "In Search of Progressivism," *Reviews in American History* 10 (December 1982), 113–32; Don S. Kirschner, "The Ambiguous Legacy: Social Justice and Social Control in the Progressive Era," *Historical Reflections* 2 (summer 1975), 69–88.

18. For a more detailed account see Mrozek, *Sport and the American Mentality.* See also Peter Levine, *A. G. Spalding and the Rise of Baseball: The Promise of American Sport* (New York: Oxford University Press, 1985), for an insightful commentary on the ways in which entrepreneurs like Spalding turned the mainstream athletic ideology into a lucrative commercial enterprise.

19. Francis Tabor, "Directed Sport as a Factor in Education," *Forum* 27 (May 1899), 321.

20. See Lester F. Ward, *Applied Sociology: A Treatise on the Conscious Improvement of Society by Society* (Boston: Ginn & Company, 1906); Herbert Croly, *The Promise of American Life* (New York: Macmillan, 1909).

21. For an enlightening portrait of the popular reception of Roosevelt's athletic gospel, see "The President's Ideas About Sports," *Ladies Home Journal* 23 (August 1906), 17. Classic pieces from the source himself include Theodore Roosevelt, "What We Can Expect of the American Boy," *St. Nicholas* 27 (May 1900), 571–74; "Commercialism, Hysteria, and Homicide," *Outlook* 99 (October 21, 1911), 409–10; "The Value of an Athletic Training," *Harper's Weekly* 27 (December 23, 1893), 1236.

22. John Corbin, "The Modern Chivalry," *Atlantic Monthly* 89 (April 1902), 601–11.

23. Lears, *No Place of Grace.*

24. Guttmann, *A Whole New Ball Game,* 5. See also Guttmann, *From Ritual to Record,* and Melvin L. Adelman, *A Sporting Time: New York City and the Rise of Modern Athletics, 1820–1870* (Urbana: University of Illinois Press, 1986).

25. Crunden, *Ministers of Reform.*

26. A. E. Colton, "What Football Does," *Independent* 57 (September 15, 1904), 605–07.

27. William Milligan Sloane, "The Greek Olympiads," *Report of the American Olympic Committee, 1920* (Greenwich, Conn.: Condé Nast Press, 1920), 59.

28. Sloane, "Modern Olympic Games," *Report of the American Olympic Committee, 1920,* 83.

29. "The Minister and Athletics: Mr. Caspar Whitney's Views," *Outlook* 55 (January 9, 1897), 181–83.

30. Tabor, "Directed Sport as a Factor in Education," 321–22.

31. Collier, "The Ethics of Ancient and Modern Athletics," 309–18.

32. For a fuller treatment of the cost of the strenuous life see Arthur Reeve, "What America Spends for Sport," *Outing* 57 (December 1910), 300–308.

33. See particularly John M. Blum, *The Republican Roosevelt* (Cambridge: Harvard University Press, 1954), and George E. Mowry, *Theodore Roosevelt and the Birth of Modern America* (New York: Harper & Row, 1958).

34. Theodore Roosevelt, "Character and Success," *Outlook* 64 (March 31, 1900), 725–27.

35. See, for instance, Leo Marx, *The Machine in the Garden: Technology and the Pastoral Ideal in America* (New York: Oxford University Press, 1964); Louis Hartz, *The Liberal Tradition in America: An Interpretation of American Political Thought Since the Revolution* (New York: Harcourt, Brace, Jovanovich, 1955); and J. G. A. Pocock, *The Machiavellian Moment: Florentine Political Thought and the Atlantic Republican Tradition* (Princeton, N.J.: Princeton University Press, 1975).

36. Roosevelt, "Character and Success," 727.

37. Collier, "Sport's Place in the Nation's Well-Being," 382–88; Whitney, "Non-Athletic China," *Harper's Weekly* 42 (February 19, 1898), 189–90.

38. Whitney, "Athletic Awakening of the Japanese," *Harper's Weekly* 42 (February 12, 1898), 165–66.

39. Carter H. Harrison, "Municipal Athletics," *Independent* 53 (November 28, 1901), 2823–24.

40. "Editor's Open Window," *Outing* 4 (May 1884), 143.

41. William Frederick Dix, "The Influence of Sport in American Life," *Independent* 55 (September 3, 1903), 2094–95.

42. Frederic L. Paxson, "The Rise of Sport," *Mississippi Valley Historical Review* 4 (September 1917), 167–68.

43. See, for instance, Anne O'Hagan, "The Athletic Girl," *Munsey's* 25 (August 1901), 729–30; "*Outing's* Health Hints for Women," *Outing* 14 (August 1889), 395; "Editor's Open Window," *Outing* 12 (June 1888), 268; Dudley Sargent, "Are Athletics Making Girls Masculine?," *Ladies Home Journal* 29 (March 1912), 11; "Women's Sports: A Symposium," *American Review of Reviews* 22 (August 1900), 232; E. Atwood, "Mother's Part in Athletics," *American Homes* 9 (June 1912), 226–28.

44. Collier, "Sport's Place in the Nation's Well-Being," 382–88.

45. Jones, *The Age of Energy*, 413.

46. "Mr. Roosevelt and the Athletes," *New York Times,* September 2, 1908: 6.

47. Whitney, "The Sportsman's View-Point," *Outing* 45 (January 1905), 493.

48. William Allen White, "Taft, A Hewer of Wood," *American Magazine* 66 (May 1908), 19–32.

49. Ralph D. Paine, "Taft at Yale," *Outing* 53 (November 1908), 135–50.

50. Reinhold Niebuhr, *The Children of Light and the Children of Darkness: A Vindication of Democracy and a Critique of Its Traditional Defense* (New York: Charles Scribner's Sons, 1944); Arendt, *The Origins of Totalitarianism.*

51. John Corbin, "A Harvard Man at Oxford," *Harper's Weekly* 42 (February 26, 1896), 212.

52. McCormick, "The Discovery That Business Corrupts Politics."

53. Richard Lipsky, "Toward a Theory of American Sports Symbolism," *Games and Sports in Cultural Context,* Janet C. Harris and Roberta J. Park, eds. (Champaign, Ill.: Human Kinetics Publishers, 1983), 83.

54. Charles Beard, *An Economic Interpretation of the Constitution of the United States* (New York: Macmillan, 1913). For the context of Beard's work and Constitution worship in early-twentieth-century America, see Richard Hofstadter, *The Progressive Historians: Turner, Beard, Parrington* (Chicago: University of Chicago Press, 1968), and Ralph Henry Gabriel, *The Course of American Democratic Thought,* 2nd ed. (New York: Ronald, 1956).

55. Woodrow Wilson, *The New Freedom: A Call for the Emancipation of the Generous Energies of a People,* comp. William Bayard Hale (New York: Doubleday, Page, 1914), 170.

56. An interesting foray into the semiotic relationship between game theory and cognition can be found in Theodore Roszak, "Forbidden Games," *Sport in the Socio-Cultural Process,* M. Marie Hart, ed. (Dubuque, Iowa: William C. Brown, 1972), 91–104.

57. Owen Wister, *The Virginian* (New York: Grosset & Dunlap, 1904), 147; Edward A. Ross, *Social Control: A Survey of the Foundations of Order* (New York: Macmillan, 1916), 34–35.

58. Wilson, *The New Freedom,* 45, 114, 105–106, 131, 153.

59. See Lears's *No Place of Grace* for a discussion of the emergence of "streamlined modern liberalism."

60. Geertz argues that the general trend in recent cultural studies has been "toward conceiving of social life as organized in terms of symbols (signs, representations, *significants, Darstellungen* . . . the terminology varies), whose meaning (sense, import, *signification, Bedeutung* . . .) we must grasp if we are to understand that organization and formulate its principles. . . . The woods are full of eager interpreters" ("Blurred Genres: The Reconfiguration of Social Thought," *Local Knowledge,* 21).

61. Wilson, "The Social Center," 3–15.

PART 2
GENDER AND THE BODY

5

Gender and Sporting Practice in Early America, 1750–1810

NANCY L. STRUNA

In the latter half of the eighteenth and the early years of the nineteenth centuries, the recreational scene in what was becoming the United States was markedly different from what had been the case 100 years earlier. Well-organized thoroughbred races on formal tracks had supplanted impromptu quarter-mile sprints in many places along the Atlantic seaboard, and race weeks drew-thousands of people to small towns and bustling cities. In the more recently settled backcountry, especially in the South, colonists constructed a variety of human and animal contests, notably baits, cockfights, and gouging matches, which tested the mettle of the contestants and appealed to the gambling interests of many. Elsewhere, foot and boat races, card games, spinning and ax-throwing matches, sledding and skating events, and even cricket games emerged, both within and outside of the context of community celebrations. The largest cities, like New York and Philadelphia, even offered commercial "pleasure gardens"; and virtually every crossroads had at least one tavern, which had been and remained the recreational center for many early Americans.[1] By 1810, a city like Baltimore, the country's third largest, had more than 300 licensed tavernkeepers, or approximately one for every 150 inhabitants.[2]

That late-eighteenth- and early-nineteenth-century Americans had begun to produce and consume more sporting practices than had their predecessors a century earlier seems certain, even from this brief description. Among the many things that are not clear about this expansionism, however, are its gender dimensions. The impressionistic evidence that undergirds the conclusion that there was an expansion in sporting practice between 1750 and 1810 suggests that it was largely a male phenomenon. Yet most of these sources—especially newspapers, diaries, and letters—were provided by men, so that is not particularly surprising. It does, however, require further testing.

The meanings of this expansion in sporting practice for gender relations and, in fact, the interplay between men and women over time constitute a second set of questions. Given that two of the major events of the era—the revolt against Britain and the transition to capitalism—did alter gender relations, particularly insofar as republican ideology, the disruption of family economies, and the changing relationship between work and leisure defined different roles and expectations for men and women, it seems possible to suggest that sporting practices may have incorporated those different roles and expectations.[3] They may even have clarified male-female relations in particular ways.

The story that emerges in the following pages focuses on two aspects of the apparent post–1750 expansion in sport and other recreational forms: consumption and production. Such a division permits one to examine more fully the dimensions of gender and gender relations. That interplay, it appears, was complex, for even though men constituted the majority of producers and consumers, they neither defined nor conducted sporting practices independently of women. Instead, men and women negotiated both the content and the meanings of recreations. The consequences were gendered practices that eventually enabled men and women to sharpen, and even redefine, their social roles and to clarify their differences.

The Expansion of Sport

Several historians have suggested that major changes in personal and popular consumption occurred on both sides of the Atlantic during the eighteenth century. Early in the century the British middle ranks began to purchase what in the previous century would have constituted luxury goods for them, including china, stylistic household goods, wallpaper, books, fabrics, and even pets.[4] By at least 1750 this "consumer revolution" had begun in the Anglo-American colonies, first with the land-owning and mercantile gentry and then among middling and lower-rank colonials. As Lois Carr, Lorena Walsh, and Gloria Main have concluded, the goods were numerous, non-essential items, and sufficiently widespread to suggest that the colonists had come to define an entirely different standard of living.[5]

The effect of this popular consumption movement on late-colonial popular culture more generally has not received any systematic attention from historians. It seems reasonable to suggest, however, that the presence of a variety of consumer goods probably underlay the broadening array of popular-culture practices evident from the middle of the eighteenth century onward.

Forms of and forums for music, theater, literary works, and art all expanded dramatically; and libraries, philosophic societies, fire and insurance companies, and academies and colleges formed. Modes of political action, forms of travel, eating and drinking facilities, and social organizations also proliferated and specialized.[6]

It also seems reasonable to suggest that the apparent expansion of sporting practices was one aspect of this expanding popular culture and popular consumption movement. J. H. Plumb in particular has put forward just such an argument for sporting and other recreational practices on the British Isles. There, horse racing became institutionalized within the social and political life of high society, cricket and boxing regularized and acquired specific ethics, and equipment and facilities became relatively common features in the lives of elite and low-born alike and the towns in which they lived.[7]

Whether Anglo-American sporting practices altered in the face of changing consumption patterns and standards of living remains a question. Using the same sources that other historians have used to document changing types and ownership patterns of consumer goods, however, we should be able to explore this possibility by focusing on sporting goods, which indicate ownership and access and perhaps even behavior. These sources are estate inventories, which list the real and personal property holdings of individuals at the time of their deaths. Estate inventories are not bias-free, particularly insofar as poorer and rural colonists tended to be underrepresented; nor do they probably register all of the goods used in sport, since not all such items were either recognizable or sport-specific. They do, however, serve as one indicator of potential consumer behavior and, hence, suffice as one gauge of sporting consumption.[8]

Table 5-1 summarizes the sporting-goods content of the inventories registered in six counties in Maryland between 1770 and 1810. Before 1770 few sport-specific goods of any kind appeared in individual inventories, even though the same inventories did register the kinds of nonessential items that early American historians have described. The timing of their appearance thus suggests that sporting goods were probably even more nonessential than were other forms of personal property, in part perhaps because people could use makeshift items and because they participated in sport away from the confines of their homes.

By 1770, as recognizable items for sporting practice began to appear, they quickly became relatively numerous and varied. Some of these items, like the varieties of gaming tables, embellished parlors and libraries in large Georgian and smaller town houses alike. Sleighs and sulkeys replaced the once-ubiquitous and multi-use sleds or sledges and wagons for winter and

Table 5-1. Sporting Goods in Maryland Estate Inventories, 1770–1810

Equipment	1770	1790	1810
Backgammon tables	1	6	5
Billiard tables	1	0	3
Card tables	0	9	45
Dice/box	0	0	1
Fishing hooks/ lines	7	4	9
Fowling pieces	3	6	15
Hunting saddles	2	2	2
Packs of cards	0	5	2
Pleasure boat	0	0	1
Shuffleboard/ checkers	0	0	4
Sleighs	1	5	7
Sulkeys	0	0	4
Totals	15	37	98
Estate *N*	239	206	361
Percent of estates with goods	6	18	27

Sources: Probate Records of Baltimore, Anne Arundel, Worcester, Frederick, Queen Anne, and St. Mary's counties, Hall of Records, Annapolis, Maryland.

summer races and recreational outings, respectively, just as fowling pieces and hunting saddles supplanted muskets and ordinary riding saddles. Moreover, more people had access to these items, as the increase from 6 percent of estates with goods to more than a quarter of all estates by 1810 suggests.

Marylanders were not the only collectors of sporting goods between 1770 and 1810, as inventories from Suffolk County, Massachusetts, described in table 5-2 indicate.

As had been the case in Maryland, the Suffolk County inventories revealed a substantial increase in the total numbers of items and the percentage of estates with sporting equipment. There are differences between the two samples, of course, and those differences are suggestive, especially about the urban/rural dimensions of ownership. By 1810 Suffolk County had essentially become Greater Boston, and consequently most of the Suffolk inventories

Table 5-2. Sporting Goods in Suffolk County Estate
Inventories, 1769–1810

Equipment	1769	1790	1810
Backgammon tables	2	3	7
Card tables	1	7	33[a]
Fishing goods	0	4	5
Fowling pieces	0	0	3
Packs of cards	0	0	9
Sleighs	1	4	6
Pigeon nets	1	2	0
"Hoyle's Games"	1	1	0
Totals	6	21	63
Estate N	108	145	93
Percent of estates with goods	6	14	68

Sources: Suffolk County Probate Records, Suffolk County Courthouse,
Boston. The 1770 inventories were missing, so the ones for 1769 were used.
a. Inventories also registered skates and sulkeys in 1790 and a pair of bar-
bells in 1810.

were Boston inventories. An examination of differences between rural and urban ownership patterns awaits a systematic analysis.

The estate inventories in both Maryland and Massachusetts help to confirm
that the expansion in sporting practice indicated in newspapers and diaries
was probably something other than a figment of contemporary imaginations.
Neither increase, either of goods or of estates with goods, signals a consumer
revolution of the dimensions evident in other consumer-behavior studies, but
the simple fact of the matter is that more people did have more sporting
goods.[9] Just as important, the owners of sporting goods were not all members
of the colonial and early national upper ranks. Indeed, by 1810 more than 60
percent of the goods registered in Suffolk and Baltimore county estates belonged to middling-rank decedents, a pattern that suggests that sporting
goods were no longer luxuries.[10]

The proliferation of sporting goods probably enabled late-eighteenth-
and early-nineteenth-century Americans to incorporate sporting practices
within their style of daily living. In doing so, such goods may have fueled the

expansion of sporting practice that contemporary diarists and newspapers described. The availability of goods does not, however, account for all or even most of that expansion, especially since many sporting practices required little or no equipment. Moreover, colonists and early nationals often engaged in sport away from the home, or the farm, or the plantation—in public places where personal holdings, or the lack thereof, would not necessarily be evident or significant.[11] Taverns in particular served as significant venues for sport. Consequently, an examination of tavern-licensing patterns may provide another gauge of the post–1750 sporting expansion.

Taverns had always been a center of social life in early America. Settlers and visitors to the colonies alike went to them for food, drink, lodging, conversation, and conviviality. Most towns and crossroads had a least one tavern, and over the course of the seventeenth and early eighteenth centuries, the numbers of taverns increased in proportion to the popular demand and an area's economic base. Tavern keepers, in turn, often acquired particular responsibilities—such as for arbitrating disputes—and respect. They also often curried the favor of local magistrates, who controlled licenses, and customers. Accommodating the latter group was, for many tavern keepers, the more critical task, for their livelihood depended on the patronage of people who came to relax and refresh themselves with food, drink, talk, and recreation. Consequently, many tavern keepers found ways either to skirt the laws concerning sporting practices, especially gambling, or to harness the popular interest in recreations by organizing and promoting particular practices. Many tavern keepers furnished tables and cards and permitted gambling, which they could limit by the amount of credit they extended. A few built cockpits and alleys, and some arranged horse races and baits. One man, Benjamin Berry, even built a business of legendary proportions in west-central Virginia by retaining locals to serve as fistfighters in bouts against all comers.[12]

There is virtually no evidence to suggest that the connection between taverns and sporting practice diminished over time in early America. In fact, particularly after the middle of the eighteenth century, as the population grew and the economy diversified, the sporting business of tavern keepers also expanded. In cities like New York, Philadelphia, and Charleston, where taverns catered to specific groups of people, to laborers or mechanics or trading and shipping magnates, the owners arranged activities ranging from baits to billiards that their clients preferred. Elsewhere, small, barely subsisting rural taverns held shooting contests; and middling-rank tavern keepers in villages and hamlets even began to import or buy from local craftspeople tables, cards, and dice.[13]

Historians may never know the full extent of sporting practice in early American taverns or even how much of the late-eighteenth- and early-nineteenth-century sporting expansion occurred in the taverns. We can begin, however, to understand the possible dimensions of what was really the producer side of this expansion by examining licensing patterns. Such patterns do not speak directly to actual sporting practice, but they may be adequate indicators of opportunity, insofar as they focus on the people who might have permitted and even promoted sport in any given colony. In the case of Maryland these patterns are made possible by the existence of county-court records, which list the names of people who obtained their licenses on a annual basis. Using the records of Baltimore County, which are more complete than are some other counties, one is able to identify who obtained licenses, when they got them, where they resided, and for how many years they kept the license. The records do not, of course, speak either to the actual use of the license or to individuals who kept unlicensed taverns.

By counting the number of licenses granted for the first time to any individual, we can chart the number of persons who first received their license in a given decade. The Baltimore County data, both actual numbers of tavern keepers licensed in each decade and scaled numbers to account for years in which the records are missing, appear in figure 5-1.[14]

Whether one examines the actual numbers of licenses given for the first time in any decade or the numbers that are scaled to account for missing years, one will see a similar and quite dramatic rise between 1750 and 1810. The actual number of licenses increased from sixty-eight in the 1750s to 1008 between 1801 and 1810, which represents a fifteen fold increase. The scaled numbers, which rose from 108 in the earliest decade to 1440 in the final one, reflect a slightly smaller rise. Either of these sets of figures, however, suggests that the number of tavern keepers receiving licenses to do business for the first time increased significantly.

Precisely why the number of tavern keepers who acquired licenses for the first time rose so dramatically, especially from 1780 onward, remains unknown. Immigration from abroad and in-migration from other parts of Maryland and other colonies probably swelled the number of prospective taverners. Both movements clearly changed the demographics of Baltimore County, which experienced approximately a tenfold rise in population. The energy and growth of Baltimore itself may also have attracted prospective tavern keepers. Little more than a village in 1760, it became the nation's second major entrepôt for goods and people, after New York City, by 1810. Other factors, including the relatively low cost of setting up a tavern, the instability of

Figure 5-1. Number of Baltimore County Tavern Keepers, First Licensed. (Baltimore County Court Minutes, Hall of Records, Annapolis, Md.)

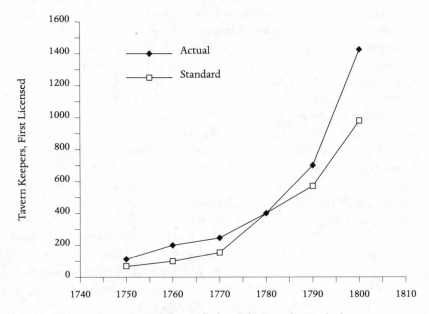

Source: Baltimore County Court Minutes, Hall of Records, Annapolis, Maryland.

the trade, the prime location of Baltimore County on the north-south travel axis, and the relatively stable economy of the region, also probably encouraged the rising tide of tavern keepers.[15]

This pattern of increasing numbers of licensed tavern keepers may have emerged in other colonies and states along the Atlantic seaboard as well. Evidence from a neighboring county, Anne Arundel, suggests precisely that, albeit on a smaller scale.[16] Anecdotal evidence from travelers and diarists also indicates that in other regions licensed taverns proliferated rapidly, as did specialized coffee and boarding houses and unlicensed taverns, between 1750 and 1810.[17]

The Dimensions of Gender

Contemporary accounts suggest that the post–1750 expansion in sporting practice was largely a white male phenomenon. Diaries and newspapers, especially, report that men arranged the matches and constituted a majority of

both participants and spectators. These sources, as well as the numerous letters and public records, also encourage one to conclude that men organized
clubs and formalized rules for sports, controlled the legislatures and courts
that continued to try to regulate sporting behavior, and determined times and
contexts for events. Even the events that engaged both sexes—such as horse
races, card games, balls, and recreational "outings" that involved things like
sleighing and fishing—appear as the products of male initiative.[18]

Is this impression fact or artifact? This question arises for the simple reason
that most of the evidence underlying this inference derives from public and
private literary sources produced by men. Women, and men of lower rank
and of color who lacked writing skills or the means of acquiring such skills,
neither constructed nor appeared in such records in proportion to their numbers. Consequently, these sources probably misrepresent the dimensions of
gender—the sex ratio was nearly equal—in many parts of late-colonial and
early-national America.[19]

Estate inventories and tavern licenses do, however, enable us to explore the
possible gender dimensions of this movement. Though not without a male
bias, both sets of records do include evidence about women. The county
courts, of course, had a vested interest in gathering the information contained
in these records from an many people as possible. Estate inventories were the
basis for inheritance taxes levied by counties, and license applicants always
paid an annual fee that went into the coffers of the county and, in some cases,
the colony or state.[20]

Because they list individuals by name, estate inventories permit us to see
who owned sporting goods. Table 5-3 compares the percentages of selected
goods registered in male and female estate inventories in Baltimore and Suffolk counties.

In both counties men owned all the registered sporting equipment in 1770
and a large majority of it in 1810. Although this pattern of ownership does not
speak to the matter of use, it does indicate access and perhaps control of the
means of participation, for in early America the owners of property held the
rights to use and conveyance.[21] In the case of sporting equipment, those owners and controllers were predominantly men.

Still, the 1790 and 1810 inventories indicate that some women did own
sporting goods. Even though the numbers are small—12 percent of the Suffolk County estates and 4 percent of the Baltimore County estates with goods
belonging to women in 1810—they encourage one to ask how women came
to own this equipment. Did they purchase or receive it as a gift and, hence, exercise control over the equipment? Or did they acquire it through inheritance

Table 5-3. Percentage of Total Selected Sporting Goods in
Baltimore and Suffolk County Inventories, by Gender

Decade	1769/70	1790	1810
% equipment in male estates			
Baltimore	100	89	96
Suffolk	100	94	88
% equipment in female estates			
Baltimore	0	11	4
Suffolk	0	6	12

Sources: Probate Records of Baltimore County, Hall of Records, Annapolis, Maryland; Suffolk County Probate Records, Suffolk County Courthouse, Boston, Massachusetts.

from their husbands?[22] If the latter case were true, the presence of equipment in women's inventories might indicate men's experience rather than their own. Historians have no way of knowing for certain how women gained possession of these goods, but one can suggest whether they acquired them by inheritance or purchase (or gift) by distinguishing the owners who were either married or widowed from those who were unmarried. Table 5-4 presents this comparison for Suffolk County.

In 1790 when women's inventories first registered sporting goods, the women who owned sporting goods were either married or widowed. Not until after the turn of the century did single women's estates in Suffolk County contain recognizable sporting goods. This pattern, coupled with the nature of the actual items, reinforces the prospect that women inherited the sporting goods registered in their estates rather than having purchased them, and that men controlled this aspect of the consumption of sport.

If records of the actual producers of sporting goods existed, we could more adequately determine whether most goods were made for and purchased by men. Unfortunately, few such records have survived the ravages of time; and the ones that have, especially ships' manifests and merchants' accounts, merely confirm what goods were for sale rather than who purchased them. Given the goods on the market, the types and percentages of that equipment in men's estates, and the kinds of events commonly described in literary sources, however, we may conclude that men were the major consumers of particular sports, especially billiards, cards, races, fishing, and hunting.[23]

Table 5-4. Percentage of Married/Unmarried Women's
Estates with Sporting Goods, Suffolk County

Decade	1790	1810
Married/widow	100	80
Single women	0	20

Source: Suffolk County Probate Records, Suffolk County Courthouse,
Boston, Massachusetts.

To understand more fully the gender dimensions of this post–1750 sporting expansion, we need to know something about men's and women's roles
as suppliers in the market. In a society undergoing a transition to capitalism,
such as late-eighteenth- and early-nineteenth-century America was, consumers and suppliers played critical and symbiotic roles in the construction of
new standards of living and new social practices. A portrait of who made
goods and organized and promoted services for whom in this emergent capitalist system, however, is just beginning to emerge. At this point, the picture
highlights men making and promoting goods and services for men, and
women often operating independently of men to provide goods and services
necessary to life but neither effectively capitalized nor efficiently incorporated
within capitalist structures. A similar pattern may have shaped the post–1750
sporting expansion as well. As owners, and presumably purchasers, men
clearly outnumbered women, but whether they dominated the market as producers remains to be seen.[24]

At this point, the only records of a supply-side group that are complete
enough to permit a systematic gender analysis are those of tavern keepers.
Figure 5-2 presents the total number of men and women who received licenses for the first time to operate taverns in Baltimore County, Maryland.

The number of both men and women licensed for the first time as tavern
keepers rose steadily across the period, an increase that reflected the general
population growth of the county. Men and women did not, however, acquire
their first licenses at the same rate. The number of women increased from
eight to ten by the 1770s, to forty-five in the 1790s, and to eighty-two in the
first decade of the nineteenth century. The number of male licensees, on the
other hand, more than tripled by the 1700s (164) and then tripled again by the
1790s (532). Finally, after the turn of the century, Baltimore County had
slightly more than eleven male first-time tavern licensees for each female who
obtained one.

Figure 5-2. Number of First-Time Tavern Licenses in Baltimore County, by Gender. (Baltimore County Court Minutes, Hall of Records, Annapolis, Md.)

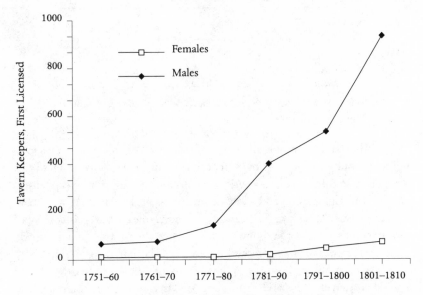

Source: Baltimore County Court Minutes, Hall of Records, Annapolis, Maryland.

This licensing pattern requires careful, even conservative interpretation. On the one hand, of course, the fact that someone obtained a license does not mean that he or she ever operated a tavern. Second, this pattern derives only from the experiences in one county, and the patterns in other places may have varied. Still, one conclusion that the Baltimore County licensing history suggests, that many more men than women were likely to obtain licenses, seems valid. Contemporary literary accounts from the period support it, as does the licensing pattern in neighboring Anne Arundel County. There, males licensed as tavern keepers increased from 67 percent of the total in the 1750s to 81 percent in the 1790s.[25] An analysis of Baltimore County tavern keepers who obtained licenses for two or more years reveals a similar pattern. Men took out 87 percent of the licenses in the 1750s and 95 percent in the first decade of the nineteenth century. Over the sixty-year period, as well, of the 1098 people who obtained licenses for at least two years, 1044 were men.[26]

It seems reasonable to suggest, then, that the tavern trade was increasingly run by men and, as the descriptions of activities in the taverns reveal, probably for men. This probability, coupled with the equipment-ownership patterns in which men also dominated, encourages one to conclude that men, at the very least, had the material base and the public presence that enabled them to define and direct much of the sporting expansion after 1750. One might also be tempted to conclude that women were minority players on this stage, particularly insofar as tavern keeping and ownership of sporting goods are gauges of their roles as suppliers and consumers, and that the post–1750 sporting expansion really was largely a male phenomenon.

Gender Relations

Prior histories of sport in early America—and, in fact, most histories of sport at other times in American life—have encouraged us to make precisely this conclusion: sporting practice has primarily been a male phenomenon. Men have constituted the majority of participants, and they have written most of the rules and created most of the organizations. Sporting practice, in turn, has been incorporated within the rituals of manhood and the institutions of men. Carried to the extreme, this nearly formulaic linking of sport and men has even produced a distinctive social type, or trope, that modernizationists define as "modern sport."[27]

As secure as this conclusion is in the writings of historians, however, it may baldly, and badly, misstate the reality of history. It surely does so in the case of early America, where women were agents in the making of sporting practices in ways and to an extent beyond what either their numbers or historians' prior readings of the literary evidence have suggested. For certain, colonial and early-national women participated in recreational forms, although not always in full view of contemporary chroniclers. But they also played a role in the construction of what have traditionally been described as men's sporting practices, particularly insofar as their labor often underlay men's leisure and insofar as their behaviors and expectations shaped those of men. Moreover, as the eighteenth century lengthened, women assumed an increasingly visible public presence in formalized and often-commercialized recreations for both sexes. Promoters targeted women as prospective participants and consumers, and organizers encouraged women to attend events.

The full extent of women's involvement in the post–1750 sporting expansion may never be known, but it seems clear that, just as did men, women participated in more numerous forms of sport. This was particularly true for middle- and upper-rank women, among whom the changing nature of work, improved modes of travel, and the tightening of kin and neighborhood bonds produced time and opportunity for recreations. Their own diaries and letters reveal that they played cards and gambled, fished, skated, ran footraces, and went sledding. Just prior to the Revolution, when domestic production became all-important, and until mechanization removed it from the domestic scene, women of all ranks transformed the necessary work of spinning into competitive contests. They divided themselves into groups, by either neighborhood or skill, and set out to produce as many skeins of yarn as possible. Invariably, as well, someone would produce a prize for the winning side.[28]

Women's participation is sport extended well beyond the confines of the home and domestic production, particularly to the era's most commonly discussed practices, horseback riding and racing. Wherever horses were common, and whether or not sidesaddles were available, girls and women took to riding as if it were an ordinary expectation. In a place like postwar Charleston, of course, it was, or so it seemed to the Venezuelan-born traveler Francisco de Miranda, who concluded that riding was the women's "favorite diversion."[29] But women did more than ride; they also raced, as German visitor Gottlieb Mittleberger noted in the 1750s, occasionally "with the best male riders for a wager" or among themselves.[30] In 1791, as the Frenchman Ferdinand Bayard observed some women challenge one another to a race near Bath, Virginia, he concluded that all of the contestants were "skillful and fearless riders."[31]

The most telling comment about late-colonial and early-national women equestrians, however, may be one made on the eve of the Revolution. Having observed the members of the Virginia family of Robert Carter, as well as their friends and relatives, for over a year in his role as tutor, Philip Fithian concluded that the females of the family "are passionately fond of Riding."[32] Contemporaries must have recognized a similar emotion and interest among the wives and daughters of other Virginia and Maryland planters and merchants, and they responded accordingly. Between the 1760s and the 1780s—as thoroughbred racing formalized, as race weeks replaced race days, and as the crowds of spectators rose from several hundred to several thousand people—jockey clubs and individual entrepreneurs changed the face of racing in the Chesapeake in substantive ways. They initiated "Ladies purses," or specific events often on the third and final day of racing.[33] They also designated seats for women and improved and expanded facilities at the course for them, even to the point of constructing "a commodious House" where women could escape inclement weather, rest, or find other entertainments.[34]

What all of this suggests, of course, is that horse racing in the Chesapeake, and eventually in other sections of the Mid-Atlantic and the Deep South, was not primarily or even predominantly a male practice. Men were the most visible, public contestants, but they were not the only ones. Nor did they alone construct the racing scene; women were evident along the rail, and women's interests shaped the structure of events. The net effect was a strikingly different sporting practice than was the case in some other places. In New England, for example, where trotting and pacing races were more common than thoroughbred events, there is no evidence that women displayed much interest in the matches, nor is there any evidence that race organizers catered to women. The same is true about the various forms of racing that emerged in the southern Piedmont and in western Pennsylvania and New York. The disinterest of women in racing in these areas, and perhaps even the disinterest in women's interests, may help to explain why horse racing, in any of its other forms, never appeared to be as popular or as important in the cultures and social lives of the people of these areas as did thoroughbred races in the Chesapeake.[35]

Recreational practices in some of these other regions did, however, incorporate women from the 1750s onward. In Salem, Massachusetts, for example, women and men went sailing and then returned to shore for supper and an evening at backgammon or cards. Wintry evenings in the Mid-Atlantic states, as well as in New England, permitted sleigh rides and races, while southerners organized balls and card parties. Rural families throughout the country regularly celebrated the end of a harvest with frolics, which included dancing and games. In northern New Jersey and the Hudson River region of New York, the "pinkster" holiday, a Dutch- and African-influenced time of dancing and drinking, among other things, became an annual event for the young and old of both sexes.[36]

In many of these events and celebrations, women's experiences extended beyond their traditional, or at least pre–1750, roles as provisioners in what were family and neighborhood gatherings. They cast the lines and drew seines, they dealt cards and rode to the hunt, and, of course, they sang and danced. They were, in effect, active participants, and perhaps even partners, in practices that may have proliferated and regularized at least in part because of women's presence in greater numbers and their interests in establishing new gender relations. For certain, the structure of these events suggests that women and men both chose to construct practices that minimized the physical differences between them and maximized shared experiences.

In the process of constructing these shared experiences, late-colonial and early-national Americans also altered the place and significance of recreational practices in general and of sports in particular. Horse races, for example, ceased to be tied to elections and court days and emerged as central rituals in the culture of the Chesapeake. Fishing parties and sleigh rides and races in many regions emerged from the shadows of ordinary food gathering and necessary travel-linked tasks, and became independent and joyful social practices. Balls, also, expanded beyond their earlier settings in official celebrations of royal anniversaries, birthdays, and military and political victories. In fact, for middle- and upper-rank early Americans after 1750, particularly those who either lived or visited for lengthy periods in urban areas, balls organized in the context of subscription assemblies became the central social events, even the hallmark, of emergent bourgeois society.[37]

This last point requires some expansion. Not all women exerted the same degree of influence in the early American sporting culture, nor did all women experience similar changes in their relationships with men. Slave women, for certain, clearly remained subject to the whims and whips of their masters, both black and white; and, except for holiday celebrations and weekend or evening breaks, they rarely had the opportunity to construct their own recreational forms. White servants, also, had little effect on the expanding sporting culture, except insofar as they, like slave women, provided the work that underlay the leisure of their mistresses and masters and insofar as they took advantage of, and were taken advantage of in, the expanding sphere of bawdy houses and laborers' commercial entertainments. Finally, women who lived on the fringes of late-colonial and early-national society, in the most recently settled frontier regions, did not find their experiences substantially different from those of their ancestors a century or more earlier. Often isolated on farmsteads and with children and farms to tend, they knew little of the outside world or its recreations. Weddings and Christmas aside, theirs was a world dominated by men and expressed in gouging and drinking and shooting.[38]

Farm women in the longer-settled and more heavily populated regions of early America, as well as the wives and daughters of village artisans and seafarers, played a more visible role in the construction of late-eighteenth- and early-nineteenth-century recreations than did any of these women who were on the margins of society. Their work, which was often independent of men's but interdependent with the family and village economy and society, frequently left them with the means and the opportunity to participate in and even to arrange frolics and quiltings and picnics and barbecues. Young women, especially, sought out or joined neighboring youths of both sexes in various recreations. Their mothers, in turn, became the managers and moral monitors of their pleasure-seeking offspring. They knew what historians of the family and women's experience have only recently begun to recognize: that recreation occasionally resulted in procreation.[39]

Neither their recreations nor their roles in shaping recreations altered as rapidly or as substantively for farm and village women, however, as both did for urban women, especially those in the middle and upper ranks. These women, of course, were the co-creators of balls and assemblies, and they had access to the card and billiard tables and the fowling pieces and sleighs that merchants sold and their husbands acquired. They also possessed the resources and the time to enjoy the increasing variety of commercial entertainments, from tumbling and equestrian exhibitions to pleasure gardens that urban entrepreneurs devised.[40]

Particularly after the Revolution, as capitalist enterprise permeated many parts of urban life, the wives and daughters of the new nation's shopkeepers, bankers, civil servants, merchants, and factory owners found themselves in a new situation. In New York, Philadelphia, Baltimore, and Charleston, the organizers of commercial recreational facilities actively pursued the participation of both women and men. The owners of buildings with rooms large enough for assemblies advertised in the papers and stressed the decorous behavior and good food that awaited dancers.[41] Charles Quinan, who operated Queen Ann's in Philadelphia, installed "flying coaches" for women and, for their escorts, "horse[s]" that whirled about—all apparently in an effort to draw customers.[42] Not surprisingly, in New York City where the competition for bourgeois customers was great, one operator of a pleasure garden went a step beyond his competitors. Having just completed a "grand Amphitheatre" for the July 4th celebration at his Vauxhall Garden, Joseph Delacroix ended his description of the proposed entertainments with this warning: "No gentleman will be admitted without [being] accompanied by a lady."[43]

Delacroix's statement suggests two expectations that men in his profession held about consumers of commercial recreations at the turn of the century. First, male patrons were not entirely trustworthy; their moral judgments were suspect, and they could be rowdy. Second, only women could effectively curb the passions of the men and prevent them from overdrinking, bothering other customers, or getting into arguments or fights. Put another way, Delacroix expected his urban female customers to assume precisely the kind of role that farm and village women had assumed: the role of moral arbiter, of social manager. He was not alone. Other men, including the members of jockey clubs, organizers of assemblies, theater managers, and exhibition and museum promoters, actively appealed to prospective female consumers, especially in the decades immediately after the Revolution.[44] They did so in part, of course, because they accepted the role for women that republican ideology expressed, the role as republican mothers, as caretakers of the new nation's virtue.[45]

———

Republicanism and capitalism thus heightened, rather than diminished, the significance and directions of male-female negotiations in the construction of post-Revolution recreations. Men owned the vast majority of sporting goods and dominated as tavern keepers, merchants, and leisure organizers, but women were clearly essential to the use of those goods and the consumption of recreations. For certain, women provided much of the labor that freed men for leisure, and they existed as a substantive body of clients to whom commercial promoters appealed. Moreover, with women responsible for the nation's virtue, they ultimately affected the definition of two different but interrelated codes of behavior evident in early-national sporting life.

The first of these codes was that of the "sportsman." In contemporary terms, a sportsman engaged only in particular sports, especially the outdoor events of hunting, fishing, quoits, and horse racing and a few indoor games like billiards and whist. He was also one who set limits on the kill—as "one brace of woodcocks and two of partridges"—kept the inevitable wager small, and displayed generosity, courtesy, and bravery.[46] The sportsman, in short, was a masculine type imbued with masculine values, and he appealed to those leading men, like John Stuart Skinner and John Randolph, who had both a political and an economic stake in distinguishing themselves from propertyless wage-laborers and servants in the young nation.[47]

Men like Skinner and Randolph also had a stake in distinguishing themselves—and their sports—from women. Rank differences with all their implications for economic and political order and power, rather than gender differences, provided the rationale; but gender provided the means, via the second code constructed by early-national middle- and upper-rank Americans: the cult of domesticity. Rooted in the image of the republican mother, which expressed virtue as a feminine characteristic and delineated what the important female virtues were, the cult of domesticity prescribed female dependency highlighted by domestic exercises and very few active, outdoor recreations. As championed by Skinner's contemporary, Catharine Beecher, the cult of domesticity envisioned forms and forums for recreations among women that were antithetical to Skinner's own tabulation of the rural ones embraced by a sportsman.[48]

This story thus ends with an ironic twist to what was a lengthy and complex series of negotiations between men and women about the content of early-national recreations and their respective roles in them. The code of the sportsman and the cult of domesticity emerged as opposing categories of experiences in a world of "separate spheres" among upper- and middle-class Anglo-Americans. Historically, however, they are not separable, for men and women like Skinner and Beecher negotiated the experiences collapsed in these social types. They did so, of course, in a social, economic, and political context that was far different from the one Mittleberger had encountered in the 1750s or even Bayard knew in the 1790s. Capitalism had penetrated more deeply into American life, and the sexual division of labor and leisure had broadened.[49] In such an era, the participant in active rural sports, the sportsman, whom Skinner championed and the domestically inclined and morally upright woman whom Beecher upheld declared the all-important differences between men and women. Each also made a statement about gender relations.

Notes

The Graduate School Research Board at the University of Maryland provided partial funding for the estate inventory and tavern keeper license research presented in this essay.

1. Nancy L. Struna, "Sport and the Awareness of Leisure," in Ronald Hoffman, Peter J. Albert, and Cary Carson, eds., *Of Consuming Interests: The Style of Life in the Eighteenth Century* (Charlottesville, Va., forthcoming); idem, "Sport and Society in Early America," *International Journal of the History of Sport* 5 (December 1988): 292–311; Elliott J. Gorn, " 'Gouge and Bite, Pull Hair and Scratch': The Social Significance of Fighting in the Southern Backcountry," *American Historical Review* 90 (February 1985): 18–43. See also note 18 below.

2. The population of Baltimore was approximately 46,600 in 1810, which is the figure used in estimating the ratio. The ratio would be lower, perhaps by two-thirds, if only males, who constituted the primary patrons of taverns, were considered; the ratio may also be reduced once the locations (either county or city) of some as-yet-untraced tavern keepers are identified. Tavern-keeper licenses appear in Baltimore County Court Minutes, 1810, Maryland Hall of Records, Annapolis.

3. See especially Ronald Hoffman and Peter J. Albert, eds., *Women in the Age of the American Revolution* (Charlottesville, Va., 1989); Linda K. Kerber, Nancy F. Cott, Robert Gross, Lynn Hunt, Carroll Smith-Rosenberg, and Christine M. Stansell, "Beyond Roles, Beyond Spheres: Thinking about Gender in the Early Republic," *William and Mary Quarterly* 46 (July 1989): 565–85; Christine Stansell, *City of Women: Sex and Class in New York, 1789–1860* (Urbana, Ill., 1987); Laurel T. Ulrich, *A Midwife's Tale: The Life of Martha Ballard, Based on Her Diary, 1785–1812* (New York, 1990); Carol Groneman and Mary Beth Norton, eds., *"To Toil the Livelong Day": America's Women at Work, 1780–1980* (Ithaca, N.Y., 1987); Jeanne Boydston, *Home and Work: Housework, Wages and the Ideology of Labor in the Early Republic* (New York, 1990).

4. Lorna Weatherill, *Consumer Behaviour & Material Culture in Britain, 1660–1760* (London, 1988); Neil McKendrick, John Brewer, and J. H. Plumb, *The Birth of a Consumer Society: The Commercialization of Eighteenth-Century England* (Bloomington, Ind., 1982); Joan Thirsk, *Economic Policies and Projects: The Development of a Consumer Society in Early Modern England* (Oxford, 1978).

5. Lois Green Carr and Lorena S. Walsh, "Changing Lifestyles and Consumer Behavior in the Colonial Chesapeake," in Hoffman, et al., eds., *Of Consuming Interests*, 59–166; Lorena S. Walsh, Gloria L. Main, and Lois Green Carr, "Toward a History of the Standard of Living in British North America," *William and Mary Quarterly* 45 (January 1988): 116–69; Lois Green Carr and Lorena S. Walsh, "Economic Diversification and Labor Organization in the Chesapeake, 1650–1820," in Stephen Innes, ed., *Work and Labor in Early America* (Chapel Hill, N.C., 1988), 144–88; Gloria L. Main and Jackson Turner Main, "Standards and Styles of Living in Southern New England, 1640–1774," *Journal of Economic History* 48 (1988): 27–46. See also Carole Shammas, "Explaining Past Changes in Consumption and Consumer Behavior," *Historical Methods* 22 (September 1989): 61–67.

6. T. H. Breen, " 'Baubles of Britain': The American and Consumer Revolutions of the Eighteenth Century," *Past and Present* 119 (May 1988): 73–104; idem, "An Empire of Goods: The Anglicization of Colonial America, 1690–1776," *Journal of British Studies* 25 (1986): 467–99; Robert Blair St. George, ed., *Material Life in America, 1600–1860* (Boston, 1988); Hoffman et al., eds., *Of Consuming Interests*.

7. J. H. Plumb, "The Commercialization of Leisure," in McKendrick et al., *The Birth of a Consumer Society*, 265–85. Support for this theme is implicit in Richard Holt, *Sport and the British: A Modern History* (Oxford, 1989), 12–73; Dennis Brailsford, "Morals and Maulers: The Ethics of Early Pugilism," *Journal of Sport History* 12 (summer 1985): 126–42; idem, "1787: An Eighteenth-Century Sporting Year," *Research Quarterly* 55 (September 1983): 217–30; Hugh Cunningham, *Leisure in the Industrial Revolution* (New York, 1980), 15–56; Robert W. Malcolmson, *Popular Recreations in English Society, 1700–1850* (Cambridge, 1973); J. M. Goldby and A. W. Purdie, *The Civilisation of the Crowd: Popular Culture in England, 1750–1900* (London, 1984), 41–87.

8. Lois Green Carr and Lorena S. Walsh, "Inventories and the Analysis of Wealth and Consumption Patterns in St. Mary's County, Maryland, 1658–1777," *Historical Methods* 8 (1980): 81–104; Gloria L. Main, "The Correction of Biases in Colonial American Probate Records," *Historical Methods Newsletter* 8 (1974): 10–28; Alice Hanson Jones, *American Colonial Wealth*, 3 vols. (New York, 1977). Most histories that rely on inventories discuss their limits as historical sources.

9. Struna, "Sport and the Awareness of Leisure." See also Stephen Hardy, " 'Adopted by All the Leading Clubs': Sporting Goods and the Shaping of Leisure, 1800–1900," in Richard Butsch, ed., *For Fun and Profit: The Transformation of Leisure into Consumption* (Philadelphia, 1990): 71–101.

10. This figure results from an analysis of estate-value totals and owners' occupations; Nancy L. Struna, "Sporting Styles and Consumer Behavior in Early

America, 1770–1810" (paper presented at the North American Society for Sport History annual conference, Tempe, Ariz., 1988).

11. In Baltimore County, middling-rank estates held 46 percent of the goods in 1790 and 66 percent in 1810; in Suffolk County, those estates held 30 percent of the goods in 1790 and 60 percent in 1810.

Newspapers, diaries, and travel accounts consistently locate most sporting events (except some practices of the gentry) at racetracks in and near towns, in fields, on roads, on village greens, and at taverns, all away from individual homes.

12. Kym S. Rice, *Early American Taverns: For the Entertainment of Friends and Strangers* (Chicago, 1983); Paton Yoder, "Melting Pot or Stewing Kettle?," *Indiana Magazine of History* 59 (June 1963): 135–51; Mark E. Lender and James Kirby Martin, eds., *Drinking in America* (New York, 1982); Patricia A. Gibbs, "Taverns in Tidewater, Virginia, 1700–1774" (M.A. thesis, William and Mary Collage, 1968); Francis M. Manges, "Women Shopkeepers, Tavernkeepers, and Artisans in Colonial Philadelphia" (Ph.D. dissertation, University of Pennsylvania, 1958); Struna, "Sport and the Awareness of Leisure." The linkage of recreation and refreshment in the taverns was not unique to eighteenth-century North America. See also Peter Clark, *The English Alehouse: A Social History, 1200–1830* (London, 1983); Thomas Brennan, *Public Drinking and Popular Culture in Eighteenth-Century Paris* (Princeton, 1988).

13. Diaries, travel accounts, and court records frequently describe and usually either praise or condemn the social life and accommodations of late-eighteenth-century taverns; see, for example, Robert Hunter, *Quebec to Carolina in 1785–1786: Being the Travel Diary and Observations of Robert Hunter, Jr., a Young Merchant of London*, ed. Louis B. Wright and Marion Tinling (San Marino, Calif., 1943), 183; Richard J. Hooker, ed., *The Carolina Backcountry on the Eve of the Revolution: The Journal and Other Writings of Charles Woodmason, Anglican Itinerant* (Chapel Hill, N.C., 1953), 129; York County, Virginia, Wills and Inventories, 20: 46–49, 22: 19–24, microfilm, Colonial Williamsburg Foundation, Williamsburg. See also Struna, "Sport and the Awareness of Leisure"; Charles G. Steffen, *The Mechanics of Baltimore: Workers and Politics in the Age of the Revolution, 1763–1812* (Urbana, Ill., 1984); Sean Wilentz, *New York City & the Rise of the American Working Class, 1788–1850* (New York, 1984); Billy G. Smith, *The "Lower Sort": Philadelphia's Laboring People, 1750–1800* (Ithaca, N.Y., 1990); Graham Russell Hodges, *New York City Cartmen, 1667–1850* (New York, 1986).

14. Numerous years of the court minutes no longer exist (1750–54, 1765–67, 1769–71, 1773–74, 1776, 1798–99, 1805–7); consequently, the scaled data are estimates (proportional within decades), helpful only in suggesting the probable number of all people who received licenses.

15. The dynamic, possibly even unstable, nature of the trade is also suggested by a comparison of the numbers of one-time tavern-keeper licenses (2,342) with the number of people who got licenses for more years: 1,098 people obtained licenses for two or more years, and 231 had licenses for six or more years. Also, tavern keepers obtained licenses for only two years on average.

On the history of Baltimore, see Steffen, *Mechanics of Baltimore*, esp. ch. 1; J. Thomas Scharf, *The Chronicles of Baltimore* (Baltimore, 1874); Sherry Olson, *Baltimore: The Building of an American City* (Baltimore, 1980).

16. Anne Arundel County licensed 162 people as tavern keepers between 1750 and 1800; Anne Arundel County Court Minutes, 1750–1800, Hall of Records, Annapolis.

17. See, for example, Henry Wansey, *Henry Wansey and His American Journal, 1794*, ed. David John Jeremy (Philadelphia, 1970), 73, 96; Johann David Schoepf, *Travels in the Confederation [1783–1784]*, trans. and ed. Alfred J. Morrison, 2 vols. (New York, 1968), 1: 46–7; Francis Baily, *Journal of a Tour in Unsettled Parts of North America in 1796 and 1797* (London, 1856), 101; Reuben G. Thwaites, ed., *Early Western Travels, 1748–1846*, 19 vols. (Cleveland, 1904), 4: 33; Mays Dramatic History of Baltimore, ms. 995, Part 6 (1747–1819), 28 February 1791, Maryland Historical Society, Baltimore; Robert Mitchell, *Commercialism and Frontier: Perspectives on the Early Shenandoah Valley* (Charlottesville, Va., 1977), 208.

18. *Maryland Gazette*, 5 February 1765, 26 September 1782, 30 October 1782; *Virginia Gazette*, 22 February 1770, 19 April 1770, 15 August 1771, 27 May 1773; Francisco de Miranda, *The New Democracy in America: Travels of Francisco de Miranda in the United States, 1783–84*, trans. Judson P. Wood, ed. John S. Ezell (Norman, Okla., 1963), 15; Hunter, *Quebec to Carolina*, 204, 210; Schoepf, *Travels in the Confederation*, 1: 361; Charles W. Janson, *The Stranger in America, 1793–1806* (New York, 1935), 309–10; John Davis, *Travels of Four Years and a Half in the United States of America During 1798, 1799, 1800, 1801, and 1802*, ed. A. J. Morrison (New York, 1909), 88–90; Thomas P. Cope, *Philadelphia Merchant: The diary of Thomas P. Cope, 1800–1851* (South Bend, Ind., 1978), 85, 253; John F. D. Smyth, *A Tour in the United States of America (1784)*, 2 vols. (New York, 1968), 1: 66–67; Isaac N. P. Stokes, *The Iconography of Manhattan Island, 1498–1909*, 6 vols, (New York, 1967), 1: 379–80; Philip V. Fithian, *Journal and Letters of Philip Vickers Fithian, 1773–1774: A Plantation Tutor of the Old Dominion*, ed. H. D. Farish (Williamsburg, Va., 1943), 198, 201–203, 212; William Dunlap, *William Dunlap (1766–1839): The Memoirs of a Dramatist, Theatrical Manager, Painter, Critic, Novelist, and Historian* (New York, 1969), 309, 321, 324, 329–39, 342–48.

19. Daniel Blake Smith, *Inside the Great House: Planter Life in the Eighteenth-Century Chesapeake Society* (Ithaca, N.Y., 1980), 80–124; Jim Potter, "Demographic Development and Family Structure," in Jack P. Greene and J. R. Pole, eds., *Colonial British America: Essays in the New History of the Early Modern Era* (Baltimore, 1984), 123–57.

20. See note 8 above. Kilty, *Laws of Maryland*, 1: March 1780, ch. xxiv provides a description of the requirements for obtaining a license.

21. Marylynn Salmon, *Women and the Law of Property in Early America* (Chapel Hill, N.C., 1986).

22. Wills are the best source of information on bequests and inheritance, but will rarely specify sporting goods. See Toby L. Ditz, "Ownership and Obligation: Inheritance and Patriarchal Households in Connecticut, 1750–1821," *William and*

Mary Quarterly 47 (April 1990): 235–65; idem, *Property and Kinship: Inheritance in Early Connecticut, 1750–1820* (Princeton, N.J., 1986); Carole Shammas, Marylynn Salmon, and Michel Dahlin, *Inheritance in America: Colonial Times to the Present* (New Brunswick, N.J., 1987); Daniel Scott Smith, "Inheritance and the Social History of Early American Women," in Hoffman and Albert, eds., *Women in the Age of the American Revolution*, 45–66.

23. Stokes, *Iconography of New York*, 5: 1182; Maryland Gazette, 20 October 1763; *Virginia Gazette*, 25 July 1766, 26 October 1769, 2 November 1769, 8 November 1770; Boston Weekly News-Letter, 17 May 1750, 27 December 1753.

24. Elizabeth Evans, *Weathering the Storm: Women of the American Revolution* (New York, 1989), 2; Laurel T. Ulrich, "Housewife and Gadder: Themes of Self-Sufficiency and Community in Eighteenth-Century New England," in Groneman and Norton, eds., "To Toil the Livelong Day," 21–34; idem, "Martha Ballard and Her Girls: Women's Work in Eighteenth-Century Maine," in Innes, ed., *Work and Labor*, 70–105; Carr and Walsh, "Economic Diversification and Labor Organization," 175–76; Harold E. Davis, *The Fledgling Province: Social and Cultural Life in Colonial Georgia, 1733–1776* (Chapel Hill, N.C., 1976); Thomas M. Doerflinger, *A Vigorous Spirit of Enterprise: Merchants and Economic Development in Revolutionary Philadelphia* (Chapel Hill, N.C., 1986).

Fragmentary evidence in newspapers and court records occasionally locates women retailers of sporting goods or animals (e.g., *New York Journal*, 29 April 1773: *New York Daily Advertiser*, 22 June 1793), but men are more commonly portrayed as salespeople, customers, and keepers (e.g., *Maryland Journal and Baltimore Advertiser*, 9 March 1790, 3; Baltimore City Court of Oyer and Terminer, Docket and Minutes, 1808/09, Series BC 0183, Maryland Hall of Records, Annapolis).

25. Anne Arundel County Court Minutes, 1750–1800, Maryland Hall of Records, Annapolis.

26. Baltimore County Court Minutes, 1755–1810, Maryland Hall of Records, Annapolis.

27. See, for example, my own "The Formalizing of Sport and the Formation of an Elite: The Chesapeake Gentry, 1650–1720s," *Journal of Sport History* 12 (winter 1986): 212–34. A later piece on women largely places women off to the side or in a separate sphere and does nothing to resolve the dilemma of gender; see, " 'Good Wives' and 'Gardeners,' Spinners and 'Fearless Riders': Middle- and Upper-Rank Women in the Early American Sporting Culture," in J. A. Mangan and Roberta J. Park, eds., *From "Fair Sex" to Feminism: Sport and the Socialization of Women in the Industrial and Post-Industrial Eras* (London, 1987); 235–55. On modernization, see Allen Guttmann, *From Ritual to Record: The Nature of Modern Sport* (New York, 1978); Melvin L. Adelman, *A Sporting Time: New York City and the Rise of Modern Athletics, 1820–70* (Urbana, Ill., 1986).

28. Anne Grant, *Memoirs of an American Lady: With Sketches of Manners and Scenery in America, as They Existed Previous to the Revolution* (New York, 1809), 54;

Anna Green Winslow, *Diary of Anna Green Winslow,* ed. Alice M. Earle (Boston, 1894), 28; "The Diary of Mrs. Mary Vial Holyoke, 1760–1800," in George Dow, ed., *The Holyoke Diaries* (Salem, Mass., 1911), 47–49, 63, 74; Ellen Spofford, "Personal Sketches of Early Inhabitants of Georgetown, Massachusetts," *Essex Institute Historical Collections* 41 (April 1905): 169–70; James Parker, "Diary," *New England Historical and Genealogical Register* 69 (January 1915): 14, 121; *Maryland Gazette,* 14 June 1753; *Essex Gazette,* 2 August 1768; *Boston Gazette and County Journal,* 16 October 1769. See also note 36 below.

29. Miranda, *The New Democracy,* 29. On a woman renowned for her riding, see Herman Mann, *The Female Review: Life of Deborah Sampson* (New York, 1972), 167. The accounts of Chief Justice John Marshall also reveal purchases of two saddles and a bridle for his wife, Polly; Herbert A. Johnson, *The Papers of John Marshall,* 3 vols. (Chapel Hill, N.C., 1974), 1:383, 485. Inventories also establish the existence of distinct "women's" saddles.

30. Gottlieb Mittleberger, *Journey to Pennsylvania,* eds. and trans. Oscar Handlin and John Clive (Cambridge, 1909), 89.

31. Ferdinand Bayard, *Travels of a Frenchman in Maryland and Virginia with a Description of Philadelphia and Baltimore in 1791,* ed. Ben C. McCary (Williamsburg, Va., 1950), 40.

32. Fithian, *Journal and Letters,* 266.

33. See for example, *Maryland Journal and Baltimore Advertiser,* 30 April 1782.

34. *Virginia Gazette and Alexandria Advertiser,* 7 October 1790.

35. Thomas Anburey, *Travels through the Interior Parts of America,* 2 vols. (Boston, 1923), 2: 227–28; John F. Watson, *Annals of Philadelphia* (Philadelphia, 1830), 238–39; *Boston Gazette,* 20 October 1760.

36. See, for example, Grant, *Memoirs,* 191; Eliza Pinckney, *The Letterbook of Eliza Lucas Pinckney, 1739–1762,* ed. Elise Pinckney (Chapel Hill, N.C., 1972), 48–49, 57; Stokes, *Inconography,* 4: 722; Fithian, *Journal and Letters,* 44–45, 140; Mittleberger, *Journey to Pennsylvania,* 85; Hunter, *Quebec to Carolina,* 245; Miranda, *The New Democracy,* 245; Dunlap, *Diary,* 64; Cope, *Diary,* 228; Anburey, *Travels,* 2: 57; John Boyle, "Boyle's Journal of Occurrences in Boston, 1759–1778," *New England Historical and Genealogical Register* 84 (October 1930): 364; James Gordon, "Diary of Colonel James Gordon of Lancaster County, Virginia," *William and Mary Quarterly,* 1st series, 11 (January 1903): 196; William Eddis, *Letter from America,* ed. Aubrey Land (Cambridge, 1969), 20–21; Julia Spruill, *Women's Life and Work in the Southern Colonies* (Chapel Hill, N.C., 1938), 85–87; Struna, "Sport and the Awareness of Leisure."

37. Robert S. Rantoul, "Historic Ball Room," *Essex Institute Historical Collections* 31 (August–December 1894): 81; Janet Schaw, *Journal of a Lady of Quality: Being the Narrative of a Journey from Scotland to the West Indies, North Carolina, and Portugal, in the Years 1774 to 1776,* eds. Evangeline W. and Charles M. Andrews (New Haven, Conn., 1931), 149, 153–54; Wilslow, *Diary,* 16–17; Thomas W. Grif-

6

Sport and the Redefinition of Middle-Class Masculinity in Victorian America

STEVEN A. RIESS

At the onset of the Victorian Era, middle-class American men had little interest in sport or physical culture. They were shopkeepers, professionals, agents, clerks, and farmers—hard-working, devout, future-oriented individuals who had little precious free time to take away from the serious business of earning a living. With the exception of clerks, generally young men were learning the business with the expectation of a future partnership or an entrepreneurial career, middle-class men were competitive workers who were their own bosses. They frowned upon the popular mass sports of the day as a waste of time, immoral, illegal, and debilitating, which should be avoided at all costs. Yet by midcentury a respectable middle-class sporting culture was beginning to evolve, and after the 1870s, it boomed. The purpose of this essay is to explain how middle-class men's concerns with their masculinity helped make sport an integral part of their lives. Sport redefined for them their sense of manliness and provided mechanisms to achieve it.

The Rise of a Respectable Middle-Class Sporting Culture, 1840–70[1]

The lives of men and women in the Victorian Era were sharply divided by gender into separate spheres in family relations, work, and leisure. Men were the breadwinners, women took care of the family, and each enjoyed their discretionary time (outside of sex) with peers of the same gender. Athletics and physical culture had historically been an almost exclusively male activity, and prowess in sporting competitions had always been regarded as a mark of manliness that meant the possession of such characteristics as courage, determination, strength, and vigor. At the start of the Victorian Era, when the United States was overwhelmingly an agrarian society, the leading sportsmen were members of a traditionally oriented male bachelor subculture who lived on the frontier, in the South, or in a few crowded urban centers. The sporting fraternity was composed of urban machine politicians, artisans, seasonal workers, Irish immigrants, and men from the dregs of society, along with young rakes from the social elite. They participated in sports for fun, to develop camaraderie, and to display their honor and manliness. Their favorite contests were blood and gambling sports that were usually illegal and reprehensible. The social ethic expressed by the premodern lifestyle and values of the male bachelor subculture was totally antithetical to the bourgeois ethos of early Victorians. A manly middle-class individual in the antebellum era gained his identity through work, not leisure, earned his money through hard work, not gambling, and was a good and steady provider for his family. He was reliable, independent, and resisted temptation. The manly middle-class American did not shun domesticity for the saloon or poolroom, but rather made family and home the centerpiece of his life.[2]

Middle-class opposition to sport and physical culture began to wane in the 1840s and 1850s at a period when the country was starting to become modernized. As the United States began to undergo the processes of urbanization, industrialization, immigration, and "civilization," the nature of sport underwent substantial changes and began to appeal to urban middle-class needs and sensibilities. This development was the product of the role-models of immigrant and upper-class sportsmen, the evolution of new sports that were congruent with the values and behavior of the middle class, and, most of all, the influence of a new positive sports creed. This ideology was popularized by Jacksonian reformers who believed that nonviolent, clean, gambling-free, outdoor physical exercise and sport would be socially functional activities that could counter the growing urban pathology and social anomie. Such sport and exercise would promote good health, sound morals, and a decent character.[3]

The concept that sports could be moral and uplifting was not novel. Back in the seventeenth century the Puritans had supported moral sports that were indulged in, in moderation, on days other than the Sabbath, and were recreational: in other words, that refreshed the body and the mind to do God's work. In the following century, Enlightenment thought that glorified Greek civilization also encouraged a positive attitude towards sport. American intellectuals like Thomas Jefferson and Dr. Benjamin Rush advocated a regular regimen of exercise in emulation of the Ancient Greeks, who believed in the unity of mind and body and consequently trained both the mental and the physical sides of man. Advanced European educational theorists of the Enlightenment such as Rousseau, and their successors in the early nineteenth century, stressed the value of physical and health education. In 1804 the great Swiss pedagogue Pestalozzi established a gymnasium in his school, while in

Sweden Ling introduced a system of free physical movements akin to calisthenics. In the 1810s *Turnplatz* schools were established in the German states by Friedrich Jahn, father of the *Turner* movement, who advocated the use of apparatus in physical training. His goals were to promote a romantic nationalistic spirit among the German peoples and build up their fitness for future conflicts with France. The work of all of these educators was publicized in the United States by the press, medical journals, and professional periodicals such as the *American Journal of Education*. Founded in 1826, the *AJE* recommended the construction of urban playgrounds and gymnasiums as well as the adoption of uplifting English sports like cricket. Gymnastics was introduced in the mid-1820s at a variety of educational settings, including Boston's progressive Round Hill School, the utopian community of New Harmony, Ind., and at Harvard and the University of Virginia, often under the auspices of German disciples of Jahn.[4]

While American sportsmen and sporting reformers were interested in classical civilization and continental reforms in physical education, they still focused their attention on England, the preeminent sporting land of the day. England had been the role-model for athletically inclined Americans since the colonial era; they copied English sporting practices, purchased their athletic equipment, and read their books, periodicals, and guides. The presence of English pedestrians and cricketers, Scottish Caledonians, and Irish pugilists in America encouraged local interest in a lively transatlantic sporting culture.[5]

American attitudes to sport were also influenced by the impact of industrialization and urbanization upon traditional English recreational patterns. Industrialization drastically altered leisure time and the pace of work, which had been formerly tied to the agricultural cycle, traditional holidays, and the farmer's self-motivation. However, the coming of the industrial revolution brought time-work discipline; the pace of work was established by the machine and the work schedule controlled by the boss. Capitalists found allies in their fight against traditional behavior and for modern work discipline in evangelicals, temperance advocates, and other social reformers who sought to promote morality and order in pathological industrial cities like Manchester by imposing social control over the urban masses. Many reformers believed that the best way to wipe out sinful amusements was by substituting useful, uplifting recreations and by shortening working weeks to enable factory operatives to revive themselves through clean, health-promoting athletics or other moral pleasures.[6]

These ideas and experiences were brought together in the United States in the 1840s and 1850s by urban reformers in a positive new sports creed. They were part of a broad-based social movement that sought to ameliorate the conditions of the common man by working for such goals as temperance, compulsory education, political democracy, economic opportunity, abolitionism, and public health. The ideology posited that participation in clean sport would improve public health, raise moral standards, and build character; that clean sport would provide a substitute for the vile practices of the sporting fraternity; and that such rational recreations would encourage the development of sport among the sedentary middle class. Supporters of this physical-fitness movement came from a wide variety of interests, and included religious leaders like the Unitarian Rev. William Ellery Channing, utopians like Robert Dale Owen, educators like Horace Mann, transcendentalists like Ralph Waldo Emerson, scientists like Dr. Lemuel Shattuck, physicians like Dr. Oliver Wendell Holmes, Sr., and health faddists like Sylvester Graham.[7]

Advocates of physical fitness sought to improve the quality of health for all urban Americans at a time when cities were undergoing their greatest rate of growth in American history. They were concerned about epidemics, the conditioning of the working class, the well-being of future mothers, and the sedentary lifestyle of the middle classes who did not engage in any physical labor, but sat at their desks all day long. Reformers pointedly chastised students and office workers for their lack of fitness. Students kept their faces buried in textbooks at the expense of their bodies, while nonmanual workers were decried for being too busy pursuing money to take care of their health. A break in these debilitating routines was encouraged to refresh the mind and body and increase productivity. As Dr. Shattuck pointed out, "intellectual culture has received too much and physical training too little attention."[8]

In 1855 the Unitarian Rev. A. A. Livermore strongly denounced the prevailing middle-class attitudes towards health, exercise, and vigorous manly activities: "O for a touch of the Olympic games rather than this pallid effeminancy! O for a return to the simple Persian elements of telling the truth, and hurling the javelin, instead of the bloodless cheeks and lifeless limbs, and throbbing brains of our first scholars in Harvard, Yale or Princeton!" The severest critic of middle-class lassitude was Dr. Holmes, a noted oarsman in his own right, who three years later in an article entitled "The Autocrat of the Breakfast Table" denounced "the vegetative life of the American," whom he compared unfavorably with the English gentry who had been a popular role-model for the American elite since the colonial era. Holmes rated American college students poorly in comparison with the vigorous Oxbridge athletes, and recommended they learn from their English brothers who rowed and engaged in other sports. The first Oxford–Cambridge boat race took place in 1829, 23 years before the first intercollegiate sports contest in America, a rowing match between Harvard and Yale. Furthermore, the British emphasis on sport extended into the public schools, where the aim was to train manly Christian gentlemen through such means as the fagging system (in which younger boys performed menial tasks for older boys) and competitive soccer and rugby. Nothing comparable existed at American schools, not even the Round Hill School, which had closed in 1834. Holmes foresaw a rapid decline of the race, certain that "such a set of black-coated, stiff-jointed, soft-muscled, paste-complexioned youth as we can boast in our American cities never before sprang from loins of Anglo-Saxon lineage." Americans had to change their ways and learn from their British cousins.[9]

Another leading proponent of middle-class physical fitness was Boston Brahmin the Rev. Thomas Wentworth Higginson, one of the most eminent antebellum social reformers. The Unitarian minister wrote a series of articles in the new *Atlantic Monthly* in 1858, outlining his philosophy that denied that "physical vigor and spiritual sanctity are incompatible." Higginson argued that the high rate of illness among nonmanual workers indicated their need to participate in either outdoor exercise or sport. He encouraged businessmen to worry less about making money and more about physical and mental well-being. Higginson recommended that they leave behind the cares of the office and join him at the gymnasium for enjoyable, healthful recreation.[10]

The advocacy of improved public health and the city's need for fresh air and space to play out-of-doors led to the development of a municipal-park movement, based largely on British antecedents. The public-health movement had begun in England in the 1830s in response to the problems created by urbanization and industrialization. In 1833 a parliamentary commission recommended the development of open spaces near large towns to improve the health and comfort of laborers, and also encouraged owners of private gardens and hunting preserves to turn over their land to local municipalities. In 1845 a park was opened in Manchester equipped with sports facilities, and two years later a suburban park was established outside Liverpool devoted to rural sports. In 1851 cricket grounds were laid out in London's Hyde Park.[11]

The American park movement, modeled after the British example, was led by journalists William Cullen Bryant and Walt Whitman, landscape architect Andrew Jackson Downing, physicians, and scientists like Dr. Shattuck, founder of the American Statistical Association (1839) and chief of the Massachusetts Board of Vital Statistics. Their primary purpose was to improve the urban public's physical and mental health by providing access to fresh air, beautiful vistas, and playing space.[12] The municipal-park movement's first major achievement was New York's Central Park, which opened in 1858. The original design by Frederick Law Olmsted and Calvert Vaux set aside space for formal gardens and wooded areas for receptive recreation, and areas for playgrounds and cricket fields for more active sports. Central Park was a huge success, and became a model for suburban parks across the country after the Civil War. However, while these were promoted primarily on behalf of the working classes living in crowded, disease-infected neighborhoods, they were all situated far from the centers of population, expensive to get to by public transport, and, at first, stressed receptive over active recreation. Consequently the new parks were for their first generation a primarily middle-class resort.[13]

The second function the new sports creed ascribed to clean sports was an ability to teach morality and promote the social order. Middle-class urbanites were confident they could transmit their high moral standards to their children, but were concerned about the more exuberant behavior of lower-class urban youth. The growing impersonality of large heterogeneous cities seemed a far cry from the close-knit communities of mythical small-town America. Rising crime rates, periodic riots, and rampant hooliganism reflected growing anomie and the erosion of basic values. Clergymen, journalists, and other self-appointed middle-class moral guardians promoted wholesome leisure activities to curtail the behavior of working-class youth who were independent of the traditional customs and social controls that regulated village life and found themselves with ample opportunities for immoral commercialized entertainments. Rational recreations like sports and physical training were expected to provide a healthy alternative to such dissipating pastimes as drinking, fornication, and gambling. Participation in athletics would raise moral standards and prepare young men for useful lives, in contrast to vile urban amusements that simply provided immediate gratification. Sports-minded reformers like the Rev. Channing, Frederick Sawyer, author of *A Plea for Amusements* (1847), and the Brahmin Unitarian Rev. Edward Everett Hale, the preeminent spokesman for rational recreation, all promoted clean sports as a viable substitute for the pernicious pleasures of the male bachelor subculture.[14]

The third element of the new sporting ideology was the presumed character-building ability of competitive sports, which was of great concern to the middle classes. Historian Melvin L. Adelman argues that this aspect of the sports creed developed in the 1850s as an adjunct to the morality thesis, but became more prominent after the Civil War when sports participation was identified as a moral equivalent of war. The key to the character-building argument was the assumption that participation in sports promoted manliness. Sport was regarded as almost inherently a male sphere, inappropriate for Victorian women, and the contemporary press described nearly all sports as manly. Advocates of the sport creed not only believed that competitive sports engendered traits that were essential to middle-class success—self-discipline, self-denial, and even courage—but also that sedentary white-collar workers could utilize sports to demonstrate manliness that was widely identified with physical labor. Real men earned their keep by the sweat of their brow and the strength of their back. Athletes were real men who had graduated from childhood and were prepared for the battles of life or death (i.e., war).[15]

The character-building qualities of sport were widely promoted by the apostles of Muscular Christianity, an English-based philosophy that sought to harmonize the mental, physical, and spiritual dimensions of man. The term is often mistakenly attributed to the English author Charles Kingsley, and the concept was popularized in America in the 1850s by Thomas Hughes's bestseller, *Tom Brown's Schooldays*. The novel depicted student life at Rugby School, which Brown had attended (1834–42) in the era of Headmaster Thomas Arnold, when a heavy emphasis was placed on the role of athletics to promote the development of Christian manliness. The book had an enormous impact on American educators, intellectuals, and average people, resulting, in the words of sport historians John A. Lucas and Ronald A. Smith, in "a kind of mysticism about robust competitive athletics." The book had a big impact on elite students and promoted a sporting boom at universities like Harvard in the late 1850s.[16]

The idea that a man who was moral and devout could and should also be physically fit tied in very well with prevailing middle-class values and the new sports creed. Hale, Higginson, Holmes, and Ralph Waldo Emerson all became leading spokesmen for Muscular Christianity. Higginson, for instance, entitled his famous essay on sports "Saints and Their Bodies," although the term Muscular Christianity did not appear there. Muscular Christianity was such a strong justification for sporting activities that it largely eliminated all but the most conservative pietistic opposition to athletics, especially when physical culture was sponsored by the evangelical Young Men's Christian Association (YMCA). The "Y" movement began in England in 1844 and was brought to America seven years later to help farm youth adjust to urban life in a moral environment. By 1860 it was supporting moral athletics and gymnastics as "a safeguard against the allurement of objectionable places of resort" and nine years later the New York branch opened a new building complete with a gymnasium, bowling alleys, and baths. In the late nineteenth century the YMCA became one of the most important facilitators of sport and physical training for middle-class youth and young men.[17]

Sexuality was an essential, if implicit, aspect of the character-building element of the spotring ideology. Muscular Christians and other mid-Victorians saw sport as both a sexual substitute and a check on effeminacy, concerns that became increasingly important over the course of the nineteenth century. Sports reformers wanted to create a manly Christian gentleman who "was the athlete of continence, not coitus, continuously testing his manliness in the fires of self-denial." The middle classes not only disdained the sexual liberties of immoral members of the male bachelor subculture, but were also worried about a loss of sexual energy and sperm, which were believed to have a finite, irreplaceable limit. Sport would provide an alternative expenditure of energy and help build manliness that would give young men the strength to resist the "secret vice" (masturbation). Moral men could earn their manhood on the playing field instead of in the bedroom.[18]

Clean sport was also viewed by contemporaries as a means to counter effeminacy. In 1859 the New York Herald attributed the feminization of culture in part to the absence of sports in America. The Times urged young men to disport themselves in "God's open air, where health, strength and manhood may be earned." Through sport men would retain such physical qualities as ruggedness and hardiness instead of degenerating into foolish fops. It was manliness the nation needed, not flabby, sick weaklings, if it was to fulfill its destiny.[19]

At midcentury middle-class young men who were convinced by the new sports creed that physical culture was an excellent and useful activity had a number of options to choose for their recreation. They nearly always preferred sports, usually competitive sorts, to mere exercise, because calisthenics were boring and no fun. Virtually any sport that did not rely on gambling for its appeal or brutalize other men or beasts was regarded as appropriate for respectable, forward-looking, middle-class men or individuals with middle-class aspirations. But unless the activity was "manly," requiring a high level of dexterity, physical skill, and courage, and not played by women, it could not be a character-building game. Sociable leisure sports like croquet and ice skating were very popular in the 1860s and perfectly acceptable, but were not manly sports because they were co-recreational. In later decades few commentators, if any, would regard golf or tennis as virile because they did not require courage or much physical exertion and were played by elite women. Bicycle riding was originally a manly sport, but became less so over time as the vehicle was modernized and roads were improved. In the late 1860s riding a velocipede, or "bone-shaker," could be construed as manly because it was so difficult to master and so uncomfortable to ride. Similarly, it took a "man" to master the ordinary bicycle, the odd-shaped vehicle introduced in 1876 with a huge front wheel and tiny rear wheel, on dangerous, poorly constructed roads. However, once technological innovations had produced the safety bicycle of the 1890s, which was light and easy to maneuver, riding become a popular fad among millions of Americans, including middle-class women. Hence cycling was only manly under certain conditions, such as when "scorching" (speeding), or participating in strenuous 100-mile outings.[20]

Given the importance of individualism for the early Victorians, a preference for individual sports would seem likely. Hunting and fishing were popular rural sports, but the growth of cities made fields and streams more distant, and sports more expensive and time-consuming. Boxing was an individualistic sport, and as Frank Queen, editor of the popular sports weekly the *New York Clipper*, wrote, "a knowledge of the science of boxing is calculated to develop and encourage the feeling of manliness, confidence, courage and love of fair play." However, Queen's readers were mainly members of the sporting fraternity, and he swayed few middle-class minds. While respectable sportsmen may have recognized that boxers had to train vigorously and lead a spartan lifestyle, the sport and its subculture stood for everything anathema to Victorian values and was consequently unacceptable.[21]

Two sports that fulfilled the desired qualities of a moral, individualistic, and manly sport were gymnastics and athletics (track and field). Gymnastics was mainly associated with the *Turner* movement that sought to promote German culture, good health, sound morals, and liberal, if not socialist, politics. In 1860 the *Turners* were identified in an article in the *American Journal of Education* as "virtuous and accomplished, pure and active, chaste and bold, truthful and warlike." They had acquired a martial reputation by organizing militia units that helped defend Germans and German institutions against nativist violence in the 1850s, and embellished it when *Turners* flocked to the Union cause during the Civil War.[22] However, the middle classes did not rush to gymnasiums to emulate these manly immigrant sportsmen because exercising on apparatus was pretty dull. They preferred agonistic activities more in line with the competitive middle-class spirit. Track and field, also originally an ethnic sport, was far more competitive than gymnastics; it started out as a professional sport dominated in the antebellum era by English pedestrians (runners) and Scottish weight-throwers. The first prominent track-and-field contests were Scottish Highland Games, beginning in 1836 under the auspices of Scottish voluntary associations. After the Civil War track and field became

Americanized as an amateur sport but it was dominated by restrictive athletic clubs and elite eastern colleges that limited middle-class participation.[23]

The main opportunity for middle-class sportsmen to participate in competitive organized sports in the antebellum era was in team ball games, which commentators regarded as particularly effective in indoctrinating respectable young men with Victorian ideals of masculinity. This was ironic because team games were not really congruent with the independent nature of middle-class work then. But over the course of the century, as white-collar jobs became less independent with the rise of bureaucratization, team games would fit in more and more with the character of nonmanual employment.[24]

Cricket was the first major team sport. It was an old, established English game played in New York during the Revolution by "Gentlemen who are Lovers of that noble and manly exercise." Very few contests were played in the United States until 1840, when English merchants, agents, and artisans in New York formed the St. George Cricket Club. A cricket fad soon developed and it was the most popular ball game until the late 1850s. But thereafter cricket was supplanted by baseball and was largely forgotten except by elite clubs along Philadelphia's Main Line. During its brief period of popularity manuals were published explaining the rules of the game, the techniques of play, and the benefits of the sport. In 1856 more than 8,000 spectators attended a two-day international match between teams from the United States and Canada, and in 1860 it was estimated that there were about 400 cricket clubs in the country with 10,000 players.[25]

Cricket eventually lost out to baseball for several reasons: it was an English game; historic rules and regulations did not readily adapt to American needs; the game took too long for busy Americans; and it was hard to play. Americans had not yet developed a ball-playing tradition, in spite of the English example, and ball playing was regarded at least until the 1840s as a child's or young boy's amusement. The English perception of cricket as a very manly game and appropriate recreation for young men and adults did not readily transfer to the United States. In the 1840s journalists working in the United States who covered the rise of a respectable sporting culture were generally strong supporters of cricket because they identified it as a masculine amusement. The Anglo-American press first identified it as a manly sport because it required physical and mental exertion that were beyond a child's capabilities, and these views were soon echoed by the sporting weeklies. The *Spirit of the Times* regarded cricket as a "manly, healthful sport," and the *New York Clipper* lauded the sport for testing mental and physical ability and strength of character. Immigrant journalist Henry Chadwick, brother of the famed English social reformer Edwin Chadwick, applauded cricket for teaching such virtues as sobriety, self-denial, fortitude, discipline, fair play, and obedience. The *Times* recommended that the sport be played in all towns and villages, and when students at New York's Free Academy started to play, the *Tribune* cheered: "Whoever started these boys to practice the game deserves great credit— it is manly, healthy and invigorating exercise and ought to be attended more or less at all schools." These comments took to task the canard that ball playing was necessarily childish (which it was not in England). Not only was playing cricket a manly activity because of the skills involved, but it also built a manly character.[26]

Baseball had an even more difficult time escaping its early identification with children's games. Various forms of baseball and ball games were played by children in the colonial era. An illustrated rhymed description of "baseball" appeared in John Newbery's *A Little Pretty Pocket-Book* (1744), republished in the colonies by 1762. A simple version of ball play was known as "one old-cat," which consisted of a batter, pitcher, and two bases. Modern baseball derived from the game of round ball, which was played on a field with four stones or posts laid out in a diamond shape, from 36 to 60 feet apart. The feeder pitched the ball to a striker who hit the ball and then ran clockwise around the bases. He was put out if the batted ball was caught on the fly or first bounce, if he was hit by the ball ("soaked") while off base, or struck out.[27]

The modern game of baseball was established in 1845 by the Knickerbocker Base Ball Club, middle-class men who played for outdoor exercise and amusement. They made little effort to secure public recognition, not surprisingly, as Adelman points out:

> After all, they were grown men of some stature playing a child's game. They could rationalize their participation by pointing to the health and recreational benefits of baseball, but their social insecurities and their personal doubts concerning the manliness of the game inhibited them from openly announcing the organization.

In the early 1850s the game began to gain popularity, at first almost exclusively among white-collar men who were probably influenced by the new sports creed and the example of cricket. Baseball soon got more press coverage, became organized with the formation of the National Association of Base Ball Players in 1858, and was spoken of as the national pastime.[28]

From 1857, journalists began describing baseball as a masculine game. *Beadle's Dime Base-Ball Player* (1860), edited by Henry Chadwick, identified the manly attributes of the game: "[Players] must possess the characteristics of true manhood. . . . Baseball to be played thoroughly, requires the possession of muscular strength, great agility, quickness of eye, readiness of hand, and many other faculties of mind and body that mark the man of nerve." Parenthetically, the guidebook also pointed out that "hissing and hooting at an umpire" was "boyish conduct" and inappropriate. Despite these views, there was still some doubt about baseball's manliness because the level of skill required was noticeably less than for cricket. Writers advocated a change in the fly rule to make the sport more difficult and less of a children's game. Instead of being allowed to catch a batted ball on the bounce, Chadwick and others recommended that it had to be on the fly. The Knickerbockers proposed such a rule change in 1857, and used it two years later for their own games. But the NABBP did not adopt the change until 1864 for fear it would make baseball too much like cricket and because players were afraid of getting hurt! This rule change persuaded Chadwick to turn his allegiance from cricket to baseball, a manly exercise valuable for American youth and more suited to the American character. Chadwick eventually became known as the father of American baseball journalism.[29]

The coming of the Civil War slowed down the rise of middle-class sport, but the necessary conditions had been established that led to an enormous boom in middle-class athletic activity soon after the war's end. The new sports creed had been so well articulated that it had become the conventional wisdom. Employers who had once criticized their workers for neglecting their duties to play baseball changed their minds. In the late 1860s, two Chicago department-store moguls, John V. Farwell and Marshall Field, became so convinced that baseball taught such Victorian values as thrift, sobriety, virtue, and hard work that they organized company teams and gave players time off for practice and games. A respectable, gambling-free sporting culture was evolving, based on behavior and attitudes consonant with Victorian values that stressed the functionalism of competitive athletics. Sport was no longer merely child's play or vile amusement for the bachelor subculture, but a useful recreational activity appropriate for respectable middle-class young men who would be transformed into manly specimens, sound of body and pure of heart.[30]

The Martial Spirit, Teamwork, and Middle-Class Sport, 1870–1900

Sport in the late nineteenth century continued to shape the middle-class sense of manliness. Middle-class masculinity was still mainly based on the role of breadwinner and head of household, but the men were undergoing a serious identity crisis that sport could help resolve. The enormous changes under way with the rise of big business and the corporate state were causing a loss of individuality and self-esteem. The expansion of the federal government in the 1870s and the rise of big business in the 1880s were accompanied by the bureaucratization of the workplace, which created a great demand for managers, professionals, salesmen, and clerks. But these salaried workers were now subordinates, no longer independent workers or entrepreneurs, and they did not enjoy the same sense of creativity and accomplishment previously enjoyed by the old middle class. A second identity crisis was that young men questioned their own courage, having been too young to have fought in the Civil War and unsure if they could measure up to the bravery of their fathers, uncles, and brothers who had worn the blue or gray. Finally, the third crisis was the feminization of American culture, which had led to the overcivilization of society. American Protestantism was becoming feminized, with church pews dominated by women and stressing feminine values like humility and meekness, and was unable to reach out to young men. The eastern elite establishment and other opinion-makers were becoming frightened that the Anglo-Saxon male had become effete, was losing his sexual identity, and was becoming impotent. For example, Congregational minister Josiah Strong in *Our Country: Its Possible Future and Present Crisis* (1885) raised the specter of native-born white Americans being overtaken in the future by hordes of fertile immigrants from eastern and southern Europe. In the 1890s concerns for manliness were epitomized by such new words as "sissy," "stuffed shirt," and "molly-coddle." Manliness was now less a stage of development out of childhood than the opposite of femininity.[31]

One important response by middle-class men to this self-questioning was to turn to vigorous physical activity as a means of proving their manliness to themselves and others. They participated in a wide variety of strenuous, clean, outdoor sports to develop their strength, courage, and virility and to regain confidence in their masculinity. The preeminent exponent of using a "strenuous life" to achieve and certify one's masculinity was the elite New York civic reformer and future president Theodore Roosevelt. Roosevelt had outgrown a sickly childhood by a regimen of daily vigorous exercise and participation in such sports as boxing, riding, and hunting. He promoted a cult of masculinity through widely read essays published in the early 1890s in such prestigious mainstream periodicals as *North American Review* and *Harper's Weekly*. Roosevelt did not advocate manly activities merely for the physical joy they brought, or even their sense of accomplishment, but because the qualities that strenuous recreation endowed would make men into leaders who would contribute significantly to the commonweal. He believed there was "a certain tendency to underestimate or overlook the needs of the virile, masterful qualities of the heart and mind," and tried to awaken public consciousness to those needs. In 1893 Roosevelt argued in "The Value of an Athletic Training" that "in a perfectly peaceful and commercial civilization such as ours there is always a danger of placing too little stress upon the more virile virtues—upon the virtues which go to make up a race of statesmen and soldiers, of pioneers and explorers." The young reformer recommended that men remedy the situation by participating in exercise and manly out-of-door sports. He was optimistic about the future, and was pleased to report a significant change for the better among well-to-do youth of the 1890s compared with their forebears at midcentury who had led effeminate and luxurious lives, a change he attributed to peer pressure.[32]

Among the sports Roosevelt recommended were big-game hunting, boxing, and football, but they had more of an appeal for the elite than the middle classes. Roosevelt was himself a boxer who sparred into his forties, and was an ardent fan of amateur boxing. He encouraged boys and young men to box because "it was a vigorous manly pastime, one of those pastimes which have a distinct moral and physical value, because they encourage such essential virtues as courage, hardihood, endurance and self-control." However, he opposed professional boxing because he believed in the amateur ideal and recognized the brutality and degradation of prizefighting. There was a brief period of elite fascination with the ring in the late nineteenth century, even though prizefighting was illegal nearly everywhere, because sportsmen admired the courage and spartan training routines of pugilists. Genteel aficionados felt that in controlled circumstances boxing would make men of their sons, teach them how to direct their aggression, maintain their cool, be courageous and quick-thinking, and learn to identify and correct their own weaknesses. However, the sport held little appeal for middle-class Victorians. Even if they respected the courage and stamina of the boxer, he still represented the values of the sporting fraternity's counterculture. Middle-class sports fans regarded John L. Sullivan as a celebrity because of his awesome athletic prowess, but not as a hero because he lacked self-control outside the ring. They did not fully accept him because of his intemperance, bullying, and sexual behavior.[33]

While hunting and boxing were individualistic sports that may have been excellent means of building manliness, few middle-class men followed those routes to character development, preferring instead team sports that were sociable, entertaining, sufficiently hazardous to promote manly qualities, and highly congruent with their future work options. The new game of football seemed particularly relevant to the needs of upper-middle-class and elite sons.

First played on an intercollegiate basis in 1869, it became Americanized from soccer and rugby and became the most prominent sport at the elite eastern universities. Football seemed the kind of game appropriate for a nation ripe for a clean, violent, virile, yet gentlemanly sport. Coming after the carnage of the Civil War in an era dominated by the social Darwinian concept of the survival of the fittest, football appeared the best sport to teach well-born young men the virtues of the martial life (sub-ordination and co-operation, presence of mind, endurance, precision, and courage) without the terror and bloodshed of war. Football was, in William James's words, a "moral equivalent of war" that would teach athletes to be "contemptuous of softness, surrendering of private interest, and obedien[t] to command." When Brahmin Civil War hero Henry Lee Higginson endowed Harvard's football field, he had it named Soldiers' Field in memory of his martyred classmates, providing a site where the next generation of proper Bostonians could test their manhood and martial spirit.[34]

College football was dominated in the 1870s and 1880s by elite institutions, especially Yale, which only lost twice to Harvard in the 1880s and 1890s, a record that resulted in a "certain loss of manhood for the Cambridge youths." Yet by the 1890s intercollegiate football had spread across the country to private institutions like the University of Chicago and Stanford, as well as to the more democratic midwestern and far western state universities. Students from all social backgrounds showed a strong preference for intercollegiate athletics over traditional extracurricular activities like debating and literary clubs because it was exciting, promoted a sense of community, and operated independently of adult supervision. Furthermore, they believed that participation in team sports would help prepare graduates for modern, bureaucratized society.[35]

The college game was extremely violent, dangerous, and at times brutal. The style of play in the 1890s emphasized mass and momentum rather than deception and wide-open offenses; passing was virtually nonexistent. The single most frightening play was the kickoff return when teams employed the flying-wedge formation, introduced by Harvard in 1892, to burst through the defense for long gains. Players wore little protection, and the number of injuries and deaths was staggering (twelve deaths in 1902 alone). Furthermore, strategy sometimes dictated that players on one squad gang up on an opposing star performer to put him out of the game. The bloodshed and such ungentlemanly behavior encouraged critics like Harvard President Charles Eliot and E. L. Godkin, mugwump editor of the Nation, to urge the banning of the sport.[36]

Proponents of football tuned several of the criticisms of the game's violence on their heads. Most sports journalists joined with coaches and the majority of athletic administrators in advocating the game, believing that its very violence and danger made it a manly sport and a moral equivalent of war. Caspar Whitney, a future editor of *Outing*, regarded football as the best game to train cadets and midshipmen.

> The game is a mimic battle-field, on which the players must reconnoiter, skirmish, advance, attack, and retreat in good order. He must exercise strategy; be prepared to meet emergencies with coolness and judgement under trying circumstances; be trustworthy, observant, vigilant, have courage, pluck, fortitude, daring, and a spirit of self sacrifice to duty. . . . [The player must] combine sobriety, common-sense, health, strength, sagacity, and espirit de corps to a marked degree; have a well-balanced manhood, a healthy mind in a sound body.

Professor Woodrow Wilson of Princeton, a former college coach, believed that football, like other sports, developed precision, presence of mind, and endurance, but particularly promoted co-operation, self-subordination, and discipline. Director Eugene L. Richards of the Yale Gymnasium described football as "the most manly and most scientific game in existence." The Harvard coach Lorin Deland, designer of the devastating flying wedge, and Yale's renowned coach Walter Camp co-authored *Football* in 1896 in which they argued that the physical and moral courage learned on the gridiron was excellent training for life.[37]

The martial values of football came to the fore in the Spanish-American War. Colonel Teddy Roosevelt purposely recruited football players as well as cowboys and other manly types for the Rough Riders. Their escapades were covered by the noted journalist Richard Harding Davis, a former Lehigh football player and ex–sports reporter who compared the Rough Riders to a football eleven. They rode "eye on the ball, and moving in obedience to the captain's signals," and their spirit was identical to that which "once sent these men down a white-washed field against their opponent's rushline."[38]

If football seemed to many upper-class and upper-middle opinion-makers the team sport that most directly prompted manliness for their sons, baseball was the game that was probably most influential in building manly characteristics among most middle-class young men. The national pastime was the most popular sport played and watched by the middle classes. Not only was it originally more prominent on college campuses, it was the preeminent sandlot sport. Besides the millions who played on a recreational basis, there were thousands who played in more organized settings; by the 1880s every city usually had an amateur white-collar workers' league. Furthermore, middle-class fans had ample opportunities to observe and learn from the manly behavior of professionals because they had sufficient leisure time to attend briskly played minor-league or major-league games, which were scheduled at convenient times at fields usually located in the vicinity of middle-class residential neighborhoods.[39]

Baseball was not only a manly game because of the courage needed to play (standing in the batter's box against a fast pitcher; sliding hard to break up the double play), it was even identified by certain commentators with a martial spirit. Morris Raphael Cohen, for instance, the noted philosopher and baseball fanatic, regarded baseball as a moral equivalent of war, although he never could convince his mentor William James. He may have been misled by the military metaphors that journalists frequently employed while discussing sports because it was a language familiar to many veterans and civilians. Far more important was that baseball was a team game highly congruent with the bureaucratic middle-class workplace, yet it also offered an opportunity to exercise one's individuality in a way that could not be done on the job. Baseball provided a milieu where traditional and contemporary values could be merged. Sedentary workers might develop a sense of team spirit and cooperation that were essential in their jobs, learning to sacrifice for the good of the team. But at the same time winning relied on nine players individually carrying their share of the load, each man doing what he did best. The result was pride and enhanced self-esteem through the *team's* success.[40]

By the end of the Victorian Era, the college athletic hero and what he represented provided an important role-model for children and adolescents. The genre of juvenile pulp fiction portrayed young athletic heroes as manly individuals who had achieved prowess in sports, yet maintained a proper balance between mind and body. These idols were of sound character and befriended and protected those who were less gifted. The prime example was Frank Merriwell, a fictional character first introduced by Burt L. Standish (Gilbert Patten) in 1896. The series, which ran for more than twenty years, followed the exploits of Frank and his brother through Fardale School and Yale. At the height of the series' popularity, more than 500,000 copies were sold per week. Merriwell excelled at all forms of athletics, and had the uncanny knack of scoring the winning touchdown on the last play of the game, or hitting a homer in the bottom of the ninth to snatch victory from defeat. Frank was a handsome, model student whose "look of manliness . . . stamped him as a fellow of lofty thoughts and ambition." In each story Merriwell usually had to overcome a villainous and jealous schoolmate while protecting a weaker classmate. Standish's readers were taught that if they participated in athletics with sportsmanship and led a righteous life just like Frank Merriwell, they would develop all the best traits of manliness and their future success was assured.[41]

The intercollegiate sports program also provided a model for secondary schools to emulate. The students at high schools in the late nineteenth century were from the middle class or above, many were college-bound, and they shared the same values as collegians. They copied many college extracurricular activities, like interschool athletic competition under the control of student organizations. Students and educators shared the conventional wisdom that athletics built character and trained values that could be readily transferred to the business world. The manly ethic of sports was most prominent, however, not at the public schools, but at the elite boarding schools, which following the lead of Groton headmaster Endicott Peabody in 1884, adopted the Muscular Christian philosophy, and made athletics compulsory. In emulation of student life at elite eastern colleges and the English public schools, competitive sports were employed to build up youths physically, morally, and spiritually as they learned to play by the rules, control their emotions, and carry out their responsibilities as members of disciplined teams. Sociologist Christopher Armstrong argues that "as games became the most popular schoolboy activity, manliness tended to overshadow Godliness and good learning." Head-masters hoped to train future leaders who would first prove themselves on the playing field and go on to "become good Christian soldiers, as prepared for moral combat or war as properly trained football players were for the big game." Once-pampered boys would leave Groton, St. Paul's, or Exeter ready for the manly playing fields of New Haven or San Juan Hill. They left school imbued with a moral code that called for playing by the rules, always trying their best, and discipline. These sportsmen were gentlemen who could now control and channel their aggression, unlike lower-class athletes who were supposedly overaggressive and out of control. Thus, as Armstrong indicates, the boarding-school youth were taught through sports a class-linked version of masculinity. Presumably many of the same lessons were also taught at Boston Latin and Brooklyn Tech.[42]

Conclusion

Sport in the Victorian Era played an important role in redefining the criterion of middle-class masculinity, moving beyond the man's relationship to his work and family to include his character and physical self. Then, once sport refined the attributes of respectable manliness, it was employed to indoctrinate proper bourgeois virtues in succeeding generations. At the onset of the Victorian Era, sport had been totally antithetical to middle-class behavior. Sports were violent, dangerous, immoral, prone to gambling, and occurred in exclusively male settings of dubious character. Sport had originally promoted a manly ethic congruent with the nature of life in premodern societies where life was harsh, hazardous, often uncivilized, and unpredictable. These values fit in well with life on the frontier, southern plantations, the open range, mining camps, and rough urban neighborhoods, but did not fit in well at all with life in settled communities or at the workplace under industrial capitalism.

The respectable urban middle classes began to participate in sport at mid-century as they learned from immigrants, social critics, health faddists, and other social reformers that physical culture could be enjoyed free of nefarious influences, and that participation was fun and uplifting at the same time. A new sport ideology developed that promoted team sports and other athletic pastimes that were consonant with the social values of hard-working, religious, future-oriented Victorians and promised to improve health, morality, and character (that is, manliness). Sedentary students and workers who were worried about their fitness and the unmanly nature of their work were drawn to sports to improve their health and gain respect for their manliness. Sport was no mere child's play, but would create Muscular Christians: rugged, disciplined, manly gentlemen would be produced out of effete, childlike youths. These men would be responsible, physically fit, moral adults who continued to live within traditional middle-class norms, abstaining from premarital sex, living within the virtues of domesticity, and serving as good providers.

Sport boomed as a middle-class recreation in the late nineteenth century and contributed significantly to the redefinition of middle-class manliness. The rise of bureaucratization, the threat posed by the new immigrants, an uncertainty of measuring up to brave ancestors, and the feminization of culture encouraged middle-class young men to test their manliness through vigorous physical activity, especially team sports. Participation in strenuous, if not dangerous, clean outdoor sports would develop strength, courage, and virility, while restoring self-confidence. Sport tested one's mettle and prepared one for adulthood. Followers of the strenuous life would grow up to become self-controlled, disciplined men of action who were team players in the workplace and bearers of the white man's burden who would protect the race against inferior immigrant strains and surmount the feminization of American culture.

Notes

1. On the formation of the nineteenth-century middle class, see Mary P. Ryan, *The Cradle of the Middle Class: The Family in Oneida County, New York, 1790–1865* (Cambridge, Mass., 1981); Burton J. Bledstein, *The Culture of Professionalism: The Middle Class and the Development of Higher Education in America* (New

York, 1976); Clyde Griffen and Sally Griffen, *Natives and Newcomers: The Ordering of Opportunity in Mid-Nineteenth Century Poughkeepsie* (Cambridge, Mass., 1978); John S. Gilkeson, Jr., *Middle-Class Providence, 1820–1940* (Princeton, 1986); and Stuart Blumin, "The Hypothesis of Middle-Class Formation in Nineteenth-Century America: A Critique and Some Proposals," *American Historical Review* 90 (April 1985), 299–338; idem, *The Emergence of the Middle Class* (Cambridge, Mass., 1989). On middle-class sport, see Melvin L. Adelman, *A Sporting Time: New York City and the Rise of Modern Athletics, 1820–1870* (Urbana, Ill., 1986), chs. 3, 5–7.

2. Nancy Cott, *The Bonds of Womanhood: "Women's Sphere" in New England, 1780–1835* (New Haven, Conn. 1977); Barbara Welcer, "The Cult of True Womanhood, 1820–1860," *American Quarterly* 18 (summer 1966), 151–74; E. Anthony Rotundo, "Body and Soul: Changing Ideals of American Middle Class Manhood, 1770–1920," *Journal of Social History* 16 (fall 1983), 23–38; Peter Stearns, *Be a Man!: Males in Modern Society* (New York, 1979); Joe L. Dubbert, *A Man's Place: Masculinity in Transition* (Englewood Cliffs, N.J., 1979). On the sporting fraternity, see Benjamin G. Rader, *American Sports: From the Age of Folk Games to the Age of Spectators* (Englewood Cliffs, N.J., 1983), pp. 30–34; Elliott J. Gorn, " 'Gouge and Bite, Pull Hair and Scratch': The Social Significance of Fighting in the Southern Backcountry," *American Historical Review* 90 (February 1985), 23–38; idem, *The Manly Art: Bare-Knuckle Prize Fighting in America* (Ithaca, N.Y., 1986); Michael T. Isenberg, *John L. Sullivan and His America* (Urbana, Ill., 1988).

3. John R. Betts, "Mind and Body in Early American Thought," *Journal of American History* 54 (March 1968), 787–805; Stephen Hardy and Jack W. Berryman, " 'Public Amusements and Public Morality': Sport and Social Reform in the American City, 1800–1860" (paper presented at the annual meeting of the Organization of American Historians, April 2, 1981, Detroit); Roberta J. Park, "Biological Thought, Athletic Attitudes on Sport and Manliness and the Formation of a 'Man of Character': 1830–1900," in J. A. Mangan and James Walvin, eds., *Manliness and Morality: Middle Class Masculinity in Britain and America, 1800–1940* (Manchester, 1987), pp. 15–42.

4. Nancy L. Struna, "Puritans and Sport: The Irretrievable Tide of Change," *Journal of Sport History* 4 (spring 1977), 1–21; Peter Wagner, "Puritan Attitudes Towards Physical Recreation in Seventeenth-Century New England," ibid., 3 (summer 1975), 139–51; Betts, "Mind and Body," 787–95.

5. John R. Betts, *America's Sporting Heritage, 1850–1950* (Reading, Mass., 1974), pp. 6, 8, 19–20, 47, 195; John Lucas and Ronald Smith, *The Saga of American Sport* (Philadelphia, 1978), pp. 96, 109, 111, 137–39; Rader, *American Sports*, pp. 35, 52, 149–50; Timothy Breen, "Horses and Gentlemen: The Cultural Significance of Gambling Among the Gentry of Virginia," *William and Mary Quarterly* 34 (April 1977), 331–33.

6. Robert W. Malcolmson, *Popular Recreations in English Society, 1700–1850* (Cambridge, U.K., 1973); Peter Bailey, *Leisure and Class in Victorian England: Ratio-*

nal Recreation and the Contest for Control, 1830–1885 (London, 1978); Hugh Cunningham, *Leisure in the Industrial Revolution c. 1780–1880* (New York, 1980); E. P. Thompson, "Time, Work-Discipline, and Industrial Capitalism," *Past and Present* 38 (December 1967), 71–86.

7. Hardy and Berryman, "Public Amusements," 608, 10–21; Betts, "Mind and Body," 787–805; Stephen W. Nissenbaum, *Sex, Diet and Debility in Jacksonian America: Sylvester Graham and Health Reform* (Westport, Conn., 1980). Excellent overviews of antebellum reform include Paul S. Boyer, *Urban Masses and Moral Order in America, 1820–1920* (Cambridge, Mass., 1978), and Ronald G. Walters, *American Reformers, 1815–1860* (New York, 1978).

8. Betts, "Mind and Body," 797–99, 802, 804–5; Roberta J. Park, " 'Embodied Selves': The Rise and Development of Concern for Physical Education, Active Games, and Recreation for American Women, 1776–1865" *Journal of Sport History* 5 (summer 1978), 5–41; Lemuel Shattuck, *Report of a General Plan for the Promotion of Public and Personal Health* (1850), quoted in John Rickard Betts, "Public Recreation, Public Parks and Public Health Before the Civil War," in Bruce L. Bennett, ed., *The History of Physical Education and Sport* (Chicago, 1972), p. 47.

9. A. A. Livermore, "Gymnastics," *North American Review* 169 (1855), 52, quoted in Park, "Formation of a 'Man of Character,' " 18; Oliver Wendell Homes, "The Autocrat of the Breakfast Table," *Atlantic Monthly* 1 (May 1858), 881. See also S. D. Kehoe, *The Indian Club Exercise, Also General Remarks on Physical Culture* (New York, 1861), 19, and Maurice Kloss, "The Dumb Bell Instructor for Parlor Gymnasts," in Dio Lewis, ed., *The New Gymnastics for Men, Women and Children* (Boston, 1862), p. 120, quoted in Harvey Green, *Fit for America: Health, Fitness, Sport and American Society* (New York, 1986), p. 183. On English school sports, see, for example, John Ford, *This Sporting Land* (London, 1977), pp. 172–85, and Eric Dunning and Kenneth Sheard, *Barbarians, Gentlemen and Players: A Sociological Study of the Development of Rugby Football* (New York, 1979), pp. 83–86, 94–96.

10. Thomas Wentworth Higginson, "Saints and Their Bodies," *Atlantic Monthly* 1 (March 1858), 582–95 (quote), 582; idem, "Gymnastics," ibid., 7 (March 1861), 283–302. See also John A. Lucas, "Thomas Wentworth Higginson: Early Apostle of Health and Fitness," *Journal of Health, Physical Education and Recreation* 42 (February 1971), 30–33; Stephen Hardy, *How Boston Played: Sport, Recreation and Community, 1865–1915* (Boston, 1982), pp. 52–53; Park, "Formation of a 'Man of Character,' " 18–20.

11. Betts, "Public Recreation," 38–41, 43.

12. Ibid. 46–48. An 1859 New York medical convention specifically recommended "that Grounds be set apart for gymnastic exercise and various manly sports." See John Bell, *Report on the Importance and Economy of Sanitary Measures to Cities* (New York, 1860), pp. 165–68, quoted in ibid., p. 48.

13. On the development of Central Park, see Ian R. Stewart, "Central Park, 1851–1871: Urban and Environmental Planning in New York City" (Ph.D.

194 STEVEN A. RIESS

dissertation, Cornell University, 1973), pp. 131–39; Frederick Law Olmsted, Jr., and Theodorak Kimball, eds., *Frederick Law Olmsted, Landscape Architect, 1822–1903* (1922–28; rep. New York, 1970), pp. 126–27, 139–40, 276–77, 421–22; Thomas Bender, *Towards an Urban Vision: Ideas and Institutions in Nineteenth Century America* (Lexington, Ky., 1975), p. 176. Roy Rosenzweig, *Eight Hours for What We Will: Workers and Leisure in an Industrial City, 1870–1920* (New York, 1983), p. 128, and Hardy, *How Boston Played*, p. 80, examine the problems of working-class urbanites seeking to use the suburban parks. On Olmsted's impact outside New York, see, for example, Glen E. Holt, "Private Plans for Public Places: The Origins of Chicago's Park System, 1850–1875," *Chicago History* 8 (fall 1979), 173–84, and Cynthia Zaitzevsky, *Frederick Law Olmsted and the Boston Park System* (Cambridge, Mass., 1983), pp. 28–32.

14. Hardy, *How Boston Played*, pp. 40–41, 45–53; Boyer, *Urban Masses*, pp. 3–120; Rader, *American Sports*, pp. 30–35.

15. Adelman, *A Sporting Time*, pp. 106, 173–74, 181–84, 186; Gorn, *Manly Art*, pp. 140–47, 198–200.

16. Lucas and Smith, *Saga of American Sport*, pp. 109 (quote), 137; Dunning and Sheard, *Barbarians, Gentlemen, and Players*, pp. 86–89; Green, *Fit for America*, ch. 8.

17. Lucas and Smith, *Saga of American Sport*, pp. 108–9, 137, 139; Hardy, *How Boston Played*, pp. 50–51; Adelman, *A Sporting Time*, pp. 279–82; Rader, *American Sports*, pp. 149–51; Christian Messenger, *Sport and the Spirit of Play in American Fiction: Hawthorne to Faulkner* (New York, 1981), pp. 149–54; Caspar Whitney, "The Minister and the Athletics: Mr. Caspar Whitney's Views," *Outlook* 55 (January 1897), 183.

18. Adelman, *A Sporting Time*, pp. 279–80; Charles S. Rosenberg, "Sexuality, Class and Role in Nineteenth Century America," *American Quarterly* 25 (May 1973), 119 (quote); Stephanie L. Twin, "Women and Sport," in Donald Spivey, ed., *Sport in America, New Historical Perspectives* (Westport, Conn., 1985), p. 198; Donald J. Mrozek, *Sport and American Mentality, 1880–1930* (Knoxville, 1983), pp. 22–27.

19. Adelman, *A Sporting Time*, p. 284; *New York Herald*, July 27, 1859; *New York Times*, June 21, 1854.

20. Adelman, *A Sporting Time*, pp. 255–59, 262–66. On golf and tennis see Caspar Whitney, "Evolution of the Country Club," *Harper's Monthly* 90 (December 1894), 16–23; George Kobbe, "The Country Club and Its Influence on American Social Life," *Outlook* 68 (June 1, 1901), 302–21; Robert Dunn, "The Country Club: A National Expression," *Outing* (1905), 160–74; Rader, *American Sports*, pp. 65–68; Ripley Hitchcock, "Country Club Life," *Chatauquan* 9 (1889), 601–13; H. W. Wind, "Golfing in and around Chicago," *Chicago History* 4 (winter 1975–1976), 44–51. On cycling, see Norman L. Dunham, "The Bicycle Era in American History" (Ph.D. dissertation, Harvard University, 1956), 47–51, 57–148; Hardy, *How Boston Played*, ch. 8; Richard Harmond, "Progress and Flight: An Interpretation of the American Cycle Craze of the 1890s," *Journal of Social History* 5 (winter 1971–1972), 253–57;

George D. Bushnell, "When Chicago Was Wheel Crazy," *Chicago History* 4 (fall 1975), 172–75.

21. Frank Queen, editor of the *New York Clipper,* established in 1853, encouraged all sports, but especially prizefighting and other working-class sports. For Queen's comments, see Gorn, *Manly Art,* p. 101.

22. Henry Metzner, *A Brief History of the American Turnerbund* (Pittsburgh, 1924), pp. 7–24; Horst Ueberhorst, *Turner Unterm Sternenbanner: Der Kampf der Deutsch-Amerikanischen Turner fur Einheit, Freiheit, und Soziale Gerechtigkeit, 1848 bis 1918* (Munich, 1978); Robert K. Barney, "Knights of Cause and Exercise: German Forty-Eighters and *Turnereine* in the United States during the Ante-Bellum Period," *Canadian Journal of the History of Sport* 13 (December 1982), 62–79; R. Von Raumer, "Physical Education," *American Journal of Education* 8 (1860), 185 (quote).

23. Rader, *American Sports,* pp. 38–41, 53–63; Lucas and Smith, *Saga of American Sports,* pp. 97–98, 107–8, 154–58, 165–66; Adelman, *A Sporting Time,* pp. 211–20; George Moss, "The Long Distance Runners of Ante-Bellum America," *Journal of Popular Culture* 8 (1970), 371–82; Gerald Redmond, *The Caledonian Games in Nineteenth Century America* (Cranbury, N.J., 1971).

24. The basic source on the early history of ball games is Adelman, *A Sporting Time,* sect. II; see also George Kirsch, *The Creation of American Team Sports: Baseball and Cricket, 1838–72* (Urbana, Ill., 1989), which is even more thorough. On the congruence argument, see Steven Gelber, "Working at Playing: The Culture of the Workplace and the Rise of Baseball," *Journal of Social History* 17 (June 1983), 3–25.

25. Alvin F. Harlow, *Old Bowery Days: The Chronicle of a Famous Street* (New York, 1931), p. 75; Adelman, *A Sporting Time,* pp. 101–4; George B. Kirsch, "American Cricket: Players and Clubs Before the Civil War," *Journal of Sport History* 11 (spring 1984), 28–29.

26. Adelman, *A Sporting Time,* pp. 91–3, 105–7, 282; *New York Tribune,* November 7, 1853, quoted in ibid., 105–6; *New York Times,* June 22, 1855. On the Anglo-American press reaction, see *Spirit of the Times,* October 15, 1842, 385; *New York Clipper,* September 3, 1853, September 13, 1856, 165, in Robert M. Lewis, "Cricket and the Beginnings of Organized Baseball in New York City," *International Journal of the History of Sport* 4 (December 1987), 323.

27. Harold Seymour, *Baseball,* vol. 1, *The Early Years* (New York, 1960), pp. 5–9.

28. Adelman, *A Sporting Time,* pp. 124 (quote), 121–37. See also Seymour, *Baseball,* chs. 1–3; Irving A. Leitner, *Baseball: Diamond in the Rough* (New York, 1972).

29. Quoted in Lewis, "Cricket and Baseball," 323; Adelman, *A Sporting Time,* pp. 127, 129–31, 173.

30. Stephen Freeman, "The Baseball Fad in Chicago, 1865–1870: An Exploration of the Role of Sport in the Nineteenth Century City," *Journal of Sport History* 5 (summer 1978), 42–64.

31. Cindy Sondik Aron, *Ladies and Gentlemen of the Civil Service: Middle-Class Workers in Victorian America* (New York, 1987), pp. 1–5; George Frederickson, *The*

Inner Civil War (New York, 1965), p. 224; Ann Douglas, *The Feminization of American Culture* (New York, 1977); Norbert Elias, *The Civilizing Process* (Oxford, 1978); Norbert Elias and Eric Dunning, *Quest for Excitement: Sport and Leisure in the Civilizing Process* (Oxford, 1986); Lucas and Smith, *Saga of American Sport*, ch. 17; Adelman, *A Sporting Time*, pp. 281–86; Rader, *American Sports*, pp. 150–51; Dubbert, *Man's Place*, ch. 6; Gerald F. Roberts, "The Strenuous Life: The Cult of Manliness in the Era of Theodore Roosevelt" (Ph.D. dissertation, Michigan State University, 1970), pp. 84–144; Twin, "Women in Sport," 199; Stephanie Twin, "Jock and Jill: Aspects of Women's Sport History in America, 1870–1940" (Ph.D. dissertation, Rutgers University, 1979), 44–65.

In John Higham's much-praised but dated speculative essay, he exaggerated the importance of regeneration among middle- and upper-class males in promoting a rise in sports in the 1890s. Higham did not realize that respectable sporting cultures had been well developed before the 1890s. See John Higham, "The Reorientation of American Culture in the 1890s," in John Weiss, ed., *The Origin of Modern Consciousness* (Detroit, 1965), pp. 25–48.

32. Theodore Roosevelt, *Theodore Roosevelt: An Autobiography* (New York, 1924), ch. 2; Edward Wagenknecht, *The Seven Worlds of Theodore Roosevelt* (New York, 1958), ch. 1; Roosevelt, "Professionalism in American Sports," *North American Review* 151 (August 1890), 187; idem, "The Value of Athletic Training," *Harper's Weekly* 37 (December 1893), 1236; idem, "The American Boy," in Theodore Roosevelt, *The Strenuous Life and Other Essays* (New York, 1956), p. 156. See also Mrozek, *Sport and American Mentality*, pp. 34–39, 43–51.

33. Theodore Roosevelt, "The Boone and Crockett Club," *Harper's Weekly* 37 (March 1893), 267; idem, "The Recent Prize Fight," *Outlook* 95 (July 16, 1910), 550; idem, *Autobiography*, pp. 28, 40–42; Gorn, *Manly Art*, pp. 196–97. On late-nineteenth-century elite fascination with pugilism, see Gorn, *Manly Art*, pp. 194–206; Dale A. Somers, *The Rise of Sports in New Orleans, 1850–1900* (Baton Rouge, 1972), pp. 174–91; Isenberg, *Sullivan*, pp. 224–35.

34. Frederickson, *Inner Civil War*, p. 224; William James, *The Moral Equivalent of War and Other Essays* (New York, 1971), pp. 6–7, 12; Higham, "Reorientation of American Culture," 25–48; Dubbert, *A Man's Place*, pp. 175–80; Messenger, *Sport and the Spirit of Play*, p. 137.

35. Lucas and Smith, *Saga of American Sport*, ch. 13; Rader, *American Sports*, pp. 75–86; John Hammond Moore, "Football's Ugly Decades, 1893–1913," *Smithsonian Journal of History* 2 (fall 1967), 49–68. See also Guy M. Lewis, "The American Intercollegiate Football Spectacle, 1869–1917" (Ph.D. dissertation, University of Maryland, 1965), and Robin Dale Lester, "The Rise, Decline, and Fall of Football at the University of Chicago, 1892–1940" (Ph.D. dissertation, University of Chicago, 1973).

36. Moore, "Football's Ugly Decades," 49–55; Lucas and Smith, *Saga of American Sport*, pp. 239–42.

37. Caspar Whitney, "The Athletic Development at West Point and Annapolis," *Harper's Weekly* 36 (May 21, 1892), 496; Moore, "Football's Ugly Decades," 50; Eugene L. Richards, Jr., "Foot-ball in America," *Outing* 6 (1885), 62–66; Walter Camp and Lorin Deland, *Football* (Boston, 1896), pp. 193–204.

38. Messenger, *Sport and the Spirit of Play*, pp. 142, 144; Richard Harding Davis, *The Cuban and Porto Rican Campaigns* (New York, 1898), pp. 152–53, quoted in ibid., p. 144.

39. Lucas and Smith, *Saga of American Sport*, pp. 199–201; Steven A. Riess, *Touching Base: Professional Baseball and American Culture in the Progressive Era* (Westport, Conn., 1980), pp. 26–30, 173–80; Freeman, "Baseball Fad," 53–61; Gelber, "Working at Playing," 8, 10–12; Steven Gelber, " 'Their Hands Are All Out Playing': Business and Amateur Baseball, 1845–1917," *Journal of Sport History* 11 (spring 1984), 5–27.

40. David Lamoreaux, "Baseball in the Late Nineteenth Century: The Sources of Its Appeal," *Journal of Popular Culture* 11 (1977), 602–8; Gelber, "Working at Playing," in Riess, *Touching Base*, pp. 22–23, 26. On the popularity of baseball at the turn of the century, and its perceived social functions, see Riess, *Touching Base*, chs. 2 and 7. For examples of the conventional wisdom about baseball's character-building capacity, see H. Addington Bruce, "Baseball and the National Life," *Outlook* 104 (May 1913), 105–6; and Henry S. Curtis, "Baseball," *Journal of Education* 82 (April 27, 1916), 466–67.

41. Messenger, *Sport and the Spirit of Play*, pp. 165–72; Dubbert, *Man's Place*, pp. 34–39; John L. Cutler, *Gilbert Patten and His Frank Merriwell Saga* (Orono, Maine, 1934), quoted in ibid., p. 38. In post-Victorian America the athlete who best epitomized the manly character of sport was Christy Mathewson, star pitcher for the New York Giants, whose total of 373 victories is still the National League record. He was a Muscular Christian who learned to play baseball at the YMCA, seldom pitched on Sundays, and almost always exhibited complete sportsmanship and honorable behavior both on and off the field. A star football player at Bucknell, Mathewson was the closest thing to a real Frank Merriwell, and was himself the role-model for a juvenile series of sports fiction. Mathewson retired from the diamond to become a manager, but resigned during World War I to serve his country. He was gassed overseas, which contributed to his untimely death seven years later. See Riess, *Touching Base*, pp. 23–24; Douglas Wallop, *Baseball: An Informal History* (New York, 1965), pp. 115–16; 129–31; *Dictionary of American Biography* s.v. "Mathewson, Christy," "Editorial," *Commonweal* 2 (October 21, 1925), 579.

42. Joseph Kett, *Rites of Passage: Adolescence in America, 1790 to the Present* (New York, 1977), pp. 138, 183–89; Jeffrey Mirel, "From State Control to Institutional Control of High School Athletics: Three Michigan Cities, 1883–1905," *Journal of Social History* 16 (winter 1982), 84–92; Hardy, *How Boston Played*, pp. 109–22; Christopher F. Armstrong, "The Lessons of Sports: Class Socialization in British and American Boarding Schools," *Sociology of Sport Journal* 1 (1984), 315, 321–24.

7

The "Amazon" and the American "Lady"
Sexual Fears of Women as Athletes

DONALD J. MROZEK

Do you blame us little animals, literally aching for the freedom of kittens, pup-
pies, and lambs, if we demand of our teachers at least five minutes gymnastic or
play-exercises at the end of every hour and a few full breaths of God's pure air?
Especially when you remember that soon it will not be proper for little girls any
longer to romp out of doors, with the boys; indeed it will be exceedingly un-
ladylike; for then we must turn up our hair, lengthen our frocks, put on corsets,
and 'we can't be "Tomboy" any longer'.

B. F. BOLLER, 1900[1]

No one seemed to realize that there is a time in the life of a girl when it is better
for her and for the community to be something of a boy rather than too much
of a girl.

DUDLEY A. SARGENT, 1927[2]

Some writers have said that . . . a big change took place in me. Their idea is that
I used to be all tomboy, with none of the usual girls' interests, and then all of a
sudden I switched over to being feminine. Well, with almost any woman athlete,
you seem to get that tomboy talk.

"BABE" DIDRIKSON ZAHARIAS, 1956[3]

The Dimensions of the Problem

The unequal development of athletic opportunities for women in America
during the nineteenth and twentieth centuries reflected many constraining
forces, but a remarkable number of them shared the underlying component
of fear. According to research undertaken in the past two decades, men feared
that they might be challenged or even displaced in governance of the basic social order. They feared dislocations in the workforce and in electoral politics.
Overall, they feared that they would lose control of public political, social, and

economic affairs, which they dominated as a special masculine realm. But once the association of public life and an active manner with masculinity had been made, the entry—or re-entry—of women into these areas and the style pervading them became exceedingly problematic. Indeed, any serious challenge to this differentiation into separate male and female spheres only contributed to the underlying fear that pervaded and united all the others—the fear of losing identity and purpose. This concern was made especially vivid and concrete in the realm of sport.

Although women engaged in sport, men still dominated it, especially competitive athletics. Overall, sport thus retained the aura of a male preserve. Not uncommonly, men boasted of their involvement in sport as a proof of masculinity, especially if their gender identity seemed threatened for other reasons. The composer Charles Ives, for example, is said to have feared that his musical interests made him seem effeminate and compensated by asserting his manhood through baseball. Asked in his youth what he played, Ives mentioned no musical instrument but replied instead, "Shortstop."[4] Ives was not unique. A prolific nineteenth-century writer of anti-masturbation literature, the Rev. John Todd, often separated himself from wife, family, and home in hunting trips out in the wild; his physical removal into "untamed" nature seems to have strengthened his sense of male identity.[5] In the years after the Civil War, health reformer James C. Jackson proposed that both girls and boys be encouraged to play outdoors so that exposure to Nature could develop their sense of "ideality" and their inclination toward "purity and truth." But such activities were also clearly intended as a curative against masturbation; and the purity that boys and girls would gain through natural play was expected to strengthen their distinctive identity as men and women.[6]

The fear that woman was by nature an excessively sexual being encouraged such separate behavior. For some men at least, as suggested by the experience of John Todd and others, there was an element of self-protection, seeing themselves as vulnerable to women rather than the reverse. The "weakness" of the "weaker sex" did not mean that they could not harm men; it meant rather that they were morally weak and, in that sense, out of control. Both ironically and appropriately, then, woman's role as moral guardian was elevated, at least as a goal and perhaps as an aid to social conformity. Yet it was this moral fragility that seemed to pose grave dangers for men.

Indeed, various forms of compensatory behavior and of self-protective hostility towards women appear deeply embedded in male experience in many cultures, as Wolfgang Lederer has suggested in *The Fear of Women*.[7] According to Lederer, the suppression of the "precarious oscillation between love and fear" in men's feelings towards women has actually strengthened the impact of the fear and given rise to pathological consequences.[8] Among the destructive impulses that followed were an intense taboo of manners among men against "doing things like a woman," as well as a deep resentment against the "Amazons," whom Lederer has sharply described as "only the church militant, the shocktroops of an ancient, world-wide system of mother-right."[9] To the extent that women challenged the stereotype of a "ladylike manner" in sport and physical leisure, they fell prey to such fear, partly by appearing to encroach upon the competitive, confrontational, shameless character that men supposedly brought to sporting events by virtue of their masculinity. The real differences between sensuality and sexuality fell largely out of view, and social convention—a matter of manners—thus edged into gender identification—a matter confused with sex and sexuality.

Cultural Differentiation and the Logic of Fear

The fear experienced by men who worried over a public role for women, even if it lacked fairness, was not without a certain logic. The rationale showed itself in matters of style and manner, which were actually matters of serious substance and consequence. The focus on the manner in which men and women acted—an evident matter of style—reflected the view, as Charles Rosenberg has put it, that "control was the basic building block of personality."[10] By the later decades of the nineteenth century, the generalized care to govern "the passions"—including gluttony, envy, and other excesses—narrowed into an insistent worry over sexuality.[11] On the one hand, this clearly suggested that excess had an intrinsically sexual undercurrent; and, on the other hand, it hinted that fears born in sexuality could falsely color activities such as sport and athletics that, though intensely sensory and sensual, were not inherently sexual.

The quest for control fostered the separation of the sexes into two parallel but not identical cultures, a division that strengthened during the nineteenth century. In the twentieth century, the male solidarity that, in Lois Banner's words, "strengthened the male tendency to see woman as a chivalric object" seemed to be challenged by the women's movement; and the male's sense of identity as well as his enjoyment of social prerogatives seemed to hinge proportionally on firm reassertion of the separate cultures.[12] To the extent that it smudged the identifying line between men and women, the emergence of women to athletic excellence could be seen as a threat to social order and as a violation of the tradition of "true womanhood." Moreover, some advocates of women's participation in sport may have been ambivalent presences. Dr. Alice B. Stockham, for example, a Chicago physician, not only praised sport and outdoor activity as a better tonic for women than medicine but also encouraged birth control and abortion.[13] This challenge to many Americans' notion of truly feminine behavior and womanly responsibility was especially troublesome because of the deeply rooted antipathy towards any suggestion of femininity in men. The late-nineteenth-century woman was said to admire in man "true *manliness*, and [she] is repelled by weakness and effeminacy. A womanish man awakens either the pity or the contempt of the fairer sex."[14] It was bad enough if a man could not manage to "behave like a man"; but his dilemma worsened if women refused to "behave like women."

Some contemporary observers regarded differentiation between men and women as inevitable in the socioeconomic circumstances of early-twentieth-century America. But its apparent causes and consequences boded ill for women's athletics. According to social scientist Anna Garlin Spencer, the "vocational divide" did not result principally from physical motherhood but from the overriding imperative, shared by men and women, that the family be sustained. In *Woman's Share in Social Culture*, first published in 1912 and reissued in 1925, Spencer said that the man's economic and professional advancement thus assumed much greater practical importance.[15] The impact on woman was to diminish her "personal achievement" and the "joy of self-expression"—hallmarks of one's commitment to sport as well as purported effects of athletic success. Apart from the fatalism that tinged Spencer's thinking, her analysis pinpointed one of the most critical distinctions—while the male's individual fulfilment was taken to further the societal interest, the female's social obligations were seen as a substitute for her individual self-expression and attainment. To the extent that such "inner-directedness" was regarded as physically inherent in women, then outer-directed activities could be regarded as deviant or suspect.

The overlays of social assumption that ultimately formed the rationale for restricting women's athletics were complex; and, although mutually supportive when seen broadly, they sometimes seemed contradictory in detail. Much of the complexity and apparent contradiction resulted from considerations of social and economic class. When commentators such as Spencer spoke of women, they most commonly meant women rather like themselves—born to some measure of comfort and to some sense of social opportunity and responsibility. In this, they resembled social commentators who spoke of sport, such as Edwyn Sandys, or political leaders who practiced sport and worried over race improvement, such as Theodore Roosevelt. These were the well-bred women, marked by a sense of self-governance and reserve. Exuberance and physical display were far more the province of the poor, the immigrant, the working-class woman, and this tendency towards display itself was often taken as a mark of moral corruption. Inadequate self-control and incompetence in domestic management, for example, coupled with the unbridling of instincts for bodily display were though to lead to such evils as prostitution.[16] To be sure, aggressive public display by women in athletics hardly constituted prostitution; but the descent into impassioned public display was suspect nonetheless. The absence of self-control that led to sexual depravity was too easily confused with the sensual expressiveness that had its outlet in sport. Since manners were thus a key sign of morality, the manner of one's sport and athletic practice also assumed a moral intonation.

In itself, the concern over propriety in female behavior was hardly new. But the concern was especially strong to protect and enforce discipline among middle- and upper-class women rather than to "redeem" the laboring poor. Discriminatory bias against poorer women had a long history, linked to suspicion of their supposed promiscuous inclinations and depreciated moral worth, whether intrinsic or induced by poverty and deprivation. As Charles Rosenberg has observed, the very fact of overt sexuality was widely regarded at the turn of the century as inimical to middle-class values. Moreover, medical practice and certainly medical prescriptions reflected class bias.[17] In addition, some historians have suggested that a disproportionate number of poorer women were subjects—or victims—of extreme surgical procedures for removal of sexual organs as a means of governing sociosexual behavior.[18] Any departure from the most restrained and proper behavioral code could be interpreted as a start down the road to depravity. But the middle class were inclined to view the tendency to wallow in such depravity as an attribute of their socioeconomic inferiors.

Middle- and upper-class Americans had long been suspicious of physical display, especially though not exclusively among women, from the colonial period through the nineteenth century. As the lower-class appreciation of physical display created a significant commercial market for entrepreneurs such as P. T. Barnum, female behavior again became a hotly debated issue.[19] When women had traditionally engaged in public displays, it had been crucial to preserve their image of moral uprightness. As Lois Banner has noted, Barnum had "cloaked Jenny Lind in a mantle of respectability" during her American tour in 1850. Even so, Barnum's effort to establish perhaps the first

thing to make money from such an oddity. But it was quite a different question how well athletically gifted women would fare when competition was more straightforward—not crossing gender barriers but allowing their exuberant athletic excellence to shine through without the protective wrapping of pagan and theatrical associations. The "Amazon" might be amusing and, perhaps, titillating as long as she remained in a realm of fantasy. But how might she be treated in the everyday world? Might not her excellence in athletics preclude her acceptance as an equal?

Recent research suggests that media accounts of prominent female athletes typically portrayed them as exceptions to the prevailing rules of femininity, regardless of the era in which they performed publicly. Eleanora Randolph Sears and Mildred "Babe" Didrikson Zaharias, for example, seemed to deviate from commonly accepted notions about the woman's role as wife and mother, her manner of dress and suitable behavior, her supposed physical limits, and the purported limits of her emotional stability.[31] There was a danger that female athletic excellence itself might be seen as a form of social and even personal deviation.

Sears shocked officials who picked her up for speeding, not only because she was driving the car but also because she wore masculine clothing. At sport, too, she sometimes adopted the masculine style. On 14 August 1910, reports were published that Sears rode astride while playing against men in a polo game. Also, descriptions of her play in the National Tennis Doubles Championships in the second decade of the century used adjectives stereotyped as male such as "hard." In the 1920s, Sears walked from Providence, Rhode Island, to Boston in 11 hours and 5 minutes. In a story in the *New York Times* on 15 December 1925, she was portrayed as superior to men. Along the way, her two male escorts began "to feel the strain. Both Cutler and Hinckley, instead of setting the pace, lagged persistently, and Miss Sears with a grin looked over her shoulders and called: 'Snap into it, boys! You offered to pace me, not chase me.' "[32] For a fragile male ego, Sears could surely be something of a test.

It may have been inevitable that some would see a connection, if not an equation, between sport and masculinity and thus look askance at those women who engaged in sport with special skill and success. Athletic clothing for women in the first decades of the century has been described by one observer as "masculinized," at least in some sports, possibly because the women "were entering the male domain—the sports world."[33] Meanwhile, the bloomer costume increasingly fell into disrepute. Advanced as a compromise between the demands of health and the strictures of Victorian social custom, the bloomer and its derivatives faltered before the "mannish" simplicity of dress for riding and before functionally determined clothing such as women's one-piece bathing suits.[34] In the latter case, dedication to athletic excellence and internalized commitment hinted at male gender identification; in the former a similar effect followed from the imitation of external style.

The social origins of those women athletes who were prominent in the first decades of the century further suggest that public excellence in women's sport lay uncomfortably on the edge of middle-class respectability. Upper-class women typically excelled in sports where the clientele was more restrictive and exclusive, such as tennis and golf. At the same time, the working class tended to provide players for games such as basketball.[35] In either case, the taste and customs of the middle class were skirted.[36]

Cases were varied. Track star Eleanor Egg, who competed in every Women's National AAU Track and Field Championship from 1923 to 1932 and set numerous track-and-field records, started as an acrobat in her parents' vaudeville act. She had already crossed the border into public entertainment long before setting foot on the cinders.[37]

But perhaps "Babe" Didrikson proved to be among the most troubling—and troublesome—cases for those who believed women to be psychologically and physiologically weaker than men and so saw highly competitive sport to be properly restricted to males. Didrikson was born on 26 June 1911, into a culture that at once boosted commercialized sport but prized the amateur ethic, especially for women. The underlying reasons for this distinctive approach towards women's sport remain the subject of debate. But it would appear that amateurism took on a powerful romantic aura, even though public attention was drawn to professional sport. At the same time, the old consensus among various elites that amateur sport genuinely transformed personal character fell into some disrepair. Didrikson broke the mold of the idealized woman amateur—not so much by actual violation of amateur rules but by a lack of concern to seem to be a part of the system. Although Didrikson defended herself against charges that she had permitted her name and photograph to be used in automobile advertisements, and forced the AAU to restore the amateur eligibility they had stripped from her, she refused reinstatement. Quoted in the *New York Times* on 6 December 1932, she said that she had preferred to make "a few playful, and I think justified, comments on the inordinate lengths and multiplicity of their rules and regulations."[38]

This was hardly the way to cultivate the fondness of men and women who thought female athleticism must be tightly circumscribed. Avery Brundage, for one, responded by saying "the Greeks were right" in barring women from sport. The problem—in a societal sense—was that Didrikson did not seem to care. Such independence conflicted with the commercial promoter's desire to exert control, with the traditionalist's gender-discriminatory limitation of women's proper sphere, and with the widely held equation of female identity with marriage and motherhood. Didrikson practiced sports that many educators in the 1920s and 1930s still believed interfered with successful pregnancy— shot put, javelin, and high jump—by supposedly making the chest "inflexible." Concerns over Didrikson's sexual identity showed themselves in frequent description of her as a "tomboy." Until her marriage to George Zaharias, the questions persisted, inspiring her to tell a reporter in January 1933: "Don't ask me whether or not I'm going to get married. That is the first question women reporters ask. And that is why I hate those darn old women reporters."[39]

Even marriage would not necessarily establish suitable sex-role identification for the woman athlete. In "Babe" Didrikson's case, the problem may have been complicated by marriage, on 23 December 1938, to a "fringe" sports entertainer, the wrestler George Zaharias. It was a moot point how much respectability Didrikson could win from a marital match with "The Weeping Greek," who played a cowardly villain in the ring.

Didrikson's manner and tone as well as her actual accomplishments in sport continued to moot her gender identification. A notable instance came in an intended boxing match with Babe Ruth. "I never met the Babe," she was quoted as saying, "but, gee, I'd like to put the gloves on with him for a while." Suggesting that she might prepare in earnest and showing no apprehension at all, she added: "Boy, how I can punch that bag." How the two contestants might have fared and whether the event would have become an incident of the "great male hope" will never be known. Ruth canceled. In a charity golf match with Didrikson, comedian Bob Hope playfully added to the portrayal of her in masculine terms. "I hit the ball like a girl," Hope said, "and she hits it like a man." As Karen Epstein has observed, Didrikson was commonly referred to as an "athlete" rather than a "girl athlete" or "lady athlete" and seemed to stand apart from other women intentionally.[40]

And Didrikson was no isolated case. The popular tennis star Helen Wills, much acclaimed for her 1924 match with Suzanne Lenglen of France, advocated shortened skirts, sleeveless blouses, and bare legs as imperative in improving the women's game. In 1928, Gertrude Ederle received a rousing ticker-tape reception in New York after swimming the English Channel, breaking the previous records of male swimmers. And Eleanor Holm was praised by sportswriter Paul Gallico as a better swimmer-athlete than any of her male counterparts. Such famous sportswomen were on the cutting edge of change, along with actresses such as Joan Crawford, Marlene Dietrich, and Katharine Hepburn, whom historian Lois Banner has called "tough" and "resilient."[41] The adoption of "masculine" dress and behavioral style widened the options for women, but it could not cancel out all the fears that females would themselves become "masculinized" and demeaned.

Although Didrikson's case was highly visible given her athletic excellence and her considerable self-possession, it still suggested the dilemma that faced women athletes more generally through much of the twentieth century. They entered a sporting world riddled with stereotypical images of female athletes and restrictive assumptions about women's physical and emotional limits. Seen one way, women's ability to perform effectively in defiance of the prevailing stereotypes should have been sufficient reason to question the stereotypes. Yet, as the treatment of Didrikson suggests, it was equally possible to question the gender identity and even the sexual character of those athletes tainted by excellence. It may be argued that, great as Didrikson's athletic achievements were, her final social acceptance came only when she had passed beyond athletic success and emerged as a *mater dolorosa* and moral paragon during her fight with cancer. Although not literally a mother, she had become the "mother of us all."

Residual Fears and Growing Opportunity

In the years after the Second World War and especially from the 1960s onward, women won broader opportunities for their self-expression and for personal and professional fulfillment. That problems remained betrayed a drag-anchor of residual fears, as well as the simple fact that perfect freedom and perfect fulfilment are overambitious aims irrespective of gender. But in one area especially, strides were made that had special and powerful significance for the reception accorded women athletes—the realm of sexual liberation. By exploring male and female sexuality, one could not only discern prejudice and bias but also discriminate between sex and gender. As a result, some diminution of the traditional bias against women athletes rooted in sex roles and in sex-related physiology proved possible.

Possible—but neither automatic nor inevitable. Often changes in views came only after a long fight. And so it was no cause for wonder that athletes sometimes felt compelled to draw attention to emblems of the prevalent mainstream notion of femininity. Even in 1961, Wilma Rudolph emphasized that, although she had occasionally played basketball with her ten brothers, "it doesn't mean that I'm a tomboy." As recorded in a *New York Times* article, she added to her affirmation of traditional femininity by "[pointing] to her bright plaid skirt for emphasis and then fingered the delicate gold buttons on her purple bodice." She "glanced apologetically" at the black slippers she wore instead of high heels, which she insisted she preferred except that "my legs get too tired if I wear them before a race."[42]

But by the end of the 1960s and certainly in the 1970s, much had been accomplished, notably by outstanding individuals such as Billie Jean King. Such persons not only proved that women could be excellent athletes but also showed themselves to be able entrepreneurs. By developing magazines devoted to women's sport, moreover, and by similar business moves, they suggested the worthiness, if not the exact parity, of women's sport applying the full apparatus of men's sport to women's. Since sport itself had achieved recognition as serious business, moreover, it could piggyback on the general ideology of women's liberation and thus avoid being boxed off as a marginal amusement, as had happened at the turn of the century.

Billie Jean King's ability to avoid total disaster upon disclosure of her lesbian relationship while maintaining a non-traditional marriage with her husband, Larry King, suggested that sexual fears concerning women athletes had been muted somewhat by the beginning of the 1980s. Meanwhile, Dr. Renee Richards overcame the initial scramble to mesh the rules of sport with the capabilities of modern medicine—for example, was a transsexual, now female, to be bound by prior experience and record in men's tennis? Relatively soon (and once it sank in that a sex-change operation was not likely to become a standard means for a mediocre male player to become a superior female athlete), Richards became widely recognized as an effective coach, associated with Martina Navratilova, and was often caught in close-up shots by television cameramen covering major tennis tournaments. Although it risks irony to say it of Richards, it was clearly true of King that she forced re-examination of what it meant to be female—and specifically what it meant to be a female and an athlete. Her aggressive style of play, still somewhat regrettably dubbed "masculine" and "a man's game," nonetheless became a model for other talented women, spreading a new definition of what a woman could be in the world of sport. The *New York Times* commented on King in this light on 15 May 1981, saying: "By her brash aggressiveness, she made it more acceptable for women to push themselves."[43] Even so, it is crucial to note that one of King's champion successors, Chris Evert Lloyd, was portrayed in the tradition of ladylike reserve and personal discipline. No single model for the woman athlete sufficed.

To be sure, the combination of women's athletic excellence and their growing activism in social, economic, and political affairs did much to expand the opportunities available to the outstanding female athlete. So, too, the legitimation of sport as a component of mass entertainment and mass culture blunted the old charges of eccentricity or freakishness. But the reduction in the sex-related fears among both men and women was at least as crucial; and this required not merely a tactical victory over male social authority but, more significantly, a substantial redirection of thinking. The "millennium" had not arrived with the likes of Billie Jean King and Martina Navratilova. But at least the residue of fear had fallen low enough so athletic excellence could hold its own against private life.

Notes

1. B. F. Boller, "Physical Training," *Mind and Body* 7 (April 1900), 25–26. The male adult Boller here was writing in the guise of an imaginary little girl eager for physical education and play outdoors.

2. Dudley Allen Sargent, *An Autobiography* (Philadelphia, 1927), p. 36. Physical educator Sargent specifically suggested that the girls' efforts in play and sport would make them less of a sexual threat to the coeval boys who would not as yet be able to resist curious advances from too-dominating females.

3. Mildred "Babe" Didrikson Zaharias, *This Life I've Lived* (London, 1956), p. 103. She also noted that Mary Lena Falk was known as "the tomboy from Thomasville, Georgia" and Patsy Berg as "the Minnesota Tomboy."

4. Frank R. Rossiter, *Charles Ives and His America* (New York, 1975), pp. 31–32.

5. A useful study of John Todd appears in G. J. Barker-Benfield, *The Horrors of the Half-Known Life: Male Attitudes Toward Women and Sexuality in Nineteenth Century America* (New York, 1976). An extended speculation on the relationship of such thinking to the gender-typing of public action and to male dominance in sport appears in Donald J. Mrozek, *Sport and American Mentality* (Knoxville, 1983), pp. 232–33.

6. James H. Jackson, *The Sexual Organism and Its Healthful Management* (Boston, 1861; reprint, New York, 1974), especially pp. 54–55 concerning play. It must be emphasized, however, that Jackson's primary remedy for masturbation was not exercise but diet, including the avoidance of horseradish and spices, which he thought confirmed the practice of "secret vice." Concerning such remedies to masturbation, see Jackson's chapter, innocently entitled, "Masturbation, How It Arises, How It Is Kept Up," pp. 60–86.

7. Wolfgang Lederer, *The Fear of Women* (New York, 1968).

8. Ibid., pp. vii–viii.

9. Lederer, *The Fear of Women*, pp. 36, 105.

10. Charles Rosenberg, "Sexuality, Class and Role," in *No Other Gods: On Science and American Social Thought* (Baltimore, 1961, 1962, 1976), p. 75.

11. Ibid.

12. Lois W. Banner, *American Beauty* (New York, 1983), p. 244.

13. Alice B. Stockham, *Tokology: A Book for Every Woman* (Chicago, 1886). Also see Stockham, *Karezza, Ethics of Marriage* (Chicago, 1896).

14. Rosenberg, *No Other Gods*, p. 79.

15. Anna Garlin Spencer, *Woman's Share in Social Culture* (Philadelphia, 1912), pp. 149–51. It should be noted that Spencer adopted a strongly accommodationist or "conservative" viewpoint; and, although she recognized the "spinster" as demonstrating female equality with men in some "specialized" tasks, she clearly agreed with the view that the mother and housewife "did something far more vital for race development" (p. 150).

16. Ibid., p. 115.

17. Rosenberg, *No Other Gods*, pp. 54–70, 80.

18. See, for example, Barker-Benfield, *The Horrors of the Half-Known Life*.

19. See, for example, Banner, *American Beauty*, pp. 254–55. It is worth noting, also, that Barnum was a key promoter of wrestling events. In making no distinction between salable sport and other commercially viable forms of entertainment, Barnum was both out of step with the sport "reformers" of the last third of the nineteenth century and a harbinger of a crucial—perhaps even predominant—thrust in sport and entertainment during the twentieth century.

20. Banner, *American Beauty*, p. 255.

21. Concerning the reluctance of prominent women to support strong athletic competition for women and girls, see Banner, *American Beauty*, pp. 286–87.

22. Inez Haynes Irwin, *Angels and Amazons: A Hundred Years of American Women* (Garden City, N.Y., 1934). Also see Margaret W. Rossiter, *Women Scientists in America: Struggles and Strategies to 1940* (Baltimore, 1982). The difficulty of pursuing "the possibilities of independence" is a theme in Peter Gabriel Filene, *Him/Her/Self: Sex Roles in Modern America* (New York, 1974), p. 52 and passim.

23. Amram Scheinfeld, *Women and Men* (New York, 1943), pp. 274–80.

24. Scheinfeld also said that menstruation severely inhibited athletic participation, and noted that the promoters of the "Aquacade" at the New York World's Fair had kept extra swimmers ready so that women could be kept out of the pool for four days during their menstrual cycles but that some women still seemed oblivious to the "fact" that they were supposed to perform badly at such times and managed somehow to overcome their purported debility. Scheinfeld, *Women and Men*, p. 281.

25. Banner, *American Beauty*, pp. 257–58.

26. Ibid., p. 278.

27. Lynn Emery, "World Renowned Champion Amazon: Jaguarina" (paper presented at the 11th annual conference of the North American Society for Sport History, Mont Alto, Pa., May 1983).

28. The use of pagan imagery as a means of exempting oneself from the strictures of Victorian culture is discussed in Mrozek, *Sport and American Mentality*, pp. 212–13.

29. Emery, "World Renowned Champion Amazon."

30. Ibid., 8.

31. See, for example, Karen V. Epstein, "Social Perceptions of Four Prominent Female Athletes during the Twentieth Century in the United States" (paper presented at the 11th annual conference of the North American Society for Sport History, Mont Alto, Pa., May 1983).

32. Ibid.

33. See Emelia-Louis Kilby, "Changing Clothes in Women's Sports: 1895–1940" (paper presented at the 11th annual conference of the North American society for Sport History, Mont Alto, Pa., May 1983).

34. Ibid.

35. See, for example, Epstein, "Social Perceptions of Four Prominent Female Athletes."

36. As Lois Banner has suggested, it was possible to stage a female beauty pageant in Rehoboth Beach, Maryland, as early as 1880 without scandal or interference, largely because it was a working-class resort. In Atlantic City, however, it took much effort and a considerable length of time before a format could be developed that fused the lower-class "carnival" and the upper-class "festival" and added the overlay of health consciousness. See Banner, *American Beauty*, especially pp. 266–67.

37. See J. Thomas Jable, "The Acrobat on the Athletic Field: Eleanor Egg, New Jersey Early Track and Field Champion and Record Holder" (paper presented at the 11th annual conference of the North American Society for Sport History, Mont Alto, Pa., May 1983).

38. See Epstein, "Social Perceptions of Four Prominent Female Athletes." Also concerning her career, see Zaharias, *This Life I've Lived;* William Oscar Johnson and Nancy P. Williamson, *Whatta-Girl: The Babe Didrikson Story* (Boston, 1975).

39. Quoted in Epstein, "Social Perceptions of Four Prominent Female Athletes."

40. Ibid.

41. Banner, *American Beauty*, pp. 275–76.

42. Quoted in Epstein, "Social Perceptions of Four Prominent Female Athletes."

43. Quoted in ibid.

8
Sports and Eros

ALLEN GUTTMANN

When Athenian youths ran races or hurled the discus, when Spartan girls wrestled one another by the banks of the Eurotas, everyone seems to have understood that physically trained bodies, in motion or at rest, can be sexually attractive. The erotic aspects of sports, welcomed by most of the ancients, have always been obvious to the *critics* of sports, then and now. Tertullian's complaints, uttered in the second century A.D., were echoed in 1934 by Cardinal Rodrigue Villeneuve of Quebec. He condemned the "pagan" cult of the body as manifested in sports and deprecated the rampant concern for "hysterical strength, sensual pleasure, and the development of the human animal." For centuries, however, lovers of sports, spectators as well as athletes, have discussed their passion as if the sensual pleasure in sports had no connection whatsoever with human sexuality. They have denied rather than defended the association of eros and sports. Whenever, for instance, outraged religious traditionalists have called attention to the erotic appeal of the female body at play, progressive reformers have blandly explained that sunlight, fresh air, and unencumbered movement were their only motives. No wonder that the interminable debates over sportswear for women left both sides frustrated and unhappy.[1]

When Protestant clergymen invented "Muscular Christianity" in the mid–nineteenth century, when Pope Pius XII decided in 1945 to affirm the value of modern sports, there was no sudden acceptance of what had been condemned, no reconsideration of the erotic element in sports. Quite the contrary. Christian propagandists for sports seemed to become blind to the sexual dimensions that had been anathema to their clerical predecessors. Ironically, once the mainstream churches took to celebrations of the joy of sports, a number of secular critics, mostly Marxists, began to deplore the "sexualization" of women's (but not of men's) sports. We seem now to be in the midst of what Margaret Hunt has aptly termed "the de-eroticization of women's liberation."[2]

While some of the more ascetic Marxist critics seem to have resurrected Tertullian's indictments of sports, social scientists of a more empirical bent seem to have entered into a conspiracy to avoid mentioning (in public) the erotic element in sports. Numerous studies have documented the fact that exercise programs result in an "improved body-image." The implications of this fact are seldom explored. European and American psychologists and sociologists have discussed an array of motivations for sports participation, including an aesthetic dimension. They are reluctant to acknowledge (in public) that "fitness" and "to be in shape" are often euphemisms for the desire to be sexually attractive. Yves LePogam edged closer to candor when he referred in a careful sociological study to the quest for "un corps conformé aux canons de beauté," at which point he, too, seemed eager to drop the epistemological hot potato.[3]

Recognition of simple truths known thousands of years ago is blocked because the topic of eros and sports is obviously, for many people, athletes and spectators both, a taboo, a source of shame and denial. To say this is most emphatically *not* to say that all sports have an erotic aspect or that all athletes are sexually attractive. The heady rediscovery of the erotic component in sports need not impel one to assert, as Christian Messenger does, that the "presentation of female athletes is . . . always eroticized by the fact that . . . any movement of the female body is erotic."[4] The sad truth is that some men and women will, inevitably, deem some male and female athletes, in motion or at rest, unattractive or even repulsive. Nonetheless, to insist that there is *no* connection between eros and sports is nonsense. Happily, the anxious denial of a connection has become less and less plausible.

When Hollywood stripped Johnny Weissmuller of his Olympic swimsuit, wrapped him in a loincloth, and filmed him in the role of Tarzan, the dreammerchants knew what they were doing. Katherine Albert, writing in *Photoplay*, marveled that "a lad who had never been in a picture before, who had been interested in nothing but swimming all his life, and who frankly admits he can't act, is the top-notch heart flutterer of the year."[5]

A generation later, Jean-Claude Killy, the French skier, became an international heartthrob. George Best, the Irish soccer star, joined the Beatles and Mick Jagger as a "teenage 'pin-up.'" Joe Namath marketed his sex appeal almost as successfully as he sold his skills as a quarterback for the New York Jets. Speaking about Canadian football players, anthropologist Robert A. Stebbins remarks mildly that they, too, are "attractive to the opposite sex." Thelma McCormack has anatomized Hollywood prizefight films as a form of "jock appeal." For the benefit of readers who have managed to remain oblivious to

their own culture, R. M. Lerner has conducted psychological research in order to prove that women find athletic men attractive.[6]

In regard to female athletes, too, there is now somewhat less hypocrisy
about sports and eros. Australian sportswriter Keith Dunston confesses, "I
think I am turned on by Martina."[7] "Men," remarks American pentathlete
Jane Frederick, "go cuckoo for me." She is obviously not offended: "As long as
I love my body, everyone else does, too."[8] Noticing that sex and sports are both
forms of physical expression, runner Lynda Huey is equally forthright: "Physical strength added to the whole sexual experience. How can anyone want
anyone but an athlete? . . . Athletes love physical expression and sex is one of
the best forms of it."[9] Ordinary women have admitted that a devotion to
sports has done more than improve their cardiovascular fitness. "Sports,"
comments a thirty-seven-year-old softball player, make "me feel more attractive . . . I feel sleeker, more fit, more feminine. And that carries over to my
marriage."[10] Women who play in the National Women's Football League say
that their game has transformed them into better lovers.[11]

In the 1980s, mainstream women's magazines became explicit about sports
and eros. In April 1983, for instance, *Cosmopolitan* crowed that body builders
are "shaplier, firmer, *sexier!*"[12] For advertisers who pay large sums for the right
to display "Flo-Jo" in full stride, the message seems equally obvious. Of course,
the advertisers have never hesitated to lure consumers with beautiful bodies,
male as well as female. Documentation of this fact is hardly necessary for anyone alive and well in the 1990s. That newspapers and magazines now have a
special penchant for sexually attractive female athletes is equally evident.

Almost as obvious is the way that sports promoters have capitalized on
men's desire to observe women's movements (as opposed to the Women's
Movement). When the movements are intrinsic to the sport, as was the case
when Colonel McCoombs dressed the "Golden Cyclones" in shorts and jerseys, feminist sensibilities are alerted; when the clothing worn and the poses
struck are no longer related to the sport in question, the ethical alarm goes off.
During the frantic attempt to keep the failing Women's Basketball League
alive, promoters marketed posters of Molly Bolin in shorts and a tank top. The
posters sold; the tickets didn't.[13] In 1981, the Ladies Professional Golf Association hired Ray Volpe to improve the appeal of women's golf with
photographs of Laura Baugh and other beautiful golfers. Australia's Jan
Stephenson suddenly appeared in *Fairway*—in bed with a seductive display of
leg.[14] *Fairway* followed this tasteless act with facsimile scenes from sexy films.
It was "a shoddy way to sell golf."[15] More abysmal yet was *Vogue's* April 1990
issue, in which tennis star Steffi Graf posed in "a black Norma Kamali maillot

dress, adjusting her high heel and aiming her décolletage lensward."[16] What the perpetrators of these travesties fail to understand is that the erotic appeal of the female athlete is to a large degree sport-specific. Bolin, Baugh, Stephenson, and Graf are unusually attractive because of the way they move and have moved—*as athletes*. The marvel of their athletic performances eroticizes them as a maillot dress cannot. In fact, an athletic body in an evening gown can cause the same kind of cognitive dissonance as obesity in a track suit.

A number of radical feminists, especially those influenced by Marxism, have waged an energetic and often-bitter campaign against the commercial exploitation of the attractiveness that, they allege, transforms women into commodities. European and American neo-Marxists have sounded variations on themes long familiar to church-goers (and to mosque-goers, too). They have, for instance, condemned the attempt of interested parties to take advantage of the female athlete's "erotic exchange value."[17] Their attack goes beyond the assault on sports promoters, media programmers, and advertisers who use women's bodies to sell tickets, boost ratings, and market products. They also deplore the efforts of women who jog, play tennis, or lift weights in order to brighten their image in the eyes of the opposite sex. Quoting poet Adrienne Rich on heterosexuality as "a beachhead of male dominance," Helen Lenskyj maintains that "a woman's conformity to male-defined standards of heterosexual attractiveness signifies her acquiescence to men's rules."[18]

While admitting that some women have benefited from sports and from the fitness fad, Nancy Theberge still alleges that programs promising enhanced sexual attractiveness represent "not the liberation of women in sport, but their continued oppression through the sexualization of physical activity."[19] After warning in an article that sports are potentially voyeuristic, Margaret Carlisle Duncan has written a sharply focused attack on the alleged "soft-core pornography" in media coverage of women's sorts. Analyzing 186 photographs from the 1984 and 1988 Olympic Games, she notes the intense media interest in sexually attractive athletes like Katarina Witt and Florence Griffith-Joyner. Such athletes are portrayed in ways that emphasize the sexual difference between men and women. Witt, for instance, is shown with "her lipsticked lips drawn up in an exaggerated pout" while four Romanian gymnasts are photographed from behind as they bend over to congratulate their Chinese rivals—a pose that according to Duncan, accentuates the gymnasts' small stature and makes them seem submissive and sexually accessible. "This is a potentially dangerous combination because it sexualizes a child image and gives viewers visual power over that image."[20] Reviewing the film *Personal Best* for *Jump Cut* magazine, Linda Williams approved of the portrayal of female athletes who were both "tough and compassionate," but she was irked that the women were presented "as so many trained seals flexing their muscles to male awe and approval."[21] (What Williams does *not* acknowledge is the film's recognition that women, too, can find athletic women sexually attractive.)

Women who allegedly acquiesce in their own humiliation have not escaped castigation by militant feminists. Margaret MacNeill, for instance, has condemned female athletes who collaborate in the repressions of patriarchal capitalism. Specifically, her ire is aroused less by Florence Griffith-Joyner's iridescent fingernails than by television's treatment of female bodybuilders whose sexuality is accentuated by voyeuristic camera angles. "Patriarchy," she charges, "is thus reproduced in a newly negotiated form that attracts women by the range of narcissistic commodities."[22] Small wonder that anger sometimes builds to the point where modern sports per se are rejected as wholly evil.

What one makes of all of this is obviously related not only to one's analytic powers and mastery of the evidence but also to one's philosophical stance and personal values. The total rejection of modern sports in the name of play, often deemed "feminine" rather than "masculine," is a topic I have discussed more than once.[23] The specific charge that sports are an exploitation of female sexuality requires comment.

I can easily imagine that we might all be better off if advertisements were purely objective statements about the availability of a newly designed automobile, the latest vintage of Beaujolais, or a long-awaited scholarly history of women's sports, but I cannot foresee an austerely rational world in which this kind of advertisement replaces the frantic hype that presently dominates the print and electronic media.

If one understands that advertisements are here to stay and that most advertisements will use physically attractive rather than unattractive models, male as well as female, one can deal with what, for me, is the root question for anyone concerned about the relationship between eros and sports. Why have so many radical feminists condemned the men who have admired physically fit women and their sports performances and why have they sought to discourage women eager for that admiration? Might they not, more logically, have demanded women's right to admire—and even to be erotically stimulated by—physically fit men and *their* sports performances? Although thoughtful scholars are properly leery of efforts to legitimize culture by references to nature, there does seem to be some biological justification for mutual attraction between men and women. Recognition of the legitimacy of this phenomenon need not be tantamount to "compulsory heterosexuality" if we are ready also to recognize, as the film *Personal Best* does, that men and women can also be moved, stirred, excited, and sometimes erotically attracted by athletes of their own sex.

Fears of violence committed against women are certainly involved in the condemnation of an erotic response to sports. Eros, it is argued, is nothing but a fancy name for lust. It motivates men to commit rape and other acts of violence against women. Since the erotic component is ineradicable, this line of argument leads logically to the inescapable conclusion that sports ought to be abolished—along with ballet, modern dance, and most other forms of physical expression. But is there any reason to believe that men who find active women attractive, as dancers or as athletes, are therefore more likely to commit violence against them or against any other woman? I doubt that there is. The undeniable fact that adolescent girls and grown women are sexually attracted to male athletes certainly does not impel *them* to seduce the first hapless male who ambles into their field of vision. The argument that eros drives us to acts of violence reduces us all to the status of Pavlovian dogs.

How can one answer the related argument that men who have erotic fantasies about female athletes are not treating these women as *persons?* The best response is that the charge is often true. The focus on the merely physical *is* partial. But modern societies require partial relationships and differentiated roles as well as the I-Thou relationships celebrated by modern piety. Admiration of Placido Domingo's disembodied voice implies no judgment whatsoever about him as a person. Humanistic philosophers urge us to treat people as ends rather than as means, but do such philosophers really want the clerk at the checkout counter and the attendant at the gas pump to take a serious interest in their personal lives? Civilization is built on civility. Intimacy is for intimates.

Some radical feminists have also, as we have seen, charged that sports spectators and sports reporters who concentrate on the appearance of female athletes neglect their performance. There is considerable truth to this accusation (as there is some truth to the related accusation that moviegoers frequently idolize bad actors with good looks). The television camera that skips over the drama of a sports contest in order to linger over "honey shots" trivializes sports. The spectator who admires the performer and ignores the performance might just as well depart from the stadium and scurry to the burlesque theater. We are not, however, trapped in an either-or situation that forces a choice between the athlete and the performance. Motivations are mixed; responses are complex. The athletic body is an inscription of the sports performance. While it may be trite to quote William Butler Yeats on the inextricability of actor from act, no one has said it better than he. How *can* we tell the dancer from the dance? Why *should* we? One can gasp at Katarina Witt's skill as a figure skater, admire her courage as a competitor, shiver with delight at the beauty of her movements, and simultaneously be stirred by the erotic appeal of her gliding, whirling, spinning, leaping figure. Why not have it all?

Notes

1. Villeneuve quoted in Jean Harvey, "Sport and the Quebec Clergy, 1930–1960," *Not Just a Game*, ed. Jean Harvey and Hart Cantelon (Ottawa: University of Ottawa Press, 1988), p. 74. On the wrangle over sportswear, see Phillis Cunnington and Alan Mansfield, *English Costume for Sports and Outdoor Recreation* (London: Adam and Charles Black, 1969); Judith Elaine Leslie, "Sports Fashions as a Reflection of the Changing Role of American Women" (Ph.D., University of North Carolina at Greensboro, 1985); Jihang Park, "Sport, Dress Reform and the Emancipation of Women in Victorian England," *International Journal of the History of Sport* (May 1989) 6(1): 10–30.

2. Margaret Hunt, "The De-Eroticization of Women's Liberation," *Feminist Review* (spring 1990) 34: 23–46.

3. Yves LePogam, *Démocratisation du Sport* (Paris: Jean-Pierre Delarge, 1979), p. 86. For a more detailed discussion, see Allen Guttmann, "Sport and Eros," *Essays in Sport History and Sport Mythology*, ed. Donald G. Kyle and Gary D. Stark (Texas A & M Press, 1990), pp. 139–54; for some tentative empirical explorations of the links between sports and sexuality, see Gordon W. Russell, Veronica E. Horn, and Mary J. Huddle, "Male Responses to Female Aggression," *Social Behavior and Personality* (1988) 16(1): 51–57; Gordon W. Russell, Sherry L. DiLullo, and Dany DiLullo, "Effects of Observing Competitive and Violent Versions of a Sport," *Current Psychology* (winter 1989) 7(4): 312–21.

4. Christian K. Messenger, "The Inscription of Women in American Sports Fictional Narrative," *Heldenmythen und Korperqualen*, ed. Handa Fischer (Clausthal-Zellerfeld: DVS, 1989), p. 83.

5. Albert quoted in Donald J. Mrozek, "Sport in American Life," *Fitness in American Culture*, ed. Kathryn Grover (Amherst: University of Massachusetts Press, 1989), p. 39.

6. Richard Holt, *Sport and the British* (Oxford: Clarendon Press, 1989), p. 324; Robert A. Stebbins, *Canadian Football* (London, Ontario: University of Western Ontario Press, 1987), p. 157; Thelma McCormack, "Hollywood's Prizefight Films," *Journal of Sport and Social Issues* (1984) 8(2): 19; R. M. Lerner, "Some Female Stereotypes of Male Bodybuild/Behavior Relations," *Perceptual and Motor Skills* (1969) 28: 363–66.

7. Dunston quoted in Claire Louise Williams, Geoffrey Lawrence, and David Rose, "Patriarchy, Media, and Sport," *Power Play: Essays in the Sociology of Australian Sport* (Sydney: Hale and Iremonger, 1986), p. 220.

8. Frederick quoted in Janice Kaplan, *Women and Sports* (New York: Viking, 1979), p. 77.

9. Lynda Huey, *A Running Start* (New York: Quadrangle Books, 1976), pp. 204, 209.

10. Quoted in Judith A. DiIorio, "Feminism, Gender, and the Ethnographic Study of Sport," *Arena Review* (May 1989) 13(1): 53.

11. John Bridges, "Women's Professional Football and the Changing Role of the Woman Athlete," *American Sport Culture*, ed. Wiley L. Umphlett (Lewisberg, Pa., 1985), p. 146.

12. *Cosmopolitan* quoted in Helen Lenskyj, *Out of Bounds* (Toronto: The Women's Press, 1986), p. 135.

13. Ted Vincent, *Mudville's Revenge* (New York: Seaview Books, 1981), p. 322.

14. Brian Stoddart, *Saturday Afternoon Fever* (North Ryde: Angus and Robertson, 1986), p. 155.

15. Adrianne Blue, *Grace Under Pressure* (London: Sidgwick and Jackson, 1987), p. 110; Jaime Diaz, "Find the Golf Here?" *Sports Illustrated* (February 13, 1989) 70: 58–64.

16. Alexander Wolff, "Oh La La, Steffi!" *Sports Illustrated* (April 23, 1990) 72(17): 45.

17. Christine Kulke, "Emanzipation oder gleiches Recht auf 'Trimm Dich?,'" *Sport in der Klassengesellschaft*, ed. Gerhard Vinnai (Frankfort: Fischer, 1972), p. 101; see also Jean-Marie Brohm, *Critiques du Sport* (Paris: Christian Bourgeois, 1976), p. 238. Michel Caillat, on the other hand, condemns sports as a bourgeois plot to "neutralize desire and assure the defeat of sexuality"; see *l'Idéologie du Sport en France* (Montreuil: Editions de la Passion, 1989), p. 151.

18. Lenskyj, *Out of Bounds*, p. 56.

19. Nancy Theberge, "Sport and Women's Empowerment," *Women's Studies International Forum* (1987) 10(4): 389.

20. Margaret Carlisle Duncan and Barry Brummett, "Types and Sources of Spectating Pleasure in Televised Sports," *Sport Sociology Journal* (September 1989) 6(3): 195–211; Margaret Carlisle Duncan, "Sports Photographs and Sexual Difference: Images of Women and Men in the 1984 and 1988 Olympic Games," *Sport Sociology Journal* (March 1990) 7(1): 22–43.

21. Williams quoted in Dorothy Kidd, "Getting Physical: Compulsory Heterosexuality and Sport," *Canadian Woman Studies* (spring 1983) 4(3): 63–64. Thelma McCormack also found the film "a travesty of liberation"; "Hollywood's Prizefight Films," 27.

22. Margaret MacNeill, "Active Women, Media Representations, and Ideology," *Not Just a Game*, p. 209. See also Michael A. Messner's fears that the vogue of women's bodybuilding will "replicate many of the more commercialized, narcissistic, and physically unhealthy aspects of men's athletics"; "Sports and Male Domination," *Sociology of Sport Journal* (September 1988) 5(3): 204.

23. Allen Guttmann, *From Ritual to Record* (New York: Columbia University Press, 1978), pp. 57–89; Allen Guttmann, "Translator's Introduction" to Bero Rigauer, *Sport and Work* (New York: Columbia University Press, 1981), p. vii–xxxi.

PART 3
CLASS, RACE, AND ETHNICITY

9

The Meanings of Prizefighting

ELLIOTT J. GORN

Working-Class Culture in Antebellum Cities

The rise of the ring was a complex phenomenon, an integral part of American social and cultural development. On one level, the great champions were not just heroes but celebrities in the sense that their fame depended at least partly on commercialized media. Newspaper stories, cheap biographies, lithographs, and photographs all helped raise public interest and disseminate the names and deeds of fistic heroes. The public personas of the champions were now marketable goods, giving them fame beyond their class and community. However, commercialized cultural production was in its embryonic stages. Even the great champions, Sullivan, Hyer, and Morrissey, were not alienated from their origins; they remained well-known figures on the urban streets, influential yet approachable men with whom one might share a bottle or play a hand of cards. Fame was not merely a product of impersonal media but was based on intimate knowledge of local customs and institutions. Heroic deeds of prowess and bravado were known firsthand.[1]

By the 1850s boxing was arguably America's preeminent sport—certainly the championship fights were among the greatest spectacles of the decade—but its popularity was not uniformly spread throughout the population. Despite the efforts of Frank Queen and his likes to argue the utility of the ring in Victorian terms, respectable native-born Americans rejected such claims. Pugilism, in other words, did not simply "mirror" American culture. Although it could be argued that boxing reflected such mainstream values as individualism, the will to succeed, and materialism, the ring remained primarily a working-class preserve and conveyed a working-class sensibility.

The ring's social isolation occurred during a period when Americans' interest in sports was expanding. Certainly influential citizens were more accepting of leisure and recreation on the eve of the Civil War than they had

226 ELLIOTT J. GORN

been twenty years earlier. The hard shell of Victorian morality remained intact, but by the late antebellum era small cracks were appearing on its brittle surface. Reformers such as Thomas Wentworth Higginson, William Ellery Channing, and even Henry War Beecher believed that man could improve himself in body as well as spirit, so they advocated fresh air and exercise as antidotes to the ills of cramped urban life. Spectator sports enjoyed newfound popularity as rowing regattas, trotting matches, and pedestrian races became very popular among diverse Americans. A few well-off men displayed their status in baseball, cricket, and yachting clubs, pastimes that required large amounts of leisure time. An occasional young rakehell, for instance Frederick Van Wyck, son of a wealthy mercantile family, even showed up at urban dives such as Tommy Norris's Livery Stable: "When you start with a dog fight as a curtain raiser," Van Wyck reminisced, "continue with a cock fight, then rat baiting, next a prize fight, then a battle of billy goats, and then a boxing match between two ladies, with nothing but trunks on—after that I think you have a night's entertainment that has enough spice—not to say tabasco sauce—to fill the most rapacious needs."[2]

Perhaps experiences like those of the young Van Wyck were more common than the surviving evidence indicates. But for most of the middle and upper classes, Victorian propriety still hedged recreations onto narrow ground, and even leisured bons vivants usually shunned the more raucous pastimes of the English sporting gentry, confining themselves to such activities as yachting and horse racing. Much of the liberalization that occurred before the Civil War gained impetus from a handful of reformers who argued for rational amusements to develop character and refresh men for labor. Parks, reading rooms, and gymnasiums, it was said, led workers away from such riotous activities as prizefighting. A few bold individuals, among them Oliver Wendell Holmes, Sr., might openly attend sparring matches, write in praise of champions' physical excellence, even speculate on the outcome of a bout. Judging by the coverage in the "respectable" press, growing numbers of men were at least willing to view the ring from afar. No doubt many in the bourgeoisie envied what they perceived as the uninhibitedness of the working class and itched to break out of their own cultural confinement. But in public, at least, Victorian strictures were still too strong and the desire openly to violate them too weak to allow much deviation. The ring remained a symbol of urban depravity, proof that the lower classes wallowed in dissipation.[3]

Despite bourgeois injunctions, working-class men—including ones in old established trades, unskilled laborers, the chronically underemployed, and those in the shadows or urban vice such as gamblers, pimps, and unlicensed liquor dealers—continued to stage their own recreations. Urban growth helped provide potential audiences for commercial spectacles. In 1820 only New York City and Philadelphia contained 100,000 people; by midcentury, Boston, Baltimore, Cincinnati, and New Orleans were over the mark. New York's 1830 population of 200,000 would increase fourfold in a mere thirty years as rural migrants and foreign immigrants came in search of work. By 1855 over half of all New Yorkers had been born abroad, and three out of ten had drawn their first breath in Ireland. This large and heterogeneous population needed leisure as well as jobs and, Victorian repressions notwithstanding, the urban working class pursued boisterous amusements.[4]

But the mere growth of cities and influx of immigrants do not wholly explain boxing's appeal. Between roughly 1820 and 1860 the economic life of urban areas was transformed. Certainly by midcentury the old apprenticeship system, in which a boy learned a trade, then worked as a journeyman and acquired the skills, property, and independence of a master, was moribund. Under the old order, shopkeepers and apprentices held mutual rights and obligations; they worked and even lived under the same roof, and their relationship was in the nature of a patriarchal family. But now the venerable ideal inherent in small-scale shops—that a craftsman was as much a father to his workers as a businessman—had dissolved. Gone too was the household economy, where labor was often performed in the home by all family members. This old social organization of work had not been without tensions; apprentices, wives, and children had often chafed under domineering masters. But it offered an ideal of mutuality, faith in the honorability of labor, and a path toward modest mobility for young men.[5]

Replacing artisan traditions in many trades was a modern system of capitalist production that tended to reduce relationships between employers and employees to questions of wages or piece rates. Most young workers no longer lived in surrogate families based on craft but in boardinghouses, seedbeds of "immoral" influences. Although many native-born tradesmen still called themselves journeymen and clung to craft traditions, most had in fact become employees, "wage slaves" in the parlance of the day. Moreover, new immigrants were filling unskilled positions in such volume that by 1850, half of all Irish males were either day laborers or cartmen. Women too, both native and immigrant, now occupied large numbers of unskilled jobs, as did the masses of native-born rural migrants pouring into the cities.[6]

This new social organization of work asked both employers and employees to exercise internalized self-restraint, to subdue their impulses and discipline their passions, if they were to accumulate wealth in increasingly

competitive markets. The old republican ideology had demanded similar behavior, but the heightened importance of profit and the fear of financial failure now elevated assertive individualism over communal welfare, giving the
emergent capitalist ethos an unmistakable harshness. The increasing emphasis on productivity brought employers to demand rigid self-control from
themselves and their workers; industriousness and frugality became litmus
tests of personal worth.[7]

Workers responded in a variety of ways, but it is probably best to think of
their reactions as points along a continuum. At one extreme were those who
accepted totally the stiffened ethic of abstemiousness. Like their bosses, many
joined evangelical sects and temperance societies, merging piety and strict
morality with industrial values. As their employers had promised, some rose
through hard work to bourgeois prosperity and independence. On the opposite end of the continuum were those who rejected the safe and sober ethic,
working so that they might play. For such lovers of street life, leisure more
than labor formed the core of personal identity and cultural values. Raucous
play offered these men a temporary escape from an oppressive working environment. In the middle were workers who adopted self-control as an imple-
ment of radical reform, a tool for building a revitalized producers' culture
centered on the values of mutuality and communal improvement. Such men
were the spiritual heirs of William Cobbett, and their assiduousness was
aimed at collective improvement rather than purely individual gain.[8]

These categories are ideal types, of course, and few individuals matched
them perfectly. The radical editor Mike Walsh, for example, wrote in the
workingman's language, mixing admonitions for labor unity with endorse-
ments of Yankee Sullivan's saloon, praise for jovial "Boss" Harrington with announcements of rat-killing contests. Similarly, one as impulsive as John
Morrissey offered his name and money to shipbuilders striking for an eight-
hour workday. But on balance, activities such as prizefighting appealed to
those in the working class inclined more toward self-indulgence than toward
constant diligence, conviviality rather than abstemiousness, "the good time
coming" instead of sober self-control.[9]

The decline of the old apprenticeship system and the new emphasis on
wages gave workers reason to value wild recreations and scope to indulge
their tastes. The capitalist economy created a sharp separation of work time
from leisure time, freeing at least a few discretionary hours and dollars. Moreover, most laborers were not becoming bosses and few journeymen would
ever be masters. For many men, the realm of play more than work now held
out the best chance for finding a sense of challenge and fulfillment. Places

such as New York's Bowery offered a kaleidoscope of plebeian pleasures. Working-class males revitalized such ancient pastimes as theatergoing, drinking, gambling, and bloodsports. They also frequented houses of prostitution, dance halls, oyster bars, minstrel shows, and circuses. Men reasserted mutuality among their compatriots in countless cliques and barrooms; they upheld a masculine honor that brooked no slighting of one's status among peers; and they demonstrated physical prowess in acts of strength and daring.[10] If not on the job, then in their free time individuals took control over their lives, found refuge from bosses, and inverted the bourgeois ethos with an antithetical assertion of rough male conviviality. Away from the impersonal workplace, where their power was ebbing, journeymen, mechanics, and laborers found alternative sources of value and esteem.[11]

Within this blossoming street culture, the new working class created a plethora of voluntary associations that engendered a sense of group autonomy. Labor unions, craft organizations, and mutual-aid societies offered hope for real social and economic change. But less respectable institutions also embodied the sensibilities of many men. Saloons, fire companies, street gangs, and political organizations all had overlapping memberships, all were deeply rooted in the social structure of mid-nineteenth-century cities, and all had ties to the prize ring.[12]

Saloons were at the heart of working-class life. Cliques of men created informal but stable brotherhoods in particular bars, where politics were argued, grievances aired, heroes toasted, sports discussed, legends told, songs sung, and friendships cemented. The tavern keeper was a businessman, but he was also the caretaker of a cultural style that emphasized camaraderie and reciprocity among peers. The line separating bars from billiard halls, gambling houses, and even brothels was not always clear, because in all of these establishments, entertainment was the order of the day. Saloon keepers promoted various recreations, including dogfights, rat-baiting contests, and boxing matches, partly to sell more liquor and arrange profitable betting pools, but also to fulfill their role as leaders of working-class culture. Foot on the rail and glass in hand, a man could momentarily feel in control of his life, for here amidst friends the harshness of labor and the moral arrogance of the middle class were left behind. From the 1840s on countless boxers made particular bars their headquarters, and the saloons that prizefighters owned, managed, or frequented were made doubly popular by their presence, because boxers symbolized the successful flouting of oppressive social and cultural norms.[13]

Volunteer fire brigades also became focal institutions of the working class. Men spent their leisure hours in the pump houses playing cards, drinking, and maintaining the equipment. Once the call for a fire went out, they rushed from their homes or shops, gathered at the station house, then dragged their gear to the blaze. For men whose working lives were prosaic and unchallenging, fighting fires offered a chance for heroic community service, a real sense of adventure, and an outlet for competitive self-assertion. Because neighborhood and ethnic conflicts often made rivals of different companies, all sought tough men who were willing to battle it out with opposing brigades, sometimes while a building burned to the ground. Boxers' fighting skills and courage were real assets to the fire companies, so Yankee Sullivan was recruited as a member of the Spartan band company, named for Mike Walsh's clique of radical workers, while Tom Hyer, Jim Jerolomon, William Poole, and John McCleester joined other brigades. Similar chances for heroics and display were offered by ubiquitous volunteer militia companies.[14]

Urban street gangs such as New York's mostly Irish "Dead Rabbits" and their archrivals, the nativist "Bowery B'hoys"—made up mainly of journeymen and apprentices—overlapped the fire companies' constituencies, and again boxers were prominent members. Middle-class commentators feared that New York, Philadelphia, and Baltimore were now overrun with gangs that were committing heinous attacks on the innocent.[15] But though some of the gangs attracted social misfits who reveled in violence, most members were workers ranging in age from their teens through their thirties. The gangs were surrogate families, based on neighborhood, occupational, and ethnic affiliation. Here, as in the volunteer fire companies, laborers and apprentices turned loose after work sought adventure with their comrades. Drinking, fighting, gambling, playing sports, attending the theater, and especially promenading in distinctive dress filled their leisure hours. Because the gangs were intent on settling scores and intimidating rivals, prizefighters often became their leaders, and the Bowery B'hoys even wore "Tom Hyer hats" as part of their garb. Undomesticated by women, loving drink, and seeking distinction among peers, members valued strength, independence, and devil-may-care audacity. Though their violence was directed mainly against one another and was much less socially disruptive than the middle-class press feared, the gangs were perceived as deeply threatening to urban peace.[16]

Politics was also a crucial part of working-class life, and political organizations often blended almost imperceptibly into gangs, fire companies, and saloons. In New York and other burgeoning cities a fierce competition for place and power characterized the antebellum era. Lacking the stability of the modern two-party system, factions came and went, and no group dominated for long. For the working class in general and ethnic Americans in particular, political life had little to do with reformers' dreams of clean and efficient government. Jobs for the unemployed, power to the ambitious, protection for those involved in vice, licensing of trades, and naturalization for the immigrant—these were the lifeblood of urban politics. With so much at stake, unorthodox electioneering methods thrived. Nominations for city office were held in open meetings, often taverns, and anyone who could pack the hall with loyal supporters and menacing toughs might carry the day. Men as diverse as Mike Walsh, the radical leader of "subterranean" laborites, and Isaiah Rynders, head of the Empire Club, which bent with any political wind, pioneered such methods, and before midcentury the regular parties retained the services of political "shoulder hitters." On election day, repeaters at the polls, ballot-box stuffers, and strong-arm boys all had their usefulness, especially in hotly contested wards.[17]

These conditions allowed politicians and pugilists to form shifting but mutually beneficial alliances. At various times John Morrissey worked for Mayor Fernando Wood, William Poole and Tom Hyer for the Know Nothings, John C. Heenan for regular Tammany, Yankee Sullivan for the Empire Club. Countless lesser fighters were employed by various parties and factions. Mike Walsh made political hay with his ties to Hyer and the Bowery B'hoys, while Poole and Morrissey used their charisma and organizational ability to raise gangs of shoulder hitters whose motives were usually a mixture of ethnic pride and self-interest. The usefulness of prizefighters to urban politicians gave the ring protection it had not enjoyed since the days of Regency England, for in case of arrest, boxers knew that men in positions of power could get them out of trouble. In New York, pugilism's mecca, aldermen regularly had their friends released from police custody, especially muscular supporters who could be counted on next election day.[18]

Political factions, youth gangs, volunteer fire companies, saloons, ethnic brotherhoods, and nativist clubs added up to more than just a handful of ad hoc organizations. These were interlocking institutions with shared memberships, focal points of a distinct working-class culture. Changes in the nature of daily labor and in the relationships between employers and employees elicited creative cultural responses. It is only in this full context of work and leisure, economics and politics, that we can begin to understand what prizefighting meant to the tens of thousands of working-class men who followed the careers of the champions or even entered the ring themselves.

Meaning in Mayhem

On the simplest level, boxing gave elemental expression to deep social conflicts, to the pervasive parochialism dividing the working class. Intense devotion to one's neighbors, shopmates, and drinking partners engendered suspicion of outsiders and the need to defend turf. Ethnic rivalries, of course, caused the deepest divisions. Boxers, saloon keeper–promoters, pool sellers, and editors all recognized that a battle between an Irish and an American fighter was good for business. But the enmity of the native-born and the Irish for each other was grounded in more than the mere manipulation of ethnic hatreds. Cultural and religious schisms ran deep, and they were exacerbated by parallel fissures in the social structure.

American-born workers bore the brunt of economic changes that destroyed old skills and crushed their autonomy. Many seized on the presence of foreigners as an explanation for their plight and accused the Irish of immiserating all laborers. Simply put, it was easier to blame one's problems on a rapacious and ruthless foreign enemy than on impersonal market forces over which one had no control. Lending credibility to nativist fears was the fact that in the competition for political power, the Irish were not passive victims but active organizers who used bloc voting as a way to secure offices and patronage. The suspicions, naturally, were reciprocal, and the Irish interpreted nativist prejudice as the source of their own special plight. Prizefighting was a means for both sides to dramatize and thereby understand these very real tensions over wealth and power. A good match focused their conflicts through the transparent symbolism of two heroes meeting under equal terms and orderly conditions. Whereas the divisions of the streets were shifting and chaotic, the ring created meaning from the chaos of existence, and the outcome of a fight offered cathartic if temporary resolution of deep social problems.[19]

Below the surface of ethnic turbulence was a less obvious battle over the nature of labor, for workplace affiliations also entered into ring loyalties. It was said of Harry Gribben, a sawyer, for example, that he had "many friends among the working classes, more especially those of his craft." Numerous native-born boxers practiced skilled trades, especially butchering. Tom Hyer, Bill Harrington, and William Poole were all members of this, one of the last bastions of the old artisan system. For young apprentice and journeyman butchers, boxing and other traditional recreations evoked the freer morality and less structured working rhythms of the preindustrial city. Better than most other tradesmen, the butchers retained their old cultural patterns centered around drinking and carousing after the markets closed.[20] But even the native monopoly on butchering was threatened in the 1840s, when Tammany politicians began selling licenses to Irish-born tradesmen. In this and other crafts the Irish were accused not simply of taking natives' jobs but of selling their labor for a pittance, aiding the extreme specialization of task that was destroying the artisan system. And indeed, impoverished, reviled, and largely unskilled, the Irish were providing cheap manpower for capitalist expansion. In this sense a fight between an American butcher and an Irish day laborer dramatized not only ethnic conflict but tensions over the nature of work as well, especially the artisan's fear of losing his trade and the laborer's envy of the craftsman's privileges.[21]

But we must not dwell exclusively on these schisms, for the ring also unified men in an expression of their lives' contradictions, momentarily resolving through a shared set of symbols the intractable conflicts of daily life. Even as it gave voice to tensions between skilled and unskilled labor, for example, prizefighting upheld the ideal of craft as a transcendent value, for pugilists demonstrated superb skill in a world that threatened labor's competence. Here, at the very beginnings of commercialized leisure, sports offered a chance for cartmen, dock workers, miners, coal stokers, and other men engaged in exhausting and dangerous jobs to supplement their meager incomes.

Equally important, spectatorship provided vicarious compensation for the destruction of traditional skills in the workplace. This can be seen in the very language of the ring. Boxing was a "profession," and pugilists were "trained" in various "schools" of fighting. Newspaper reports regularly used such phrases as "they went to work," or "he did good work," in their round-by-round coverage. "Art," "science," "craft"—such words were constantly invoked to describe boxers' abilities. Symbolically, the ring was a surrogate workplace. In an environment that rapidly eroded the skills of many laborers, prizefighters retained their autonomy and traditions, their sense of craftsmanship. Sullivan, Hyer, Heenan, and Morrissey did not submit to the rigid regularity of industrial working rhythms: they might train diligently for a fight, but once it was over, they returned to their old, free-and-easy ways. In other words, prizefighters controlled the rhythms of their "work," enjoying precisely that independence which was sorely lacking in most men's lives. And even for less-than-famous boxers, the ring offered not only a chance to make a few extra dollars but a compensatory sense of accomplishment, of pride in one's own courage, grace, and skill that the work world denied.[22]

This shared sense of craft highlights the fact that even while prizefighting dramatized the parochial social conflicts of the streets, it also bound men together with their own cultural style. Despite political, ethnic, and occupational schisms, despite the intense rivalries of urban cliques, boxers and their fans shared values and behaviors. Tom Hyer helping raise Yankee Sullivan's bail, John Morrissey giving a benefit for Bill Harrington's widow, pugilists acting as pallbearers at their comrades' funerals, all reveal that a sense of unity often transcended the volatility of working-class culture. Boarding the trains or steamboats for a fight, the sporting crowd sought a neutral space where its social divisions could be dramatized even as the rites of the ring brought it together into a larger whole.[23]

The overarching unities of pugilism derived from the shared ethos of a large segment of the working class, and boxing's symbolism, in turn, reinforced that ethos. Prizefighting inverted Victorian norms, not necessarily rejecting them but adapting, transforming, even parodying them. Boxers and their backers were all ambitious men, seeking to make money with their skills. Saloon keeper–promoters prospered when new patrons flocked to their drinking establishments, and gamblers thrived when fans bought into their betting pools. Pugilists not only profited from taking a share of the stakes plus side bets, but the glory they gained in the ring also opened up new opportunities. Like John Morrissey, Irish-born Mike Norton parlayed his prize-ring fame into local political power, becoming a Tammany district leader, state assemblyman and senator, and municipal-court judge. When he died in 1889 he left $20,000 in real estate to his family, property purchased with profits from his liquor and hotel businesses. Men such as Norton attained wealth and respect, but they did so on terms acceptable to the culture they came from. By their example they proved that bourgeois propriety and evangelical piety were not the only routes to success.[24]

Boxers, then, embodied a distinctly working-class version of the American dream, providing models of upward mobility within bounds acceptable to the street culture. Alone in the ring with only his own skills, the prizefighter refracted the American cult of individualism through the norms of his peers. As we have seen, training regimens, with their temperance, chastity, and self-discipline, read like Victorian manuals on upright behavior. Boxers who underwent such preparation temporarily accepted a kind of middle-class, goal-oriented behavior, a version of the delayed gratification that is the hallmark of the modern personality in industrial society. In this narrow sense, plebeian culture incorporated elements of bourgeois culture.[25]

But no one claimed, as observers would in the twentieth century, that the success of oppressed peoples in sports was evidence that social mobility was available to all who sought it, proof that any poor boy might "make it" in America. Quite the contrary, the very word "sport" implied social deviance. The gambler's bold wager, the drinker's revelry, the gang leader's profane boast—these were central to ring culture, and they offended middle-class sensibilities profoundly. A boxer who trained assiduously in order to mutilate another man mocked the goals of a society that deemed itself earnest, productive, and humane. Large crowds who set off on riotous excursions in the middle of the week implicitly denied the sanctity of the work ethic. Sinful excess, vulgar conviviality, open dissipation, fanciful pageantry, and unvarnished violence all sharply contradicted the ways good men were supposed to behave. And the fact that steamboats and railroads—charged symbols of social progress—carried the rowdies to their destinations stoked higher the flames of middle-class resentment.[26]

The centrality of money to prizefighting gives further evidence of the ring's inversion of evangelical and bourgeois ways. When a prizefighter or gambler flaunted his earnings, he was inherently attacking the cherished hope of the middle class that prosperity, piety, and hard work flowed together. Working-class men who marveled at the $10,000 Tom Hyer and his backers won against Yankee Sullivan accepted the importance of wealth as a sign of success. But they valued money as a means to conviviality more than as a reward for sober self-control, or a sign of God's grace, or a vehicle of progress. Liquor sellers, gamblers, politicians, and boxers were not just petty entrepreneurs who, given the chance, would have chosen more respectable occupations. These men were successful by the standards of their communities, and they were leaders and heroes because their lives expressed the values of a large segment of the working class.[27]

Indeed, the revenues from liquor sales and gambling were the engines driving the sports boom of the 1850s. It would be an exaggeration to say that prizefighting existed solely so men could gamble, but without betting the ring would have stirred far less excitement. When a man wagered on a boxer—perhaps in a seemingly irrational amount—he risked not only his money but also his self-esteem. Choosing to bet on a particular fighter was a statement of ethnic, neighborhood, or occupational pride. Gambling brought excitement to a prosaic world, and shrewd wagering offered an alternative display of skill for men whose working lives too often denied them a sense of craft.[28]

Above all, both the small bettor and the professional gambler reversed the Victorian meaning of money. Rather than sanctifying wealth by putting it to prudent use, those who risked a high-stakes loss found in the risk itself what made gambling attractive. A man who put his money on a fighter gained status among his peers because he revealed his willingness to lose all in an effort to win big; gambling was a mark of courage. Of course, men wagering on a prizefight did not want to lose. Businessmen and gamblers both sought to increase their resources, and both assumed that agreements must be binding. But while the businessman argued that personal enrichment went hand-in-glove with material betterment for all, the gambler made no claim that his deeds brought social improvement. He was content to enjoy the thrill of the moment, thereby mocking middle-class ideals of thrift and progress. In this way the successful bettor was more dangerous than the failed one, for the latter merely jeopardized his own and his family's security, where the former was rewarded, encouraging him and others to continue their immoral behavior. As a stimulant to gambling, then, prizefighting undermined the Victorian meaning of wealth, transforming it from a sign of virtue into a source of corruption.[29]

Within the magic circle of the ring, not only were concepts of wealth altered, but gender too became inverted. With the breakdown of the household-based artisan economy, sexual identity grew increasingly bifurcated. Moreover, men and women were encouraged to moderate their passions and keep them from interfering with the goal of economic success. In the bourgeois canon, masculinity meant, above all, taking responsibility, controlling one's impulses, and working hard in order to support a family. Being a good provider was the touchstone of being a man, so probity, dependability, and resistance to temptation defined a middle-class male ideal. The very word manly was usually conjoined with "independence" or "self-reliance," thus linking the bourgeois concept of masculinity with autonomy and self-possession, key elements of Victorian character that flowed from diligent labor. Not all Victorian men fulfilled the role; many slid back into less morally rigid ways. The sporting underworld could stir the envy of those who felt themselves deprived of the freedom and openness they perceived in working-class culture. Despite these deep feelings of ambivalence, however, the bourgeois male ideal remained compelling, and it was reinforced by a new female role. For middle-class women, the home became a separate sphere, not a place of production but a haven where their superior morality refined men, nurtured children, and inculcated tender emotions. This domestic ideal placed women at the center of moral life, freeing men to go into the corrupting world, then return to a purifying sanctuary.[30]

If the fundamental test of masculinity was, by Victorian lights, being a good breadwinner, if work was a man's primary source of self-definition, the measure of his worth, and proof of his manhood, then many working-class men in industrializing cities were doomed to failure. Of course, those who performed heavy or dangerous tasks could take pride in their strength and stamina. But fathers now had diminishing legacies of wealth or skill to pass on to sons, and for most men, earnings were small and opportunities limited. Put simply, daily labor undermined rather than buttressed masculinity. It made sense, then, that many workers turned to a more elemental concept of manhood, one they could demonstrate during leisure hours. Toughness, ferocity, prowess, honor—these became the touchstones of maleness, and boxing along with other sports upheld this alternative definition of manhood. The *manly* art defined masculinity not by how responsible or upright an individual was but by his sensitivity to insult, his coolness in the face of danger, and his ability to give and take punishment.[31]

Sociologists have talked of a "bachelor subculture" to capture a phenomenon so common to nineteenth- and early-twentieth-century cities: large numbers of unmarried males finding their primary human contact in one another's company. In some large cities unweddedness was so common that at midcentury, 40 percent of the men between twenty-five and thirty-five years of age were single. Irish immigrants contributed to this tendency, bringing a tradition of late marriage and high rates of bachelorhood to America, but even among the native-born, working men in the nineteenth century tended not to marry until their late twenties. The bachelor subculture, however, included betrothed men as well as unattached ones. Sullivan, Hyer, and Morrissey, for example, were all married, but their wives seemed almost tangential to their lives as the champions passed their nights drinking and carousing among friends. With the breakdown of the household economy, men and women spent diminishing amounts of their work time together, and many chose to take their leisure too in gender-segregated realms. In saloons, pool halls, and lodges as well as in gangs, firehouses, and political clubs, men gathered to seek companionship, garner one another's esteem, and compete for status.[32]

Here, implicitly, was a rejection of the cult of domesticity so characteristic of bourgeois Victorian life. Members of the bachelor subculture expected women to be submissive; they also tended to view them as either pure and virginal or exciting and whorish. Women were both exploitable and less than central to men's affective lives. Rather than spend their nonworking hours within the confines of the family circle—where women's allegedly superior moral nature and "instinctive" sense of self-sacrifice tamed men and elevated children—members of the sporting fraternity chose to seek rough male companionship. It was not only men, however, who felt stifled by the domestic ideal. The Victorian home emotionally suffocated many middle-class women as well, and to compensate for the deprivations caused by their gender-based role, they sought one another's company. The homoerotic tone of letters women wrote to each other and the sensual descriptions of their meetings at spas where they went for physical and emotional therapy had less to do with simple homosexuality (though no doubt homosexual acts and relationships occurred) than with women reaching out for the warmth, love, and emotional contact that home life denied.[33]

There was a parallel in the bachelor subculture that supported the ring. Of course heterosexual prowess was an important element of masculinity; fathering a family, picking up unattached women, and frequenting prostitutes all demonstrated virility. But maleness seemed most emphatically confirmed in the company not of women, but of other men. The loving descriptions of boxers' bodies so common in antebellum fight reports grew less from narrowly defined homosexuality than from a common male aesthetic. Men perceived men as creatures of beauty because they focused so much emotional attention on one another. In the saloon, the firehouse, or the gang, many working-class males found their deepest sense of companionship and human connectedness. The boxer's physique was a palpable expression of such masculine values as strength, power, and stamina. With his body alone the prizefighter attained financial autonomy. Conversely, women were associated with those family responsibilities made so onerous by low pay and lack of economic opportunity. Rather than accept domesticity as the highest good—and domesticity, after all, was a bourgeois luxury; working-class women often toiled in factories or as laundresses or maids—many laboring men sought refuge from the family in all-male peer groups where heroic prizefighters symbolized independence through physical prowess.[34]

Here the concept of male honor helps us understand the culture of the ring. Honor, as historians have recently applied the term, is distinct from the more modern ideals of conscience and dignity. The Victorian man of character possessed a particularly well-developed conscience (an internalized sense of morality stressing strict self-control) and a profound belief in human dignity (especially faith in the fundamental equality of all men). Thus each Christian faced God alone, businessmen were responsible for the fulfillment of their contracts, and good citizens acted on inviolable principles to perfect society. Although the approbation of others was gratifying for such men, good deeds brought their own internal satisfactions and immoral acts evoked a sense of guilt.[35]

But honor more than conscience or dignity depended on external ratification. It was conferred when men acknowledged one another as peers, often in symbolic acts such as buying drinks, spending money lavishly, or toasting one another's accomplishments. Honor had no existence outside group life, for only reputation and the esteem of others conferred it. Honorific societies have tended to be tightly knit and nonbureaucratic, placing special emphasis not on inward virtues but on outward signs that must be approved or rejected by one's status equals. The objects of honor have varied across time and cultures. They have included the protection of the chastity of wives and daughters, grand displays of hospitality, and tests of male prowess. But regardless of the specifics, an individual had honor only when his kin or his fellows said he did. Honor was denied him when his peers refused to acknowledge his status as an equal, and no amount of arguing could restore it. Only acts of valor, especially violent retribution, expunged the sense of shame, proved one's mettle, and reasserted one's claim to honor.[36]

The fights between boxers and the collectivities they belonged to—fire brigades, gangs, political factions, saloon cliques, militia companies, and so forth—were often animated by a sense of lost honor, of having had one's status impugned. Stake money for fighters, turf between gangs, and elected office for political parties were tangible objects to contend over, but the real battle was for peer recognition, for a sense of distinction that made a man first among equals in the small male cliques of working-class society. Saloons were so central to the culture of the ring in part because here, with alcohol lowering inhibitions, men affirmed their right to drink together or, alternatively, to cast aspersions that only blood could redeem. The ethic of honor had roots in the Old World, but it continued to thrive where individuals were concerned less with morality or piety, more with flaunting their status among peers through acts of masculine prowess. In mid-nineteenth-century America, then, character, conscience, and dignity were hallmarks of middle-class culture, while honor remained central to the lives of the poor and marginal, the acid test of personal worth in the male peer society.

The Rites of Violence

Perhaps most important, the bloodiness displayed in the ring was symptomatic of the violence endemic to urban working-class life. Unemployment and poverty were constant threats, and a cycle of alternating depression and inflation made the antebellum years particularly unstable. New York City's per capita wages fell by roughly 25 percent in the decade before midcentury. Moreover, the *New York Times* estimated in the middle of the 1850s that a family of four needed a minimum yearly income of $600, double the salary of many laborers and well over what the majority of working-class men earned. In the impersonal market economy, lack of job security and inequalities of wealth and power were becoming intractable problems. And it was not only underemployment, poverty, and powerlessness but occupational hazards that hit the working class with unrelieved force. Staggering numbers of men were killed or maimed on the job. Indeed, by 1860 there were four Irishwomen for every three Irishmen in New York City, partly because of desertions, partly because of breadwinners' need to travel in search of work, but also because of brutally high job-related mortality rates. In addition, poor diet, overcrowding, and lack of modern sanitation contributed to waves of deadly epidemics. Between 1840 and 1855 the city's mortality rates rose from one in forty to one in twenty-seven, and nearly half of all New York children died before reaching age six.[37]

The death sounds of livestock slaughtered in public markets, the smell of open sewers, the feverish cries of children during cholera season, the sight of countless men maimed on the job: all were part of day-to-day street life. The poor lived as their ancestors had, in a world that did little to shield them from pain. Men tolerated violence—created violence—because high death rates, horrible accidents, and senseless acts of brutality were a psychological burden that only stoicism or bravado helped lighten.[38]

This context makes sense of the ring's violence. Boxing, as well as cockfighting, bull baiting, and ratting, did not just reflect the bloodiness of life. Rather, these and similar sports shaped violence into art, pared away its maddening arbitrariness, and thereby gave it order and meaning. Here, ideally, was true equality of opportunity, a pure meritocracy free of favoritism and special influence. At their best, the ring and the pit rendered mayhem rule-bound instead of anarchic, voluntary rather than random. Boxers, like fighting cocks and trained bulldogs, made bloodshed comprehensible and thus offered models of honorable conduct. They taught men to face danger with courage, to be impervious to pain, and to return violence rather than passively accept it.[39]

As members of male peer societies steeped in the conflicts of their day, prizefighters embodied community values, giving them concentrated symbolic expression. Often harsh and brutal, working-class life required a dramatic form to express its reality. Boxing acknowledged rather than denied life's cruelty, even celebrated it. In the midst of nagging hatreds and festering rivalries, often unleashed by flowing alcohol and blustering attacks on masculine honor, the cool restraint needed to sign articles, train, organize excursions, and bring off matches made bloodletting comprehensible. A properly carried-out fight was a performance, a pageant, a ritual, that momentarily imposed meaning on the savage irrationalities of life. Out of chaos the ring created an aesthetic of violence based on bodily development, fighting skills, and controlled brutality.

This is not to argue that boxing and similar sports supplanted real with vicarious brutality. On the contrary, as recent research reveals, symbolic displays of violence tend to promote further violence.[40] Even as pugilism brought order to bloodiness, made it comprehensible by confining it to two men who represented larger collectivities and fought by rules, the ring also upheld, indeed gloried in the fact that brutishness was part of man's fate. Not the pious homilies of evangelicals, the sentimental humanitarianism of reformers, or the optimistic progressivism of the middle class, prizefighting as a metaphor declared that there was limited good in this world, that every man's victory implied another's loss, that the way was harsh and bloody for all, and that hardship, even death, were the soulmates of life. The ring thus expressed an outlook in which pain and defeat were ineluctable parts of living, a notion almost heretical in this rationalistic age.[41]

Despite the divisions among sporting men, then, all were united by disruptive change in their patterns of work, alienation from bourgeois or evangelical ways, and shared attitudes toward wealth, labor, leisure, masculinity, and honor. Working-class men adopted their own forms of expressive culture, and prizefighting symbolically affirmed their distinct ethos. If not a political threat to new alignments of social and economic power, the ring at least offered cultural opposition; if not a challenge to evangelical or bourgeois authority, here at least was a denial of the values that undergirded oppressive social relationships.

Above all, the manly art gave men a way to get a symbolic grip on the contradictions in their lives, to see these conflicts neatly arranged and played out. It offered an alternative to the Victorian vision of an ever-improving world, stressing instead a constant balance between victory and defeat. As drama, the prizefight depicted pain as the portion for both winner and loser, violence as a necessary means to human ends, and loyalty to one's communal group along with honor in defending one's good name as the very highest human ideals. The ring celebrated the high-stakes gamble, the outrageous boast, the love of strife. Prizefighting made Old World virtues such as prowess, courage, and virility the essence of manhood, while loving descriptions of muscles and sinews gave palpable expression to naked physical beauty as a source of masculine pride.

Of course the culture of the ring had an ugly, disturbing side. Bare-knuckle fighting attracted some social misfits who reveled in brutality. Boxing could become an outlet for bully boys who enjoyed inflicting pain, sociopaths who responded only to their own pleasure at others' suffering. The special order of the ring, moreover, sometimes broke down under the tensions it symbolically reconciled, unleashing further violence. Prizefighting also defined masculinity in a narrow way that encouraged male exploitation of women and alienated men from a whole range of softer emotions within themselves. But at its best the ring dramatized a world of victory for the socially downtrodden, realistically counterposed to defeat any bloodshed. It offered colorful, satisfying rituals that embodied the most profound human strivings but always presented them in mercilessly unsentimental terms. Boxers responded to a violent world by embracing violence, by accepting brutality and returning it with interest, by being as tough and savage as life itself.

In all of these ways bare-knuckle prizefighting was woven into the texture of working-class culture during the antebellum era. A plethora of urban street institutions supported the ring, as boxing helped crystallize the ethos of laboring men. Pugilism gave controlled expression to the schisms of working-class life, not in order to drain away violent passions but to make those divisions comprehensible and thereby transform chaos into meaning. Divided by neighborhood, ethnic, and workplace tensions, large segments of the lower classes were nonetheless united in opposition to key Victorian values, values on which an onerous new social system was built. Every bout inverted bourgeois and evangelical assumptions about such fundamental social phenomena as money, gender, and violence. More, the prize ring conveyed its own alternative outlook. Pugilism was an autonomous expressive form that symbolically opposed the drift of modern society. In crucial ways, then, boxing during the age of heroes captured the values, the ethos, the distinct culture of countless working men who felt dispossessed amidst the Victorian Era's heady optimism.

Notes

1. Peter George Buckley, "To the Opera House: Culture and Society in New York City, 1820–1869" (Ph.D. dissertation, State University of New York at Stony Brook, 1984), 505–10, raises the crucial issue in a very sophisticated way. We must be careful, however, not to read the present into the past. Today's celebrity possesses an aura of media-created intimacy that is fraudulent and alienating. We never personally touch the media-created celebrity, and he or she is oblivious to fans as individuals. But this was not the case for the first generation of great bare-knucklers.

2. Frederick Van Wyck, *Recollections of an Old New Yorker* (New York, 1932), 100–114. On the development of sports in the antebellum era see Benjamin G. Rader, "The Quest for Subcommunities and the Rise of American Sports," *Ameri-*

can Quarterly 29 (1977), 307–21; Roberta J. Park, "The Attitudes of Leading New England Transcendentalists toward Healthful Exercise, Active Recreations, and Proper Care of the Body, 1830–1860," *Journal of Sport History* 4 (1977), 34–50; Melvin Adelman, "The Development of Modern Athletics: Sport in New York City, 1820–1870" (Ph.D. dissertation, University of Illinois, 1980), esp. chs. 9–11; John Rickard Betts, "Mind and Body in Early American Thought," *Journal of American History* 54 (1968), 790–801; John Rickard Betts, "Sporting Journalism in Nineteenth Century America, 1819–1900," *American Quarterly* 5 (1953), 39–56; John Rickard Betts, *America's Sporting Heritage, 1850–1950* (Reading, Mass., 1974), pt. 1; Stephen Hardy and Jack Berryman, " 'Public Amusements and Public Morality': Sport and Social Reform in the American City, 1800–1860" (paper presented at the annual meeting of the Organization of American Historians, Detroit, April 1–4, 1981); Peter Levine, "The Promise of Sport in Antebellum America," *Journal of American Culture* 2 (winter 1980), 623–34; Benjamin G. Rader, *American Sports: From the Age of Folk Games to the Age of Spectators* (Englewood Cliffs, N.J., 1983), pt. 1.

3. On the bourgeois response to the poor of mid-nineteenth-century cities see Paul Boyer, *Urban Masses and Moral Order in America* (Cambridge, Mass., 1978), pts. 2 and 3; Carroll Smith-Rosenberg, *Religion and the Rise of the American City* (Ithaca, N.Y., 1971). For examples of Victorian responses to sport, see John Dizikes, *Sportsmen and Gamesmen* (Boston, 1981), chs. 1–5, 8; Buckley, "To the Opera House," 591–604; Edward K. Spann, *The New Metropolis: New York City, 1840–1857* (New York, 1981), 164–73; Rader, *American Sports,* 30–43. Stow Persons captures the earnest tone of Victorian life in *The Decline of American Gentility* (New York, 1973). On the growing bifurcation of American culture—elite vs. plebeian—see Buckley, "To the Opera House," esp. 160–61. Excellent discussion of the underlying assumptions in Victorian culture is contained in Daniel T. Rodgers, *The Work Ethic in Industrial America, 1850–1900* (Chicago, 1978); Daniel Walker Howe, ed., *Victorian America* (Philadelphia, 1976); and Daniel Walker Howe, *The Political Culture of the American Whigs* (Chicago, 1979).

4. For demographic change, see Spann, *New Metropolis,* ch. 1; Amy Bridges, *A City in the Republic* (Cambridge, Mass., 1984), 39–45; Sean Wilentz, *Chants Democratic: New York City and the Rise of the American Working Class, 1788–1850* (New York, 1984), 18–24, 192; Allen Stanley Horlick, *Country Boys and Merchant Princes: The Social Control of Young Men in New York* (Lewisburg, Pa., 1975), ch. 1; George Rogers Taylor, "American Urban Growth Preceding the Railroad Age," *Journal of Economic History* 27 (1967), 309–39; Douglass C. North, *The Economic Growth of the United States, 1790–1860* (New York, 1966), pt. 2; Philip A. M. Taylor, *The Distant Magnet: European Migration to the United States of America* (London, 1971), 34–37. Frank Queen claimed that audiences for sparring matches ranged from dealers in Wall Street to dealers in faro, from Broadway dandies to sellers of lozenges. However, he mentioned nothing of shopkeepers, businessmen, or industrialists. *New York Clipper,* February 4, 1854.

5. For a fine discussion of the moral economy of the old artisan culture, its rootedness in republican ideology and collective welfare, see Wilentz, *Chants Democratic*, chs. 2 and 3. For changes in the relations of work, see Wilentz, *Chants Democratic*, 108–10, 119, 134; Paul Faler, *Mechanics and Manufacturers in the Early Industrial Revolution: Lynn, Massachusetts, 1760–1860* (Albany, 1981), ch. 7; Bruce Laurie, "'Nothing on Compulsion': Life Styles of Philadelphia Artisans, 1820–1850," *Labor History* 15 (1974), 337–66; Susan Hirsch, *Roots of the American Working Class* (Philadelphia, 1978), chs. 1, 2, and 5; Joseph F. Kett, *Rites of Passage: Adolescence in America, 1790 to the Present* (New York, 1977), ch. 6; Bridges, *A City in the Republic*, ch. 3; Paul Johnson, *A Shopkeeper's Millennium: Society and Revivals in Rochester, New York, 1815–1837* (New York, 1978), ch. 2. On wealth distribution see, for example, Stephan Thernstrom, *Poverty and Progress: Social Mobility in a Nineteenth Century City* (New York, 1975); Edward Pessen, *Riches, Class and Power before the Civil War* (Lexington, Mass., 1973); Lee Soltow, "Economic Inequality in the United States in the Period from 1790–1860," *Journal of Economic History* 31 (1971), 833–39.

6. For some of the social and cultural implications of the transformation from an artisan to an industrial economy, see the works of Wilentz, Faler, Johnson, Laurie, Hirsch, and Horlick cited above, in addition to Laurie, "Fire Companies and Gangs in Southwark: The 1840s," in Allen F. Davis and Mark H. Haller, eds., *The Peoples of Philadelphia: A History of Ethnic Groups and Lower-Class Life, 1790–1940* (Philadelphia, 1973), 71–87; J. Thomas Jable, "Aspects of Moral Reform in Early Nineteenth Century Pennsylvania," *Pennsylvania Magazine of History and Biography* 102 (1978), 344–63; Susan G. Davis, "'Making Night Hideous': Christmas Revelry and Public Order in Nineteenth Century Philadelphia," *American Quarterly* 34 (1982), 185–99; Rodgers, *Work Ethic*, 15–22; Jill Siegel Dodd, "The Working Classes and the Temperance Movement in Antebellum Boston," *Labor History* 19 (1978), 510–31; David Montgomery, "The Working Classes of the Pre-Industrial American City, 1780–1830," *Labor History* 9 (1968), 3–22; Karen Halttunen, *Confidence Men and Painted Women: A Study of Middle-Class Culture in America* (New Haven, Conn., 1982), esp. 8–37.

7. The social stress created by the expansion of markets is a central theme in the work of Wilentz, Johnson, Faler, Laurie, Horlick, Rodgers, and Hirsch.

8. Ibid.

9. Raised on the radical republicanism of the preindustrial city, editor George Wilkes also merged support for labor with interest in sporting events. See Alexander Saxton, "George Wilkes: The Transformation of a Radical Ideology," *American Quarterly* 33 (1981), 437–58. Wilkes's devotion to radicalism waned as his desire to acquire wealth grew. Wilentz argues that historians have exaggerated the inherent contradiction of labor radicalism and street life; *Chants Democratic*, 255–56, 270–71, 326–35. Also see Bridges, *A City in the Republic*, 152; *Subterranean*, January 31, February 28, and May 23, 1846, and October 25, 1845.

10. As Buckley reveals in "To the Opera House," surprising numbers of these men migrated to California in search of adventure. War also provided a test of masculine honor. Several boxers and their backers signed an open letter to *Subterranean* (July 11, 1846), for example, declaring their intention to enlist and fight in Mexico. For an alternative interpretation of sports and work, one emphasizing "congruence" between labor and leisure values, see Steven M. Gelber, "Working at Playing: The Culture of the Workplace and the Rise of Baseball," *Journal of Social History* 16 (1983), 3–22. For two pathbreaking studies of nineteenth-century theater, see Robert Toll, *Blacking Up: The Minstrel Show in Nineteenth Century America* (New York, 1974), and David Grimsted, *Melodrama Unveiled: American Theater and Culture, 1800–1850* (Chicago, 1968).

11. Wilentz argues persuasively that the street culture was not purely traditionalist—seeking to restore the recreations of the past—but a hybrid, mixing old and new social and cultural patterns; *Chants Democratic,* 53–60, 257–63. Also see Joshua Brown, "The 'Dead-Rabbit'-Bowery Boy Riot: An Analysis of the Antebellum New York Gang" (Ph.D. dissertation, Columbia University, 1976), 155–56; Spann, *New Metropolis,* 248–56; Hirsch, *Roots of the American Working Class,* 74–75; Howard B. Rock, *Artisans of the New Republic* (New York, 1979), 295–319; Buckley, "To the Opera House," 319–35; Bruce Laurie, *The Working Peoples of Philadelphia, 1800–1850* (Philadelphia, 1980), 53–58.

12. Brown, Spann, Wilentz, Buckley, Rock, Hirsch, and Laurie all touch on these points. The desire to form voluntary associations was part of the larger tendency of Americans to band together in pursuit of specific goals, a tendency engendered by the atomization of market- and contract-based society. As Rader observes, sports organizations such as early baseball clubs were another way that men countered social isolation with voluntary consocation. See "Quest for Subcommunities," 355–69. The Irish also brought their heritage of secret societies and faction fighting—the poor man's tools for influencing elections and tempering the power of landlords and bosses—all of which fed the gangs, fire companies, political clubs, and other working-class institutions in American cities. See Brown, "The 'Dead Rabbit'-Bowery Boy Riot," 117–47.

13. Stonecutter and Bowery B'hoy David Broderick also opened a tavern, named it in honor of Mike Walsh's radical newspaper, and there entertained the editor along with the likes of Yankee Sullivan, William Poole, and John Morrissey. Another saloon keeper, Tom McGuire, a man whose roots were in the radical republicanism of the preindustrial city, grew to moderate wealth-promoting prizefights as well as blackfaced minstrelsy, and even grand opera in New York and San Francisco. J. Frank Kernan, *Reminiscences of the Old Fire Laddies and Volunteer Departments of New York and Brooklyn* (New York, 1885), 114–19; Saxton, "George Wilkes," 437–38, 442. For a typically judgmental account of these "degraded" characters, see Browne, *Great Metropolis,* ch. 6. On the centrality of the saloon to working-class culture see Jon M. Kingsdale, " 'The Poor Man's Club': Social Func-

tions of the Urban Working-Class Saloon," *American Quarterly* 25 (1973), 472–89; Michael T. Isenberg, "John L. Sullivan and His America," draft manuscript (Annapolis, 1985), ch. 2; Roy Rosenzweig, *Eight Hours for What We Will: Workers and Leisure in an Industrial City, 1870–1920* (Cambridge, Mass., 1983), pt. 2, ch. 2.

14. Laurie, *Working Peoples of Philadelphia,* 58–62; Herbert Asbury, *Ye Olde Fire Laddies* (New York, 1930), 154–55, 171–84; Wilentz, *Chants Democratic,* 259–63; Kernan, *Reminiscences,* 19; Buckley, "To the Opera House," 333–42; Adelman, "Development of Modern Athletics," 569–74; Alvin F. Harlow, *Old Bowery Days* (New York, 1931), ch. 12; Leo Hershkowitz, *Tweed's New York* (Garden City, N.Y., 1977), chs. 1–6; Kett, *Rites of Passage,* 90–93; Ed James, "Lives and Battles of the Irish Champions" (1883), in a scrapbook of clippings on nineteenth-century American sports, New York Public Library Annex.

15. See, for example, anon., *London and New York: Their Crime and Police* (New York, 1853), reprinted from articles in the *New York Journal of Commerce,* February 1853; Harlow, *Old Bowery Days,* chs. 11 and 16; Herbert Asbury, *The Gangs of New York* (New York, 1928), 37–45; Jerome Mushkat, *Tammany: The Evolution of a Political Machine, 1789–1865* (Syracuse, 1971), 208; Gustavus Myers, *The History of Tammany Hall* (New York, 1901), 154–63; and M. R. Werner, *Tammany Hall* (New York, 1928), 44–65.

16. Saxton, "George Wilkes," 437–58, does a fine job of revealing the juncture of politics, street life, and working-class culture. Also see Kett, *Rites of Passage,* 8–90; Wilentz, *Chants Democratic,* 255–64, 300–301; Brown, "The 'Dead Rabbit'-Bowery Boy Riot," 60–61, 144–56; George G. Foster, *New York by Gaslight* (New York, 1850), ch. 12; George G. Foster, *New York in Slices by an Experienced Carver* (New York, 1849), ch. 9; Laurie, *Peoples of Philadelphia,* 151–58; Harlow, *Old Bowery Days,* chs.11 and 16; Asbury, *Gangs of New York,* 37–45; Mushkat, *Tammany,* 208; Myers, *History of Tammany Hall,* 154–63; and Werner, *Tammany Hall,* 44–65. For an alternative interpretation of gang behavior—one stressing antisocial acts more than group norms—see Leonard Berkowitz, "Violence and Rule Following Behavior," in Peter Marsh and Anne Campbell, eds., *Aggression and Violence* (Oxford, 1982), 91–101.

17. Spann, *New Metropolis,* 319, 326–29, 344–50, 352–53; Wilentz, *Chants Democratic,* 255–64, 326–35; Brown, "The 'Dead Rabbit'-Bowery Boy Riot," 78–95; Bridges, *A City in the Republic,* 61–62, 110–13, 132–35. Rynders, for example, brought such fighters as Bill Ford and John McCleester to sixth-ward primary meetings, trying to use muscle to broaden his political base beyond the fifth ward. Kernan, *Reminiscences,* 52–54. On violence as a political tool in artisan culture see Michael Feldberg, "Urbanization as a Cause of Violence: Philadelphia as a Test Case," in Davis and Haller, eds., *The Peoples of Philadelphia,* 56, 66. For ties between urban vice, gambling, and politics, see Haller, "Recurring Themes," conclusion to Davis and Haller, 277–90.

18. For more on street politics, see George Walling, *Recollections of a New York Chief of Police* (n.p., 1890), 375–76; *New York Daily Tribune*, "The Poole Tragedy," March 10, 1855; Spann, *New Metropolis*, 318–19; Fred Harvey Harrington, "Gamblers, Politicians and the World of Sport, 1840–1870" (paper read at the Organization of American Historians meeting, April 8, 1983). As Buckley points out, several of the most influential individuals in working-class culture, such as editors George Wilkes and Mike Walsh, politician Isaiah Rynders, and promoter David Broderick, became wealthy men and ultimately cut themselves off from the very culture they helped create. "To the Opera House," 406–9.

19. On nativism and politics in New York see Robert Ernst, "Economic Nativism in New York City during the 1840s," *New York History* 29 (April 1948), 170–86; Ira M. Leonard, "The Rise and Fall of the American Republican Party in New York City," *New York Historical Society Quarterly* 50 (April 1966), 150–92; Wilentz, *Chants Democratic*, 315–25, 343–49. Several historians have argued that ethnic conflict was the major formative influence in the politics of the antebellum era. For this "ethnocultural" school, see Michael F. Holt, *Forging a Majority: The Formation of the Republican Party in Pittsburgh, 1848–1860* (New Haven, Conn., 1969); Michael F. Holt, *The Political Crisis of the 1850s* (New York, 1978); Joel H. Silbey, *The Transformation of American Politics, 1840–1860* (Englewood Cliffs, N.J., 1967); Robert Kelly, *The Cultural Pattern in American Politics: The First Century* (New York, 1979); Paul Kleppner, *The Cross of Culture: A Social Analysis of Midwestern Politics, 1850–1900* (New York, 1970); Paul Kleppner, *The Third Electoral System, 1853–1892: Parties, Voters and Political Cultures* (Chapel Hill, N.C., 1979).

20. Wilentz, *Chants Democratic*, 137–39; Buckley, "To the Opera House," 342–49; *New York Clipper*, April 29, 1854.

21. See Wilentz and Buckley, passim.

22. For examples, see *New York Clipper*, October 15 and December 10, 1853.

23. The most comprehensive work on street culture is Buckley, "To the Opera House."

24. On symbolic inversion see Barbara A. Babcock, ed., *The Reversible World: Symbolic Inversion in Art and Society* (Ithaca, N.Y., 1978). Police Captain Petty referred to Norton's fifth-ward clique as "a gang of rowdies composed of thieves, gamblers, pimps, bounty jumpers, fighters, and rum sellers." The president of the police board called Norton "the champion of the desperate and dangerous classes," including thieves, murderers, and prostitutes. Other boxers also found success on their own terms. Ed Price became an attorney after retiring from the ring, building his practice with the aid of his street contacts, while Orville "Awful" Gardner—a few years after biting off part of William "Dublin Tricks" Hasting's ear in a brawl—was converted to Christianity and preached to others of his background in the language and style of the Bowery. Quotations from Edwin P. Kilroe, comp., "Skeleton Outline of the Activities of Michael Norton," New York

Historical Society manuscript dated April 1, 1938. See also Charles Loring Brace, *The Dangerous Classes of New York and Twenty Years Work Among Them* (New York, 1872), 288–97.

25. On "modern" personality see Richard D. Brown, *Modernization: The Transformation of American Life, 1600–1865* (New York, 1976), chs. 5 and 6, and Wilbur Zelinsky, *A Cultural Geography of the United States* (Englewood Cliffs, N.J., 1973), ch. 2. My considerable debt to Clifford Geertz should be obvious in these pages. See his *Interpretation of Cultures* (New York, 1973).

26. Contrast the behavior of men at a fight with Victorian propriety as elucidated by Howe et al. in *Victorian America* and by Halttunen in *Confidence Men and Painted Women*.

27. On gambling see Ann Fabian, "Rascals and Gentlemen: The Meaning of American Gambling, 1820–1890" (Ph.D. dissertation, Yale University, 1983).

28. On the centrality of gambling to the rise of sport see Harrington, "Gamblers, Politicians, and the World of Sport." Labor radical Mike Walsh seems to have taken a live-and-let-live attitude toward gambling; see *Subterranean*, December 27, 1845. The ring depended on professional gamblers for stake money and to facilitate wagering among other bettors. Jake Somerendyke, for example, was a regular at the Empire Club, where fights were discussed and arranged. He earned his money from his expertise at the ring and track, handicapping horses and fighters and selling "pools" to other gamblers. See Ed James, *The Life and Battles of Tom Hyer* (New York, 1879), 2.

29. Fabian, "Rascals and Gentlemen"; Harrington, "Gamblers, Politicians and the World of Sport." Also see Haller, "Recurring Themes," 277–90.

30. On gender roles in Victorian America see Rader, *American Sports*, 34; Peter Stearns, *Be a Man: Males in Modern Society* (New York, 1979), ch. 5; Edward Anthony Rotundo, "Body and Soul: Changing Ideals of American Middle Class Manhood," *Journal of Social History* 16 (summer 1983), 23–38; Rotundo, "Manhood in America: The Northern Middle Class, 1770–1920" (Ph.D. dissertation, Brandeis University, 1982), chs. 4–6; Mary P. Ryan, *Cradle of the Middle Class: The Family in Oneida County, New York, 1790–1865* (Cambridge, Mass., 1981); Charles E. Rosenberg, "Sexuality, Class and Role in Nineteenth-Century America," in Joseph and Elizabeth Pleck, eds., *The American Man* (Englewood Cliffs, N.J., 1980), 219–54; Michael Gordon, "The Ideal Husband as Depicted in the Nineteenth Century Marriage Manual," in Pleck and Pleck, *The American Man*, 145–57; Joe L. Dubbert, *A Man's Place: Masculinity in Transition* (Englewood Cliffs, N.J., 1979), ch. 2; Pleck and Pleck, "Introduction," *The American Man*, 14–15; Nancy F. Cott, *The Bonds of Womanhood: "Woman's Sphere" in New England, 1780–1835* (New Haven, Conn., 1977); Ann Douglas, *The Feminization of American Culture* (New York, 1977); William H. Chafe, *Women and Equality: Changing Patterns in American Culture* (Oxford, 1979), ch. 2; Peter G. Filene, *Him/Her/Self: Sex Roles in Modern America* (New York, 1974), chs. 1 and 2; Nancy F. Cott and Elizabeth H. Pleck, eds., *A Heritage of*

Her Own: Toward a New Social History of American Women (New York, 1979), chs. 6–14.

31. Spann captures the male basis of this culture. *New Metropolis,* 344–50. Rotundo's dissertation is particularly helpful here, especially chs. 2–6. Also see Jonathan Katz, ed., *Gay American History: Lesbians and Gay Men in the USA* (New York, 1976). Joseph H . Pleck, *The Myth of Masculinity* (Cambridge, Mass., 1981), 140–42, uses the terms "traditional" and "modern" to differentiate male-centered from female-centered masculinity, a class-biased formulation. Peter Stearns is quite sensitive to the problem of how class and gender roles interact: *Be a Man,* 41–46, 59–60, 62–63, 70–71.

32. Rader, *American Sports,* 34; Hirsch, *Roots of the American Working Class,* 54–55; Kernan, *Reminiscences,* 165; Stearns, *Be a Man,* 52–53, 85; Kingsdale, "The 'Poor Man's Club,' " 472–89; Brace, *Dangerous Classes of New York,* 286–97; Ned Polsky, *Hustlers, Beats and Others* (Chicago, 1967), esp. 31–37, 72–73, 85–115; Adelman, *Development of Modern Athletics,* 582–89; Boyer, *Urban Masses and Moral Order,* 7; David R. Johnson, *Policing the Urban Underworld* (Philadelphia, 1979), esp. 29–40, 78–89, 126–81.

33. Carroll Smith-Rosenberg, "The Female World of Love and Ritual: Relations between Women in Nineteenth Century America," *Signs* 1 (autumn 1975), 1–29.

34. *New York Clipper,* December 10, 1853. Joseph and Elizabeth Pleck point out that eighteenth-century men were intensely intimate in their interactions with one another. *American Man,* 13.

35. On the concept of honor see Bertram Wyatt-Brown, *Southern Honor: Ethics and Behavior in the Old South* (New York, 1982), esp. pt. 1; Bertram Wyatt-Brown, *Yankee Saints and Southern Sinners* (Baton Rouge, 1985); Edward L. Ayers, *Vengeance and Justice, Crime and Punishment in the Nineteenth Century American South* (New York, 1984), esp. ch. 1; Gorn, " 'Gouge and Bite, Pull Hair and Scratch': The Social Significance of Fighting in the Southern Backcountry," *American Historical Review* 90 (1985), 38–42; Peter Berger et al., *The Homeless Mind* (New York, 1973), 83–94; Julio Caro-Baroja, "Honour and Shame: An Historical Account of Several Conflicts," trans. R. Johnson, and Julian Pitt-Rivers, "Honour and Social Status," both in J. G. Peristiani, ed., *Honour and Shame* (Chicago, 1966), 88–91, 19–77; "Honor," in David Sills, ed., *The International Encyclopedia of the Social Sciences* 6 (New York, 1968), 503–10.

36. See references in note 14 above.

37. Wyatt-Brown, 113–17; Bridges, *A City in the Republic,* 116; Spann, *New Metropolis,* 25–28, 71, 134–51; Wilentz, *Chants Democratic,* 117–19, 363–64; Roger Lane, *Violent Death in the City* (Cambridge, Mass., 1979), 59–64, 117–24. The human environment could be as threatening as the natural one. Mobbing and rioting were common, traditional forms of protest aimed at attaining particular social or economic goals. Moreover, street crime—though comparatively infrequent by

modern standards—was perceived as growing out of control. See Feldberg, "Urbanization as a Cause of Violence," 53–69.

38. Wilentz, *Chants Democratic,* ch. 7, esp. 262–66; Leonard L. Richards, *Gentlemen of Property and Standing: Anti-Abolition Mobs in Jacksonian America* (New York, 1970). Traditional use of violence is a pervasive theme in Buckley, "To the Opera House," and Joshua Brown, "The 'Dead Rabbit'-Bowery Boy Riot." Also see Harlow, *Old Bowery Days,* 146–51, and Charles N. Glabb and Theodore Brown, *A History of Urban America* (New York, 1967), 87–88.

39. Even though the rules of the ring sometimes broke down, it was the *ideal* of fair combat that gave boxing symbolic power. After a barroom misunderstanding in 1859, John C. Heenan was set upon in the streets of Boston, kicked down from behind, shot at, and left bleeding with injuries to his back and knee. Contrast such brutality—not uncommon in street life—with the controlled passions of the ring. Ed James, *Life and Battles of John C. Heenan* (New York, 1879), 3. For a fascinating discussion of the verbal violence in English youth gangs, see Peter Marsh, "The Rhetorics of Violence," in Marsh and Anne Campbell, eds., *Aggression and Violence* (Oxford, 1982), 102–17.

40. The best evidence indicates that violent spectacles such as boxing matches do not have a cathartic effect but tend to promote violence. See, for example, David P. Phillips, "The Werther Effect," *The Sciences* (July–August 1985), 33–39; George Gaskill and Robert Pearton, ch. 10 of Jeffrey H. Goldstein, ed., *Sports, Games and Play: Social and Psychological Viewpoints* (Hillsdale, N.J., 1979), 263–91; Jeffrey Goldstein, ed., *Sports Violence* (New York, 1983); Richard G. Sipes, "War, Sports and Aggression: An Empirical Test of Two Rival Theories," *American Anthropologist,* n.s. 751 (February 1973), 64–86.

41. For an excellent survey of sociological theories on youth-gang violence, see David Downes, "The Language of Violence," in Marsh and Campbell, *Aggression and Violence,* ch. 3.

10

"Oy Such a Fighter!"
Boxing and the American Jewish Experience

PETER LEVINE

Benny Leonard was the lightweight champion of the world between 1917 and 1925, one of the greatest boxers of all time, and folk hero to many East European Jewish immigrants and their children. Early in his career he knocked out one Ah Chung during a six-round bout in New York's Chinatown on the Chinese New Year in 1913. Chung, in fact, was a Jewish boxer named Rosenberg. Determined to attract immigrant Chinese fight fans, the bout's promoters convinced him to put on eye makeup and apply yellow body paint to match his billing as a "Peking native" and the "only Chinese boxer in the world." At least one Chinese spectator was not fooled by the hoax. As Rosenberg rested between rounds, a distinguished-looking Chinese gentleman, dressed in a purple-and-gold mandarin robe, questioned the fighter in rapid-fire Chinese. The fighter, totally ignorant of what the man was saying, perfunctorily nodded "yes." As it turned out, Rosenberg answered correctly. According to one sportswriter, our Chinese patron demanded that the fighter admit he was an imposter. "You no China boy, you fake," he insisted. "China boy got more sense than to stand up and get licking when he can iron shirts and collars."[1]

Laced with its own racist stereotyping of Chinese in the United States common to the early twentieth century, this column suggests something of boxing's popularity among immigrants and of the number of Jewish boys who put on gloves. Although this Jew didn't even have a "Chinaman's chance," many second-generation young men from East European immigrant working-class families did. Between 1910 and 1940, Jewish boxers more than held their own in the professional ranks. Prior to 1916 most title contenders in the eight weight divisions ranging from heavyweight to flyweight were either Irish, German, or Italian. By 1928, Jewish fighters constituted the largest total. Only two Jews held titles between 1900 and 1909, but then the numbers increased dramatically: four between 1910 and 1919, eight between 1920 and 1929, and ten between 1930 and 1939. Some, like Al Singer, didn't last long: "The Bronx Beauty" lost his lightweight crown after four months. But he was the exception to the reasonably long tenures of Jewish champions. Benny Leonard reigned as lightweight king for eight years. "Slapsie" Maxie Rosenbloom and "Battling" Levinsky both held their light-heavyweight crowns for five years. And Barney Ross topped the welterweight division for five consecutive years and the light-weight division for three—two overlapping with his welterweight crowns in 1934 and 1935.

Ross was the only Jewish champion to hold titles in two divisions at the same time. But Jewish fighters commonly held more than one world title in any given year. The only year between 1910 and 1939 when there was not a single Jewish champion was 1913. In seventeen of the remaining twenty-nine years, at least two Jewish boxers were world champions in the same year. In seven years, including 1930, 1932, 1934, and 1935, Jews held three titles simultaneously. In 1933, light-heavyweight Maxie Rosenbloom, middleweight Ben Jeby, welterweight Jackie Fields, and lightweight Barney Ross held four of the eight championship belts. At one time or another, Jews on Chicago's Maxwell Street or in its Lawndale section, on New York's Lower East Side or the Bronx's Pelham Parkway, around Boston's Commonwealth Avenue, or in south Philadelphia could all claim one of their own as contenders or champions. New York, with the largest concentration of East European Jews in the United States, produced nine of the sixteen Jewish titleholders in these years. So prominent were Jewish boxers in certain weight divisions that nine times between 1920 and 1934, Jews fought each other in championship bouts. Three times Benny Leonard successfully defended his lightweight crown against Jewish challengers. "Corporal" Izzy Schwartz won the flyweight belt in 1927 from "Newsboy" Brown. And "Slapsie" Rosenbloom defended his light-heavyweight title against Abie Bain in 1930, then lost it four years later to Bob Olin.[2]

Statistics provide a map of Jewish involvement in boxing, marking out a period between 1910 and 1940 when Jews were a major presence. But they do not explain the significance of this participation, both for those who fought and for those who followed the sport. More so than baseball or basketball, boxing combined opportunity for symbolic connection to nationally recognized individuals with intimate, community involvement in local sporting activity. Baseball was America's National Game but boxing, with its quest for world championships, permitted its own opportunities for focusing national attention on individual Jewish athletes. Although disdainfully labeled as an activity fit only for society's lower classes, boxing possessed a long history in the United States as a local community experience that had served other immigrants well in their quest for stability, place, and identity. Whether appropriated as public symbols or as part of their neighborhood's social world, flamboyant Jewish boxers, more than any other group of athletes, confirmed Jewish toughness and the will to survive, while providing vivid counterpoint to popular anti-Semitic stereotypes. They also served as a touchstone for attempts to reconcile traditional, ethnic values with mainstream American culture while making their own special contribution to defining an American Jewish identity in the face of real threats to Jewish existence both at home and abroad.

I

Surrounded by his fellow Jewish immigrant workers in a sweatshop on New York's Lower East Side at the turn of the century, Abraham Cahan's "Yekl" searches for a badge of his new American identity and finds it in boxing. Asked by a presser if John L. Sullivan is still heavyweight champion of the world, he responds as Jake, with all the American enthusiasm he can muster:

> "Oh no!" . . . Jake responded with what he considered a Yankee jerk of the head. "Why don't you know? Jimmie Corbett *leaked* him, and Jimmy *leaked* Cholly Meetchel, too. You can *betch you' bootsh!* Johnnie could not *leak* Chollie, *becaush* he is a big *bluffer*, Chollie is," he pursued, his clean-shaven florid face beaming with enthusiasm for his subject, and with pride in the diminutive proper nouns he flaunted. "But Jimmie pundished him. *Oh, didn't he knock him out off shight!* He came near making a meat ball of him"—with a chuckle, "He *tzettled* him in three *roynds.*"[3]

Asked what a round is, Jake offers an explanation proudly embroidered with his knowledge of the ring. Not everyone, however, is as taken with his American interest as he is. His newspaper reading interrupted by Jake's reply, Bernstein, described by Cahan as "the rabbinical-looking man" usually addressed by his shopmates as "Mr.," suggests that any "burly Russian peasant . . . would crunch the bones of Corbett himself." Besides, Bernstein adds, "My grandma's last care it is who can fight best." When Jake persists, however, even his shopmate realizes how important boxing is to Jake's emerging American identity. Referring to Jake's passion for boxing and baseball he remarks: "And you Jake, cannot do without 'these things,' can you? I do not see how you manage to live without them."[4]

Jake's choice of the "Great John L." and "Gentleman" Jim Corbett as reference points for his infatuation with boxing and his own identification as an

American is not surprising. Sullivan, the "Boston strong boy," won the heavy-weight championship of the world in 1882 and held the title until defeated by Corbett ten years later. Both men reached prominence at a time when boxing was considered corrupt, violent, disreputable, and, in many places, illegal sport. Nevertheless, these Irish champions found a special place not only in Jake's heart but especially in the hearts of working-class Irish immigrants desperate for some positive sign of their own American future in a life that offered them little control over their time or destiny. As Elliott Gorn tells us, limited to menial employment, with little prospect for advancement in the workplace, first- and second-generation Irish male immigrants found opportunities for fulfillment only in their leisure world. Centered on the saloon and ring and with a special interest in the success of their own kind, they created a subculture replete with violence that bound them together in a world of mutuality and ethnic pride far removed from mainstream America. Boxing, to both participants and spectators, was an integral part of that world, and the presence of Irish champions only reinforced allegiance to it.

At the same time, however, the success and bravado of a Sullivan, the country's first national sports hero, who liked to introduce himself by boasting that he could "lick any son-of-a-bitch alive," endeared him to Irish-Americans as well as to other immigrants for more obvious reasons. His rise from beginnings no better than their own affirmed their own American possibilities, especially since few activities seemed so obviously American as sport. Where else were the values of competition and individual effort so transparently important? What other activity more easily provided opportunities for immigrants to participate as American consumers, to learn about something identified as distinctly American, or to witness the American triumphs of their own kind in the flesh or boldly announced on billboards or in the press?[5]

Writing in 1896, Abraham Cahan recognized similar possibilities for his own people when he announced Jake's knowledge and adoration of Irish champions. Sullivan and Corbett were not Jewish, but their immigrant working-class backgrounds as well as their champion status made them better symbols of immigrant aspiration than any Jewish fighter then available to him.

When Cahan wrote his novel, America's first Jewish world champions, Abe Attell and Harry Harris, had yet to capture their crowns or approach the prominence accorded Sullivan or Corbett. Cahan's best Jewish bet would have been San Francisco's "Chrysanthemum" Joe Choynski. But Joe, despite his reputation as a solid heavyweight who fought several memorable battles with Corbett in the late 1880s as well as a staged exhibition with his hero, John L. Sullivan, in 1891, never achieved their glorious heights. More important, little in his background provided any immediate source of identification for the hundreds of thousands of working-class East European immigrants that Cahan addressed in his stories and newspapers.

Joe Choynski did have one thing in common with many of the East European Jews who came to America at the turn of the century: he was Polish, at least on his father's side. Born in San Francisco in 1868 to a middle-class family of intellectuals, he had an upbringing far removed from the experience of later waves of Polish immigrants. Although anti-Semitism certainly existed for San Francisco's small Jewish population, by all accounts this burgeoning West Coast community offered far more freedom and tolerance than larger midwestern and East Coast cities with their immigrant working-class ghettoes. Especially so for the Choynskis, whose class and social position found them among San Francisco's Jewish elite.

By the time Joe was born, his father, Isadore, one of the first Jews to attend Yale, had established himself as the West Coast correspondent of the *American Israelite*, Isaac Mayer Wise's organ of reformed Judaism and, at the time, the chief Jewish publication in the United States. He also wrote columns for local San Francisco newspapers and operated an antiquarian book store. Along with his wife, Harriet, known for her interests in poetry and music, Choynski was a member of Congregation Sherith Israel. Prominent in San Francisco's Jewish community, Isadore served as president of the local YMHA and even won election to the same post of a local chapter of B'nai B'rith.[6]

Despite this background, Joe dropped out of high school, took jobs as a candy puller and as a blacksmith, and pursued his boxing aspirations as an amateur under the auspices of the Golden Gate Athletic Club. Fighting at a time when there was no light-heavyweight class, Joe, who earned his nickname "Chrysanthemum" for his shock of white hair, competed in the heavyweight division, despite the fact that he never weighed more than 165 pounds. Undeterred, by the age of nineteen he captured and successfully defended the California amateur heavyweight crown and made the decision to pursue a professional career in the ring. Over the next fifteen years, he fought in 77 bouts, compiling a record of 50 wins, 14 losses, 6 draws, and 7 no-decisions. Although he was small for a heavyweight, half of his victories came by knockouts.

Joe's father occasionally championed his son's physical prowess in ways that anticipated later interest in the connection between Jewish muscle and Jewish survival. For the most part, however, little attention was given by Joe, Abraham Cahan, or anyone else to his Jewish connections.[7] If only *Yekl* had been written twenty years later, Cahan would have had no trouble finding

Jewish boxers to take the place of Sullivan and Corbett as ethnic heroes and symbols of American aspiration. By World War I, Jewish boxers reigned as world champions, and boxing, as survival skill and neighborhood sport, was commonplace in Jewish immigrant urban ghettoes.

II

Whether they learned their trade in Hester Street or Maxwell Street, Jewish champions, would-be contenders, and many of their followers shared one thing in common: the importance of streets and settlement houses in teaching them how to fight. Jackie Fields, who was born in Chicago in 1908 and went on to a boxing career that included a gold medal in the featherweight division in the 1924 Olympics and the world welterweight title in the early 1930s, vividly recalls that for himself and his friends, fighting was a familiar part of everyday life. Talking about his Chicago childhood, he observes:

> We didn't know the difference of a good neighborhood or a bad neighborhood. Pushcarts on one side, pushcarts on the other. We'd play in the streets, play in the alleys. We had Stanford Park three blocks away where you had to fight your way to the swimming pool because the Italians, the Polish, the Irish, the Lithuanians were there. The Jews were surrounded by all of 'em. So in order to go to the pool you had to fight. "What are you doin' here, you Jew bastard?" "Hey, Kike." You know. We'd start fighting right away.

Once at the pool, Fields and his friends jockeyed for position on the waiting benches closest to the pool entrance. As Jackie put it, "You start[ed] a fight again . . . we were always fighting for position."

Territorial imperative and anti-Semitism were not the only reasons to learn how to fight. Place and pocketbook also provided incentive. "In that neighborhood," Fields remembers, "you had to be tough. A kid that couldn't take it—you'd call him a sissy. We wouldn't let him with us." Constant challenges and fights among his friends established a pecking order and honed their boxing skills. Occasionally, with towels wrapped around their fists for protection, Jackie and his gang staged fights in the streets, hopeful that people passing by would applaud their efforts by giving up their loose change.[8]

Growing up in a predominantly Irish neighborhood in Philadelphia, Benny Bass, world featherweight champion in 1927 and 1928, also learned to fight in the streets. When he was fourteen, as one sportswriter told it, his Irish peers demanded that he fight each of them if he wanted to live. "It is a matter of neighborhood record," the reporter noted, "that Bass fought one fight every day for a period of three months. At the end of that time he was wearing a slightly swollen nose, eyes that had a deeper surrounding color than nature bestowed—and also 92 Irish scalps." Confident in his ability, Bass proceeded to enter an amateur tournament and "beat up on Bohemians, Germans, Italians, Greeks, more Irish, a few English and some folks from his own race." Soon after, he became a professional boxer.[9]

Ninety-two Irish scalps! An impressive if unlikely start, even for a future world champion. Exaggerated though this tale may be, the existence of so many comparable stories confirms its basic truth. Benny Leonard certainly recalls a similar introduction to boxing. The son of Gershon and Minnie Leiner, Russian immigrants who raised eight children on tailor sweatshop wages, Benny grew up in a Jewish neighborhood in New York's East Village near Eighth Street and Second Avenue. As a skinny, frail youngster he remembered being "the butt of Irish 'Micks,' Italian 'Wops,' and the hoodlums of a dozen different races." Whether "going to the store or to the public baths," fighting between his Jewish friends and other ethnic groups of adolescents was an everyday experience. As he told it: "In the winter we fought with snowballs packed tightly around pieces of coal and soaked with water until they were as hard as cannon balls. Then we used baseball bats, stones and loaded canes. These were real brawls. There was many a boy who suffered permanent injury from an encounter with the warriors from the next block."[10] After Benny had suffered one particularly fierce beating at the hands of the "6th Street Boys," Benny's uncle, who clearly was not orthodox, took his nephew to a boxing club on Saturdays to teach him how to protect himself. Within a short time his protégé had become the champion of his block.[11]

Leonard's formal training was a bit unusual for Jewish boys who became professional boxers. Most developed skills initially learned on the streets, in settlement houses, and at YMHAs. Jackie Fields's first organized instruction took place at the Henry Booth Settlement in Chicago. Here, as well as in a downtown gym where professional boxers worked out and where he often visited instead of going to school, Fields began learning his trade. Ruby Goldstein, better known as a boxing referee than for his brief career as a middleweight, dedicated his autobiography to New York's "Henry Street Settlement and the Educational Alliance for starting me out on the right foot and paving my way." Describing the Lower East Side's Henry Street in much the same fashion that Jackie Fields remembers Maxwell Street, Goldstein recalls growing up in a poor family whose widowed mother took in sewing and wash and whose grandfather worked in a sweatshop as a finisher of men's clothes. Taken to the settlement house by his older brother, Ruby discovered boxing, feeling too small for baseball or basketball. "With its divisions to suit every size boy, it offered an opportunity for me to advance. Suddenly it had become my favorite sport." Forced to travel uptown, away from his friends, to the annex of the High School of Commerce on West Eighty-ninth Street and Amsterdam Avenue, Ruby dealt with his loneliness by cutting school and watching Joe Gans, Jack Britton, and other professional boxers train at Grupp's Gym in Harlem. At fourteen he quit school, got a job as an office boy for $12 a week, and continued boxing in the evenings at Henry Street. There he met Hymie Cantor, a former boxer who coached kids at the Educational Alliance. Under Cantor's guidance, Goldstein turned to boxing as a profession.[12]

Similar stories belong to boxers as well known as world champions like bantamweight Abie Goldstein and light-heavyweight "Slapsie" Maxie Rosenbloom, who learned their craft respectively at the Ninety-second Street YMHA and Harlem's Union Settlement House, as well as to lesser-known pugilists. New Yorker Sammy Dorfman, a ranking junior lightweight in 1929, took up boxing at Clark House. Lou Bloom, who came to Columbus, Ohio, as a youngster from Minsk in 1908, studied the manly art at the Schoenthal Center, the city's Jewish community center. Known locally as the "Little Heb," he won several amateur state boxing titles before becoming a professional boxer and an Australian national champion. For every Goldstein, Rosenbloom, Dorfman, and Bloom who actually enjoyed success as professional boxers, countless other children of Jewish immigrants learned the sport in similar settings.[13]

At least for one Jewish boxer, the settlement house served a different purpose. Louis Wallach, better known in the boxing world as Leach Cross, used it to keep his father from learning of his passion for the sport. Born in 1886, Louis and his friends on New York's Lower East Side learned to fight in the streets and at the Clark Settlement House in order to protect themselves from Irish kids as they walked to school. Wallach attended CCNY, where he became friendly with a boy whose father owned the Long Acre Athletic Club. Here Wallach worked the concessions, all the while nurturing his love of boxing by fighting in preliminary bouts.[14]

The Long Acre was no different from innumerable neighborhood boxing clubs located in New York and other cities. At a time when many states, including New York, prohibited prizefighting, these clubs held "exhibitions" and no-decision bouts for their members and became the chief venues of what passed for professional boxing. Money provided to fighters under the table, lucrative gambling on the outcome of bouts on the side, and "membership" for virtually anyone who wanted to attend kept the sport alive.[15]

Within two years, Wallach advanced to main events and determined to make boxing a career even as he completed his education by obtaining a degree in dentistry from NYU. Knowing that his parents, Chaim and Rosa, would disapprove, Wallach fought professionally under the name of Leach Cross. Questioned at home about his occasional black eyes and bruised face, he covered his tracks by recounting his exploits on the basketball court at Clark House rather than on the canvas at Long Acre.

The ruse eventually caught up with him in 1908 when the young lightweight put away Joe Bernstein in four rounds. Bernstein, billed as "the pride of the ghetto," was at the very end of his long career as one of the great featherweights of the 1890s and early 1900s. Although never a world champion, he contested with the best of his division and emerged as the first Jewish boxer born on the Lower East Side to win the attention of East European Jewish immigrants eager for some recognition of their American existence. As Sam Wallach, one of Louis's brothers, tells it, their father learned of his son's triumph one Friday evening when his neighbors stopped him on his way home from work to congratulate him on the news. When the patriarch of the Wallach family came to the Sabbath table in his orthodox Jewish home, he made his feelings on the subject quite clear to his son the boxer: "So a prize fighter you are. I believe you when you come home with a black eye and tell me you got it playing basketball at Clark House. Now I learn you are a prize fighter! A loafer! A nebbish!"[16] This father's disgust with his son's decision is clear. Like other Jewish immigrant parents who came to the United States in hopes that they, and especially their children, would be able to improve their economic lot, Chaim Wallach could not fathom how his well-educated boy could throw away a worthwhile career to become a boxer. Conflict over economic and social aspiration rather than concern that his son's love of boxing broke with Jewish religious tradition occasioned his ire. Embedded in the elder Wallach's reaction is the fact that many of his generation had difficulty comprehending that the Golden Medinah offered more than the possibility of a better economic future for their children. Obviously, few immigrant children turned to boxing as one of those choices. Nevertheless, this story, like others already told, underlines that much of the conflict engendered between the first and second generation turned on a myriad of daily decisions by children to participate in an American culture on their own terms.

Even boys less prepared than Louis Wallach to take advantage of what America had to offer met parental disapproval when they devoted themselves to the ring. Abe Attell, the "Little Hebrew" who held the world featherweight crown between 1901 and 1912, remembered an impoverished San Francisco childhood where his Russian immigrant parents struggled to put food on the table for their twelve children. Born on Washington's birthday but named after Abraham Lincoln, he recalled that growing up in a predominantly Irish neighborhood introduced him to fighting at an early age. When Abe was thirteen, his father died. His mother sent him to Los Angeles for a year to stay with an uncle. Returning to San Francisco in 1897, Abe sold newspapers in front of the Mechanics' Pavilion on Eighth and Market. He also watched boxing matches there and began fighting in amateur bouts.[17]

Abe's mother was not happy about his interest in pugilism. In August 1900, Attell signed for his first professional fight. Knowing that she would be displeased with his decision, he kept it a secret. But one week before the match, she heard about it from a neighbor. As Attell recalls, "She grabbed me by the neck and laid down the law." Only after Abe promised that this would be his "first and last fight" did she agree to let him in the ring. Attell knocked out his opponent in the second round and earned $15 for his efforts. When he returned home he gave his mother his purse. As he recalled, "She looked at the money, but didn't touch it. Then she looked at my face very carefully. 'You mean the fight is all over and you got this $15.00?' she asked. 'And you don't have no cuts on you at all.' I smiled and nodded my head. . . . She stood up and patted me on the head and in a slow voice asked, 'Abie, when are you going to fight again?' "[18]

Benny Leonard also overcame his parents' opposition to his boxing aspirations. Leonard knew how anxious his mother was that no harm come to him and of her belief that boxing went against Jewish tradition. So, early in his career, Benny lied about how he spent his time. Although his real last name was Leiner, he fought under the name of Leonard in case his mother read news of his bouts in the *Jewish Daily Forward*. Like Leach Cross and Abe Attell, Leonard eventually told his parents the truth. Returning home from a fight with a black eye, he admitted he had been hurt in the ring. He also gave his parents his victory purse of $20. "My mother," Benny recalled, "looked at my black eye and wept. My father, who had to work all week for $20, said, 'All right Benny, keep on fighting. It's worth getting a black eye for $20; I am getting verschwartzt [blackened] for $20 a week.' "[19]

Gershon Leiner's reasoning, developed out of his own sense of exploitation and economic hardship working as a sweatshop tailor, won out over Minnie Leiner's fears. Like Abe Attell's mother, the fruits of his son's labors overrode objections to how it had been earned. By 1916, so successful had their boy become that Benny was able to move his family to a better neighborhood up in Harlem. But he never forgot his mother's concern. In 1925, he retired as undefeated champion of the world, announcing that he had promised his sick mother that he would fight no more. "My love for her," he told a New York *Evening Telegram* reporter, "is greater than my love for the game that has made me independently wealthy, and to which I owe all I now possess."[20] Only the stock-market crash in 1929, which wiped out Leonard's fortune earned from boxing, real estate, and vaudeville, forced him back into the ring.

III

Not all Jewish boxers fared as well as Benny Leonard. Nor could they totally escape legitimate protest that their sport often fell prey to criminals and gamblers who rigged fights and threatened fighters with their own brand of violence if they refused to go along. Barely any Jewish fighter avoided such temptation or threat. For instance, Abe Attell's proclivity for the fast buck, which eventually involved him with Arnold Rothstein and the attempt to fix the 1919 World Series, emerged first in his career as a boxer. The "Little Hebrew" was frequently accused of carrying lesser opponents for a few extra rounds and even of throwing fights in order to cover bets or hustle a bigger-paying rematch. Commenting on his tenure as world featherweight champion, one journalist noted that "during the time Attell held the title he engaged in more crooked bouts than all the champions in the country put together in the last decade. It got so that during the last four or five years no one could tell what was going to happen when Attell stepped into the ring."[21] And though Ruby Goldstein denied he ever gave less than his best in the ring, there's no question that at one time or another, Charlie Rosenhouse and Waxie Gordon, prominent members of New York's Jewish underworld, owned his contract.[22]

Connections to crime and corruption, however, did not diminish the importance of Jewish boxers to their communities. For those looking for quick routes to success, cocky, tough fighters who consorted with well-known gangsters likely provided their own attraction. Either way, Jewish boxers provided a special source of ethnic pride and acceptance. Like Jewish basketball players who came in for their own share of adulation, boxers often lived in the very neighborhoods where they plied their trade. In much the same spirit that basketball games between local teams were transformed into ethnic celebrations, boxing matches became community events. Yet boxers, unlike basketball players, were also part of a larger national sports culture that awarded public attention and praise to those who competed for world championships. Although never as reputable as the few Jewish baseball players who made it into the major leagues, their large numbers, assertive stance, and public presence still made them attractive as symbols of American success and Jewish toughness. Some boxers were popular enough with Americans of all backgrounds that they even received praise for their ability to defuse ethnic tension. Recollections of childhood heroes, countless newspaper stories describing the triumphs of Jewish fighters and their loyal followers, and even the fiction of American Jewish writers richly embroider the importance of Jewish boxers as middle ground and the place of boxing in Jewish community life.

Prior to the Great Depression, Benny Leonard personified all that these men meant to their fellow Jews. When "The Great Bennah" died refereeing a fight in 1947, Al Lurie of the Philadelphia *Jewish Exponent* captured a sense of his appeal. Leonard's years as lightweight champion of the world between 1917 and 1925, he wrote, made him "the most famous Jew in America . . . beloved by thin-faced little Jewish boys who, in their poverty, dreamed of themselves as champions of the world." More than inspiration and pride, Leonard also offered hope of their own acceptance as Americans. As Lurie put it:

> When a people is beaten, persecuted and frustrated, it finds more than mere solace in its champions. Thus, when Benny Leonard reached the heights in boxing, he aided not only himself, but the entire American Jewish community. When Leonard was accepted and admired by the entire fair-minded American community, the Jews of America felt they, themselves, were being accepted and admired. Leonard, therefore, symbolized all Jewry. And he knew it.[23]

Leonard's contemporaries also recognized that the great champion was both a hero to Jews and a positive force in fostering Jewish acceptance by mainstream America. Commenting on Leonard's recent retirement from the ring in 1925, New York's *New Warheit* provided an interesting measure of his popularity among Jews and Gentiles. Comparing him to Albert Einstein, the paper noted that Benny

> is, perhaps, even greater than Einstein, for when Einstein was in America only thousands knew of him but Benny is known by millions. It is said that only twelve people or at the most twelve times twelve the world over understand Einstein, but Benny is being understood by tens of millions in America; and just as we need a country so as to be the equal of other peoples, so we must have a fist to become their peers.[24]

Writing in the midst of sport's so-called golden age, when even boxing gained respectability and Jack Dempsey reigned supreme with Babe Ruth as America's greatest heroes, this Jewish journalist recognized the growing importance of sport as part of American popular culture and the place of sports celebrities in it. As he understood it, Leonard's fistic triumphs were more likely to provide Jews in America both ethnic pride and American acceptance than Einstein's genius. At least in this commentary, the importance of Jewish muscle enhanced the possibility of assimilation without diminishing Jewish pride or identity.

In that same year, the *Jewish Morning Journal* carried similar sentiments in a column devoted to Jewish boxers and other Jewish athletes. Confessing both ignorance of and a lack of interest in the news of Jewish boxers in the sports pages of the regular press, the paper admitted it was on even shakier grounds when it came to sports such as squash. "It may be a Passover dish of the Reform Jews as far as we are concerned." Nevertheless, news of the triumph of Jewish players over their Gentile opponents, be it in the ring or on the court, filled the paper's reporter with "hope for the Jewish future." "We claim the distinction," he intoned, "of having discovered a Hebrew page in American newspapers."[25]

Over half a century after Leonard's tenure as middleweight champion, novelist Budd Schulberg could still recall in vivid detail the importance of Leonard to Jewish immigrants and their children engaged in their own American struggles. Writing in the boxing magazine *Ring*, Schulberg remembers that when he was a young boy, his hero was "neither the new cowboy star Tom Mix nor the acrobatic Doug Fairbanks. . . . Babe Ruth could hit fifty-four homers that year and I really didn't care." Not even the "legendary Ty Cobb brought a chill . . . to my skin at the mention of his name. That sensation," Schulberg insists, "was reserved for Benny Leonard." For himself and Jewish boys like him who "tasted the fists and felt the shoe-leather of righteous Irish and Italian Christian children" who accused them of killing Christ while they walked to "shul on the Sabbath . . . The Great Benny Leonard" was their "superhero."[26]

Nor were they alone in their admiration. Before Schulberg was old enough to read, his father known as B. P., himself only four years older than Leonard, gave him a scrapbook full of pictures and articles about the young Jewish champion. B. P. already was making his mark in motion pictures, splitting his time between New York and Los Angeles. Eventually he moved his family to the West Coast, served as production head for Paramount Pictures, and became one of the Jewish Hollywood moguls who dominated the industry. Although described by one Hollywood historian as a man whose Jewishness consisted of eating delicatessen on Sunday nights, B. P. reveled as a Jew in his admiration of Benny Leonard.[27] As Schulberg put it, "All up-and-coming young Jews in New York," like his father, "knew Benny Leonard personally. They would take time off from their lunch hour . . . to watch him train. They bet hundreds of thousands of dollars on him" and relished his boast that no matter how hard the battle no one ever "mussed" his thick black hair "plastered down and combed back in the approved style of the day." As Schulberg recalls, when Leonard's "hand was raised in victory, he would run his hand over his sleek black hair, and my father, and Al Kaufman, and Al Lichtman, and the rest of the Jewish rooting section would roar in delight." Much like the thousands of Jewish followers who crowded the Harlem street where Benny lived with his mother the night he first won the lightweight crown and cheered him by waving American flags and shouting his name, for B. P. and his friends, "The Great Bennah" symbolized the possibility of their own American success. As Schulberg reminds us, he also allowed them "to share in his invincibility" and to retaliate against all those who had demeaned them and their children because they were Jews. In Schulberg's words, "To see him climb in the ring sporting the six-pointed Jewish star on his fighting trunks was to anticipate sweet revenge for all the bloody noses, split lips, and mocking laughter at pale little Jewish boys who had run the neighborhood gauntlet."

In 1921, Schulberg almost got a chance to see and feel such things for himself. As he recalls it, approaching his seventh birthday, he had two ambitions in life: to become a world champion like his hero and "to see the Great Benny in action." While the first possibility remained remote, news that his father would take him to a championship bout between Leonard and the Irish contender Richie Mitchell filled him with great anticipation. Nor was he alone. According to one sportswriter, the fight, staged in Madison Square Garden on January 14, 1921, less than a year after the New York State legislature legalized boxing, would help the sport's reputation. The fact that the Garden's promoter, Tex Rickard, planned to stage it as a benefit to help raise money for a war-torn France and that governors, philanthropists, and members of high society were all expected to attend, figured in his assessment. Arnold Rothstein, still embroiled in the Black Sox scandal, also was excited about the bout. According to one story, his friend Benny Leonard had told him he would knock Mitchell out in the first round. Accordingly, Rothstein bet $25,000 on Benny and an additional $2,500 on behalf of the champion. Rumor had it that Leonard himself wagered his own $10,000 on the fight.

Schulberg never made it to ringside. When he and his father arrived at the Garden on East Twenty-third Street, ticket takers informed them that no one under the age of sixteen would be allowed into the arena. Heartbroken, the young Schulberg was rushed home by his father in a taxi. B. P. then hurried back downtown while his young son wallowed in miserable realization that by the time he turned sixteen his hero would long since have retired from the ring.

Although Schulberg missed the fight, his father recreated every detail for him. Mitchell's surprising knockdown of Leonard in the third round that made "thousands of young Jews" in attendance will their champion up off the canvas received less attention than B. P.'s vivid description of the bloody sixth round. In it Benny unmercifully bloodied and shredded Mitchell's face until the Irishman's corner threw in the towel.

As it turned out, little more than a decade later, Schulberg did get to see his hero fight. Despite earning lots of money through boxing, real-estate investments, and an occasional turn on the vaudeville circuit, Leonard lost it all in the Depression and came out of retirement in 1931. After a series of unimpressive victories against run-of-the-mill opponents, he signed to fight Jimmy McClarnin, a promising Irish welterweight contender who boasted a string of victories against Jewish boxers. Schulberg, then a freshman at Dartmouth, drove to New York to witness the bout.

Benny's return to the ring once again evoked Jewish admiration and pride. "There is scarcely a Jew whose blood runs red," as one sportswriter for Los Angeles's *B'nai B'rith Messenger* put it on the eve of the bout, "who is not vitally interested in the outcome of the long-looked-forward-to Benny Leonard–Jimmy McClarnin set-to." Admitting that Leonard was a decided underdog, he recognized that, as a "sportswriter," he felt Benny didn't have a chance. But, he insisted, as "the JEWISH man on the streets, I give this fight to Benny Leonard. Tomorrow morning," he continued, "I will know just how wrong I really am. But at least I will know that no matter how wrong I was, I was still right in believing that Benny Leonard would win—FOR win, loss, or draw, this compatriot of mine will have shown the world that he was a true fighting man."[28]

The fight was a mismatch. As Schulberg recalls, McClarnin toyed with his balding, overweight hero before knocking him out in "six of the saddest rounds I ever saw." When it was over, he didn't have the heart to call his father back in Los Angeles who awaited news of the outcome. Instead, then, and in later life, Schulberg preferred to think of that famous "Round Six" that he had only heard about in order to recreate the memory of Leonard's importance and place among his Jewish constituents.

Irving Rudd's memories of Benny Leonard and of Jewish involvement in boxing evoke similar responses. Although at different times in his career he worked as publicity director for the Brooklyn Dodgers and for Yonkers

Raceway, he began his trade promoting local fight cards in Queens and Brooklyn. Today, in his seventies, Rudd does the same job for Top Rank Boxing. Growing up in the Brownsville section of Brooklyn in the 1920s, Irving recalls that in his neighborhood, Leonard was a "deity." If his memory is correct, even McClarnin's knockout could not tarnish Benny's image. Given the chance to interview the great champion for his school newspaper, Irving remembers going backstage at a New York vaudeville theater to talk to him. There he also received Benny's photograph, on which Leonard wrote: "To My Friend Irving Rudd. If anyone wants to hit you, just send for me. Your friend, Benny Leonard." Needless to say, the next day at the local candy store, Irving was the envy of all his friends.[29]

For Rudd and countless other Jewish boys and men, Leonard was the greatest but hardly the only Jewish boxer in these years who evoked their passion, loyalty, and pride. In New York, Detroit, Boston, Chicago, or Los Angeles, every Jewish neighborhood boasted its own heroes whose names frequently appeared on posters in neighborhood store windows, on the marquees of local boxing clubs, or in newspaper stories describing their fights. Examples are endless. Jewish boys in Providence, Rhode Island, kept track of the exploits of their local hero, Maurice Billingkoff, a Russian immigrant who moved from Montreal to Providence at the age of seven in 1904 and who fought as a bantamweight. A newspaper cartoon of his knockout of one Kid Moran in March 1916 must have delighted local Jewish followers with its caption: "Oy! Such a fighter!" Chicago papers kept careful track of "ghetto boy" Morrie Bloom as he fought his way through the Midwest and West Coast in the decade before World War I. Reporting on the whereabouts of this middleweight in 1929, the Chicago *Jewish Chronicle* noted that "one of the greatest Jewish fighters ever turned out in the midwest" now trained businessmen and their sons in the manly art. Announcing world featherweight champion Louis "Kid" Kaplan's upcoming Chicago fight with Frankie Schaeffer in June 1925, the Chicago *Tribune* also informed "Jewish followers of the boxing racket" of the chance to see one King Solomon fight Gene Tunney in July. Pages of the *New York Times* throughout the 1920s catalogued the accomplishments of Jewish boxers on almost a daily basis. In similar fashion the Los Angeles *B'nai B'rith Messenger* kept its readers in touch with the exploits of local Jewish favorites such as welterweight Mushy Callahan. Jackie Fields, who spent part of his childhood in Chicago but who lived in Los Angeles as an adult, found himself claimed by Jewish fans in both cities as their local hero. Newspaper advertisements in Yiddish featuring boxers engaged in combat praising the virtues of Old Gold cigarettes confirm the popularity of the sport among Jews. Even the *American*

Hebrew kept its more sophisticated German-Jewish audience aware of the "many Jews in professional pugilism."[30]

In fact, as Irving Rudd recalls, in crowded urban Jewish neighborhoods like his own, it was impossible not be be aware of the presence of Jewish boxers and the feelings they evoked. Memories of his childhood friendship with Bernie Friedkin, who, like Budd Schulberg, dreamed of becoming a Jewish boxing champion, poignantly capture this sense.[31] Friedkin actually fought with moderate success as a lightweight in the late 1930s and early 1940s, at times promoted by Rudd himself. But as an adolescent, Bernie's dream jarred with images of the future held out to Rudd by his hard-working immigrant parents who hoped that "their designated genius," as Irving put it, would become "chief surgeon at Mount Sinai hospital" or at worst an orthodox rabbi. As an adult, Rudd served as his friend's promoter. As a boy, Irving filled in as a punching bag. Friedkin, whose basement was set up as a boxing ring and who learned to read by consuming *Ring,* once took Rudd on a tour of his East New York neighborhood. There, Irving remembers, "in the windows of the kosher butcher, the candy store, the hardware store . . . [were] big cardboard posters advertising professional boxing bouts at local clubs—the Broadway Arena and Ridgewood Grove. I [saw] names that [were] neither Irish, Polack, or German: "Pal" Silvers, Lou Feldman, Georgie Goldberg, and Marty Fox." Anxious to impress him with his knowledge of Jewish fighters, Friedkin revel[ed] him with stories of Ruby Goldstein, declaring that when the "Jewel of the Ghetto" loses a fight, the whole Jewish community "sits shiva."

Although he never claimed that all Jews mourned his defeats, Ruby Goldstein also remember how important he was to his loyal Lower East Side Jewish fans. "In that crowded neighborhood," he wrote, "I walked in a crowd of my own. . . . My social club was still Steinberg's candy store. Placards announcing my fights were hung in the windows of the store. Pictures were on the walls. Tickets for my fights were sold there. After every fight, it was jammed with 'members' waiting to see me." Even more impressive to the New York lightweight was the nickname the sportswriters gave him. Known as the "Jewel of the Ghetto," Goldstein recalled that the handle evoked memories of Joe Bernstein, the "Pride of the Ghetto." In Ruby's words, Bernstein remained "a figure in our folklore" and a name that even "bearded patriarchs who had never seen a fight . . . and who couldn't have named the name of another fighter, still spoke of." The fact that his own nickname might evoke similar responses from the same people filled him with immense pride.[32]

Goldstein's hope that even Old World Jewish patriarchs might identify with his success should not obscure the fact that for every one of them who came to the United States between 1881 and 1924, far more Yekls made the trip. Clearly many East European Jewish immigrants and their children were avid followers of the ring. Like Irish, Italians, and blacks, they came out to cheer on their landsmen, wager on the outcome, and enjoy a sense of independence and freedom in a separate male world of fierce loyalties to athletes that personified both ethnic pride and, however crudely and starkly, the importance of individual effort, hard work, discipline, and competition as keys to succeeding as Americans.

Fight promoters were not conscious of their own role in providing entertainment that implicitly educated immigrants in American ways, but they were keenly aware of the ethnic and neighborhood loyalties of their faithful patrons. Bouts arranged by astute entrepreneurs that emphasized ethnic conflict brought out working-class Jewish fans anxious to prove their superiority over their Irish and Italian neighbors who also filled local arenas. Leach Cross, for example, who fought over 150 times between 1908 and 1918, recalled that many of his fights in neighborhood boxing clubs like the Manhattan Casino and the Empire Athletic Club pitted him against Irish fighters. "The Irish used to come to see me get licked," he noted, and "the Jewish fans came to see me win."[33] So strong was his following among New York's East European Jewish community that after he had defeated Frankie Madden on St. Patrick's Day in 1908, the Jewish Daily Forward devoted part of its front page to a description of the fight and to a picture of the triumphant Jewish boxer. Five years later, when Cross traveled to New Orleans to take on Joe Mandot, the "Louisiana Wildcat," a special telegraph line was set up in front of the Western Union office on Rivington Street so that his loyal Jewish fans could follow the fight. Nat Fleischer, a childhood friend of Cross's and later founder and editor of Ring, suggests that "through Leachie, 1000s of New Yorkers who might never have followed boxing, became ardent fans."[34] Some 20 years later, matches between Chicago's lightweight Davey Day and his crosstown Italian rivals Frankie Siglio and Nick Castiglione regularly packed Chicago Stadium with 13,000 Jews and Italians eager for each other's throats. As one reporter noted, fans "cared more about a boxer's national or religious persuasion than his weight."[35]

While such matchups appeared to inflame ethnic hatred, some commentators suggested that they allowed Jewish boxers to act as a middle ground in the service of assimilation and ethnic harmony. Just as Abraham Cahan realized that Irish champions could also be Jewish heroes, several columnists argued that champions like Benny Leonard were popular with all people. Ted Carroll, for instance, told his Ring audience that Benny's "immense following was drawn from every segment and strata of society." And Arthur Brisbane, writing for the Hearst newspapers, noted that Leonard's reputation as a tough boxer as well as his participation in exhibition bouts to raise money for Catholic charities did "more to conquer anti-Semitism than 1,000 textbooks." Benny, as Brisbane put it, has "done more to evoke the respect of the non-Jew for the Jew than all the brilliant Jewish writers combined."[36]

Boxing promoters were also aware of the potential in pitting Jewish boxers against each other. Leach Cross's victory over Joe Bernstein that so enraged his father was only one of many such bouts that brought together neighborhood rivals as the unofficial standard bearers of different Jewish neighborhoods. Benny Leonard's two fights with Lou Tendler, the son of a sweatshop tailor who came out of Philadelphia's Market Street Jewish ghetto to challenge the great lightweight champion, stand out here. The first bout, billed as the Jewish lightweight championship of the world, took place at Boyles Thirty Acres in Jersey City on July 27, 1922. In a savage display that left both boxers bloodied at the end, Leonard held on to his title in a no-decision bout before a crowd of some 60,000 fans, many of whom were Jewish. One year later, the two met again, this time in Yankee Stadium before some 58,000 spectators who paid $452,648, then a record for a lightweight bout. Anticipating the battle for its fight fans, the *Jewish Daily Forward* commented that "while only one of the two combatants will exit the arena a champion, neither will leave the place unmarked." According to Heywood Broun, who covered the fight for the New York *World,* Leonard won a decisive victory. His description vividly captures the sport's visceral appeal to Jewish fight fans from Philadelphia and New York who came to cheer on their favorite. As Broun put it:

> The wonder is that Tendler still had a head. Rights and lefts, hooks and jabs rocked him from the beginning. Water cascaded from the top of the Philadelphian's pompadour as if he had been Old Faithful, the Geyser. Now his head went back. Next it sagged, but mostly was doubled from side to side as Leonard landed first with one hand and then with the other. . . . Distinctly this was highbrow entertainment, for it was boxing developed to its most lofty phase as a fine art. The only trouble was that it was not a contest between two masters. The participants were professor and pupil.[37]

Whether fighting against each other or against other ethnic foes, Jewish boxers occasionally showed their appreciation of Jewish support by sacrificing their own profits for Jewish causes. Much like Jewish basketball players who played ball in the spirit of the Jewish tradition of tzedakah, Ruby Goldstein, Charlie Phil Rosenberg, Art Lasky, and Maxie Rosenbloom fought exhibitions to raise money for the Palestine Relief Fund or for local Jewish charities. In July 1925, for instance, Rosenberg, then world bantamweight champion, "K.O." Phil Kaplan, and Abie Goldstein appeared before 13,000 on a card at New York's Velodrome that raised over $63,000 for the Hunt's Point Jewish hospital.[38]

Participation in such events endeared Jewish boxers to their Jewish fans. Name-changing also played a part here. Although Benny Leonard, Leach Cross, Mushy Callahan, and a number of other Jewish fighter anglicized their Jewish names either to disguise their occupation from disapproving parents or because they thought it would promote their careers, others emphasized Jewish monikers in hopes of attracting ethnic audiences. Charlie Phil Rosenberg's given name, for instance, was Charles Green. Born on the Lower East Side in 1902, he grew up in Harlem, where his mother struggled to survive as a pushcart peddler. One of his friends, Phil Rosenberg, made a few extra dollars as a boxer. One day Rosenberg became ill and unable to make a scheduled fight. Green took his license, convinced the promoter that he was Phil Rosenberg, and earned $15 for his effort. Green kept his newfound professional name and went on to become world bantamweight champion in 1925.[39]

Even more telling is Barney Lebrowitz's story. Born in Philadelphia in 1891, Lebrowitz began his boxing career in 1906 under the name of Barney Williams. After seven mediocre years in New York clubs as a light-heavy-weight, he became the property of "Dumb" Dan Morgan. More astute than his nickname implied, Morgan immediately arranged a fight for him with Dan "Porky" Flynn at New York's St. Nicholas arena. Aware that bouts between Jews and Irish were moneymakers, he persuaded the arena's promoter to advertise his fighter as Battling Levinsky, the Jewish boxer ready to take on any Irishman in the country. Levinsky handled Flynn and quickly became a favorite with Jewish fight fans, not only for his name but for his success in the ring. During a career that spanned three decades, he reigned as light-heavyweight champion between 1916 and 1920, fought in 272 bouts, and took on all comers, including Georges Carpentier, Jack Dempsey, and Gene Tunney. Along with Leach Cross, Benny Leonard, Davey Day, and a host of other Jewish boxers, Levinsky wore a Star of David on his trunks in case Jewish fight fans forgot his Jewish name.[40]

Name changing one way or another did not always guarantee boxers their desired results. The Leiners and the Wallachs knew who Benny Leonard and Leach Cross were, just as Los Angeles Jewish fight fans recognized that Mushy Callahan was their beloved Vincent Morris Schneer. So too did the faithful in Chicago and Los Angeles who claimed Jackie Fields as their own. Field's birth name was Jacob Finkelstein. When he began his career as an amateur boxer in Los Angeles, he changed it because promoters thought his Jewish name would present the wrong image for him. As he told it, "A Jew wasn't supposed to be a tough fighter. A Jew is supposed to be a guy for the books." Searching for a "high-class name," Finkelstein remembered his Chicago roots and picked Fields, naming himself after Chicago businessman and philanthropist Marshall Field, who owned the department store of the same name. Jackie, "just American for Jacob," Fields remembered, took less thought.[41]

That's how most Americans who took any interest in boxing first came to know the young Jewish boxer. At a time when the Olympic Games hardly captured the public's attention as they do today, Fields traveled to Paris in 1924 as part of the American Olympic team. After a series of elimination bouts he won the welterweight championship from one of his own teammates, becoming, at sixteen, the youngest boxer ever to win an Olympic gold medal. In its brief coverage of the boxing competition, the *New York Times* identified Fields either as an "American" or as a "Californian," making no mention of his Jewish immigrant roots. Regardless of his name, by the time he concluded his professional career in 1933, this colorful welterweight who won 73 of 87 bouts and who reigned as world champion in 1929 and 1930 and again between 1932 and 1933 was better known as a tough Jewish fighter and a popular favorite of Jewish fight fans.[42]

IV

Two stories about Jewish fighters and their names suggest another reason why Jewish fighters were so important to Jews growing up in America in the first part of the twentieth century. One, handed down by Irving Rudd, tells of a match in a western coal-mining town between Benny Leonard and one "Irish" Eddie Finnegan. Unfortunately for Eddie, cries from spectators urging him to "kill the kike" or "murder the Yid" enraged Benny. In Rudd's telling, Leonard attacked his opponent with a furious flurry of jabs, stabs, and moves, busting up Finnegan's eyes and lips. Holding on for dear life, "Irish" Eddie grabbed Leonard in a clinch and pled for mercy, gasping in Yiddish that his real name was Seymour Rosenbaum.[43] The other story appeared in Elias Lieberman's "Melting Pot" column for the *American Hebrew* in June 1919. Titled "Irony," it told the saga of "slugger Kid Cohen's" fight with a boxer named Kid Paul. As Lieberman presented it, depressed over news of pogroms in his Polish homeland, Izzy Cohen fought listlessly against a much lesser opponent "who would have failed miserably were it not for the Jew's obvious lack of interest." Between rounds Cohen told his handlers that the news made him wonder "if I'm any earthly use to either my people or myself." A Jewish voice from the crowd shook Izzy out of his lethargy, urging him to destroy Kid Paul because he is a "Polack." With "childhood memories of Kiev flamed before his eyes" and "boyhood tales of Kishineff . . . in his ears," Cohen proceeded to clobber his opponent, symbolically offering retribution for the punishment Polish Jews endured from their own countrymen. "Praise God, thundered the avenger, in purest Hebrew, as he flung aloft his mittened hands." And "from his feet came the same cry in weaker tones: Praise God, Oh, Israel!"[44]

In both stories, Jewish fighters disguise their identities only to incur the wrath of superior Jewish figures who use their fists to challenge anti-Semitism directed at themselves and against other Jews. Even respectable organs of Jewish public opinion like the *American Hebrew*, which at other times disapproved of boxing as proper sport for assimilating Jews, could appreciate the positive effect of such stories in demonstrating that Jews were fit to be Americans and in developing an American Jewish identity that embraced physicality and toughness as necessary for Jewish survival. Although Jewish advocates of sport and Jewish baseball players like Hank Greenberg make their own contributions to these connected strands of American Jewish history, Jewish dominance in a sport defined by physical violence, strength, and toughness brought them together in special ways. Despite its reputation as a disreputable sport, no other activity provided such a clear way to refute stereotypes of the weak, cowardly Jew that anti-Semites employed to deny Jewish immigrants and their children full access to American opportunities. Nor did any other sport that Jews engaged in provide better connection to a historical tradition of Jewish physical strength and power employed in behalf of Jewish protection and survival in a hostile world.

Boxing's role in challenging anti-Semitic stereotypes and in shaping a Jewish-American identity emerged most fully in the years between the wars. We know, however, that some Jewish spokesmen at the turn of the century, in the spirit of Max Nordau's European cries for "muscular Jews," urged East European Jewish immigrants to participate in all sports for similar reasons. Even earlier, at least one Jewish writer anticipated boxing's special potential in this respect. Writing at a time when East European Jewish immigrants first began coming to America, Isadore Choynski used the pages of the *American Israelite* to inform his German-Jewish readers of his son's ring triumphs. In 1885, when Joe Choynski, the first great Jewish-American boxer, was only 17, Isadore boasted that his boy was "able to knock Sullivan out . . . in a single round."[45] Just in case this assertion failed to impress the great John L., the elder Choynski provided additional evidence after Joe won the California amateur heavyweight crown two years later. With references to a Union Civil War marching song that identified his American attachments, his own father's orthodox Jewish disdain for physical violence, and a distinguished boxing heritage of European Jews, Isadore announced his son's victory to his readers:

> We are coming Father Abraham! The boys of the Jewish persuasion are getting heavy on muscle. Many of them are training to knock out J. L. and it may come to pass. It is almost an everyday occurrence to read in our papers that a disciple of Mendoza ... has knocked out the best of sluggers. . . . This week a youngster who calls himself J. B. Choynski, 19 years old, native of this city, weighing 160 pounds, fought for the championship and gold medal with one named Connelly, and the lad with the Polish name knocked out the well-knitted Irish lad of much experience in three rounds, and carried off the medal and the applause triumphantly. . . . I knew that boy's grandfather quite well. He is dead several years but if the pious, learned grandfather could lift his head from the grave and look upon the arena where mostly the scum of society congregate and behold his grandson slugging and sparring, fighting and dodging . . . he would hang his head and exclaim, "What is this horrible show for?"[46]

In one brief paragraph Choynski captured contradictory themes about Jewish physicality that became increasingly relevant to future generations of East European Jews and their children. Recognition of a heritage of Jewish boxing ability dating back to England's Daniel Mendoza, disdain for involvement in questionable activity even by standards of American respectability coupled with traditional Jewish disgust with such behavior, and yet pride in this display of Jewish physicality that helped Jewish boys establish their American place anticipated the range of responses that accompanied later Jewish involvement in the ring.

Several months later, when Joe successfully defended his title by knocking out an Irish blacksmith named William Keneally, Choynski connected his son's victory to a tradition of tough Jews willing and able to risk their lives in behalf of Jewish survival. As he reported: "The Choynski boy fairly wiped the floor with the Irish gentleman, and finished him in four hard contested rounds. The Jews, who take little stock in slugging, are glad that there is one Maccabee among them, and that the Irish will no longer boast that there is not a Jew who can stand up to the racket and receive punishment according to the rules of Queensberry."[47]

Sportswriters, sportsmen, Jewish boxers, and their fans continually drew the same lessons about the importance of Jewish boxers in the 1920s and 1930s. Some even made direct connections to other Jewish heroes who risked their lives defending their own people. Reporting on the victories of Cleveland boxers Henry Goldberg, George Levine, and Sammy Aaronson, one reporter for Cleveland's *Jewish Independent* in 1926 scoffed at those people who expressed surprise in "the prowess of the Jew in athletics." "A perusal of the ancient records," he noted, "will prove beyond question that even in antiquity, athletics and physical development were qualities that were sought and encouraged among Jewish men." Any doubters only needed to remember that "Samson the Strong is still the ideal of the strong men of the world."[48]

Several years later, Bill Miller, a sportswriter and boxing publicist, added another voice to a growing chorus that underlined the critical role Jewish boxers played in refuting charges of Jewish inferiority and weakness. Looking back on his childhood, Miller reminded his Los Angeles *B'nai B'rith Messenger* readers of a story that always brought " a belly laugh" when Jewish comics told it on the vaudeville circuit. "Vell, vun time," the comic began, "me und mine brodder, und mine oncle, und nine uff mine relations, ve nerly licked a Irishman vunce!" Now, however, thanks to the glorious achievements of Jewish boxers that Miller briefly recounted, charges of Jewish impotence were "inane and pointless." Never again, he insisted, will there be a recurrence of the "excruciating jest" about a bunch of weak Jews and an Irishman that so pained him as a child. Now, he concluded, "it's pretty nearly the other way around."[49]

H. P. Hollander, an English welterweight and member of the British Maccabi Association, presented a similar if more measured account of the same theme for readers of the Detroit *Jewish Chronicle*. In an article entitled "Why Jews Make Good Boxers," Hollander noted that throughout their history Jews found "few opportunities for play" in their "desperate struggle for existence." With time only for infrequent recreation at night, their "amusements were more intellectual than physical, more of the brain than of the body." Emphasizing the popular theories of human development and the environment, he continued that such practice, coupled with living conditions that were often unhealthy, not surprisingly failed to develop a people with "recognized athletic slender build," but rather built ones who are "generally short, muscular and broad." Even with these handicaps, however, Jews "spread thinly all over the face of the world," and although "outnumbered and downtrodden," also inherited from their ancient ancestors "pride of birth and virile instincts." Resentful of "slurs" and "sneers" about "their small stature and lack of skills in many sports," the result of circumstances that prohibited opportunity for participation, the individual Jewish boxer, Hollander suggested, vindicated what had been denied his people. "Once he could get into the ring, The Jew could show the world that he could fight—and fight with brain and with strength and with courage. Then no one could deny him that he was a man amongst men, for few sports appeal more to the general imagination than boxing." Jewish history, the Englishman concluded, "has made him a boxer of purpose and determination."[50]

The praise of Jewish toughness and physical strength appeared in a Jewish newspaper that in the same year reported news of the Nuremberg Laws, Father Coughlin, and the plight of the Palestinian homeland movement. Although Hollander did not explicitly connect his appreciation of the physically tough Jewish boxer to everyday concern about Jewish survival, others did. Bill Kadison, a sportswriter for the Los Angeles *B'nai B'rith Messenger,* offered his own contribution by recounting a string of triumphs of American Jewish boxers over German opponents in the early 1930s. "Ever since Herr Hitler inaugurated his 'rid Germany of the Jew' campaign," Kadison wrote in 1933, "his boys have suffered defeat every time they stepped out against ring warriors of the 'faith.' "[51]

Benny Leonard echoed similar views even before Adolf Hitler's rise to power. Interviewed by David Barzell, a reporter for the *Jewish Tribune,* at the height of his career, "The Great Bennah" reviewed Jewish history and concluded that "the Jew has always been a fighter when he has a fair chance." Talking about his own sport and his own times, Leonard insisted that of all nationalities represented in the ring, the Jew was the "most fightingest of them all." Leonard, Barzell concluded, believed that the Jewish people are judged "as a whole" by the actions of individual prominent Jews. As one of those people, Benny took "his responsibility for the rest of Jewry" seriously. "A Jew has no right to be mean or puny," Barzell noted, "and Leonard seeks to live up to this ideal."[52]

Three years later Leonard extended his commitment to Jewish strength and survival in a most explicit way by associating himself with Camp Hakoah, a summer athletic camp designed to prepare Jews for potential combat with their enemies. Situated on Sackett Lake near Monticello, New York, in an area fast becoming the vacation grounds for New York City's large Jewish population, the camp, as advertised in the *American Hebrew,* was named after "the mighty and heroic Hakoah Soccer Team, which is the standard bearer of Jewish strength." There, Benny Leonard, "our own national hero," whose picture appeared in the advertisement, would head the physical-training department. Developing Jewish "children to the highest degree of physical perfection," the camp hoped to "produce Jewish men of brawn who will form the vanguard of the Jewish people with a view of protecting them against attacks." Added inducement for signing up included the prospect of receiving periodic recommendations throughout the year about diet and exercise from Benny and the chance to write him about individual needs.[53]

There is no record of how much Leonard earned for his participation in this venture or whether it involved any more than brief, symbolic appearances by the athlete as celebrity so common to sports camps today. Moreover, even at the advertised reduced rate of $175 (marked down from $300), this summer experience was well beyond the reach of most of New York's East European Jewish population. Still, the stated purpose of the camp undeniably emphasizes the constancy with which the success of Jewish boxers remained tied to concerns about the need for physical, tough Jews able and willing to resist all threats to Jewish existence.

Certainly not everyone embraced Jewish involvement in boxing as a positive contribution to either Jewish survival or Jewish assimilation. But even here, writers did not dispute a tradition of Jewish strength. Chicago's Yiddish-language *Daily Jewish Courier,* for instance, in 1923 took issue with a local "gentile newspaperman" who argued that "the number of Jewish pugilists in the front ranks of this country's fighting fraternity" demonstrates the falseness of "the theory that Jews are physical cowards." While voicing approval of Jewish participation in sport, the *Courier*'s correspondent doubted that it was "proof of the physical courage . . . let alone the spiritual courage of that people." "The Jews," he proclaimed, "have never been lacking in either." As for Jewish boxers, the writer's disgust both for their sport and for their claims as Jews was clear:

> As for our highly honored members of the fighting fraternity, we may say that if the Jewish people has anything to contribute to the common civilization and culture of the race, such contributions are rather to be sought in the realm of their intellects than in their fists. . . . As a matter of fact none of these pugilists may be said to be Jews except in the accident of their birth. We should certainly encourage clean athletics but we need not bother about the pugilists. Let them take care of themselves. They believe they can very well do so.[54]

The *Courier*'s criticism recognized the importance of a Jewish tradition of physical courage, but only when tied intimately to Jewish spirituality and intellect. As John Hoberman argues, even physical-culture enthusiasts like Max Nordau praised and encouraged Jewish muscularity only when managed by what he considered to be a superior Jewish intellect.[55] Characterizing all Jewish boxers as unconnected to a Jewish tradition where mind ruled over muscle, the *Courier* excluded them as part of an important and heroic heritage of Jewish physicality. Implicit in its remarks is a disdain for these men and their backgrounds—Jews by "accident of their birth" who came primarily from immigrant working-class families where the daily struggle for existence and the personal aspirations of many left little room for intellectual concerns or formal religious practice.

Within this framework it's also reasonable to assume that the *Courier*'s editorialist would not have been swayed by stories of Jewish boxing triumphs that linked victory not only to their physical strength but also to their intellect. Accounts of Benny Leonard's triumphs, for instance, invariably commented on "his brains" as being as important to his success as his strength. Nat Fleischer described him as a man "with a pair of dark brown eyes that sparkled intelligence" who "combined the boxing ingenuity of Young Griffo; the masterful technique of James J. Corbett; the clout of Jack Dempsey; the alertness of Gene Tunney; and the speed of Mike Gibbons." Above all, he noted, "Leonard had a hair-trigger brain. As he shifted about the ring, the fans could almost read his thoughts as he mapped out his plan of attack." Leonard, himself, dubbed the "king of scientific fighters" by one reporter, argued that "it was the Jewish fighters who put the science in the game." Even more emphatic about the intelligence of the Jewish boxer was Johnny Ray, the manager of the great Irish heavyweight Billy Conn. Commenting on his fighter's defeat by knockout at the hands of the immortal Joe Louis in a championship fight where the Irishman seemed well ahead on points, Ray bemoaned Conn's ill-fated decision to go for the kill. "If he had a Jewish head instead of an Irish one, he'd be the champ."[56]

Jewish immigrants struggling to escape their working-class roots, and their children, who were to enjoy the economic success that their parents only dreamed about, no doubt read these accounts in their newspapers. Some may even have chuckled over a *Jewish Daily Forward* piece that identified those who believed in the "congenital cowardice of the Jewish race" as the same people who "pass laws to banish Darwin from college textbooks." "We can afford," the *Forward* concluded, "to be in the same boat with the author of the *Origin of Species*."[57] For many of them, reading about Jewish boxers, going to the fights, betting on their heroes, and celebrating their victories as local and world champions allowed opportunities to vicariously challenge anti-Semitic stereotypes and to identify with Jewish boxers who personified the necessity of Jewish toughness in a threatening world.

Despite the *Courier*'s concerns, the very fact that Jewish boxers often came from the same backgrounds as their Jewish constituents and appeared in public in particular ways only heightened their appeal. Delighting in the often-flamboyant lifestyles and public immodesty of uneducated Jewish men from their same streets, other Jews recognized them as symbols of redemption and possibility in an America that, for all of its freedom, offered no guarantees of success. Much like the ways in which John L. Sullivan appealed to Irish immigrants or black champions like Jack Johnson and Joe Louis lifted the spirits and hopes of their own people, the manner in which the Jewish fighters made their way was just as important as their victories. Whether in the ring, on the vaudeville circuit, or in the company of notorious gangsters and beautiful women, amassing huge earnings with their fists and losing it all in the stock-market crash, Benny Leonard and a host of other Jewish boxers offered their own appeal. Although newspaper columnists rarely commented on such themes, a Jewish playwright and a Jewish novelist writing fifty years apart capture measures of this attraction in their own commentaries on American immigrant life.

Some thirty years after *Yekl* appeared in print, a Jewish playwright with the unlikely name of Clifford Odets rehearsed variations of Cahan's themes with immigrants of a different nationality that could just as well have been Jewish. In *Golden Boy*, first produced in 1937, Joe Bonaparte, a second-generation son of an Italian immigrant, gives up a promising career as a violinist to become a prizefighter. Although ignoring his father's hope that he would become a musician, Joe, like Jake, remains torn about his decision throughout the play—a conflict that eventually contributes to his tragic death in a car accident. For him, a career in the ring becomes a way of reaching for the American dream in the midst of Depression America. Telling his father of his decision to take up boxing on the eve of his twenty-first birthday, he declares:

> Now's a time for standing. Poppa, I have to tell you—I don't like myself, past, present and future. Do you know there are men who have wonderful things from life? Do you think they're better than me? Do you think I like this feeling of no possessions? . . . You don't know what it means to sit around here and watch the months go ticking by! Do you think that's a life for a boy my age? Tomorrow's my birthday! I change my life![58]

Opportunity for economic advancement and escape from the ethnic, immigrant working-class world of his youth alone do not move Joe to pugilism. Odets is far more sophisticated than that. But they are issues that also motivated a number of Jewish youth to seek their fortunes on the canvas. Once committed, symbolized by a ring triumph in which Joe breaks his hand in a ferocious display of punching that simultaneously damages any aspirations toward the violin while alleviating his trainer's fears that he isn't aggressive enough, Joe displays a new sense of himself as a tough, strong, fearless man. Talking to a newspaper reporter on the eve of his big fight with the Choco-

late Drop Kid, Joe reminds the skeptical writer that he now has what it takes
to be a winner:

> I don't blush and stammer these days. Bonaparte goes in and slugs with the
> best. In the bargain his brain is *better* than the best. That's the truth. Why
> deny it? . . . What good is modesty? I'm a fighter! The whole essence of
> prizefighting is immodesty! "I'm better than you are—I'll prove it by break-
> ing your face in!" What do you expect? A conscience and a meek smile? I
> don't believe that bull the meek will inherit the earth![59]

A generation removed from Yekl, Joe not only reaffirms the children of immigrants as tough and strong but also adds another significant ingredient—
immodesty. Here is a man by trade and by choice who people notice for his
style in the ring and out. Although Odets has other concerns, his characteri-
zation of Joe in this way hints at some of the reasons why successful boxers
from immigrant backgrounds became public heroes to their ethnic constituencies. Here was a style, if not a career, to aspire to: one that encouraged
young men to step outside their familiar ethnic world and assert their American right to opportunity and success. The fact that risks were inherent in such
choices, including the possible abandonment of that world and its values or,
at the least, the problem of reconciling it with mainstream American culture,
challenged the American-born children of East European Jewish immigrants
as surely as it did Joe Bonaparte. In part, their interest in boxing, both as fighters and as interested spectators, remained driven by such matters.

As E. L. Doctorow's *Billy Bathgate* reminds us, the whole matter of risk-
taking was further complicated in the 1930s, when economic depression shat-
tered the dreams of many Americans, immigrants and native-born alike.
Recreating the poverty and richness of a 1930s working-class Bronx neighborhood as seen through the eyes of a fifteen-year old member of Dutch
Schultz's faltering band of criminals, Doctorow, although talking about gangsters, not pugilists, suggests something of the appeal that Jewish boxers must
have had among their own people as well as others who were struggling to
make the most of an American dream gone sour. In a long passage he describes how his young protagonist, Billy Bathgate, feels about himself and his
own neighborhood when he returns for the first time as an acknowledged
member of the Schultz mob. Wearing a new satin jacket of a sports team
known as the Shadows and his new sneakers, Billy realizes:

> I represented another kind of arithmetic to everyone on the block, not just
> the kids but the grown-ups too, and it was peculiar because I wanted every-
> one to know what they figured out easily enough, that it was just not given

to a punk to find easy money except one way, but at the same time I didn't want them to know. I didn't want to be changed from what I was, which was a boy alive in the suspension of the judgment of childhood, that I was the wild kid of a well-known crazy woman, but there was something in me that might grow into the lineaments of honor, so that a discerning teacher or some other act of God, might turn up the voltage of this one brain to a power of future life that everyone in the Bronx could be proud of. I mean that to the more discerning adult, the man I didn't know and didn't know ever noticed me who might be living in the building or see me in the candy store, or in the schoolyard. I would be one of the possibilities of redemption, that there was some wit in the way I moved, some lovely intelligence in an unconscious gesture of the game, that would give him this objective sense of hope for a moment, quite unattached to any loyalty of his own, that there was a chance, bad as things were, America was a big juggling act and that we could all be kept up in the air somehow, and go around not from hand to hand, but from light to dark, from night to day, in the universe of God after all.[60]

Billy Bathgate could well be Jewish; Doctorow doesn't tell us. Dutch Schultz, born Arthur Flegenheimer, certainly was. Neither Billy nor Dutch was a boxer. Nor did careers as boxers or gangsters signify Jewish arrival within the American economic or social mainstream. Boxing was at best considered a marginal sport, and the life of crime, by definition, unacceptable. But as the fictional Bathgate suggests, in dire times the escapades and accomplishments of even boxers and criminals offered hope of an American future and confirmation that the decision involved in leaving old ways behind, however ambivalent, might still be worth it. Even without this special attraction, however, Jewish boxers challenged stereotypes of the weak Jew and helped define an American Jewish identity that included physical toughness as an acceptable trait. Both as symbols of possibility and as part of Jewish community experience, they offered their own contributions to how immigrants became Americans.

Notes

1. Cleveland *Press,* January 12, 1924.
2. Steven A. Riess, "A Fighting Chance: The Jewish-American Boxing Experience, 1890–1940," *American Jewish History* 74 (March 1985), 234, and Ken Blady, *The Jewish Boxers' Hall of Fame* (New York, 1988), are the sources for this information.
3. Abraham Cahan, *Yekl and the Imported Bridegroom* (New York, 1970), 2.

4. Ibid., 2–5.

5. Elliott Gorn, *The Manly Art: Bare-Knuckle Prize Fighting in America* (Ithaca, N.Y., 1986), 132–41, 224–49.

6. Unless otherwise noted, information on Choynski's family and career comes from William Kramer and Norton B. Stern, "San Francisco's Fighting Jew," *California History* 53 (winter 1974), 333–45. Also see Blady, *The Jewish Boxers' Hall of Fame* 27–38. On San Francisco, see Irena Narell, *Our City, The Jews of San Francisco* (San Diego, 1981).

7. Kramer and Stern, "San Francisco's Fighting Jew," 336.

8. All of Fields's quotations are from Ira Berkow, *Maxwell Street* (New York, 1977), 142–43.

9. Unnamed 1934 newspaper clip by Frank Menke called "Benny Bass Started as Pug by Beating up Irish Kids," Jews and Sports collection, AJA.

10. Blady, *The Jewish Boxers' Hall of Fame*, 112–113.

11. Ibid.

12. Bernard Postal, Jesse Silver, Roy Silver, *Encyclopedia of Jews in Sport* (New York, 1965) 154 (hereafter *Encyclopedia*); Ruby Goldstein, *Third Man in the Ring* (New York, 1959), 6, 16–18, 23.

13. Cleveland *Press*, March 22, 1924; *Encyclopedia*, 171; Cleveland *Jewish Independent*, October 30, 1925; Marc Raphael, *Jews and Judaism in a Midwestern Community, Columbus, Ohio* (Columbus, 1979); Detroit *Jewish Chronicle*, November 2, 1934.

14. Blady, *The Jewish Boxers' Hall of Fame*, 81–90, covers Cross's career. Also see Riess, "A Fighting Chance," 230, and *Encyclopedia* 152.

15. Jeffrey T. Sammons, *Beyond the Ring: The Role of Boxing in American Society* (Urbana, Ill., 1988), provides an overview of the history of boxing in the United States.

16. Riess, "A Fighting Chance," 230.

17. For information on Attell see Blady, *The Jewish Boxers' Hall of Fame*, 39–48. Also see Riess, "A Fighting Chance," 232–34.

18. Blady, *The Jewish Boxers' Hall of Fame*, 41–42.

19. *Jewish Tribune*, October 5, 1923; Nat Fleischer, *Leonard the Magnificent* (Norwalk, Conn., 1947), 96; *Encyclopedia*, 162–65; Blady, *The Jewish Boxers' Hall of Fame*, 109–28; all provide information on Leonard and repeat this story.

20. Fleischer, *Leonard the Magnificent*, 87.

21. Riess, "A Fighting Chance," 233. For connections between Jewish gangsters and boxing see Albert Fried, *The Rise and Fall of the Jewish Gangster in America* (New York, 1980), and Jenna Joselit, *Our Gang: Jewish Crime and the New York Jewish Community, 1900–1940* (Bloomington, Ind., 1983).

22. Goldstein, *Third Man in the Ring*, 31–35.

23. Philadelphia *Jewish Exponent*, April 25, 1947.

24. New York *Jewish Daily Bulletin*, March 25, 1925, reprints the column.

25. Ibid.

26. Budd Schulberg, "The Great Benny Leonard," *Ring Magazine* (May 1980), 32–37, is the source for the following account and the quotations.

27. Neal Gabler, *An Empire of Their Own: How the Jews Invented Hollywood* (New York, 1988), 283.

28. Los Angeles *B'nai B'rith Messenger*, October 7, 1932.

29. Irving Rudd interview, July 5, 1988.

30. Benton Rosen, "Some Outstanding Jewish Athletes and Sportsmen in Rhode Island, 1916–1964," *Rhode Island Historical Society Notes* 5 (November 1968), 153–67; Chicago *Jewish Chronicle*, March 30, 1929; Morrie Bloom Scrapbooks, Chicago Jewish Archives, Spertus College of Judaica; Chicago *Tribune*, June 21, 1925; *American Hebrew*, January 20, 1928. The Detroit *Free Press*, Detroit *Jewish Chronicle*, Chicago *Tribune*, New York *Times*, *American Hebrew*, and Los Angeles *B'nai B'rith Messenger* provide an abundance of other examples.

31. Rudd interview, July 5, 1988.

32. Goldstein, *Third Man in the Ring*, 45–46.

33. Riess, "A Fighting Chance," 230. *Encyclopedia*, 152.

34. Nat Fleischer, *Fifty Years at Ringside* (New York, 1958), 163.

35. Chicago *Herald American*, March 3, 1941; Chicago *Tribune*, November 18, 1982.

36. Blady, *The Jewish Boxers' Hall of Fame*, 111; *Jewish Tribune*, October 5, 1923.

37. Riess, "A Fighting Chance," 239–40. Broun quotation in New York *World*, July 23, 1923.

38. *American History*, July 31, 1925; Chicago *Tribune*, July 22, 1925. For other examples see Los Angeles *B'nai B'rith Messenger*, October 25, 1929, August 28, 1931, November 29, 1935, June 26, 1936; Goldstein, *Third Man in the Ring*, 90–91.

39. Blady, *The Jewish Boxers' Hall of Fame*, 185–89.

40. Ibid, 99–104.

41. Berkow, *Maxwell Street*, 141–42.

42. New York *Times*, July 19, 20, 21, 1924.

43. Rudd interview, July 5, 1988.

44. *American Hebrew*, June 6, 1919.

45. *American Israelite*, June 30, 1885.

46. Ibid., December 16, 1887.

47. Kramer and Stern, "San Francisco's Fighting Jew," 336.

48. *Jewish Independent*, July 30, 1926.

49. Los Angeles *B'nai B'rith Messenger*, November 20, 1931.

50. Detroit *Jewish Chronicle*, March 15, 1935.

51. Los Angeles *B'nai B'rith Messenger*, June 23, 1933.

52. *Jewish Tribune*, October 5, 1923.

53. *American Hebrew*, June 4, 1926.

54. Chicago *Daily Jewish Courier*, February 16, 1923.

55. John Hoberman, "Sport and the Myth of the Jewish Body," paper presented at NASSH conference, May 27, 1989.

56. Fleischer, *Leonard the Magnificent*, 1–2; *Jewish Tribune*, October 5, 1923; Cleveland *Press*, January 11, 1924. Johnny Ray quotation is in Christopher Mead, *Champion, Joe Louis: Black Hero in White America* (New York, 1985), 180–81.

57. *Encyclopedia*, 138, has *Jewish Daily Forward* quotation.

58. Clifford Odets, *Six Plays of Clifford Odets* (New York, 1933), 252.

59. Ibid., 305.

60. E. L. Doctorow, *Billy Bathgate* (New York, 1989), 94–95.

11
Muscular Marxism and the Chicago Counter-Olympics of 1932

WILLIAM J. BAKER

At Barcelona in 1936, the games did not go on. The People's Olympics, scheduled as a protest against the Nazi Olympics in Berlin, became the first victims of the Spanish Civil War. Fascists and Loyalists began fighting on the very day the games were to have begun.[1] Perhaps it was just as well. Cancellation allows us to imagine a grand athletic festival in honor of the human spirit and progressive values, sparing us a ludic version of George Orwell's *Homage to Catalonia* where liberals and socialists squabble endlessly and everybody hates the Bolsheviks.[2] In truth, the idealism behind the Barcelona Games might well have self-destructed in the heat of nationalistic competition between, say, German and French foes, not to mention British and American (or Polish and Russian) athletes.

By comparison, the Chicago Counter-Olympics of 1932 were politically simple and geographically parochial. Sponsored by the Communist Party USA (CPUSA) as a protest against the Los Angeles Games and the prolonged imprisonment of a labor activist, they were held 28 July–1 August at Stagg Field on the campus of the University of Chicago. Officially called the International Workers Athletic Meet, they featured athletes mostly from the urban industrial belt of the northeastern and upper-midwestern United States. Far from being lionized and later idealized, the Chicago Counter-Olympics were largely ignored, then quickly forgotten.

Yet they are worth remembering because they, like the Barcelona Games, represent a unique, alternative vision of sport in society. These Chicago Games of 60 years ago stand as a distant forerunner of the Olympic boycotts and counterattractions that have become common within the past three decades. Most important, they represent a newly emergent interaction of American radical politics and popular culture. "Nothing like this has ever been seen on this continent," said Arthur Stein, one of the organizers of the event. "These types of events are known to the European labor sports movement but are practically unknown here." The observer quickly gave way to the optimist in Stein, who promised "that this tradition will find a place among the real amateur sportsmen in the United States, the athlete who is at the same time a worker and who has no juicy 'expense accounts'."[3]

Despite his unrealistic prediction, Stein rightly called attention to the connection of the Chicago Games to the workers' sport movement in Europe. Hostile to the elitism, militaristic chauvinism, and commercial exploitation of bourgeois sport, European trade unionists and politically left sportsmen agitated throughout the interwar era for working-class athletic clubs, meets, and sporting values. By 1928 the combined membership of the Socialist Workers' Sport International and the rival Red Sports International totaled over four million people. From 1921 to 1937 numerous workers' festivals, olympiads, and spartakiads were held in places such as Leipzig, Nuremburg, Paris, Frankfurt, Berlin, Prague, Vienna, Antwerp, and Moscow, with winter workers' games at Schrieberhau, Johannesbad, Munzzuschlag, and Oslo. In the summer of 1931, just a year before the Chicago Games, more than 250,000 people watched some 1,400 athletes from twenty-six countries compete at Vienna in the second Workers' Olympiad. A rich pool of European experience was available to American enthusiasts for workers' sport.[4]

The Chicago Counter-Olympics originated, however, in peculiarly American terms. They were the brainchild of the Labor Sports Union of America, an organization formed in 1927 by old Wobblies, Socialists, and Communists. In 1928 the Communists expelled the Wobblies and Socialists, and in August 1929, the Labor Sports Union affiliated with the Red Sports International.[5] Within the month the Labor Sports Union announced plans for "a monster athletic carnival" of worker-athletes in New York City, and a rousing reception for a visiting soccer team, the Soviet Flyers, featuring "a march of all the athletes, a mass drill and then the formation of a huge hammer and sickle."[6] The Labor Sports Union was one of the several "intermediary mechanisms" between the Communist Party and the American people during the aggressive "third period" of Comintern policy. Scarcely a month went by from 1929 to 1934 without some new organization being created. The Labor Sports Union took its place beside the John Reed Clubs, the Workers' Defense Corps, the Workers' International Relief, and the United Farmers League, all designed "to reach many thousands of workers not yet prepared for Party membership" as Minnesota's Communist Party leader, Clarence Hathaway, put it. "Through these organizations," Hathaway (a former semiprofessional baseball player) explained, "the Party must necessarily find its training and recruiting ground."[7]

In the promotion of Counter-Olympic Games in Chicago, the Labor Sports Union found something else: a means of calling attention to an apparent miscarriage of justice. Sixteen years earlier, radical socialist Thomas Mooney had been convicted, largely on perjured testimony, of murder in a San Francisco bombing. Originally sentenced to death and then to life imprisonment at San Quentin, he was not forgotten by his friends of labor and the left, who periodically protested against the frame-up by demonstrating in the streets and petitioning the governor of California.[8] At the Provincetown Theater in New York, a play called *Precedent* dramatized the episode in the early 1930s. Politically sympathetic members of the audience hissed the villains and cheered the hero, but despite numerous attempts to get him freed, the Mooney character remained offstage, behind bars, in the play's final scene. The curtain fell just as a friend said to Mooney's stage wife, "Yes, we must try something new."[9]

The use of sport for radical political ends certainly qualified as "something new" to the American scene. In 1913 a young woman by the name of Emily Davison desperately threw herself into the path of racehorses as a means of calling attention to suffragette concerns. But the king of England, not the president of the United States, owned the horse at the head of the pack; Miss Davison was British, not American.[10] In August, 1931, some 1,800 Swedes signed a petition urging a boycott of the Los Angeles Olympics unless California released Mooney and fellow defendant Warren K. Billings. But those Swedes were residents of Goteburg, not Minneapolis. They mailed the document to the American embassy in Stockholm.[11]

In October 1931, Tom Mooney himself called for a boycott of the 1932 Los Angeles Olympics as a protest against his continued imprisonment. The Labor Sports Union rose to the challenge, endorsing Mooney's appeal and suggesting that he serve as honorary chairman of a committee being formed to air the possibility of sponsoring Counter-Olympic Games in Chicago, the birthplace of the Communist Party, USA.[12] Just three months later the Labor Sports Union, headed by Simon Gerson (who had played freshman baseball at the City College of New York), created a National Provisional Counter-Olympic Committee with headquarters at 16 West 21st Street in New York City. The committee first met on 10 January, and immediately announced its plans for "Tom Mooney Street Runs" in various cities throughout the country. Participants would wear front and back signs demanding the release of Mooney and Billings. These races would constitute the preliminary heats for the selection of track competitors at the Chicago Games. Local soccer, swimming, and basketball tournaments would also be held, all leading up to the International Workers Athletic Meet in Chicago.[13]

Much of this information simply never made its way into the public domain. The Counter-Olympic Committee regularly distributed news releases to the nation's print media, and by early March turned out weekly newsletters, but editors apparently filed them in the nearest wastepaper baskets.[14] Even the central Communist Party organ, the *Daily Worker,* found it difficult to take a sporting event seriously. In 1932 a reporter for the *Daily Worker,* B. K. Gebert, observed that sport was "one of the very important factors in the lives of the working class of the United States,"[15] but not until four years later did the *Daily Worker* produce a "sports page"; its coverage of the Chicago Counter-Olympics was spasmodic at best.[16] Far more regular and complete announcements could be found in the *Young Worker,* a weekly organ of the Young Communist League.

Several years earlier, the Labor Sports Union had produced a short-lived little newsletter called *Sport and Play.* Its successor, *The New Sport and Play,* first appeared in March 1932, primarily for the promotion of the Chicago Counter-Olympics. "How can we explain the real nature of the Olympics?" editor Si Gerson asked his readers. "How can we show worker athletes what the Labor Sports Union stands for? *The New Sport and Play* is the best weapon we have for this. It is our voice; it is also our mirror. It explains our program; it reflects our activity."[17] Unfortunately, not even Gerson (now a spry activist in his mid-eighties, who still commutes regularly from his home in Brooklyn to party offices in New York) knows where any copies of *New Sport and Play* can be found; nor can the knowledgeable staff at the labor-history archives in the Tamiment Library at New York University help in this matter. Apparently only one issue of *New Sport and Play* has survived, appropriately tucked away in the Thomas Mooney Papers at the Bancroft Library on the campus of the University of California, Berkeley. One would be ill-advised to generalize solely from those mere sixteen pages, but a complete run of the *Young Worker* in the Tamiment, a stack of press releases and pamphlets in the Mooney Papers, and occasional items in the *Daily Worker* fill out the picture of Communist sports reportage and commentary in the early 1930s.

Three themes recur regularly. First, and most pervasive, is an outright denunciation of bourgeois sport in all its YMCA, CYO, NCAA, AAU, and IOC guises. As Communists saw it, organized sport customarily catered to a few pampered superstars rather than mass participation, whetted nationalist appetites for imperialistic war, and diverted public attention away from the more pressing problems of wage cuts and unemployment. In the early 1930s, of course, millions of hungry people stood in soup queues while "a few, self-appointed millionaires, counts, army officers, and Amateur Athletic Union job holders" refined plans for the Los Angeles Olympics. "The Olympic Games are a glorified racket," declared Si Gerson. "Our contention is that the Olympic Games are used to prepare the masses of sport-loving youth for Wall Street wars. It is also used to make Bill Worker forget about trouble at home, about the fact that he's out of a job or, if he still has one, is getting one wage cut after another."[18]

The Winter Olympics at Lake Placid inevitably came under red fire. The Games at that "ritzy" resort provided thrills mostly for "some jaded millionaires and their mistresses," insisted Gerson. "Thar's gold in them there Olympic hills—particularly when the hills have to be covered with snow," he noted with reference to the need to bring truckloads of snow from Canada for the cross-country races. Gerson broke down the million-dollar budget, item by expensive item. "Read 'em," he urged his readers, "and see why A.A.U. officials can stay on the pie lines while most of us can't stay off the bread line."[19] If bourgeois sport was an evil to be avoided, the Olympics were a quadrennial visitation of the devil.

A second dominant theme in the Communist sports program was a passionate concern for the full equality of "Negro" athletes in all clubs and competitive meets. Despite the Party's preponderance of foreign-born, working-class immigrants, for whom the African-American posed competition in the marketplace, the Party followed the lead of the Comintern in the late 1920s in attempting to win black support.[20] High on the agenda of the Counter-Olympic Committee was the rejection of "Jim Crowism" in all its various southern and northern forms, and the "full equality of Negro athletes and all colored athletes in all sports organizations and meets."[21]

In mid-April 1932, a workers' sports club in Detroit voted to bar African-American athletes from membership. Shortly afterwards, the club applied for admission to the Labor Sports Union only to receive word that it was deemed "unfit for membership": "No club which bars Negroes, which Jim-Crows the Negro athletes, can join the Labor Sports Union of America. The Labor Sports Union will absolutely not compromise on this question."[22] Nor would the National Counter-Olympic Committee, which insisted that participation in the Chicago Games be entirely open to people of color, unlike the "boss policy that dominates the A.A.U., the Y.M.C.A., and the colleges from whose ranks come the big shots of the Olympic Games."[23]

A third item of great importance to the Communist Party was a breaking of the "sport blockade against the Soviet Union." Not since the Stockholm Games of 1912 had the Russians competed in the official Olympics. The 1916 Games were canceled because of the First World War, of course. In the midst of the war, the Bolshevik Revolution occurred, making the Soviet Union a pariah among Western nations. Despite all its rhetorical protestations against the politicization of sport, the International Olympic Committee simply refused to invite Soviet athletes to Antwerp in 1920, to Paris in 1924, to Amsterdam in 1928, and to Los Angeles in 1932.[24]

American Communists viewed that policy as a mere extension of capitalist political and economic attempts to quarantine and ultimately to undermine the Soviet Union. "The rich businessmen and generals who run the Olympics," complained a writer for *New Sport and Play*, "are carrying out on the sport fields the same policy of blockade against the U.S.S.R. as their governments on the political and economic fields."[25] Worse still, the persistent refusal to recognize the Soviet Union athletically seemed the flip side of the diplomatic coin of nonrecognition, a policy that provided "direct aid to the war-mongers who want war against the Soviet Union." In 1932 Japanese armies stood poised "at the gates of Siberia ready to invade and to attempt destruction of the Soviet Union," warned Tom Mooney from his San Quentin cell. "You must do all that you can," Mooney urged a group of Counter-Olympic enthusiasts in Fresno, "to rally the youth of the country, not only to participate and support the workers' sports movement against the bosses' Olympics, but to expose and defeat the new war being hatched by the Imperialists."[26] As a means of dramatizing the exclusion of Soviet athletes from the Los Angeles Games, the Counter-Olympic Committee offered to pay all expenses for five track athletes to travel from the USSR to the Chicago Counter-Olympics. In early March the Committee received a letter from the Soviet Supreme Council of Physical Culture, accepting the offer.[27]

During the early months of 1932 political demonstrations accompanied "Free Tom Mooney Runs" in more than a dozen cities. In New York twenty-four red-shirted athletes toed the mark at Rutgers Square at 2:30 on a Saturday afternoon, and charged off toward Union Square led by a police car. By prior arrangement, five female competitors ran only one mile; nineteen men ran a "miniature marathon" of two-and-one-half miles. Ben Tucker, a member of the Red Sparks Athletic Club, won the event in 13:15 minutes. At Union Square several hundred workers convened to hear speeches denouncing the Amateur Athletic Union and the "boss Olympics" movement, and calling for support of the forthcoming International Workers Athletic Meet in Chicago.[28]

The road to Chicago quickly became pockmarked with frustration. The city of Boston adamantly refused permission for a "Free Tom Mooney Run" through its streets, and the school boards of Buffalo and Detroit rejected requests for the free use of school gyms in order for worker-athletes to train during the winter months. Elsewhere the forces of nature combined with media silence to negate the effect of one preliminary event after another. A torrential downpour wiped out the Cleveland run; lack of mainstream newspaper coverage made other turnouts of both athletes and spectators exceedingly small. Worse still, the AAU refused to sanction the Chicago Games, and threatened to ban for life any athlete who participated even in the preliminary runs.[29]

Yet more serious problems were soon to surface. In early April the National Counter-Olympic Committee announced that the athletic complex at Loyola University would serve as the site for the Chicago Games. In early May, however, Loyola officials withdrew their agreement to host the event. According to the *Young Worker*, Athletic Director McCabe reacted harshly against the "class prejudice" in a pamphlet released by the Counter-Olympic Committee, and broke the contract he had earlier signed. Various Communist spokesmen blamed the American Olympic Committee, the AAU, and Chicago philanthropist Samuel Insull for putting pressure on Loyola officials.[30] Unfortunately, not a single mention of this issue can be found in the Loyola archives.[31]

Whatever the causes, Loyola's withdrawal sent the organizing committee scampering for a new site. Curiously, they turned to the University of Chicago, an institution recently built on the abundant wealth of the ultimate in late-nineteenth-century capitalism, John D. Rockefeller. However incongruous it might have been for such an opulent, elite place to host a working-class, Communist-sponsored athletic event, the campus had certainly been exposed to issues represented in the Counter-Olympic crusade. On the evening of 26 May 1932, a socialist candidate for the mayorship of Los Angeles, William Busick, addressed a campus Socialist Club, urging a general boycott of California products to protest the continued imprisonment of Tom Mooney. Just five days later the Communist Party's presidential candidate, William Z. Foster, castigated the economic failures of capitalism and insisted on a movement "towards a Soviet America" to a crowd of 1,000 students and faculty at Mandel Hall. [32]

At noon on the very day of Foster's visit, Chicago's old Muscular Christian football coach and athletic director, Amos Alonzo Stagg, spoke at Bond Chapel on "What my Religion Has Meant to Me." His religion had taught him to live confidently and non-materialistically, he insisted, and to be broadminded in judging people fairly.[33] Presumably that self-proclaimed broadmindedness was soon to be sorely tested when confronted by Communists requesting the use of the university's athletic stadium for anti-Olympic activity. Stagg, after all, represented the National Collegiate Athletic Association on the Executive Committee of the American Olympic Committee, and for more than a year had served on the American Olympic Track and Field Committee.[34] As Chicago's director of athletics, he had turned over all the profits of the spring intrasquad football game to support the United States Olympic team.[35] He planned shortly to board a train bound for the Los Angeles Games.[36]

In truth, Stagg apparently never questioned the motives behind the request to use the field. According to Communist newspaper accounts, Counter-Olympic facilities coordinator A. L. Harris wrote to Stagg, and received an affirmative reply. Si Gerson relates a more personal touch. As he now remembers it, he, Harris, and another colleague approached "the quiet home of Stagg—yes, the great Stagg," and stated their request. "Stagg was a bit puzzled but friendly," says Gerson. "He agreed to lend us the stadium for free and even provided the hurdles, cross bars, etc. but made one proviso: No hard liquor." Gerson's group truthfully swore that they were "life-long prohibitionists" themselves, and would allow no liquor on the premises. That declaration satisfied Stagg, as Gerson remembers it, "and we concluded the deal with a handshake."[37]

They found the Department of State much less agreeable. For several months, officers of the Labor Sports Union attempted to obtain visas for two German worker-athletes as well as the five Russians who wanted to compete at Chicago. A registered letter finally stirred the State Department to explain that consular officials abroad handled visa applications without interference from Washington.[38] Behind the scenes, however, the director of the Division of Eastern European Affairs passed the word on to consulates in Berlin and Riga, Latvia (which handled Soviet-related issues), that the essential "purpose, scope and activities of the so-called workers' sports movement" was the spread of communism throughout the West. Finally, in late June, the Labor Sports Union was informed that visas would simply not be given to Soviet and German applicants in order for them to participate in an event "supported and furthered by the American Communist Party."[39] The *Daily Worker* observed that the secretary of state, Henry Stimson, just happened to be the honorary vice-president of the American Olympic Committee.[40]

On the eve of the Counter-Olympics, Chicago buzzed with athletic excitement. The White Sox languished in seventh place, but the Cubs (who were to win the National League pennant that year) narrowly trailed the Pirates. On 22 July, British, South African, Hungarian, and Canadian Olympic teams on their way to Los Angeles all stopped over in Chicago as guests of the Lake Shore Athletic Club. Germany's Olympic boxing team stayed in town for an entire week. They trained hard, attended a couple of civic-club luncheons, and provided local sportswriters with colorful copy to hype a one-night bout against Chicago's Golden Gloves champions. Scheduled outdoors at Soldier Field on 26 July, that event had to be postponed because of rain. On the following evening, 27 July, some 40,000 people turned out to watch the Germans and Americans fight to a 4-4 draw.[41]

On the very next morning, the International Workers Athletic Meet opened at Stagg Field. Never were so many hopes for so great a political impact dashed so decisively. The *Young Worker* told of workers riding boxcars and hitchhiking to Chicago; forty-two iron-ore miners from the Upper Peninsula of Michigan reportedly rode to the meet in a couple of large trucks, eating bread and milk on the way.[42] But in truth the turnout of both spectators and athletes was disappointingly small. The *Daily Worker* reported crowds of 5,000 in the stands; Si Gerson insists that no more then 2,000 spectators ever attended, despite a daily admission fee of merely 25 cents, with children admitted free of charge.[43] Earlier predictions of 1,000 athletes were as ill-founded as was a later low tally of 112. The truth probably lay somewhere between the *Daily Worker's* report of 200 and the *Young Worker's* estimate of 400 competitors, considerably fewer than the 1,500 or so athletes who competed at Los Angeles.[44]

The program itself was radically pruned from its original design. Swimming and basketball finals were planned so long as Loyola's gymnasium and indoor swimming pool were available. Without those facilities, track and field dominated the athletic portion of the program. Outdoor gymnastic exhibitions, choral presentations, mass singing of revolutionary songs, and art exhibits filled out the program around some boxing and wrestling bouts. The single "big indoor affair" (held on the opening night in a rented hall in South Chicago) was no athletic contest at all, but rather "a big protest meeting against the continued imprisonment of Tom Mooney." In the final event, the Red Sparks soccer team from New York City appropriately won the soccer final, 2-0.[45]

The prominence of European track-and-field athletics, gymnastics, and soccer reflected the immigrant flavor of the International Workers Athletic Meet, which in turn accurately represented the ethnic demography of the Communist Party USA. Just ten years earlier, only 5–10 percent of all American Communists spoke English; by 1932 still more than half of all Party members were foreign-born. Most were Finns; others were Russians, Lithuanians, Yugoslavians, Bulgarians, and Germans, in that order.[46] Names such as Kujanpaa, Luelle, Mahi, Kuosen, Bolog, Duletski, Groos, Heikkila, Kuokkanen, Meissner, Koch, and Jalo dominated the list of winners at Chicago, with an occasional Murphy and Gustafson and an even rarer Brown and Wilson thrown in.[47] For four days in the summer of 1932, the stadium at Stagg Field was a veritable tower of babble.

To what end, with what results? The National Counter-Olympic Committee planned the games primarily to land "a powerful blow to the Olympic Games and [to] the jailers of Tom Mooney,"[48] but failed dismally at both those points. Not even an imaginative demonstration on behalf of Tom Mooney on that final day of the Los Angeles Olympics could diminish the glitter of that event. In the closing ceremonies, four men and two women leaped from the stands and circled the track carrying "Free Tom Mooney" signs. As they were seized by police, the band immediately began playing the "Star-Spangled Banner" and the final parade of Olympic athletes began.[49] Neither that demonstration nor the Chicago Games made a dent, much less delivered a damaging blow, to the official Olympic Games. Nor did the Chicago Counter-Olympics secure the release of Tom Mooney from San Quentin. Fully seven years later (1939), Mooney was pardoned by a new governor of California who had probably never even heard of the International Workers Athletic Meet in Chicago.

The relative failure of the Counter-Olympics of 1932 mirrored the marginal position of the Communist Party in the United States. Within the past three years, one Communist-organized strike after another had met resounding defeat—among textile operatives in North Carolina and Massachusetts, automobile workers in Michigan, field hands in California, miners in southern Illinois, Kentucky, and Alabama, and steel-workers in Pittsburgh and Alabama. Even the Depression had failed to send Americans flocking into the Communist Party. After thirteen years of aggressive recruitment, Party membership in 1932 numbered only 18,000. In the presidential election shortly after the Chicago Games, the Communist Party USA attracted just over 100,000 votes for its candidate, William Z. Foster, while the Socialist Party candidate, Norman Thomas, received almost 900,000 votes.[50]

Lack of funds was both a cause and an effect of these dismal showings, athletically as well as politically. "Especially during the Depression," recalls Si Gerson, "we lived and did our Party work on a shoestring."[51] Certainly the Counter-Olympics got planned and promoted with lots of zeal and hard work, but little money. The paucity of funds came awkwardly to the fore over the question of awards for the winning athletes. At first, the organizers of the event planned to give silver-plated cups to each victor, but in the end decided they could afford only three cups—one to the individual scoring the highest number of points, one to the team that scored the most points, and one to the winner of the special Tom Mooney Relay. All the other victorious athletes received an autographed photograph of Tom Mooney and presumably were happy to get that when complaints of the organizing committee ranged from "penniless" to "a desperate financial situation."[52] Whatever the combination of causative factors, the unsteady preparations, inadequate press coverage, and slim audiences for the Chicago Counter-Olympics simply reinforced the sense of marginality that permeated the Communist Party in the early 1930s.

It also underscored the weakness of the workers' sport movement in the United States. More subtly, it hinted at the impossible dilemma of the Communist Party in relation to the politics of sport. To cater to the immigrant core of the party was to stick with track and field, soccer, and gymnastics, activities that had scant appeal for mainstream Americans in the era of Babe Ruth, Bronko Nagurski, and Frank Luisetti. To turn to baseball, football, and basketball, however, was to plunge headlong into problems of cash nexus and class consciousness. Actually, the choice never really had to be made. In the 1930s, the All-American tandem of public school- and company-sponsored sports programs floored workers' sport for the count.[53]

On a more positive note, the Chicago Games afforded an occasion for the Communist Party to begin its crusade to end racial segregation in American sport. Mark Naison has documented Communist agitations on behalf of American black athletes in the late 1930s and 1940s,[54] but that activity began around the time of the 1932 Counter-Olympics. Unlike most athletic patrons of that day, the organizers of the Tom Mooney street runs welcomed "all young workers and amateur athletes," as a San Francisco entry blank phrased it, "regardless of race, color or creed." In addition to the "Free Tom Mooney" signs on the front and back of runners in the street runs, "Free the Scottsboro Boys" signs flourished.[55] By several accounts, about a quarter to a third of the athletes at Stagg Field were black, at a time when only four blacks could be found in the entire American Olympic track-and-field squad in Los Angeles. Given his name, one might think "A. Abraham" was a Jewish immigrant. In fact, he was a black steelworker from Gary, Indiana, who won the Counter-Olympics' 110-meter hurdles in 13.7 seconds. A fellow black resident of Gary, A. Tracy of the Spartan Athletic Club, won the pole vault.[56]

At the end of the games, the Labor Sports Union used the occasion to hold a National Convention in Chicago on 2–4 August, to discuss and plan more fully the politically beneficial use of sport. Undaunted by Depression economics, Labor Sports Union leaders announced their intentions to sponsor several dozen athletes' attendance at a forthcoming World Spartakiade in Moscow, in August 1933, in honor of the conclusion of the Soviet Union's first Five-Year Plan.[57] An American, too, would be honored in Moscow. According to a spokesman for the Labor Sports Union, there would be "a special relay event—the International Tom Mooney Relay."[58]

No doubt some of those Chicago competitors also made their way to Barcelona in 1936, and exchanged their athletic togs for military weaponry. Finally attentive to workers' sport, the American Communist press reported athletic contests behind Loyalist lines. Fittingly, a "Tom Mooney Company" fought in the Abraham Lincoln Brigade.[59]

Notes

1. Richard D. Mandell, *The Nazi Olympics* (New York: Macmillan, 1971), barely mentions the Barcelona Games (81): for more details, see Duff Hart-Davis, *Hitler's Games: The 1936 Olympics* (New York: Harper & Row, 1986), 123–24, 130.

2. George Orwell, *Homage to Catalonia and Looking Back on the Spanish War* (London: Secker & Warburg, 1938).

3. Press release, National Counter-Olympic Committee, 29 June 1932, Mooney Papers, Bancroft Library, University of California, Berkeley.

4. Until now, little of this information has been available except in German sources: Arnd Kruger and James Riordan (eds.), *Der Internationale Arbeitersport: Der Schlussel zum Arbeitersport in 10 Landern* (Cologne, 1985); Horst Ueberhorst, *Frisch, Frei, Stark, und Freu: Die Arbeitersportbewegung in Deutschland, 1983–1933* (Dusseldorf, 1973); Heinz Timmermann, *Geschichte und Struktur der Deutschen Arbeitersportbewegung, 1893–1933* (Ahrensburg, 1973); Helmut Wagner, *Sport und Arbeitersport* (Cologne, 1973); Seppo Hentila, "Zur Geschichte des Arbeitersports in Finland," *Stadion: International Journal of the History of Sport*, 11 (1985), 71–91. Notable but brief treatments of workers' sport in English are Robert F. Wheeler, "Organized Sport and Organized Labour: The Workers' Sports Movement," *Journal of Contemporary History* 13 (1978), 191–210; David A. Steinberg, "The Workers' Sport Internationals, 1920–28," *Journal of Contemporary History*, 13 (1978), 233–51; William J. Murray, "Sport and Politics in France in the 1930s: The Workers' Sports Federations on the Eve of the Popular Front," in Wray Vamplew (ed.), *Sport, Nationalism and Internationalism* (Adelaide: Australian Society of Sport History, 1987), 32–90, and "The French Workers' Sports Movement and the Victory of the Popular Front in 1936," *International Journal of the History of Sport*, 4 (1987), 203–30. A more complete study, Stephen G. Jones, *Workers at Play: A Social and Economic History of Leisure, 1918–1939* (London: Routledge & Kegan Paul, 1986), focuses entirely on insular interwar Britain. Soon to be published is a compilation of essays in English surveying the international scene more thoroughly than could Arnd Kruger in "The Rise and Fall of the International Worker Sports Movement," *Proceedings of the 11th HISPA Congress* (Glasgow, 1985), 225–28. Edited in English by Kruger and Riordan, it is tentatively entitled *The International Workers Sport* (Champaign, Ill.: Human Kinetics Publishers).

5. Si Gerson, "Six Years of Workers Sport in America," *International Press Correspondence*, 13 (19 January 1933); Theodore Draper, *American Communism and Soviet Russia* (New York: Viking Press, 1960), 179–80.

6. *Daily Worker*, 19 September 1929.

7. Harvey Klehr, *The Heyday of American Communism: The Depression Decade* (New York: Basic Books, 1984), 104. For an excellent analysis of the changing relation of the Communist Party to sport in the interwar period, see Mark Naison, "Lefties & Righties: The Communist Party and Sports during the Great Depression," *Radical America*, 13 (July–August 1979), 47–59.

8. For the political and legal issues surrounding the Mooney case, see Richard H. Frost, *The Mooney Case* (Stanford, Calif.: Stanford University Press, 1968); Estolv E. Ward, *The Gentle Dynamiter: A Biography of Tom Mooney* (Palo Alto, Calif.: Ramparts Press, 1983); Curt Gentry, *Frame-Up: The Incredible Case of Tom Mooney and Warren Billings* (New York: Norton, 1967).

9. Myra Page, "The Mooney-Billings Frameup," *New Masses*, 6 (May 1931), 21.

10. See William J. Baker, *Sports in the Western World* (Urbana: University of Illinois Press, 1988), 189.

11. Letter from G. A. Karisson to the American Legation, August 1931: 811.4063 Olympic Games/175, National Archives, Washington, D.C.

12. Si Gerson, "Olympics versus Counter-Olympics," *International Press Correspondence*, 12 (2 June 1932), 498.

13. Press release, National Provisional Counter-Olympic Committee, 5 January, 1932, Mooney Papers; *Daily Worker*, 11 January 1932; *Young Worker*, 11 January, 1932.

14. Press release, National Counter-Olympic Committee, 8 March 1932, Mooney Papers; typescript letter, Edwin Rolfe to Anna Mooney, 18 March 1932, Mooney Papers.

15. *Daily Worker*, 27 July 1932.

16. See Naison, "Lefties & Righties," 49, 54. For the *Daily Worker*'s later treatment of sport, see Harvey A. Levenstein's entry in Joseph R. Conlin (ed.), *The American Radical Press, 1880–1960* (Westport, Conn.: Greenwood Press, 1974) 1:231–33; "Sports for the Daily Worker: An Interview with Lester Rodney," *In These Times*, 12–18 October 1977.

17. *Young Worker*, 11 April 1932; *New Sport and Play*, 1 (April 1932), 2.

18. Press release, National Counter-Olympic Committee, n.d. (February 1932?), Mooney Papers; Si Gerson, "The Olympics Racket," *New Sport and Play*, 1 (April 1932), 3. See p. 12: " 'The policies by which the Olympics are being guided are exactly the policies of the boss class generally,' a Cleveland branch of the Labor Sports Union announced shortly after a conference in late December 1931. Los Angeles would be 'an anti-working class' meet 'where no real workers will compete. It will be a jingo festival that must be fought by all real amateur athletes, workers, farmers, students and all honest intellectuals.' "

19. Gerson, "Olympics Racket," 3. For further criticism of the Lake Placid Games ("a war move of the bosses"), see *Young Worker*, 8 February 1932.

20. For the party's unsteady policy shift in this direction, see Klehr, *Heyday*, 324–48.

21. "Boycott the Anti-Labor Olympics!" flyer circulated by the Eastern Olympic Provisional Counter-Olympic Committee, Mooney Papers. For a ringing indictment of the Jim-Crowism of the Olympic Games," see *Young Worker,* 11 April 1932.

22. Press release, National Counter-Olympic Committee, 27 April 1932, Mooney Papers.

23. Robert Smith, "The Olympics and the Negro Athlete," *New Sport and Play,* 1 (April 1932), 6. The Counter-Olympic Committee was especially critical of the AAU's handling of an incident during an American track team's visit to South Africa in the previous summer, 1931, when the AAU capitulated to the barring of American black runner Eddie Tolan from competition against white South Africans. Press release, National Counter-Olympic Committee, 18 March 1932, Mooney Papers.

24. See William J. Baker and John M. Carroll, "The Politics of the Olympics," in Baker and Carroll (eds.), *Sports in Modern America* (St. Louis: River City Publishers, 1981), 160–61. Not until the Helsinki Olympics of 1952 did the Soviets send a team; see Baker, *Sports in the Western World,* 264–68, and Richard Espy, *The Politics of the Olympic Games, with an Epilogue, 1976–1980* (Berkeley: University of California Press, 1981), 31–39.

25. Mac Gordon, "The Olympics and the Soviet Union," *New Sport and Play,* 1 (April 1932), 7.

26. Letter (typescript) from Tom Mooney to Counter-Olympic State Elimination Meet, Fresno, California, 1 July 1932, Mooney Papers.

27. Press release, National Counter-Olympic Committee, 10 March 1932, Mooney Papers.

28. *Young Worker,* 21 March 1932; "Roamin' the Districts," *New Sport and Play,* 1 (April 1932), 8.

29. *Young Worker,* 18 January, 29 February, and 14 March 1932.

30. Ibid., 9 and 30 May 1932; Press release, National Counter-Olympic Committee, 19 May 1932, Mooney Papers. Insull, as Si Gerson put it, was a "utility magnate and purchaser of Senators," and "a heavy contributor to the Loyola University fund and to the Olympics Fund."

31. Letter from Loyola University archivist Brother Michael Grace, S.J., to William J. Baker, 13 February 1991.

32. *The Daily Maroon* (University of Chicago student newspaper), 27 May and 1 June 1932.

33. *Daily Maroon,* 1 June 1932.

34. Letters from Joseph Townsend England to Amos Alonzo Stagg, 30 August 1932, and from George W. Graves to Stagg, 17 November 1932, Stagg Papers, Box 82, folder 1A, Joseph Regenstein Library Archives, University of Chicago.

35. *Daily Maroon,* 13 May 1932.

36. *Chicago Tribune,* 23 July 1932.

37. Letter from Si Gerson to William J. Baker, 1988. According to the *Young Worker*, 20 June 1932, A. L. Harris wrote to Stagg in late May and received a reply on 1 June. Otherwise, the details are remarkably similar to Gerson's: Stagg granted permission to use Stagg Field free of charge but with "bottled goods" prohibited.

38. Press releases, National Counter-Olympic Committee, 27 April, 20 May, and 16 June 1932; Mooney Papers.

39. For this information I am grateful to Barbara Pinto for sharing notes taken from letters in the Olympic Games section 811.4063, nos. 264, 279, 325, 327, National Archives.

40. *Daily Worker*, 27 July 1932.

41. *Chicago Tribune*, 19, 23, 27, and 28 July 1932; *New York Herald Tribune*, 28 July 1932.

42. *Young Worker*, 22 August 1932.

43. *Daily Worker*, 2 August 1932; Gerson to Baker, 1988.

44. M. S. Mayer, "Chicago: City of Unrest," *Forum and Century*, 89 (January 1933), 49; *Daily Worker*, 2 August 1932; *Young Worker*, 22 August 1932.

45. Letter from Si Gerson to Tom Mooney Molders' Defense Committee, 22 July 1932, Mooney Papers; *Chicago Defender*, 30 July 1932; *Daily Worker*, 2 August 1932.

46. Theodore Draper, *The Roots of American Communism* (New York: Viking, 1957), 392; Theodore Draper, *American Communism and Soviet Russia*, 190.

47. In the Mooney Papers is a three-page typewritten list of first-, second-, and third-place winners in all the track-and-field events.

48. Press release, National Counter-Olympic Committee, undated (May 1932?), Mooney Papers.

49. *Young Worker*, 22 August 1932.

50. For an explanation of the limited size, resources, and successes of the Communist Party USA in the late 1920s and early 1930s, see Fraser M. Ottanelli, *The Communist Party of the United States: From the Depression to World War II* (New Brunswick, N.J.: Rutgers University Press, 1991), 17–48; cf. Paul Buhle and Dan Georgakas, "Communist Party, USA," in Mari Jo Buhle, Paul Buhle, and Dan Georgakas (eds.), *Encyclopedia of the American Left* (New York: Garland, 1990), 150.

51. Author's interview with Simon Gerson, 7 November 1990.

52. Letters (typescripts) from the Tom Mooney Molders' Defense Committee to Louis J. LaVenture, 12 April 1932; to Ed Black, 1 July 1932; and to the National Counter-Olympic Committee, 23 July 1932, Mooney Papers.

53. This story has yet to be told satisfactorily. For now, see the useful but undigested information in John R. Betts, *America's Sporting Heritage: 1850–1950* (Reading, Mass.: Addison-Wesley, 1974), 181, 263–66, 278; cf. the more polished account of school and industrial sponsorship of sport in Frederick W. Cozens and Florence Scovil Stumpf, *Sports in American Life* (Chicago: University of Chicago Press, 1953),

52–92. For focus on a specific sport, see Harold Seymour, *Baseball: The People's Game* (New York: Oxford University Press, 1990), 50–105, 213–57. By way of contrast, Roland Naul provides a brief summary of the absence of school-sponsored sport in relation to working-class sports clubs in Germany: "The Renaissance of the History of School Sports: Back to the Future?," *Journal of Sport History,* 17 (summer 1990), 199–213.

54. Naison, "Lefties & Righties," 56–57.

55. Press release, National Counter-Olympic Committee, 13 May 1932, Mooney Papers; *Young Worker,* 18 and 25 April 1932. "The Scottsboro Boys Must Not Die!" and "Scottsboro-Tom Mooney Street Run!" announced an advertisement flyer for an event on 16 April, sponsored by the Vesa Athletic Club of New York City; Mooney Papers.

56. *Young Worker,* 22 August 1932; winners' list (typescript) in the Mooney Papers.

57. Gerson, "Olympics versus Counter-Olympics," 499; press release, National Counter-Olympic Committee, 17 August 1933, Mooney Papers.

58. Letter (typescript) from Gerson to Tom Mooney, 8 December 1932, Mooney Papers.

59. *New Masses,* 14 February, 1939.

12

Selling Sport and Religion in American Society
Bishop Sheil and the Catholic Youth Organization

GERALD R. GEMS

American sport historians have often analyzed the role of race, ethnicity, and class and their effect on sporting practices, while religion in the modern era has been relatively neglected. Religion, in fact, transcended and linked each of these variables. In the case of the Catholic Youth Organization (CYO), a religious agency brought a synthesis to these previously divergent cultural factors and merged them with patriotic values. This process of cohesive Americanization took place during the particularly troublesome period of the Great Depression, and it succeeded when previous efforts had failed.[1]

Like the CYO, progressive reformers utilized sports in an attempt to homogenize various constituencies with only limited success. Despite the success of African-American teams, Rube Foster removed his baseball Giants from the Chicago City League after the race riot of 1919 took thirty-eight lives. Despite the promotional savvy of a white agent, Abe Saperstein, the black Savoy Five basketball team found greater opportunity on the road as the Harlem Globetrotters. In the parks and playgrounds blacks fought whites, and whites fought whites, as racial and ethnic groups clashed over territorial rights. By the end of the decade gangs seemingly ruled the city, and the youth idealized gangsters such as Al Capone. In 1929 the stock market crashed, and in the midst of such social upheaval the CYO was born.[2]

Bishop Bernard J. Sheil, the legendary and controversial sponsor of the Catholic Youth Organization, officially founded the program in Chicago in June 1930, allegedly with the following quote: "We'll knock the hoodlum off his pedestal and we'll put another neighborhood boy in his place. He'll be dressed in C.Y.O. boxing shorts and a pair of leather mitts, and he'll make a new hero. Those kids love to fight. We'll let them fight. We'll find champions right in the neighborhood."[3]

Within a few short years the program reached international proportions and, combined with Sheil's humanitarian and labor activities, enhanced his image as a national figure. Sheil's stature as a promoter and as an activist rose over the next two decades; but time, the destruction of the early CYO records, and the glorified products of his biographers have obscured the truth and magnified the myth. Several important questions remain unanswered. How and why did the program expand so rapidly in the midst of the Depression to include blacks, Asians, Jews, and a multitude of other ethnic groups? Why did Sheil choose boxing to initiate the program? More important, what was the role of the clergy in sport and how did such religious programs affect their participants and the larger society?[4]

The initial questions are more easily answered. In Europe, Catholics' leisure activities had long centered on the Church and were often tied to religious feasts. Religion and leisure coincided, and parishioners looked to the clergy for leadership in such matters. Upon transplantation to America, Catholic recreational activities still revolved around the parish church; but the American Church was dominated by an Irish hierarchy and fractured by ethnic concerns and nationalistic issues. Clergy tended to parishioners' leisure interests in an autonomous, often-domineering fashion that reinforced traditional gender roles and particular value systems. When Polish and Czech women became involved in the suffrage movement and clamored for greater independence in the 1890s, priests soon quelled their efforts.[5] Likewise, from the 1880s through the 1920s, clergy subdued the dance fads that attracted youthful parishioners.[6]

The religious flock consisted of a largely ethnic, immigrant, and working-class constituency, whose isolation from mainstream society led them to look to parish priests to serve traditional leadership roles. By virtue of their position and education, priests emerged as "organic intellectuals" who shaped and directed ideologies within their own domains.[7] In the nineteenth and early twentieth centuries clerical leadership reinforced religious and ethnic nationalistic values that were often at odds with the dominant American culture, but by World War I the Catholic hierarchy sought greater inclusion in American society.

The process of transition occurred on the heels of the Progressive movement that failed to fully incorporate the myriad ethnic groups into an American melting pot. This study describes and analyzes the role of religion, sport, and clerical leadership in effecting a more successful outcome during a period when the American capitalist system faced its greatest challenge. The merger of sport, religion, and politics in the vision of one man effectively curtailed any potential threat as it Americanized the proletarian masses, who felt the hardships of the Depression most acutely and might have been swayed to more radical alternatives by Communist organizers and labor unionizers.

302 GERALD R. GEMS

Progressive reformers had previously felt that sport offered alternative and more wholesome forms of leisure, and sporting practices eventually brought divergent groups to some accommodation.[8] By the turn of the century the Knights of Columbus began organizing previously informal activities into regular tournaments. By 1910 Chicago's Catholics boasted of the largest religious baseball league in the United States.[9] The *New World*, the official publication of the Chicago archdiocese, offered uniforms to parish and parochial school teams in return for subscriptions.[10] Priests actively organized and administered such teams to maintain religious influences as the Americanized offspring of immigrants sought greater inclusion in the secular world. The National Catholic Athletic Association joined the Amateur Athletic Union in 1911, and previously independent semipro teams became subject to the sanction of both clerical and native governing bodies.[11] Within a decade Catholics had established other parish-centered leagues, and Catholic teams engaged in football, soccer, track, indoor baseball, and gymnastics competition against Protestant, Jewish, fraternal, and independent foes in a widespread athletic network.[12] Athletic victories often bolstered ethnic and religious pride and fostered cohesiveness as World War I brought nativist attacks. The Notre Dame football squad symbolically carried the Catholic banner into its contests and the *New World* extolled the spotless 37-0 record of the DePaul basketball team against secular opponents.[13] Sport associations and Catholic victories brought identity and some sense of stability to local religious affairs wracked by internal dissent. Upon his accession to the Chicago archbishopric in 1916, George Mundelein embarked upon a comprehensive program of Americanization that met with steadfast resistance in ethnic parishes. Mundelein won his battle by centralizing the bureaucracy, limiting parish autonomy, and placing young, American-born clergy as assistant pastors to serve a watchdog function.[14]

Bernard J. Sheil proved one of the most talented of the priestly corps, and he soon became a protégé of Mundelein. Born in 1888 to James Sheil, a coal merchant who never utilized his two professional degrees, and his wife, Rosalie, caretaker of the neighborhood needy, Bernie Sheil enjoyed a middle-class upbringing that emphasized commercial opportunities and humanitarian concerns. As a pitcher for the St. Viator team, his no-hitter against the University of Illinois and his performances for the semipro Logan Squares attracted professional scouts. Sheil turned down their contract offers to pursue the priesthood, but maintained his love for, and belief in, sport as a means to character development and success. After his ordination in 1910 Sheil served seven years at the parish level before assignments at Great Lakes Naval Station and as Cook County Jail chaplain. Administrative duties at the archdiocese office brought him to the attention of Mundelein, who nurtured Sheil's career thereafter. In 1924, when Mundelein accepted the cardinal's hat in Rome, Sheil traveled with him to be named chancellor of the Chicago archdiocese. Both nurtured grandiose plans for American Catholicism, and Chicago was to serve as its headquarters. Their organization of the International Eucharistic Congress of 1926 brought each further fame and titles. Sheil was named a bishop and vicar general in 1928.[15]

Using religion as a pretext for unity, Mundelein had ordered that Holy Name societies be established in each parish during World War I, but membership in the religious clubs languished until they assumed an athletic organizational function.[16] As general director of the Holy Name Society and a special commissioner of the Boy Scouts of America, Bishop Sheil had a vested interest in the organization of youth groups. The Catholic Youth Organization developed through such efforts; however, it was not the overnight sensation of lore. According to legend, Sheil's merger of sport, religion, and social activism in the CYO emanated from an anguished conversation with a condemned prisoner in the Cook County Jail during his chaplaincy there. He brooded over the possibilities for saving such wayward youth until, inspired by the CYO concept, he solicited Cardinal Mundelein's approval for such a project on a chauffeured limousine ride through one of Chicago's ravaged ghettoes. In reality, Sheil founded the CYO upon an already-well-established framework of sport, religious, and administrative structures at the parish and archdiocesan levels, such as the Holy Name Societies. Although histories of the CYO depict Sheil as a human dynamo who organized, promoted, sponsored, and directed activities in imperial fashion, such accounts fail to credit other important figures. Ellen Skerrett claims that Sheil used the sports program of Visitation Parish as the model for the CYO. Her contention is supported by the selection of a Visitation Parish priest, Father Thomas Tormey, as the first CYO athletic director.[17] Even the *New World* initially acknowledged Father Raphael "Ray" Ashenden as the "sponsor and controlling factor of the CYO."[18] In February 1931 Ashenden was killed by a car, and Sheil quickly solidified his own control of the organization. His leadership signaled a transition from Catholic isolationism to greater inclusion in American society. At that point Catholic schools had already been competing in their own baseball, basketball (for both boys and girls), track, tennis, and football leagues, along with swimming, bowling, and boxing tournaments. The CYO basketball program featured a national tournament hosted by Loyola University, and Sheil claimed the largest basketball league in the world with 120 teams in 1931. Boxing, however, enjoyed the spotlight.[19]

Borrowing heavily from the *Chicago Tribune*'s Golden Gloves format, the initial CYO boxing tournament occurred in the fall of 1931 amidst fanfare and promotional gimmicks. The program featured championship bouts at the Chicago Stadium in eight weight classes, with winners awarded four-year college scholarships, and gold medals commissioned from the papal sculptor in Rome. Sheil operated in conjunction with his friend, Arch Ward, the powerful sports editor of the *Tribune*. The match proved mutually beneficial. As a successful promoter of the Golden Gloves boxing tournament and an ardent Catholic, Ward had entrepreneurial knowledge, contacts with influential people, and the power of the media. In a largely Catholic city, the *Tribune*'s support and promotion of CYO activities resulted in avid readers. The sporting alliance between the archconservative *Tribune*, owned by the powerful McCormick family, and the liberal Catholics hierarchy, headed by Mundelein, bridged significant social and political groups in the city.[20]

At the height of the Depression the CYO provided not only the opportunity for college, but also free medical care and all equipment and instruction for participants. Thousands of working-class youths responded to the call with representation by all ethnic groups. Eighteen thousand fans, including Al Capone, witnessed the finals and a grand spectacle. Chicago dignitaries fêted the semifinalists at a lavish banquet. Contenders passed through an honor guard of 1,000 CYO boy scouts, and champions formed a traveling team touring across the country in a chartered railroad car to challenge opponents in California. Future trips included international bouts in exotic locales such as Panama and Hawaii. Even runners-up accompanied the squad as alternates and the boxers were treated to a full suit of clothes and shoes, including ties, hats, and underwear. They ate a special diet, enjoyed bottled water, and stayed at the finest hotels. Three CYO boxers made the 1936 Olympic team, while many others turned pro. The CYO managed the latter as well, paying their expenses and investing their winnings.[21]

For many young, working-class youths facing destitution during the Depression, the CYO offered the American dream of stardom, fame, and social mobility. There was, however, a price to pay. As Ernie "Blackie" Giovangelo, director of the West Side CYO Center, stated, "Sport is not the answer, just the bait."[22] The merger of sport and religion brought the secularization process under clerical control and allowed the Church to retain a hold on youth. For those who chose professionalism the CYO had exclusive rights to the first year of their contract. More important, all CYO athletes were required to take a public pledge of sportsmanship and loyalty to God and Church, and to forgo the use of vulgar language. Students had to maintain passing grades to compete, and Catholics had to partake of the sacraments. Intercity teams demonstrated their allegiance by attending church services before setting out on their road work.[23] Sheil had chosen boxing because of its appeal to the working class, who valued toughness and physical prowess. He offered education and social mobility for the adoption of middle-class values. In the process he hoped to create neighborhood role-models to counteract street life, delinquency, and the fascination with gangsters. The bargain proved an attractive one. Tony Motisi, a high-school dropout, but a member of the CYO intercity and international teams, claimed that the trip to Hawaii was the thrill of his life. He planned to turn pro thereafter.[24] But it was Jimmy Christy, Sheil's personal favorite, who exemplified his ideal type. The CYO rescued Christy from the streets. As a young ruffian enamored of the fight game, he persevered to become a CYO champion and entered the professional ranks. His patriotism led him to forgo pugilism to serve his country in World War II, in which he gave his life as a fighter pilot.[25]

The CYO launched its boxing program at a particularly opportune time, as the hardships of the Depression caused many Americans to question the capitalist system. From 1927 to 1932 Chicago hosted the athletic competitions of radical labor groups, including the Communist-sponsored Counter-Olympics of 1932. The Church greatly feared such movements, which were often sponsored by atheistic and socialistic organizations.[26] The CYO boxing program attracted those most likely to heed the call of the radicals. Sheil provided an outlet for the aggressions of the disenchanted. He answered critics of the organized violence by stating that youthful offenders simply weren't interested in checkers. In so doing, he performed an important function as an intermediary between classes. By creating class, racial, and ethnic heroes who operated within the established system, he gave hope and directed hostility internally. Rather than fight the system, CYO athletes and their supporters concentrated their energies on ethnic or racial opponents within the working class.[27]

As Elliott Gorn has shown, boxers and their fans bonded in a sense of craftsmanship and autonomy in opposition to dominant group values.[28] Sport, and its inherent gambling, became a means to money for Jewish and Italian boys, while Eastern Europeans so idolized champions Leo Rodak and Max Marek, who had defeated Joe Louis, that they named teams after them.[29] This was particularly important during the state of uncertainty and expendability occasioned by the Depression. As young men lost their livelihood, boxing still allowed them to retain their masculinity. The *Tribune* even asserted that one proved his manhood with a tournament entry card.[30] Boxing reinforced such working-class values as physical prowess as it muted working-class consciousness within middle-class structures and aspirations. Participants continued to believe in the American promise of opportunity and the work ethic. The vast majority of boxers vented their frustrations in the ring and returned to their jobs. CYO athletes were required to make a public statement of patriotism and religious beliefs that reinforced the status quo. Moreover, a wide variety of ethnic groups were represented on the traveling teams, and international bouts promoted a sense of inclusion in American society, thereby effecting a transition from ethnic to American nationalism and support for the established system. In the face of such acquiescence the radical Labor Olympiad in Ohio proved a dismal failure in 1936.[31] Working-class ethnics wanted to believe in the American dream and the CYO reaffirmed their hopes during a critical period of instability. By mid-decade the CYO program claimed 200,000 participants.[32]

Lucrative sport promotions provided the springboard for larger efforts. Sheil's widely publicized social activism in support of African-Americans, Jews, and labor groups presented him as the clerical champion of the underclass and the disenfranchised. The CYO not only accepted Jewish fighters, but recruited Benny Leonard, former lightweight champion and a Jew, as one of its boxing instructors. The CYO also engaged in competitive ventures with its Jewish counterpart, the B'nai B'rith Youth Organization; and Sheil's own battles against anti-Semitism earned him a place on a presidential commission that addressed the problem. Bishop Sheil became the first Gentile to be honored with the B'nai Brith's humanitarian award. The bishop also founded Sheil House, a settlement house in the African-American community headed by Joe Robichaux. In addition to providing much-needed child care, Robichaux's athletic program produced a highly successful track team. The CYO men's team won the Central AAU meet four consecutive years, while the women's team, featuring 1952 Olympian Mabel Landry, captured the national title. While African-Americans protested their exclusion from mainstream society, Sheil offered assistance and a means to sustain racial pride.[33]

Sheil provided similar community centers for the Nisei, Italian, Puerto Rican, and Navajo Indian communities. In areas where the CYO did not have a center it operated in conjunction with the neighborhood parks to administer twenty-four vacation schools taught by parochial-school teachers and Catholic college students. The Chicago Welfare Council questioned religious proselytism in the use of the public facilities; nevertheless, it provided funding for CYO programs over the next two decades. Sheil's reputation and political contacts were undoubtedly helpful in securing such funds.[34]

Bishop Sheil's outspoken attacks on bigots and in support of laborers earned him a national reputation but nearly cost him his life when an attacker fired upon him preceding a 1939 rally for the Congress of Industrial Organizations. In the succeeding years Sheil achieved international recognition as he engaged in European studies for President Truman and Pope Pius XII, claimed a hand in the Marshall Plan, and chaired a national commission on the minimum wage. The CYO program stretched to international proportions as well. CYO athletes competed with European and South American opponents. Media services included an international agency, publications in Polish, French, and German, and a radio station. On the home front Sheil financed and directed the National League of Decency, conducted charity drives, and provided social services to veterans, parolees, the poor, the sick, the blind, and the uneducated. He even founded two institutions of higher learning. In 1953 Sheil celebrated his twenty-fifth anniversary as a bishop with a dinner that included testimonials from two U.S. presidents, several members of Congress, at least thirteen foreign statesmen, a United Nations representative, five Supreme Court Justices, two generals of the army, J. Edgar Hoover, and a host of local dignitaries and labor leaders, including John L. Lewis.[35]

Sheil's contacts were indeed widespread and reached both ends of the political spectrum. Such an influential network proved of little help in the clandestine affairs of the Church, however. While Sheil's star burned brightly on the international stage, it glimmered faintly in his clerical world. After the death of Cardinal Mundelein in 1939, Sheil had fully expected to assume the reins of leadership, and perhaps a cardinal's hat; but promotions ceased with the death of his mentor. Instead, Samuel Cardinal Stritch of Milwaukee replaced Mundelein as head of the Chicago archdiocese. Still revered by his working-class constituents, but feeling frustrated and unappreciated, Sheil retreated in seclusion to a small parish. The flamboyant and increasingly egocentric bishop still operated too autonomously for his superiors. The scope of the CYO program stepped well beyond its budget, and the Welfare Council stopped its contributions when the CYO failed to pay its membership dues. Considered somewhat of a scoundrel and less than a team player by archdiocesan powers, Sheil abruptly and publicly resigned when confronted with allegations of mismanagement and erratic financing. In his last bit of grandstanding he announced the fact to the media before he even informed Stritch.[36]

Monsignor Edward Kelly, the new CYO director, curtailed many of its social services, decentralized the bureaucracy, and de-emphasized boxing.[37] The CYO lost much of its preeminence among sports organizations in Chicago; but the legend of Bishop Sheil only grew larger. Despite his fall from grace within the Church, Sheil had a lasting effect on American society. The CYO programs brought a greater degree of unity to diverse factions, as African-Americans, Jews, Asians, Hispanics, and European ethnics all found a common purpose in athletics and a champion in Sheil. With such a leader, and sustained by New Deal welfare programs, Catholic laborers saw little need to follow more radical elements. Sheil gave them hope and a means to express their own cultural values in the CYO cornerstone, the boxing program. In so doing he allowed workers to maintain a sense of class without provoking class consciousness during a particularly delicate period. He inspired American patriotism in conjunction with, rather than opposed to, ethnic pride, in contrast to the nativist attacks of the 1920s. He brought Catholics closer to the mainstream by demonstrating that religion, particularly when combined with sport, had greater influence than class, race, or ethnicity. The CYO left a legacy of faith and obedience to God and country. It would be another generation before Vietnam-era Catholic youth dared to question authority and government.[38]

Notes

1. Nancy Struna, "Puritans and Sport: The Irretrievable Tide of Change," *Journal of Sport History* 4:1 (spring 1977), 1–21, and Thomas Jable, "Pennsylvania's Early Blue Laws: A Quaker Experiment in the Suppression of Sport and Amusements, 1682–1740," *Journal of Sport History* 1:2 (November 1974), 107–21, have addressed religious influences during the colonial period. Among historical works that treat religion, see Roy Rosenzweig, *Eight Hours for What We Will* (Cambridge: Cambridge University Press, 1983).

2. William L. Katz, ed., *The Negro in Chicago, 1922* (reprint, New York: Arno Press, 1968); William M. Tuttle, *Race Riot: Chicago in the Red Summer of 1919* (New York: Atheneum, 1978); Frederic M. Thrasher, *The Gang, 1927* (reprint, Chicago: University of Chicago Press, 1963); Robert E. Park, Ernest W. Burgess, and Roderick D. McKenzie, *The City* (Chicago: University of Chicago Press, 1925), 112.

3. *The New World*, February 6, 1931, 9; February 20, 1931, 1; Bishop Bernard J. Sheil, ed., *CYO Survey*, 2:6 (June 1953), 8.

4. Nancy Struna addresses such questions in her book review of Patricia Click, *The Spirit of the Times: Amusements in Nineteenth-Century Baltimore, Norfolk, and Richmond*, in *Journal of Sport History* 17:3 (winter 1990), 369–71.

5. See Gerald R. Gems, "Sport and the Americanization of Ethnic Women," in George Eisen and David Wiggins, eds., *Ethnic Experiences in North American Sport* (Westport, Conn.: Greenwood Press, 1994), 177–200.

6. Archdiocesan letter to Rev. Kruszas, January 28, 1921, and *St. Augustine's Parish Golden Jubilee Program and Chronological History* (Chicago, 1936), at the Chicago Archdiocese Archives.

7. The term "organic intellectual" is used by Antonio Gramsci to describe leaders within a particular class who may influence group ideology. Quintin Hoare and Geoffrey N. Smith, eds., *Selections from the Prison Notebooks of Antonio Gramsci* (New York: International Publishers, 1971), 3–6, 57–59.

8. Clarence E. Rainwater, *The Play Movement in the United States* (Washington, D.C.: McGrath, 1922). Among the multitude of studies involving sport during the era, see Dominick Cavallo, *Muscles and Morals: Organized Playgrounds and Urban Reform, 1880–1920* (Philadelphia: University of Pennsylvania Press, 1981); Cary Goodman, *Choosing Sides: Playground and Street Life on the Lower East Side* (New York: Schocken Books, 1979); Stephen H. Hardy, *How Boston Played: Sport, Recreation, and Community, 1865–1915* (Boston: Northeastern University Press, 1982); Rosenzweig, *Eight Hours for What We Will.*

9. *New World,* April 16, 1910, 8.

10. *New World,* April 23, 1910, 8.

11. *New World,* March 19, 1910, 8; April 16, 1910, 8; April 23, 1910, 8; October 1, 1910, 8; January 28, 1911, 8; October 31, 1919, 6; January 9, 1920, 6.

12. *New World,* January 28, 1911, 8; June 17, 1911, 8; September 26, 1919, 6; October 10, 1919, 6; October 17, 1919, 6; October 31, 1919, 6.

13. *New World,* March 23, 1912, 8; January 16, 1920, 6; April 16, 1920, 6.

14. Edward R. Kantowicz, *Corporation Sole: Cardinal Mundelein and Chicago Catholicism* (Notre Dame, Ind.: Notre Dame University Press, 1983), 49–83; Robert A. Slayton, *Back of the Yards: The Making of a Local Democracy* (Chicago: University of Chicago Press, 1986), 135–36, 138; Charles Shanabruch, "The Catholic Church's Role in the Americanization of Chicago's Immigrants, 1833–1928," Ph.D. dissertation, University of Chicago, 1975.

15. Program, "Silver Episcopal Jubilee of His Excellency, the Most Reverend Bernard J. Sheil, D.D., April 29, 1953" (n.p.); Roger L. Treat, *Bishop Sheil and the CYO* (New York: Julian Messner, Inc., 1951), 12–43.

16. The *New World* continually petitioned for membership in the Holy Name and bemoaned the lack of participation throughout the 1920s. See *New World,* April 16, 1920, 6, on the influence of sports on membership.

17. Treat, *Bishop Sheil and the CYO*; Ellen Skerrett, "The Catholic Dimension," in Lawrence J. McCaffrey et al., *The Irish in Chicago* (Urbana: University of Illinois Press, 1987), 22–60.

18. *New World,* January 24, 1930, 10; February 20, 1931, 1, 11. Sheil apparently destroyed some CYO records during his seclusion after his resignation in 1954. Other early records were destroyed in a fire.

19. *New World,* June 6, 1930, 10, 16; June 20, 1930, 10; February 6, 1931, 9; November 10, 1933, 14. The Knights of Columbus, with a forty-nine-team league, claimed to be the second-largest.

20. Thomas B. Littlewood, *Arch, a Promoter, Not a Poet: The Story of Arch Ward* (Ames: Iowa State University Press, 1990), 49–59, 81, 85, 88, 115, 117; Treat, *Bishop Sheil and the CYO,* 59; Kantowicz, *Corporation Sole,* 181–82.

310   GERALD R. GEMS

21. Alexander Ropchan, Report on Medical and Dental Department of the CYO, December 1, 1938, Municipal Welfare Council Papers, Box 257, Folder 3, at the Chicago Historical Society (CHS). Treat, *Bishop Sheil and the CYO*, 59, 67–96, 119; *New World*, December 11, 1931, 12; January 6, 1933, 1, 10; January 13, 1933, 10; November 17, 1933, 15; November 29, 1935, 10; October 16, 1936, 12; November 20, 1936, 12; *Chicago Tribune*, December 3, 1931, 21; December 1, 1936, 27; December 1, 1936, 31; November 26, 1937, 19.

22. Treat, *Bishop Sheil and the CYO*, 120–21.

23. *Chicago Tribune*, March 25, 1934, pt. 2: 1–2; *New World*, January 6, 1933, 1.

24. *Chicago Tribune*, November 25, 1937, 37.

25. Treat, *Bishop Sheil and the CYO*, 46, 65, 71, 109–19; St. Sebastian's Parish, "Silver Jubilee, 1912–1937," (n.p.); *New World*, November 10, 1933, 14; December 1, 1933, 1; December 8, 1933, 13; *Chicago Tribune*, Dec. 1, 1936, 31.

26. Lizabeth Cohen, *Making a New Deal: Industrial Workers in Chicago, 1919–1939* (New York: Cambridge University Press, 1990), 252–53; 261–67; Mark Naison, "Righties & Lefties: The Communist Party and Sports During the Great Depression," *Radical America* 13 (July–August 1979), 47–59; William J. Baker, "Muscular Marxism and the Chicago Counter-Olympics of 1932," *International Journal of the History of Sport* 9:3 (December 1992), 397–410; Ronald H. Bayor, *Neighbors in Conflict: The Irish, Germans, Jews, and Italians of New York City, 1929–1941* (Baltimore: Johns Hopkins University Press, 1978), 40–41, 85–90.

27. Hoare and Smith, eds., *Selections from the Prison Notebooks*, 3, 210. Littlewood, *Arch*, 51–52, 79–81.

28. In addition to Elliott J. Gorn, *The Manly Art: Bare-Knuckle Prize Fighting in America* (Ithaca, N.Y.: Cornell University Press, 1986), see testimonials to boxers in Herbert J. Graffis, ed., *Esquire's First Sports Reader* (New York: A. S. Barnes & Co., 1945), 55–62, 112–20; Benjamin G. Rader, "Compensatory Sport Heroes: Ruth, Grange and Dempsey," *Journal of Popular Culture* 16:4 (spring 1983), 11–22; Randy Roberts, "Jack Dempsey: An American Hero in the 1920s," *Journal of Popular Culture* 8:2 (fall 1974), 410–26; Stephen H. Hardy, "One Future Direction: Toward a Theory of Sport," presentation delivered at the North American Society for Sport History convention, Chicago, May 25, 1991.

29. Raymond Sayler, "A Study of Behavior Problems of Boys in Lower North Community," and S. Kirson Weinberg, "Jewish Youth in the Lawndale Community: A Sociological Study," both in Burgess Papers at the University of Chicago, Box 135, Folder 4, and Box 139, Folder 4, respectively. *New World*, December 8, 1933, 13; March 23, 1934, 13; *Chicago Tribune*, January 17, 1933, 7; February 16, 1934, 27; February 18, 1934, Pt. 2:1; February 26, 1934, 17, 21; February 28, 1934, 19; March 29, 1934, 22; November 28, 1936, 19.

30. *Chicago Tribune*, December 3, 1931, 21.

31. Joseph Chada, "A Survey of Radicalism in the Bohemian-American Community," 1954, ms. at Chicago Historical Society.

32. *New World,* December 1, 1933, 11; January 12, 1934, 1.

33. Peter Berger, "Social Sources of Secularization," in Jeffrey C. Alexander and Steven Seidman, eds., *Culture and Society: Contemporary Debate* (New York: Cambridge University Press, 1990), 239–48. Ken Blady, *The Jewish Boxers' Hall of Fame* (New York: Shapolsky, 1988), 109–11; program, "BBYO-CYO All-Star Basketball Classic, 1957" (n.p.), states twenty-three years of friendly rivalry; program, "Silver Episcopal Jubilee of His Excellency, The Most Reverend Bernard J. Sheil, D.D., April 29, 1953" (n.p.); "1948 CYO Delinquency Prevention Program" and "CYO Report to the Welfare Council, January 1954," in Box 257, Folder 3 of Welfare Council Papers, CHS.

34. Welfare Council Papers, Box 257, Folder 3, CHS. Sheil's secretary, Father Peter Meeghan, who also served as CYO vice-president and treasurer, was the brother of Joseph Meeghan, a park director and a leader of the Back of the Yards Neighborhood Council. See Slayton, *Back of the Yards.*

35. Mary Elizabeth Carroll, "Bishop Sheil: Prophet without Honor," *Harper's Magazine* 211:1266 (1954), 45–51; program, "Silver Episcopal Jubilee."

36. Carroll, "Bishop Sheil." The reasons for the resignation were not announced and the media speculated that Sheil's recent inflammatory speech versus McCarthyism proved his undoing. On budget problems and program changes, see "CYO Report to the Welfare Council, January, 1954," Welfare Council Papers.

37. Catherine V. Richards's interview with Monsignor Kelly, January 9, 1958, in Welfare Council Papers, Box 257, Folder 3, CHS.

38. Antonio Gramsci, "Culture and Ideological Hemegony," in Jeffrey C. Alexander and Steven Seidman, eds., *Culture and Society,* 47–54, discusses the hegemonic process of socialization and conformity and the role of religion in political passivity.

13

"Great Speed but Little Stamina"
The Historical Debate over Black
Athletic Superiority

DAVID K. WIGGINS

"Environmental factors have a great deal to do with excellence in sport," wrote Martin Kane, a senior editor for *Sports Illustrated*, in a 1971 article entitled "An Assessment of Black Is Best," "but so do physical differences and there is an increasing body of scientific opinion which suggests that physical differences in the races might well have enhanced the athletic potential of the Negro in certain sports." The assertion by Kane that black athletic superiority in sport was perhaps due to innate racial characteristics caused a furor among many people because of its lack of scientific proof and by virtue of the fact that it came out during a period of intense interest in black Americans and appeared in one of this country's most popular and highly circulated magazines. Kane's comments resulted in a flurry of responses that ranged from outright rejection of the claim that black athletes were innately superior athletically to a grudging acceptance that blacks were much better than their white counterparts in some sports and decidedly inferior in others.[1]

This essay traces the ongoing debate waged over black athletic superiority, charting the various arguments and theories espoused by individuals who have sought to explain black dominance in sport. Martin Kane was hardly the first person to raise the question of black athletic superiority. At least since the latter part of the nineteenth century, people from all walks of life—coaches, athletes, trainers, cultural anthropologists, psychologists, sociologists, physical educators, biologists, medical doctors, and sportscasters—have put forth their own theories regarding racial differences and their possible effects on sport performance. Certain trends were evident in their comments, and the issue of black athletic superiority had different ramifications for whites and blacks. Notwithstanding, the weight of the evidence indicates that the differences between participation patterns of black and white athletes is primarily a consequence of different historical experiences that individuals and their particular racial group underwent. While elite championship athletes are blessed with a certain genetic makeup that contributes to their success in sport, these inherited attributes transcend any racial groupings.

Early Scientific Principles and the Black Athlete

Edwin B. Henderson, the noted physical educator and early historian of the black athlete, claimed that the question of black athletic superiority was first advanced when John B. Taylor, the great track star from the University of Pennsylvania, was capturing collegiate championships in the quarter-mile during the first decade of this century. Henderson wrote that some people of the era attributed Taylor's outstanding track performances to the fact that he was built more like a white runner, possessing larger gastrocnemius and soleus muscles than are found in the "African Negro."[2]

While Henderson was correct in acknowledging the debate over Taylor's prominence in track and field, there is little question that discussion of the black athlete's special talents occurred long before the University of Pennsylvania track star came on the scene. In the latter half of the nineteenth century, a number of outstanding black athletes distinguished themselves in predominantly white organized sport, which did not escape the attention of contemporary white academicians and social commentators who were already busily involved in studying racial differences. Investigators on both sides of the Atlantic were intent on determining the hierarchy of races and distinguishing one from another by examining such things as skull sizes, human brains, facial angles, skin color, structure of human hair, and the different varieties of body lice. The upshot of the various investigations—even when the results did not withstand the testing methods of science—was that blacks were physically different from whites and possessed an accompanying character and temperament that was unique to their species.[3]

One of the first black athletes who was talked about in terms of the scientific principles of the day was Peter Jackson, the great Australian boxer, probably best known as the man John L. Sullivan refused to fight. Many people in boxing tried to explain Jackson's dominance over his opponents by depicting him as a natural-born fighter who was more skilled at physical combat than the majority of white pugilists. Jackson was reminiscent of the primitive man, whose essential attribute was physical power. He was, in the words of one contemporary newspaper, a "human fighting animal," a personification of precivilized days when African men had to survive on strength alone.[4] However, in keeping with the scientific theories of the period, Jackson also possessed certain weaknesses that were indigenous to other black fighters. The common opinion in boxing circles was that Jackson could be beaten if you forced him to go the distance because he lacked stamina. In addition, Jackson could be taken out by a blow to the stomach, an inherent weak spot of all black fighters. The secret to beating Jackson was to "pummel his ribs" and he would soon lose his willingness to fight.[5]

The use of racial theories to explain athletic performance spilled over into the twentieth century. In 1901 Marshall "Major" Taylor, the famous bicycle racer from Indianapolis, was examined by a group of medical doctors at the Academy of Sciences in Bordeaux, France, in an attempt to test the racial stereotypes of the period. The doctors examined his heart, took anthropometric measurements, x-rayed him, and concluded by stating that Taylor "could be said to be absolutely perfect were it not for the fact that because of his bicycle racing, which has exaggerated the size of certain of his leg muscles, his thighs were a little over developed."[6]

The discussion of Taylor's special talents was followed by additional comments over the next few years about the abilities of runner John B. Taylor, heavyweight boxing champion Jack Johnson, and occasionally other outstanding black athletes. However, there was a noticeable decline in the amount of attention given to the question of black athletic superiority over the first and second decades of this century. The reason for the decline is easy to understand. By this time the majority of black athletes had been successfully shunted behind segregated walls and eliminated from white organized sport. With the occasional exception of some outstanding performances turned in by black athletes in Olympic competition, on predominantly white university campuses, and in professional boxing, most black athletes were left to compete among themselves on their own amateur and professional teams.[7]

Jesse Owens and Other "Black Auxiliaries" Intensify Debate

The discussion of black athletic superiority resurfaced following the 1932 Olympic Games in Los Angeles and then accelerated after Jesse Owens's record-breaking performances at the Big Ten Track Championships in 1935. The exploits of Owens and other black track stars such as Eddie Tolan, Ralph Metcalfe, Ed Gordon, Eulace Peacock, and Ben Johnson resulted in a number of comments from various people who ascribed the success of these athletes in the sprints and jumping events either to a longer heel bone or stronger Achilles tendon than those of their white competitors, or implied that in some way it was due to racial characteristics. In 1936, for example, Frederick Lewis Allen, in *Harper's Monthly Magazine,* noted that one of the most intriguing "athletic phenomena of our time is the emergence of American negroes as the best sprinters and jumpers in the world." Allen speculated that the rise to athletic supremacy by black Americans was primarily a sociological phenomenon. He added, however, that blacks were perhaps particularly "well fitted emotionally for the sort of brief, terrific effort which sprints and jumps require." Yale track coach Albert McGall suggested that maybe black sprinters got better leverage—and a little advantage over white sprinters—because of the projecting heel bone that was frequently found among blacks. Dean Cromwell, the well-known University of Southern California and Olympic track coach, felt that blacks excelled as sprinters and jumpers because they were closer to the primitive than white men. "It was not long ago," said Cromwell, "that his [a black man's] ability to sprint and jump was a life-and-death matter to him in the jungle. His muscles are pliable, and his easy-going disposition is a valuable aid to the mental and physical relaxation that a runner and a jumper must have."[8]

These kinds of speculations caught the interest of W. Montague Cobb, the well-known black physical anthropologist from Howard University. Cobb, who had a long interest in the physical constitutions of American blacks, refuted the claims that athletic success was based on racial characteristics. In a 1936 article in the *Journal of Health and Physical Education* entitled "Race and Runners," Cobb argued that no particular racial group had ever exercised a monopoly or supremacy in a particular kind of event in track and field. He acknowledged that certain events might continue to be more popular among particular kinds of people, but noted that "split-second differences" in the performances of the great black and white sprinters were insignificant from an anthropological standpoint. The physiques of champion black and white sprinters in general and Jesse Owens in particular revealed no indications that "Negroid physical characteristics are anatomically concerned with the present dominance of Negro athletes in national competition in the short dashes and the broad jump."[9]

Cobb also questioned, as have many cultural anthropologists, whether there was even such a thing as a racial group considering the enormous lack of racial homogeneity within both the black and white cultures. He noted that Howard Drew, the former sprinter from the University of Southern California, was "usually taken for a white man by those not in the know." Ed Gourdin, the great sprinter and long jumper from Harvard, had dark straight hair, no distinctly black features, and a light-brown complexion. Cobb pointed out that Jesse Owens did not even possess what was generally but erroneously considered the "Negroid type of calf, foot and heel bone." The measurement of Owens's gastrocnemius, in fact, was more in line with that of a "caucasoid type rather than the negroid." Cobb suggested that proper training and incentive were the key factors in the making of a champion, and implied that black athletes, like their white counterparts, were stimulated by a "desire to emulate their predecessors."[10] In essence, Cobb was similar to other prominent intellectuals of the decade in that he espoused the theory that environment, not race, determined the individual capabilities of man. This was certainly the underlying thesis of E. Franklin Frazier's *The Negro Family,* Richard Wright's *Native Son,* and Ann Petry's *The Street.*

Cobb was not the only scientist during the 1930s to examine the physical differences between the races and determine the possible effects they had on athletic performance. Eleanor Metheny, the noted physical educator from the State University of Iowa, was intrigued by the debate being waged over the prominence of black athletes in track and field. In 1939, Metheny conducted a study in which she attempted to determine if there were some differences between blacks and whites in proportions of the body that gave blacks an advantage in certain types of athletic performances. She first took anthropometric measurements of fifty-one black and fifty-one white male students at the State University of Iowa and analyzed the differences between the two groups, then compared the findings with those of other investigators. Metheny found statistically significant differences in bodily proportions between the black and white students.[11]

On the basis of her anthropometric measurements of the black and white students, Metheny presented several kinesiological implications for athletic performance. While careful to point out that her findings were only tentative and that such things as reaction time, muscle viscosity, and various psychological factors played an important role in determining success in particular activities, Metheny offered, nonetheless, the possible effects that different body types could have on sport participation. She suggested, for example, that blacks could be at an advantage in throwing and jumping events because of their longer forearms and hands. In jumping, the longer, heavier arm is able to develop greater momentum, and this momentum, when transmitted to the body as a whole, would assist blacks in jumping. She also noted that the longer legs and narrower hips of blacks would aid them in running because they permitted longer strides and less angular reaction to the forward stride. On the other hand, the chest construction and markedly lower breathing capacity of blacks would handicap them in distance running and other events of longer duration.[12]

Clinical psychiatrist Laynard Holloman presented several theories about black athletic superiority in a 1943 essay entitled "On the Supremacy of the Negro Athlete in White Athletic Competition." He implied that hatred and a desire for revenge against whites was one reason for the supremacy of black athletes in certain American sports. Black fighters dominated boxing, for instance, because it was an ideal way for them to express their hatred for the white man through getting revenge. Unable to discharge their hatred toward the white man directly, black boxers fought against white opponents with a kind of savageness they did not exhibit when fighting members of their own race. In the squared ring, black boxers expressed their pent-up emotions, discharged latent energies, satisfied their restless ego, and healed their wounded narcissism. Holloman also hypothesized that blacks strove for excellence in sport because it was a means to compensate for their feelings of inferiority. Black athletes, said Holloman, sought "victory with a drive that is much more forceful and insistent than that for a medal or the plaudits of the crowd." What they fought for on the playing fields was a "quieting of the strife that goes on in the mind that thinks itself inferior, to quiet the yelling of a group that claims itself superior."[13]

Black Dominance in the Manly Art

Much of the discussion about black athletic superiority during the 1950s centered on boxing. Especially during the early part of the decade there was a good deal of speculation about why blacks ruled boxing and whether their overrepresentation in the sport would lead to its demise. The black-owned journal *Our World* asserted in 1951 that blacks ruled boxing because it was a way to make big money, fast. The large majority of black boxers were "underprivileged kids" who discovered they could capture their "pot of gold" by using their fists. Former heavyweight champion Jack Dempsey offered his own explanations as to why blacks dominated the fight game. An unlikely candidate to discuss black dominance since he had supposedly ducked the great black boxer Harry Wills, Dempsey argued that other things besides money accounted for the preponderance of black boxing champions. He noted, in tones not typically reserved for blacks, that one reason black boxers dominated the sport was their penchant for hard work. Black fighters were willing to pay the price necessary to become champions. As a group, they trained more diligently and more conscientiously than whites. Mike Jacobs, the famous boxing promoter, echoed Dempsey's comments, arguing that black boxers worked harder than their white counterparts. Generally coming from underprivileged backgrounds, black boxers learned early in life that they had to fight hard to survive and to succeed.[14]

The comments of Dempsey and Jacobs seem important for two reasons. First of all, both men used terms to describe black boxers that were antithetical to white America's stereotype of blacks. While whites variously characterized blacks as docile, lazy, irresponsible, and childlike, Dempsey and Jacobs utilized such terms as "hard working" and "progressive" to depict black fighters of the period. This seems significant because the implication in any discussion of black athletic superiority was that blacks achieved success in sport by virtue of their naturally endowed physical skills and not through hard work, sacrifice, self-discipline, and other admirable character traits. Perhaps nowhere was this stereotypical image of the black athlete more fully expressed than by the Harlem Globetrotters, the famous all-black basketball team founded by Abe Saperstein in 1927. The Globetrotters perpetuated the black Sambo stereotype with all its negative connotations, coming across as frivolous, somewhat dishonest children who were lazy and given to wild bursts of laughter. Running about the court emitting shrill jungle sounds and shouting in thick southern accents, the Globetrotters reflected all the prejudices that the dominant culture had built up about blacks in this country. The Globetrotters had innate physical skills and exhibited "natural rhythm," but were in need of "mature white handling." Sportswriter Jack Olsen noted that "the white man's encapsulated view of the whole negro race [was] set to the rhythm of Sweet Georgia Brown."[15]

Mike Jacobs's comments were also noteworthy in that they were followed closely by a lengthy debate about boxing's future and whether the overrepresentation of blacks in the sport would cause its ultimate demise. Certainly one of the underlying fears associated with the discussion of black athletic superiority was that the preponderance of blacks in sport diminished fan interest, cut gate receipts, and seriously jeopardized the future of individual sport franchises. Club owners were certainly aware of the potential problems when white spectators were asked to identify with a racial minority they had historically rejected.[16]

Olympic Competition and Resurgence of the Debate

The discussion of racial differences and sport performance waned somewhat during the latter 1950s but resurfaced again the following decade. In fact, during the 1960s the debate seemed to rise and fall in every Olympic year. The outstanding performances of black athletes in Olympic competition and their increased involvement in professional sport refueled the debate over black athletic superiority. The British physician James M. Tanner garnered some attention at the beginning of the period with his book *The Physique of the Olympic Athlete*. He admitted that "economic and social circumstances" probably accounted for the large number of blacks in competitive sport, but noted that the different body types of black track-and-field performers were perhaps responsible for their tremendous success in certain events. Based on anthropometric measurements of 137 athletes at the Rome Olympics in 1960 and earlier at the British Empire and Commonwealth Games, Tanner and his associates concluded that there were large and significant racial differences among track-and-field performers that might well have enhanced the athletic potential of blacks in particular events like the sprints, high jump, and long jump, while inhibiting their performance in events such as the marathon.[17]

Like Eleanor Metheny some twenty years earlier, each time the performance of black athletes contradicted Tanner's theory of physical differences, he offered either an alternative explanation or said that more research needed to be done on the topic. He noted, for example, that the body type of blacks should make them particularly well-suited for the pole vault. But blacks did not distinguish themselves in the event, said Tanner, "perhaps only for reasons of tradition."[18] Tanner, like Metheny and a host of other academicians, never illustrated exactly how physiological differences translate into outstanding athletic performances. He presented no evidence that success in sprinting is influenced by slimmer calves per se or that the ability to achieve great heights in the pole vault is directly related to arm length.

In 1964, the writer Marshall Smith published an article in *Life* magazine entitled "Giving the Olympics an Anthropological Once-Over," where he summarized the various opinions given on the questions of racial differences and athletic performance. Smith relied to a great extent on the expertise of Carleton S. Coon, a former Harvard and University of Pennsylvania anthropologist, and Edward E. Hunt, Jr., an anthropologist from Harvard, who both believed that inherited physical adaptations seemed to play a part in the abilities of certain members of particular races to excel in different sports. They admitted that social factors and/or motivation played a part in the success of black athletes, but contended that the particular body type of blacks made them more suitable for certain sports. Coon, for example, described the feet of black men, with their longer heel bone and thicker fat pads, as a "marvelous organ for mobility, leaping, jumping and landing with a minimum of shock." In addition, the black man's slender calves, with tendons proportionately longer than those of whites and with an overall appearance of loose jointed-ness, were characteristic, said Coon, of "living things (cheetahs, for instance) known for their speed and leaping ability."[19]

One of the more thorough examinations of the topic was undertaken by sportswriter Charles Maher in a five-part series on the black athlete written in 1968 for the *Los Angeles Times*.[20] In two separate articles entitled "Blacks Physically Superior? Some Say They're Hungrier," and "Do Blacks Have a Physical Advantage? Scientists Differ," Maher presented the various arguments given concerning racial differences and athletic performance. Besides citing the work of Montague Cobb, Carleton S. Coon, and other experts, he contributed additional insights by quoting opinions of well-known sport scientists, coaches, and athletes. By and large, the people Maher quoted attributed the success of black athletes to factors other than physical superiority. Thomas K. Cureton, a well-known professor of physical education at the University of Illinois who spent a lifetime studying the physical characteristics of champion athletes, said that performance differentials were not the result of race. "Because of years of training, yes," noted Cureton. "Because of motivation, yes. Because of social goals, yes. Those make a difference. But not race." John Wooden, the legendary basketball coach at UCLA, said he doubted that the athletic success of blacks had anything to do with physical superiority. "I think he [the black athlete] has just a little more ambition to excel in sports," noted Wooden, "because there aren't enough other avenues open to him." Tommy Hawkins, the well-known black basketball player for the Los Angeles Lakers, probably came close to the truth when he noted that the black athlete's pre-occupation with sports in this country was a self-perpetuating condition. "From an early age," said Hawkins, "you identify with people who have been successful. From a Negro standpoint, those people would be in sports and entertainment."[21]

Serious Dialogue between Kane and Edwards

Three years after Maher's series of articles appeared, Martin Kane published his previously mentioned essay in *Sports Illustrated*, detailing the numerous arguments given about possible black athletic superiority. Kane attempted to present evidence supporting the notion that outstanding athletic performances in particular sports were based on racial characteristics indigenous to the black population. Utilizing the expertise of coaches, black athletes, athletic researchers, and medical doctors, Kane suggested that racially linked physical, psychological, and historical factors have given rise to black dominance in sport.[22] There were a number of interesting speculations made by various people in Kane's article, but perhaps the strongest comments on the subject came from James Counsilman, the Indiana University and former United States Olympic swimming coach. Counsilman argued that black athletes were markedly superior to white athletes in those sports that required speed and power because they had more white muscle fibers. Commenting that exercise physiologists were afraid to admit this fact publicly, Counsilman pointed out that the white muscle fibers so prominent in black athletes were adapted for speed and power, while red muscle fibers, which white athletes had in abundance, were adapted for endurance. At the same time, Counsilman asserted that the lack of great black swimmers resulted primarily from socioeconomic factors. Blacks did not have the opportunity to be good swimmers because they generally lacked the money and did not have access to the facilities that were necessary to achieve excellence in the sport.[23]

Kane's article drew an angry response from Harry Edwards, who refuted all of the sportswriter's proposed theories.[24] Edwards noted that Kane's attempt to establish a connection between racially linked physical characteristics and black athletic superiority suffered from serious methodological problems and debatable assumptions about the differences between the races of men. Edwards pointed out, like Montague Cobb and other scholars earlier, that there exist "more differences between individual members of any one racial group than between any two groups as a whole." This fact precluded any assertion by Kane that particular racial groups were predisposed to certain physical activities. Edwards also disputed Kane's assertion that blacks had a peculiar psychological disposition that contributed to their overwhelming success in sport. Specifically, the notion that black athletes are better able to relax under pressure than white athletes not only lacked scientific foundation but was "ludicrous as even a common sense assumption." Lastly, Edwards refuted Kane's suggestion that slavery had weeded out the "hereditarily and congenitally weak" among the black population and created a physically superior group of people. He argued that the major implication of Kane's assertion was that "it opens the door for at least an informal acceptance of the idea that whites are intellectually superior to blacks." The white population lost nothing by supporting the idea of black physical superiority. If anything, it reinforced the old stereotype that blacks were "little removed from the apes in their evolutionary development."[25]

Edwards concluded by asserting that a variety of societal conditions were responsible for the high value black youths placed on sport and the resultant channeling of a disproportionate number of talented blacks into sport participation. While whites had more visible role-models and greater job alternatives, black Americans were restricted to a very narrow range of occupational choices. Sport and, to a lesser extent, entertainment appeared to be the most achievable goals for blacks, and as long as that remained the same, black athletic superiority would go unchallenged. This circumstance was most unfortunate, said Edwards, because it encouraged blacks to strive for success in a highly competitive profession that left only so much room for athletes of any color. The vast majority of black aspirants ended up back in the ghetto, either because they lacked the talent to become a superstar, or because they were unwilling to accommodate themselves to the oppressive tendencies of the American sport establishment. The dream of athletic success became a reality for only a small number of black youths. The large majority were left with unfulfilled fantasies of stardom, glamour, and wealth.[26]

Coinciding with the debate over black athletic superiority during this period was an equally controversial discussion taking place in academic circles regarding differences between black and white intellectual ability. Just two years prior to the appearance of Kane's article, Arthur R. Jensen, a psychologist from the University of California at Berkeley, rekindled the age-old debate over black and white intelligence differences with the publication of a 123-page study in the *Harvard Educational Review* entitled "How Much Can We Boost IQ and Scholastic Achievement?" Jensen, who apparently was influenced by William B. Shockley, a well-known professor at Stanford and Nobel Laureate in Physics, caused an uproar by arguing that "it is not an unreasonable hypothesis that genetic factors are strongly implicated in the average, negro-white intelligence difference." Jensen pointed out that heritability measures indicated that about 80 percent of the determinance of intelligence was due to genes and some 20 percent to environment. Jensen noted that after having several discussions with well-known geneticists he could safely conclude that "any groups which have been geographically or socially isolated from one another for many generations are practically certain to differ in their gene pools, and consequently are likely to show differences in any phenotypic characteristics having a high heritability." In addition, said Jensen, "genetic differences are manifested in virtually every anatomical, physiological, and biochemical comparison one can make between representative samples of identifiable racial groups. There is no reason why the brain should be exempt from this generalization."[27]

Jensen's ideas caused such an uproar that the *Harvard Educational Review* reprinted his entire article in its very next issue, along with critiques by theorists of education, psychologists, and a population geneticist.[28] This issue was in turn followed by a number of articles on the subject in various academic journals, a book in 1975 edited by Ashley Montagu devoted specifically to Jensen's ideas, and a myriad of essays since that time on the topic, which is sometimes referred to as "creeping Jensenism."[29] The rebuttals took many forms, but the most general criticism came from scholars who viewed Jensen's work with skepticism because of illogical claims in his presentation and his rather naive conception of the interplay between genetic and environmental factors in behavior. Stephen Jay Gould argued, for example, that Jensen had no new data on the subject of intelligence testing and that "what he did present was flawed beyond repair by inconsistencies in the data itself and by inconsistent claims in his presentation."[30]

The Jensen affair was similar in many ways to the debate over black athletic superiority. Both debates were centered on some controversial research studies, were concerned with trying to distinguish environmental from genetic factors and the possible effects they had on performance, and were marked by volatile responses from many members of both the white and black communities who feared that the discussion led to a perpetuation of longstanding stereotypes rather than an enlightened perspective on racial issues. In essence, the debates were nearly one and the same. Jensen and his cohorts could not fail to discuss physiological differences between the races when speaking of intelligence abilities, while individuals involved in the debate over black athletic superiority could not avoid the implication that blacks were somehow inferior to whites intellectually.

Impact of the Debate in America's Black Community

The increasing number of blacks participating in sport combined with the burgeoning interest in blacks in general throughout the decade of the 1970s caused much speculation about the special skills of black athletes. Much of the discussion was taken up by people from within this country's black community. Black Americans were obviously interested in a debate that concerned them most. In 1972, black Harvard psychiatrist Alvin F. Poussaint argued that black men, stripped of their social power, focused their energies on other symbols of masculinity, particularly physical power. Writing in an *Ebony* article attractively titled "Sex and the Black Male," Poussaint noted that the need of many black men to display physical power has produced impressive athletic achievements. He pointed out that whites like to be entertained by athletically gifted black men, "as long as it doesn't take the form of having sexual intercourse with white women. Whites want black men to be virile on the work gang and on the playing field, but impotent everywhere else." Unfortunately for whites, argued Poussaint, the success of blacks in athletic competition has enhanced their sexual image. Black men want to "outclass whites on the ball-field, on the dance floor, and in the boxing ring. Black men have an image to maintain and a great psychological victory to win." One of the regrettable consequences of the need to be physically superior, noted Poussaint, "has been the contempt in which many young blacks hold their peers who have opted for success in more sedate activities."[31]

In 1974, Jesse Owens, a man whose performances contributed to the debate over black athletic superiority, told members of the American Medical Association that physical differences had no bearing on the overrepresentation of blacks in American sport. Citing the anthropometric measurements that Montague Cobb had taken of him some 40 years earlier, Owens argued that desire rather than physiological differences accounted for the large number of blacks in competitive sport.[32]

In the same year that Owens addressed the American Medical Association, sportswriter Bill Rhoden wrote an extended article in *Ebony* titled "Are Black Athletes Naturally Superior?" Rhoden added nothing new to the debate, but reiterated the various theories espoused by Cobb, Edwards, Metheny, Poussaint, and others. In 1977 *Time* magazine ran an article titled "Black Dominance" in which the opinions of well-known black athletes, among others, were given concerning the question of black athletic superiority. Almost to a man, the black athletes quoted argued that physical differences accounted for the superior performances of blacks in sport. O. J. Simpson, the great running back of the Buffalo Bills, said that blacks were physically geared to speed, an important attribute considering that the majority of sports were geared to speed. "We are built a little differently," noted Simpson, "built for speed—skinny calves, long legs, high asses are all characteristics of blacks." Echoing similar feelings was Joe Morgan, the outstanding second baseman of the Cincinnati Reds. "I think blacks, for physiological reasons, have better speed, quickness, and ability," said Morgan. "Baseball, football, and basketball put a premium on those skills."[33]

In 1980 Legrand Clegg published an essay in *Sepia* magazine titled "Why Black Athletes Run Faster," in which he reported the research studies being conducted on the question of black athletic superiority by several black sci-entists on the West Coast. Clegg explained that Malachi Andrews, an associate professor in physical education at California State University, Hayward, along with several black scholars in the School of Ethnic Studies at San Fran-cisco State, was convinced that the abundance of melanin in blacks was re-

sponsible for their outstanding athletic performances. The researchers believed that melanin, rather than being a fairly inert pigment important only
for its ability to protect the skin from harmful effects of the sun, was capable
of absorbing a great deal of energy, which blacks utilized to achieve superior
speed in running events.[34]

The above comments seemed to be accounted for by ethnic pride and the
symbolic importance of athletic success more than anything else. Decidedly
image-conscious, members of America's black community had often expressed the belief that the success of individual black athletes could possibly
quicken the advancement of the whole race. Blacks saw accomplishment as
ammunition in the barrage against unreasonable barriers. A great deal of attention was always directed at those blacks who achieved prominence in
American life—particularly in those fields in which they excelled in competition with whites—because it presumably helped break down the prevailing
opinions of the black man's inferiority and had an uplifting effect on blacks
themselves. Every act of a black man that came to public attention—such as
a rushing title by Simpson or most valuable player award for Morgan—had expressive connotations far beyond the importance of the act itself.[35]

The irony was that the same people who were proudly pointing out the
success of black athletes in American sport were also emphasizing that blacks
should strive for success in other fields of endeavor. One of the important facts
about the escalating debate over black athletic superiority during the 1970s
was that the more blacks were recognized for their special athletic abilities, the
more America's black intelligentsia stressed how essential it was that younger
blacks develop their "brains" as well as their "brawn." Like Harry Edwards,
the more learned members of this country's black community were forever
trying to reverse the stereotype that blacks were intellectually inferior to
whites and fearing that the channeling of a disproportionate number of blacks
into sport and other forms of entertainment could possibly delimit the conditions of black identity within American culture and guarantee the continu-
ation of those limits. Well-informed members of the black community also
realized that the chance of a black athlete (or white athlete, for that matter)
ever playing professional sport was very small. And rather than slavishly as-
piring to a career in professional sport, blacks would be better served by hon-
ing those skills necessary to achieve success in other professional fields.

America's black intelligentsia recognized, moreover, that success in sport
would never completely eradicate the problems of the race. However psychologically satisfying or however materially advantageous to a few, success
in athletics was not a satisfactory solution to the problem of discrimination,

because the political and economic dominance still remained in white hands. In large measure, then, America's learned blacks were rather ambivalent toward sport. While they believed sport was a worthy activity, viewed athletic success as a legitimate goal, and proudly pointed to the achievements of individual black athletes, America's black intelligentsia continually cautioned against an overemphasis on sport and stressed the importance of preparing for life after basketball.[36]

Examples of this ambivalent attitude toward sport are numerous. Earl Graves, publisher of *Black Enterprise* magazine, said he understood why black children would be attracted to sport. The lure of frame and chance to make large sums of money had a seductive effect on black children in the ghetto. Graves pointed out, however, that at best only one out of every 4,000 black children ever participates in professional sport. Considering these sobering statistics, black children are foolish to throw their "heart and soul into the pursuit of an athletic career."[37] Perhaps no one expressed more eloquently the black community's ambivalent attitude towards sport than Arthur Ashe, the black tennis star from Richmond, Virginia. In a frequently cited open letter to black parents in the *New York Times* titled "Send Your Children to the Libraries," Ashe argued that "black culture expends too much time, energy and effort raising, praising, and teasing our black children as to the dubious glories of professional sport." He pointed out that blacks have been on the sports and entertainment road for too long. "We need to pull over," said Ashe, "fill up at the library and speed away to congress and the supreme court, the unions and the business world."[38] More recently, Alan Page, former defensive lineman of the Minnesota Vikings and Chicago Bears, used the occasion of his induction into Pro Football's Hall of Fame to express his feelings about the overemphasis on sport and the importance of education in America's black community.[39]

Sport Sociologists Examine the Overrepresentation of Black Athletes

The question of black athletic superiority caught the interest not only of Edwards and other black Americans, but also of sport sociologists, who were busily studying various aspects of black athletes' involvement in American sport. Virtually every sport-sociology text and anthology that came out during the 1970s and early 1980s included a discussion of the topic. While many of these books merely summarized the oft-repeated arguments of Kane and Edwards, some of them offered additional insights into the controversy. For example, Stanley Eitzen and George Sage suggested in *Sociology of Sport* (1978) that two of the more likely reasons for black dominance in sport were occupational discrimination and the sports opportunity social structure within American society. The authors pointed out that black athletes may be more determined and motivated to succeed in sport because their opportunities for vertical mobility are limited in American society. Blacks may perceive athletics as one of the areas in which they can realize a measure of success in American culture.[40]

The reason that black athletes tended to gravitate towards certain sports and were underrepresented in others, said Eitzen and Sage, perhaps stemmed from what sociologist John Phillips has called the sports opportunity social structure. Simply stated, black athletes tended to be successful in those sports where they had access to coaching, facilities, and competition, while being underrepresented in those activities where such items were unavailable to them. This accounted for the success of black athletes in such sports as basketball because the skills necessary to achieve a level of proficiency in this activity could be learned in school and community recreation programs. This also accounted for the dearth of black athletes in golf, tennis, and other sports typically taught in private clubs, which have historically denied membership to certain minority groups for economic and social reasons.[41]

Jay Coakley furnished some possible insights into the question of black athletic superiority by discussing the notion of racial differences and their effect on sport performance in his widely cited book *Sport in Society: Issues and Controversies*. Coakley argued that racial differences in sport were not the result of genetic factors but caused by a combination of the different characteristics of particular kinds of sport activities, the patterns of discrimination, and the motivation of individual athletes. Coakley pointed out, for example, that black athletes' selection of sports was predicated on how they defined their chances for success. Like anyone else, black youngsters were likely to adopt highly successful athletes as their role-models who would play a part in their career goals and future aspirations in sport. Because the vast majority of these role-models participated in a selected number of sports, the chances were good that younger black athletes would elect to take part in the same sports.[42]

Coakley also suggested that the level of involvement of black athletes in sport was contingent on both the needs of those individuals who controlled sport and "the amount of off-the-field social contact" that was prevalent in a particular sport. He argued that the lure of big profits on the part of owners in professional sport has caused them to become less concerned about the race of particular athletes and more interested in their skills. Black athletes with requisite skills can gain access to particular sports if they are viewed as potentially big winners and profitable gate attractions. Lastly, Coakley pointed out that blacks were most often found in those sports where social distance was increased (boxing, track, baseball, football, and basketball) and underrepresented in those sports that were closely associated with "informal, personal, and often sexually mixed relationships" (golf, bowling, tennis, and swimming).[43]

Among the more thought-provoking discussions of black athletic superiority was a 1982 essay by sociologist James LeFlore entitled "Athleticism Among American Blacks." LeFlore acknowledged that genetic, environmental, and economic factors certainly played a part in the athletic success of black athletes, but believed that a more comprehensive explanation for black dominance in sport was grounded in what he termed "subcultural and informational poolings." He argued that the disproportionate number of black athletes in certain sports was contingent on both the cultural setting in which black athletes found themselves and the information that was available to both them and their subculture group. Generally speaking, black athletes arranged their world based upon available information, interpreted the feedback, and eventually made decisions that hopefully resulted in social reward.[44]

LeFlore pointed out that members of the black subculture interpreted their social system through a generalized and specific pool of information. Participation in sports that fostered disapproval from the larger social system was typically avoided by black athletes, while those sports in which blacks were expected to take part attracted a disproportionate number of participants. At the same time, argued LeFlore, black athletes' decision to participate in some sports but not others was, to a great extent, determined by the subculture's perception of those sports. Blacks who choose to participate in fencing or golf, for example, have to confront the perceived status of these sports within their subculture. If perception of those sports is negative, because they are viewed as unmanly, deemed unworthy, or seen as elitist and of a snobbish nature, then the black athlete must deal with this negativism. Continued participation in these sports may have a decided effect on the relationship between black athletes and other members of the subculture.[45]

"Of Mandingo and Jimmy 'The Greek' "

LeFlore's 1982 article did not signal the end of the debate over black athletic superiority. The last few years have been marked by a continuing discussion of the black athlete's special talents and overrepresentation in particular sports. Perhaps the best example of the current status of the debate over black athletic superiority can be gleaned from the recent incident involving Jimmy

"The Greek" Snyder, a twelve-year veteran on CBS's "The NFL Today" show, who received national attention on January 15, 1988, when he told a local television interviewer in Washington, D.C., that blacks were better athletes than whites because they were "bred to be that way since the days of slavery" and that if more blacks became coaches "there's not going to be anything left for the white people."[46] Responding to a question by Ed Hotaling about the progress of blacks in sports, Snyder argued that the beginnings of black athletic superiority occurred during the Civil War period when "the slave owner would breed his big black with his big woman so that he could have a big black kid." Black athletes can "jump higher and run faster," said Snyder, because of their "thigh size and big size." White athletes will never be able to overcome those physical advantages, continued Snyder, because they are lazy and less motivated than their black counterparts.[47]

Snyder's comments caused a great deal of controversy and drew heated responses from various people. The editors of *Sports Illustrated* said that "Snyder's ramblings betrayed an ignorance of both U.S. history and sport." The sports prognosticator "was also guilty of the sort of sweeping generalizations on which racial stereotypes and prejudices are built." Harry Edwards called Snyder "obviously incompetent and abysmally ignorant." "I'm not sure that his [Snyder's] views in this regard necessarily disqualify him for choosing a betting line," said Edwards later, "but I think a more overriding concern is that he is a disgrace to the network." John Jacob, president and chief executive officer of the Urban League, said that "one would expect a man like Jimmy the Greek or anyone who has this kind of exposure on the national media involving athletics not to deal with myths but empirical data. It's dumb for Jimmy the Greek to make such a ludicrous comment." Susan Kerr, spokeswoman for CBS, issued a statement just an hour after Snyder's interview was aired locally in Washington, D.C., stating that CBS Sports deeply regretted the remarks made by Snyder and emphasized that they did not reflect the views of the network.[48] One day after Kerr issued her statement, CBS made it perfectly clear how they felt about Snyder's comments by firing the well-known sports prognosticator.[49]

Snyder made several mistakes during his interview for which he would later apologize and seek forgiveness. As noted by his critics, Snyder's remarks displayed an ignorance of both sport and American society. He left himself open for criticism by insisting that the preponderance of blacks in certain sports resulted from physical differences between the races and not acknowledging that other factors perhaps contributed to the outstanding performances of black athletes. His views that blacks had bigger thighs than their

white counterparts would certainly not hold up under scrutiny by physical anthropologists. While blacks suffered cruel indignities during slavery, Snyder's
notion of selective reproduction was certainly not one of them. Snyder also
did not endear himself to anyone when he complained that blacks would soon
take control of sport.

Perhaps more than anything else, however, Snyder was criticized not so
much for what he said, but for what he didn't say. Dorothy Gilliam, a writer
for the *Washington Post,* poignantly noted that many people reacted to the "implications and unstated assumptions that lie behind the Greek's statements."
Gilliam made it clear that for many people, including individuals like Harry
Edwards, the flip side of any discussion about black athletic superiority was
the implication that blacks were intellectually inferior. In large part, Snyder's
comments were interpreted more as an indictment of black intellectual ability than as an acknowledgment of black athletic superiority.[50]

Genetic Freaks or Well-Trained Gladiators? Continuous Questions in an Unending Debate

The "Snyder bashing," as one writer referred to the incident, was followed by
yet another series of comments about possible racial differences and their effects on sport performance. For example, Arthur Ashe recently noted that he
would like to see more research completed on the subject. He noted, as he has
on a number of occasions, that he thinks blacks are especially gifted at such
activities as running.[51] Brooks Johnson, the black track coach at Stanford, was
quoted as saying in a recent edition of the *New York Times* that the domination
of black sprinters reflected "racism in society in general." He compared the
instant gratification of sprint races to a sense of urgency felt by many blacks
because of their lowly economic conditions. Calvin Hill, the former star football player with the Dallas Cowboys and one of the most frequently quoted
athletes on the subject of black athletic superiority, recently stated in the *Journal of Sport History* that the outstanding performances of black athletes have
resulted from the large number of positive black role-models in particular
sports, the emphasis on instant gratification in America's black community,
and the fact that black athletes were descendants of the physically gifted slaves
who survived the harsh middle passage to this country.[52] In April 1988 Tom
Brokaw hosted an NBC special devoted to the question of black athletic superiority that included guests such as Harry Edwards, Arthur Ashe, anthropologist Robert Malina, and Richard Lapchick, director of the Center for the
Study of Sport and Society at Northeastern University. The special received

front-page headlines in American newspapers and caused widespread reaction that ranged from outright disgust that the program was even aired to acknowledgment that the subject must be broached if stereotypes were to be eliminated.[53]

The aforementioned comments are an indication that the subject of black athletic superiority continues to fascinate people from various backgrounds, and that one of the most glaring aspects of the debate down through the years has been the divergent opinions and theories expressed not only between the black and white communities in this country but among the two groups themselves. This is accounted for by the fact that a person's race was seemingly less influential than educational background or any number of other variables in determining their particular philosophy of black athletic superiority. Harry Edwards's position on the subject was, for example, more aligned with Jay Coakley than it was with either Arthur Ashe or Calvin Hill. As academically trained sociologists, Edwards and Coakley could be expected to have different views from the two black athletic stars, possessing perhaps a more critical understanding of American society and a better ability to understand the reasons for the abject powerlessness of many blacks in this country.

While race seemed to be less influential than other factors in determining an individual's view of black athletic superiority, there seems little question that there were certain trends evident in the comments emanating from within this country's black and white communities, and that the topic had differing ramifications for the two groups. For many in the black community, the overrepresentation of blacks in competitive sport was a source of both pride and concern. On the one hand, black Americans took great satisfaction in the fact that black athletes dominated certain sports because it would give the black community a new sense of dignity and self-esteem, ingredients that were not only inspiring in and of themselves, but necessary for the ultimate destruction of discrimination in this country. Great black athletes served as role-models and could become symbols of possibility and much-needed examples of black achievement. At the same time, the black intelligentsia recognized that success in sport would never completely eradicate the problems of the race. The preponderance of blacks in competitive sport could possibly delimit the conditions of black identity within American culture and contribute to the stereotypical notion that blacks could excel in physical pursuits, but not in the life of the mind.

White Americans perhaps had even more at stake in the discussion of black athletic superiority. They were both fascinated and troubled by the dominance of black athletes in particular sports. By and large, the dominant culture in this country leaned towards a physiological explanation for black athletic superiority and was reluctant to acknowledge possible sociological reasons for the phenomenon. By acknowledging a physiological basis for black athletic superiority, whites in this country could more easily maintain the broad range of black character they found acceptable and had marked off so carefully. Acknowledgment of physical superiority did nothing to disrupt the feeling among a large segment of the white population that blacks were either docile or savage, faithful or tricky, pathetic or comical, childish or oversexed. In large measure, believing that physical differences accounted for the overrepresentation of black athletes in certain sports seemed quite natural considering that the dominant culture's stereotype of blacks was traditionally opposite to the Protestant ethic. The notions of hard work, dedication, and sacrifice were rarely used by white commentators to describe the efforts of such athletes as John B. Taylor, Eddie Tolan, Ralph Metcalfe, Jesse Owens, and Isiah Thomas.

Perhaps the best indication of the dominant culture's attitude about black dominance in sport can be gleaned by noting the comparatively little attention paid to the overrepresentation of white ethnic groups in particular sports throughout American history. Unlike the numerous studies completed on the black athlete, very little time has been given over to questioning such things as the possible physiological basis for the high proportion of Jewish basketball players in the early part of the twentieth century, the disproportionate number of Slavic football players in line positions during the 1930s and 1940s, or the one-time dominance of Irish, Jewish, or Italian fighters. There might be occasional comments about the physical strength, speed, or stamina of these athletes, but more often than not their success was accounted for by such factors as low economic background, pride in performance, work habits, intelligence, and the commitment and discipline they brought to each contest. Commentators certainly had stereotypical notions about these athletes, but spoke of them in more complimentary terms than they used for black athletes and in a spirit that reflected more deeply ingrained American virtues held most dear by the dominant culture.[54]

The argument that black athletic superiority was the result of innate physical differences was not only made by some white Americans, but by many blacks as well. Some people in this country's black community expressed the belief that inherent physical differences accounted for the overrepresentation of blacks in certain sports. While racial pride, educational background, social class, and any number of other factors accounted for this reasoning, the fact remains that some blacks tried to explain black athletic superiority along racial lines. Many blacks unthinkingly accepted the ethnic and racial stereotypes cre-ated by the dominant culture, and thus helped perpetuate the idea that black athletic superiority was largely the result of physical differences between the races. The notion of race undoubtedly had different connotations for blacks but it was still a convenient way for them to explain the complex phenome-non of black athletic superiority. Perhaps this tells us nothing more than that portions of the black community were similar to their white counterparts in that they were sometimes guilty of prejudicial assumptions and had a pen-chant for using a simple explanation to account for a phenomenon that was not easily explainable.

For all that, the question still remains: Why are black athletes dominant in certain sports and underrepresented in others? Certainly one of the things that can be said with a degree of assurance is that there is no scientific evidence of genetic association or linkage between genes for individual and group athletic achievement among black Americans. We know as little about the contribu-tion of genes to athletic ability as we do about the genetics of intelligence. Ath-letic ability is clearly a function of many genes in interaction with a number of other variables such as economic background, motivation, facilities, and coaching. How many genes may be involved in athletic ability is difficult, if not impossible, to determine since there is no way to separate out the contribu-tions made by the aforementioned variables to sport performance.

Drawing links between genetic makeup and athletic ability is highly sus-pect, moreover, because, as Cobb, Edwards, and other academicians have made plain through the years, it is highly questionable whether there is such a thing as a racial group considering the enormous lack of racial homogene-ity within this country's black and white communities. The anthropometric differences found between racial groups are usually nothing more than cen-tral tendencies, and do not take into account wide variations within these groups or the overlap among members of different races. This fact not only negates any reliable physiological comparisons of athletes along racial lines, but makes the whole notion of racially distinctive physiological abilities a moot point.

The weight of the evidence indicates that the differences between partici-pation patterns of black and white athletes are primarily due to differences in the history of experiences that individuals and their particular racial group have undergone. Blacks in this country have traditionally not enjoyed equal cultural and socioeconomic opportunities, having been oppressed, discrimi-nated against, impoverished, and generally excluded from the good things in life. The result is that blacks have shown both a preference and an inclination for different sports than their white counterparts. The lack of other job opportunities is partly to blame for the considerable importance attached to sport by many black Americans. The lower-class black community's religious fervor for sport is directly proportional to the disillusionment it feels over inadequate employment opportunities. If blacks place a decided premium on physical virtuosity through sport, as many people have claimed, it is caused more by their particular station in life than by any hereditary factors.

Lacking money and access to certain equipment and facilities has guaranteed that black athletes will focus their attention on certain accessible sports and disregard others. It takes very little in the way of equipment and facilities to participate in basketball and track and field, while such activities as golf and tennis demand resources that are out of reach for a majority of blacks. The participation patterns of black athletes have also remained remarkably similar through the years largely because of the stereotyping of black athletes by the dominant culture and the fact that younger blacks tend to emulate and follow in the footsteps of their athletic forebears. There is no reason to believe this situation will change in the near future. The economic plight of black Americans has not changed dramatically enough, nor has the basic structure of organized sport evolved to the point where black athletes would suddenly find themselves overrepresented in golf and excluded from basketball.

The overrepresentation of black athletes in particular sports will certainly continue to draw attention from academicians and various other people in society. Let us trust that these people will not treat black athletes as though a stereotype were sufficient and as though the individual could be ignored. This would only contribute to a continued escape from consideration of the effect of social and economic inequities upon black sport participation, and to an insistence on attributing the outstanding performances of black athletes to inherent racial differences. The spirit of science necessitates, however, that academicians continue their research to determine if the success of black athletes is somehow the consequence of racially distinctive chromosomes. The worst thing to happen would be for researchers to refrain from examining the possible physical differences between black and white athletes for fear that they would be transgressing an established political line or be labeled racist. Like all areas of research, the topic of black athletic superiority needs to be examined from a broad perspective and not from a preconceived and narrowly focused vantage point. If the truth is to be known about outstanding black athletic performances, scholars need to investigate the topic from a biosocial perspective while at once recognizing the inequities in our pluralistic society and acknowledging that the overrepresentation of black athletes in certain sports had its counterpart among white athletes who excelled in their own activities without fear of being branded as genetic freaks.

Notes

1. Martin Kane, "An Assessment of Black Is Best," *Sports Illustrated,* January 18, 1971, 72–83.

2. Edwin B. Henderson, "Physical Education and Athletics Among Negroes," in *The History of Physical Education and Sport,* ed. Bruce L. Bennett (Chicago, 1972), 82–83.

3. See Thomas P. Gossett, *Race: The History of an Idea* (Dallas, 1963); George M. Frederickson, *The Black Image in the White Mind* (New York, 1971); John S. Haller, *Outcasts from Evolution* (Urbana, Ill., 1971).

4. *San Francisco Examiner,* May 31, 1892.

5. See David K. Wiggins, "Peter Jackson and the Elusive Heavyweight Championship: A Black Athlete's Struggle Against the Late Nineteenth Century Color Line," *Journal of Sport History* 12 (summer 1985), 143–68. Randy Roberts discusses the stereotype of black boxers in his biography of Jack Johnson, *Papa Jack: Jack Johnson and the Era of White Hopes* (New York, 1983), 61, 63.

6. Andrew Ritchie, *Marshall "Major" Taylor* (San Francisco, 1988), 174.

7. See, for example, Edwin B. Henderson, *The Negro in Sports* (Washington, D.C., 1939); A. S. "Doc" Young, *Negro Firsts in Sports* (Chicago, 1963); Jack Orr, *The Black Athlete: His Story in American History* (New York, 1969).

8. Frederick Lewis Allen, "Breaking World Records," *Harper's Monthly Magazine* 173 (August 1936), 302–10; Marshall Smith, "Giving the Olympics an Anthropological Once-over," *Life,* October 23, 1964, 81–84; Dean B. Cromwell and Al Wesson, *Championship Techniques in Track and Field* (New York, 1941), 6.

9. W. Montague Cobb, "Race and Runners," *Journal of Health and Physical Education* 7 (January 1936), 3–7, 52–56.

10. Ibid.; see also Cobb, "The Physical Constitution of the American Negro," *Journal of Negro Education* 3 (1934), 340–88. The contemporary version of Cobb's article might be James H. Jordan's "Physiological and Anthropometrical Comparisons of Negroes and Whites," *Journal of Health, Physical Education, and Recreation* 40 (November–December 1969), 93–99.

11. Eleanor Metheny, "Some Differences in Bodily Proportions between American Negro and White Male College Students as Related to Athletic Performance," *Research Quarterly* 10 (December 1939), 41–53.

12. Ibid.

13. Laynard L. Holloman, "On the Supremacy of the Negro Athlete in White Athletic Competition," *Psychoanalytic Review* 30 (April 1943), 157–62.

14. "Why Negroes Rule Boxing," *Our World* 6 (November 1951), 48–52; Jack Dempsey, "Why Negroes Rule Boxing," *Ebony* 7 (May 1950), 29–32; Mike Jacobs, "Have Negroes Killed Boxing?" *Ebony* 7 (May 1950), 29–32.

15. See Ben Lombardo, "The Harlem Globetrotters and the Perpetuation of the Black Stereotype," *Physical Educator* 35 (May 1978), 60–63.

16. See Frank T. Bannister, Jr., "Search for 'White Hopes' Threatens Black Athletes," *Ebony* 35 (February 1980), 130–34; Frank Deford, "The Big Game Is Over: This Way to the Exit, Bwana," *Ovi* (spring 1973), 51, 132, 134; Harry Edwards, *Sociology of Sport* (Homewood, Ill., 1973), 214.

17. James M. Tanner, *The Physique of the Olympic Athlete: A Study of 137 Track and Field Athletes at the XVII Olympic Games, Rome, 1960* (London, 1964).

18. Abrahams, "Race and Athletics," 107. Olympic athletes have received much attention down through the years from sport scientists interested in anthropometric measurements. See for example, Alfonso L. de Garay et al., *Genetic and Anthropological Studies of Olympic Athletes* (New York, 1974); T. K. Cureton, *Physical Fitness of Champion Athletes* (Urbana, Ill., 1951); Ernst Jokl, "Essay on Medical Sociology of Sports," in Jokl, *Medical Sociology and Cultural Anthropology of Sport and Physical Education* (Springfield, Ill., 1964), 65–71.

19. Smith, "Giving the Olympics an Anthropological Once-over," 81–84 (quotes, 83).

20. See *Los Angeles Times*, March 24 and 29, 1968.

21. Ibid., March 25, 1968.

22. Kane, "An Assessment of Black Is Best," 72–83.

23. Ibid., 72–73. It is a common perception in this country's dominant culture that blacks make terrible swimmers because of their "unique" anthropological makeup. For a discussion of blacks in swimming, see John A. Faulkner, "Physiology of Swimming," *Swimming Technique* 6 (April 1970), 14–20, and Malachi Cunningham, Jr., "Blacks in Competitive Swimming," *Swimming Technique* 9 (1973), 107–8.

24. See particularly Edwards's articles: "The Sources of the Black Athlete's Superiority," *Black Scholar* 3 (November 1971), 32–41; "The Myth of the Racially Superior Athlete," *Intellectual Digest* 2 (March 1972), 58–60; and "20th Century Gladiators for White America," *Psychology Today* 7 (November 1973), 43–52.

25. Edwards, "The Sources of the Black Athlete's Superiority," 35, 37–39.

26. Ibid., 39–41.

27. Arthur R. Jensen, "How Much Can We Boost IQ and Scholastic Achievement?," *Harvard Educational Review* 39 (winter 1969), 1–123.

28. See *Harvard Educational Review* 39 (spring 1969).

29. See, for example, Ashley Montagu, ed., *Race and IQ* (New York, 1975); C. L. Brace and F. B. Livingstone, "On Creeping Jensenism," *Race and Intelligence,* ed. C. L. Brace, G. R. Gamble, and J. T. Bonds (Washington, D.C., 1971).

30. Stephen Jay Gould, "Racist Arguments and IQ," in Montagu, *Race and IQ*, 145–50.

31. Alvin F. Poussaint, "Sex and the Black Male," *Ebony* 27 (August 1972), 114–20 (quotes, 115–16).

32. *New York Times*, December 2, 1974.

33. Bill Rhoden, "Are Black Athletes Naturally Superior?," *Ebony* 30 (December 2, 1974), 136–38, and "Black Dominance," *Time* 109 (May 9, 1977), 57–60.

34. Legrand H. Clegg, II, "Why Black Athletes Run Faster," *Sepia* 29 (July 1980), 18–22, and "Is Black Fastest?," *Black Sports* 4 (May 1975), 18–24.

35. David K. Wiggins, "The Quest for Identity: The Dialectic of Black Consciousness and the Involvement of Black Athletes in American Sport," paper presented at the annual meeting of the North American Society for Sport History, Columbus, Ohio, May 27, 1987.

36. This attitude has been prevalent in the black community for a long time. Black newspapers in the latter half of the nineteenth century, for example, expressed the importance of developing both "brain" and "brawn." See, for example, *Indianapolis Freeman*, September 18, 1890; *The New York Age*, December 20, 1890.

37. Earl Graves, "The Right Kind of Excellence," *Black Enterprise* 10 (November 1979), 9.

38. *New York Times*, February 6, 1977. See also ibid., May 1, 1977.

39. Ibid., July 31, 1988. See also Anthony Leroy Fisher, "The Best Way Out of the Ghetto," *Phi Delta Kappan* 60 (November 1978), 240.

40. D. Stanley Eitzen and George Sage, *Sociology of Sport*, 2nd ed. (Dubuque, Iowa, 1978), 300.

41. Ibid., 301; John C. Phillips, "Toward an Explanation of Racial Variations in Top-Level Sports Participation," *International Review of Sport Sociology* 3 (1976), 39–55.

42. Jay Coakley, *Sport in Society: Issues and Controversies*, 3rd ed. (St. Louis, 1986), 146–50.

43. Ibid. For other discussion about black athletes from a sociological perspective, see Wilbert Marcellus Leonard, II, *A Sociological Perspective of Sport*, 3rd ed. (New York, 1988), 214–55; George Sage, *Sport and American Society: Selected Readings*, 3rd ed. (Reading, Mass., 1980), 313–47; D. Stanley Eitzen, ed., *Sport in Contemporary Society* (New York, 1979), 356–408; Barry D. McPherson, "The Black Athlete: An Overview and Analysis," in *Social Problems in Athletics*, ed. Daniel M. Landers (Urbana, Ill., 1976), 122–50; Morgan Worthy and Allan Markle, "Racial Differences in Reactive Versus Self-Paced Sports Activities," *Journal of Personality and Social Psychology* 16 (1970), 439–43; James M. Jones and Adrian Ruth Hochner, "Racial Differences in Sports Activities: A Look at the Self-Paced Versus Reactive Hypothesis," *Journal of Personality and Social Psychology* 27 (1973), 86–95.

44. James LeFlore, "Athleticism Among American Blacks," in *Social Approaches to Sport*, ed. Robert M. Pankin (Toronto, 1982), 104–21. Two other articles that furnish an insightful look at the black experience in sport are Larry E. Jordan, "Black Markets and Future Superstars: An Instrumental Approach to Opportunity in Sport Forms," *Journal of Black Studies* 11 (March 1981), 289–306, and Hal A. Lawson, "Physical Education and Sport in the Black Community: The Hidden Perspective," *Journal of Negro Education* 48 (spring 1979), 187–95.

45. LeFlore, "Athleticism Among American Blacks," 104–21.

46. See, for example, *New York Times*, January 16 and 17, 1988; Jonathan Rowe, "The Greek Chorus: Jimmy the Greek Got It Wrong But So Did His Critics," *Washington Monthly* 20 (April 1988), 31–34; Jack E. White, "Of Mandingo and Jimmy 'The Greek,' " *Time* (February 1, 1988), 70; Peter Ross Range, "What We Say, What We Think," *U.S. News & World Report* 104 (February 1, 1988), 27–28.

47. *New York Times*, January 16 and 17, 1988.

48. Susan Ballard, "An Oddsmaker's Odd Views," *Sports Illustrated* 68 (January 25, 1988), 7; *New York Times*, January 16, 1988.

49. *New York Times*, January 17, 1988; ibid., January 19, 21, and 24, 1988.

50. *Washington Post*, January 21, 1988.

51. John Underwood, "On the Playground: Troubling Thoughts about Top Athletes—and Too Much Success," *Life* 11 (spring 1988), 107. Arthur Ashe also comments on the questions of black athletic superiority in *A Hard Road to Glory: A History of the Afro-American Athlete*, 3 vols. (New York, 1989).

52. *New York Times*, July 17, 1988; David Zang, "Calvin Hill Interview," *Journal of Sport History* 15 (winter 1988), 334–55.

53. *New York Times*, April 26, 1989; *Los Angeles Times*, April 26 and 27, 1989; *Washington Post*, April 26, 1989; *USA Today*, April 26, 1989.

54. See for example, William M. Kramer and Norton B. Stern, "San Francisco's Fighting Jew," *California Historical Quarterly* 53 (winter 1974), 333–46; Dennis P. Ryan, *Beyond the Ballot Box: A Social History of the Boston Irish, 1845–1917* (Rutherford, N.J., 1983); Harold U. Riablow, *The Jew in American Sports* (New York, 1948); Ralph C. Wilcox, "In or Out of the Melting Pot? Sport and the Immigrant in Nineteenth Century America," in *Olympic Scientific Congress, 1984 Official Report: Sport History*, ed. Norbert Muller and Joachim K. Ruhl (Niedernhausen, 1985); Kirson S. Weinberg and Henry Arond, "The Occupational Culture of the Boxer," *American Journal of Sociology* 57 (winter 1952), 460–69.

PART 4
MARKETS
AND AUDIENCES

14

Entrepreneurs, Organizations, and the Sports Marketplace

STEPHEN H. HARDY

The Sport Industry: New Questions and New Approaches

Last year the *Chronicle of Higher Education* ran a feature story explaining that sport history has gained "new respectability." As noted in this article, no longer will the chancellor of the University of Wisconsin at LaCrosse suspect that sport historians spend their time trading baseball cards! Such veiled praise notwithstanding, these are heady times for the field. Quality articles and monographs on sport and leisure are on the increase. New lines of research have branched out to such an extent that Nancy Struna recently characterized the literature as a "glorious disarray."[1]

While I agree with the thrust of Struna's perceptive essay, on closer inspection one finds that most of the recent work may be synthesized under the rubric of social history. This has resulted in publications that focus on two, often complementary, elements of interpretation: long-term *social forces* that have nudged sporting practices in certain directions and the *social functions* of sport within this context. Among the former one finds the rise of cities, technological revolutions, immigration, the changing roles of women, and the maturing of capitalism. Among the latter, status, ethnic identity, social control, and boosterism.[2]

The result of this research has been a greater appreciation of both the context and the significance of baseball, football, hockey, tennis, horse racing, boxing, and other sports as they were experienced in history. At the same time, however, it is important to remember that the social history of sport does not constitute the totality of sport history. As this essay attempts to outline, a number of important topics demand attention from perspectives that are closer to business and economic history. These topics require a shift in attention from the significance of consumption to the structures of production, from the broad sweep of social forces to the minute elements of decision-making. In general, they focus on the ways in which entrepreneurs have developed a special, perhaps singular, industry that has produced a particular part of the past. They demand a closer look at why certain organizational forms have grown to dominate the production and distribution of games and sports to their consumers; how these organizations have merged into systems of interdependence, wherein some units clearly dominate others; and, finally, what rules, resources, and practices have constituted the structure or logic of the sport industry over time. In short, they call for an appreciation of sport as a special industry, like agriculture, steel, or medicine.[3]

Naturally, such analysis must pay close attention to social and cultural developments in the wider environment of suppliers, creditors, consumers, and critics. Yet this will be important not only to clarify the sport industry's submission to some wider *mentalité,* but also to explore the ways in which entrepreneurs may have insulated themselves from outside forces and thereby either filtered, misread, or distorted the arguments of their constituents. Indeed, even the most successful entrepreneurs like Albert Spalding faced endlessly complex decisions about game rules, contract negotiations, stadium leases, and interleague wars. As simple as Spalding tried to paint reality, he and his colleagues could not hope to understand or control the full consequences that their steady stream of decisions would have on the patterns of sport production and consumption. Neil Harris has made similar observations about the organizers of cultural institutions like libraries, museums, and universities. As Harris maintains, one cannot easily pigeonhole their motives into compartments of "social control" or "nationalism," because they were too often consumed with a struggle to understand, if not govern, their complex organizations. The same may be said about the sport industry. To use Harris's words, historians will not appreciate its development until they begin to "clearly reconstruct the old alternatives" and "suggest the kinds of choices [these] institutions represented." Only by reconstructing the old alternatives that decision-makers faced can historians begin to understand how and why baseball, football, golf, tennis, hockey, and other sports developed along the lines they have, and why the industry's system and structure took on its particular shape and logic.[4]

Reconstructing the history of sport as a productive industry will, first, require an inversion of the dominant process of inquiry. Instead of analyzing sport from the outside in, the researcher must consider developments from the inside out. In other words, the starting point will not be the broad processes that concern social historians—developments in social class, urban life, or racism. Rather, the initial focus will be on the central issues as the sport organizations defined them. While only greater research can clarify these, it is a reasonable assumption that they center upon the acquisition and maintenance of facilities, supplies, and players; the staging of events, the minimization of costs, the garnering of publicity: in short, the concerns of a business. In turn, these will probably revolve around the key functions of management—planning, coordinating, and controlling human, material, and financial resources in order to reach some objectives, either clear or hazy. The historian's questions then become woven less around changing issues in the social environment and more around standard, ongoing issues within the sport industry. Seen in this light, Jules Tygiel's masterful study of the integration of major-league baseball is as much an analysis of problems in strategic planning, talent acquisition, and public relations as it is a thorough if specialized study of American racism. The brilliance of Tygiel's book lies in its ability to do both.[5]

What follow are suggestions for historical research into the development of the sport industry. These revolve around three main topics: 1. the sport product; 2. the role of entrepreneurs and investors in developing the product; 3. the types of individual organizations and networks of organizations that entrepreneurs created. Scholars in economics and sport management have already provided important insights into the contemporary industry. Their work, however, often lacks historical perspective.[6] While historians have uncovered considerable evidence about the past business of sports, especially baseball, their research needs synthesis. But this essay seeks not to supplant any approach to research. Rather, it offers a supplemental framework for analysis. Readers will note its limitations: a focus on team sports and, more particularly, team sports in America. At the same time, some of the discussion and sources suggest the potential for wider applications.

The Sport Product: A Triple Commodity

Sport history, from the "inside out," begins with an analysis of the sport product, since a particular product's nature usually influences the organizations that produce it.[7] On close inspection, the sport product unfolds as a triple or three-part commodity, and the sport industry divides into segments that generate or distribute one or more of the parts. These parts, which can exist in isolation but which reach full expression in combination, are as follows: the activity or game form, the service, and the goods.

The term "commodity" demands some consideration here since it must be understood historically. A commodity, as Marx noted, is "in the first place, an object outside us, a thing that by its properties satisfies human wants of some sort or another." But all products are not necessarily commodities. "To become a commodity," Marx explained, "a product must be transferred to another whom it will serve as a use-value, by means of exchange."[8] Sport, then, becomes a commodity when its producers transfer it, via exchange, to a separate group of consumers. Clearly, even today not all sports exist in commodity form. Stickball flourishes largely as use-value, consumed only by its producers. But even here, components of the activity—balls, special bats— may be commodities if they are purchased at Woolworth's or K-Mart. The job of historians is to uncover the process by which the sport product evolved and by which its triple components edged ever closer to pure commodities.[9]

Now, if one considers the game form first, one can sense the subtlety of this evolution. As a game form, the sport product consists of activities embodied in the rules defining the way the game is played, or the "game occurrence," to use John Loy's phrase.[10] Of course anyone can make up a game, as Professor Naismith demonstrated. But this is of little consequence until rule-making is organized and controlled by particular groups who regulate the game form's distribution, or who try to regulate it. Can game forms ever exist as a commodity? Indeed they can and they do, especially at the level of high-performance sport. For while sandlotters animate their competition with arguments about unwritten rules, organized leagues resort to published rule books, purchased annually by officials, administrators, coaches, players, and fans. This is no mere cottage industry. *Beadle's Dime Base-Ball Player* sold 50,000 copies annually in the 1860s, and it receives due credit for its part in making the New York game the national pastime. A few years later, "guides" (including rules and statistics) for all sports constituted a substantial segment of Albert Spalding's empire, both netting him vast profits and supporting the influence of governing bodies whose rules he published. Sales of this commodity continue to be strong. In 1984, NCAA Publishing alone sold approximately $50,000 worth of rule books for college sports.[11]

Sandlotters of course play on, in blissful ignorance of technicalities; but the game form has been a commodity for some time. Rule-making itself has become more and more difficult, subject to pressures from lobbies like the American Medical Association. Obviously, the particular forms of any sport, in any historical period, are hardly inevitable derivatives of some *zeitgeist*. They are the products of conscious decision-making that cries out for more historical investigation.[12]

If rulemakers create a special product—the game form—that may exist as a commodity, it is also true that their product seldom exists in isolation. Without disregarding sandlotters, it is clear that game forms are usually played in a situation that involves more than simple, expressive use-value for the players. Some utility beyond competition—not expressed or implied in the rules— is appended to the game performance. This utility is the sport service, the second component of the triple commodity.[13]

Sport services have existed historically in many aspects, including education, status, military preparation, urban boosterism, political propaganda, and, most extensively, entertainment. Those familiar with the literature quickly recognize the complex histories of these different service utilities: slow and steady accretions over centuries (recognition of games as military preparation and education dates to the ancients) coupled with flashing, revelatory episodes of growth (the use of the Modern Olympics as political propaganda). Further confounding this history, several services have often wrapped around the same game form. Indeed, one could easily argue that the most popular team games have been fertile ground for every conceivable service. And of course this provides a clue to their popularity.[14]

While historians have chronicled and interpreted sport services for some time—usually as "social functions"—a reconsideration will be valuable on several theoretical grounds. For instance, it appears that special organizations have emerged to promote and capture the service utilities, and that these service organizations are often distinct from those controlling the game form. This may result in pressure tactics, negotiations, and accommodations between organizations. A case in point would be the 1905–6 football controversy. At one level, this episode became a power struggle between the old rules committee and the emerging organization, the Intercollegiate Athletic Association, whose avowed mission was to shape both the game form and the educational service. The results of these and other conflicts and their consequences for the contemporary sports product can only be understood through careful historical reconstruction of decision-making from the inside out.[15]

Such research may also explain more clearly the movement of sport services toward commodity forms. Social functions are not always free. If we want to enjoy the status value associated with the game of tennis, we pay for membership in an exclusive club. If we want the (sometimes dubious) educational values of soccer for our children, we pay the registration fee for the youth league. If we want entertainment from football, we pay for a Steeler ticket. But this all is not the result of a natural or inevitable process. Every sport has experienced a period of discovery when players, sponsors, and promoters have recognized that others might pay to watch or play a game, in essence exchanging money for the chance to derive their personal use-value from their own form of involvement. Historians are especially equipped to uncover the effects of this discovery on the production of the sport product and on the structure of the sport industry.

The third component of the unified sport product involves the goods, the physical objects necessary to the game form that are recognized or regulated in the rules. Balls, goals, sticks, bats, protective equipment, and uniforms normally fall into this category. So do facilities that are requisite to the contest or exercise, such as swimming pools, or lined fields, or running tracks. Nonessential facilities like bleachers, grandstands, or press boxes fall under the province of services. Although this segment of the sport industry has received almost total neglect from historians, it appears that sporting goods reached full-blown commodity status faster than either the game form or the service. The consequences of this sprint are considered later in this essay.[16]

As this brief excursus on the sport product reveals, simple definitions of "sport" run a risk of distorting historical reality. This is especially true since different segments of the sport industry must combine to fuse multiple components into a laminated product that embraces a game form, services, and goods. Such orchestration between organizations has never been smooth, nor has it been static. Indeed, it is the dynamic nature of the industry and its products that renders simple definitions of sport historically hazardous.

Entrepreneurs and Investors

This complexity has intensified in the last two centuries, not surprisingly the same time period that saw the movement of the sport product ever closer to a pure commodity. In reassessing these developments, it will make sense to focus initially on the activities of entrepreneurs, whose role was first outlined by Arthur Cole, Fritz Redlich, and Sebastian DeGrazia. All three suggested that profit-seeking entrepreneurs had altered the direction of leisure and sport in the nineteenth century. As Cole put it. "One man's curiosity may become another man's profit." Or as Redlich argued, "What was originally an autonomous trend favorable to business was consciously developed by business so that in the end business domination of leisure time activities was the result." What these authors emphasized was the commercialization of sport and leisure in the increasingly urbanized culture of nineteenth-century America. A logic that promoted spectacle and profit overwhelmed an earlier, more rural ethos of home-backed, wholesome fun.[17]

While there is much to learn by rereading these still-insightful works, there is too easy a sweep to their interpretations. Their speculative nature and their

limited sources do not allow for a clear investigation of the motives of entrepreneurs in sport or leisure. And while the profit motive has surely nudged
sport in certain directions, one cannot say that it has dominated or even controlled the industry's structure. Sports entrepreneurs have often been like
Robert Wiebe's version of the Robber Barons: "Yet as shrewdly as some of
them pursued the main chance, they were also trapped by the present, scurrying where they appeared to stalk." One only needs to think of Chris Von der
Ahe or Andrew Freedman to see a scurrying sports magnate.[18]

Indeed, one senses that profit-seeking and risk-taking—normally central
dimensions of entrepreneurship—have not always been so pivotal in an industry whose production process has often been heavily subsidized by state
and philanthropic agencies (think of high-school athletics or YMCAs). Although profit and risk have been and remain important, the hallmark of the
sport entrepreneur has more likely been the innovative activity that Joseph
Schumpeter emphasized in his *Theory of Economic Development*. This includes:
1. the introduction of a new good or new quality of a good (or service); 2. the
introduction of a new method of production or a new way of handling a commodity; 3. the opening of a new market; 4. the acquisition of a new source of
raw materials or unfinished goods; 5. the crafting of a new organizational
structure. Any of these activities results in a "new combination" of production. The parallels in the sport industry are instructive.[19]

In Schumpeter's sense, Walter Camp was an entrepreneur, not because he
sought profits for Yale, but because he aggressively created and introduced a
new game form, resulting in a product that was attractive *and* profitable.
Naismith's creation of basketball was similarly an entrepreneurial activity; but
so also was Senda Berenson's introduction of a new quality to the sport. Further, she opened a new market. Along this last line, massive research is needed
to identify the obscure entrepreneurial figures who introduced eastern-born
football and baseball to new southern and western markets in the nineteenth
century. Easier to assess are the entrepreneurial efforts of Branch Rickey,
whose minor-league system represented a new source of supply, or William
Hulbert, who helped effect a radical reorganization of the baseball industry in
1876. Hulbert's accomplice, Albert Spalding, was thereafter an entrepreneur
in all phases of Schumpeter's definition. Indeed, one of the many strengths of
Peter Levine's splendid biography of Spalding is its focus on the many moments of innovation that "A. G." orchestrated in all three components of the
baseball product. If historians are to uncover the development of the sport industry as a special, perhaps unique, system and structure, it will be necessary
to outline the key moments of innovation and the key innovators in any given

segment or activity. And doubtless these will diverge from commonplace notions about "great moments" or "great heroes" in sport.

While innovation may be a useful starting place, there are other activities often associated with entrepreneurs—risk-taking and profit-seeking. After all, most innovative projects involve risk and financing, and risk-takers usually expect some utility or profit if the project is successful. Who have been the risk-takers and financiers of the sport industry?

In his new book, Richard Mandell claims that one foundation for the rise of American sport was "the country's banking system," which he says "was flexibly capable of supplying venture capital."[20] Unfortunately, Mandell does not support this assertion, and it is extremely doubtful that banks were assuming the risks for ventures as tenuous as nineteenth-century sports. Nonetheless, Mandell does prompt a useful question: When did banks begin to accept some risk in financing sport organizations, wherein they recognized as collateral an organization's franchise values or expected profits and not simply its tangible assets? This would mark a significant moment of legitimacy for individual firms, for networks of firms, and for the industry as a whole.

Although historians have not examined bank financing, they have uncovered the early investors and risk-takers for many sports and recreations. Basically they may be sorted into three groups: private sponsors, commercial promoters, and the state. Of the three, it appears that private sponsors played the crucial role early in the history of most sports. This term denotes individuals or groups primarily and initially interested in pursuing games as pure fun or as services unrelated to gate receipts. White-collar and elite groups come quickly to mind: Knickerbocker ball-players, Harvard footballers, New York Athletic Club leaders, members of the Country Club. As baseball historians demonstrate, however, petit bourgeois, working-class, and ethnic groups were also early sponsors of sport.[21]

While private sponsors soon recognized the financial benefits of gate receipts and concessions, and thus often contributed to the "commercialization" of sports, they must be distinguished from commercial promoters as long as their central concerns lay in areas other than profits. For the commercial promoter, on the other hand, sport (in any of its commodity forms) has principally been a means to personal or corporate profit. As one might expect, the distinction between private sponsor and commercial promoter has often been hazy. The motivations of magnates like Henry V. Lucas of St. Louis, Deacon White of Edmonton, or the young Art Rooney, Sr.—owners of sports operations that were marginally (if at all) profitable—surely included civic duty, egotism, and a love of sport as well as a concern for some profit. Other historical figures however, are more clearly painted as commercial promoters: John I. Rogers of the Phillies, who swindled his fellow owners out of gate receipts; Cadwallader Colden, who first tried in 1829 to run the Union Course and horse racing on the basis of gate receipts: or Horace Bigelow, who transformed Lake Quinsigamond into a showcase of salable sports and recreation.[22]

The third major investor in sport development has been the state in its many forms of legislative bodies, appointed commissions, and regulatory agencies. Beginning with its mid-nineteenth-century investments in public parks and, later, playgrounds, the state slowly grew (often through public education) to control stadiums, arenas, vast equipment inventories, leagues of teams, and playing and eligibility rules. At its heart, the state's interest in sport has always been its contribution to social order. As recent works on public recreation suggest, however, although state-controlled sport and recreation have probably served the interests of dominant social groups, it is by no means clear that this occurred to the exclusion of the interests of subordinate groups. Workers and ethnic communities found the play areas to be a fertile ground for contention over the control of leisure, if not of work.[23]

Several questions arise about the relationship of special investor and interest groups to the developing sport product. To begin, have private sponsors, commercial promoters, or the state imposed their own particular *stamp* on game forms, services, or goods under their control? What happens to football, for example, when commercial promoters borrow its form from private and state sponsors (colleges and schools) in order to establish their own venture (ultimately, the NFL)? Are there major alterations in the game form, in associated services, or in goods? Are the tendencies similar in other sports? How have investor groups opposed or accommodated each other's interests? One intersection of interests in need of greater research is the expansion of sports facilities in the first half of the twentieth century. Here was a fertile ground for tradeoffs between private or commercial sponsors and the state. Here began the precedents that make public subsidy of private gain a contemporary expectation.[24]

Besides the interaction between investor groups, what about the social composition *within* them? Has this changed over time, with corresponding effects on sport? Ted Vincent has raised this important issue in his provocative (if lamentably unfootnoted) book *Mudville's Revenge*. According to Vincent, the early years of professional baseball and basketball were a "democratic and pluralistic era . . . in which a grocer or saloon keeper had as much chance as a millionaire of producing an event that grabbed headlines in the national sporting magazines."[25] Without providing closely detailed evidence, Vincent suggests that the earliest owners of professional teams tended to be petit bourgeois—liquor dealers, pawnbrokers, attorneys, and the like—who had much closer, organic ties with their communities of fans and players. This group was gradually squeezed out by the higher capital requirements of larger, more permanent facilities, by players' demands for higher salaries, and by the design of rivals. Similarly, Steven Riess has shown that by the early 1900s big-league baseball was controlled by "new men of affluence," the owners of traction companies, large breweries, and construction firms. Lyle Hallowell maintains that a similar process occurred in ice hockey, particularly after 1912, when the advent of artificial ice rinks brought both higher capital requirements and higher potential profits to those wishing to try the big-league game. Petit bourgeois would be hereafter relegated to investing in the minor leagues.[26]

Did social and economic backgrounds affect the work "styles" of entrepreneurs and investors? Were "new men of affluence" apt to be more conservative or innovative with the sport product? More exploitive with labor? Clearly, more detailed prosopography is needed across sports, but it appears that the greatest innovations (for better or worse) came from the petit bourgeois. This certainly occurred in track and field, if one can believe the account of James Brendan Connolly, America's first Olympic gold medalist. In 1910, Connolly wrote an exposé called "The Capitalization of Amateur Athletics" in which he accused the AAU—purportedly the guardian of amateurism—of leading the wave of commercialization that threatened pure sport. Connolly traced the problem to the material interests of the printers, jewelers, and politicians who ran various regional and local branches of the AAU. Ultimately, Connolly claimed, all of them were beholden to Albert Spalding and his employee, James Sullivan, who doubled as the president of the AAU.[27]

Connolly's article challenges a commonplace notion about the control of track and field by elite gentlemen. But it reinforces the idea that any one entrepreneur, investor, or group could not hope to achieve unopposed mastery of any part of the sport industry. "Interlopers," to use the language of baseball, regularly have sought their own share of the market through some innovative combination in game form, service, or good. Their challenges were often the seeds of change.

Organizational Change: Shaping Firms for Expanding Markets

Innovative entrepreneurs have developed salable sport products through countless disputes, decisions, and deals. At the same time, however, they have nurtured extended networks of organizations that produce and distribute these products. Unfortunately, historians have not yet begun to investigate systematically the types of organizations that germinated from the seeds of entrepreneurial decisions. This must be remedied, since organizations are often more enduring than the individuals who create them. Indeed they are the skeletons of the industry (although sometimes only in fossil form). As such, they provide an obvious framework for analysis.

Alfred Chandler and others have demonstrated that organizational forms and structures in any industry are influenced by the nature of the product, the nature of the market, and what Chandler aptly calls the "visible hand" of strategy.[28] If any sport is, in fact, a tripartite product composed of a game form, associated services, and associated goods, one may begin by examining the different types of organizations operating in the three product segments.

Although there is considerable overlap between the organizations producing and controlling game forms and services, there are also important historical distinctions that await clarification. Thus, while both game forms and services tend now to be controlled by regional or national regulatory agencies (e.g., NCAA, NAIA, NFSHSA, NFL), this has not always been true. As noted earlier, Walter Camp's Rules Committee was concerned with the game form. Its successor, the NCAA, is concerned with both game forms and services. The growth patterns of other regulatory agencies demand scrutiny. Has expansion typically been local to regional to national? Has control extended in a regular fashion from game rules into services and ultimately into goods? Promising research already exists in these areas, but it has not been synthesized.[29]

One thing, however, is historically certain. In team sports, the production of the consumable game form or service has always been tied to a local firm, which is tied in turn to a basically local market. Sport, as we know it, exists as a "joint inverted product"—a single product (the game and its associated services) that is the result of interaction between two separate firms (each team). This fact alone distinguishes football, hockey, baseball, and the like from other commodities. Even more distinctive are the firms producing the game. They have remained essentially local firms, even as their once strictly local markets have sometimes extended to regional or national dimensions. Teams like the Dallas Cowboys and the Pittsburgh Steelers, which compete to create the most commercialized and modernized games, have persisted as what Alfred Chandler calls "traditional" firms—consisting usually as a single unit or single office, with a single owner or small group of owners, with a single product line, in a single geographic area. One can't stress locality enough, despite the wider distribution of broadcasts and novelties.[30]

For historians interested in examining the production of sport, a central question now emerges. Is it natural or inevitable that the game should have persisted as a by-product of competition between distinct, local, traditional firms? Was there no logical alternative? Of course there was, and it may be credited with spreading the popularity of virtually every modern sport. This was the barnstorming model, in which the competing teams were part of the same "firm" that viewed an entire region, nation, or, in Al Spalding's case, the world as its market. Most team sports have experienced barnstorming along these lines, yet this model of product ownership and distribution has never thrived or endured.[31]

But why not? Single or common ownership of multiple teams, even if they are anchored in different localities, makes greater economic sense than the wasteful competition between separate firms that has long dominated the team-sport industry. Surprisingly, however the great "concentration move-ment" that swept American industry in the late nineteenth century never se-riously threatened the structure of team sports. Sports magnates have suffered severe public scorn when they have been caught investing in more than one franchise in the same league. Andrew Freedman's ill-fated though eminently logical attempt to form a major-league baseball trust stands in virtual isola-tion. Albert Spalding led the fight against Freedman and he had the press and the public on his side. But neither the press nor the public cared much about the "Freedmanism" that Spalding pursued in sporting goods. Why all the con-cern about a *team's* autonomy?[32]

While only detailed historical analysis across sports can answer this ques-tion, it is likely that the persistence of the traditional firm in team sports is the result of historical conditioning over centuries. As entrepreneurs developed rounders, stoolball, and baseball, or soccer, rugby, and American football, they extended the logic of team competition so that these games became "repre-sentational" as well as "recreational." That is to say, the actual competitors not only enjoyed a form of recreation, but they often bore the burden of repre-senting the interests of a larger group of patrons and general followers. Now, this is not simply a nineteenth-century phenomenon. Descriptions of folk football in fourteenth-century Britain or *calcio* in sixteenth-century Italy reveal the deep roots of representational sports. The frequent manipulation of mod-ern games by urban or other community boosters in the last century has been a matter of degree, not revelation.[33]

Indeed, it appears that the very structure of modern team sports is in im-portant ways "premodern," imbued with a communal or community logic that has supported the persistence of the traditional firm. Even at the most commercialized levels, where homegrown talent is a rarity, there is a sense of suspicion about the absentee owner, but little concern about players hired from the outside. The whole firm, not just the collection of players, has become the representative of community interests. It *must* remain separate and distinct from its competitors or it can no longer be truly representative. Therefore, although it might have been eminently logical for ownership of multiple teams to have concentrated into the hands of a few, the longer history of sport itself included a premodern sense of community that sometimes rebuffed the modern logic of capitalism.[34]

Rather than a consolidation of firms, there developed *networks* of separate, traditional firms attempting to create, control, and apportion networks of local markets. This evolution has occurred at all levels of game forms and services, from the pee-wee to the professional. It has occurred both vertically within a single sport (Pop Warner Football, the NFL) and horizontally across sports (the NCAA, NFSHSA).

At least three areas merit attention as historians examine the interaction of firms and the tensions between capital and community that lay therein. The first concerns the disputes over product and market control between firms and between networks of firms. As Guy Lewis and Ronald Smith have ably demonstrated, the 1905–6 football controversy was more than a general question of violence in the game form. It was also a question of who would control the game form: the entrenched eastern interests so well symbolized in Walter Camp, or the emerging Midwest. The well-documented battles between rival leagues in professional baseball, football, and basketball have similarly been part of long-lasting wars for market control.[35]

The results of these struggles present the second subject that merits attention. This consists of the stratification or layering of firms and markets. It appears that every sport has undergone a "shakeout" by which firms have been layered into sets or networks of relatively equal strength. As Edward Gross argues in his seminal paper on the subject, this process is a necessity if the weaker firms are to survive at all, because it allows the chance for victory that is so demanded in representational sport.[36]

But while the outcomes are manifest now—competitive divisions in school, college, and amateur sports; layers of minor leagues in professional sports—the decisions that drove these shakeouts largely lie hidden in the shrouds of history. To what extent has stratification been the result of the "invisible hand" of the market, by which entrepreneurs succumb to the odds of population density, per capita wealth, existing modes of transportation, alternative services, or entrenched tasks? To what extent has stratification been forced by the "visible hand" of power and manipulation? The quiet death of the Canton Bulldogs or the Syracuse Nationals reflects the former. The flashing birth of the National League in 1876 exemplifies the latter. Economists often compare sports leagues to cartels. This can be a useful model, but cartels are only one product of a larger process of stratification that will be fully understood only when historians examine it through the lens of local sources in a variety of locales: small towns, regional entrepots, dominant metropolises.[37]

At the same time, as the National League's endurance prompts, scholars may profit from a closer look at the third and related subject of stratification studies. This is the creation and growth of the central administrative offices that coordinate the activities of individual firms in a given network. As Robert Stern outlines in his brilliant studies of the NCAA, the history of such offices has often involved a quest for autonomy from the network of firms that gave them birth. Eugene Murdock's recent study of Ban Johnson provides an excellent glimpse of the central administrator thirsting, groping, and battling for control of the network. One of Johnson's important contributions was his strengthening of the central umpire's bureau, an important source of autonomy and a hallmark of administrative power. His ultimate pathetic demise reflects how fleeting network control can be. For every Judge Landis there are ten Happy Chandlers.[38]

Despite their apparent weaknesses, the central offices of the myriad leagues, conferences, and associations dotting the historical landscape of sports have helped to bring order to the marketplace. Without stable systems of competition, sports firms generally die a-borning, a baseball's graveyard amply demonstrates. The structure of firms producing game forms and services is largely composed of complex molecules—benzene rings of compatible atoms. Free-floating atoms like the Harlem Globetrotters are exceptions that prove the rule.

Sporting goods present something different. Rather than networks of traditional, local firms, one finds instead the rapid emergence of what Chandler calls the "modern" firm: multiunit, multifunction, multiproduct, multimarket. Whereas thousands of tiny organizations compete to produce and distribute game forms and services, a relative handful of firms supply the material components of that competition. While individual communities feel a special, sometimes-passionate attachment to their local team, there is no such sentiment for the sporting-goods manufacturer or dealer. Why has this occurred and with what consequences for the integrated sport product?[39]

To date, few historians have considered the sporting-goods industry in any depth or breadth. A quick glimpse at the sources, however, suggests that production and distribution were traditional and slow until after the Civil War. Athletes and sportsmen often fashioned their own utensils or balls. Some equipment—largely for hunting and fishing—was imported or manufactured by specialized firms. More frequently, however, one probably found production in the hands of local artisans in metal, leather, or woodworking, who crafted sporting goods as a sidelight. Indeed, one current product leader, Hillerich and Bradsby Co. of "Louisville Slugger" fame, began this way. J. Frederich Hillerich started his woodturning business in 1859, making bedposts and handrails as well as some tenpins and bowling balls. Only his son Bud's affection for baseball got the firm slowly involved in the turning of bats, and even then (1880) the elder Hillerich resisted such frivolity because he saw better profits in the current market for butter-churn booms![40]

While larger-scale manufacture of baseball goods appears to have risen in the late 1860s, football remained at a primitive stage. As one annalist tells us, the first Yale-Princeton game (1873) "was delayed an hour and a half because of the failure to obtain a ball. Another delay occurred during the game when the precious ball burst and had to be repaired."[41] These conditions would change rapidly, however, as entrepreneurs saw the potential for profits in supplying and fueling the demand for sports. The surge of participation in the next decade was the result of as much as the cause of concentrated ownership in sporting-goods production and distribution.

Peter Levine's recent biography of Albert Spalding provides important information on this process, as Spalding's firm represents a classic example of expansion and integration. Spalding opened his first store in Chicago in 1876. By 1899 his empire had extended worldwide, his company had integrated both backward into manufacturing and horizontally into marketing and retail. Along the way he had gobbled up numerous competitors. He had 3,500 employees toiling in five large manufacturing plants around the country, each with product specialties: bicycles and steel products in Massachusetts, boats and canoes in upstate New York, uniforms in New York City and Chicago, bats and wooden materials in Chicago, balls and leather goods in Philadelphia. At the other end, he had dispensed with jobbers and begun selling directly to retailers under what his brother called the "Spalding one-price policy." The 20,000 accounts now dealing with Spalding could not cut Spalding prices or they would risk losing their supply of these popular goods. The empire was fully integrated, from Michigan lumber mills to retail outlets. It paralleled the developments in other industries.[42]

While Spalding's was perhaps the dominant company, buying out Reach, Wright & Ditson, and others, it was not a monopolist. Competitors developed by a similar process of horizontal and vertical integration. The Rawlings Brothers began a retail store in St. Louis in 1888, acting as "exclusive agent" for distribution of Reach products in the South and West. Even before reorganizing in 1898, Rawlings moved into manufacturing. On the other hand, P. Goldsmith and Sons started in the Cincinnati area in 1875, making toys and baseball goods. Steady expansion in manufacturing, marketing, and acquisitions created the firm now known as MacGregor. Wilson began its operation turning out goods from a little red schoolhouse in Chicago. These were capable competitors for Spalding in the team-sports field, but rivals were even stronger for the bicycle market of the 1890s. Here Spalding was an also-ran to the giant Pope and Western manufacturing works.[43]

Much more research is needed before we can safely say that the production and distribution of sporting goods was oligopolistic. Intense competition by newcomers eroded Pope's bicycle profits in the later 1890s. The combination of severe price cutting and high capital costs was ruinous: the attempt at a trust failed. Developments in team sports are even less clear. Nevertheless, it appears that considerable concentration of control occurred there in the five decades after the Civil War. (This of course has continued so that several sporting-goods giants are now owned by even larger conglomerates.)

The effects were enormous. Manufacturers, retailers, and the networks between them formed the vast material foundation for the rise of sport. By 1899, the Reach plant in Philadelphia produced an estimated 18,000 baseballs a day. Machines cut and shaped twenty brands of balls for handstitching, including a "Deadball," a "Bounding Ball," and "Out of Sight Ball," a "King of the Field Ball," and a "Cock of the Walk Ball." Similar scales of manufacturing existed for other sports products. As the British magazine *Field* explained in 1904, American golf clubs began to dominate the British market, probably because of "the painstaking care with which the American balances, finishes, and constructs the club according to a standardized average pattern in lie, weight, and form." Standardization and mass production were important aspects of the growing industry, but so was marketing. Companies didn't simply meet demand, as Betts has maintained, they created demand.[44]

As Albert Pope wrote in 1895, bicycle manufacturers knew "at the outset" that they must "educate the people to the advantage of this invigorating sport, and with this end in view, the best literature that was to be had on the subject was gratuitously distributed." Bicycle advertising included colorful posters and witty copy distributed through dozens of general and trade magazines. Albert Spalding went a step further, with the creation of the American Sports Publishing Company, through which he published and distributed guidebooks on dozens of sports. These guides included not only the rules of the leading governing bodies but also important statistics on the participation and records of individuals and teams around the country. Throughout, Spalding's editors sprinkled reminders that Spalding products were the "official" products of the sport in question. When one remembers that by 1899 Spalding claimed to have 20,000 retail accounts, it is clear how significant this distribution system was for the total sport product. Basketball historian Albert Applin is doubtless correct in crediting Spalding's marketing arrangement for much of the dramatic spread of basketball in the 1890s.[45]

If the sporting-goods industry influenced participation rates, it is equally probable that their innovations in equipment influenced styles of play and, hence, the rules themselves. In 1902, Rawlings ran advertisements for their new line of football equipment designed by their product genius William P. Whitley. Aptly named, "Whitley's Football Armor" included an "armor" jacket "reinforced with cane ribs which, when struck, equally distributes the force of the blow, thus preventing injury to the player." But as with the boxing glove, protective equipment might equally result in more brutal play. This seems to have occurred in football. Lyle Hallowell has made a similar suggestion about hockey, for which protective equipment was developed in the early 1900s, the same period as the slashing, hard-checking "Ottawa" style of play. The precise relationships between sporting goods, playing styles, and playing rules await detailed research, but it is clear that playing styles and rules don't always determine the goods. The sporting-goods industry, especially the manufacturers, has had greater capital investments and greater stakes involved than most franchises. The manufacturers have seldom been passive observers.[46]

Conclusion: The Sport Industry and Its Impact

I have covered a fair amount of ground in this essay, all in order to offer a framework for research into the development of sport as an industry. Whether the sport is football, hockey, golf, or boxing, my framework focuses on the decisions of entrepreneurs who developed organizations to produce and distribute three-part commodities.

If I have argued for the need to reconstruct sport industry through the perspective of entrepreneurs—or from the "inside out." This is not to say that these men or women have ever enjoyed autonomy from the forces and issues in the environments that swirl around them. As one historian of entrepreneurs has argued, even the most powerful magnates like Rockefeller and Carnegie "made history only within those external constraints they could not change." Given these constraints, however, entrepreneurs have achieved much. I conclude with some questions and propositions about their achievements in sport.[47]

To begin, there appears to be a process of structural development—for products and organizations—that is unique to sport and that may be common to all sports. Loy, Ingham, and Gruneau have all offered important theoretical suggestions about the transformation of *a* set of rules to *the* set of rules. Gruneau has recently extended his model (based on Canadian history) to include stages of bourgeois, corporate, and state control. Guttmann, Ingham, and Adelman had earlier offered notable insights into the organizational differences between premodern or folk sports and their modern, rationalized counterparts.[48]

But while these authors capture much of the larger framework of development, there is need for much closer morphology. For instance, have all sports developed initially under the aegis of private sponsors—often the players themselves—who have been concerned chiefly with noncommercial utilities? Has each sport experienced a transition in which players have lost control of both the process and the product of their labor? Has this transition come before, after, or simultaneous to the moment of commercialization?[49] Has every sport had a "shakeout" and subsequent stratification of firms and markets into sets of similar power and capacity? Have these sets regrouped into even more compatible networks of markets, and have they then fashioned central offices to regulate their activities?

It appears that similar life cycles have prevailed. Since these life cycles have been staggered, however, historians may have to rethink their periodizing of the "rise of sport." For instance, professional baseball had assumed much of its modern structure by 1903, at the very time when football, hockey, and basketball were still very much at a primitive stage of development. And despite the presence of the baseball model, the other sports spent decades working through or replicating similar struggles in the marketplace. At what stage, then, is it appropriate to call any of these sports "modern," to use Adelman's term?[50]

Even as one recognizes the distinct chronologies that have accompanied the life cycles of sports networks, one must also recognize a more pervasive process at work: the concentration of control over the product itself. Thus, although the marketplace has remained formally free (anyone can invent a game), the nature of the product (particularly game forms and goods) has since the early 1900s been determined by a narrow range of firms. A handful of rules committees controls the game forms played by most people; a few manufacturers supply the goods at all levels; a limited number of professional groups establish guidelines on coaching, training, playing, and management techniques. As Raymond Williams describes this phenomenon of product convergence, "The general effect is of a relatively formed market, within which the buyer's choice—the original rationale of the market—has been displaced to operate, in majority, within an already selected range."[51]

Ultimately, then, one must ask to what extent the rise of an integrated industry of sport, encompassing both production and distribution, has limited our choices of consumption, both in terms of the range of sports we play and in terms of the way we play that limited range. Has the rise of sport as a commodity meant the strangulation of sport as play? Have the fleeting or enduring "alternatives"—sandlot activities, governance by women, the Labor Sports Union—had any impact on this process?[52]

All of these questions merit further attention from historians. For some time we have recognized the outlines of modern sport and we have learned much about its social and cultural significance. But we still need more detailed research in many areas, including rules formation, the life cycles of teams and leagues, and the introduction of new goods and services. Many of these topics may be profitably explored by concentrating on the activities of entrepreneurs and, following Neil Harris's advice, reconstructing their alternatives and the choices they made.

Notes

1. Nancy Struna, "In Glorious Disarray: The Literature of American Sport History," *Research Quarterly* 56 (1985), 151–60; Karen J. Winkler, "A Lot More Than Trading Baseball Cards: Sport History Gains a New Respectability," *Chronicle of Higher Education,* June 5, 1985, 5, 9. For an opposite view—that serious analysis obfuscates the essence of sport—see Michael Hirschorn, "Eggheads Strike Out: Why Intellectuals Miss Baseball's Pitch," *New Republic,* September 9, 1985, 8–10.

2. The social history perspective is evident in the best surveys and in literature reviews. See Benjamin Rader, *American Sports: From the Age of Folk Games to the Age of Spectators* (Englewood Cliffs, N.J., 1983), v; John Lucas and Ronald Smith, *Saga of American Sport* (Philadelphia, 1978), vi; Donald Mrozek, *Sport and American Mentality, 1880–1910* (Knoxville, 1983), xvi; Melvin Adelman, "Academicians and American Athletics: A Decade of Progress," *Journal of Sport History* 10 (spring 1983), 80–106; Stephen Hardy, "The City and the Rise of American Sport, 1820–1920," *Exercise and Sport Sciences Review* 9 (1981), 183–219. For an earlier treatment of this issue, see Jack Berryman, "Sport History as Social History?" *Quest* 20 (June 1973), 65–73.

3. My orientation in this essay has been especially influenced by several readings of Raymond Williams, *The Sociology of Culture* (New York, 1982); Thomas Cochran, *Business in American Life: A History* (New York, 1972); Louis Galambos, "The Emerging Organizational Synthesis in Modern American History," *Business History Review* 44 (autumn 1970); idem, "Technology, Political Economy, and

Professionalization: Central Themes of the Organizational Synthesis," ibid. 57 (winter 1983), 471–93; Melvin Adelman, *A Sporting Time: New York City and the Rise of Modern Athletics, 1820–70* (Urbana, Ill., 1986).

4. Neil Harris, "Cultural Institutions and American Modernization," *Journal of Library History* 16 (winter 1981), 38–39. For a similar argument, see David C. Hammack, "Problems in the Historical Study of Power in the Cities and Towns of the United States," *American Historical Review* 83 (1978), 323–49.

5. Jules Tygiel, *Baseball's Great Experiment: Jackie Robinson and His Legacy* (New York, 1983). For comprehensive views on management and sport management see Peter Drucker, *Management: Tasks, Responsibilities, Practices* (New York, 1974), and Guy Lewis and Herb Appenzeller, eds., *Successful Sport Management* (Charlottesville, Va., 1985).

6. Economic analysis includes Roger Noll, ed., *Government and the Sports Business* (Washington, D.C., 1974); idem, "Major League Sports," in *The Structure of American Industry,* 6th ed., ed. Walter Adams (New York, 1982); Ralph Adreano, *No Joy in Mudville: The Dilemma of Major League Baseball* (Cambridge, Mass., 1965); Jesse Markham and Paul Teplitz, *Baseball, Economics, and Public Policy* (Lexington, Mass., 1981); Henry Demmert, *The Economics of Professional League Sports* (Lexington, Mass., 1971). Studies from sport management include Guy Lewis, "The Sports Enterprise," *Arena Newsletter* 4 (October 1980), 1–11; idem, "Characteristics of Sport Marketing," in Lewis and Appenzeller, *Successful Sport Management,* 101–24.

7. Drucker, *Management,* 61–65, 77–78; Arthur Thompson and A. J. Strickland, *Strategy Formulation and Implementation* (Plano, Texas, 1983), 16.

8. Karl Marx, *Capital,* vol. 1, ed. Friedrich Engels (1887; reprint, Moscow, 1954), 43, 48; "Commodity," *Dictionary of Marxist Thought,* ed. Tom Bottomore et al. (Cambridge, Mass., 1983), 86.

9. I am indebted to the pioneering effort of Richard Butsch, "The Commodification of Leisure: The Case of the Model Airplane Hobby and Industry," *Qualitative Sociology* 7 (1984), 217–35. See also Chris Rojek, *Capitalism and Leisure Theory* (London, 1985), ch. 5, which summarizes earlier work by the Frankfurt School on this question, and Robert Goldman, "We Make Weekends: Leisure and the Commodity Form," *Social Text* 8 (1984), 84–103.

10. John Loy, "The Nature of Sport: A Definitional Effort," *Quest* 10 (May 1968), 1–15; see also Allen Guttmann's chapter on definitions in *From Ritual to Record: The Nature of Modern Sports* (New York, 1978), 1–14.

11. On the Beadle book see Harold Seymour, *Baseball: The Early Years* (New York, 1960), 44. On Spalding see Peter Levine, *A. G. Spalding and the Rise of Baseball* (New York, 1985).

12. See Richard Gruneau's comments on the social construction of rule-making in *Class, Sports and Social Development* (Amherst, Mass., 1983), 19–52. For two interpretations of one rule change—baseball's "fly rule"—see Adelman, *A Sport-*

ing Time, 129–31, and Warren Jay Goldstein, "Playing for Keeps: A History of American Baseball, 1857–1876" (Ph.D. dissertation, Yale University, 1983), 80ff.

13. On utilities and services see Max Weber, *Economy and Society,* ed. Guenther Roth and Claus Wittich (Berkeley, 1978), 68. On recreation and sport as a service see Louis Mariciani, "A New Era in Recreation Marketing," *Athletic Business* 9 (October 1985), 31.

14. Fine studies of sport services include J. A. Mangan, *Athleticism in the Victorian and Edwardian Public School: The Emergence and Consolidation of an Educational Ideology* (Cambridge, Mass., 1981); Greg Lee Carter, "Baseball in St. Louis, 1867–1875: An Historical Case Study in Civic Pride," *Missouri Historical Society Bulletin* 34 (July 1975), 253–63; Richard Mandell, *The Nazi Olympics* (New York, 1971).

15. See Guy M. Lewis, "Theodore Roosevelt's Role in the 1905 Football Controversy," *Research Quarterly* 40 (1969), 717–24. Ronald Smith has corrected Lewis on several points in "Harvard and Columbia and a Reconsideration of the 1905–6 Football Crisis," *Journal of Sport History* 8 (winter 1981), 5–19.

16. John Rickard Betts gave scattered attention to sporting goods in *America's Sporting Heritage* (Reading, Mass., 1974), and Peter Levine has excellent material on Spalding in *Spalding,* but in general this subject has been neglected.

17. See Arthur Cole, "Perspectives on Leisure-Time Business," *Explorations in Entrepreneurial History,* 2nd ser. 1 (summer 1964), 6; Fritz Redlich, "Leisure-Time Activities: A Historical, Sociological, and Economic Analysis," ibid. 3 (1965), 3–24; reprinted in idem, *Steeped in Two Cultures* (New York, 1971), 299. See also Sebastian DeGrazia, *Of Time, Work, and Leisure* (Garden City, N.Y., 1964), 189–211.

18. Robert H. Wiebe, *The Search for Order, 1877–1930* (New York, 1967), 18. Indeed, the centrality of the profit motive has been questioned in Carl Betke, "Sports Promotion in the Western Canadian City: The Example of Edmonton," *Urban History Review* 12 (October 1983), 47–56, and Wray Vamplew, "The Economics of a Sport Industry: Scottish Gate-Money Football, 1890–1914," *Economic History Review* 35 (1982), 549–67. American magnates may have been more profit-oriented, but their activities demand closer scrutiny.

19. Joseph A. Schumpeter, *The Theory of Economic Development* (1934; reprint, Cambridge, Mass., 1961), 66. For discussion of Schumpeter and other theorists, see Jonathan Hughes, "Entrepreneurship," in *Encyclopedia of American Economic History,* ed. Glenn Porter (New York, 1980), 214–28; Joseph C. Pusateri, *A History of American Business* (Arlington Heights, Ill., 1984), 182.

20. Richard Mandell, *Sport: A Cultural History* (New York, 1984), 182.

21. See Adelman, *A Sporting Time,* chs. 6, 7; Stephen Freedman, "The Baseball Fad in Chicago, 1865–1870; An Exploration of the Role of Sport in the Nineteenth-Century City," *Journal of Sport History* 5 (summer 1978), 42–64.

22. On Rodgers, see Seymour, *Baseball* 293. On Colden, see Adelman, *A Sporting Time,* 51, 53. On Bigelow, see Roy Rosenzweig, *Eight Hours for What We Will: Workers and Leisure in an Industrial City, 1870–1920* (New York, 1983), 172–83.

23. The best introduction to questions on sport and the state is Hart Cantelon and Richard Gruneau, eds., *Sport, Culture, and the Modern State* (Toronto, 1982).

24. For an excellent investigation into the question of state-supported facilities, see Alan Metcalfe, "Urban Response to Demand for Sporting Facilities: A Study of Ten Ontario Towns/Cities, 1919–1939," *Urban History Review* 12 (October 1983), 31–45. See also Judith Davidson, "The Federal Government and the Democratization of Public Recreational Sport: New York City, 1933–1945" (Ph.D. dissertation, University of Massachusetts, 1983); Steven A. Riess, "Power Without Authority: Los Angeles Elites and the Construction of the Coliseum," *Journal of Sport History* 8 (spring 1981), 50–65.

25. Ted Vincent, *Mudville's Revenge: The Rise and Fall of American Sport* (New York, 1981), 13.

26. Riess, *Touching Base: Professional Baseball and American Culture in the Progressive Era* (Westport, Conn., 1980), 76; Lyle Hallowell, "The Political Economy of Violence and Control: A Sociological History of Professional Ice Hockey" (Ph.D. dissertation, University of Minnesota, 1981), 106–10.

27. James B. Connolly, "The Capitalization of Amateur Athletics," *Metropolitan Magazine*, July 1910, 443–54, cited in Levine, *Spalding*, 172. For a model useful to sport historians, see Lary May's analysis of early movie moguls in *Screening Out the Past: The Birth of Mass Culture and the Motion Picture Industry* (Chicago, 1983), 167–99. DeGrazia, *On Work, Time, and Leisure*, 148, suggests that the leisure industry had special appeal to immigrants.

28. Alfred D. Chandler, Jr., *The Visible Hand: The Managerial Revolution in American Business* (Cambridge, Mass, 1977); Glenn Porter and Harold Livesay, *Merchants and Manufacturers: Studies in the Changing Structure of Nineteenth-Century Marketing* (Baltimore, 1971).

29. See, for instance, Robert N. Stern, "The Development of an Interorganizational Control Network: The Case of Intercollegiate Athletics," *Administrative Science Quarterly* 24 (June 1979), 242–65; idem, "Competitive Influences on the Interorganizational Regulation of College Athletics," ibid. 26 (March 1981), 15–31; Alan Metcalfe, "Sport and Athletics: A Case Study of Lacrosse in Canada, 1840–1889," *Journal of Sport History* 3 (spring 1976), 1–19; Richard Gruneau, "Elites, Class, and Corporate Power in Canadian Sport: Some Preliminary Findings," in *Sociology of Sport*, ed. F. Landry and W. Orban (Miami, 1978), 201–42; Don Morrow, "The Little Men of Iron: The 1902 Montreal Hockey Club," *Canadian Journal of History of Sport* 12 (May 1981), 51–65.

30. Chandler, *Visible Hand*, 3. On the nature of the market, see Philip Kotler, *Marketing Management*, 5th ed. (Englewood Cliffs, N.J., 1984). For a useful introduction to mainstream economic theory of sports see Noll, "Major League Sports," 348–87.

31. Besides the standard histories of baseball, see Donn Rogosin, *Invisible Men: Life in Baseball's Negro Leagues* (New York, 1983), which outlines the continued im-

portance of barnstorming to black players. Ronald Ladwig, "A History of Public Entertainments in Ada, Ohio, 1850–1920" (Ph.D. dissertation, Bowling Green State University, 1978), shows the importance of barnstorming from the viewpoint of the small town.

32. On the concentration movement see Naomi R. Lamoreaux, *The Great Merger Movement in American Business, 1895–1904* (Cambridge, Mass., 1985), which contains an excellent bibliography. On the baseball "trust" and on the duplicity of magnates like Spalding, see Seymour, *Baseball*, 317–22, and Levine, *Spalding*, 66–69.

33. A valuable and well-written introduction to early representational sports is William J. Baker, *Sports in the Western World* (Totowa, N.J., 1982), 43–98; see also his excellent bibliographic essay.

34. On the importance of long-term structures, see Fernand Braudel, *On History*, trans. Sara Matthews (Chicago, 1980). Alan Ingham and I have argued for the centrality of a tension between capital and community in the history of modern sport. See our "Sport: Structuration, Subjugation and Hegemony," *Theory, Culture, and Society* 2 (1984), 85–103.

35. On football, see Lewis, "Theodore Roosevelt's Role," 717–24; Smith, "Harvard and Columbia," 5–19; Lucas and Smith, *Saga*, 229–49. Sources for the baseball wars are Seymour, *Baseball*, 135–61, 221–62, 307–24; David Q. Voigt, *American Baseball: From Gentlemen's Sport to the Commissioner System* (Norman, Okla., 1966), 121–69. On basketball, see Albert Applin, "From Muscular Christianity to the Marketplace: The History of Men's and Boy's Basketball in the United States, 1891–1957" (Ph.D. dissertation, University of Massachusetts, 1982).

36. Edward Gross, "Sports Leagues: A Model for a Theory of Organizational Stratification," *International Review of Sport Sociology* 14 (1979), 103–12.

37. An excellent study of the need for networking is Morris Mott, "The first Pro Sports League on the Prairies: The Manitoba Baseball League of 1886," *Canadian Journal of History of Sport* 15 (December 1984), 62–69. See also Harold Evans, "Baseball in Kansas, 1867–1940," *Kansas Historical Quarterly* 9 (May 1940), 175–92. Myron Cope has material on the NFL's shakeout in *The Game That Was* (New York, 1974).

38. Stern, "The Development of a Control Network"; idem, "Competitive Influences"; Eugene Murdock, *Ban Johnson: Czar of Baseball* (Westport, Conn., 1982). *The Sporting News* had regular stories on the umpiring problem; the paper also editorialized at times on important administrative skills. See *The Sporting News*, June 25, 1887, on qualities needed for the presidency of the association.

39. On the nature of the "modern firm," see Chandler, *Visible Hand*, 3, 347, 373–74.

40. "Hillerich & Bradsby Co. Incorporated" (unpublished, undated release from H & B, in author's possession). For comments on the early days of home and artisan crafting, see John Krider, *Krider's Sporting Anecdotes* (1853; reprint, New

York, 1966), foreword, 70 ff; Seymour, *Baseball,* 7–8, 18; William Clarke, *Boy's Own Book* (New York, 1864), 17, 264; Patricia Click, "Leisure in the Upper South in the Nineteenth Century: A Study of Trends in Baltimore, Norfolk, and Richmond" (Ph.D. dissertation, University of Virginia, 1980), 187. One exception to this ante-bellum situation was the billiard industry, dominated by Michael Phelan; see Adelman, *A Sporting Time,* 220–29.

41. Alexander Weyand, *American Football* (New York, 1926), 4.

42. See Levine, *Spalding,* 71–96. Levine found articles of use to me in *The Sporting News:* March 30, 1895; March 31, 1896; July 1, 1899.

43. *The Sporting Goods Dealer,* a trade journal, had histories in the following issues: July 1948 (Rawlings), September 1946 (Wilson), February 1951 (Spalding). On the bicycle industry see David Hounshell, *From the American System to Mass Production, 1800–1932: The Development of Manufacturing Technology in the United States* (Baltimore, 1984), 189–216. The Brunswick Company has recently published a history: Rick Kogan, *Brunswick: The Story of an American Company from 1845 to 1985* (Skokie, Ill., 1985). I would like to thank Mr. Grant Burden and Miss Alice Flint for help in gathering material on the sporting-goods industry.

44. Betts, *America's Sporting Heritage,* 76; Reach plant statistics in *Sporting Goods Dealer,* October 1899, 4–5; 1904 *Field* article reprinted in special 75th anniversary issue of ibid., October 1974, 110. On the technical meaning of mass production, see Hounshell, *American System.*

45. Applin, "From Muscular Christianity to the Marketplace," 55; Levine, *Spalding,* 75–78; Albert A. Pope, "The Bicycle Industry," in *One Hundred Years of American Commerce,* ed. Chauncey M. DePew (New York, 1895), 551. On the relationship between manufacturers, advertising, and American culture, see Daniel Boorstin, *The Americans: The Democratic Experience* (New York, 1973), 89–164, 307–448, 525–56; Stuart Ewen, *Captains of Consciousness: Advertising and the Roots of American Consumer Culture* (New York, 1976); Richard Wightman Fox and T. J. Jackson Lears, eds., *The Culture of Consumption: Critical Essays in American History, 1880–1980* (New York, 1983).

46. *The Sporting News,* September 22, 1902; Hollowell, "Political Economy of Violence and Control," 131. On the brutalizing aspects of boxing gloves, see Elliott Gorn, "The Manly Art: Bare-Knuckle Prize Fighting and the Rise of American Sports" (Ph.D. dissertation, Yale University, 1983), 480–81. For comments on exercise equipment and physical culture, see Mrozek, *Sport and American Mentality,* 84–88.

47. Hughes, "Entrepreneurship," 214. For an excellent look at how the political environment could constrain as well as enable cagey promoters, see Riess, "In the Ring and Out: Professional Boxing in New York, 1896–1920," in *Sport in America,* ed. Donald Spivey (Westport, Conn., 1985), 95–120.

48. Guttmann, *From Ritual to Record;* Alan Ingham and John Loy, "The Social System of Sport: A Humanistic Perspective," *Quest* 19 (1973), 3–23; Gruneau, *Class,*

Sports and Social Development; Alan Ingham, "Methodology in the Sociology of Sport: From Symptoms of Malaise to Weber for a Cure," *Quest* 3 (1979), 187–215; Rob Beamish, "Sport and the Logic of Capitalism," in Cantelon and Gruneau, *Sport, Culture and the Modern State,* 141–98; Adelman, *A Sporting Time,* 3–10.

49. The links between commercialization and the erosion of player control are quite complex. Beamish and Hallowell provide suggestions about hockey, while Adelman and Goldstein consider baseball.

50. Adelman, *A Sporting Time,* 115. On the notion of life cycles, see John Kimberly and Robert Miles, *The Organizational Life-Cycle* (San Francisco, 1980); Henry Mintzberg, "Power and Organization LIfe Cycles," *Academy of Management Review* 9 (1984), 207–24.

51. Williams, *Sociology of Culture,* 105. Limited space prevented me from exploring here the emergence of professional organizations. Their role in the industry has been significant in the twentieth century, since professional organizations have had much to say about playing styles, rules, and equipment. For useful works on professions see Burton Bledstein, *The Culture of Professionalism* (New York, 1976); Thomas Haskell, ed., *The Authority of Experts* (Bloomington, Ind., 1984). For interpretations of the sport professions see Mrozek, *Sport and American Mentality,* 67–102; Hal Lawson, "Problem Setting for Physical Education and Sport," *Quest* 36 (1984), 48–60.

52. The question of freedom versus constraint in sport has been ably outlined in the dialogue between Richard Gruneau and Allen Guttmann in the *Journal of Sport History* 7 (winter 1980), 68–86, and ibid. 11 (spring 1984), 97–99. Works dealing with alternatives include Rob Ruck, "Sandlot Seasons: Sport in Black Pittsburgh" (Ph.D. dissertation, University of Pittsburgh, 1983); Joan Hult, "The Governance of Athletics for Girls and Women: Leadership by Women Physical Educators," *Research Quarterly* 56 (centennial issue, 1985), 64–77; Mark Naison, "Righties & Lefties: The Communist Party and Sports During the Great Depression," *Radical America* 13 (July–August 1979), 47–59.

15

Mediated Spectatorship

ALLEN GUTTMANN

Shifting Methodological Gears

The sports spectators of the 1930s took the streetcar or the subway to the stadium, bought a ticket at the kiosk, and made their way through the turnstile. Fifty years later, the spectators either have a season ticket or, in the case of one-time events, dial Ticketron (or its equivalents) for a computer-assisted reservation. If assured of a place to park, they are more likely to drive than to take public transportation. Where spectators once came dressed in straw hats or derbies, or in white dresses and feathered hats, their grandsons and daughters are likely to show up in blue jeans and leather jackets or in shorts and T-shirts. Baseball fans are liable nowadays to loll bare-chested in the sun and even Wimbledon crowds are liable to cause grim lips among the straitlaced.

Spectators of the 1930s knew that each sport had its season. Today's fans can look forward to, or dread, the day when soccer, football, baseball, basketball, hockey, golf, and tennis compete simultaneously for their attention. Although the phenomenon has not yet afflicted Europe, American spectators experience anew the kind of organizational instability that marked the first decades of modern sports: "gypsy" franchises that move suddenly from one city to another, entire leagues that appear, announce their challenge to the established circuits, and collapse. Wholly new sports, like hang gliding, float into place along with modern versions of the martial arts, like judo and karate. Pseudosports like Roller Derby have suddenly attracted immense numbers of lower-class female fans and have just as suddenly disappeared, leaving behind banked tracks and a film with Raquel Welch.[1]

Among the established sports, there are constant shifts in relative popularity. Professional football, American style, became far more popular in the postwar period than it had been. In the same years, basketball arenas began to dot the European landscape and American blacks suddenly found themselves household names in cities like Milano and Napoli. Tickets to women's gymnastics became intensely sought-after Olympic prizes and club fights now attract crowds so small that some have begun to fear (and others hope) that pugilism might die a natural death.

How can any scholar, immersed in modernity's plethora of data and buffeted by a welter of contradictory trends, tendencies, and fads, sensibly discuss anything as complex as sports spectatorship in the latter half of the twentieth century? How can one avoid both the Scylla of triviality (the economics of the concessions booth) and the Charybdis of otiosity (a sport-by-sport and country-by-country analysis of the demographic composition of the contemporary sports crowd)? The dilemma is familiar. Equally familiar is the response. We seek the field of investigation that seems important to us, devote years to our research, and hope that others will agree that the game was worth the candle.

Since most of the basic patterns of spectatorship were established by the end of the 1930s, some fundamental questions may be asked about contemporary sports spectators. One in particular seems to justify sustained consideration: What have been the consequences of modern communications, especially television?

Modern Sports Journalism

Now that an entire generation has grown up assuming that life without television is an impossibility, it may be useful to remind ourselves that sportscasting began with radio, not with TV, and that sports journalism in print is older still. A few comments on sports magazines and on the golden age of radio sports are in order.

Beyond the obvious fact that the audience for the earliest printed reports had to be literate (or to rely on someone able to read aloud), we know next to nothing about those who read early periodicals like *The Sporting Magazine* and *The Spirit of the Times*. Internal evidence, always circumstantial, suggests a fairly affluent and educated audience able to understand literary references and Latin tags but also cognizant of the Fancy's fancy slang. Presumably, the purchaser of such a journal was not destitute, but even this is a presumption; twentieth-century fans have been known to deprive themselves of "necessities" in order to buy tickets to a game. Since the tastes and preferences of the readers inevitably exert strong pressure on the editors, one can assume that early-nineteenth-century British and American readers were especially enthusiastic about horse races, field sports, and pugilism. By the middle of the century, popular journals in the United States featured stories about baseball, while their British and German counterparts opted for soccer and French periodicals began to follow *le vélocipède* on its merry career. By the end of the century, there was an audience for magazines like *Outing*, which reported on regattas and Derby Day, on bicycle tours of the Far East, and on hunting expeditions in the Wild West.

Since different sports appeal to different social strata, the spectrum of specialized magazines corresponds to the class structure of modern society, but it should be emphasized that the readers of sports magazines are, in general, likely to be better off economically than the average person. While 9 percent of upper-class Germans read the distinguished intellectual weekly *Die Zeit*, 7 percent of them also read Germany's most popular sports magazine, *Der Kicker*.[2] Statistics on the readership of *L'Equipe* also indicate an appeal to the advantaged members of French society.[3] *Runner's World* reports periodically on the advanced education and affluence of its readers.[4] It is no surprise when *Boating* boasts that 73 percent of its subscribers are college-educated, but *Bowling*, struggling to convince advertisers that its subscribers are not all waitresses and housewives, claims 55.6 percent of them are college-educated, which suggests that American bowlers are better educated than golfers (*Golf Digest*'s subscribers are a mere 52 percent college-educated).[5]

No periodical that pretends to cover sports in general has ever devoted as much attention to female as to male athletes. Popular journals appealing to the lower classes, like *The Police Gazette*, were to be found not on the library tables of elegant homes but rather in bars, barber shops, and fire stations. Their readership was predominantly male (and their interest in women's sports tended to be confined to voyeuristic accounts of "lady" wrestlers). General sports magazines appealing to the better educated and more affluent devote more space to women's sports. From the 1880s to the 1920s, *Outing* published numerous essays reporting on and strongly advocating women's participation in sports; from 1954 to the present, *Sports Illustrated* has gradually increased its coverage of, and its covers featuring, women's sports. It seems reasonable to assume that significant numbers of middle-class and upper-class women once perused Outing and now read Sports Illustrated. In fact, women now account for approximately 13 percent of *Sports Illustrated's* readership. The similarity of European to American patterns of readership is striking. In 1962, 18 percent of the readers of *L'Equipe* were women.[6] A decade later, a German scholar of the sporting press reported identical results: 18 percent of the German readers were women.[7] The readership of Rio de Janeiro's

Jornal dos Sports is 19 percent female, which seems remarkable in a society even more patriarchal than those of Europe and North America.[8]

Inevitably, journals specializing in male-dominated sports like soccer have mostly male readers. *Fussballwoche* has eleven male readers for every female.[9] This seems appropriate for a game played mostly by males, but other statistics require interpretation. Although *Boating* reports that 97.7 percent of its subscribers are male, one cannot conclude that only a handful of women actually read the magazine; one must assume that many women who love to sail are content to have their male relatives do the actual subscribing. One's suspicions about a mismatch between reported data and the real world increases when *Bowling* maintains that only 17.6 percent of *its* readers are women.

If we look not at the gender of the subscribers but at the reading habits of the public at large, we have a somewhat different picture. Scientific survey data indicate that 43 percent of all German men but only 14 percent of the women read about sports (which corresponds to the fact that 39 percent of the men and only 11 percent of the women actually attend sporting events on a regular basis).[10] These credible data imply that one-third of the readers of German sports magazines must be women.

Adolescents are the age group most likely to participate in sports and they are certainly readers of sports magazines, but they are less likely than their more financially secure elders to be subscribers. The median ages for subscribers are: *Boating* 46 years, *Golf Digest* 39.8 years, *Bowling* 26.1 years. Since *Bowling* also asserts that there are as many five-to-eleven-year-old bowlers as there are those over fifty years of age, one must distrust either one's impressions or the stereotype-shattering statistics.

Although we have some data on the social class, gender, and age of sports-magazine readers, we skate toward thin ice when we speculate about their racial identity. The evidence is almost entirely inferential. Since the racial minorities of Europe and the United States are less likely, for economic as well as cultural reasons, to participate in sports, it is probable that they are also underrepresented as readers. Then, too, racial minorities are in general less literate than the white majority. On the other hand, the salience of sports heroes for disadvantaged groups is a reason for general magazines, like *Ebony,* to pay what may seem disproportionate attention to athletic achievement.

On the whole, scholars (as opposed to advertisers) know little about the readership of sports magazines. This should not surprise literary historians because it is a truism among them that there is almost no empirical evidence pertinent to the readers of fiction about whom scholars have been making confident statements for approximately 200 years. What we do know about sports-magazine readers tends to come from internal evidence (the literary scholar's favorite source) or from self-interested surveys conducted with an eye on advertisers. The internal evidence may or may not tell us something about the readers: Do teenagers focus on stories about teenagers? Are essays about women's sports read only by women? The survey data, which many editors are reluctant to release, are a help, but skepticism is called for.[11] An editor must be superhumanly honest to report to potential advertisers that his readers are young, poorly educated, and unemployed. It is best to admit that our picture is a blurred one.

Radio Sports

Some of the same methodological problems appear when we look at radio. The medium was most deeply involved in sportscasting in the 1930s and 1940s, after which time it more or less abandoned the national market to television, while still playing an important role in broadcasting games of local franchises. Since statistically sophisticated audience surveys were practically unknown in radio's heyday, and we seldom have a record now of what was actually said then, we know even less about the radio fan than about the newspaper and magazine reader. The A. C. Nielsen Company has made a science of finding out exactly who is tuned in to what television program, but one can only conjecture about the radio audience of the twenties, thirties, and forties.

On July 2, 1921, the era of network sports broadcasting was inaugurated when RCA's WJZ broadcast the Dempsey-Carpentier fight from Boyle's Thirty Acres in Jersey City. A month later, on August 5, KDKA Pittsburgh did a play-by-play of the Pirates versus the Phillies at Forbes Field.[12] There must have been some initial skepticism about the receptivity of the audience. Listening to a game of baseball or soccer is obviously a mild form of sensual deprivation. Skepticism proved unfounded. Millions of people tuned in to hear the crack of unseen bats and to hear about the hooks, jabs, and uppercuts of invisible boxers. Two years after Dempsey battled Carpentier, an estimated 2 million people heard the Firpo-Willard fight. By 1927, 50 million listened to Graham McNamee's blow-by-blow account of the second Dempsey-Tunney bout.[13] German fans had to wait until 1925 for "live" broadcasts; in July of that year Sender Muenster reported on a crew contest and then, in November, a soccer match between Arminia Bielefeld and Muenster Preussen.[14] Because the BBC had signed restrictive contracts with the news agencies, British listeners had to wait until 1927 for the first running commentaries on sports.[15]

Some hallowed British institutions, like the Henley Regatta, resisted the temptation even then and opted for exclusivity. The National Olympic Committee of the Netherlands refused to allow broadcasts from the Games held at Amsterdam in 1928, and financial problems hindered broadcasts of the Games from Los Angeles in 1932, but the Berlin Olympics of 1936 provided the basis for a "monumental radio show."[16]

Inevitably, at least in the United States and other countries choosing privately owned rather than state-run broadcasting, corporate sponsors moved in to exploit the commercial possibilities of an eager audience. By 1934, Henry Ford paid $100,000 for the rights to baseball's World Series. By 1945, all the clubs had overcome their initial reluctance to "give away" their product. By that time, sportscasters like Mel Allen (the New York Yankees) and Red Barber (the Brooklyn Dodgers) had become local heroes whose voices were instantly recognized by millions of people.

Assuming correctly that the sports audience was predominantly male, the Gillette Safety Razor Company played a major role in sports-related radio advertising. Brewers were quick to follow.[17]

The impressionistic evidence from Europe indicates the same demographic pattern as in the United States. Radio audiences were disproportionately male. Unless this audience was a sociological anomaly within the structure of organized sports, the audiences contained disproportionately few older people, poor people, and members of racial or ethnic minorities.

Radio differs from the print media in many ways. One important difference is its immediacy. Most newspapers are read within the space of a few hours, but it is impossible to imagine that millions of readers have ever read their papers at *exactly* the same moment. With radio, however, we can be sure of simultaneity: apart from the possibilities of taped replay, everyone listens at the same time. This may seem like an obvious and trivial point to make, but it is a point that helps to explain regional and national outbursts of sports-related violence. Radio made it possible for millions of people simultaneously to experience the thrill of a game. Radio made it possible for *all* black Americans to exult while Joe Louis pounded his white opponents. Small wonder that celebrations broke out across the length and breadth of the land. Small wonder that some of them turned violent. Had radio rather than the telegraph flashed the news of Jack Johnson's victory over Jim Jeffries in 1910, the appalling toll of killed and injured would probably have been even higher than it was.

On a smaller scale, radio made possible the kind of instant citywide celebration of victory by the local college team or professional franchise. In a model study, a pair of political scientists have shown how the broadcast of an away-game triumph set the stage for a celebration, how the radio announcement of the team's arrival time enabled thousands of physically distant people to converge upon the airport, and how radio in a certain sense caused the violence that ensued when the celebration became too boisterous.[18] Each season now brings repetitions of the pattern.

The Wide World of Television Sports

Television represents—at least at present—the ultimate stage of mediated experience (and the last word in audience monitoring).[19] Indeed, the illusion of immediacy is so powerful that today's journalists can plausibly tell us that we are really *there*. Whether one agrees or disagrees with Marshall McLuhan's notorious theories about "hot" (radio) and "cool" (television) media, one fact is indisputable: the new electronic medium displaced the radio in the lives of sports fans.[20] In the 1930s radio was an essential part of almost everyone's daily life; by the end of the 1940s, the average American listened to the radio for only twenty-four minutes a day.[21]

Although the French began to experiment in 1935 with a transmitter placed upon the Eiffel Tower, the first regular telecasts began in Berlin on January 15, 1936.[22] The Olympic Games, held in Berlin that summer, became the world's first major television event, in which 150,000 people were able to watch the flickering picture transmitted to 27 *Fernsehstuben* ("TV locales") scattered through the city.[23] The BBC began to experiment with television in late 1936 and covered the Oxford-Cambridge boat race of 1937.[24] The United States entered the era of sports television on May 17, 1939, when NBC affiliate W2XBS New York sent Bill Stern to telecast a baseball encounter between Columbia and Princeton on the former's field.[25] An estimated 200 sets were already in place in the New York area.[26] The poor quality of the picture disguised the potential of the medium, but NBC was pleased enough with the outcome of the experiment to offer the viewers a boxing match, two weeks later, in which Lou Nova defeated Max Baer and thus won the dubious privilege of facing Joe Louis. Further telecasts followed in 1940, but the immense popularity of televised sports came after the war, when larger screens, improved pictures, closeups, slow motion, color, instant replays, and split screens provided an experience rivaling and in some ways surpassing that to be had in the stadium.

In the earlier years of televised sports, however, technical limitations strongly influenced the networks' selection of events to be offered to the public. The large size of the baseball field and the smallness of the ball and the swiftness of its motion, plus the fact that the ball is likely to go in one direction while the runner goes in another, make the game relatively unsuited for television. Boxing, on the other hand, seemed ideal for the TV camera, which could be trained on two men in a small space. The result was a glut of matches, which reduced the live audience at Madison Square Garden by as much as 80 percent and eventually provided the television viewers with more fisticuffs than they wanted. (In 1952, boxing was able to attract 31 percent of the prime-time audience; by 1959, the share had sunk to 10.6 percent and the networks began to bail out.)[27]

Initially, no one seemed to realize what the new medium was destined to do to sports as an institution. The Fédération Internationale de Football Association, which sponsors the quadrennial World Cup soccer championship, gave away the rights to its 1954 spectacle in Bern, Switzerland, and considered itself lucky to get the publicity.[28] Forty-five stations in eight European countries allowed most of the continent to watch the German team carry off the trophy. In 1982, FIFA received over 100 million German marks for radio and TV rights.[29] Avery Brundage, president of the International Olympic Committee from 1952 to 1972, doubted that the networks would be willing to pay for the rights to the Games. (When he discovered that the contrary was true, he was farsighted enough to worry about the impending transformation of "amateur" sports by the influx of huge sums of media money.)[30]

Brundage was unquestionably wrong about the reluctance of the networks to pay. After experiments with the Winter Games in Cortina d'Ampezzo in 1956 proved the feasibility of Olympic television, the National Olympic Committee of Italy sold the rights to the 1960 Games, which were held in Rome. NBC agreed in 1961 to pay $600,000 for the rights to the 1964 games in Tokyo. Although European networks, including those of the Soviet bloc, have paid millions of dollars for television rights, the commercially operated American networks are the major source of this particular variety of Olympic gold. For the Olympic spectacles of 1984, Eurovision managed to come up with less than $20 million, while ABC paid $92 million for the Winter Games in Sarajevo and $225 million for rights to the Summer Games in Los Angeles. ABC spent an additional $100 million to produce its coverage. The huge investment was economically sound. The network found sponsors who were ready to pay as much as $520,000 a minute for the right to interrupt the athletic action with their advertisements. While the runners, swimmers, and gymnasts reaped their golden, silver, and bronze harvest, ABC gleaned an estimated $650 million. (Olympians like Carl Lewis, Edwin Moses, Mary Decker, and Joan Benoit have also earned hundreds of thousands of dollars as a result of their vividly televised performances in Los Angeles.) Supported by the sale of TV rights,

Table 15-1. Attendance at British Soccer Matches

Season	Attendance
1948–1949	41,250,000
1960–1961	28,500,000
1982–1983	18,750,000

direct contributions from some of the nation's largest corporations, and an army of volunteer workers, the financially astute organizers of the Los Angeles Games closed out their affairs with a net profit of approximately $250 million, the first surplus since the last time the Olympics had been staged in Los Angeles in 1932. Whether or not ABC will recoup the $309 million it has offered for the Winter Games in Calgary in 1988 remains to be seen (as is the case with NBC's similar offer for the 1988 Summer Games in South Korea), but the offer itself is evidence that the most experienced of Olympic televisers have faith that the bubble is not going to burst—at least not yet.[31]

At the dawn of the Age of Television, the owners of American sports franchises were not more prescient than Brundage was. Their initial reaction was to protect their "gate" from the threat of "free" entertainment at home. They sought, at a very minimum, to prevent the transmission of home games. There seemed to be good reason for apprehension. Minor-league baseball attendance declined from a peak of 42 million in 1949 to a scant 10 million twenty years later, at which time fifty-one leagues had shrunk to twenty. In England, the introduction of the new medium seemed to threaten the end of professional soccer as a spectator sport. The attendance figures in table 15-1 tell the story.[32] There was no guarantee that TV would not have a similar effect on American football attendance. When the Los Angeles Rams of the National Football League allowed their games to be televised in 1950, their attendance plummeted from 205,109 the previous year to 110,162. When home games were blacked out in 1951, attendance figures bounced back.[33] It was not until the arrival of Alvin "Pete" Rozelle as NFL commissioner in 1960 that suspicions were overcome and the league became firmly committed to television.[34]

For their part, the networks were also surprisingly slow to consummate the marriage that has transformed the world's spectator sports. In retrospect, the hesitation of the networks seems almost comical. DuMont, which was then a serious rival to the major networks, televised five NFL games in 1951 and twelve (plus the championship) in 1954, for a mere $95,000! Only two years later, CBS paid over a million dollars for the season. By the 1980s, the NFL's annual Super Bowl was attracting over 130 million viewers, more than half of the entire population of the United States. Commercials cost $800,000 a minute and "cabinet members, corporate executives, and celebrities of all sorts vied for the tickets." In 1982, the NFL played hard to get and was cajoled with the promise of $2 billion over five years, a sum so enormous that the three major networks agreed to share the rights (and the costs). Under this contract, each team was guaranteed $15 million a year before the first ticket was sold. In 1983, baseball, despite its unsuitability for the screen and its alleged demise as the "national game," was still attractive enough for the networks to pool their resources and sign a four-year contract for $1 billion.[35] In comparison, the sum of 38 million marks paid by the German TV networks for rights to the 1974 World Cup, which was hosted by the Deutscher Fussball Verband, seems like a real bargain (but one must remember that the publicly owned German networks had to carry their advertisements indirectly, by training the camera on advertisements displayed in the stadia).[36]

For the owners of American sports franchises, infusions of television money make a life-or-death difference. Challenging the established NFL, the American Football League was on the brink of bankruptcy in 1964 when television came galloping to the rescue. The situation was a rather dramatic one. On January 24, 1964, CBS unexpectedly outbid NBC and won the rights to do the NFL games. Two hours later, NBC offered the AFL $42 million for a five-year contract. With this bankroll, the league was able to offer Joe Namath, the first of its superstars, $420,000 over three years, the first of the extravagant salaries.[37] The AFL lived to merge with the NFL in 1966 (thanks also to a generous antitrust exemption granted by the sports-obsessed United States Congress). Last-minute rescues make good TV shows, but bad business. Before it played a single game of its first season, the United States Football League had already arranged to sell TV rights to ABC for $9 million and to cable TV's Entertainment and Sports Network (ESPN) for $11 million.[38]

Televised sports can also make, and perhaps break, a network. In 1959, NBC decided to discontinue prizefights, which had lost most of their TV popularity, but which the Gillette Company wished to continue to sponsor. Louis Maxon, whose advertising agency handled the Gillette account, called ABC's Thomas Moore and offered him Gillette's entire TV advertising budget of $8 million. With the windfall, ABC was able to acquire the rights to intercollegiate football from the National Collegiate Athletic Association (NCAA). Under the direction of Roone Arledge, ABC's sports division went on to purchase the rights to professional golf and a variety of amateur sports then controlled by the Amateur Athletic Union (AAU). These rights enabled the network in 1961 to inaugurate the technically innovative and spectacularly successful series "Wide World of Sports," which entranced its 25 million viewers with slow motion, zoom lenses, stop action, hand-held and underwater cameras, mug shots, and split screen, with track meets, cliff divers, and the stunts of R. C. "Evel" Knievel. The next step in ABC's drive to TV sports hegemony came when the network bought the rights to the 1968 Olympics for $7 million. (The Games, held in Mexico City, were the first covered by means of satellite transmission.) A year later, ABC launched the prodigiously successful series "Monday Night Football." It was Arledge who introduced "honey shots" of attractive female spectators and who established Howard Cosell as "the man you love to hate," the volubly opinionated sports commentator simultaneously most liked and disliked by TV fans. It was also Arledge who defied the International Olympic Committee in 1968 and sent Cosell to interview Tommie Smith after his clenched-fist black-power demonstration, and it was Arledge who decided at Munich in 1972 that ponytailed Olga Korbut was the gymnast most likely to attract American viewers to what was, until then, an almost-unknown spectator sport. (When Korbut slipped, fell, and wept, Arledge ordered a close-up and sent "a shudder of empathy through America.")[39] In 1976, shortly after the Montreal Olympics, ABC topped CBS for its share of the TV audience *for all shows*.[40]

The popularity of televised sports has also had an enormous influence, mostly nefarious, upon intercollegiate athletics. Although complaints about the commercialization of campus sports are a century old, television has drastically upped the ante. More than school pride is at skate when TV appearances can bring a school as much as a million dollars (and make its athletic recruitment infinitely easier). In 1983, NBC paid $7 million for a single event—the Rose Bowl. In 1984, the NCAA, which oversees and vainly attempts to control collegiate sports, was busy distributing some $60 million a year to its members when the University of Georgia and the University of Oklahoma, unhappy about their share of the money, sued successfully to break up the NCAA's monopoly.[41]

As the universities' sports programs become increasingly dependent upon TV revenue, paid directly or distributed through athletic conferences and the NCAA, coaches come under increased pressure to put together bowl-bound telegenic teams. When success can bring adulation and a quarter-million-dollar-a-year contract while failure brings contempt, contumely, and dismissal, the temptation to win at any price is hard to resist. Coaches demand more and more of "student-athletes" who are recruited with less and less regard for the NCAA's mostly unenforced rules. The athletes are well aware that many coaches and alumni have broken the rules in order to recruit them and keep them in school. (Cash delivered in a shoebox and a grade of "A" for a course not taken do stimulate awareness.) The "student-athletes" cannot be severely blamed if they decide that they are badly rewarded for their athletic efforts. They become prime targets for gamblers who prefer fixed games to the charms of Lady Luck. Since most of the abuses from which we presently suffer date from the 1890s, it is obvious that television has not created them, but television, and the spectators who turn their sets on every autumnal Saturday, have made the disease incurable.[42]

If tens of millions of ordinary Americans were not as sports-obsessed as their political representatives in Washington, manufacturers of automobiles, beer, and computers would not purchase halftime spots at $15,000 a second. Quite plainly, however, major corporations—the only ones that can afford largess on this gargantuan scale—are persuaded that these millions of dollars are well spent, and the A. C. Nielsen Company assures them that they are correct. In the 1970s, 31 percent of the nation's viewers watched ABC's "Monday Night Football," listened to the histrionics of Howard Cosell, and—presumably—rushed out the next day to purchase whatever products appeared between the plays. That the viewers did *not* rush to work the next day can be seen in the fact that Tuesday supplanted Monday as the peak of absenteeism in Detroit's automobile factories.[43]

Since most Europeans watch state-run rather than commercial television networks, the economics of sports and the mass media are less clear than in the United States. What *is* clear is that sports are as attractive to European as to American viewers. In fact, some data indicate that German television offers its viewers as much sport as do the American networks—i.e., about 10 percent of the total program content—while the figures for French and British television have soared as high as 15 percent (RDF) and 25 percent (BBC).[44] In Germany, soccer matches can draw upwards of 80 percent of the audience, and track-and-field meets, a rarity on American television, can attract as many as 36 percent of the viewers.[45] The Olympic Games are even more popular than in the United States, which means that Eurovision (the organization formed by the Western European networks) is ready to pay sizable amounts of the taxpayers' money for the right to offer the quadrennial spectacle to the French, the Germans, the Italians, et cetera.

Now that most American sports leagues (including the major collegiate sports conferences) have become dependent upon television money, subtle and not-so-subtle changes have occurred. When the networks commit themselves to handing over billions of dollars, there is an explicit or implicit expectation that he who pays the piper will at least be allowed to request the tune. Examples of influence are many. Athletes have accepted the fact that they must shoot their baskets or trade their punches at times suitable for East Coast viewers. The Ali-Foreman fight took place at 2:00 A.M., the Ali-Bugner fight at 6:00 A.M. Baseball players shiver their way through the World Series because the networks want them to play during prime time—i.e., evenings. Popular golfers tee off in prime time while the unknowns drive and putt through morning mists and evening shadows. Soccer matches are sprinkled with penalties and "injuries" so that the advertisements can be inserted. Boxers toy with their opponents for round after round for the same reason. There were "adjustments" in the daily schedule of events in Seoul in 1988—to provide the American viewers with prime-time coverage of their favorite sports.

Just as significant is the change in the economic status of the players. While the great athletes of the past often received princely salaries, such as Babe Ruth's $80,000 a year in the midst of the Great Depression, the stream of network gold that has poured into the hands of contemporary owners has aroused passionate demands that at least some of the flow be diverted into the pockets of those who put their bodies on the line (and on the screen). It is inconceivable that basketball players performing in arenas holding 15,000 spectators could earn $500,000 a year if their owners did not have lucrative television contracts. On March 4, 1985, the cover of *Sports Illustrated* listed the names of thirty-six baseball players earning over a million dollars a year. No matter how many fans thronged to see the Phillies, no matter how many hot dogs they consumed, they alone were too few to pay Mike Schmidt's $2,130,000. At best, ballpark spectators have become the equivalent of studio guests; at worst, they are background, mere television props.

Does any of this bother the television viewer? Ironically, three quarters of the fans questioned in a 1983 poll complained about the high salaries that their addiction has made possible.[46] When athletes go on strike, no matter what the cause, in Europe as in the United States, the fans almost invariably side with the owners. Disgruntled, they gripe loudly about high salaries and greed, yet they have only themselves to blame. If Marvin Hagler earns $7 million a year as the best middleweight in the business, it is because the American people have made their values known—whether they realize the fact or not. If Americans supported opera as they support spectator sports, tenors and mezzo-sopranos would have incomes comparable to those of boxers and basketball players.

Although occasionally bothered by the modern players' business acumen, American spectators acquiesce supinely in the advertisers' interruptions of

the game. If sports spectacles are a species of drama, as numerous theorists
have proclaimed, they are unquestionably mutilated dramas whose mutila-
tion arouses little protest. Edwin Cady's comment is unusual: "The cameras
and directors fragment, skew, and impoverish the potential esthetic experience. . . . The television fan does not know the game; he has never seen it."[47]
Popular programs like ABC's "Wide World of Sports" or German television's
"Sport Aktuell" shift disruptively from sport to sport and oscillate between
gymnastics and a demolition derby. What does the popularity of such programs say about theories of "dramatic unity"? About the psychology of the
viewer? Have commercial radio and television "programmed" their American
audience to expect and enjoy experiences that a theatergoer would find absolutely intolerable? These are questions that have been scarcely raised, much
less answered.

It is somewhat easier to say that *some* sort of satiety or disillusion has begun to set in. During the 1984 football season, all three networks suffered a decline in the Nielsen ratings. CBS was down 16 percent while ABC and NBC
were down 6 percent and 4 percent. Over a five-year period, telecasts of the
NCAA basketball final, the Super Bowl, college bowl games, the Indianapolis
500, the Masters golf tournament, the Kentucky Derby, and Wimbledon all
attracted a diminishing number of viewers. Network executives like Arthur
Watson of NBC and journalists like William Taafe of *Sports Illustrated* attribute the dropoff to the glut of televised sports available to the beleaguered
(in several senses of the word) fan. In the ten years between 1973 and 1983,
CBS more than doubled the hours of sports it offered the public and the three
networks together boosted their sports telecasts by 63 percent. This suggests
saturation. On the other hand, the 1984 Super Bowl had the eleventh largest
audience in American history and the Los Angeles Olympics averaged 23.5
percent of the prime-time viewers. While there has certainly been a dip in the
curve, the graph of TV sports popularity does not yet prove that the public's
hunger has finally been sated.[48]

It is much easier to indicate who watches what. On the whole, American
viewers prefer sports to newscasts, documentaries, situation comedies, and
every other standard category except movies.[49] German viewers seem to rank
their preferences differently; 66 percent of them told pollsters they were very
interested in newscasts and only 44 percent admitted to a strong interest in
televised sports. (Since people tend to give socially acceptable answers to pollsters' questions, and Germans still tend to believe in high-mindedness, some
skepticism about German viewing habits is necessary.)[50]

Men watch more TV sports than women do. In the United States, 90 percent of the former and "only" 75 percent of the latter say they watch.[51] For

some sports, like football and basketball, the gender gap is very large, which is why one rarely sees a halftime ad for perfume. In 1963, when the A. C. Nielsen Company began to provide advertisers with precise and accurate data on the demographics of TV sports, the five most popular sports all showed a preponderance of male viewers even though women make up a slightly larger percent of the total U.S. population (see table 15-2). Twenty years later, in its survey of the 1983 season, A. C. Nielsen found a very similar pattern (table 15-3).[52]

There are, of course, some spectator sports that attract more women than men. Although track and field is not as popular in the United States as in Europe, women made up a larger share of its small 1969–1970 audience than men did. In 1980, women were more likely than men to have watched ABC do the Winter Olympics from Lake Placid, a very popular event that drew an average audience of 21.6 percent of all TV households (compared with 44.4 percent for the NFL Super Bowl and 32.8 percent for the World Series).[53] In 1983, more women than men watched CBS do the NCAA gymnastics championships.

One reason for the popularity of gymnastics among women is, of course, that the sport has almost as many female champions as male. (Men have more events.) In general, men are more likely to watch men perform while women are a more reliable audience for female athletes. There may, however, be some erosion of this gender-determined pattern as females are increasingly accepted as authentic athletes and not as "bimbos" or "cheesecake." Shortly before the Los Angeles Olympics of 1984, both men and women who were asked to name members of the American team were more likely to respond with "Mary Decker" than with any other name; both men and women indicated that they looked forward most intensely to the gymnastics contests.[54]

In regard to the gender of TV spectators, European data strongly confirm the American pattern. In Norway, 64 percent of the men and only 49 percent

Table 15-2. Percent of 1963 TV Audience

Sport	Adult Males	Adult Females	Teenagers	Children
Football	50	27	11	12
Boxing	46	37	7	10
Baseball	44	33	10	13
Bowling	44	37	8	11
Golf	38	29	11	22

Table 15-3. Average 1983 TV Audience as Percent of U.S. Population

Sport	Adult Males	Adult Females
NFL Football	16.3	7.4
USFL Football	6.1	2.6
NCAA Football	11.2	5.1
Baseball	9.0	5.2
NBA Basketball	6.3	2.6
NCAA Basketball	5.5	2.6
Golf	3.9	2.7
Tennis	2.1	1.9
Bowling	4.6	4.1
Auto Races	6.9	2.7
Horse Races	6.9	6.7
Boxing	4.9	2.2

of the women follow the country's most popular sports telecast. Norwegian women, however, are more likely than men to watch gymnastics and swimming.[55] In Germany, 75 percent of the men and 52 percent of the women are regular consumers of TV sports. Soccer is "seen gladly" by 86 percent of the men (and a surprising 52 percent of the women), while the proportions are reversed for the second most popular sport, figure skating (81 percent of the women, 58 percent of the men). Considering the American preference for team sports, one should note that the Germans polled indicated that skiing, gymnastics, and track and field were what they most wanted to see after their lust for soccer and figure skating was satisfied. Since German television is state-run and not dependent on commercial sponsorship, there is no guarantee that the spectators will actually see what they most want to see. In 1974, for instance, the two networks (ARD and ZDF) telecast forty-four soccer shows that captured an average of 36 percent of all sets and twenty-two tennis shows that occupied a miserable 4 percent of all sets. Women clamoring for figure skaters had to be content with ten shows.[56]

Television has had a mostly unnoticed effect on the age of the fans who actually go to the sports events. Photographs prove beyond question that pretelevision crowds for baseball, cricket, and soccer were composed mostly of adults. When, however, the television camera zeroes in on the spectators, one sees a much younger crowd. This perception is amply supported by an admirably detailed study of the soccer crowd in Cologne, West Germany, where 52.6 percent of those who show up in the stadium, fair weather or foul, are twenty-one or younger. (And 88.2 percent of them are male.) Clearly, the older fans of 1.FC Koeln have decided that it is easier to turn on the TV set than to battle the traffic on Aachenerstrasse or squeeze into the streetcar for Muengersdorf.[57]

It is no surprise that social class also makes a difference in the audience. Almost from its origins in the 1840s, baseball has attracted lower-class fans. In Europe, despite its derivation from games played at Oxford, Cambridge, and the elitist "public schools," soccer is identified as the "people's game." American football was once strongly associated with institutions of higher education, but the advent of television has unquestionably made a difference. Certainly, the stereotypical image of the football fan has changed: the college boy in raccoon coat and with a whisky flask in his pocket has been replaced by the truckdriver in his T-shirt and with a beer bottle in his hand. Conventional imagery set the collegian in the stadium, where he cheered drunkenly for his team, while the truckdriver was plopped down before the television screen, where he cheered drunkenly for his team.

The new stereotypes are exaggerations. The traditional associations bear up rather well. In fact, A. C. Nielsen Company's data reveal that televised baseball consistently attracts a disproportionate number of the poor and the elderly while football telecasts continue to appeal to younger and wealthier spectators. Precise survey data also confirm the conventional wisdom that says that bowling is for the workers. Economic relationships are neatly captured in the price tags; although the average audience for bowling is 42 percent of that for NFL football (6.6 percent versus 15.8 percent of all households in 1983), bowling's commercials cost less than one-sixth as much as football's.

The European situation is unambiguous. Cycling remains immensely popular, and lower-class French and Italian fans continue to be mad about the Tour de France and the Giro d'Italia. The television audience for tennis and golf is growing, but these sports are still perceived as expensive elitist pastimes of very little interest for ordinary men and women. Although numerous European intellectuals have fallen in love with soccer, as many once did with boxing, televised soccer continues to be "the people's game."

Notes

1. On the history and demographics of Roller Derby, see Frank Deford, *Five Strides on the Banked Track* (Boston: Little, Brown, 1971).

2. Siegfried Weischenberg, *Die Aussenseiter der Redaktion* (Bochum: N. Brockmeyer, 1976), 169.

3. Edouard Seidler, *Le sport et la presse* (Paris: Armand Colin, 1964), 239–43.

4. "Who Is the American Runner?" *Runner's World* (August 1984) 19 (8): 46–51, 156–68.

5. These and subsequent data are from subscriber surveys conducted in 1982 (*Boating*), 1983 (*Bowling*), and 1984 (*Golf Digest*).

6. Seidler, *Le sport et la presse,* 260.

7. Weischenberg, *Aussenseiter,* 169.

8. Janet Lever, *Soccer Madness* (Chicago: University of Chicago Press, 1983), 82.

9. Brigitte Hammer and Mechthild Kock, "Sportzeitschriften," *Sport und Massenmedien,* Josef Hackforth and Siegfried Weischenberg, eds. (Frankfurt: Limpert, 1978), 49.

10. Klaus Wehmeier, "Publikum," in Hackforth and Weischenberg, *Sport und Massenmedien,* 116.

11. Apropos of editorial reluctance, I must add that in no phase of my research did I receive less cooperation than in my request for data on magazine readership.

12. Erik Barnouw, *A Tower in Babel* (New York: Oxford University Press, 1966), 80; Ron Powers, *Supertube: The Rise of Television Sports* (New York: Coward-McCann, 1984), 37.

13. Benjamin G. Rader, *In Its Own Image: How Television Has Transformed Sports* (New York: Free Press, 1984), 25.

14. Weischenberg, *Aussenseiter,* 141–42; Peter Goedeke, "Sport und Hoerfunk," in Hackforth and Weischenberg, *Sport und Massenmedien,* 20–28.

15. John Ford, *This Sporting Land* (London: New English Library, 1977), 223.

16. Weischenberg, *Aussenseiter,* 143–44.

17. Rader, *In Its Own Image,* 25; Powers, *Supertube,* 23–30.

18. Clark McPhail and David Miller, "This Assembling Process," *American Sociological Review* (1973) 38: 721–35.

19. My statistics on the TV audience, unless otherwise documented, are taken from data generously supplied me by the A. C. Nielsen Company.

20. On McLuhan, see Susan Birrell and John Loy, "Media Sport: Hot and Cool," *International Journal of Sport Sociology* (1979) 14(1): 5–19.

21. Phil Patton, *Razzle-Dazzle* (Garden City, N.Y.: Dial, 1984), 28.

22. Raymond Marcillac and Christian Quidet, *Sport et Television* (Paris: Albin Michel, 1963), 150; Josef Hackworth, *Sport im Fernsehen* (Muenster: Verlag Regensberg, 1975), 14.

23. Weischenberg, *Aussenseiter,* 145.

24. Ibid.

25. Powers, *Supertube,* 33.

26. Patton, *Razzle-Dazzle,* 30.

27. Rader, *In Its Own Image,* 45.

28. Hackforth, *Sport im Fernsehen,* 295.

29. Weischenberg, *Aussenseiter,* 152; Knute Hickethier, "Klammergriffe," in Rolf Lindner, ed., *Der Satz "Der Ball Ist Rund" Hat Eine Gewisse Philosophische Tiefe* (Berlin: Transit, 1983), 68.

30. Allen Guttmann, *The Games Must Go On: Avery Brundage and the Olympic Movement* (New York: Columbia University Press, 1984), 218–19.

31. Josef Hackworth, "Fernsehen," in Hackforth and Weischenberg, eds., *Sport und Massenmedien*, 73–86; Powers, *Supertube*, 18–22, 204–20; Horst Seifart, "Sport and Economy: The Commercialization of Olympic Sport by the Media," *International Review of Sport Sociology* (1984) 19(1): 15.

32. Rader, *In Its Own Image*, 59; Charles Critcher, "Der Fussballfan," Wilhelm Hopf, ed., *Fussball* (Bensheim: Paedagogischer Extra Buchverlag, 1979), 150; Ian Taylor, "Professional Sport and Recession," *International Review of Sport Sociology* (1984) 19(1): 15.

33. Rader, *In Its Own Image*, 86; Patton, *Razzle-Dazzle*, 31.

34. Powers, *Supertube*, 173.

35. Rader, *In Its Own Image*, 99, 117–37; Powers, *Supertube*, 172–82.

36. Weischenberg, *Aussenseiter*, 177.

37. Powers, *Supertube*, 152–59; Patton, *Razzle-Dazzle*, 86–99; Rader, *In Its Own Image*, 91. That such salaries were economically rational, at least in the 1970s, is shown by Roger G. Noll, "Attendance and Price Setting," in Noll, ed., *Government and the Sports Business* (Washington: The Brookings Institute, 1974), 115–58.

38. Rader, *In Its Own Image*, 154.

39. Powers, *Supertube*, 107–71, 212; Patton, *Razzle-Dazzle*, 105–12; Don Kowett, "TV Sports," *TV Guide* (August 19, 1978), 2–8.

40. Rader, *In Its Own Image*, 110–113; Patton, *Razzle-Dazzle*, 60–61, 82; Powers, *Supertube*, 18–19, 209–12.

41. *New York Times,* June 28, 1984.

42. On some of the abuses of college sports, see Allen Guttmann, "The Tiger Devours the Literary Magazine, or, Intercollegiate Athletics in America," James H. Frey, ed., *The Governance of Intercollegiate Athletics* (West Point, N.C.: Leisure Press, 1982), 71–79.

43. Patton, *Razzle-Dazzle*, 111.

44. Marcillac and Quidet, *Sport et television*, 26; Weischenberg, *Aussenseiter,* 174; Hackforth, *Sport im Fernsehen*, 98; Hackforth, "Fernsehen," 80; Robert T. Bower, *Television and the Public* (New York: Holt, Rinehart and Winston, 1973), 131.

45. Hackforth, *Sport im Fernsehen*, 261.

46. Rader, *In Its Own Image*, 191; see also Randall Poe, "The Angry Fan," *Harper's* (November 1975) 151: 86–95.

47. Edwin H. Cady, *The Big Game* (Knoxville: University of Tennessee Press, 1978), 95.

48. William Taafe, "Perspective," *Sports Illustrated* (February 11, 1985) 62(6): 170–90; *New York Times,* October 15, 1984.

49. George Comstock et al., *Television and Human Behavior* (New York: Columbia University Press, 1978), 143. Similar results appear in Bower, *Television and the Public*, 131.

50. Wehmeier, "Publikum," 120–21.

51. Kowett, "TV Sports," 2–8.

52. These may seem like suspiciously low figures, but one must remember that they are averages. In the case of NFL football, there were ninety-four telecasts.

53. The Winter Olympics peaked on Saturdays with nearly 28 percent of the audience. It is likely that female spectators were most attracted by figure skating and skiing.

54. *New York Times,* June 6, 1984.

55. Kari Fasting and Jan Tangen, "Gender and Sport in Norwegian Mass Media," *International Review of Sport Sociology* (1983) 18(1): 66–67.

56. Wehmeier, "Publikum," 115–31.

57. Hans J. Stollenwerk, "Zur Sozialpsychologie des Fussballpublikums," Dirk Albrecht, ed., *Fussballsport* (Berlin: Bartels and Wernitz, 1979), 199.

16

The "Visible Hand" on the Footrace
Fred Lebow and the Marketing of the Marathon

PAMELA L. COOPER

During the decade of the 1970s, marathon participation increased dramatically. In 1969, there were fewer than forty marathons in the United States; by 1977, there were nearly 200. The Boston Marathon zoomed from 890 starters in 1968 to 4,391 in 1978. More significantly, the New York City Marathon increased from 126 starters in 1970 to 16,005 in 1980.[1] This was the result of innovations and changes in the New York City Marathon that served the purposes of managerial capitalism, the "visible hand," which, in this case, used capital and technology to meet a demand that was as much created by road-racing administrators and sponsors as determined by the market. The New York City Marathon became a business enterprise, which, as Alfred Chandler explains, "did not . . . replace the market as the primary force in generating goods and services," but did "take over from the market the coordination and integration of the flow of goods and services." In the early 1980s, the New York Road Runners Club was given not-for-profit corporation status, and the club's financial statements were registered with the New York State Department of State. These financial statements show "a hierarchy of salaried executives" and indicate the growth and presence of "distinct operating units," both characteristics of Chandler's modern business enterprise.[2]

The New York City Marathon led the way for a nationwide change, not only in number of participants, but also in restructuring the marathon to validate the presence of many runners of little athletic potential. Before the "marathon boom" of the 1970s, marathoners were competitors who hoped, if not to win, at least to place in the top ten or to compete for age-group awards. Marathon courses were often closed after four hours, and the times of late finishers went unrecorded.[3] However, in the 1981 New York City Marathon, about one-third of the field, over 4,000 people, finished after four hours. Race officials stayed to record their times, crowds remained to cheer them, and each finisher was awarded a marathon medal.

New marathon runners often perceived the event less as a competition than as a ritual whose subjective reward was spiritual achievement, "a special sensation that attunes them closer to the world yet also raises their consciousness and provides a sense of elation"; others ran for good health or to relieve tension.[4] For those less inner-directed, the New York City Marathon provided a festival atmosphere and symbols, such as finishers' medals and race T-shirts, which assured all who actually completed the course, no matter how slowly, that they were part of an elite group. The New York City Marathon found ways to accommodate and sanction a wide variety of reasons for entering a 26.2-mile footrace.

A single entrepreneur, Fred Lebow, seized control of the New York City Marathon in the mid-1970s,[5] and enhanced its potential to attract corporate funding by increasing the number of participants—regardless of their athletic ability. When marathon fields were small, they comprised serious runners who were generally blue-collar men; however, a study of the 1980 New York City Marathon field showed those runners to be mostly upper-status men and women.[6] The history of the New York City Marathon from 1970 to 1980 suggests that the marathon's directors consciously sought this comparatively affluent population for the purpose of attracting corporate sponsors. In creating new services and presenting the marathon to appeal to upper-status, recreational runners, Lebow changed the nature of the New York Road Runners Club, which administers the New York City Marathon, from a volunteer organization serving the athletic interests of its members to a business enterprise with a staff of salaried managers.[7]

The new upper-status runners were most concerned with personal well-being. Having time and money to expend on their health, they were likely to be informed on the matter. Their interest in marathon running was often ascribed to the marathon's alleged health-enhancing properties. "It does improve the efficiency of the heart," a 1977 *Fortune* magazine article reported on the running and marathoning interest among corporate officers. "Other executives and their wives claim even larger benefits: running has improved their sex lives, made them stop smoking, cured hangovers, jet lag, ulcers, constipation, alcoholism, depression, and insomnia, and prevented the common cold."[8]

The association of running with such values as health, fitness, and feminism made marathoning attractive to upper-status individuals. Sociologist James Curtis, of the University of Waterloo, Ontario, and William McTeer, of Wilfrid Laurier University's Health and Physical Education Department, use the positive correlation of health consciousness with social status to explain their findings of higher-status backgrounds among marathoners surveyed for a 1981 sociological study of the sport. Certainly New York Road Runners Club members were predominantly upper-middle class. A 1983 study of its 21,696 members revealed that almost 90 percent were college graduates, and that their average income was $40,000.[9]

The new women marathoners also contributed to the overall change in socioeconomic status among runners. In 1977, 2,000 women participated in a relay that conveyed a torch from Seneca Falls, New York, to the National Women's Conference in Houston. When the torch arrived, New York politician Bella Abzug accompanied the runner into the convention hall. The woman runner became a feminist symbol at a time when feminism was mainly a middle-class protest movement concerned with bettering women's educations, opening the professions to them, and protecting their property after marriage. These opportunities were assumed to be for all women, but often only middle- and upper-class women could take advantage of them. Similarly, upper-status women would be most likely to have the leisure for a time-consuming, financially unproductive amateur sport such as marathon running.[10]

In the past, the marathon footrace had been a lower-status event, not only in the economic class of its participants, but also within the amateur sport bureaucracy.[11] The principal governing body for intercollegiate athletics, the National Collegiate Athletic Association, ignored marathon running. The Amateur Athletic Union, which managed Olympic sports in the United States until the Amateur Sports Act of 1978, was scarcely better. AAU meets often neglected events such as the hammer throw and the marathon because they were not traditionally profitable as spectator sports.[12]

Dissatisfaction with the AAU's treatment of long-distance runners led to the creation of the Road Runners Club of America (RRCA) by former Olympic steeplechaser H. Browning Ross in December 1957. Interest in jogging in the 1960s strengthened the RRCA's position by creating a new pool of potential long-distance runners who were of higher socioeconomic status than the traditional club runners. While RRCA clubs staged AAU-sanctioned road races, the RRCA also produced "closed" events—for members only—that could be held without AAU sanctioning. Often joggers were introduced to racing by low-key Road Runners events rather than high-pressure AAU competitions. The New York Association of the RRCA, which became the New York Road Runners Club (NYRRC), was organized in June 1958 in order to provide more long-distance races in the area governed by the Metropolitan AAU. The NYRRC was denied affiliation with the Metropolitan AAU, until NYRRC president Aldo Scandurra ran for Metropolitan AAU office and was elected second vice-president, a tactic that he and the RRCA continued and carried through at the national level. The AAU, responsible for ensuring that athletes were eligible for international competition, remained the governing body of marathoning, but, by infiltrating the AAU bureaucracy, the RRCA increasingly controlled domestic aspects of long-distance racing.[13]

During the 1960s and 1970s, the New York Road Runners Club became the pivotal section of the RRCA by moving into all three of the components that Stephen Hardy identifies as constituting the "sport product": the game form, the goods, and the services. Much of Hardy's explanation of the sport product refers to the economic and business history of sport. He defines the game form as "the rules defining the way the game is played," adding, "Of course, anyone can make up a game, as Professor Naismith demonstrated. But this is of little consequence until rule-making is organized and controlled by particular groups." The NYRRC was one of those groups. It extended its authority over the game form by standardizing course-measurement methods. Theodore Corbitt, who became the NYRRC's first president in 1958, published a pamphlet on the topic *Measuring Road Racing Courses,* and the NYRRC supplied expertise and sanctioning on course calibration.[14]

The second part of the sport product comprises goods. Hardy lists "Balls, goals, sticks, bats, protective equipment and uniforms" as well as facilities, such as running tracks, that are essential to the contest. The New York Road Runners Club was among the pioneers in the use of computerized finish-line equipment directed at accurately scoring large fields of runners, particularly when several runners would finish at the same time.[15]

Although sport services are traditionally defined in terms of such social functions as "education, status, military preparation, urban boosterism, political propaganda, and most extensively, entertainment," Hardy adds that special organizations to promote the sport, and to serve it in ways apart from the game form, are also sport services. One such special organization was the United States Age Group Competitions for boys and girls, originated by NYRRC members Ann and Nat Cirulnick, Barry Geisler, and Joe Kleinerman. This was a significant program for women, because mothers were encouraged to jog with their children in noncompetitive Fun Runs. According to Aldo Scandurra, "This was the breakthrough that led to LDR [long distance running] scheduled programs for women."[16]

With the rebirth of active feminism in the mid-1960s, as well as the events leading up to the passage of Title IX in 1973, there was increased overall interest in women's athletics. No group has done more to promote long-distance running for women than the Road Runners Club of America. Throughout the 1960s, the RRCA repeatedly challenged the AAU's ban on women's long-distance races. Women were finally allowed to participate in an AAU-sanctioned marathon in Atlantic City on 25 October 1970. Six female RRCA members officially entered through the usual RRCA device: the marathon was a "closed" competition, sponsored by the RRCA.[17]

Women runners may have been the first to present the possibilities of the marathon as a profit-making enterprise. In 1972, Fred Lebow of the New York Road Runners Club was approached by the public relations firm of S. C. Johnson & Son, Inc., about staging a marathon for women. Lebow had originally been a textile consultant in New York City's garment industry. He was elected president of the NYRRC in 1972, and still holds that position, once voluntary but now salaried. He left his career as consultant in the late 1970s and now devotes himself to managing the NYRRC. Lebow recognized the attractiveness of a women-only marathon but was also cognizant of the scarcity of women capable of running 26.2 miles. Instead he suggested, and the sponsor accepted, a women's road race of six miles.[18]

The public-relations firm mailed thousands of invitations to women in local high schools and colleges, while Lebow demonstrated his own aptitude for promotion, handing out entry blanks and flyers all over Manhattan, occasionally taping them to light poles. He encouraged six Playboy Bunnies to run in the race, and recruited the patrons of a rock-music nightclub. The result of this feverish activity was a field of seventy-eight women.[19]

This was the first running of what would become a prestigious annual ten-kilometer competition: the Women's Mini-Marathon, popularly known as "the Mini." By the late 1970s the event would draw over 6,000 participants to a single 6.2-mile race, but in 1972 it was memorable mainly for its farcical elements. The sponsor insisted that the runners wear identical white T-shirts with their numbers stamped below the name of the product—"Crazy Legs," a shaving cream for women. A male runner decided to pace first woman Jackie Dixon through the race, leading what Tom Derderian (husband of second woman Charlotte Lettis) said "looked more like a comic refugee regiment slowly plodding around the park in identical jerseys." Denied her right to break a tape, Dixon had to burst through a huge paper banner advertising Crazy Legs, her win subjugated to the needs of the sponsor's product. Promoting long-distance running for women was going to require even more effort and imagination, or perhaps a little less.[20]

In 1973 and 1974, Olympic Airways gave some financial support to the New York City Marathon in return for race-day publicity. In 1975, however, the marathon lost that sponsor and had to rely on numerous small donations from members. The *New York Times* commented on the incongruity of the loss of

corporate sponsorship "at a time when more New Yorkers than ever are embracing a run-for-fun philosophy." In responding to its need to attract sponsorship, the New York Road Runners Club became an entrepreneurial
organization, "one with a high motivation," as Philip Kotler explains in *Marketing for Nonprofit Organizations,* "and capability to identify new opportunities
and convert them into successful businesses."[21]

The New York City Marathon's limited spectatorship and low number of
participants (just over 500 in 1974 and 1975) influenced sponsors' perceptions
of the marathon as an event that would have little commercial value. On the
positive side, joggers and, increasingly, competitive long-distance runners were
already considered upper-status individuals, important as consumers. Frank
Shorter's gold medal in the 1972 Munich Olympic Marathon was a form of tes-
timonial: the twenty-four-year-old, Yale-educated law student on the winners'
stand provided a role-model for young professionals interested in marathoning. Affluent earners could, and would, be enticed to recreational running
through careful presentation of the services of the sport: cardiovascular fitness, weight control, and the companionship of other upper-status persons.[22]
In order to be recruited for the marathon, the well-to-do had to be made aware
of the event as an attractive achievement that was accessible to them.

The New York City Marathon had been an inconspicuous event for the first
six years of its running, held within the confines of Central Park, comprising
a bit over four laps of the Central Park road. In 1975, even though the New
York City Marathon was also the Women's National AAU Championships, it
still was given very little attention. Horseback riders, bicyclists, pedestrians,
and dogs freely crossed the runners' lane. To the media, the marathon was a
sport eccentricity; the marathon coverage on one television station devoted
most footage to a chance spectator who shouted, "Look at all these crazy people!"[23] Certainly the New York City Marathon directors were looking for
some way to enhance the prestige of their event, and to associate marathon
running with serious achievement.

The prestige came the next year, when two of the 1976 United States
Olympic marathoners competed in the race. In 1976, with Bicentennial com-
memorations under way throughout the country, the New York Road Runners Club, in keeping with the Bicentennial spirit, proposed that the upcoming
New York City Marathon be taken out of Central Park and run through all
five boroughs on the streets of New York. Frank Shorter had won the silver
medal in the marathon at the Montreal Games; Bill Rodgers, winner of the
1975 Boston Marathon, had placed fortieth in the Olympics. Both attractive
men in their late twenties and graduates of highly regarded universities, they

were fine examples of marathon runners for affluent earners in their twenties and thirties.[24]

The five-borough marathon was endorsed by New York City Mayor Abraham Beame and by Manhattan Borough President Percy Sutton, and the Rudin family, founders of a major New York City real-estate firm, offered $25,000 to sponsor the race. Through Lebow's promotional efforts, the event picked up other sponsors, including Manufacturers Hanover Trust Company, *New Times* magazine, Finnair, and Bonne Bell cosmetics. The New York Academy of Sciences' "Conference on the Marathon" was scheduled October 25–28. Advertisements for the marathon included announcements for the conference that implied a connection between the marathon and medical approval. As the race drew near, colorful posters appeared all over the city. Entrants poured in, half of whom had never run a marathon before.[25]

The success of the 1976 New York City Marathon was to a great extent due to Rodgers and Shorter. "Under-the-table money," the illicit payment of amateur athletes, underscored the vital role of top runners. According to Lebow, Rodgers was paid $2,000 for this race, and Shorter was also "treated . . . fairly." The guaranteed appearances of famous, world-class runners attracted the attention of the media that publicized the race, and of sponsors who paid for the banners, T-shirts, and other paraphernalia of the festival. The acclaim and the spectacle were necessary to draw enough spectators to provide sufficient public-relations value to the event's sponsors.[26]

The payment of athletes by the New York City Marathon is difficult to trace, partly due to the manner in which the payments were made. In 1976, Rodgers probably received a cash payment. In 1979, Jon Anderson ran in the New York City Marathon and finished ninth. He did not give lectures or appearances; in his own words, he "simply ran the race and finished ninth." New York Road Runners Club treasurer Peter Roth arranged for Anderson to receive a $1,500 check from New York City Marathon sponsor Great Waters of France (Perrier). Officially, there was nothing but Anderson's word to connect the New York City Marathon with the payment of an athlete in violation of the amateur code.[27]

Events in 1976 also marked a major change in the New York Road Runners Club from a democratic organization to one in which all authority was vested in Lebow.[28] According to Hardy, when a sport is not subsidized by the state or by a philanthropic agency, it is important that the sport have an entrepreneur willing to engage in profit-seeking and risk-taking and other innovative activity, such as introducing a new service or opening a new market. Lebow fit this description as he spearheaded the New York City Marathon and did much of the negotiating himself directly with sponsors and city officials.[29]

Although the more than 2,000 entrants made the 1976 New York City Marathon the world's largest, in many ways this race seemed to be aimed at runners who would enter the marathon in 1977 and after. The first five-borough marathon provided a general awareness of the event, especially to those with the leisure time to train for the next year's race. The 1976 New York City Marathon attempted to target the upscale market of health-conscious joggers through the personal appearance of Shorter and Rodgers; inhabitants of the affluent Upper East Side saw two twenty-nine-year-old Olympians racing, followed by ordinary, thirtyish men and women much like themselves.

Two days after the marathon, an article appeared in the *New York Times* entitled "Want to Run Marathon? Take It Easy, Doctor Warns Hopeful Novices." The piece contained extensive advice on training and referred to the Academy of Sciences conference. The author concluded with a statement from Fred Lebow that the city would like "to make the five-borough marathon an annual event." According to Lebow, "The New York Road Runners Club raised $40,000 from various corporate sponsors, but still will wind up with a $20,000 deficit for the race." This article summed up the situation nicely: Lebow was calling out to next year's runners and next year's sponsors.[30]

The 4 June 1977 ten-kilometer Women's Mini-Marathon, which increased to 2,000 entrants from 408 in 1976, indicated the direction the marathon would be taking. First, finish-line timing and scoring procedures were computerized to enable the staff to accurately score four or five finishers per second. This ten-kilometer women's race became a test run for the technology that would permit a greatly increased field at the upcoming marathon. The modification had marked commercial value; larger fields were important to sponsors, since they meant that many more people would be exposed to advertising for sponsors' products. Second, the directors of the Mini-Marathon improved public and press relations. According to the *Runner's World* coverage of the event, the 1977 Mini-Marathon's success could be attributed "to a bit of marketing genius." The *Runner's World* article gave an account of fun runs and clinics for members of the press, mass mailings of schedules and flyers, and advertisements of the race in upscale magazines such as *Vogue* and *Harper's,* as well as in magazines geared to young adults with significant disposable incomes, such as *Seventeen* and *Glamour.* The April 1977 edition of *Vogue* and the May 1977 edition of *Mademoiselle* carried articles by medical doctors explaining the benefits of jogging.[31]

By August, 5,000 entrants had been accepted for the upcoming 1977 New York City Marathon. The marathon course had been changed slightly, so that now the runners would travel up First Avenue, past the trendy singles bars. Perrier became a marathon sponsor, and on 23 October 1977, the young, upwardly mobile professionals of the late 1970s became the object of Perrier's American advertising campaign as they watched Bill Rodgers and Garry Bjorklund in an impressive duel up First Avenue.[32]

Rodgers, the winner of the 1977 and 1978 New York City Marathons, appeared on the cover of *Sports Illustrated* on 30 October 1978 during a New York City newspaper strike. His racing number, along with the printed name of sponsor Manufacturers Hanover, was clearly visible. *Forbes* magazine quoted Manufacturers Hanover Vice President Charles McCabe as saying, "You can't buy advertising like that." But even without *Sports Illustrated* and the newspaper strike, sponsors such as Perrier were reaching a suitable consumer audience through the New York City Marathon. The commemorative T-shirts given to the entrants were ideal for corporate trademarks and other advertising.[33]

The race T-shirts had many functions. They were a motivation for participation in road events where enormous fields meant few runners could win a trophy. According to sociologist Jeffrey Nash of Macalester College, "The common practice of awarding T-shirts to all finishers symbolized the individual conquest of failure."[34] Running togs became a fashion statement as well, and the commemorative T-shirt implied the wearer was a clean-living individual. On 1 April 1978, Perrier co-sponsored a ten-kilometer race with Bloomingdale's. Race tank tops and T-shirts were distributed at a check-in held in Bloomingdale's new running-wear department. "Can't we get these people to move any faster?" a Road Runners official reportedly asked a Bloomingdale's sales clerk as runners wavered in their choice between the tank tops and the T-shirts. "How can you possibly give the Bloomingdale's customer a fashion decision to make and expect them to make it quickly?" the clerk replied.[35]

While runners and non-runners alike recognized the social and psychological advantages of wearing a marathon T-shirt, marketing vice-presidents acknowledged the race T-shirt's value as "unsolicited" advertising. "The sight of a smiling corporate vp is not unfamiliar these days at running races," said a 1979 *Advertising Age* article that began with a few paragraphs on the potential of race T-shirts imprinted with a company's name and logo: "All those runners undoubtedly would take those T-shirts home and wear them another day."[36]

A 1978 *Runner's World* survey conducted by market-research firm Yankelovich, Skelly, and White indicated that runners were mostly white-collar people with yearly incomes much higher than the national average. Journalist Neil Amdur, in *The Runner*, made a connection between the new marathoners and the possibilities for corporate sponsorship. Amdur noted the significance of the New York City Marathon in "changing the image of long-distance running from one of personal struggle to a joyous one shared by an entire city," and, especially, in creating an "expanded constituency" for what was formerly an event of limited participation. "Corporations . . . saw the up-beat, middle-income, college-educated market moving onto the roads. What better way to sell an image than by identifying with a healthy amateur sport?"[37] A large part of the sponsoring corporation's image would be determined by the presentation of the New York City Marathon: by the overall organization, the facility of procedures, the services offered, and the care of individual runner.[38]

The New York Road Runners Club was originally concerned with the politics of road racing: developing opportunities for competition, sanctioning races, and representing long-distance runners' interests in a track-dominated athletics culture. Administrative and other tasks were carried out through the cooperative efforts of runners and non-competing members, generally in a private home or temporarily donated office space. When the NYRRC finally obtained its first permanent office in the West Side YMCA, it was intended to be run on a "family basis," with members expected to "drop in to help out" as the need arose. But the staging of the first five-borough marathon necessitated the establishment of formal committees, over a dozen of them, each little more than a chairperson dependent on sporadic volunteer help, all under the direct control of Fred Lebow. The system was barely workable and often chaotic.[39]

The five-borough marathon also required the use of city services, such as police, coordinated by Lebow but clearly under their own direction. This set an important precedent as race production became the NYRRC's main product and the various committees achieved increasing autonomy. For example, the medical committee, chaired by an NYRRC-member physician, but staffed by volunteer residents, interns, and medical students, was self-contained due to the professional nature of its work. The Medical Committee also filled an important public-relations role, as noted in the minutes of the 25 July 1977 meeting of the Marathon Committee: "If two or three people drop dead then we will be placed in a position of answering a lot of questions. We will have to be able to say that we acted like responsible citizens in allowing people to run twenty-six miles."[40]

The Technical Committee, responsible for the finish-line structure and timing and recording devices, was another unit that quickly achieved autonomy, again in Chandlerian fashion, as a reflection of its highly specialized knowledge and function. As time and road racing progressed, the Technical

Committee fulfilled its Chandlerian destiny, essentially becoming "separated from its ownership," the members of the NYRRC. By 1980, the NYRRC was renting out its equipment and personnel as consultants to other races, some far from the area served by the NYRRC. Rather than merely sponsoring an NYRRC race, other organizations could produce their own events, using NYRRC technology and expertise.[41]

Within a few years of the first five-borough marathon, responsibility for the race was shared among established committees. The committees were headed by coordinators, salaried managers who developed their own systems of handling different aspects of marathon production and staging. These autonomous units called upon a pool of thousands of NYRRC volunteers for labor. As the systems evolved their own rule-bound procedures, the volunteers required formal training for their tasks. In October 1983, *Successful Meetings*, a management periodical, described the bureaucratic experience of volunteering for the New York City Marathon: filling out application blanks, attending classes, putting in time to gain seniority, and learning new skills required for a promotion. At a meeting about two weeks before race day, "volunteers meet their supervisors, get to know each other, learn the necessary procedures, and receive their race credentials. An additional two-hour training session in peace-keeping and crowd control is required for those volunteers whose jobs demand it," according to *Successful Meetings's* interview with Jolene Roberts, the coordinator of volunteers.[42]

In the early days of the NYRRC, race-course and finish-line tasks were performed by member runners who expected reciprocity when it was their turn to compete. But many of the new volunteers never ran competitively or even assisted in any other NYRRC event. Volunteering became their way of participating in the marathon, a position the NYRRC validated by stressing the "basic, life supportive things" volunteers do for the runners. "How many times do you give someone a drink of water who may get sick or even die without it?" Roberts asked. The NYRRC also recognized the volunteers' contributions with awards and small gifts, the most prized of which were the specially designed "Marathon Volunteer" T-shirts.[43]

As the number of paid employees of the New York Road Runners Club grew, the administration of the New York City Marathon became a separate entity that was capable of functioning independently of other NYRRC activities. The New York Road Runners Club now had all the characteristics of a modern business enterprise. Its state-of-the-art product, the New York City Marathon, could most efficiently be produced by the cooperative effort of a series of autonomous systems run by a professionalized managerial hierarchy, using the labor of a controlled workforce. Major decisions of the NYRRC, such as the purchase of a building in 1981, promoted the long-term goals of the organization and provided for its stability, often before they answered the needs of its competing members.[44] In 1982, the Athletics Congress permitted cash prizes for top finishers, and another managerial role of the New York City Marathon, allocating the funds of its wealthy corporate sponsors to the world's greatest runners, was now openly acknowledged.[45]

The directors of the New York City Marathon used personal appearances and popular concern with fitness to present their event in a manner that appealed to young, upper-status individuals. Through a change of venue, they modified the game form to make the marathon more accessible. They created auxiliary organizations, sport services, to attract specific groups. They provided sport apparatus such as the computerized finish line that could accommodate the increasing numbers of participants the marathon attracted. Just as important, the New York Road Runners Club produced commemorative T-shirts—race T-shirts, volunteer T-shirts, T-shirts for the medical corps, and T-shirts in which to train for next year's race—tangible and lasting reminders that managerial capitalism, the "visible hand," had united athletic achievement and economic production.

Notes

1. "More People, More Speed," *Runner's World* 10 (February 1975): 23; Joe Henderson, "Seven Big Issues for '77," *Runner's World* 12 (February 1977): 19; David E. Martin and Roger W. H. Gynn, *The Marathon Footrace: Performers and Performances* (Springfield, Ill.: Charles C. Thomas, 1979), 254, 339; "Demographics—1980 NYC Marathon," *New York Running News* 24, 5 (1980): 134.

2. Alfred D. Chandler, *The Visible Hand: The Managerial Revolution in American Business* (Cambridge, Mass: The Belknap Press of Harvard University Press, 1977), 1, 4, 6, 11, 498; James Texas, "Take the Money and Run," *The Runner* 1 (January 1979): 16, 19. The financial statements of the New York Road Runners Club are public record since 1982. Copies are available from the New York State Department of State, Office of Charities Registration, Albany, New York, 12231–0001.

3. Hal Higdon, "The AAU: Kingdom in Crisis," *The Runner* 1 (September 1979): 57. Higdon first ran the Boston Marathon in 1959. "Those marathoners in 1959 either were more talented or more dedicated than those of 1979. . . . While winning times may seem slow by today's standards, almost everybody was capable of marks near 3:00. For someone to run slower than 4:00—unheard of! The officials, none of whom were runners and all of whom smoked cigars, would never wait around that long anyway."

4. Ian T. Macauley, "Marathon Men and Women on Their Marks," *New York Times*, 22 October 1976, C22.

5. Paul Milvy, "Milvy to Lebow," letter from Paul Milvy to Fred Lebow, printed in *Road Runners Club New York Association Newsletter* no. 71 (spring 1977): 6. Paul Milvy, a biophysicist affiliated with the Mount Sinai School of Medicine, was a runner who assisted the NYRRC with technical matters. In this letter, Milvy, then a member of the NYRRC Executive Committee, decried Lebow's authoritarian administrative practices.

6. James Curtis and William McTeer, "Toward a Sociology of Marathoning," *Journal of Sport Behavior* 4, 2 (1981): 79. For the lower-status origin of the marathon in social terms, see Pamela Cooper, "Community, Ethnicity, Status: The Origins of the Marathon in the United States," *International Journal of the History of Sport* 9 (April 1992): 50–62.

7. Thomas O'Donnell with Jinny St. Goar, "Marathon Money Matters," *Forbes* 132 (24 October 1983): 37. See also New York State Department of State, New York Road Runners Club, Inc. Annual Report—Charitable Organization, for the years ended 31 December 1982 and 31 December 1985; and Milvy, "Milvy to Lebow," 6.

8. Benjamin G. Rader, "The Quest for Self-Sufficiency and the New Strenuosity: Reflections on the Strenuous Life of the 1970s and the 1980s," *Journal of Sport History* 18, 2 (1991): 258–60; Marilyn Wellemeyer, "Addicted to Perpetual Motion," *Fortune* 95 (June 1977): 58.

9. Curtis and McTeer, "Sociology of Marathoning," 79; Frank Litsky, "A Second Wind in the Running Room," *New York Times*, 16 April 1983, C6.

10. Olive Banks, *Faces of Feminism: A Study of Feminism as a Social Movement* (New York: St. Martin's Press, 1981), 250; William J. Baker, *Sports in the Western World* (Totowa, N.J.: Rowman and Littlefield, 1982), 295.

11. Pamela Cooper, "How the AAU Suppressed the Marathon," *Footnotes* 11, 1 (1983): 14.

12. United States, Congress, Senate, Committee on Commerce, *NCAA-AAU Dispute: Hearing before the Committee on Commerce*, 89th Cong., 1st sess., 16–27 August 1965, 523–24, (hereafter cited as *NCAA-AAU Dispute*). This was part of the statement submitted by Hugh D. Jascourt, then president of the Road Runners Club of America.

13. *NCAA-AAU Dispute*, 523–24; "Jogging for Heart and Health—It's Catching On," *U.S. News and World Report* 62 (25 December 1967): 49; Aldo Scandurra, "History of Long Distance and Road Racing," *Long Island Running News* 1 (3) (1981): 11. Scandurra joined the Road Runners Club New York Association (as the NYRRC was then called) in 1960. He also held a number of offices in the AAU, among them chairman of the National LDR Committee. Scandurra devised the tactic of infiltration of the AAU by the RRCA. See also "Who Is the American Runner?" *Runner's World* 19 (August 1984): 49.

14. Stephen H. Hardy, "Entrepreneurs, Organizations, and the Sport Marketplace: Subjects in Search of Historians," *Journal of Sport History* 13 (1986): 17; Scandurra, "History of Long Distance," 12; John Chodes, *Corbitt: The Story of Ted Corbitt, Long Distance Runner* (Los Altos, Calif.: Tafnews Press, 1974), 147. Theodore Corbitt, an African-American runner, was an Olympic marathoner in 1952.

15. Hardy, "Entrepreneurs," 19; Paul Milvy, "How the Mini Kept Score," *Runner's World* 12 (August 1977): 51–53.

16. Hardy, "Entrepreneurs," 18–19; Scandurra, "History of Long Distance," 16.

17. Scandurra, "History of Long Distance," 15–16; Pat Tarnawsky, "What's This? Women Welcome!" *Runner's World* 6 (January 1971): 22. Title IX of the 1972 Educational Amendments Act requires that all high schools and colleges receiving federal monies do not discriminate against students and employees on the basis of gender. In sports, this meant theoretically equal opportunities and facilities.

18. Fred Lebow with Richard Woodley, *Inside the World of Big-Time Marathoning* (New York: Rawson Associates, 1984), 61–62. David G. Santry, "The Business of Running," *New York Running News* 21 (December 1979): 11.

19. Lebow with Woodley, *Big-Time Marathoning*, 45–46.

20. Tom Derderian, "Women's Day in Central Park," *Runner's World* 12 (August 1977): 49; Charlotte Lettis, "Promoting Women's Running?" *Runner's World* 7 (September 1972): 44.

21. Neil Amdur, "Area Marathons Feel Money Squeeze," *New York Times,* 3 June 1975, 38; Philip Kotler, *Marketing for Nonprofit Organizations* (Englewood Cliffs, N.J.: Prentice Hall, 1975), 113.

22. *U.S. News and World Report* 62 (25 December 1967): 49; P. Rosenfeld, "Cooper's Cohorts Run Down Heart Disease," *Saturday Evening Post* 249 (September 1977): 18–20. See also Dave Prokop, "Frank Shorter," *Runner's World* 11 (January 1976): 46.

23. Joan Ullyot, *Women's Running* (Mountain View, Calif.: World, 1976), 145–47.

24. Neil Amdur, "New York's First Citywide Marathon Draws Some of World's Top Runners," *New York Times,* 25 October 1976, 31.

25. Lebow with Woodley, *Big-Time Marathoning*, 64; Ted Brock, "All Around the Town," *Runner's World* 11 (December 1976): 22; *Runner's World* 11 (August 1976): 26; Amdur, "First Citywide Marathon," 31.

26. Montieth M. Illingworth, "Run for the Money," *Manhattan, Inc.* 2 (October 1985): 129.

27. Lebow with Woodley, *Big-Time Marathoning*, 15; Jon P. Anderson, "Lebow," letter to the editor, *The Runner* 4 (January 1982): 6.

28. Milvy, "Milvy to Lebow," 6. The following is an excerpt from this letter of March 1977: "Just look at where we stand today: we have a President and an

Executive, neither of which was ever elected by the membership. And as undemocratic as this may be, from a purely practical point of view, it doesn't matter at all: the Exec. never even convenes! From time to time, authority to work independently is given to various individuals with one hand, too often taken away with the other. Their decisions may well be made after careful thought, yet all to likely they are countermanded by the President's personal whim."

29. Hardy, "Entrepreneurs," 20; Lebow with Woodley, Big-Time Marathoning, 63–69.

30. Neil Amdur, "Want to Run Marathon? Take It Easy, Doctor Warns Hopeful Novices," New York Times, 26 October 1976, 33.

31. Milvy, "How the Mini Kept Score," 51–53; Derderian, "Women's Day in Central Park," 49; George Sheehan, "Fitness Rx," Vogue 167 (April 1977): 136–37; Arthur Frank and Stuart Frank, "Jogging," Mademoiselle 83 (May 1977): 92–95.

32. Lebow with Woodley, Big-Time Marathoning, 82–83.

33. O'Donnell with St. Goar, "Marathon Money," 37.

34. Jeffrey E. Nash, "Weekend Racing as an Eventful Experience: Understanding the Accomplishment of Well-Being," Urban Life 8, 1 (1979): 212.

35. Neil Amdur, "Running Boom: Too Much Too Soon?" New York Times, 17 April 1978, C1, C8.

36. Carol Galginaitis, "To Corporations, Name's the Game," Advertising Age 50 (27 August 1979): S-2; Ullyot, Women's Running, 70.

37. "Who Is the American Runner?" Runner's World 15 (December 1980): 37; Neil Amdur, "What Makes the Seventies Run," The Runner 1 (October 1978): 14.

38. Texas, "Take the Money," 19; Santry, "The Business of Running," 12–13.

39. Road Runners Club New York Association Newsletter no. 1 (?1959): 1; Road Runners Club New York Association Newsletter no. 67 (spring 1976): 8; Paul Milvy, "The Definitive Short History of the New York City Five-Borough Marathon," New York City Five-Borough Marathon (?1976): n.p. This undated, unpaginated publication was the program for the 1976 New York City Marathon. See also Lebow with Woodley, Big-Time Marathoning, 70, 72, 80.

40. Milvy, "Short History"; Lebow with Woodley, Big-Time Marathoning, 64, 71; Kathleen Macomber, Minutes, 25 July 1977 Meeting, Marathon Committee, New York City Marathon for the Samuel Rudin Trophy, 3.

41. Chandler, The Visible Hand, 6–10. See also Art Jahnke, "The Boss," Running 8 (September/October 1982): 34–40; Milvy, "How the Mini Kept Score," 51–53; Texas, "Take the Money," 16.

42. Michael Adams, "The New York City Marathon: How It's Run," Successful Meetings 32 (October 1983): 29–30. For the bureaucratization of labor, see Sanford M. Jacoby, Employing Bureaucracy: Managers, Unions, and the Transformation of Work in American Industry, 1900–1945 (New York: Columbia University Press, 1985), 2. For the significance of standardized procedures and job descriptions, see Daniel Nelson, Managers and Workers: Origins of the New Factory System in the United States,

1880–1920 (Madison: University of Wisconsin Press, 1975), 151–55. See also Chandler, *The Visible Hand*, 124.

43. Adams, "How It's Run," 30, 32.

44. Chandler, *The Visible Hand*, 1–10, 107. That the newsletter *Road Race Management* began publication in 1982 was a clear statement of the professionalization of race directors. *Road Race Management* gave advice on race organization and sponsorship, legal and medical issues, etc.

45. Illingworth, "Run for the Money," 124.

17

The Quest for Self-Sufficiency and the New Strenuosity

BENJAMIN G. RADER

In the 1970s and the 1980s evidence of a preoccupation with strenuous living was widespread.[1] One of its dimensions was the popularity of physical fitness.[2] Even in bone-chilling Nebraska winters, runners grimly pounded out the miles needed to reach their weekly quotas. At the local gymnasiums of the Young Men's and Women's Christian Associations and hundreds of special health centers, women did exhausting aerobic dance routines and both sexes grunted under the weights of Nautilus machines.[3] Specialists designed individualized fitness programs, complete with elaborate quantifications of performances. Millions gave up cigarettes, reduced or eliminated the consumption of red meats, and cut down on or quit drinking alcoholic beverages.

A second dimension of the strenuous life, which became increasingly manifest in the 1980s, entailed the presentation of a particular self.[4] Physical vigor and a sinewy or, conversely, a muscle-bound body became extremely important as a means of self-presentation. In scorching summers, women revealed their fitness in loose-fitting runners, T-shirts or in shorts over form-fitting leotards, and men donned short shorts and muscle-revealing T-shirts. Stylish jogging suits became de rigueur for weekend excursions to the supermarket as well as the local fitness center. In newspaper personals men and women presented themselves to each other as dedicated fitness freaks. Energetic, strong, willowy young men and women filled the television screens in both commercials and rock videos. Perhaps no sign of the times was more important than the decision to update the marketing of Barbie, "the ultimate Yuppie doll," by including with the doll a workout center, complete with exercise cycle, dumbbells, slant boards, and locker room with towel.[5]

Obviously, the most direct predecessor of the modern concern with vigorous living was Theodore Roosevelt's call for the strenuous life at the turn of the twentieth century.[6] Like more recent exponents of strenuosity, Roosevelt was convinced that fitness could contribute to improved health, but in other respects his position differed fundamentally from the movement of the 1970s and 1980s. First, Roosevelt and his followers would have been shocked at the sheer intensity and degree of physical activity characteristic of the new strenuosity. Although in his forties Roosevelt went on long, fast walks over hill and dale along the Potomac River, neither he nor his friends ran in marathons, or ran at all, for that matter. Second, while Roosevelt wanted genteel women to be stronger so that they could bear large broods of white, Anglo-Saxon children, he certainly would have been surprised if not shocked at the conspicuous role of women in the modern strenuous-life movement.

Finally, the goal of Roosevelt's strenuosity was social. Through more strenuous living, he hoped to rejuvenate his own social class, which he believed had become too soft and effeminate. Once physically strengthened, they could provide capable national leadership. Social goals, especially becoming fit enough to meet the perceived threat of the Soviet Union, also informed the President's Council on Physical Fitness, organized in 1956.[7] Although the President's Council remains in existence today, it has had a negligible relationship to the modern fitness crusade. Indeed, the focus of the new strenuosity has been upon the self, upon the individual rather than upon society or the community.

The stress on the self leads to the main theme of this essay, namely that the preoccupation with the strenuous life in the 1970s and 1980s was part of a wide-ranging quest for greater self-sufficiency among the "successful." In general, the successful were the "Baby Boomers," those born between 1945 and 1960, who had higher incomes than the national average and lived in the suburbs; more specifically in the 1980s they frequently fit the definition of the "Yuppies," a term applied to the young, upwardly mobile professionals.[8]

Although this group enjoyed more material success than did most Americans, ill-defined and only partly understood dissatisfactions within its ranks arose from other quarters. One of the least contestable was a growing awareness that modern medicine had no panaceas for extending life or preventing aging. Less conclusive was the absence of adequate satisfactions in work, consumption, and personal relationships. As society became more rationalized and systematized and more people worked in bureaucracies, the importance of the individual seemed to diminish. Many, especially those in white-collar occupations, experienced powerlessness and anonymity in their jobs. Neither did greater consumption seem to satisfy yearnings arising from material wants, impotency, meaningless work, loneliness, or sexual deprivation. Apart from the issue of whether consumption has the capacity to satisfy the deepest needs of the human species, the very existence of the advertising industry

depended on its ability to convince people that they could not achieve fulfillment unless they purchased an ever-greater quantity of goods or services.
Whatever the sources of anxiety and unfulfillment, the postwar successful increasingly turned to the self to nurture the resources needed to cope with
modern life.

———

A growing recognition of the limits of modern medicine provided the
most obvious impetus for the new quest for greater self-sufficiency.[9] Americans have long been skeptical of the claims of the professional practitioners of
medicine. Alternative forms of medicine flourished in the nineteenth century;
reformers in the antebellum era claimed that particular diets and exercises
would promote better health. The great sanitary reforms of the second half
of the nineteenth century, since they proved highly effective in reducing the
incidence of contagious diseases, represented measurable progress in preventive medicine.

Then in the twentieth century came the sudden medical breakthroughs, in
particular the antibiotic revolution in the 1940s and 1950s, which seemed to
suggest that humans could safely rely on the "wonder drugs" to protect their
health and increase their longevity without worrying so much about sanita-
tion, diet, or exercise. American confidence in the medical profession suddenly soared to undreamed-of heights. Just as enthusiasm for wonder drugs
had reached a crescendo in the mid-1960s, however, Americans learned about
the dangerous side effects of such powerful drugs as thalidomide and antibi-
otics. "The result," Norman Cousins has written, "was a growing distrust not
just of the highly sophisticated new drugs but of almost all medications in
general."[10] The percentage of the population expressing high confidence in
medicine fell, according to national public-opinion polls, in a descending curve
from a high of 73 percent in 1966 to only 34 percent in 1980.[11]

With the success of the antibiotic revolution in reducing or eliminating
many dreaded killers, the main health concern transferred to the degeneration of the body rather than control of contagious diseases. Increasing
longevity and a growing obsession with youthfulness made Americans all the
more aware of body degeneration. In the 1960s cardiovascular diseases and
cancer replaced contagious diseases as the main human killers. In both cases
modern medicine offered no wonder drugs. Simultaneously, a growing body
of epidemiological evidence indicated that the way persons lived directly affected their health. Indeed, according to this evidence, "lifestyle items," such

as the absence of exercise, obesity, smoking, fat intake, and heavy drinking, greatly increased the risks of cardiovascular problems and possibly cancer as well.[12] The result was that growing numbers of Americans tried to alter their lifestyles. They watched what they ate, tried to control their diet, exercised more, stopped smoking, and tried to reduce stress in their lives. All of these behavioral changes could be accomplished by the self. With little or no reliance upon society, the individual seemed to be able to forestall the arrival of the Grim Reaper. Such thinking dovetailed nicely with American traditions of individualism and self-help.

———

Into this favorable climate stepped a new guru of exercise, Air Force physician Kenneth Cooper. In the late 1960s, at the very time that disillusionment with the Great Society and the Vietnam War had set in, Cooper developed measurable standards of ideal conditioning, thereby giving fitness the illusion of resting on proven experimentation. Unlike earlier apostles of fitness, Cooper insisted that only exceptionally strenuous activities, such as jogging, running, racquetball, cycling, or swimming raised the pulse rate to sustained levels adequate for one to become what he called "aerobically fit." Only then could the exerciser gain significant cardiovascular benefits. Cooper personally brought to his "aerobics" movement an intensity and moral earnestness befitting his evangelical Protestant origins.[13]

Fed partly by Cooper's claims but even more by media hype, a popular runners' movement blossomed in the late 1960s and early 1970s. First the public learned that astronaut-hero John Glenn followed Cooper's regimen of aerobic fitness. Then came ABC television's coverage of the marathon at the 1972 Olympic Games in Munich. Before the marathon took place, monumental blunders, sparkling heroes, and genuine tragedy at the Games had already glued the entire nation to the television spectacle. With an emotionally charged commentary provided by Eric Segal, the author of the sentimental, bestselling novel *Love Story*, American Frank Shorter came from far behind the pack to whip the world's best. Shorter became an instant hero. No other specific event did more to encourage the running mania.

But Shorter's victory coincided in time with a turning away from society to the self as well. Growing recognition of the limits of expertise and disillusionment with the government's ability to deal with race, poverty, stagflation, pollution, energy shortages, and foreign affairs all encouraged the coming of what social commentator Tom Wolfe labeled the "Me Decade." Many Americans sought greater control over their lives and greater personal satisfaction in arenas other than jobs, consumption, or social movements. They became converts to charismatic religions, experimented with vegetarianism, hallucinatory drugs, psychotherapy, EST, or became apostles of the new fitness cult.[14]

After 1972 jogging and running "took off" in popularity. While many jogged for short distances only a few times weekly, an astonishing number of Americans took up regular long-distance running. In 1970 only 126 men entered the first New York Marathon, but by the mid-1980s the organizers accepted a maximum of 20,000 "official" entries from both men and women while rejecting thousands of others. By then hundreds of cities scheduled marathons in all parts of the nation. Again television contributed to the popularity of long-distance running. To the surprise of media watchers, millions watched the telecasts of the New York and Boston Marathons. As if running twenty-six miles were not enough exercise, the apostles of running invented the triathlon, which included a two-mile swim, a 112-mile bicycle race, and a twenty-six mile run. In 1986 more than a million Americans competed in one or another version of this grueling event.[15]

The runners claimed for their activity much more than aerobic benefits. Apart from building additional energy and reducing anxieties, running, according to its proponents, released endorphins, producing a mystical-like "runner's high," a trancelike euphoria that could be addictive. Running and other vigorous exercises that induced burning pain, pounding hearts, and gasping lungs also helped satisfy human yearnings for concentrated awareness, a focused consciousness that drove away all distractions. "Your mind is consumed by the motion of what you are trying to do and by the pain factor," explained Paul Karlin, a restaurant owner and weight lifter from Bethesda, Maryland. "When you stop, it's like coming down from a high," but in this instance a high without hangovers or presumably the permanent disabilities associated with drug use.[16]

Runners as often as not candidly confessed that their activity was self-centered. "I am a nervous, shy non-combatant who has no feeling for people," wrote Dr. George A. Sheehan, running's self-appointed chief philosopher. "I do not hunger or thirst after justice. I find no happiness in carnival, no joy in community."[17] Sheehan found joy only in the self, in pushing the self to the limits. Like religious converts, runners frequently took on new identities. They made new friends while shedding old ones; they divorced spouses in record numbers; and they rejected smokers. "I abandoned the non-running world," was a typical comment of a convert.[18]

A distinctive runner's culture emerged, one that revolved not only around running, but clubs, special diets, in-group understandings and behaviors, running magazines and books, running celebrities, and a flourishing equipment industry. Even though running required no special physical talents (which was one of its attractions), it separated populations into groups who regularly ran ten miles or so several times a week and those who did not or could not. It furnished the former with at least one unambiguous source of superiority that they might not enjoy in other arenas of their lives. So important was running to individual well-being, according to a *Runners Magazine* poll in 1983, that 23.3 percent of the men and 38.1 percent of the women readers said that they would give up sex before they would abandon running.[19]

———

Although by and large serious runners sought satisfactions within themselves or within their special culture, running, as well as weight lifting, Jazzercise, and other kinds of vigorous exercise, might contribute to feelings of self-sufficiency in other ways. In short, strenuous activity could be instrumental as well as compensatory. Like the top-flight football or basketball player who lifted weights in order to play more effectively, the fit claimed that they worked out so that they could have an edge in both personal relationships and in the workplace over their more sluggish colleagues. They worked harder or were more mentally alert, they said, than non-exercisers. Corporate executives frequently agreed. They not only hoped to have harder-working, more efficient employees but to reduce their insurance premiums and absenteeism as well. In the late 1970s a "wellness" movement swept through the corporate world. Larger corporations provided their employees with stress management and dietary counseling and set up fully equipped gymnasiums with indoor tracks, saunas, and exercise cycles.[20]

Professional women reported that physical fitness relieved them of feelings of inadequacy. Physical strength and endurance could assert gender equality as well as aid women in resisting male oppression. "I enjoy being strong," said Houston librarian Anne Mollberg, who lifted weights. "I have a sense of security knowing that I have the stamina and strength to do almost anything I want to do, physically."[21] "I want to be lean and mean," a weight-lifting librarian told me in 1988. Success in physical fitness encouraged in some women a greater sense of mastery, of control over their destiny, that extended beyond fitness to other parts of their lives.

———

Perhaps the most intriguing facet of the new strenuosity was how it became in the late 1970s and in the 1980s an integral component in self-presentation. To be sure, in all cultures the shape of the body, its adornments, and its movements have been an important means of communication, especially in the rituals of mating and matrimony as well as evidence of status and power. But in modern America self-presentation became more important than ever before. Even in the early part of this century, observers noted that individual success in bureaucracies arose as much—perhaps even more—from the impressions that one made on others as it did from what one created or the actual decisions one made while at work. Thus the management of impressions as represented supremely in the salesperson replaced the making of things as represented supremely in the skilled artisan as the most frequented avenue to success.

The modern preoccupation with appearances arose from other sources as well. As the fear of sudden death from epidemics or plagues vanished, as advertisers promoted the excitement of a youth culture, and as modern persons devoted less of their lives to the perpetuation of their families and/or communities, a person's self-esteem became increasingly dependent upon the impressions that he made on others. Given this context, body shape and physical expression could be of the utmost importance for one obtaining validation of his or her raison d'être. "Part of what provides confidence," reported the editors of Vogue, an avant-garde magazine of the Yuppies in 1988, "is physical appearance, which is why—in this decade of the body—the removal of body fat by liposuction has increased in the past two years by 78%."[22]

In the 1980s the new strenuosity became one of the important symbols of Yuppie status and power. It joined such items as owning one's own business, frequent travel to foreign countries, trusteeship in cultural institutions, and conspicuous but tasteful consumption as evidence of success. It was no longer enough for the "beautiful people" of Southern California to be "just plain rich and/or successful," concluded Jody Jacobs in the Los Angeles Times in 1983.[23] They had to be tanned, sleek, lean, and physically fit. The celebrities regularly took off for a week or more to "fat farms" located in Palm Springs or Scottsdale in preparation for the fall party season. And they employed personal fitness trainers who led them through exercises three or four times a week. Ordinary Yuppies usually had to be satisfied with something a bit less, such as membership and participation in a chic health club. The number of fitness clubs multiplied from 350 in 1968 to more than 7,000 in 1986. By 1986 Americans spent more money on exercise devices in the home than they did on golf, camping, and racquet sports combined.[24]

The presentation of the self through fitness by no means included a denial of either consumption or competition. Indeed, instead of escaping the rigors of competition in the workplace or in consumption, fitness followers took it with them to the health spas, the tennis courts, and their exercise-equipped bedrooms. Fitness itself became competitive, not only with others but even with the self. Neither were the disciples of fitness ascetics. The pressures of consumption frequently extended into the fitness arena; one had to exhibit the most fashionable exercise clothing and belong to the appropriate clubs. In Southern California, it even included fitness centers for the six-month- to three-year-old toddlers of the professional classes.[25]

Physical display in health clubs could be a means of attracting the opposite sex. While many health clubs catered mainly to members of the same sex or to families, others openly made themselves into "meat markets" for Yuppies. "Health clubs are becoming the singles' bars of the 80's," said Ronald Gasaway, the manager of the American Fitness Center in suburban Atlanta, in 1981. Everyone not only shared a common interest in getting into shape, but "when everyone's groaning together" it lowers people's "barriers," explained Victoria Horne, an official of the New York Health and Racquet Club.[26] Along with facilities for fitness, the clubs frequently provided restaurants, bars, lounges, and a social calendar of dances, ski trips, and other events tailored more to enhancing courtship than to losing pounds or toning muscles. Apparently women in particular felt more comfortably meeting strangers of the opposite sex in a fitness center than in a singles bar. "You . . . don't meet as many low-life creeps and insistent drunks. It's safer," explained a New York woman.[27]

———

Changing notions of the ideal male and female also encouraged the commitment to the strenuous life.[28] Part of the ideal was a matter of physical appearance. For women in the 1960s the anorexia look promoted by fashion photographers and glamorized by Jacqueline Kennedy, Twiggy, and rock musicians had replaced the more voluptuous and sometimes imperious movie queens of the 1930–1960 era as the American ideal of female beauty. By the 1970s nearly everyone agreed that Marilyn Monroe could have lost a few pounds. American women grew to despise fat. To be fat in the United States became the greatest sign of personal failure. "Eating has become the last bona fide sin left in America," concluded columnist Ellen Goodman.[29] Obviously exercise, when joined by dieting, drugs, and ultimately plastic surgery, could aid one in achieving the anorexia ideal as well as feelings of greater self-sufficiency.[30] Unalloyed with other characteristics, the anorexia look suggested frailty and vulnerability, a parallel to Victorian notions of womanhood, rather than power and competence.

In the late 1970s a new ideal woman began to emerge, one who was thin but physically fit, energetic, possessing some muscle definition, and who was more assertive (even in intimate relations between the sexes) than her predecessors. The movie 10, which was released in 1979 and featured the body of Bo Derek, helped bring the new model to the attention of the public. Someone associated with the film ingeniously invented the title 10, thereby not only tying it to the modern fascination with numbers but also the inexact ratings systems employed in gymnastics, diving, and skating, sports made enormously popular by television. Only three years earlier, Nadia Comaneci had scored a series of spectacular "10s" in gymnastics at the Olympic Games.

Derek, unlike her anorexia predecessors, was conspicuously fit and active. In order to develop tautness and body tone, she had gone into weight training with a Nautilus machine three months before filming commenced.[31] The movie also suggested a new gender relationship. The 42-year-old insecure George Webber (played by Dudley Moore) could barely generate enough resolve to move beyond fantasies about the younger and much taller Jennifer Miles (Derek). It was Miles who bluntly proposed: "Wanna fuck?" And when the relationship was about to be sexually consummated, Webber was brought to his senses by a telephone call that reminded him that Miles was a married woman. Perhaps because of the overpowering images of Derek, movie fans seldom recalled or perhaps failed to realize that it was in fact the far more old-fashioned Julie Andrews who director Blake Edwards intended to be the perfect "10."

Soon other movies and dozens of television shows, rock videos, and commercials employed Derek prototypes. Perhaps it reached a final expression in Jennifer Beals as Alex (note the unisexual name) in Flashdance (1983).[32] In the film, Alex has an inexhaustible supply of energy. In the opening scene, she is doing man-sized work as a welder; after work she returns to her warehouse apartment over the steep Pittsburgh hills by bicycle; then by night she "works" as a dancer at a local club, which, astonishingly, is depicted as a place for good clean fun in which even Pittsburgh's steelworkers do not leer. She dances to the hard-driving beat of rock music, the kind of dancing that soon prevailed on rock videos. The sheer intensity of her life does not end there. Then we learn that Alex engages in heavy aerobics and weight lifting in order to achieve her long-held dream of becoming a ballerina.

The film and Alex had something for everyone. Although it employed the Cinderella, poor-girl-wins-rich-man formula of success, Alex did it without startling physical beauty but in large part with the projection of a new kind of unself-conscious eroticism. At the nightclub none of the dancers were full-figured and all revealed muscle definition, though certainly falling far short of professional female body-builders. Although the dances included spectacular gymnastic-like routines, they were punctuated throughout by sexual suggestiveness. A more blatant statement of female sensuality was portrayed in *Perfect* (1985), in which the aerobics instructor, Jamie Lee Curtis, led her class through a series of pelvic thrusts. Only the seemingly innocent setting of the class and the club prevented the scenes from being manifestly pornographic.[33]

To a far more pronounced degree than in the past, the popular culture depicted the strenuous women as the sexual aggressors. It was the women who more often used the naughty four-letter words. No longer did the females coyly entice the male into making the first move. "I'm Goin' on a Manhunt," the revealing title of a song in *Flashdance,* included in the lyrics: "Turn it around. Women have been hunted but now we are huntin' around." Similar movies, literally hundreds of rock videos, and nearly an equal number of commercials (especially for diet foods) revealed a new female eroticism, assertiveness, and perhaps ultimately self-sufficiency.[34]

As the population as a whole became more elderly, heroines of the popular culture seemed to be those women who resisted most effectively the process of aging by exhibiting strong bodies. In 1988 *People* magazine asked its male readers to rate the best female bodies. In descending order they chose Cher, Raquel Welch, Loni Anderson, Joan Collins, Vanna White, Jane Fonda, Christie Brinkley, and Linda Evans. When the poll was taken, six of these women were more than forty years old, and at least four of them had exercise videos on the market.[35]

The popular culture also produced archetypes of physically fit ideal males. The anorexic male found in the long-distance runner won few admirers, though runners invariably took great personal satisfaction in the stamina and manifest healthiness found in their lean, sometimes-gaunt bodies. At the opposite pole was the professional body-builder, who used weight lifting and frequently anabolic steroids to obtain body mass. The main, uncamouflaged point of body building was physical display; professional body builders did not build bodies to engage more effectively in sports. Instead of considering Sylvester Stallone in terms of a model for good health or as a potential star of the NFL, one was supposed to admire his well-oiled nude upper torso as he marched through the jungles of Southeast Asia as Rambo. In a time of female challenges to male hegemony and a time of diminished individual power else-where, body builders may have hoped to convey through rippling muscles continued male potency. At any rate, a 1988 survey revealed that far more high-school boys tried to achieve muscle mass by taking anabolic steroids to impress the girls rather than to enhance their prospects of becoming varsity athletes.[36]

But neither the exceptionally thin nor the body builders may have repre-sented the most popular male figure. John Travolta in *Saturday Night Fever* (1977) was the male counterpart of Bo Derek; in fact, appropriately, he played opposite of Curtis in *Perfect*. Travolta's spectacular dancing in the film touched off a disco fever that soon became a worldwide phenomenon. Dark, hand-some, and lithe, Travolta embodied a relentless physical energy and a pre-sumably wholesome eroticism similar to Beals's. Like Derek, Travolta soon had a host of celebrity imitators: Michael Jackson, Tom Cruise, and Pierce Brosnan, for example.

In the 1980s, the ideal male often entailed statements of cool, expensive el-egance as well as physical fitness.[37] The new Beau Brummels were full-scale participants in the unembarrassed return to luxurious ostentation embodied in the Reagan White House. They frequently employed fashion consultants, subscribed to *Gentleman's Quarterly*, supported a thriving skin-care business, and had their hair permed. Upon leaving prison in the final scene of *Perfect*, John Travolta drove away with Jamie Lee Curtis in a BMW—what else?

The Beau Brummels of the 1980s suggested a potentially new relationship between the sexes. Pierce Brosnan, the star of the NBC television series "Rem-ington Steele," and Brian Bosworth, a star linebacker with the Seattle Sea-hawks and the star of Right Guard men's deodorant commercials, seemed hardly to need women at all. Brosnan and Bosworth were so satisfied with their self-statement that women were an additional adornment, perhaps ultimately unnecessary or even a distraction from themselves. "The only problem here is that a lot of these people [men] look like they'd rather go home and look at themselves than somebody else [i.e., women]," was how a female New York Yuppie put it about the men in her exercise club in 1984.[38] No celebrities, men or women, seemed their equals as representatives of a new narcissism.

On the other hand, the presentation of a well-groomed, elegantly dressed, smooth-skinned, physically fit, energetic male may have been part of a new, largely unconscious strategy in attracting the opposite sex. In the past men had so exclusively controlled society's resources that women could not easily reject the advances of men. In the 1980s, with women far less dependent on men for physical or psychological essentials, attracting mates (at least those of the Yuppie sort) may have required the presentation of a less aggressive and more attractive self. In the 1980s the popular culture suggested something of a reversal in traditional gender relationships.

———

To recapitulate, the new strenuosity of the 1970s and 1980s entailed a common effort to nurture a more sufficient self in two general ways. One stressed physical fitness; it was epitomized by aerobics, but particularly by long-distance running, and by abstention. Not only did its adherents usually abstain from lavish equipment in luxurious surroundings, but they frequently refrained entirely from, or cut back on, their consumption of "unhealthy" food and drink. Second was the use of physical robustness and energy to present a more attractive self. These participants in the new strenuosity eschewed neither consumption nor competition. Indeed, they employed fitness as part of a larger strategy to gain status, power, and greater control over their personal relationships.

Although trying to comprehend recent history is an extremely treacherous enterprise, evidence suggests that by the late 1980s the new strenuous-life movement may have passed its zenith. In 1988 *Newsweek* claimed that participation in marathons had dropped by more than 15,000 through 1987 and that the number of persons doing aerobics had fallen 4 million below the peak year of 1985. The magazine even predicted that the "anorexic look" might be waning in popularity.[39] That such unanorexic-looking women as Roseanne, Oprah, and (perhaps) Barbara Bush became media celebrities lent support to *Newsweek*'s prognostication. In addition, in the late 1980s the media introduced "the couch potato" as a popular-culture species who conspicuously rejected the strenuous life.

Notes

1. There is no general history of the new strenuosity, but see especially Patricia A. Eisenman and C. Robert Barnett, "Physical Fitness in the 1950s and 1970s: Why Did One Fail and The Other Boom?" *Quest* 31 (1979): 114–22; Randy Roberts and James Olson, *Winning Is the Only Thing: Sports in America Since 1945* (Baltimore, 1989), 213–34; Marc Leepson, "Physical Fitness Boom," *Editorial Research Reports*, April 14, 1978: 263–80; series of articles in *New York Times*, January 3, 1988: III, 13.

2. Despite polls reporting frequent exercise and other manifestations of a concern for fitness, one should keep in mind that the overwhelming majority of Americans were not physically fit by any of the standard definitions of fitness. See, for example, Robert Sullivan "The Unfitness Boom," *Sports Illustrated* 70 (March 13, 1989): 13.

3. For the fascinating relationship between equipment and strenuosity, see, among others, "The Case for Nautilus: 'Full Range' Exercise," *New York Times,* July 10, 1978: III, 10. For individualized fitness programs, see Lynn Langway, "Fitness with a Personal Touch," *Newsweek* 101 (June 27, 1983): 83.

4. See Erving Goffman, *The Presentation of the Self in Everyday Life* (New York, 1959); Mary Jo Deegan, *American Ritual Dramas: Social Rules and Cultural Meanings* (New York, 1989); Stanley B. Woll and Peter Young, "Looking for Mr. and Ms. Right: Self-presentation in Videodating," *Journal of Marriage and the Family* 51 (1989): 109–14.

5. See Anastasia Toufexis, "The Shape of the Nation," *Time* 126 (October 7, 1985): 60–61.

6. For the intricate connections between the new strenuosity and earlier movements, see James C. Whorton, *Crusaders for Fitness: The History of American Health Reformers* (Princeton, N.J., 1982); Hillel Schwartz, *Never Satisfied: A Cultural History of Diets, Fantasies, and Fat* (New York, 1986); Donald J. Mrozek, *Sport and the American Mentality, 1880–1920* (Knoxville, 1983); Elliott J. Gorn, *The Manly Art: Bare-Knuckle Prize Fighting in America* (Ithaca, N.Y., 1986), 185–206; Harvey Green, *Fit for America: Health, Fitness, and American Society* (New York, 1988); Kathryn Grover, ed., *Fitness in American Culture: Images of Health, Sport, and Body, 1830–1940* (Amherst, Mass., 1989); Gerald F. Roberts, "The Strenuous Life: The Cult of Manliness in the Era of Theodore Roosevelt" (Ph.D. dissertation, Michigan State University, 1970).

7. During the President's Council's existence, schoolchildren have improved little if any in their level of fitness. On the creation of the President's Council, see Dorothy Stull, "A Measure of Fitness," *Sports Illustrated* 7 (August 5, 1957): 28–33; on the recent fitness of children, Karin DeVenuta, "Future Stars Aren't Ready," *Wall Street Journal,* February 26, 1988.

8. See, for example, Martin E. P. Seligman, "Boomer Blues," *Psychology Today,* October 1988: 50–55; Roger Thompson, "Baby Boom's Mid-Life Crisis," *Editorial Research Reports,* January 8, 1988: 2–11.

9. See especially John C. Burnham, "Change in the Popularization of Health in the United States," *Bulletin of the History of Medicine,* 58 (1984): 183–97; Mark Leepson, "Staying Healthy," *Editorial Research Reports,* August 26, 1983: 635–52; Paul Starr, *The Social Transformation of American Medicine* (New York, 1982).

10. Norman Cousins, *Anatomy of an Illness as Perceived by the Patient* (New York, 1979), 113–14.

11. ABC News–Harris Survey, November 24, 1980.

12. See John Grossman, "Inside the Wellness Movement," *Health* 13 (December 1981): 10–15.

13. Kenneth H. Cooper, *Aerobics* (New York, 1968); Kenneth H. Cooper, *The Aerobics Way* (New York, 1977). For Cooper and his influence, see Edwin McDowell, "Publishing: 'Aerobics' Scores a Hit," *New York Times,* December 3, 1982:

III, 29; and Robert Reinhold, "Has the Aerobics Movement Peaked? An Interview with Kenneth Cooper," ibid., March 29, 1987: VI, 14.

14. See especially Christopher Lasch, *The Culture of Narcissism: American Life in an Age of Diminishing Expectations* (New York, 1978).

15. Melvin Durslag, "1st Prize: Surgery, 2nd Prize: Divorce, 3rd Prize: A Mugging," *TV Guide*, October 23, 1982: 14–15; Meg Lukens, "Three Sports Are Better Than One," *Good Health Magazine*, March 26, 1987: 26–27. For the running boom, see also Rory Donaldson, *Guidelines for Successful Jogging* (New York, 1977); James F. Fixx, *The Complete Book of Running* (New York, 1977). Among the relevant periodicals, see *Jogger* and *Runner's World*.

16. Quotations in Michael Walsh, "Make Way for the Spartans," *Time*, September 19, 1983: 90–92. See also Shirley James Longshore, "Fitness: A Universal Goal," *Advertising Age*, July 18, 1983: 9, 29.

17. George A. Sheehan, *Being and Running: A Total Experience* (New York, 1978), 9.

18. See Charles and Betty Edgely and Ronny Turner, "The Rhetoric of Aerobics: Physical Fitness as Religion," *Free Inquiry in Creative Sociology* 10 (November 1982): 187–91, 196.

19. Leepson, "Physical Fitness Boom," 273–74; Eileen Norris, "Kansas Boy Grabs an Idea and Runs With It," *Advertising Age*, July 18, 1983: 14, 16.

20. Philip Whitten and Elizabeth J. Whiteside, "Can Exercise Make You Sexier?" *Psychology Today*, April 1989: 42–44; Marc Leepson, *Executive Fitness* (New York, 1983); Leepson, "Physical Fitness Boom," 271–73; Leslie Bennetts, "American Capitalism Sees the Profit in Exercise," *New York Times*, June 12, 1978: II, B14; John Cavanaugh, "On the Corporate Treadmill," ibid., March 11, 1979; XXIII, 1, 9; "Companies Pour Millions into Programs Aimed at Keeping Workers Well," ibid., October 14, 1984: I, 36; Jack Martin, "The New Business Boom—Employee Fitness," *Nation's Business*, February 1978: 17–18; Patty Beutler, "Wellness Activities Welcomed in Workplaces," *Lincoln (Neb.) Star*, April 17, 1989.

21. See, for example, such advertisements as "The Power Broker" of realtors Shannon & Luchs, featuring a woman in her thirties wearing a padded suit jacket and lifting a weight symbolizing her strength in the *Washington Post*, March 5, 1989: D29. I am indebted to Patrick Miller for this and several other advertisements reflecting themes in the new strenuosity.

22. *Vogue* 178 (October 1988): 198.

23. Jody Jacobs, "For the Beautiful People of L.A. Fitness Is More Than a Fad," *Los Angeles Times*, September 2, 1983: V, 1, 4–5. See also Lisa Bercovici, "Golden Door: Enter Fat, Exit Wiser," *New York Times*, December 27, 1973: 50; T. George Harris and Daniel Yankelvich, "What Good Are the Rich?" *Psychology Today*, April 1989: 37–39.

24. Nancy Giges, "Health Trend Hits Life-Style Mainstream," *Advertising Age* 57 (February 17, 1986): 58; "Exercise Industry Sees Spurt in Sales to Homes," *New York Times*, May 21, 1984: IV, 1; Jack McCallum, "Everybody's Doin' It," *Sports Illustrated* 61 (December 3, 1984): 72–86.

25. Keith Bradsher, "You've Come a Long Way, Baby; Designer Jeans, Sleek Strollers, Exercise Gyms: Toddlers Have a Choice in the Booming Market," *Los Angeles Times*, October 19, 1987: IV, 5; Stuart Copperman, "Do Toddlers Need Exercise?" *Washington Post*, June 9, 1987: 17; Sam Hose Verhovek, "A Little Joyful Exercise: Are Exercise Classes for Infants Helpful, Harmful, or Just Fun?" *New York Times Magazine* 137 (April 17, 1988): S22.

26. Quoted in Robert Lindsey, "Health Clubs Thrive as Meeting Places for Young Single People," *New York Times*, December 4, 1981: 18.

27. Quoted in William E. Geist, "The Mating Game and Other Exercises at the Vertical Club," *New York Times*, May 19, 1984: I, 25.

28. For the history of female beauty in the United States, see Lois W. Banner, *American Beauty* (New York, 1983). Unfortunately, no equivalent book exists for the history of male beauty.

29. Quoted in Schwartz, *Never Satisfied*, 308. See also Kim Chernin, *The Obsessions: Reflections on the Tyranny of Slenderness* (New York, 1981), and Jean Rosenblatt and Sandra Stencil, "Weight Control: A National Obsession," *Editorial Research Reports* 19 (November 19, 1982): 853–68.

30. Advertisements suggested that plastic surgery improved feelings of self-sufficiency. "Sometimes cosmetic surgery shows more on the inside than the outside," read an advertisement of the Lincoln General Hospital, Lincoln, Nebraska, *Lincoln (Neb.) Star*, March 21, 1989.

31. Jacobs, "For the Beautiful People," 4.

32. See Janet Maslin, "Under the 1983 Chic, Movies Still Leer at Women," *New York Times*, May 21, 1983: II, 5.

33. See Vincent Canby's review in the *New York Times*, June 7, 1985: C18.

34. A systematic study of the content of commercials, rock videos, and exercise videos is much needed.

35. *People*, September 19, 1988: 109; Craig Wolff, "Videotapes to Divert Exercises," *New York Times*, August 8, 1987: I, 52.

36. See Janet Maslin, "Musclebound Movies," *New York Times Film Review (1985–1986)* (New York, 1987), 83–84, and the provocative interpretations of Alan M. Klein, "Fear and Self-Loathing in Southern California: Narcissism and Fascism in Bodybuilding Subculture," *Journal of Psychoanalytic Anthropology* 10 (1987): 117–37.

37. See Jerry Adler, "You're So Vain," *Newsweek* 107 (April 14, 1986): 48–55.

38. Quoted in Geist, "The Mating Game."

39. Bill Barol, "The Eighties Are Over," *Newsweek* 111 (January 4, 1988): 40–48. The strenuous-life movement had never been popular with the working class. Those whose jobs required physical toil might play softball, bowl, hunt, or pursue water sports in their spare time, but they rarely altered their diets and drinking habits, took up jogging, or engaged in any systematic program of physical exercise. See especially Bennett M. Berger, *Working-Class Suburb* (Berkeley and Los Angeles, 1969), chapter 5, and David Halle, *America's Working Man* (Chicago, 1984), chapter 2.

Contributors

MELVIN L. ADELMAN, an associate professor in the College of Education at Ohio State University, is the author of *A Sporting Time: New York City and the Rise of Modern Athletics, 1820–70* (1986). He is working on a book that explores professional football in the immediate post-World War II period, focusing on the factors that led to the rise and fall of the All-American Football Conference.

WILLIAM J. BAKER is a professor in and chair of the Department of History at the University of Maine. The author of *Jesse Owens: An American Life* (1986) and *Sports in the Western World* (1988), he is completing a book, *Washed in the Blood: Religion and the Rise of Sport*, which will be published in 1997.

PAMELA L. COOPER is an assistant professor of history at Texas A&M University at Corpus Christi. She is completing a book on the history of the marathon footrace in the United States, tentatively titled *Twenty-six Miles in America*.

MARK DYRESON, an associate professor of history at Weber State University, has published essays on American culture and sport in the *Journal of Sport History, Olympika, International Journal of Sports History,* and several other journals. He is completing work on a book tentatively titled *Inventing the Sporting Republic: American Sport, Political Culture, and the Olympic Experience, 1877–1919,* to be published by the University of Illinois Press.

GERALD R. GEMS is chair of the Department of Health and Physical Education at North Central College, in Naperville, Illinois. He is the editor of *The Organization and Rationalization of Sport* (vol. 5, forthcoming) in the series Sports in North America: A Documentary History, and the author of a forthcoming book on sport in Chicago.

ELLIOTT J. GORN is a professor of history and American studies at Miami University, in Oxford, Ohio. He is the author of *The Manly Art* (1986), the coauthor (with Warren Goldstein) of *A Brief History of American Sports* (1993), and the editor of *Muhammad Ali, the People's Champ* (1995).

ALLEN GUTTMANN is a professor of American studies at Amherst College. Among his books in the field of sport history are *The Games Must Go On: Avery Brundage and the Olympic Movement* (1983), *From Ritual to Record: The Nature of Modern Sports* (1979), *Women's Sports: A History* (1991), *The Olympics: A History of the Modern Games* (1992), and *Games and Empires: Modern Sports and Cultural Imperialism* (1994).

STEPHEN H. HARDY the coeditor of *Sport Marketing Quarterly,* teaches sport studies at the University of New Hampshire. He is the coauthor (with Bernard J. Mullin and William Sutton) of *Sport Marketing* (1993) and the author of *How Boston Played* (1982), as well as numerous book chapters and journal articles.

PETER LEVINE is a professor of history and director of American studies at Michigan State University. His most recent book, coauthored with Robert Lipsyte, is *Idols of the Game: A Sporting History of 20th Century America* (1995).

DONALD J. MROZEK is a professor in and chair of the Department of History at Kansas State University. The author of *Sport and American Mentality* (1983), he is working on a book about sports, film, and reshaping of myth in America in the twentieth century.

MICHAEL ORIARD is a professor of English at Oregon State University. The author of *Reading Football: How the Popular Press Created an American Spectacle* (1993), he is working on a second volume in his cultural history of football, dealing with the 1920s through the 1960s.

S. W. POPE is an editor of the *Journal of Sport History* and the author of *Patriotic Games: Sporting Traditions in the National Imagination, 1876–1926* (1996). He is currently working on a cultural history of radio sportscasting.

BENJAMIN G. RADER is a professor of history at the University of Nebraska at Lincoln and the author of *American Sports: From the Age of Folk Games to the Age of Televised Sports* (3d ed., 1995) and *Baseball: A History of America's Game* (1993), among other works.

STEVEN A. RIESS is a professor of history at Northeastern Illinois University. The former editor of the *Journal of Sport History*, he is the author of *Touching Base: Professional Baseball and American Culture in the Progressive Era* (1980), *City Games: The Evolution of American Urban Society and the Rise of Sports* (1991), and *Sport in Industrial America, 1850–1920* (1995).

NANCY L. STRUNA, an associate professor of kinesiology at the University of Maryland at College Park, serves as president of the North American Society for Sport History. She is the author of *People of Prowess: Sport, Leisure, and Labor in Early Anglo-America* (1996).

DAVID K. WIGGINS, a professor of physical education in the Human Service Programs at George Mason University, has published numerous articles on African Americans in sport in the *Journal of Sport History*, the *International Journal of the History of Sport*, and *Research Quarterly for Exercise and Sport*, among others. He is the editor of *Sport in America: From Wicked Amusement to National Obsession* (1995) and the coeditor, with George Eisen, of *Ethnicity and Sport in North American History and Culture* (1994).

Index

Books in the Series Sport and Society

A Sporting Time: New York City and the Rise of Modern Athletics, 1820–70
Melvin L. Adelman

Sandlot Seasons: Sport in Black Pittsburgh   *Rob Ruck*

West Ham United: The Making of a Football Club   *Charles Korr*

Beyond the Ring: The Role of Boxing in American Society   *Jeffrey T. Sammons*

John L. Sullivan and His America   *Michael T. Isenberg*

Television and National Sport: The United States and Britain   *Joan M. Chandler*

The Creation of American Team Sports: Baseball and Cricket, 1838–72   *George B. Kirsch*

City Games: The Evolution of American Urban Society and the Rise of Sports
Steven A. Riess

The Brawn Drain: Foreign Student-Athletes in American Universities   *John Bale*

The Business of Professional Sports   *Edited by Paul D. Staudohar and James A. Mangan*

Fritz Pollard: Pioneer in Racial Advancement   *John M. Carroll*

Go Big Red! The Story of a Nebraska Football Player   *George Mills*

Sport and Exercise Science: Essays in the History of Sports Medicine   *Edited by Jack W. Berryman and Roberta J. Park*

Minor League Baseball and Local Economic Development   *Arthur T. Johnson*

Harry Hooper: An American Baseball Life   *Paul J. Zingg*

Cowgirls of the Rodeo: Pioneer Professional Athletes   *Mary Lou LeCompte*

Sandow the Magnificent: Eugen Sandow and the Beginnings of Bodybuilding
David Chapman

Big-Time Football at Harvard, 1905: The Diary of Coach Bill Reid   *Ronald A. Smith*

Leftist Theories of Sport: A Critique and Reconstruction   *William J. Morgan*

Babe: The Life and Legend of Babe Didrikson Zaharias   *Susan E. Cayleff*

Stagg's University: The Rise, Decline, and Fall of Big-Time Football at Chicago
Robin Lester

Muhammad Ali, the People's Champ   *Edited by Elliott J. Gorn*

People of Prowess: Sport, Leisure, and Labor in Early Anglo-America   *Nancy L. Struna*

The New American Sport History: Recent Approaches and Perspectives
Edited by S. W. Pope

REPRINT EDITIONS

The Nazi Olympics   *Richard D. Mandell*

Sports in the Western World (Second Edition)   *William J. Baker*

The new American sport
history : recent approaches
and perspectives